UP IS UP
BUT SO IS DOWN

New York's Downtown Literary Scene, 1974–1992

Edited by Brandon Stosuy

Afterword by Dennis Cooper and Eileen Myles

New York University Press

New York and London

New York University Press
New York and London
www.nyupress.org

Library of Congress Cataloging-in-Publication Data
Up is up, but so is down : New York's downtown literary scene,
1974-1992 / edited by Brandon Stosuy.
p. cm.
Includes bibliographical references.
ISBN-13: 978-0-8147-4010-1 (cloth : alk. paper)
ISBN-10: 0-8147-4010-3 (cloth : alk. paper)
ISBN-13: 978-0-8147-4011-8 (pbk. : alk. paper)
ISBN-10: 0-8147-4011-1 (pbk. : alk. paper)
1. American literature--New York (State)--New York. 2. Authors, American--Homes and
haunts--New York (State)--New York. 3. American literature--20th century. 4. Arts, American-
-New York (State)--New York--20th century. 5. SoHo (New York, N.Y.)--Intellectual life.
6. Lower East Side (New York, N.Y.)--Intellectual life. I. Stosuy, Brandon.
PS549.N5U65   2006
810.9'9747109045--dc22   2006002277

New York University Press books are printed on acid-free paper,
and their binding materials are chosen for strength and durability.

Book & cover design: Yolanda Cuomo Design, NYC
Designer: Angela Lidderdale

Printed in China

C 10 9 8 7 6 5 4 3 2 1
P 10 9 8 7 6 5 4 3 2 1

The urban artist's "sense of place" is not rooted in

rolling hills and nostalgia. It's already once removed.

It skins its knees on the pavement, steps in dog shit,

and stumbles in the gutters as it is chased from one place

to another by debts and developers.

—LUCY R. LIPPARD, FROM "HOMELESS AT HOME," 1986

CONTENTS (TEXT)

PART THREE:
THE 1990S

CONTENTS (ART)

PART THREE:
THE 1990S

ACKNOWLEDGMENTS

MOST OF the texts in this volume are from the Downtown Collection at the Fales Library, New York University. The Downtown Collection, which began in 1993, documents the Downtown scene in SoHo and the Lower East Side during the 1970s through the early 1990s, providing primary resources for scholars interested in the history and culture of downtown New York.

I'd like to thank Marvin Taylor, Director of the Fales Library, for hiring me when I first landed in New York, recommending me to NYU Press after I'd left the library, generously allowing me full access to the collection, and tirelessly passing along key suggestions throughout the anthology's production process.

Fales's entire desk staff was essential to the book's completion. Thank you for putting up with my requests. Additionally, I could never have cobbled this together if not for the expertise of Fales archivist Ann Butler and the library's curator of books, Mike Kelly.

Eric Zinner, editor in chief at NYU Press, allowed me the space to turn *Up Is Up, but So Is Down* into an idiosyncratic document, but knew when to intervene and set me back on course. Emily Park, assistant editor at NYU Press, answered the most random questions graciously, caught errors before we went to print, and engaged me in discussions about pigeons and Will Oldham.

Jennifer Vinopal and the rest of staff at New York University's digital lab made sure scans were up to snuff.

Joseph Ketner III transcribed Dennis Cooper and Eileen Myles's afterword discussion quickly and accurately with zero advance notice.

Entering the Downtown proper, I want to thank everyone who gave me permission to reprint materials. A special tip of the hat to those who loaned out-of-print objects, reminisced about their own particular scenes, and passed along constructive criticism: Penny Arcade, Holly Anderson, Allan Bealy, Bruce Benderson, Max Blagg, Lisa Blaushild, Edmund Cardoni, Michael Carter, Peter Cherches, Susan Daitch, Steve Dalachinsky, Constance DeJong, Maggie Dubris, Denise Duhamel, Janice Eidus, Barbara Ess, Lisa B. Falour, Kevin Killian, Tuli Kupferberg, Lydia Lunch, Tsaurah Litzky, Joe Maynard, Sharon Mesmer, Thurston Moore, Scott Neary, Deborah Pintonelli, Anselm Berrigan (and the Poetry Project), James Romberger, Ed Sanders, Walter Sipser, Esther K. Smith (and Purgatory Pie Press), Patti Smith,

Sparrow, David Trinidad, Margarite Van Cook, Matias Viegener, Carl Watson, Bruce Weber, and Emily XYZ. (My apologies to anyone I have forgotten to mention.)

Sarah Schulman assisted me with the paragraphs on AIDS activism. Chris Kraus wrote the Cookie Mueller and David Rattray bios and helped me with Semiotext(e)/Native Agents facts. Wendy Olsoff at P.P.O.W. Gallery forwarded biographical details about David Wojnarowicz.

Besides offering his insights, Richard Hell chased down a handful of photo permissions. bart plantenga gave early assistance with the table of contents. Lynne Tillman supplied continual advice, friendship, and conceptual assistance. From my tentative inquiries up to the hour or so before deadline, Mike Golden ably fielded my queries. (After much deliberation, he also came up with the book's title.) Robert Glück kindly read my introduction, improving it greatly with his spot-on suggestions. Thanks, Bob. A major thank you to Ron Kolm, who sent me on my way with piles of books, zines, and flyers every time we met for coffee (even if he showed up late).

For their expansive and highly readable dialogue as well as continued friendship and mentorship, I can't thank Dennis Cooper and Eileen Myles enough.

This book would feel like a fragment without their contributions.

Robert Siegle's *Suburban Ambush: Downtown Writing and the Fiction of Insurgency* (1989, John Hopkins) has proven wonderful company and remains the essential close reading of New York City's textual territory. Allan Tannenbaum's *New York in the 70s: Soho Blues* (2003, Feierabend Verlag) is a great pictorial resource.

My always patient editors at *Pitchfork, Rhino,* and the *Village Voice* allowed me to repeatedly push deadlines around when I hit crunch time.

I am also indebted to my family and friends for their understanding and support throughout the year it took to turn scraps into a book. My parents deserve a special commendation for fostering my early interest in experimental writing by helping me photocopy my own zine when I was sporting bad blue hair in high school.

Finally, thanks to Jane Lea, who spent weeks scanning materials, provided around-the-clock, on-the-spot pep talks, and put up with the transformation of our tiny Brooklyn apartment into a disheveled Downtown archive. You've been amazingly patient, Jane: this book is for you.

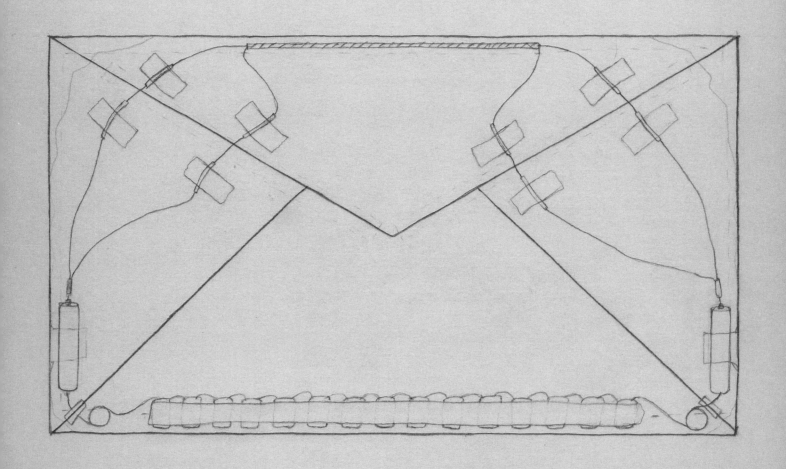

INTRODUCTION

BRANDON STOSUY

WHAT MAKES writing "Downtown"? In the context of *Up Is Up, but So Is Down*, the term refers variously to an agglomeration of noncommercial literary and not-so-literary prose, poetry, guerrilla journalism, and undefined hybrids that emerged in the mid-1970s in homegrown periodicals, newsprint weeklies, xeroxed zines, semigloss monthlies, and small presses in New York City more or less below Fourteenth Street, covering Tribeca to the Lower East Side. Within the Downtown region of that time, maps proved only so helpful, though, and exact boundaries remained pleasingly impossible to chart.

Downtown writing not only served as an alternative to mainstream publishing; it presented writers with a shadowy, shifting, often ad hoc blueprint of how to create works that breathed freely and remained connected significantly to the everyday, circulating like samizdat. Reversing Oscar Wilde's maxim of looking at the stars with feet planted in the trenches, Downtown writers located inspiration by keeping eyes firmly focused on the muck, only occasionally gazing towards that vastness of astrological space, a star-bitten purity unimaginable in a cramped New York tenement.

After scanning this book's table of contents, you might wonder why you haven't heard of many of these urban archivists. Simply put, in a town of zero eye contact, it can prove difficult to leave a permanent mark, and the Big Apple is prime real estate for those hoping to disappear. The decision to produce experimental, noncommercial literature in the corporate publishing industry's stomping ground points to punk-influenced, low-key self-control. Even for those who want to be seen, New York City's ever-shifting urban palimpsest can prove a cutthroat graveyard: monthly flavors are forgotten, style wars have no winners, and entire social scenes duck furtively into alleys, skulking into the critical laboratory when nostalgia beckons for reassessment.

Aiding in the anonymous-seeming free flow was the fact that there was no *one* scene; often each group possessed its own audience: you could enjoy notoriety within one group and remain entirely obscure outside of it. The split between St. Mark's Poetry Project's New Year's marathon and Bruce Weber's Alternative New Year's readings at Cafe Nico (a space above the Pyramid), CBGB's, and ABC No Rio offers a good example of these micro divisions. In fact, Weber started the series after taking a seminar with Bernadette Mayer, then director of the Poetry Project, in the fall of 1990. Feeling stifled by what he perceived as her lack of enthusiasm regarding his sound experiments, he has said his event exists for voices not represented by St. Mark's.[1]

Unlike Dadaists, Beats, or even the second generation New York School poets whom many saw as forerunners, Downtown writers partook in a catch-phrase-free aesthetic; on the relatively small Manhattan island, divergent (and sometimes linked) subscenes gathered around both day-old friendships and complex agendas at institutions and

"Letter Bomb" (1992)
Walter Sipser

anti-institutions such as 8BC, ABC No Rio, Biblios, CBGB's (a biker bar on the Bowery turned no-wave/punk headquarters), Cafe No Bar, Cedar Tavern, Club 57, Danceteria, Darinka, Ear Inn, Fez, the Gas Station, Knitting Factory, Life Cafe, Living Theater, Max's Kansas City, the Mudd Club, Nuyorican Poets Cafe, the Pyramid, and St. Mark's Poetry Project.

Though talk still revolves around the myriad differences between SoHo and the East Village, more intriguing than simplified neighborhood demarcations was the felt character of the urban environs as a whole—a graffiti-covered subway car's subterranean rumble, a sidewalk's familiarly uneven surface, the cumin and clove scent of one street or the urine and wine stink of another—and the way it was experienced by these often willfully unpolished, subversively intelligent authors.

Anyone who's lived in New York City knows it isn't advisable to negotiate Manhattan's stained and mucked-up terrain without remaining alert, as even a simple jaunt to the corner bodega involves an obstacle course of discarded circulars and gamey refuse. Imagine these authors, then, as your guides.

Post-Giuliani New York City is different from the location described and narrated in this book, but even with the mini-mall airbrushing of Astor Place, the attempt to turn CBGB's into a tourist museum (or worse), and the theme-park vibe of Times Square, New York still has its share of filth. Without a doubt, though, it was dirtier and more dangerous in the 1970s and 1980s, a time when American cities were limping out of longtime decline after the suburban migration or "white flight" of the 1950s and 1960s. What remained in the wake of this exodus were inadequate city schools, a lack of well-paying blue-collar jobs, widespread crime, desperation, fear, and anger.

Downtown author Ron Kolm's account gives a first-hand feel for the city at that time:

In 1972 I was working in the Strand Bookstore. Richard Hell and Tom Verlaine had left by then, but Patti Smith was there for one summer. She got a gig doing a reading on a loft-building rooftop in SoHo, so we all trooped down there after work to support her. Afterwards, as we stumbled back towards 14th Street, we noticed how totally empty that part of the city was. We passed a bunch of cast-iron buildings with their doors propped open and, looking in, were amazed to see these old guys stamping-out plastic parts on ancient machines. In the East Village, on the other hand, you simply got mugged if you ventured east of Avenue A after dark.[2]

Participants swear aesthetic, economic, and sociological differences exist between glossier SoHo and the grubbier Lower East Side. This makes sense on a large scale, but content-wise, despite neighborhood allegiances, Downtown voices can't always be easily relegated to either corner. In fact, a number of New York's most compelling writers weren't entirely associated with the Big Apple: Kathy Acker was raised in New York, where she became known as the ex-stripper punk bad girl, but is linked to San Francisco New Narrative for her use of theory, cut-ups, and appropriation (though she moved also between New York and London). Dennis Cooper, the coauthor of this book's afterword, left New York City in the mid-1980s for Amsterdam and then Los Angeles, where he remains a major champion of West Coast writing and art. The list goes on.

Because zip codes aren't a reliable demarcation, one way to connect Downtown writers is through the situations encountered in their texts. As the reader of this collection will notice, subject matter was diverse, though it often involved a fluid take on desire and sexuality and high and low culture, a subversive approach to belles lettres, warped naturalism, and a focus on community and class interaction.

Besides engaging and trying to unpack pop or underground cultures, authors rewrote the texts and lives of others (including the "classics"), cobbling a vast collage of dream language, body and textual modification (whether Bataille or Iggy Pop), mail art, foreign languages, punk flyers, diary excerpts, tattoos, and pornographic romance novels.

A number of these writers ably picked on the squeaky-clean narratives of the mainstream: combining the casual first person of the irreverent New York School poets (most visibly, the hirsute Pepsi addict, editor of *C* magazine, and author of the vastly influential *Sonnets*, Ted Berrigan) with punk's anti-art salvos, Downtown writers found inspiration in the lives of their friends (and lovers) as well as those who came before them, including the scene surrounding Andy Warhol's Factory, experimental filmmaker Jack Smith's *Flaming Creatures*, the minimalist drone of the Dream Syndicate, and the Pop collaborations of lifelong friends Ron Padgett and Joe Brainard.

Texts reinscribed the intellectual provocations of the Dadaists and Fluxists, the pre-Gap Beats' commingling of jazz and dusty rambles, Marxist economic critique, a deconstructionist's sense of indeterminacy, and countless transgressive thinkers and outsiders who escaped categorization. Of course, some writers just as easily rejected these things, too.

Though obviously open to various stylistic avenues, Downtown experimentation avoided the so-called "Brat Pack" and the "dirty realism" of *Bright Lights, Big City*, a polished revision of Downtown reality. Often attacking the stiff literariness and bourgeois irony epitomized by the *New Yorker*'s short fiction and poetry and the "well written" workshop tales of MFA programs, Downtown writers played ebulliently with form and content, sex and language, and produced work depicting the underbelly of real life, no matter how unsavory.

In his introduction to the *Blatant Artifice* anthology

of short fiction, Edmund Cardoni of Hallwalls, a Buffalo-based center for contemporary art founded by Robert Longo, Cindy Sherman and Charles Clough in 1974, discussed the importance of privileging structural play, noting that trendy (though quite good) authors like Jay McInerney "could do with a little more dirt and a lot less realism" and colorfully made it known that the straightforward narratives of David Leavitt, among others, were anything but challenging:

If this stuff is on the cutting edge of anything, it's of a sterling silver butter spreader resting on the gilt edge of a white china bread plate on a thickly padded white linen tablecloth on the table in the family dining room, with father at the head and the writers' napkins in their laps. And the butter had better be *real* soft.[3]

Beginning in 1983 and continuing publication until 1990, Joel Rose and Catherine Texier's *Between C & D* presented one of the strongest forums for the work Cardoni championed. The periodical was named for the location of Rose and Texier's apartment complex on East Seventh Street between Avenues C and D, and they laid each issue out at home on an Epson computer. Copies were printed individually on a dot-matrix printer, decorated by artists like Kiki Smith, Rick Prol, Art Spiegelman, and David Wojnarowicz (with multiple cover variations for each issue), and packaged in a Ziploc bag to imitate the dime bags of drugs passed between dealers and users in their Lower East Side neighborhood.

Between C&D is best known for its 1988 Penguin anthology, which showcased materials published previously in the magazine. It included work by David Wojnarowicz, Darius James, Lisa Blaushild, Dennis Cooper, Gary Indiana, Ron Kolm, Bruce Benderson, Lynne Tillman, Patrick McGrath, Peter Cherches, and Tama Janowitz, among others. In the anthology's introduction, Rose and Texier offered a cogent overview of Downtown writing, which they correctly saw as quite different from "sensitive" fiction "teeming with believable characters a reader could care for throughout the length of a novel":

[T]hey owe more to Burroughs, Miller, Genet, or Céline or even to Barthes and Foucault or J. G. Ballard, than they do to Updike or Cheever. In the classic tradition of the avant-garde, they use sex, violence, shock value, parody, cynicism, irony, and black humor to attack the complacency of established literature and its middle-class values. . . . These writers are closer to urban archaeologists than to landscape artists or campus sociologists, and regardless of their backgrounds, they choose to explore the underside of life—the frontier where the urban fabric is wearing thin and splitting open. . . . What these writers share is a common passion for exploring the limits of fiction in this the late twentieth century and a rebelliousness against the established order of traditional narrative. You won't find any middle-class family dramas or cute college tales in these stories. Nor are there coy, slickly portrayed vignettes of modern life.

The work is sometimes shocking in its frank sexuality or violence, in its absence of sentimentality, in the deliberate sketchiness of the characters. And even the most polished stories have a gritty, jagged edge, as they attempt to break through the slick surface and hypocrisy of smooth, airtight contemporary fiction, desperately seeking to expose what lies beneath the cracks.[4]

Rose and Texier point to John Cheever and John Updike as stylistically incompatible, but Downtown literature also differed from the more playful metawriting of John Barth, William Gaddis, and their postmodern brethren. Instead, the nineteenthcentury French poet Arthur Rimbaud remained at least an early touchstone.

In addition to being a general poster boy for flyers and a theme for readings, Rimbaud figured prominently in work by such personalities as Dennis Cooper, Kathy Acker, Patti Smith, and David Wojnarowicz. Richard Hell especially glanced backwards at French artistic culture, suggesting at one point that his spiked hair was inspired by the scruffy bard. (A flyer found on page 50 of this book announces his post-Television band, the Voidoids, with a quote from Comte de Lautréamont.)

In 1988, to celebrate the publication of the second issue of his magazine, *Cuz*, Hell decided to have a Poets' Banquet at St. Mark's Church. The invitation list included David Trinidad, Ishmael Houston-Jones, Dennis Cooper, Susie Timmons, Eileen Myles, Lee Ann Brown, Bernadette Mayer, and Cookie Mueller. Hell explains the event as follows:

I was thinking of the poor poets/ painters' dinners in Paris at the turn of the century: Picasso, Max Jacob, Apollinaire. I'd made the acquaintance of a good chef or two, and my girlfriend at the time—the clothing designer Amanda Uprichard—loved to have parties. We served hare and venison and mead (fermented honey) and genuine absinthe (courtesy an upstate moonshine purveyor of the real thing, and it was very real). All invitees could bring a guest but the invitations went exclusively to contributors to the magazine, plus the staff of the Poetry Project and two photographers (Roberta Bayley, who brought Glenn O'Brien, and Chris Stein who brought Debby Harry).[5]

But by and large, Downtown writing itself wasn't as decadent as this evening might suggest. Given that Thomas Pynchon's

New York City
in 1979,
Cover (1981)
Photo:
Anne Turyn

Between C & D,
Vol. 2 No. 2,
Cover (1985)
Art:
Barbara Kruger

Portable
Lower East Side,
Vol. 4 No. 1,
Cover (1987)
Art: Kurt
Hollander

Gravity's Rainbow was released in 1973 (the same year Lou Reed's "Walk on the Wild Side" hit popular radio), Downtown work can feel remarkably minimalist and even pithy in comparison, resembling punk lyrics or a manifesto's euphorically scribbled demands.

Some followed in the path of the Fugs. Founded in 1964, Tuli Kupferberg, Ed Sanders, and Ken Weaver's band recorded satirical antiwar (and anti-everything) songs like "Slum Goddess of the Lower East Side," providing another irreverent aesthetic template.

All in all, these writers have more in common with Reed and his Velvet Underground, the tight three-chord anthems of the Ramones, or the jagged sounds of Suicide and DNA than baroque Pynchon and his V-2 missiles.

In line with their punk (or no wave or proto-punk or Beat-punk) influences—look at Joe Maynard and Nick Zedd in this anthology,

for instance—Downtown literature often presented warts-and-all protagonists who nonetheless (now and again) won over the reader through their flawed natures. The artist Greer Lankton explained this punk/underground camaraderie especially well: "New York has got this underground; it attracted us and all our friends." She continues, "Everyone we know is someone who was the wildest from wherever they were from. I don't want my art to shock, but to be understood."[6]

Punk was also apparent in the ad hoc venues that popped up to host literary events. Gary Ray, an actor who had a part in *Desperately Seeking Susan*, opened Darinka in a basement apartment on East First Street near Avenue A. It remained active from 1984 until 1987 and hosted a number of readings that doubled as parties, including

a potluck hosted by performance artist/writer Karen Finley.

Another alternative gathering place was Tin Pan Alley, a pimp's bar near Times Square with the Sex Pistols on its jukebox and a bloodstained pool table. Tin Pan Alley is associated with a group of writers, the Unbearables, who since 1985 have taken advantage of the city's inexpensive beers in its working-class pubs. The original Tin Pan Alley group consisted of Max Blagg, Peter Lamborn Wilson, bart plantenga, Mike Golden, a tattoo artist named Matty Jankowski, and Ron Kolm. Since then, the Unbearables have grown to include dozens and still exist, in one form or another. The tongue-in-cheek neo-Beat crew was originally christened the Unbearable Beatniks of Life by David Life, during a reading series at his Life Cafe on Tenth Street and Avenue B, for which he created a semi-

Woolens   Silks
G. + F. Fabrics, Inc.
Cottons   Notions
"No Smoking"

ironic logo depicting goatee-wearing participants sporting berets but sans bongos (see page 262).

LIKE PUNKS, Downtown writers took an active role in the production process, starting magazines, small and occasional presses, galleries, activist organizations, theaters, and clubs. These endeavors are reflected today in photocopied suburban fanzines, low-fidelity four-track recordings, cassette-only labels, and rustbelt artist-run collectives. Their varied activities reflected both DIY (do-it-yourself) culture and the openness of artistic production of the scene.

An archetypal punk author, the leather-jacket-clad Kathy Acker changed her hair colors as often as she switched perspectives in her narratives; besides writing hugely influential novels, over the course of her thirty-year career, she performed in a sex show at the Fake on Forty-second Street, hung out at St. Mark's Poetry Project, made Hi-8 videos with Alan Sondheim, charted dream maps, collaborated with the Mekons on a rock album, worked with Richard Foreman on a play version of *My Life, My Death,* and illustrated her own books. A beanpole with a cigarette and a bemused look, David Wojnarowicz painted, drew, sculpted, shot film and video, took photographs, wrote essays, memoirs, and stories, was a major AIDS activist, and played in the band 3 Teens Kill 4.

Interestingly, the scarcity of Downtown materials often comes as a direct result of an adherence to DIY culture. Due to limited editions and self-distribution, many publications were sold out within weeks of their first (and only) printings. James Romberger and Marguerite Van Cook intentionally serialized installments of their comic strip, *Ground Zero,* in different publications, forcing diehards to search through any number of weeklies, monthlies, and one-offs if they wished to continue the story.

Other contributions to Downtown writing showed up in the *East Village Eye, Cover, Downtown, Soho News,* and *Soho Arts Weekly* or irregulars like Allan Bealy's *Benzene,* Peter Cherches' *Zone,* Brian Wallis and Phil Mariani's *Wedge,* Bob Witz's *Appearances,* Lucio Pozzi's *New Observations,* Jeffrey Isaac's *Public Illumination* (still in publication), and Anne Turyn's *Top Stories.* (These and other periodicals are described more fully in the addendum's "Downtown Publication Roundup" on page 457.)

The main distribution points for Downtown publications were local bookstores. As Ron Kolm, who currently works at Coliseum Books on Forty-second Street, put it,

If you wanted the new Kathy Acker, or a copy of *ZAP #4,* you had to visit the Eastside Bookstore on St. Mark's Place. The walls were covered with flyers announcing readings, apartments for rent and political rallies. That was in the mid-Seventies. By the end of that decade the center of hipster gravity had moved to New Morning Bookstore on Spring Street in SoHo. That was pre–tourist trap SoHo. In the Eighties, if you wanted a book by Barthes, or some language poetry, you had to frequent St. Mark's Bookshop.

Kolm terms bookstores **"the crossroads of the counter-culture,"** viewing them as equally important as the clubs that housed the readings. **"Any artist who wanted to get his or her artifact, whether it was a zine or a chapbook, into circulation, had to place it in at least one of them—the more the better."**[7]

THUS FAR this introduction has stressed the underground nature of Downtown writing, but focusing on obscurity is misleading, because a number of writers managed significant success despite the lack of a general audience for experimental writing in the United States.

Boutiques

Peter Cooper Nursing Home "Aid for the Feeble" "Comfort for the Aged" Dentists along here.

A gay second-storey porch, the tiniest here.

fertilizer by innumerable dogs.

"did Leon buy the sign Co." Min. "Buk-"

dence of Wystan Hugh Au-den for over thirty years. "Roman Between Them." "Roman, Law Offices" Diesnicki!, Diesi-

stand, pointing right, Pizza

The area's handsomest "pol-"

A misplaced bodega that fits

ST. MARK'S PLACE

SECOND AVENUE

Taking advantage of the popularity of cabaret, Eric Bogosian pioneered avant-garde standup; eventually his *Talk Radio* was adapted for film by Oliver Stone and he retooled his own *subUrbia* for the silver screen. Initially notorious for her nude performances and wrangles with religion and patriarchy, Karen Finley became a well-respected educator and an artistic (and feminist) icon after her clash with the NEA. When he committed suicide in 2004, Spalding Gray was memorialized on a large scale in the popular as well as underground press. His performance of *Swimming to Cambodia* and other film work as well as his touring one-man shows are contemporary stage classics. Gray started with the Wooster Group, a troupe of multidisciplinary provocateurs who remain prolific and daring today, with members like Willem Dafoe moonlighting as Hollywood stars.

The Nuyorican poet Miguel Piñero's life became a Hollywood biopic; Patrick McGrath's *Spider* was transformed into a film by David Cronenberg; Mary Gaitskill received the big-screen treatment in *Secretary*; one-time poet Peter Schjeldahl is the *New Yorker*'s art critic; the novelist Gary Indiana's journalism has been nominated for the Pulitzer Prize on four occasions; Bruce Benderson won France's 2004 Prix Le Flore; Lynne Tillman, whose *No Lease on Life* was nominated for a National Book Critics Circle Award in fiction in 1988, is cited as an influence on a new generation of New York writers like Jonathan Lethem and Jonathan Safran Foer; and Dennis Cooper and Eileen Myles (among others) have become major culture figures.

THOUGH MUCH of it is out of print and difficult to locate, Downtown writing has never been more relevant. While in recent years there have been myriad safety-pin-chic punk monographs, Lower East Side group retrospectives, hyperbolic *New York Times Magazine* features, '80s-inspired acid-disco productions, and shredded hipster fash-

ions, Downtown literature itself remains conspicuously overlooked. The underground writing of this period has received far less airtime than Club 57's cocaine-fueled dance marathons, graffiti's entrance and exit from the gallery system, performance art's much ballyhooed yam-stained outbursts, and "dirty realist" representations by New York City's glitterati. In fact, so much of this work is out of print that many young writers and artists have only a second-hand knowledge of their influences.

To help remedy this unfortunate trend, *Up Is Up, but So Is Down* gathers almost twenty years of downtown New York City's smartest and most explosive writing, mixing standards with lesser known but equally essential materials. Because the East Village art scene has already been well served by a number of retrospectives and catalogues, an effort was made not to use gallery art, but instead to include visual work that emerged from some sort of literary collaboration, whether as an illustrated manifesto from a zine, a punk-inflected chapbook cover, or a complex flyer for a reading. In this forum, New York City's rich underground literary history is presented more completely than it would be in just another slim and underwhelming "best of."

Other anthologies exist, but none states the reason behind its specific starting point. And though some would disagree, there is no codified Downtown canon. Alan Moore and Josh Gosciak's *A Day in the Life: Tales from the Lower East Side* (1990) samples fifty years of Lower East Side writing, from 1940 to 1990, including work by Peter Cherches, Gary Indiana, Ron Kolm, Lynne Tillman, Emily XYZ, Ted Berrigan, Herbert Huncke, Ed Sanders, and Enid Dame. *ABC No Rio Dinero*, edited by Moore with Marc Miller, centered on the alternative performance space ABC No Rio, located on Rivington Street in the Lower East Side. In 1991, Anne Turyn collected pieces from her *Top Stories* series in *Top Top Stories*.

Though often as difficult to locate as the authors' original editions, the best anthologies came out in the '80s. Some of the strongest were Barbara Ess and Glenn Branca's *Just Another Asshole* No. 6 (1983), Brian Wallis's *Blasted Allegories* (1987), and Hallwalls's *Blatant Artifice* No. 2/3 (1988).

The sharpest was *Wild History* (1985), edited by Richard Prince for Reese Williams's Tanam Press. In *Wild History*, Prince paired contributions with black-and-white photos of the authors. As might be expected, some of the authors look stiff, but Peter Downsborough's noir photo of Constance DeJong, Cookie Mueller's playful self-portrait, and Prince's take on Williams as a cowboy are downright glamorous. As is Lynne Tillman's, whose section of *Haunted Houses* (on page 257) is accompanied by an existential-seeming Nan Goldin photo of the author taken in the bar from the film *The Verdict* on Seventh and Avenue B. (The photo is reproduced on page 261 of this anthology for the first time in its complete, uncropped form.) Among the authors Prince corralled are Roberta Allen, Peter Nadin, Gary Indiana, Kathy Acker, Spalding Gray, and Wharton Tiers.

The Downtown literary scene's single full-length critical study remains Robert Siegle's excellent 1989 *Suburban Ambush*, which was named after a brief poem by Ron Kolm, reproduced as a collaboration with the visual artist Michael Madore in this anthology. Though written far from the Big Apple at Virginia Polytechnic Institute and State University, Siegle's treatise is a Downtown project in and of itself. Ending its coverage in 1989, Siegle's study analyzes major authors such as Kathy Acker, Lynne Tillman, Spalding Gray, and Eric Bogosian, but it's more interesting to experience Siegle's takes on less well-known SoHo and East Village writers such as Judy Lopatin, Anne Turyn, Constance DeJong, Reese Williams, and Peter Cherches because nowhere else do they receive anything approaching Siegle's detailed exegesis. Caught in the flurry of the moment, Siegle bravely gambled on what would and wouldn't last, imparting valuable insight into some forgotten authors and in turn a glimpse at what it was like in New York City at that time amid **"[b]uildings burned out by junkies so that they can sell the copper piping, boarded-up dead stores with their graffiti-laced steel shutters, post-nuclear vacant lots, jumpy-eyed adolescent males and twelve-year-old girls with Mona Lisa smiles, scruffy winos and children ex-** ploding out of school into sidewalk tag-team mayhem."[8]

EXPANDING ON and updating these precursors, *Up Is Up, but So Is Down* offers the most expansive snapshot of the era's most relevant works, offering direct contact with the work and saving readers the effort of wading through the innumerable fragments the period produced.

Beginning in 1974 and arranged chronologically, *Up Is Up, but So Is Down* attempts to put this hugely varied material in productive juxtaposition. In doing so, it gives the reader a sense of the views, agendas, and movements at play during the book's period.

The book focuses on writers and poets. A few performance artists are included, but only those who chiseled a significant body of written work published alongside more recognizable poetry and prose writers. The visuals tend toward flyers, zine covers, newsprint weeklies, photographs (of people and the city), artist/writer collaborations, book covers, and letterpress broadsides. Though virtually none of the art is gallery work, the collection includes some of the most enduring visuals of the period. Manhattan looms in the background throughout, punctuated with the words and images of

Flyer for a Reading by Michael La Bombarda, Robert Lunday, Ron Kolm, Hal Sirowitz (1983)/
Portable Lower East Side No. 1, Cover, Front/Back (1984) Art/Design: Kurt Hollander/
Between C & D Reading at Darinka/ABC No Rio, Flyer (1985)/
Dennis Cooper and Alice Notley, The Poetry Project, Flyer (1984)/
Big Cigars, no. 3, Cover (1988) Artist/Designer: Michael Randall/
"Suburban Ambush" (ca. 1990)Art: Michael Madore; Text: Ron Kolm

Top to Bottom:

New Yorkers living and working in the shadows of the skyline.

Each section is introduced briefly to present a context, and an addendum rounds up publications of that time period, offering a pre-Internet map of DIY distribution. Also looking at this era (and charting the region's rise, fall, and revival), Dennis Cooper and Eileen Myles provide a valuable afterword.

Why 1974 to 1992? Downtown writing lacks a spectacular beginning blast, but a timeline can be scribbled. Before these writers, there were the Beats and the New York School poets. Those camps were influential, but not a part of the scene that ultimately flowered in the '80s. The book begins in the early 1970s, when artists and writers started flocking to the Downtown for low rent and space to work. In 1973 and 1974 Kathy Acker began publishing a number of hyper-Sadian texts as the Black Tarantula, circulating them via the mail and by hand. Her concerns with the body and language and the anonymous, cut-up, fanzine style in which she presented her subject matter presented an important template for works to come, separating her from the New York School before her and aligning her more closely with punk rock and a nonacademic, nonbourgeois

approach. A similar development took place in 1974–1975 when Sylvère Lotringer founded Semiotext(e), a small independent journal and press that turned theory into something potentially sexy to nonacademics, especially in its 1981 Polysexuality issue.

And 1992? Purists often claim the scene was over by 1988, but that's too early, especially considering the concentration of important novels released in 1987 or the continued publication of major works in zines like *Redtape* through the 1990s. Admittedly, much like the beginning, it is difficult to place an exact moment when one Downtown scene ended and a different sensibility emerged, but by 1992 AIDS had ravaged the Downtown community, high rents had forced most writers and artists from their lofts, and the Seattle-based grunge band Nirvana reached number one on *Billboard*'s album chart with *Nevermind,* temporarily shifting the focus away from New York City as *the* cultural center. Presently, a new generation of young artists, writers, and musicians is moving to Brooklyn.

Regardless of exact beginnings and endings, as a repackaged version of the early Downtown scene becomes an object of fascination for today's art makers and as New York City's cultural scenes

develop and twist into newer and more bizarre and alien shapes, this master copy and primary documentation of what came before will not only provide historical footing; it will also lay down some bread-crumb clues as to how things were, where things may go, and, more importantly, how they got there in the first place.

NOTES

1. Bruce Weber, email to the editor, November 28, 2004.

2. Ron Kolm, email to the editor, April 3, 2005.

3. Edmund Cardoni, "Introduction," *Blatant Artifice: An Annual Anthology of Short Fiction, Visiting Writers, 1984–1985*, edited by Edmund Cardoni (Buffalo: Hallwalls, 1986), 9–10.

4. Joel Rose and Catherine Texier, "Introduction," *Between C & D: New Writing from the Lower East Side Fiction Magazine*, edited by Joel Rose and Catherine Texier (New York: Penguin, 1988), ix, xi.

5. Richard Hell, email to the editor, January 14, 2005.

6. Qtd. in "Greer Lankton: My Life Is Art" by Carlo McCormick, *East Village Eye*, vol. 5, no. 49, November 1984, 19.

7. Ron Kolm, email to the editor, December 10, 2004.

8. Robert Siegle, *Suburban Ambush: Downtown Writing and the Fiction of Insurgency* (Baltimore, Md.: Johns Hopkins University Press, 1989), 1.

PART ONE
THE 1970S

INTRODUCTION TO THE 1970S

THE EARLY 1970s was a time of transition: Richard Nixon resigned in 1974 and the Vietnam War ended a year later. In June 1974 the Loft Law was passed and, accordingly, mostly postwar-born New York City–based artists and writers relocated to the low-rent lofts, tenements, and warehouses of SoHo and the Lower East Side, pecked away at typewriters, organized readings, and published their fictions.

Around these authors, punk rockers also spilled into the streets, sweaty communal crash pads, and eventually the high-end boutiques. Today, fan-boys need only hearken to the Ramones' 1974 CBGB's debut and an oft-documented story unfurls. There is no single analogous event for Downtown writing.

Eileen Myles's first New York reading at CBGB's also occurred in 1974, but that event alone cannot be cited as having jumpstarted Downtown writing. Even devoted fans of New York's underground will he hard-pressed to name a watershed literary moment.

Still, there are some factors that helped establish the zeitgeist. In the early '70s, Kathy Acker as the Black Tarantula took publication into her own hands—combining punk, mail art, Sade, and Charles Dickens—by mimeographing her own words and the appropriated texts of others and passing along the textual assemblage via subscription and to individuals on the artist Eleanor Antin's mailing list. (An excerpt is reprinted on page 31.)

FIRST AVENUE

ST. MARK'S PLACE

ST. MARK'S PLACE

SECOND AVENUE

The area's handsomest houses, with several residents of uptown eminence.

The remainder of the white building seems suspiciously unused. "House of Musical Traditions." Exotic instruments. Upstairs, Charlie Brown. "You're a good man, Charlie Brown."

Woolens   Silks
G. + F. Fabrics, Inc.
Cottons   Notions
"No Smoking"

Pizza stand, pointing north.

Night, people going west.

Now the basement sign reads "Luna Printing Co." Upstairs (Ukrainian): Residence of Wystan Hugh Auden for over thirty years. "Roman Diesnicki, Law Offices." Between them.

Now they publish Trotsky and Nicholai! "Novy Mir." But— In #77, in 1916-7, did Leon Trotsky and Nicholai Bukharin publish "Novy Mir."

Odiferous trees and shrubs, most of them privately planted and fertilized by innumerable dogs.

People are walked at night.

Now a movie house where teenagers out front and the sound of rock inside.

Unmarked building with lively teenagers out front and the sound of rock inside.

At #80 played interminably, "You're a good man, Charlie Brown." Upstairs.

St. Cyril's R.C. (for Slovenes)

Holy Cross Polish National Catholic Church

The German Methodist Church

The first facaded, yet richly brownstones, narrow as churches

A misplaced bodega that does little perceptible business.

All tall bank. Hip clinics.

Remodeled prestigious buildings commanding uptown rents. Most prestigious address "The Eleventh Room" "Tales of Hoffman"

After midnight, snappily dressed couples, mostly black, returning to their parked automobiles.

Between 5 & 7 p.m. girls off in their work clothes, sprint home "to put on something comfortable."

Peter Cooper Nursing Home "Aid for the Feeble" "Comfort for the Aged"

A gay second-storey porch.

The skinniest house here.

Beyond, left, right

Dentists along here.

An ancient lady continuously perched atop a garbage can.

"The Legal Front" "Pomegranate" "The Ham Man" "Kurtas" "Lotus Shop." "Instant Pants" "Scorpiana" "The Him" "Sal, Ann" "Poor Pearl"

Boutiques, mostly in basements, generally too expensive for local folk; their names as striking and transient as rock groups:

Gems Spa — newspapers, ice cream, magazines, drugs (?), egg cream, ci- garettes, candy and telephones — open 24 hours, re- portedly the most profitable store of its kind in N.Y.C.

Where revolutions are most conspic- uously planned.

"Got any spare change?"

"A dime?"

them away.
chase them
cops
until
sitting
on the
sidewalk
people
street people

"(cigarette?)"

East Side Bookstore. Inventory of literate preoccupations; black rock, feminism, astrology, poetry, etc.

A dissonant chorus of honking cars particularly on Saturday night.

Black and white conversing with each other, rather than apart. Integrated.

"Change?"

Klarissabbe picking rather than apart.

Men Women
"Paul McGregor's Hair House"

"Spare en obstacle"

Mary a prostitute, but

"Charles Czalzynski Carroll Adwokat Lawyer Abogado"

Slick with clean windows, neat displays of "hip" clothing and jewelry, 2 or more affluent cruisers-by.

shops selling of

Psychedelicatessen

Under the Circus, also is "The Dom," Polish by ancestry, once a "literary" discotheque, now strictly a "spade" club with jazz and a spruced-up black clientele.

familiar neighbor- hood fixture. Comes, like so much else so foreign, a at first quickly be- seemed vulgarly alien new clientele, and a blue facade, decor, a bright an awning, psyche- delic formed radically by National Home, trans- formerly "The Polish The "Electric Circus,"

Boys and girls more together than apart, all over a psychedelicatessen

St. MARK'S PLACE

Little shops set back from the property line filled with strolling customers — posters, records, buttons, books, art supplies, clothes, art supplies, bowls, ice cream, alco- hol and what-not over a psychedelicatessen. "Change?"

Bus stop going north.

The street's fashion show is a sensual feast. "Change?"

course.

The genuine bums in for hirsute guys, both join- Long-haired girls waiting for merous patrolling police. against cars eyeing the nu- place. subway kids leaning streaming out of "Astor roadside stands, with wide sidewalks land) with wide sidewalks The main drag of head-band

ST. MARK'S PLACE

"Ralph Basel & Co., Kosher Meats & Poultry"

"Main Street to some here, Hell's Hole to others."

"Nick's Pub"
"Chas. Hon's plumbing" "Bath" walking #17 preserves a revival facade, #20 was recently the Schaefzen Gesellschaft, Deutsche-Americanische straight-laced passers-by

ST. MARK'S PLACE

Here do the com- munity's kings and queens hold court, guys who really do resemble gals.

pontificating their messages, coming...here. Intimations of violence explode

The most popular pizza street palace

On February 10, 1971, poet-rocker Patti Smith gave her first reading. It took place at the Poetry Project, where she opened for Gerard Malanga and was accompanied onstage by Lenny Kaye, eventual lead guitarist for the Patti Smith Group. In 1974, Smith signed to a major label; it was the first such contract for the first wave of CBGB's bands. Her debut album, *Horses,* was not released until 1975, but the signing immediately focused media attention on the sounds coming out of the Lower East Side. During the same period of Smith's jump to a major and the release of *Horses,* Sylvère Lotringer founded Semiotext(e), the Ramones inked a deal with Sire, and like Acker author and visual artist Constance DeJong mailed her first novel, *Modern Love,* to subscribers in serial form. A multimedia project, the text was presented as live performances and a radio piece scored by Philip Glass. (In 1977 *Modern Love* appeared as a book on the Standard Editions imprint, an excerpt from which is reprinted on page 39.)

In 1975 DeJong and Acker joined forces at the performance space the Kitchen. DeJong describes the event:

It was the first reading for the Kitchen; their first time presenting writers. Neither Kathy nor I actually read texts. Without consultation we each prepared a performance. Kathy enlisted a number of performers to deliver sections of her text, a kind of ensemble act. The performers were on the floor either sitting or laying on their stomachs. They did read from white pages of paper but no one would call their presentation a reading … Beforehand, I was busy going over my text, recording it and listening to my delivery at my kitchen table and, in the process, inadvertently memorizing thirty minutes of text. Being able to speak text from memory became an idea, a way to produce language in real time; no paper between me and the audience and no end of control to the velocity, volume and syntax of the text.[1]

All of these occurrences contributed to the formation of a punk-lit hybrid, wherein the literary/rock club circuit overlapped in ways it hasn't since. Writers and musicians invaded CBGB's and Max's Kansas City; when the Mudd Club and Club 57 opened their doors, filmmakers, artists, performance provocateurs, and fashionistas mingled. Danceteria, which only lasted from 1982 to 1986, functioned as a multidisciplinary venue during its brief tenure. Straddling the club scene as well as the realm of poetry and performance, Laurie Anderson, Glenn Branca, Richard Hell, Lydia Lunch, Thurston Moore, and Tom Verlaine have become bona-fide taste-making/shifting legends.

Beginning in 1979 Richard Hell's "Slum Journal" appeared in Leonard Abrams's *East Village Eye.* Mixing texts and graphics, Hell used the tabloid format to maximum effect, especially in the April 13, 1980, issue (reprinted here on page 96) wherein an S & M photo of a bound woman's lower body took over the entire page except for a tiny text box at the bottom center. For a time, new *East Village Eye* subscribers received a copy of Glen Branca's *Symphony No. 1* or a sampler including Patti Smith, Richard Hell, and Television. Those who opted for the latter were treated to a shirtless poster of Hell.

Due to his rocker background in Television, the Heartbreakers, and the Voidoids, Hell met some resistance as a writer. Later, in 1992, he teamed up with another rocker/writer Thurston Moore in the Dim Stars, along with Steve Shelley and Don Fleming. But the "Slum Journals" weren't simply a diversion from his bass playing; in fact, Hell has remained as prolific as any author in this book. He initially moved to New York City as a poet and later founded the excellent literary journal *Cuz* and his own press, Cuz Editions, through which he's published the work of Maggie Dubris (one of the editors of *Koff*), Eileen Myles, Ron Padgett, and Nick Tosches, among others. His literary output includes a collection of poems, prose, drawings, and ephemera called *Hot and Cold* and a pair of novels, *Go Now* and *Godlike*.

No-Wave icon and Teenage Jesus and the Jerks frontwoman Lydia Lunch crossed into the literary world through a book of poetry, various collections of her performance texts, and a well-received novel, *Paradoxia*. (An excerpt from Lunch's "Between the Hammer and the Anvil" is reprinted on page 425, in the 1990s section of this collection.)

Other Downtown musicians who contributed to the anticanon include the inimitable GG Allin, Talking Heads' David Byrne, Rhys Chatham, Tony Conrad, Arthur Russell, DNA's Arto Lindsay, memoir-happy members of the Ramones, and Sonic Youth's Lee Renaldo. M. Gira of Swans shows up in early Downtown collections like *Just Another Asshole No. 6*, has a collection of stories and tales called *The Consumer*,

records haunting music as Angels of Light, and runs a successful label, Young God Records. Static member Barbara Ess curated the *Just Another Asshole* series with Glenn Branca, who first performed his Symphony No. 2 in 1982 at St. Mark's Church.

The highest-profile musician in this collection, Thurston Moore, has published his own fanzines, *Killer* and *Ecstatic Peace* (the latter also an experimental record label) and continues to play in Sonic Youth, which collaborated with Lunch on 1984's *Death Valley '69*. Though Sonic Youth has now graduated to stadiums, Moore and bandmates perform in small clubs regularly with various avant-garde musical side projects. Showing Hell-style crossover capabilities, Moore published *Alabama Wildman*, a compilation book of poetry and miscellaneous writings, contributes poetry regularly to Cleveland's poetry-and-noise-fusing Slow Toe press, writes liner notes for bands like Wooden Wand and the Vanishing Voice (and poems for Magik Markers), and has a column with Byron Coley in *Arthur* magazine. In 2005 he edited *Mixtape: The Art of Cassette Culture*.

It could be argued that the fusion of power chords and words started happening here.

NOTES

1. Constance DeJong, email to the editor, April 16, 2005.

FROM *I DREAMT I WAS A NYMPHOMANIAC!:*
IMAGINING (1974) BY THE BLACK TARANTULA

I TOLD the guy I was living with I no longer wanted to fuck him. He told me to fuck or split. Then he started beating me up. I had to split fast. Either I could get a new apartment in New York City or split to California, the only other place I had friends. Either way I needed a lot of money. I was broke.

I was a nice shopgirl, working in Barnes and Noble eight to nine hours a day answering phone-calls. Eighty dollars a week takehome. I was a nice girl earning nice money. Nice money doesn't exist. I needed a lot of money. I figured I could sell my body, a resource open to most young women, not for a lot of money but at least for more than eighty dollars a week and less than eight hours a day. My friends were all respectable (i.e. had minimum money): I couldn't ask them shit. So I opened the back pages of the Village Voice. In less than three hours I became a go-go dancer. A go-go dancer is a strip-tease artist, midway in the hierarchy between a high-class call girl and a streetwalker.

I waited on the corner of 178th and Broadway, near the George Washington Bridge. It was a cold and windy night. A large car, a Chevy or Impala, pulled up; a white hand motioned me to get in. I didn't know if I was going to make money or get raped. I didn't have any choice. A guy got out of the car: a cheap Broadway crook. "Come on, get in the car. We've got a time schedule. Do'ya have an outfit?" he mumbled. Gee, I was scared.

The owner of the bar handed me five quarters and told me to put them in the juke box. Dance to 10 songs, rest an equal amount of time. I did what he told me. When I got off the dance floor, I didn't know what to do, I couldn't see anywhere to escape. I sat at an empty table. It was a crummy bar: all men no women. The men were working-class creeps. A man came up to the table started to talk to me. I told him to go away. The bartender came up to me told me it was my job to talk to the men get them to buy me drinks. He told me I looked terrible. I walked up to the bar sat between two bearable-looking men. Turned out they were younger than me. They told me I was O.K. except my hair-cut made me look like a nigger. I had short curly hair all over my head. The bartender told me he was going to call up my agent to come get me because I was a creep. The men said he shouldn't do that they liked me. My agent told me I needed a costume then I'd be O.K. Gee, I was crying.

It was a sleazy Bronx tenement a high-rise made out of special New York plastic. I thought one of the kids was going to throw a bomb then I'd see a big hole. My agent rang the doorbell again and again. A woman with partly bald head partly grey hair wooshing all over the place dirty nightgown over her body tells us to come in. My agent should stay outside: she doesn't like men. My agent wants to come inside so he does. She tells me to take off all my clothes except for my stockings. Stockings make a girl feel more confident. I have a good body, she touches my breasts, if I work hard, I'll go far. I feel terrific. I tell her I like silver best. She has hundreds of costumes: two bra cups held together by almost invisible elastic, a G-string (or an almost G-string), that is: a triangle of cloth covering the cunt (and part of the asscrack) held together by slightly thicker elastic: all this covered by gorgeous elaborate layers of pearls silver beads silver metal disks. These are the simplest costumes: each one costs eighty dollars.

It's a strange history.

UNTITLED (1973)

THERESA STERN

How come no one forces me to do what I won't do?

All the boys and girls lie down in the boulevard

and hug and cry for a long time

on receipt of my subliminal apology.

The person you don't know whispers goodbye to you on his deathbed

the waves from his eyes caress my swollen back

in return you strip the outer paper from your tongue

revealing the chaw of pulp.

Then I unbuckled his trousers

I saw that he was not a man

Between his legs was the Addams Family mansion

. . . no . . . maybe this is what men look like!

I thought they looked like herons entangled in airplane propellors

and I'm never wrong

3170 **BROADWAY** (1974)

PEDRO PIETRI

we took the elevator to our eyes
we got off at the wrong floor
we knocked on the wrong door
we enter without moving an inch
we hear the apartment bleeding
we jump out the window of our mind
we wake up inside mail boxes
we are attacked by airmail stamps
we hide inside our back pockets
we swallow obsolete calendars
we discover snow in our sweat
we get bored with so much darkness

the radio that was not on
was playing loud enough
to be heard from the 1st floor
to the 21st floor & the roof
but all the tenants had turned
on their television sets
and stereo record players
at full blast from the 1st day
they moved into the projects
making hearing impossible

in a matter of seconds
our father which art in the backseat
of a lincoln continental limousine
known in some circles as Mister Clean
will give the housing authority
the middle finger sign
and all the tenants will find
themselves on the 21st floor
and the only way you will be able
to see the streets again

will be by jumping out the window

isolation is the name of the game
you do not know
your next door neighbors name
your next door neighbor
does not know your name
you have been living on
the same floor since this
so-called promisedland opened
the only way you get to know each other
is after one or the other dies

everybody has a headache
in these human file cabinets
known as the housing projects
when the night comes
those who were not mugged
were stuck in the elevator
for a couple of hours
others fell down the stairs
chasing their minds
to bring it back to jesus
the bookie is the only one
who loves the projects

you go to sleep on the 17th floor
you wake up on the 13th floor
you walk down to the 7th floor
to borrow aspirins from somebody
who borrowed them on the 15th floor
from somebody who found them
on the 20th floor after somebody
on the 8th floor lost them

the night they lost everything
playing cards on the 2nd floor

muggers and junkies and pushers
succeed in life in the projects
the housing police cannot stop them
because the housing police
does not exist everyday of the week
they only come around once
every other ten weeks to tell you
not to stand in the lobby
of the building you have been living
and dying in for the past fifteen years

when the elevators
are finally fixed
they only function properly
for a couple of minutes
before the buttons
start hallucinating again
and you find yourself moving
up & down & sidewards
when the elevator stops
you get off on the same floor
you got on
like you have to get high
on something else
if you want to get
to the floor you came down from

somedays the sun comes out
& the tenants say to each other
"nice day" & nothing else
the only other time they talk
to each other is to find out
what number came out   somebody
is always attending a funeral

in the projects   death brings
the tenants closer to each other
until whoever died is buried

the pope
will never go near
the projects
regardless of
how many tenants
are members
of his fan club
the housing authority
employees will
not be caught dead
in the projects
after the sun
that never came out
goes down and
the deadly
weapon wind
blows backwards

from the 1st floor
to the 21st floor
everybody is saving money
to move to a better neighborhood
because the buildings
look worse than the buildings
they moved you out from
the promisedland
has become the garbage can

THE AGE (1975)

EDWARD SANDERS

This is the Age of Investigation, and every citizen must
      investigate! For the pallid tracks of guilt and death,
      slight as they are, suffuse upon the retentive
      electromagnetic data-retrieval systems of our era.
      And let th' investigators not back away one micro-unit
      from their investigations — for the fascist hirelings
      of gore await in the darkness to shoot away the
      product of the ballot box

      And if full millions do not investigate, we will see the
      Age of Gore, and the criminals of the right will rise up
      drooling with shellfish toxin, to send their berserker
      blitz of mod manchurian malefactors mumbling with
      motorized beowulfian trance-instructions, to chop
      up candidates in the name of some person-with-a-serotonin-
      imbalance's moan of national security

And this is the Age of Investigative Poetry, when verse-froth
      again will assume its prior role as a vehicle for the
      description of history—and this will be a golden era
      for the public performance of poetry: when the Diogenes
      Liberation Squadron of Strolling Troubadours and Muckrakers
      will roam through the citadels of America to sing
      opposition to the military hit men whose vision of the
      U.S.A. is a permanent War Caste & a coast-to-coast cancer
      farm & a withered, metal-backed hostile America forever

And this is the age of left-wing epics with happy endings! of
      left-wing tales/movies/ poems/ songs/ tractata/ manifestoes/
      epigrams/calligrammes/graffiti/neonics and Georges
      Braque frottage-collage-assemblage Data Clusters which
      dangle from their cliffs the purest lyricals e'er
      to hang down a hummingbird's singingbird throat

This is the age of Garbage (pronounced Garbájzhe). And we're not talking here about
　　　Garbage Self-Garbage—but an era of robotic querulousness—
　　　how at the onset of a time when the power of a country
　　　is up for grabs, the Garbage Hurlers, attired in robes
　　　of military-industrial silk, arise to hurl, as swift
　　　in their machinations as a chorus in the Ice Capades:

and none of us will trudge this era without a smirch-face
　　　waft of thrilly offal dumped upon our brows of social
　　　zeal—and the pus-suck provocateurs armed with orbiting
　　　plates of dog vomit will leap at us while we stand
　　　chanting our clue-ridden dactyls of KNOW THE NEW FACTS
　　　EARLY! Know-the-new-facts-early, know-the-new-facts
　　　early! And do not back away one micro-unit just because
　　　some C.I.A. weirdomorph whose control agents never ended
　　　WW II invades your life with a mouthful of curdled
　　　exudate from the head of the Confederate Intelligence
　　　Agency &

This is the Age of Nuclear Disarmament—when the roamers of
　　　the Hills join hands with the nesters of the Valley
　　　Wild, to put an end to nuke puke w/ a zero-waver total
　　　transworld Peace Walk—that the War Caste wave no
　　　more their wands of plutonium and the dirks
　　　in the nuclear mists no longer chop
　　　　　　　　up the code of life

And this is the Age of the Triumph of Beatnik Messages of Social
　　　Foment Coded into the Clatter of the Mass Media over
　　　20 Years Ago!　　Ha! Ha! Ha! How do we fall down to salute
　　　with peals of Heh heh hehhh! That the Beats created change
　　　without a drop of blood!

In 1965 it was all we could do to force-cajole the writers
　　　for *Time* Magazine not to reinforce the spurious Anslinger
　　　synapse, that pot puff leads to the poppy fields—
　　　but now the states are setting hemp free! Ten years of
　　　coded foment! Heh! Heh! Heh!

Yesterday: the freeing of verse

Today: pot

Tomorrow: free food in the supermarket

Heh! heh! heh!

And finally let us ne'r forget that this is the Age of Ha Ha Hee!
    Ha Ha Hee is such a valuable tool
    in the tides of social transformation!

    Ha Ha Hee will set you free from worm-farm angst
    Ha Ha Hee will even curdle the fires of jealousy!

    Ha Ha Hee outvotes the Warrior Caste
    Ha Ha Hee doth whelm the self-devouring quarrel

    Ha Ha Hee peals out through all the cosmos
        mandorla'd with

            poet angels holding Plato's
            7 single syllables
            in a tighter harmony than the
            early Beach boys—

This is the poets' era
and we shall all walk
crinkle-toed upon the smooth
cold thrill of Botticelli's shell.

            Written for
            the New Year's
            Reading at
            St. Mark's Church
            January 1, 1975

MODERN LOVE

CONSTANCE DE JONG

STANDARD

EDITIONS

FROM *MODERN LOVE* (1975/7)

CONSTANCE DeJONG

PART ONE

Everywhere I go I see losers. Misfits like myself who can't make it in the world. In London, New York, Morocco, Rome, India, Paris, Germany. I've started seeing the same people. I think I'm seeing the same people. I wander around staring at strangers thinking I know you from somewhere. I don't know where. The streets are always crowded and narrow, full of men. It's always night and all strangers are men.

I hear talk of a new world. Everywhere I go: eco-paleo-psycho-electro-cosmo talk. Of course, men do all the talking. I don't get the message, my ears ache; my eyes are falling out, I don't see these street talkers as the makers of a new world. Anyway, they're not real losers. And the new world's an old dream.

They said, "Wait till you're twenty-seven, then you'll be sorry." I'm twenty-seven. I'm not sorry.

Who are "they"? Not answered.

And the new world? I've heard tell; seen no evidence; been looking.

I saw people in India with no arms, no legs, no clothes, no food, no money, no place, no nothing but other people, people, people. Real losers. I talked to very serious people in Europe who were, were not my own age because they saw themselves in perspective. More abstract losers, but losers just as real. They saw: a convergence in the distant present coming out of the recent past: themselves. I saw the historical bogeyman coming around the corner hustling for a place to crash. It scared me, made me run around Paris, Rome, Germany being noisy. Being pushy. Slamming around making up stories as fast as I could go. "The world spins and I go around in circles ha ha I'm a dizzy blonde gibbering off into the sun setting behind the

Arc de Distrust. . . ." Running off at the mouth. At the feet. Here today, not there tomorrow, gone leaving no incriminating evidence of my unpopular half-baked world view. That's a good girl.

"I wonder if I'll always be alone," I think to myself.

The misfits I've been seeing everywhere, they aren't real losers. They all have bank accounts: can afford to be losers. I'm broke. What's the exchange rate for my wealth of information? I'll drop pearls on the sidewalk, the page. I'll be drippy: "The new world's an old dream and I'm tired of dreams. Come upstairs," I whisper in the ears of passing strangers.

I was a seven-year dreamer. . . .

I think I have to have a past. I think too much. A common malady. I make a vow: restrain yourself, become more or less observant, use fewer French and/or fancy words. I have to watch myself. I was a seven-year dreamer. I live two, three, four, multiple lives; I get distracted in these crowded narrow passages. I have to watch myself; it's not safe for a woman to be alone on the streets. Have to get off. I'll take someone home. "Hey honey, come up to my place, I'll show you my best recipes. Do you have a lot of cash?" Shameless at last. It's 1975 and I can say and do anything I want. I want to prove this. Obviously, by saying and doing anything I want. "Hey honey. . . ."

I want this guy to fit into my plans. I wonder, "Maybe he's a murderer, a cop." I'll find out:

"Do you spell 'they' with a capital or a small 't'?" I ask.

He's grinning. "All caps, toots."

Whew. He got my message. He's not one of them. Two misfits. Just like I planned it. I call him Roderigo, my favorite romantic name. All strangers are men with romantic names. And romantic pasts.

We're in my room. I think I have to prove something, I don't know what. I have to make up my mind: two cells collide and twenty-seven years later I'm sitting on my Persian rug. With Roderigo. Now I have a past. Now Roderigo will see me like I want. I want Roderigo to think I'm fabulous. I want to be like broken glass on the sidewalk; diamonds on black velvet; glitter against the ground. It turns out I want to control people. That's no good. I better watch myself.

See me. See me. From behind, sideways, above, below, from every angle I'm the same. See, I'm every-where; no different from the rug the furniture the floor ceiling walls bookshelves. See how it all fits to-gether. Everything from the ritual objects to the easy chair is immaculately arranged, sort of a Victorian-style shrine. There's no room for accident, or an event. That's no good.

I've been seeing too many artists. I can't go through life looking at how objects are colored, cut out, and arranged. I'm no painter.

I am wearing a red sweater. Holding a blue cup. Sitting on a Persian rug. This is where I belong. This room is self-sufficient, the universe. Everything can take place here, I have everything I need: I live here.

"I can see right through you, baby. I could write your diary," says Roderigo.

I'm shattered. I don't want to be like broken glass. I don't want to be a metaphor.

We're in my room. I can do anything I want. I want Roderigo. I want him to do everything to me. I want him to feel easy with me and my possessions and my burning desires. I have to turn my self and my place inside-out so he'll enter into the deep, dark, hidden secretive, mysterious, fabulous magic inner meanings of my life. So he'll disappear. With me.

"Take this cup: it's a magic vessel that transmits legends from lip to lip. Hold it next to your ear and listen to the sweet rustle of the mysteries of the universe as they unfold. Hear the sweet angel voices come across the ages, hear the thunder. Sit on this rug: it's been handed down from generation to generation. Whole lifetimes leap up from every stain, every worn spot. Sit over here where Lady Mirabelle dropped her wine glass fainting in ecstasy into the arms of Monsieur Le Prince. See this sweater: it's my favorite. I bought it from an old lady at the Paris flea market who sold gypsy scarves and fuzzy sweaters. It's a sacred red. A deep, dark red to match the color of the blood that's zooming through my veins."

Two cells collide and twenty-seven years later I come back with Roderigo. I want him to feel at home. I'll make some coffee.

"I'll make some coffee. You make yourself at home."

"Okay."

Roderigo leans against the wall. His fingers are twitchy. There are colors around his head. He reaches without reaching. I turn without turning, we yes each other without speaking, then we fuck like maniacs. I have no graphic images. Roderigo does everything to me. He touches me everywhere. We do everything from behind, sideways, above, below. I come from every angle. I never had it so good; he says it's the same for him.

"I gotta go now," says Roderigo. "Maybe I'll see you around."

That's modern love: short, hot and sweet.

I want to tell you my life story. It's a very interest-ing story. One midnight I was transported all at once from my solitude in La Soho by a stranger who came tapping at my door. His name's Monsieur Le Prince. For seven years I'd been . . .

"You don't have to tell me anything. I can see right through you. I could write your diary. I feel like I've known you all my life. Don't talk. Come next to me," Roderigo whispers.

He reaches without reaching, I turn without turning, we yes each other without speaking, then we tumble together, we disappear together, down down down the deep dark, magic mysterious love tunnel. I have no graphic images. He reaches, I turn, then we fuck. He reaches, I turn, then we fuck. He reaches, I turn then we fuck. He reaches, I turn then we fuck. He reaches I turn then we fuck.

People used to tell me, if you keep on writing maybe you'll make a name for yourself. They were right: My name's Constance DeJong. My name's Fifi Corday. My name's Lady Mirabelle, Monsieur Le Prince, and Roderigo, Roderigo's my favorite name. First I had my father's name, then my husband's, then another's. I don't know, don't want to know the cause of anything. They said, "You'll see when you're thirty." When I was thirty I was standing at the Gate of India. I saw nothing. I'm still thirty. I want to tell you my life story.

First I had the name John Henry. Until I was born, I was a boy: a typical father's assumption. Then I became my father's second choice, a very romantic name. Then I took my husband's, now another's name. I'm still writing. Obviously, nothing's been changed. I keep on seeing the same people everywhere I go. I go up and down, burning with the desires of my age. Flames leap up at every corner. Die down, flame up. I drop my control and my vow, my pretensions for inner and outer order. Ashes swirl around my feet as I tiptoe out the door. The door,

my doors all open to the light. Are passages into the heart, the substance. It's an emotional association.

I was wandering around Soho one night. The streets were very crowded: it must have been Saturday. People were walking in twos and threes, laughing, talking, going from bar to bar. I was looking at the books in a window display, thinking to myself. People were shouting to each other: "Hey, Henri!" "Hello, Pablo, how's it going?" "Hey, there's Guillaume and Marie." "How ya doing, Gertrude? Are you coming to Rousseau's party?" "Seen Eric? What's doing with him anyway? I hear he left town." Dark currents darted around the street. Flickering colors, big shadows, vapory voices brushed against me. Brushed over me. I felt the wool against the back, the blood against the vein; my head swelled with circles inside of squares, intricate structures, rhomboids, cups of coffee, pieces of furniture, parts of bodies, lists, broken-off sentences. . . . I saw Roderigo duck around a corner. He's out looking for a little coke and sympathy: his name's Mick Jagger. It ain't me you're looking for, babe. He thinks modern love isn't worth repeating. I think I saw Roderigo. It must have been my imagination. Anyway, he never was very interested in my fucking visions.

One midnight I was transported all at once from the depths of my solitude by a stranger. . . .

Tap. Tap. Tap.

"Lady Mirabelle?"

"Why yes," I answered.

"I hope I'm not intruding. But, I happened to be passing by and, noticing the light in your window, I thought . . ."

At first I had difficulty placing him. He appeared to be of Oriental extraction. A Tartar, or perhaps a Persian. We spoke in French. He explained that he'd seen my light burning as he passed beneath my window. It was the only bright spot on the otherwise dreary Rue Fermat. It was a long walk to his apartment on the Rue du Dragon and he thought perhaps he could rest for a moment and perhaps if it wasn't too much trouble have a bit of wine to refresh himself before he continued on his journey home. As my maid had just brought up my nightly claret, I easily obliged the stranger without having to disturb the slumbering household. Before I knew it, I had charmed the pants off Monsieur Le Prince. I heard the faint rustle of my taffeta skirts as we slid—meeting by chance, but loving as if by design—into each other's arms.

Many's the time while walking in the gardens or sitting in the window or attending to one of my endless tasks, my sewing, my letters, my salon, my accounts, my friends; many's the time I've been startled by the memory of this amorous event in my life. It catches me from behind. I feel his touch. I turn. Then I tumble down, disappear into the dark passage. I know this passage. I know where it leads. Still, I cannot restrain myself. My daily efforts, the trivial tasks and the tidy lessons, all my orderly preoccupations, everything scatters. My pearls are soap bubbles floating over the roof and out to sea. I watch them vanish; let them go. Only a child would pursue these fleeting visions. I know better. I know it's a transparent allusion. I see through it: can see a diamond burning in the night. Diamonds are forever. I can always turn to them when everything else seen, heard, touched begins to make me blind, deaf, insensitive. When I feel his fatal touch, then I let myself go. I return. I feel the hand against my heart, a tapping at my door. I don't have to keep on chipping and polishing and guarding my treasure, my memory. I have a permanent impression. Monsieur Le Prince is inside me. Forever. There's a place where the emotions are intact. A room. A permanent association. Whole days scatter

into the blue when Monsieur Le Prince reaches out: then my favorite lover condenses into a single, mythical moment. An instant can be an event. An instant can be a fatal event. An instant is sufficient. I'm not fooling: that's all it took. All at once my heart became a place full of light. All aflame. A brilliant shine. A star. It's still a heart. It's 1975 and I'm not sorry I've died for love.

Many years have passed and time after time I startle over. I use fancy words to envelop my vivid impressions. I get wrapped up in the ageless pursuit of naming an emotion as if it were an object. Monsieur Le Prince stands for love, truth, wisdom, honesty, etc. His memory, my memory jumps up involuntarily, like a reflex. It startles me. Makes me run through my inside-out versions of love of death of. . . . "Even in this day and age," I say to myself. Even in this age of insight? I say, yes, there's still room for a love story. I don't need, don't want to need a perfect, sacred explanation. I always go where these abrupt passages lead me. Rainbow-colored bubbles swirl into the sky. I told Monsieur Le Prince, words are just rollers that spread the emotions around. As for me, I have everything I need: diamonds are always bright. They're reliable. It's true: I'll gladly drop down when the trap door springs open at a touch. I go down once, twice, countless times. It's always pretty interesting. And, that's sufficient. No. I'm not sorry I once died for love. Now, I have a second, a better chance.

Here's the story. I'm in my room. It's a long sentence: I sit, I stand, I drift back and forth between these walls, flitting over the floorboards, wearing myself to a shadow, comparing myself to the flickering gleams on the ceiling the walls, attempting to merge with the background, trying to become anonymous, hoping to stay forever in the total freedom of obscurity, I'm imprisoned, dreaming hard. This goes on for seven years. It was a long sentence. I'm recalling it as a time of solitary refinement. I'm free to say whatever I want. I tell Roderigo, I want to be a guard at the gate of indecision. Want to know the cause of everything, all things. I've an inkling he doesn't get my drift. He doesn't have time on his hands. No time for long pretty intricate explanations. He twitches when I talk. Probably all he ever thinks about is fucking. I think he's fabulous, I want to find him flawless, I'm ready to kneel at his feet. I think men tire me. I'll show him. I place you in a picture flooded with moonlight. That's where you belong. Permanently framed in a romantic episode. I'll tell you more.

There are two strangers in the room. Three strangers in the room. In the seven-year dream, I two, four, six; I multiply. The room's crowded. I'm running around in hot pursuit, attempting to find, attempting to be the originating cause of everything. I don't believe in numbers. I'm after a total effect, wanting to see how it all fits together. There are presences in the room. Vague. But presences just the same. As real as numbers. They're my visitors: station masters, generals, writers, artists, countless corpses, editors, nurses, lost children, various animals, a long procession of the living and dead. I don't actually look for them. They come to me like guests who have rights of a sort. They come, I accept them. When they sit, I stand. When I talk, they listen. When they stand, I turn around. When I look, they stare back. When I've had enough of this, I create situations in which they'll leave me: I tell them, "My name's Étoile, I come from France, I live here in the Eiffel Tower, I'm the center of the universe, ha ha I'm a star, the world revolves around me." When they leave me, I wonder if I'll always be left alone.

I think, "Maybe I read too much."

One day I exclaim, "I'm surrounded by fools and foolish ideas! I want a better world!" I'll make up a better image. This is my idea: I place the earth on the back of an enormous elephant in order to hold it up in space. The elephant is supported by a tortoise which in turn is floating in a sea contained in some sort of vessel.

That was one day's total effort.

The next day, I'm sitting, reading a book on Hindu mythology. I read: "In Hindu mythology, the earth is placed on the back of an enormous elephant in order to hold it up in space. The elephant is supported by a tortoise, which in turn is floating in a sea contained in a vessel." That was depressing.

I don't like seeing myself in other words; I feel foolish.

The next day, I am sitting, standing, drifting around, moaning and sighing, feeling sorry talking to myself:

"Will the world come to me or will I go to it?" she said.

"You have to make up your mind," she said.

I flit over to the bookcase. I reach without choosing. I'm reading: "I view her," he said, "with a certain unaccountable excitement, living in her tower, supplied with telephones, telegraphs, phonographs, wireless sets, motion picture screens, slide projectors, video monitors, glossaries, timetables, and bulletins. She has everything she needs. She wears an Egyptian ring. It sparkles when she speaks. For a woman so equipped, actual travel is superfluous. Our twentieth century has inverted the story of Mohammed and the mountain; nowadays the mountain comes to the modern Mohammed."

I hated that description.

I read it; felt no deep emotion; the dream ended.

In other words, I saw the light.

That night, I sat at my desk writing: (1) THE ECLECTIC IS NOT UNIVERSAL. (2) NOT ALL COINCIDENCES ARE INTERESTING. These were the daily lessons: seven years wrapped up in two sentences. I better think this over. I worry that my messages are cryptic; too obscure and/or too personal. I pinned them to the refrigerator door and went out for a walk.

It must have been a Saturday. Everyone was on the street. I ran into Jorge Luis Borges. A likely coincidence. . . .

I ran into Bob Dylan.

I ran into Jorge Luis Borges and asked him if it was okay to quote him in my book.

"Is it okay, Jorge? I want to use the part about the person who's confined. You know, the modern dreamer. I'm writing a prison novel. I'll just make a few changesfrom your original words. Add a little here and there. What do you say? Is it okay?" "It's okay, darling. Many times I've said, 'All collaborations are mysterious.' Just remember, always write what you know about." "Okay."

I'll write about the past. In the past, everything is immaculately arranged. All things have the same value: people, books, events, chairs, numbers, me, love, New York are of equal value. Are interchangeable. A little of this, a little of that; everything is coincidental, is interconnected. It's so simple, it all fits: events are things; people are things; objects are colored, cut out, arranged; are simply things following from/ leading to other things. That's all very nice. I hate this dream. This modern dream, love of complexity. I had this dream. It had me. In it I become a fixture in a crowded, airless setting. No different from the rug, the furniture floor ceiling, etc. My head was filled with intricate nonsense which made all coincidences so interesting. I'm remembering: "There are stains and worn spots all over this rug. If I connect the individual marks, I can map the generations who walked off their lives across this Persian landscape. I can graph

an image of the procession of life. It'll be called The Shape of Time. I'll be famous for my insight." My visions images ideas, my vows, my burning desires, my thinking, my occupation: I was dreaming hard.

"Hey, honey, I want to tell you a secret."
"Great."
"See this cup? I want you to have it."
"Is it worth anything?"
"All you ever think about is money!"
"That's right."
"Don't you know money isn't everything? You're famous and that's what counts."
"Right."
"Can't you just appreciate my precious cup? I want you to have it because it means something very special to me."
"Oh."
"Because you're someone special to me. You're my real friend. Do you know what I mean? Do you know how hard it is to find a really dependable, true blue friend in the world?"
"Sure I know. That's no secret."
"Oh."
"I gotta go now." I don't know: "Can a young girl really find happiness in the world trusting only me and objects?"

When he leaves me, I invent reasons to keep on living. I remember people always told me, write what you know about. I know a lot of artists. I'm surrounded by people making art; misfits like myself. I don't really believe this. Actually, I believe there's something to art. And, I even know what it is. Art is . . .

"No, no, no!" scream the editors. "SEX. REVOLUTION. VIOLENCE. The big stuff. All caps, sweetheart. We can't sell art, your friends, your

crummy insights. Listen, angel, don't you want to
make a name for yourself?"

"Yes," I murmur. "I want a lot of money. But
what's a poor girl to do?"
"Come upstairs," they said. "You'll see."
The People are screaming, "No! We want
Education, Food, Houses. We want our rights!"
People are shouting, "Don't sell out to the Man."
"Yes, yes, you're right, your rights," I stutter,
I stumble. I have to run run run, have to work
hard, have to get off the streets. Threats and
accusations and insults rain down; my head swims;
the street's whirling with blood and dirty water,
broken-up furniture and parts of bodies. It's dark,
it's crowded, I'm running fast, it's a narrow escape.

Gosh, I made it. I'm safe in my room. (1) The Universe
is a mythological expression: I read that somewhere.
(2) The universe is a great big soap bubble that starts
in a jar, ends up in bubble heaven. There are people
up in Nova Scotia who send their kids to Bubble Island
instead of college. Let them go; maybe they'll have a
better chance. Maybe not. I'm no parent. Me, I'm self-
sufficient. That means: I'm off in some remote corner.
Pacing off the safety zone. Wearing myself to a shadow.
Holding onto my precious integrity, worrying: I can't
spend my whole life trusting only artists. I need to see
more of the world, to get in touch with better energy.
Can I take a big chance? Can I afford a ticket to India?

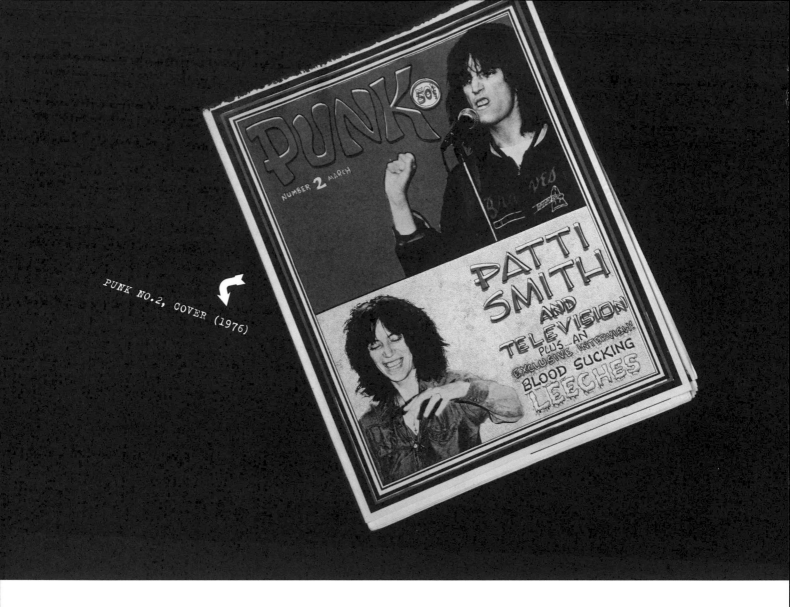

PUNK NO.2, COVER (1976)

PISS FACTORY (1974)

PATTI SMITH

Sixteen and time to pay off
I get this job in a piss factory
inspecting pipe
forty hours, thirty-six dollars a week
but it's a paycheck, Jack
it's so hot in here, hot like Sahara
you could faint in the heat
but these bitches are just too lame to understand
too goddamned grateful to get this job
to know they're getting screwed up the ass
all these women they got no teeth or gum or cranium
and the way they suck hot sausage

but me well I wasn't sayin' too much neither
I was moral schoolgirl, hard-working asshole
I figured I was speedo motorcycle
I had to earn my dough, had to earn my dough
but no you gotta relate right
you gotta find the rhythm within
floor boss slides up to me and he says
"Hey sister, you just movin' too fast,
you screwin' up the quota,
you doin' your piece work too fast,
now you get off your mustang sally
you ain't goin' nowhere, you ain't goin' nowhere."

I lay back. I get my nerve up. I take a swig of Romilar
and walk up to hot shit Dot Hook and I say
"Hey, hey sister it don't matter
whether I do labor fast or slow,
there's always more labor after."
she's real Catholic, see.
she fingers her cross and she says
"There's one reason, there's one reason.
You do it my way or I push your face in
we knee you in the john if you don't
get off your get off your mustang Sally
if you don't shape it up baby."
"Shake it up, baby. Twist & shout"
oh would that I could will a radio here.
James Brown singing "I Lost Someone"
the Jesters and the Paragons
Georgie Woods—the guy with the goods
and Guided Missiles
But no, I got nothin', no diversion, no window,
nothing here but a porthole in the plaster
where I look down at sweet Theresa's convent
all those nurses, all those nuns scattin' 'round
in their bloom hoods like cats in mourning
oh to me they, you know,
to me they look pretty damn free down there
not having to smooth those hands against hot steel
not having to worry about the inspeed
the dogma the inspeed of labor
they look pretty damn free down there,
and the way they smell, the way they smell
and here I gotta be up here smellin'
Dot Hook's midwife sweat
I would rather smell the way boys smell
oh those schoolboys the way their legs
flap under the desks in study hall
that odor rising roses and ammonia
and the way their dicks droop like lilacs
or the way they smell that forbidden acrid smell

but no I got, I got pink clammy lady in my nostril
her against the wheel me against the wheel
oh slow motion inspection is drivin' me insane
in steel next to Dot Hook—oh we may look the same—
shoulder to shoulder sweatin' 110 degrees
but I will never faint, I will never faint
they laugh and they expect me to faint
but I will never faint
I refuse to lose, I refuse to fall down
because you see it's the monotony that's got to me
every afternoon like the last one
every afternoon like a rerun next to Dot Hook
and yeah we look the same
both pumpin' steel, both sweatin'
but you know she got nothin' to hide
and I got something to hide here called desire
I got something to hide here called desire
I will get out of here, I will get here
you know the fiery potion is just about to come
in my nose is the taste of sugar
and I got nothin' to hide here save desire
and I'm gonna go, I'm gonna get out of here
I'm gonna get out of here, I'm gonna get on that train
I'm gonna go on that train and go to New York City
I'm gonna be somebody, I'm gonna get on that train
go to New York City
I'm gonna be so bad so big
and I will never return
never return, no, never return
to burn out in this piss factory

And I will travel light.
Oh, watch me now.

An oral poem
patti smith
June 6, 1974, version of a piece first drafted in 1970.

dodgems

BLANK GENERATION (1977)

RICHARD HELL

I was sayin let me out of here before I was
even born. It's such a gamble when you get a face.
It's fascinatin to observe what the mirror does
but when I dine it's for the wall that I set a place.

I belong to the blank generation and
I can take it or leave it each time.
I belong to the ——— generation but
I can take it or leave it each time.

Triangles were fallin at the window as the doctor cursed—
He was a cartoon long forsaken by the public eye.
The nurse adjusted her garters as I breathed my first . . .
The doctor grabbed my throat and yelled, "God's consolation prize!"

I belong to the blank generation and
I can take it or leave it each time.
I belong to the ——— generation but
I can take it or leave it each time.

To hold the TV to my lips, the air so packed with cash
then carry it up flights of stairs and drop it in the vacant lot.
To lose my train of thought and fall into your arms' tracks
and watch beneath the eyelids every passing dot.

I belong to the blank generation and
I can take it or leave it each time.
I belong to the ——— generation but
I can take it or leave it each time.

RICHARD HELL &
THE VOIDOIDS

Pic: Roberta Bayley

I hear in the distance prolonged shrieks of the most poignant agony.

"Heaven grant that his birth be not a calamity for his country, which has thrust him from its bosom. He wanders from land to land, hated by all. Some say that he has been a victim of some special kind of madness since childhood. Others believe that he is of an extreme and instinctive cruelty, of which he himself is ashamed, and that his parents died of grief because of it. There are those who maintain that in his youth he was branded with an epithet and that he has been inconsolable for the rest of his existence because his wounded dignity perceives there a flagrant proof of the wickedness of mankind, which manifests itself during their earliest years and grows continually. This epithet was The Voidoid!"

I hear in the distance prolonged shrieks of the most poignant agony.

"They add that night and day without rest nor respite horrible nightmares cause him to bleed through the ears and mouth; and that ghosts sit at the head of his bed and, driven despite themselves by an unknown force, fling in his face, now softly, now in tones like the roar of battle, and with implacable persistence, that loathsome and persistent epithet, which will perish only when the universe perishes. Some say that love brought him to this state; or that his cries are the expression of remorse for some crime, shrouded in the night of his mysterious past. But most think that he is tortured by incommensurable pride, as Satan was, and that he would like to be God's equal."

I hear in the distance prolonged shrieks of the most poignant agony.

Lautréamont

with the ERASERS and the GHOSTS
at CBGB'S April 20, 21, 22
315 Bowery @ Bleecker 982 4052   Thursday, Friday, Saturday

IT'S ALL TRUE (1979)

RICHARD HELL

To Orson Welles, Knut Hamsun, and Edgar Allen Poe

The train I arrived on that early Autumn night might as well have been a bicycle—I was the only passenger getting off, I felt anxious and awkward as I would have on a bike, and, most of all, I've always had a strong sense of fantasy.

It was very late at night, though comfortably warm, and I began walking away from the center of the small village towards the hilly forest that surrounded it. I wasn't exactly afraid in the unfamiliar darkness but my senses felt extraordinarily acute. Actually I was never so happy to be completely alone and a stranger. I'd taken the ride from New York on an inspired whim and didn't know where I'd gotten to. Tears came to my eyes once or twice simply because there was nothing to prevent them from doing so. I was glad to be still capable of sensitivity.

I was following a grassy path in the open misty woods. The moon was very bright. Ahead of me I saw an animal. It was a young doe but it actually had antlers! And it was white. Sexually mutated and albino as well! I want with all my heart for you to believe that this is really true. A thoughtful and sophisticated human mind or one that's utterly naive realizes that anything it can conceive must exist. (The universe is certainly as large as a human mind.[1]) But I won't humiliate myself any further with pleas for your confidence. The highest art form is the meditative joke.

I fell for that doe the minute I laid eyes on it. I've never been able to fall in love in public or with a creature that can talk. This is my innermost self . . . but it doesn't take much courage to reveal inasmuch as I admit I realize you're not likely to take it very seriously. I approached the pale doe with eyes half closed and with very weak feeling knees, as if I were gliding, and the only other muscles moving were in the rise and fall of my chest. The deer gazed at me motionlessly. It gazed at me devoid of tension as if it were invulnerable. Did its brain get the wrong genes too? No, it could never have survived the slightest mental deficiency on top of all the rest. I looked her over and she seemed to be practically aglow with alert intelligence. Considering the handicap of her glaring visibility, not to mention the sad and confusing effect her possession of antlers must

RICHARD HELL &
THE VOIDOIDS AT CBGB'S,
FLYER (1978)

have had on all the other deer, the apparently excellent condition of her health suggested she probably possessed quite *superior* intelligence.

How long shall I dwell on this incident? So many things happened that night. I was never so happy. I gently put my arms around the creamy neck of the calm animal and my head against the soft fur of its side. I stroked it, hardly breathing. I felt completely abstract, as if my being were a force of desire to please the doe. Paradoxically, this feeling increased my own excitement as I found myself automatically further elaborating my act of tenderness toward the exquisite animal with a gentle sexual caress certainly known only among deer until discovered by me in those moments spent engulfed in the dreamy billows of utter sensuality that seemed to clothe the white doe, blurring the boundaries between us and combining and replacing our surfaces with mist. . . . We came at the same time. The doe's vagina would taste like warm folds of liquefying bubblegum and then like lobster-meat drenched in lemon butter sauce. The alternating flavors shifted like shafts of light reflected from the facets of a giant diamond, colored pink. I was never so grateful. I was a flood of gratitude, pleasure and happiness.

As I lay in the grass with the stars overhead, the doe wandered away. Soon after, I arose and continued my walk.

---

1. Could be said to be untrue. There are more "states" of the brain than there are atoms in the universe.

KOFF MANIFESTO

THE ARTISTS. THEY ABANDON THE WORLD
ON YOUR DOORSTEP. THEY SHOW YOU THE THINGS
YOU LIVE AMONG SO YOU MAY KNOW
YOURSELF. THEY COUGH IN YOUR FACE,
THEY SPIT BY YOUR ELBOW. THE ARTISTS.
THEY LEAVE THEIR GARBAGE IN YOUR HALLWAY.
THEY THROW THEIR HEARTS IN FRONT OF THE A TRAIN.
DISEASE IS LOVE TRANSFORMED. THEY
UGH. THEY SPIT IN YOUR SILENT MUSEUMS.
THEY HURL THEIR SOULS IN YOUR
DIRECTION LIKE A
STONE THROUGH

POLISHED GLASS.
THEY DIE IN YOUR
LANDSCAPE. THEY MESS UP YOUR BANQUETS.
YOU CAN'T TURN AWAY. THE ARTISTS.

FROM KOFF NO. 2:
LETTERS TO THE EDITOR
(1978)

Letters to the Editor

March 27 1978

Dear KOFFers,

Hello, I am president (national) of the International Fuck Frank O'hara Movement, & it has come to our x attention that you have misappropriated & otherwise ripped off our slogan, demeaning attitudes, & so forth. However, in the interests of killing off vestigial interest in this (faggot) & paean of the "people" (unverified) we wd gladly join forces for a giant burn-in', or, a suck-THAT-cock-baybee day, or, screw you too you little greeps & if you think yr gonna get away w/ that kinda crap well you gottanother fuckin THINK coming & I for one (2) hope it comes SOON & then you drop dead too you little bastards.

Thank you for yr kind attention to this problem of mutual concern to all of us here at the Baptist Con-vention, & hoping for a speedy resolution of the matt-er,

I am,
Most sincerely,
Yours,

Ms. M. Mancini

* * * * *

Dear Editor:

Ahhh Poetry is life and art is desire in its purest form. One can only marvel at the flawless intersection of distant planes; the sky with the earth, or the 707 with the plunging B-15. I ask you, what is beauty if not this sudden collision of separate entities; where does life lead us if not into death?

Respectfully,
F.F. O'Hara

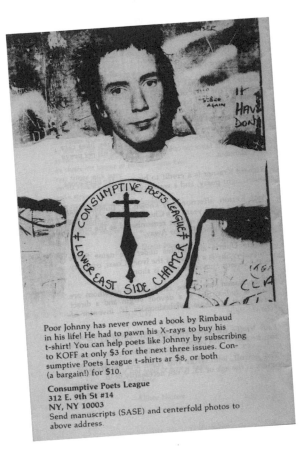

Poor Johnny has never owned a book by Rimbaud in his life! He had to pawn his X-rays to buy his t-shirt! You can help poets like Johnny by subscribing to KOFF at only $3 for the next three issues. Consumptive Poets League t-shirts ar $8, or both (a bargain!) for $10.

Consumptive Poets League
312 E. 9th St #14
NY, NY 10003
Send manuscripts (SASE) and centerfold photos to above address.

I MISSED PUNK (1979)

PETER SCHJELDAHL

FROM KOFF NO. 1:
CONSUMPTIVE POETS
LEAGUE T-SHIRT
(1977)

I missed punk

because my record player was broken

because I was suddenly older

because I can stand only so much distraction

only so much excitement and elation

but mainly because my record player was broken

and none of my friends cared much about new music

(Back in the '60s the thought that I'd missed something

would depress me terribly

Now it's one of those things that happen)

Who are we anyway

any of us

who care about new music or anything?

We are ones who care about their own skins, certainly

about saving them

and not being totally crazy and alone, in pain

We will go through a lot of incidental pain

as long as it keeps us in company

even ridiculous company, which most company is

We certainly don't want to be alone

and this makes us ridiculous

What I want to be is virtuous and noticed

What good is virtue if no one notices?

You don't know it's virtuous unless someone says so

I missed punk

but it brushed past me in the cultural bazaar

and seemed to drop a hint about virtue

being what I'd always thought:

a readiness to lose, to let go

because only in loss is one not ridiculous

(if anyone notices)

Never resist an idea

Never say no to a contradiction

They have come to help you

smash the ego

which always reconstitutes

(and if it doesn't, well,

your worries are over)

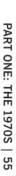

WORDS IN REVERSE (1979)

LAURIE ANDERSON

The following texts are extracts from "Like A Stream" (1978)—a piece for string ensemble, tape bow Instruments, and voice—and "Americans On The Move" (1979)—an extended series for voice, electronics, film, and instruments.

It was the night flight from Houston—almost perfect visibility. You could see the lights from all the little Texas towns far below. I was sitting next to a fifty-two year old woman who had never been on a plane before. Her son had sent her a ticket and said, "Mom, you've raised ten kids, it's time you got on a plane." She was sitting in the window seat, staring out. She kept talking about the Big Dipper and the Little Dipper and pointing. Suddenly I realized she thought we were in Outer Space, looking down at the stars. I said, "You know, I think those lights down there are the lights from little towns."

I saw a photograph of Tesla who invented the Tesla Coil. He also invented a pair of shoes with soles four inches thick to ground him while he worked in the laboratory. In the picture, Tesla was sitting in his lab, wearing the shoes, and reading a book by the light of the long streamer-like sparks shooting out of his transformers.

I went to the movies and I saw a dog thirty feet high. And this dog was made entirely of light. And he filled up the whole screen. And his eyes were long hallways. He had those long, echoing, hallway eyes.

He thought of space that way . . . as something you could fall into . . . Falling for miles . . . sideways.

I met a man in Canada and every day he had the same thing for lunch. He had a carrot and he had a bowl of chocolate pudding. First he ate the carrot into the shape of a spoon. Then he ate the pudding with the carrot shaped spoon. And then he ate the carrot.

There are Eskimos who live above the timber line. There's no wood there for the runners of their sleds. So instead, they use long frozen fish, which they strap to the bottoms of their sleds to slip across the snow.

I saw a man on the Bowery and he was wearing ancient, greasy clothes and brand new bright white socks . . . and no shoes. Instead, he was standing on two small pieces of plywood and as he moved along the block, he bent down, moved one of the pieces slightly ahead and stepped on it. Then he moved the other piece slightly ahead and stepped on it.

You're walking . . . and you don't always realize it but you're always falling. With each step . . . you fall. You fall forward a short way and then catch yourself. Over and over . . . you are falling . . . and then catch yourself. You keep falling and catching yourself falling. And this is how you are walking and falling at the same time.

It was the Fourth of July and a parade of ships from all over the world sailed slowly by. Each was "camou-flaged" by a particular shade of blue, gray, blue-gray or gray-blue. Bright blue for Greece, pale blue for Portugal, silver-gray with white trim for France, steel-gray for the United States. Strictly local colors. Regional ideas about the ocean. No one could have sneak-attacked anywhere but off their own coasts. This is the trouble with the transparency of water.

It was a room full of people. They had all arrived at the same building at approximately the same time. They were all free and they were all asking themselves the same question: **What is behind that curtain?**

(Peter says the thing he likes best about bowling is that you can see exactly what shoe sizes people wear.)

Outside the theater showing the Jane Fonda movie, the lights are bright. The movie is over and the crowd moves slowly out the glass doors. Most of the moviegoers are squinting, temporarily disoriented by three-dimensional space. All told, about seventy Jane Fondas stride through the doors—heads set at jaunty new angles, wise-cracking over their shoulders, brand new memories. Even the short-legged have new, jive, long ones. This is one of the effects of light.

No one has ever looked at me like this for so long. No one has ever **stared** at me like this for such a long time. This is the first time anyone has ever looked at me like this, **stared** at me like this for such a long time . . . for so long . . . for such a long time. . . .

Dan said he was on a plane flying over Greenland with a bunch of Texans. And they had binoculars. They were looking for polar bears down on the ice. White bears down on the white ice. From approximately 10,000 feet. And they said, "Look! I think I see one now! Down there . . . I think I see one down there. Maybe that's one right there! Well, it **could** be one. . . ."

Oh. Oh. I like the way you look. Oh. Oh. Oh. I like the way you talk. Oh. I like the way you walk. But most of all I like the way you look (at me).

In my dream, I am your customer.

He didn't know **what** to do. So he decided to watch the government, and see what the government was doing, and then kind of scale it down to size and run his life that way.

It was an ancient Japanese pot, incised with grooves. Thin-ridged grooves. Grooves all around it. It looked like one of those collapsible paper lanterns. It was an experiment. The pot was placed on a turntable and the turntable began to revolve. A needle was set into the groove. A stereo needle. They were waiting to hear the voice of the potter potting the pot 2,000 years ago. They were hoping the sounds of the potter had somehow been embedded into the wet clay. And stayed there, intact, clinging to the ridges of the clay. The pot turned around and around, like a record being treadled into the third dimension. It turned. They listened. They were listening. Some of them heard an unidentifiable Japanese dialect, rapid and high. Some of them heard high-pitched static. The needle dug into the pot. The needle was getting blunt. More and more blunt. It was that scientific. Blunter and scientific. More blunt . . . and more scientific.

I can draw you so that you have no ears. I can draw you so that you have no ears at all. So that where your ears would be, there is only blank paper.

Looking into his eyes was like walking into a large municipal building. He had perfected an arrangement of his features that suggested International Style architecture: a subtle yet daring blend of American industry's most durable yet flexible materials. His expression seemed to suggest he had just finished saying, "That's the way things will be in the year 2,000."

A certain American sect has completed its research on the patterns of winds, tides, and currents during the Flood. According to their calculations, during the Flood, the winds, tides, and currents were in an overall south-easterly direction. This would then mean that in order for the Ark to have landed on Mount Ararat, it would had to have started out several thousand miles to the west. This would then locate pre-Flood history somewhere in the area of Upstate New York, and the Garden of Eden roughly in Genesee County.

I am in my body the way most people drive in their cars.

I went to a palm reader and the odd thing about the reading was that everything she told me was totally wrong. But she seemed so sure of the information that I began to feel like I'd been walking around with these false documents permanently tattooed to my hands. It was very noisy in the parlor and members of her family kept running in and out. They were speaking a high, clicking kind of language that sounded a lot like Arabic. Books and magazines in Arabic were strewn all over the floor. It suddenly occurred to me that maybe there was a translation problem—that maybe she was reading my hand from right to left instead of left to right. Thinking of mirrors, I gave her my other hand. Then she put her hand out and we sat there for several minutes in what I assumed was some sort of participatory ritual. Finally I realized that her hand was out because she was waiting for money.

A couple of weeks ago, an earthquake was reported in parts of the Bronx and New Jersey. The quake measured roughly 3.5 on the Richter scale and its epicenter was pinpointed to an ancient New Jersey bog. It was the first quake of this magnitude in the area since 1927. The scientists at nearby Princeton, however, missed the quake. They said, "At the time of the earthquake, we were changing our chart paper."

You know, you look a lot like a car. From a distance, say, from a few blocks away, you look exactly like a car. You look like a car from a distance.

The detective novel is the only type of novel truly invented in the twentieth century. In the detective novel, the hero is dead in the very beginning. So you don't have to deal with human nature at all. . . . Only the slow accumulation of facts—of data. You must put the hero together yourself.

In science fiction novels, the hero just flies in at the very beginning. Nothing is explained. He can forge steel with his bare hands. He can walk in zero gravity. And they say, "Look! He can walk in zero gravity!" So you don't have to deal with human nature at all.

I wanted you. . . . And I was looking for you. . . . But I couldn't find you. I wanted you. . . . And I was looking for you all day. . . . But I couldn't find you. . . . I couldn't find you. . . .

He explained his career in filmmaking this way—his mother had always had a hobby of cutting out pictures of hamsters from magazines. She would make frames for the photographs by gluing the wood chips from the bottoms of hamster cages into rectangles. She hung these over the fireplace, which was how he got the Idea for using light.

Dad said last spring there were a lot of geese in his wheat field. The geese grew and the wheat grew; the geese grew and the wheat kept growing. But the geese always grew just slightly faster than the wheat. And all you could see were their long necks waving above the fields of grain. And he said, "Look! They look like cobras out there in that wheat field."

If you can't talk about it, point to it.

Last night I dreamed I was lying in bed sleeping. Last night I dreamed all night that I was just lying in bed dreaming I was sleeping. Last night I dreamed I was sleeping.

When Bobby got back from his first trip to Las Vegas, he said he noticed he was pausing just a little longer than usual after putting his money into parking meters and xerox machines.

TOP STORIES

WORDS IN REVERSE

LAURIE ANDERSON

Words In Reverse, Cover (1979)
Photograph by Marcia Resnick

I met a writer at a cocktail party. This writer used "I" in all his books. He was famous for the way he used "I" in all the books he wrote. At the party, people kept coming up to him and saying, "Gee! I really like your work!" And he kept saying, "Thanks, but I'm not very representative of myself."

I read about a rabbit in a laboratory. The experimenters held the rabbit's head, eyes open, pointed towards an open window. For twenty minutes, staring at the bright window. Then they took a knife and cut the rabbit's head off, peeled the tissue off its eyes, dyed it, and under the microscope, like film, the tissue developed. There were two windows imprinted on the rabbit's eyes. And they said, "Look! This rabbit has windows on its eyes!"

The reason you always think there are fires at riots is because that's the only place at the scene of the riot where there is enough light for the video camera. Actually, maybe this fire is only something happening **near** the riot . . . incidental to the riot. Someone's trash is on fire or someone is having a barbeque near the riot but not as **part** of the riot. But that's why you think there are always fires at riots when sometimes there aren't any fires at riots, or in any case, not at every riot.

Steven Weed wrote in his autobiography that he was asked by the FBI to come in and answer a few questions. He said It wasn't like an interrogation room at all—there were no bright lights. . . . But he said they had it set up so that there was an agent on his right and an agent on his left and they alternated questions so that he had to keep turning his head back and forth, back and forth, to answer them. He said that after a few hours of doing this, he realized that no matter what answer he gave, It always looked like "no" . . . "no" . . . "no." . . .

From "IT Song"—A song for a man and a woman who can't agree on what the word "it" refers to

She said: It looks. Don't you think it looks a lot like rain?

He said: Isn't it . . . isn't it just like a woman?

She said: It's hard. It's just kind of hard to say.

He said: Isn't it just . . . isn't it just like a woman?

She said: It goes. That's the way it goes. It goes that way.

He said: Isn't it just . . . just like a woman?

She said: It takes. It takes one. It takes one to know one.

He said: Isn't it just like . . . just like a woman?

She said: It takes one. It takes one, two. It takes one to know one.

She said it. She said it to know. She said it to no one.

Isn't it, isn't it just, isn't it just like a woman?

***

From "Closed Circuits"—A Song for Voice, Microphone Boom, and Electronics

Well I know who you are baby. I've seen you go into that meditative state. You're the snake charmer, baby. And you're also the snake. You're a closed circuit baby. You've got the answers in the palms of your hands.

Well, I met a blind judge and he said, "I know who you are," and I said, "Who?" And he said, "You're a closed circuit, baby." He said, "You know the world is divided into two kinds of things. There's luck . . . and there's the law. There's a knock on wood that says 'it might' and there's the long arm of the law that says 'it's right.' And it's a tricky balancing act between the two because **both** are equally true. Cause might makes right and anything could happen, que sera sera . . . am I right?"

Well, I saw a couple of hula dancers hula-ing down the street and they were saying, "I wonder which way the tide's gonna roll in tonight?" And I said, "Hold up hula dancers! You know the tide's gonna roll in . . . then it's gonna roll right out again. Cause it's a closed circuit baby. We've got rules for that kind of thing and the moon is so bright tonight."

And don't think I haven't seen all those blind Arabs around. I've seen 'em around! And I've watched them charm that oil right out of the ground. Long black streams of that dark, electric light. And they said, "One day the sun went down and it went way down . . . into the ground. Three thousand years go by . . . and we pump it right back up again. Cause it's a closed circuit baby. We can change the dark into the light . . . and vice versa."

Well I know who you are, baby. I've watched you count yourself to sleep. You're the shepherd, baby. And you're also 1-2-3-hundred sheep. I've watched you fall asleep.

In one of the spacecraft we sent to Jupiter, there were two identical computers—one active and the other quiescent, "asleep," a fail-safe back-up. For some unknown reason, NASA engineers had left out one program. They hadn't told the computers that at blast-off there would be a temporary adjustment period. At the moment of lift-off, the first computer began to get strange read-outs. Nothing seemed to calibrate. What should have read zero read 2,000 and vice versa. Whole systems went out. The computer began to troubleshoot, scanning all systems. ". . . Inoperative . . . Inoperative . . . Inoperative. . . ." It concluded that since **all** systems seemed inoperative, the computer itself was defective. It woke up the second computer which in turn scanned the craft. ". . . Inoperative . . . Inoperative. . . ." It concluded that it **too** was non-functional and that the spacecraft would have to return to earth.

In Houston, programmers suddenly realized the omission. The new message flashed off, brief, simplified by emergency. **#1—Reactivate . . . #2—Resume quiescence . . . Now: Shock; . . . Now: Illusory, temporary inoperative state. . . . Now: Birth.**

It was that way for him. Some days he was flying. Flying easily. White light. Great ideas. He could do no wrong. And then one day, it would all leave him. For no reason, it left and suddenly nothing worked. He burned the toast. Dented the car. He was clumsy. Depressed. And then it would change again. It would be easy again. It changed fast and for no reason, it changed. And he went to the doctor and the doctor said, ". . . chemical imbalance . . ." and gave him some chemicals and cured him. Cured him until it was all evened out—every day same thing. And he was so relieved to find out that "he" wasn't crazy. "It's not me . . . it's my biochemistry. . . ."

When TV signals are sent out, they don't stop. They keep going. They pick up speed as they leave the solar system. By now, the first TV programs ever made have been traveling for thirty years. They are well beyond our solar system now. All those characters from cowboy serials, variety hours, and quiz shows are sailing out. They are the first true voyagers into deep space. And they sail farther and farther, intact, still talking.

And as we listen with our instruments, as we learn to listen farther and farther into space, we can hear them. We listen farther and that is what we hear. They are jamming the lines. We listen and we hear them talking, traveling faster and faster, getting fainter and fainter. And as our instruments get more sophisticated we can hear them better . . . speeding away . . . the sound of speeding away . . . like a phone continuously ringing.

East Village Eye,
Vol. 1 No. 1, Cover (1979)
Artwork: Dana Gilbert;
Christof Kohlhoefer, Art Director:

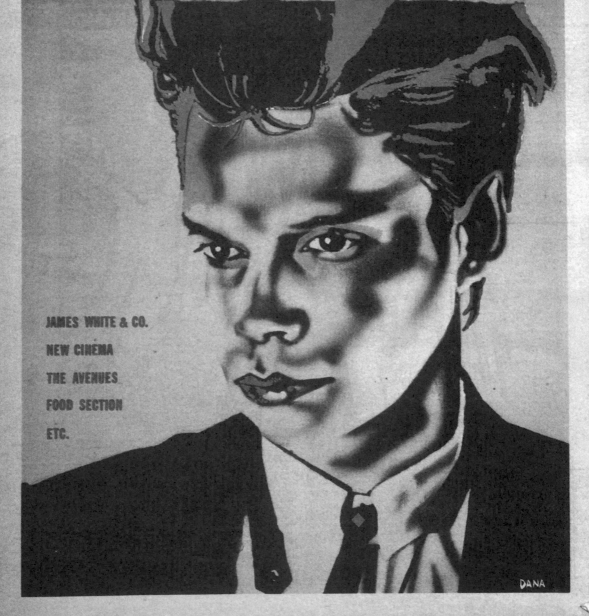

EAST VILLAGE

MAY 1979   VOL. 1 No. 1   "It's all true." $1.00 outside Manhattan $.50

JAMES WHITE & CO.

NEW CINEMA

THE AVENUES

FOOD SECTION

ETC.

DANA

A solitary drawing (printed on a page) the bravery of which provokes a surging and dying desire to cry . . .

Let me remind you of the feeling . . . No, they've all been replaced by

The wall with deliberation raises its eyelids and lowers its rolledback irises to speak.

. . . dreams or personal precision or more likely by a horrible nostalgia, the result of realizing that your worth is completely determined by your appraisal of it . . .

One gets wall-eyed, so blank. While any new presence on the screen is terrific, the attention it demands can render you vulnerable to everyday dangers again . . .

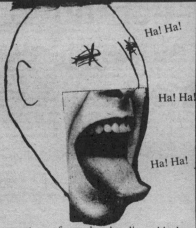

A huge percentage of people who die suddenly are laughing at the time and . . .

Each humans eternity is comprised of the last act of his brain before death.

© Richard Hell

Slum Journal No. 1, First Page, From the East Village Eye (1979), Richard Hell

FROM *EPIPHANIES* (1979)

RICHARD KOSTELANETZ

I.

In white sheets of paper he found the beginning of his story and in black sheets the end/no ambition he had was deeper than his desire to seduce a set of twins/it was his taste to crush his penis between her breasts and come all over her chest and neck/he could make his penis pop up and down with the precision of a baton/he hung crucifixes from her nipples/they peed in the sink, vomited on the tables, and defecated on my rug/you can find epiphanies anywhere, even in garbage cans/he bolted from the table clutching his stomach/knee-deep in sewage, he held his nose as he slogged through the tunnel/he could faintly discern in the desert darkness a naked woman masturbating against a plant/he woke to the pain of a hypodermic needle plunging into his arm/ah, yes/am I getting better, doc; am I getting any better?/profundity in art is impossible without acknowledgment of God/I wish my backside were not so protuberant/in place of the oriental carpets that had once lined his apartment, he now had wall-to-wall foam/an elastic band, ripped from his underpants, was the only bond between/ them/love/I'm probably the only man in the world who can suck himself off/he drank and drank and drank/his daily lunch consisted entirely of rutabagas/for ten whole years there were only blank pages in his diaries/ he buried his chicken-livers in the cold, cold ground/ after courting his demise in innumerable spectacular ways, he died from a fish bone lodged in his throat/ what begins in noise ends in nervousness.

II.

She rearranged her lover's photographs into a continuous chronological order/like other women her size, she liked to push men around/she invariably answered the question before you finished asking it/he taught her about love-making as they shifted gears in the driver-education car/whenever she spread her legs he saw only lavender underpants/she was long where most of us are short, and short where many of us are long/one could see her body bulging, both over and under her girdle/he was the first of her lovers that she could not lift over her shoulders/there appeared to be no limits to her enthusiasm for housekeeping/ she continually spelled *there* "their"/every day she would rewrite the same sentences over and over again, believing they were better every evening, but then deciding otherwise the following morning/the garbage that she touched instantly turned into a pile of gold/always looking for tokens by which to compare herself with others, she estimated that she had gained higher marks, received more extracurricular honors, won richer scholarships and rejected more seductive men, than any of her classmates/"Balls," she said, was her middle name/she tried to radiate sensuality, even in the dark/she changed her outfit seven times a day/as she snuffed her old cigarette with her left hand, she picked up a new one with her right/she envied anyone who had written the novel she was never able to complete/in all her complaints against "men," she actually had in mind only one or two.

III.

When someone strange touched her nipple, she
screamed and screamed and screamed and screamed/
she cried continuously for seventy-two minutes and
thirty-seven seconds/she walked in a daze for seven
full years/night and day she was haunted by desires
for revenge/red medicine gurgled out of her mouth/she
bellowed like a moose/perhaps because she could not
control her hysteria, her voice became by turns too
loud and too soft/she filled her house with mirrors not
because she was narcissistic but because she could
not tolerate being alone/she danced before us dressed,
as usual, in a sheer turquoise nightgown/caught in
the whirl of the crowd, she feared suffocation/she
painted trees to look like penises and leaves to look like
vulvas/she liked to take off her clothes while staring
directly at an audience of strangers/she smelled of tar
and fish/she feared that in the hysteria of repacking
she had lost her husband's ashes/she could feel her
control over things, important things, slipping away/
though normal and reasonable in most respects she
was sexually paranoid, thinking everyone, both male
and female, wanted to seduce her/she wore a jacket to
conceal her breasts and diaphanous slacks to reveal her
bottom/from behind she looked like a princess; from in
front, a prince/she seemed angry for reasons that were
not visible/the figure before me had the undeveloped
breasts of a girl and the undeveloped penis of a boy/I
was reluctant to tell her that the quiche she had cooked
especially for us tasted like rust.

TOP STORIES #9

$2.50

NEW YORK CITY IN 1979   by Kathy Acker

New York City in 1979, Cover (1981)
Photo: Anne Turyn

FROM *NEW YORK CITY IN* 1979 (1979, 1981)

KATHY ACKER

The Whores in Jail at Night

—Well, my man's gonna get me out of here as soon as he can.

—When's that gonna be, honey?

—So what? Your man pays so he can put you back on the street as soon as possible.

—Well, what if he wants me back on the street? That's where I belong. I make him good money, don't I? He knows that I'm a good girl.

—Your man ain't anything! Johnny says that if I don't work my ass off for him, he's not going to let me back in the house.

—I have to earn two hundred before I can go back.

—Two hundred? That ain't shit! You can earn two hundred in less than a night. I have to earn four hundred or I might just as well forget sleeping, and there's no running away from Him. My baby is the toughest there is.

—Well, shit girl, if I don't come back with eight hundred I get my ass whupped off.

—That's cause you're junk.

—I ain't no stiff! All of you are junkies. I know what you do!

—What's the matter, honey?

—You've been sitting on that thing for an hour.

—The pains are getting bad. OOgh. I've been bleeding two days now.

—OOgh OOgh OOgh.

—She's gonna bang her head off. She needs a shot.

—Tie a sweater around her head. She's gonna break her head open.

—You should see a doctor, honey.

—The doctor told me I'm having an abortion.

—Matron. Goddamnit. Get your ass over here matron!

—I haven't been bleeding this bad. Maybe this is the real abortion.

—Matron! This little girl is having an abortion! You do something. Where the hell is that asshole woman? (The matron throws an open piece of Kotex to the girl.) The service here is getting worse and worse!

—You're not in a hotel, honey.

—It used to be better than this. There's not even any goddamn food. This place is definitely going downhill.

—Oh, shutup. I'm trying to sleep. I need my sleep, unlike you girls, cause I'm going back to work tomorrow.

—Now what the hell do you need sleep for? This is a party. You sleep on your job.

—I sure know this is the only time I get any rest. Tomorrow it's back on the street again.

—If we're lucky.

LESBIANS are women who prefer their own ways to male ways.

LESBIANS prefer the convoluting halls of sensuality to direct goal-pursuing mores.

LESBIANS have made a small world deep within and separated from the world. What has usually been called the world is the male world.

Convoluting halls of sensuality lead to dependence on illusions. Lies and silence are realer than truth.

Either you're in love with someone or you're not. The one thing about being in love with someone is you know you're in love: You're either flying or you're about to kill yourself.

I don't know anyone I'm in love with or I don't know if I'm in love. I have all these memories. I remember that as soon as I've gotten fucked, like a dog I no longer care about the man who just fucked me who I was madly in love with.

So why should I spend a hundred dollars to fly to Toronto to get laid by someone I don't know if I love I don't know if I can love I'm an abortion? I mean a hundred dollars and once I get laid I'll be in agony: I won't be doing exactly what I want. I can't live normally i.e. with love so: there is no more life.

The world is gray afterbirth. Fake. All of New York City is fake is going to go all my friends are going crazy all my friends know they're going crazy disaster is the only thing that's happening.

Suddenly these outbursts in the fake, cause they're so open, spawn a new growth. I'm waiting to see this growth.

I want more and more horrible disaster in New York cause I desperately want to see that new thing that is going to happen this year.

JANEY is a woman who has sexually hurt and been sexually hurt so much she's now frigid.

She doesn't want to see her husband anymore. There's nothing between them.

Her husband agrees with her that there's nothing more between them.

But there's no such thing as nothingness. Not here. Only death whatever that is is nothing. All the ways people are talking to her now mean nothing. She doesn't want to speak words that are meaningless.

Janey doesn't want to see her husband again.

The quality of life in this city stinks. Is almost nothing. Most people now are deaf-mutes only inside they're screaming. BLOOD. A lot of blood inside is going to fall. MORE and MORE because inside is outside.

New York City will become alive again when the people begin to speak to each other again not information but real emotion. A grave is spreading its legs and BEGGING FOR LOVE.

Robert, Janey's husband, is almost a zombie.

He walks talks plays his saxophone pays for groceries almost like every other human. There's no past. The last six years didn't exist. Janey hates him. He made her a hole. He blasted into her. He has no feeling. The light blue eyes he gave her; the gentle hands; the adoration: AREN'T. NO CRIME. NO BLOOD. THE NEW CITY. Like in Fritz Lang's *Metropolis*.

This year suffering has so blasted all feelings out of her she's become a person. Janey believes it's necessary to blast open her mind constantly and destroy EVERY PARTICLE OF MEMORY THAT SHE LIKES.

A sleeveless black T-shirt binds Janey's breasts. Pleated black fake-leather pants hide her cocklessness. A thin leopard tie winds around her neck. One gold-plated watch, the only remembrance of the dead mother, binds one wrist. A thin black leather band binds the other. The head is almost shaved. Two round prescription mirrors mask the eyes.

Johnny is a man who don't want to be living so he doesn't appear to be a man. All his life everyone wanted him to be something. His Jewish mother wanted him to be famous so he wouldn't live the life she was living. The two main girlfriends he has had wanted him to support them in the manner to which they certainly weren't accustomed even though he couldn't put his flabby hands on a penny. His father wanted him to shut up.

All Johnny wants to do is make music. He wants to keep everyone and everything who takes him away from his music off him. Since he can't afford human contact, he can't afford desire. Therefore he hangs around with rich zombies who never have anything to do with feelings. This is a typical New York artist attitude.

New York City is a pit-hole: Since the United States government, having decided that New York City is no longer part of the United States of America, is dumping all the laws the rich people want such as anti-rent-control laws and all the people they don't want (artists, poor minorities, and the media in general) on the city and refusing the city Federal funds; the American bourgeoisie has left. Only the poor: artists, Puerto Ricans who can't afford to move . . . and rich Europeans who fleeing the terrorists don't give a shit about New York . . . inhabit this city.

Meanwhile the temperature is getting hotter and hotter so no one can think clearly. No one perceives. No one cares. Insane madness come out like life is a terrific party.

In Front of the Mudd Club, 77 White Street

Two rich couples drop out of a limousine. The women are wearing outfits the poor people who were in ten years ago wore ten years ago. The men are just neutral. All the poor people who're making this club fashionable so the rich want to hang out here, even though the poor still never make a buck off the rich pleasure, are sitting on cars, watching the rich people walk up to the club.

Some creeps around the club's entrance. An open-shirted skinny guy who says he's just an artist is choosing who he'll let into the club. Since it's 3:30 A.M. there aren't many creeps. The artist won't let the rich hippies into the club.

—Look at that car.

—Jesus. It's those rich hippies' car.

—Let's take it.

—That's the chauffeur over there.

—Let's kidnap him.

—Let's knock him over the head with a bottle.

—I don't want no terrorism. I wanna go for a ride.

—That's right. We've got nothing to do with terrorism. We'll just explain we want to borrow the car for an hour.

—Maybe he'll lend us the car if we explain we're terrorists-in-training. We want to use that car to tryout terrorist tricks.

After 45 minutes the rich people climb back into their limousine and their chauffeur drives them away.

A girl who has gobs of brown hair like the foam on a cappuccino in Little Italy, black patent leather S&M heels, two unfashionable tits stuffed into a pale green corset, and extremely fashionable black fake-leather tights heaves her large self off a car top. She's holding an empty bottle.

Diego senses there's going to be trouble. He gets off his car top. Is walking slowly toward the girl.

The bottle keeps waving. Finally the girl finds some courage heaves the bottle at the skinny entrance artist.

The girl and the artist battle it out up the street. Some of the people who are sitting on cars separate them. We see the girl throw herself back on a car top. Her tits are bouncing so hard she must want our attention and she's getting insecure, maybe violent, cause she isn't getting enough. Better give us a better show. She sticks her middle finger into the air as far as she can. She writhes around on the top of the car. Her movements are so spasmodic she must be nuts.

A yellow taxicab is slowly making its way to the club. On one side of this taxicab's the club entrance. The other side is the girl writ(h)ing away

on the black car. Three girls who are pretending
to be transvestites are lifting themselves out of the
cab elegantly around the big girl's body. The first
body is encased into a translucent white girdle.
A series of diagonal panels leads directly to her cunt.
The other two dresses are tight and white. They are
wriggling their way toward the club. The big girl,
whom the taxi driver refused to let in his cab,
wriggling because she's been rejected but not
wriggling as much, is bumping into them. They're
tottering away from her because she has syphilis.

Now the big girl is unsuccessfully trying to climb
through a private white car's window now she's
running hips hooking even faster into an alleyway taxi
whose driver is locking his doors and windows against
her. She's offering him a blowjob. Now an ugly boy
with a huge safety pin stuck through his upper lip,
walking up and down the street, is shooting at us with
his watergun.

The dyke sitting next to me is saying earlier in the
evening she pulled at this safety pin.

It's four o'clock A.M. It's still too hot. Wet heat's
squeezing this city. The air's mist. The liquid that's
seeping out of human flesh pores is gonna harden
into a smooth shiny shell so we're going to become
reptiles.

No one wants to move anymore. No one wants to
be in a body. Physical possessions can go to hell even
in this night.

Johnny like all other New York inhabitants doesn't
want anything to do with sex. He hates sex because
the air's hot, because feelings are dull, and because
humans are repulsive.

Like all the other New Yorkers he's telling females
he's strictly gay and males all faggots ought to burn
in hell and they are. He's doing this because when he
was sixteen years old his parents who wanted him
to die stuck him in the Merchant Marines and all the
marines cause this is what they do raped his ass off
with many doses of coke.

Baudelaire doesn't go directly toward self-
satisfaction cause of the following mechanism: X
wants Y and, for whatever reasons reasons, thinks it
shouldn't want Y. X thinks it is BAD because it wants
Y. What X wants is Y and to be GOOD.

Baudelaire does the following to solve this
dilemma: He understands that some agency (his
parents, society, his mistress, etc.) is saying
that wanting Y is BAD. This agency is authority is
right. The authority will punish him because
he's BAD. The authority will punish him as much
as possible, punish me punish me, more than
is necessary till it has to be obvious to everyone
that the punishment is unjust. Punishers are unjust.
All authority right now stinks to high hell. Therefore
there is no GOOD and BAD. X cannot be BAD.

It's necessary to go to as many extremes
as possible.

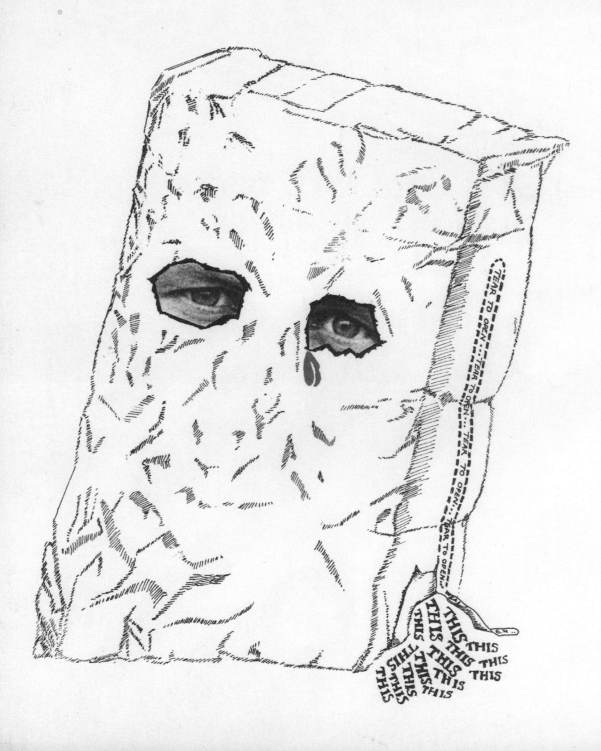

BIKINI GIRL

THIS ISSUE:

FREEDOM FROM CHOICE!

SOIREE– CAR RECORDS

FABREGA– FRENZY!

LOWER EAST SIDE LIVING

CULTS

MANHATTAN'S CLUB MUDD

SWIMWEAR FUN

B-52s CUT-OUTS

VICIOUS GOSSIP

五風製新方

MORE MADNESS INSIDE (–AND HOW TO COPE WITH IT)

BIKINI GIRL

Bikini Girl, Vol. 1 No. 2, Cover (1979)

Bikini Girl, Vol. 1 No. 3, Cover (1979)

FROM *BIKINI GIRL* NO. 8 (1981)

LISA B. FALOUR

Fourteenth Street, NYC. A visit to Gerard Malanga. Tortuous walkup—he lives on the top floor, wouldn't you know?

(Knocking.)

GERARD: Justa minute!

LISA: Hi! What's shakin'? Hey, you look alright, for someone with a "bad back."

G: My "bad back" is over now.

L: I got stuck uptown. I couldn't get a cab . . . no more money. Had to subway it. (Peering into wallet.) It's not a bottomless pit, y'know, it *does* have its *limits*. . . !

LYNNE TILLMAN: It's the only thing I spend money on, is taxis . . .

L: TAXES?

LT: *Taxis.*

G: Would either of you ladies like some tea?

L: Tea would be great. (To Lynne) How ya doin'? (Doesn't give her a chance to respond.) I overdid it today. I thought I'd be "cute" and take a calisthenics class at the gym.

LT: Oh, you know, when I called you last time, your husband seemed very friendly.

L: I know. He tried *real* hard. I was right there when you called, and he got this very evil look on his face, then it sort of disappeared and he said (very sweetly), "*How* are *you*. . . ?"

LT: You see, I'm not being cynical.

L: Yeah, right. He's still not very good over the phone. He has a habit of walking into a room when I'm on the phone and making these statements, and when I ask him to be quiet, he says, "Are you trying to humiliate me?" But believe me, I wouldn't waste my time.

LT: Did you cut your hair?

L: No, I haven't, it's just falling out. (Takes out an artist's book titled "Come Back, Kitty Kitty Kitty!" by Judy Malloy—Pathological Press, Berkeley—a gift from Lynne several weeks previous. Shows it to Lynne.) I carry this with me where ever I go. I have these *horrible* nightmares about my cats, Dot and Spot! I have these dreams that I forgot to feed my cats, and . . .

G: (to his black kitty) Evan, did you hear that, sweetheart?

L: . . . and I showed this little book to my psychiatrist today. He wasn't *too* impressed . . . I started to tell him about a dream I had about him, but I didn't want to finish it, because it . . . got embarrassing. I had to LIE about how it ended.

LT: "And they all lived happily ever after . . ."

L: It was my fault, bringing up the dream at all. I should know better. See, I said to him, "Did you have a mustache when we first met?" and he said, "No," then I said, "Oh, but you had one in my *dreams* . . ." His eyes lit up and he said, "Oh, what dream was THAT?" Uh-oh!

LT: How's it going with him?

L: Fine. I got some tranquilizers.

LT: Feeling better?

L: Oh, sure. It was just a "spell." Those things pass . . .

LT: It was probably from your parents visiting.

L: Oh, no. It was even before that.

G: What happened?

L: I started having trouble functioning. I was always upset. Things were getting blown out of proportion.

G: Where did your parents visit from?

L: Cleveland . . .

LT: Did they meet your husband?

L: Yeah, yeah. I didn't tell them that he was completely tattooed.

G: Your husband is completely tattooed?

L: . . . I married him very, very suddenly.

G: (fascinated) *Completely tattooed?*

L: Well, his *face* isn't . . .

G: From the neck down?

L: Yeah.

G: Completely tattooed?

L: Yeah. Even his feet. But not his hands . . . He's wearing some of Spider Webb's best work! But I . . . don't know if I *like* tattoos . . .

LT: Then why did you marry him?

L: (vaguely) Well . . . beauty's only skin deep . . .

G: You're married!

L: Yes, I am! It's incredible! But he wouldn't meet my parents. Finally I pleaded with him. "Grant me just this!" So he took us all out to dinner, and everything was going so well . . .

G: Till he opened his shirt.

L: (To Lynne) So what have you been up to?

LT: Argh, running around like *crazy*. The interview with Charles Henri Ford . . . you wanted me to introduce you to him, didn't you?

L: Yeah, I'm very intrigued by him.

G: I can picture Charles Henri shrugging, saying, "Why do all these *girls* want to meet me?"

L: He doesn't *mind* girls, does he? He's not one of *those*?

LT: Oh, no . . .

G: Bill *Burroughs* doesn't like girls . . . shouldn't you turn on your tape recorder?

L: Huh? It IS on? It's ALWAYS on!

G: Oh no! Charles! I take everything back!

L: . . . You know, William Burroughs will *not* answer my mail! And I've tried everything to get him to respond! (Thoughtfully . . .) . . . Maybe it's the pink stationery . . .

LT: Why don't you send him an offer he can't refuse?

G: Is this tape recorder really on?

L: (aghast) It's always on!

G: Even in the subway?

L: Always.

LT: (shaking her head) . . . These children of Warhol . . .

L: It has nothing to DO with Warhol! It has to do with um . . . and you know . . . I don't listen to them . . .

LT: When you transcribe, you don't listen to them?

L: No, I usually just . . . fake it.

G: (to his black kitty, sitting up on his shoulder) Evan, you're gonna be on the tape recorder!

LT: I'm not gonna ask why you even *make* a tape if you're not gonna . . .

L: Remember when I told you I loved making soundsheets? I want to record my different shoes, going down stairs, going up stairs, the sounds of people, moving around . . .

LT: But you never listen to them?

L: No. Why should I?

G: You're in school? What are you studying?

L: That's a very good question. (Long, thoughtful pause.) Art.

G: What, drawing classes and all that?

L: No, I don't do that anymore.

G: Art history?

L: Mm. Byzantine art. Really cool teacher. All I can do is stare at his crotch . . . it's HIS fault, for dressing "that way!"

LT: Is he tall?

L: Stop teasing me! (A handsome youth enters the apartment, carrying bags that say MACY'S. He's staying with Gerard.) (We are introduced. He sits down shyly.)

LT: Gerard, were you really hurt when VINYL was made?

G: *Hurt?!* Oh, you mean in the movie?

LT: Yeah, physically!

L: No—emotionally!

G: It did get a little out of hand, I wasn't prepared for (to his young Swedish guest)—you can pull up a chair.

L: Had you ever had one of those black leather bondage hoods on before that?

G: No.

L: Scary, isn't it?

G: It *got* scary, because as the film progressed, I became less and less . . . what do you call it . . . free. You know? Like, all of a sudden my hands were tied, the hood was on . . . Tosh stuffed this orange strainer in my mouth and started breaking amyl nitrates and it was getting really out of hand.

L: Wow.

LT: And Andy was just—

G: —dizzy. At the end of the film, I was *very* dizzy. Swaying back and forth on my knees, and—

L: And the *best* moment was when the hood came off.

G: Ah, yes, that was my Artaud moment.

LT: I never actually lasted long enough to see that. I nearly fainted during the film. I had to walk out.

L: (very surprised) Why? Why?

LT: Because I couldn't stand to see Gerard get . . . tortured.

L: But—it wasn't . . . *that bad* . . .

LT: Well, I faint easily.

L: I guess I'm more used to seeing people tied up with those black leather hoods on. That's terrible that you left, you missed a great scene.

LT: I miss a great deal in life.

L: I was newly-arrived in Manhattan when I first saw VINYL . . . hopped up on speed . . . it is a brilliant film.

G: (proudly) It was written for *me*.

LT: You should have a print of it, Gerard.

L: You don't own a print of it? How come Ondine has one?

G: Because he borrowed it, and never returned it.

LT: Lisa, these people have been calling me about WEIRD FUCKS (LT's novel) in the latest BIKINI GIRL . . .

L: Y'know, these kinky guys who want to be slaves look up the names of BIKINI GIRL's contributors in the Manhattan directory—and they don't want MY phone number, they want *Deena's.* That Deena's quite an item. I get a lot of invitations to suspicious parties addressed to her. She's quite an item.

G: Who's Deena?

L: Well, it's a pseudonym for me. Deena does all the things I wouldn't want my parents to know about. This one guy from Queens calls for Deena. He says he's rich, he has a trust fund, and he wants to set up a "BIKINI GIRL Deficit." I told him I'd meet him for a drink next week.

G: Yeah, I wanna meet him too.

LT: Don't we all. Gerard'll even wear a bikini!

L: —but this guy wants to be treated horribly. He wants to be, like, abused.

LT: Like, what's his name, that servant of yours?

L: Angelo?

LT: Yeah, Angelo. Y'know, Gerard, Lisa did the funniest thing, she had this sick party, she called it a "Hen Party." Only women.

G: Pillow fights?

LT: This was kind of a high Catholic party. Angelo was serving hours d'oeuvres. Pleated skirts . . . a sort of punk Catholic party. Punk is such a Catholic movement. So these girls are reading marriage and motherhood magazines from 1962 and they're quite bright, and Angelo, the servant who does Lisa's laundry and stuff, comes over with drinks on a tray, and we're sitting on this weird Victorian couch . . . but the guy's so dumb, he's holding the tray up high, and nobody can see what's on it, anyway. So nobody wants anything.

L: And all these girls start yelling at him, ordering him around.

LT: That party taught me how easy it would be to become a Sadist.

L: Of course!

G: I photographed a little Catholic girl on the street about three weeks ago. I ran into her— I had to stop her. I only got two shots, though, and she ran away. She was really scared, and didn't want to stop to begin with.

L: Oh, Catholic girls . . . in the city . . . they are *so* HARASSED. They're just so . . . desirable!

(Laughter)

L: I mean, everyone wants to look at them, and talk to them . . . and molest them . . .

G: Where did I put that contact sheet? We had this GREAT conversation . . . I'm doing a new series called SIGHTINGS. There's the copy printed below the photograph, and it's blown up to three by four feet.

LT: These are women you just . . . encounter?

G: (reading) "SHARK BAIT. SHARK BAIT! October 6, 1980, approximately 1:30 PM, first name Debbie, last name not given, navy blue school uniform skirt, sweatshirt logo: SHARK BAIT. Lineage presumably Italian, age 14, sighting West Broadway between Spring and Prince, subject walking North on West side of street. Conversation: Shark Bait! Shark Bait! Can I take a picture of your sweatshirt?"

"I'M IN A HURRY."

"It'll only take a minute, please!"

"I'M IN A HURRY."

"Here! Come over here! It'll only take a second!"

"WADDYA WANNA TAKE A PICTURE OF MY SWEATSHIRT FOR?"

"Because it looks good on you!"

"(The *nerve* of a parochial school student wearing a sweatshirt with the logo SHARK BAIT!)"

(He shows us the contact sheet proudly.) And I got this great photograph of her.

LT: Do you think the men who read this are going to go to the points where you found these women?

G: Little Sharkey. The AUDACITY of her!

L: Yeah, look, she's wearing Dr. Scholl's Exercise Sandals.

LT: . . . Sort of a mixed metaphor.

L: Gerard, where do you come from?

G: MMMM, New York. Riverdale. I was in Europe when I was very young. Till I was 7 years. Italy. It-al-y.

L: What's it like not being a star anymore?

G: "Everyone is a star!"

L: No, they're NOT.

G: In the future, everyone will be famous for 15 minutes . . .

LT: How democratic. The saneness of it all.

L: I see him EVERYwhere. I always have in the city. Everywhere I look, it seems. On the street.

G: You see him up by Hunter, right? He lives two blocks from where you go to school.

L: Union Square . . .

G: That's where the Factory is. His mansion is . . . 67th Street between Park and Lex . . . 67 or 66, I forget . . .

LT: So if there are any Andy watchers out there . . .

L: What for?

LT: Well, for nothing, I think . . .

L: I would never say anything to him on the street.

G: I stopped a girl on the street yesterday—

L: Another one?

LT: It's all for art, Gerard.

G: This one is a girl who has posed for OUI magazine . . . naked, and she's a *top* fashion model.

L: She's rare, then, cuz most of them won't do that.

G: I know. Well, she did it before she was a top fashion model.

L: I'm afraid to say anything to anybody! I'm afraid they're going to set me on fire because they "feel like it." Did you see that girl on TV? The one who set somebody on fire cuz she felt like it? That fucking Canarsie train . . .

G: I need some girl models.

L: Where's your studio?

G: Right here.

L: What kind of models do you want?

G: Well, beautiful ones.

L: I know a few fashion models who'll test. I'll tell them.

G: They'll pose nude?

L: NUDE. Gerard, *nobody'll* do that.

G: Dancer types will do that.

L: But fashion models, NO, Gerard! How can you get them in your own home, and get them to take off their clothes as well? Are you that persuasive?

G: (Thoughtfully) Well, I got a Stewart Model last week . . . as long as they know they're coming over to do that, then there's no problem . . .

this is the trip: I'm included in this book—that this friend of mine is doing, which Horst is gonna be in, and Robert Mapplethorpe, and Debbie Turbeville, and uh, a whole bunch of fashion photographers. It's called "SMALL-BREASTED WOMEN."

LT: (giggles)

L: You're kidding.

G: No, I'm not kidding.

L: Okay, you're not.

G: So long as they know there's a kind of credibility involved in it . . .

L: What will they think of next?

G: That's the premise to get models to come over and take their clothes off.

(Gerard fumbles with the Swedish youth. Something about a Velvet Underground record for sale for fifty dollars.)

G: Lynne's a friend of John Cale's—

L: A *friend*? (Laughter)

G: Isn't he in your book?

LT: No, I'm saving him.

L: For a whole book.

LT: Well, I don't think it would take up a whole book. (Embarrassed.)

G: Here, Lisa. Look at my photos. They're not from the small-breasted women book, these are from my erotic voyeuristic series.

(Lynne and Lisa look at the photos and giggle.)

LT: Isn't he *obsessive*?

L: Hee-hee! This one of a woman's fingernails is really ugly!

LT: Gerard used to carry a whip in the 60's. When I saw him in Crete, he wore all white. I said, "Gerard, when you used to dress in black leather and carry a whip, you used to frighten me. Why'd you do that?" He said, "Oh, it was my image of a poet."

G: I was such a romantic then.

L: (looking at Gerard's photos) These are so strange!

G: What's "so strange?"

L: They're DIRTY (Gerard gasps.)

G: You're the first person who's said these photographs are dirty.

L: They're dirty to me! Armpits and teeth! And fingernails with chipped polish!

LT: You're such a mixture of innocence and something else, Gerard, I can't figure out what. I guess you're not innocent.

G: I'm guilty!

LT: Lisa says you're very big in the Midwest.

G: I am?

L: Yeah!

G: Well what the fuck am I doing sitting in New York? I should be giving readings out there!

L: Yeah. I remember at my first college, I had to go to the special collections archive to even look at your book PRELUDE TO INTERNATIONAL VELVET DEBUTANTE. They wouldn't even let me *touch* the book. (Pause.) I'd like to have children.

G: and **LT:** Oh, Lisa!

L: Well, I don't really want to, but my astrologer says I'm gonna get pregnant no matter what I do. I might as well get myself into . . . into . . . into looking forward to it.

LT: You could always have an abortion.

L: It doesn't do any good!

G: You could be pregnant right now!

L: Not after what I went through today. I get hysterical pregnancies often, though.

LT: I had TWO defective diaphragms.

G: At least you can say you tried!

L: I tried.

LT: One time when abortions were illegal in New York . . .

G: They may be again—

LT: Yeah, I know. THAT I'll take to the streets.

L: They can't do that. They wouldn't get away with it. People would get very violent, that's like cutting off Food Stamps in New York . . . there'd be . . . like . . . wars.

LT: Yeah, can you imagine it? The Abortion Wars.

G: Pregnant women cutting their bellies open with—Like Vietnam.

L: I remember when girls used to mail coat hangers to Washington . . .

LT: That's better than in Holland! There, they mail you their shit! Surprising Amsterdam! Nobody puts *that* in the tourist guides.

G: Lisa, are you a bad girl? What kind of sexual fantasies do you have?

L: None. I-I-I've turned frigid. It's my new thing. What are yours? Hey, how come you look better now than you did in VINYL?

G: Well, my hair was dyed silver, I had on a lot of makeup . . .

L: Did you get a nose job?

G: No, but I *give* nose jobs.

L: People who've known Andy Warhol don't seem to age well.

G: They jump out of windows . . .

L: Poor Andrea.

G: Well, I won't compromise myself by taking a 9 to 5 job. I'm an artist. I have a good jawline.

L: How do you like Fourteenth Street?

G: I HATE it.

L: But the shopping is so good. You can get flaming apple green clothes for a dollar.

G: I'm waiting for Miss Right.

L: Or Mrs. Right?

LT: Do you get involved with married women?

G: Once or twice, when I was younger. But no, not usually. I don't have time for coquettes. (He pronounces it "cockettes.") Do you have any more questions?

L: Yes, but they are more existential. I've been drinking a lot lately. Have you? I think there's something going around.

LT: Bottles of liquor. Where's the bathroom?

L: You didn't ask permission to go!

LT: I'm not your slave!

G: Wow. (phone rings) Hello! Oh it's Pete!

LT: Wanna eat?

L: Yeah, I'll eat. But it's gotta be something cheap.

G: I'm being interviewed . . . that was a good guess . . . that's nice . . .

L: Where does Charles Henri live?

LT: The Dakota.

L: Is he rich?

LT: No . . .

L: Isn't it expensive to live there?

LT: Well, I think he's got a *fair* income . . .

L: I like discussing people's incomes. I can't *help* it! (fiddling with bits of pink paper.)

G: Bye. (hangs up) What are those pink papers? Questions?

L: Oh, no, a letter from Angelo. A sad letter. He really doesn't think too well of himself. I took him out one night, and people did some really mean things to him. Like, they threw him on the floor, they poured beer down his throat . . .

G: Where was this?

L: Some S and M club.

G: S and M? Sincerity and Malice?

L: I wasn't keeping a close enough eye on Angelo, and some dominants got 'im.

G: Who's doing the next cover for BIKINI GIRL?

L: I told you you could do it, Gerard. Lynne can be on the cover.

G: Only if you feel comfortable in a bikini, Lynne . . .

LT: On my head?

G: No, Lisa, you should get somebody who looks really *fantastic* in a bikini . . .

LT: Fuck you, Gerard! I'm going to the bathroom— IF I'm not too afraid to pull down my pants! I read a great interview with Lou Reed and William S. Burroughs. Lou says, "Y'know, Bill, there's something I can't understand about Kerouac. How could such a great writer turn into such a slob, sitting in front of the TV at his mother's house, drinking beer?" And Burroughs said, "He never changed much. First he was a young slob sitting in front of the TV at his mother's house, drinking beer, and then he was an *old* slob sitting in front of the TV at his mother's house and drinking beer."

G: We should go out for a drink.

L: Amen.

ON THE LOOSE (1994)

THURSTON MOORE

In '77 I was nineteen living on East 13th Street in New York and paying, or trying to pay, $110 a month rent. I was bonkers, alone, with no social life. I met this girl and became obsessed with being in love with her. She was fucking this older writer poet guy who lived in my building on the top floor. I would hang out my window from afternoon to evening hoping and waiting for her to turn the corner. One day she knocked, came in and I knew we were gonna have to be together forever. Five minutes later the writer guy knocked and walked in all innocent and smiling and I realized the two of them had plans that day and she said, "OK, see y'later!" and I was like, "OK" and then I blanked out. It wasn't so tragic cuz I did eventually score some quality time with her (she was Swedish!) but too many stupid hours were spent walking from the East Village to Tribeca, back and forth, chanting punker mantras of unrequited desire, hoping to run into this incredible on-the-loose girl.

I moved to New York early '77. I had planned it for the last couple of years, I fantasized about it constantly. My fantasies were fueled by the progressive development of punk. It was David Johansen to Patti Smith to John Cale to the Ramones to the Dictators to Punk Magazine to New York Rocker to Rock Scene to St. Mark's Place to Bleecker Bobs to Manic Panic to Gem Spa to Max's to CBGB, etc. I was playing in a Television/T. Heads–influenced art-rock band called the Coachmen. They were Rhode Island School of Design graduates (same school David Byrne went to) and they were older than me (early 20's). I met the leader guy in my hometown record store and he told me he was moving to New York to start a punk band. We pen-palled and I moved in and joined them.

Sid was on the loose. Someone stabbed Nancy a week or two prior and Sid was bombing around town. He would come see Judy Nylon at CBGB cuz he was friends with her. We (the Coachmen, the only friends I had) would go to the gig cuz we knew the drummer and the place would be pretty empty. Judy wasn't super popular but she was rad, doing a real slow punky version of "Jailhouse Rock". But fucking Sid would walk in and sit right near us. He was the skinniest. His skin was totally white. And he had the looks and mannerisms that you knew he just had to have. My dream was to start a band with him that would totally kill. He was down and out and I was ready to immerse myself in him. Total punk rock. But I was in an art-rock band. He was into heroin, murder and weird sex from after-hours hell. When he died it was one of the most intense moments of my life. I watched the TV reports like it was Kennedy being assassinated. I collected and have to this day every newspaper clipping there was (unfortunately there was a newspaper strike in New York which limited the amount of super schlock coverage).

I used to walk the streets looking for pennies so I could save up 200 of them and then go to St. Mark's Cinema (2nd Ave. & 8th—the Gap's there now) and see the second-run double-feature. The audience was a mixture of artist downtowners, East Village Puerto Rican dudes, luminaries (Divine, Richard Hell, etc.) and new-wave loners (myself). The lobby was a cloud of cigarette and pot smoke. I remember Richard Hell sitting down with his then girlfriend Susan Springfield and I got up and sat in front of them as if I was a disheveled poet punk hoping to impress them. I met Richard many years later and he had no recollection of this.

I spent a glorious March weekend with the Swedish girl I was obsessed with and I figured she would just stay in my apartment forever from that moment on but she left Monday morning wearing my overcoat. She actually said she'd be right back but she never returned. I ran into her a couple of weeks later and she refused to address the issue and I told her I needed my coat back. I actually almost cried in front of her and told her I loved her and all I wanted was a girlfriend to live with and all the while a fire engine was screaming past us. She knew what I was saying and just kind of smiled compassionately because of all the noise around us. We were both a little embarrassed.

I lived on 13th street between A & B. In '77/78 there weren't so many skinny white kids in the area and I'd get harassed and chased sometimes. The only person I was aware of living on that street was Lydia Lunch. At first I was anti-Lydia because there was an interview with her in Soho Weekly News where she called Patti Smith a barefoot hippie chick and Television a bunch of old men playing wanky guitar solos. Seeing as how punk rock defined itself by trashing Led Zep, Floyd et al, I was amazed there was a new punk person trashing Patti Smith! I moved to New York to fucking marry Patti Smith and now Lydia was saying Patti was most definitely uncool. Patti had moved away anyway. And Television was over. And the Voidoids were over. I saw Lydia standing on the corner of 13th and A and she had a nose ring. Nobody had a nose ring in those days. I thought she was exquisite. Later I saw her on the platform of the L train at 1st Avenue. I came barreling down the stairs through the turnstile and nearly ran her over. She stared at me very wide-eyed and I continued on. I became good friends with Lydia many years later and she told me she was obsessed with tall skinny white guys at the time and we were both of the age and demeanor where something wild could've definitely developed. Who knows what would've happened if I had become Lydia's lover at 18.

The Coachmen broke up and I decided to play the guitar as if I existed in a pure state of mind and could attack it with flowing mindful sensitive energy/expression. I knew nothing of jazz, free jazz, or any studied musical concept of improvisation. I had a ratty skinny-lapel suit jacket (all East Village poor-boy punk rockers had one) and no job. I jammed with this girl Miranda who asked me after our first 'session,' "Do you always play like that?" I wasn't sure. It was new to me. She said her best friend was this beautiful artist named Kim. They played music together in a group called CKM which was the two of them and the drummer Christine Hahn from Glenn Branca's trio The Static. I was duly impressed and even more exciting was that they were trying to get Nina Canal from UT to play with them.

Kim wore glasses with flip-up shades and had an Australian sheepdog named Egan. She had an off-center ponytail and wore a blue and white striped shirt and pants outfit.

She had beautiful eyes and the most beautiful smile and was very intelligent and seemed to have a sensitive/spiritual intellect. She seemed to really like me. I definitely liked her but was scared as always to make a move. I was afraid to kiss her. We walked around a couple of times. One night it got late and we were eating at Leshko's and I think she wanted me to ask her over. I only lived up the street. So we parted.

She would take the subway way the fuck up to the west side in the 100's somewhere. She was staying at gallery owner Anina Nosei's place. Before she split she actually touched my arm(!) and said, "See you later." She moved into a raw railway apartment on Eldridge Street below Grand Street. The artist Dan Graham lived upstairs and had acquired the place for her. She invited me over one evening and I played this beat up guitar she had. I knew the guitar because it belonged to David Bowes, an associate of the Coachmen gang, who left it at Jenny Holzer's loft where Kim stayed and somehow it passed on to her. All she had was the guitar and a foam rubber cushion for sleeping. That night was the first time we kissed. The end.

PART TWO

THE 1980S

INTRODUCTION TO THE 1980S

SIMILAR TO the punk-scene parallels of the 1970s, the Downtown literary scene may be read through the more documented art explosion that ran alongside it in the 1980s.

A definite cross-pollination occurred: artists and writers published in the same magazines, got drunk at the same parties, lived in the same tenements, and collaborated on intriguing visual/textual enjambments whether as comics, Purgatory Pie Press's broadsides and artist books, flyers, or single-page illustrations. As the art scene boomed and rapidly burst, though, many poets and novelists ultimately enjoyed less trendy, but more quietly sustained artistic life spans.

A brief history of the East Village art world is helpful in conveying an idea of New York City's atmosphere in the '80s. Though it can be debated, some look to the opening of Fun Gallery by Patti Astor and Bill Stelling in 1981 as the beginning of the East Village scene. Astor and Stelling's stable of artists included Jean-Michel Basquiat, Keith Haring, Kenny Scharf, and Futura 2000. Because money was (and is) a major factor, depending on whom

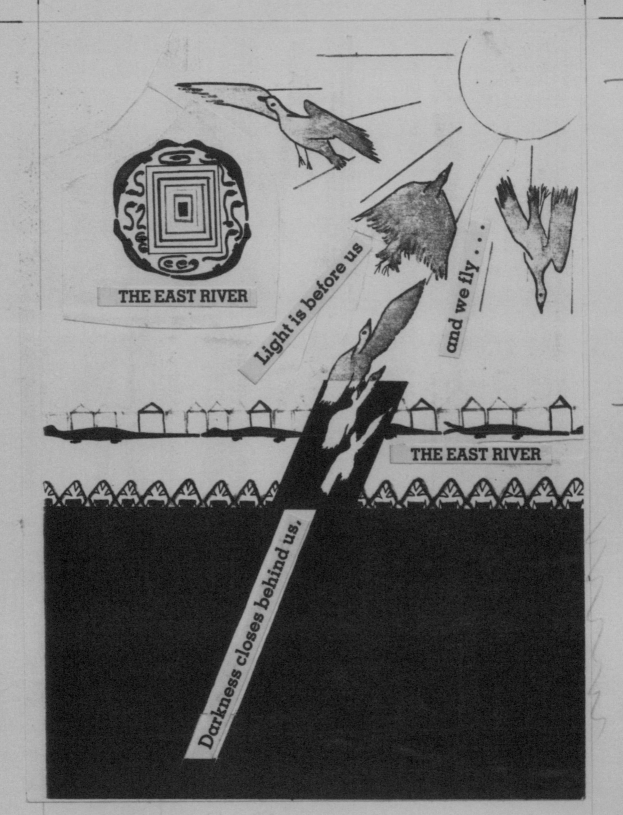

THE EAST RIVER

Light is before us

and we fly . . . .

THE EAST RIVER

Darkness closes behind us,

There are no more judges, there are only thieves, murderers, firebrands.

Wild horses

A forgotten city,

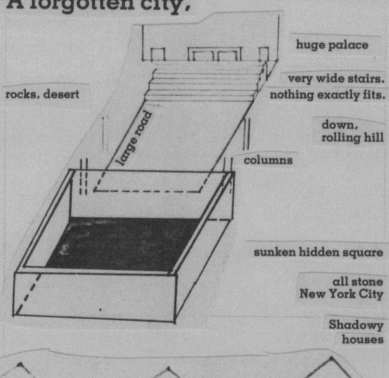

huge palace

very wide stairs.
nothing exactly fits.

rocks, desert

down,
rolling hill

columns

sunken hidden square

all stone
New York City

Shadowy
houses

[Ayco

you ask and to what aesthetic they subscribe, the East Village art scene could also be pinned to Nature Morte, Group Material, Gracie Mansion, Civilian Warfare, or any of the almost 200 new galleries that popped up in the area until the grand exodus back to SoHo, and then Chelsea, less than a decade later.

With the arrival of this crop of art spaces came the full-scale gentrification of the area. Lower East Side neighborhoods were often wrongly viewed as unlivable, war-torn territories and fetishized for their crumbling poverty, but there were working-class immigrants and minorities living there before artists and writers arrived and kick-started the so-called process of revitalization. Presciently, Lower East Side artist Martin Wong once referred to abandoned buildings and structures as "the fashion of the future."[1] The avaricious real estate world is depicted in Joel Rose's *Kill the Poor*, an excerpt of which is included on page 287 in this section.

Such were the issues at events like ABC No Rio's Real Estate show at 123 Delancey Street, which opened on January 1, 1980, and was shut down on January 2 when the city repossessed the building where it was housed. In the Real Estate Show's "Manifesto or Statement of Intent," the committee behind the exhibition said the "action" was put together to draw attention to "the way artists get used as pawns by greedy white developers" and "to show that artists are willing and able to place themselves and their work squarely in a context which shows solidarity with oppressed people . . . and a recognition that artists, living and working in depressed

communities, are compradors in the revaluation of property and the 'whitening' of neighborhoods."[2]

The month-long *Times Square Show* organized by Collaborative Artists Inc. (Colab) in 1980 was also an attempt to communicate with portions of society (and the community) unfamiliar with art galleries as well as with regular art goers. As the artist John Ahern said about the show's "crossroad" location, an area outside of the gallery system where diverse types of people could intermingle: "There has always been a misdirected consciousness that art belongs to a certain class or intelligence. This show proves there are no classes in art, no differentiation."[3]

A debate of these and other issues was initiated in the pages of *Art in America* in 1984. In the June issue, an extensive East Village scene report by Carlo McCormick and Walter Robinson titled "Slouching Toward Avenue D" was followed by contributing editor Craig Owens's "The Problem with Puerilism." Owens's brief, but harsh, rejoinder played on the idea of a false bohemia and false pluralism, stating that what existed in the East Village was "a simulacrum of the *social* formation from which the modernist avant-garde first emerged."[4] Discussing the scene's economic role and his opinion that East Village artists had surrendered themselves to "the means-end rationality of the marketplace," he concluded, "The appropriation of the forms whereby subcultures resist assimilation is part of, rather than an antidote to, the general leveling of real sexual, regional, and cultural differences and their replacement with the culture industry's artificial, mass-produced, generic signifiers for 'Difference'—in the

East Village Eye, Vol. 2 No. 12,
"Death of Punk" (1980)
Art: John Holmstrom;
Art Director: Gaby Moritz

present instance, the empty diversity and puerilism of the East Village 'avant-garde.'"[5]

In his *East Village Eye* "Art Seen" column, McCormick rebuffed Owens for the attack, and he also cocurated a show called "Puerilism" with Robinson at the Kamikaze nightclub. Fifteen years later, McCormick reflected that because Owens's critique "of our unwilling, or at least unwitting, role in the gentrification not only of the neighborhood but of the avant-garde as such came from one far more empowered than any of us hurt and offended in ways I'd like to think the author never intended. But they also furthered our intuitive disgust with the institutional left presiding from the ivory tower."[6]

At the time, offering a sociological response to this battle, Rosalyn Deutsche and Cara Gendel Ryan wrote convincingly of the situation in "The Fine Art of Gentrification," first published in the winter 1984 issue of the journal *October* (and later reprinted in the *Portable Lower East Side*). They analyzed the aestheticization of poverty "as a metaphor for the artist's own purported refusal of bourgeois convention" and asserted that "the figure of the bum provide[d] the requisite identification with marginal figures and social outcasts by which avant-garde and the bohemian glamour accrues to the East Village scene despite its embrace of conventional values."[7]

When the dust settled in 1985, it was Carlo McCormick who sarcastically announced the scene's demise in the pages of the *East Village Eye*. He evoked the *Village Voice*'s Gary Indiana, C. Carr, and Robert Hughes along with Owens's "simulacrum," lamenting that "our once-radiant beauty is but a fading flower:

the art world is finally ready to preserve our youth like the glamorous visage of the internally decrepit Dorian Gray. . . . Uncle! But just know that someday you won't have the East Village to kick around anymore."[8] Fittingly, he titled the piece "East Village, R.I.P.," with the epitaph printed in an especially large font.

Amid this tête-à-tête, postpunks bred some anti-intellectual (or at least anti-academic) sentiments in the heart of the Downtown literary scene, but when theory came to town in the hands of the right people, suddenly the words of French theorists like Michel Foucault and Gilles Deleuze (with Felix Guattari) offered another, fairly punk, way of subverting narrative and decoding culture.

Semiotext(e) founder Sylvère Lotringer believes the '80s started in 1983 with Jean Buadrillard's *Simulations*, "which propelled a kind of weightless nebula into culture just before a charge of Orwellian paranoia took over. . . . The society of the spectacle had already become a society of spectators, and Foucault's panopticon a Möbius strip."[9]

Debuting in 1974–75 with an issue featuring general linguistics' founding father, Ferdinand de Saussure, Semiotext(e) provided many Downtown writers their first taste of theory they could stomach. From his decision to mix American popular culture with French theory to the low-fi design of the books—"small, black, and thin; footnotes or other academic commentary were conspicuously absent. . . . They could be read on the subway, a few pages at a time, like the newspaper: Their place was in the pockets of spiked leather jackets as much as on the shelves"[10]—Lotringer gave even the densest concepts

EAST VILLAGE EYE

1ST ANNIVERSARY ISSUE!

CHRIS BURDEN
SLUGGER ANN
U.S. APE
WERNER SCHROE—
TER
RAYBEATS
CLUBS
.....

50¢

"It's all true."

June 1980

JOHN HOLMSTROM AND THE DEATH OF PUNK
THE ORIGINAL

SUPER-HIP NEW WAVE DISCO SUPPER CLUB
TONIGHT: BLONDIE!
CORBETT MONACA
SUZANNE FELLINI
WAYNE NEWTON

$50 COVER

WHO ARE YOU?

WELL, LEGS, WE BLEW IT!

HEY, YOU! SPARE A CIGARETTE?

OH, ICK! MY GOD!

DEAD BOY

PUNK
NEW WAVE

PUNK

©JOHN 1980 HOLMSTROM

PUNK THE ORIGINAL

SLUM

JOURNAL #5

by Richard Hell

East Village Eye April 13, 1980

a Downtown feel. And in 1975 at the Schizo-Culture conference on prisons and madness at Columbia, at which two thousand showed up to partake in heated exchanges with Foucault, Deleuze and Guattari, Lyotard, R. D. Laing, William Burroughs, and John Cage, Semiotext(e) presented its strongest theory-meets-pop-culture coup.

Sensing a strong connection between French theory and the New Narrative writing being practiced in New York and San Francisco during the 1980s, Chris Kraus began the Native Agents New Fiction series for Semiotext(e) in 1989. Kraus hoped to show that female first-person writing need not be read as confessional memoir: that it could have the humor, universality, and weight of underground classicists Céline or Henry Miller. The series continued for more than a decade, publishing books by Kathy Acker, Lynne Tillman, Michelle Tea, Kraus herself, and Jane Delynn.

Semiotext(e)'s theories of the body and the thrust of its 1981 *Polysexuality* issue took on different tones with the emergence of AIDS. Looming large at the end of the '80s, AIDS led to the death of prominent community literary and art figures like Cookie Mueller in 1989, Jack Smith in 1989, Tim Dlugos in 1990, and David Wojnarowicz in 1992.

The AIDS crisis destroyed people's lives emotionally, while leading to a stronger sense of the political within the community. Political and service organizations including the PWA Coalition, the Lavender Hill Mob, and others began responding to the crisis in the early '80s; radical activist arts groups like the Silence Equals Death Project followed. They

brought the image of the upside-down pink triangle logo to the newly formed ACT UP, the AIDS Coalition to Unleash Power, in February 1987 and offered it to them as a fundraiser and organizing tool. Later, Gran Fury, ACT UP's internal Art Collective, began with a window in the New Museum bringing together trained and untrained artists to create graphics and public art projects for ACT UP. Other gay arts collectives like Group Material turned their attention to AIDS.

Film and video artist Gregg Bordowitz says of that frenetic time, "We changed the way patients are viewed. We changed the way drugs are developed, tested, and sold. Our uncompromising demand to give people with AIDS power over decisions affecting their lives is *the* lasting historical contribution of ACT UP."[11]

After David Wojnarowicz was diagnosed as HIV positive in 1987, he turned out some of his strongest work, most famously "Post Cards from America: X-Rays from Hell." This polemical piece indicts the United States government's nontreatment of AIDS and John Cardinal O'Connor's refusal to endorse the teaching of safe sex in the New York public schools. First published in *Witnesses: Against Our Vanishing*, a show of artists' reaction to AIDS curated by Nan Goldin at Artists Space from November 16, 1989 to January 6, 1990, Wojnarowicz's piece led the NEA to revoke a ten-thousand-dollar grant awarded to Artists Space, though due to community protest the grant was eventually restored. As novelist, playwright and activist Sarah Schulman remarked in conversation, "In the late '80s, artists who received government funds became subject to withholding of those funds because of their content, usually sexual in some

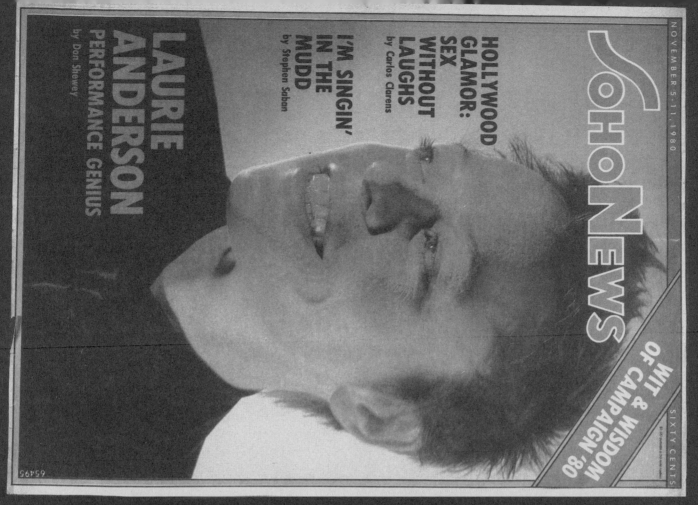

SoHoNEWS

NOVEMBER 5-11, 1980

WIT & WISDOM
OF CAMPAIGN '80

SIXTY CENTS

HOLLYWOOD GLAMOR: SEX WITHOUT LAUGHS
by Carlos Clarens

I'M SINGIN' IN THE MUDD
by Stephen Saban

LAURIE ANDERSON
PERFORMANCE GENIUS
by Don Shewey

65495

Soho News, November 5-11,
Photo of Laurie Anderson (1980)
Photo: Jimmy DeSana

Soho News, October 22, 1980,
Cover (1980) Photo: Allan Tannenbaum

SoHoNEWS

OCTOBER 22-28, 1980

BOOKS!
PRIZE FICTION

SIXTY CENTS

THE NEW EAST VILLAGE

GAYS, GOYS, AND GOURMETS
David Hershkovits

CITY OPERA'S AMERICAN FLOPS
......Tim Page

PVT. BENJAMIN' IS ALL WOMAN
......Veronica Geng

65495

way. This inflated some careers, ended many others by creating a 'chilling effect' within institutions, and drove more people towards commodity product."[12]

Amid this activity, in the late '80s, a Hollywood version of Downtown living showed up on the big screen via the film adaptation of Tama Janowitz's short story collection, *Slaves of New York*. Alongside the glitz, in response to the AIDS crisis, there were personal poems dedicated to dead friends or heroes, as in Denise Duhamel's ode to Cookie Mueller, "Beauties Who Live Only for an Afternoon," and Max Blagg's poem for Mueller, "Gathering Bruises"—both composed in 1989 and included in this section.

The 1980s were the bustling central moment of the Downtown scene. The disparately lively writing in this section reflects that frenetic period.

NOTES

1. Martin Wong, "Martin Wong: Writing in the Sky," interview with Yasmin R. Harwood, *East Village Eye*, October 1984, vol. 5, no. 48, 25.

2. Committee for the Real Estate Show, "Manifesto or Statement of Intent," 1980, http://www.abcnorio.org/about/history/res_manifesto.html.

3. John Ahern quoted in Susana Sedgwick, "Times Square Show," *East Village Eye*, vol. 2, no. 13, Summer 1980, 21.

4. Craig Owens, "The Problem with Puerilism," *Beyond Recognition: Representation, Power, and Culture*, edited by Scott Bryson; introduction by Simon Watney (Berkeley: University of California Press, 1992), 263.

5. Craig Owens, "The Problem With Puerilism," *Beyond Recognition: Representation, Power, and Culture*, edited by Scott Bryson; introduction by Simon Watney (Berkeley: University of California Press, 1992), 266.

6. Carlo McCormick, "Boy in the Hood" (The Wild East: The Rise and Fall of the East Village), *Artforum*, vol. 38, no. 2, October 1999, 159.

7. Rosalyn Deutsche and Cara Gendel Ryan, "The Fine Art of Gentrification," *October,* no. 31, Winter 1984; reprinted in *Portable Lower East Side*, vol. 4, no. 1, Spring 1987, http://www.abcnorio.org/about/history/fine_art.html.

8. Carlo McCormick. "East Village, R.I.P.," *East Village Eye*, vol. 7, no. 59, October 1985, 23.

9. Sylvère Lotringer, "My '80s: Better Than Life," *Artforum*, vol. 41, no. 8, April 2003, 194.

10. Sylvère Lotringer, "My '80s: Better Than Life," *Artforum*, vol. 41, no. 8, April 2003, 197.

11. Gregg Bordowitz, "My '80s: My Postermodernism," *Artforum*, vol. 41, no. 7, March 2003, 274.

12. Sarah Schulman, email to the editor, April 1, 2005.

A LOWER EAST SIDE POEM (1980)

MIGUEL PIÑERO

Just once before I die
I want to climb up on a
tenement sky
to dream my lungs out till
I cry
then scatter my ashes thru
the Lower East Side.

So let me sing my song tonight
let me feel out of sight
and let all eyes be dry
when they scatter my ashes thru
the Lower East Side.

From Houston to 14th Street
from Second Avenue to the mighty D
here the hustlers & suckers meet
the faggots and freaks will all get
high
on the ashes that have been scattered
thru the Lower East Side.

There's no other place for me to be
there's no other place that I can see
there's no other town around that
brings you up or keeps you down
no food little heat sweeps by
fancy cars & pimps' bars & juke saloons
& greasy spoons make my spirits fly
with my ashes scattered thru the
Lower East Side. . .

A thief, a junkie I've been
committed every known sin
Jews and Gentiles. . . Bums and Men
of style. . . run away child
police shooting wild. . .

mother's futile wail. . . pushers
making sales. . . dope wheelers
& cocaine dealers. . . smoking pot
streets are hot & feed off those who bleed to
death. . .

all that's true
all that's true
all that is true
but this ain't no lie
when I ask that my ashes be scattered thru
the Lower East Side.

So here I am, look at me
I stand proud as you can see
pleased to be from the Lower East
a street fighting man
a problem of this land
I am the Philosopher of the Criminal Mind
a dweller of prison time
a cancer of Rockefeller's ghettocide
this concrete tomb is my home
to belong to survive you gotta be strong
you can't be shy less without request
someone will scatter your ashes thru
the Lower East Side.

I don't wanna be buried in Puerto Rico
I don't wanna rest in long island cemetery
I wanna be near the stabbing shooting
gambling fighting & unnatural dying
& new birth crying
so please when I die. . .
don't take me far away
keep me near by
take my ashes and scatter them thru out
the Lower East Side. . .

LOWER EAST SIDE MESOSTICS 81–82 (1981–1982)

HOLLY ANDERSON

it's gristLe and
bOnes here:
the lIfe. can comfort come
from needleS or
night trAin? you hunch, you
shIver at 3, four a.m.
anD 5. "where's the
bAg? the bottle? the bed?"

Late may, a
cOncrete yard
In ragged bloom.
look at that roSe. look too,
the womAn who strolled,
now sleepIng alone on
the Dirty
wAlk.

she was eLegant
a year agO; her pearls,
her perpetual cIgarette
the woolen Suit worn
every dAy. her
hIgh heels are
fasteneD to swollen feet
with scrAps now.

six dirty bLack
dOgs and
theIr
maSter
wAlk slowly,
dInner over, those
6 gorgeD on
neighbors' trAsh

garbage garLands
snake rOund a
fIre hydrant.
treeS in full
leAf.
glItter of broken
bottles anD beer
cAns.

bruised appLes and
brOwn lettuce,
crates In the gutter
may feed Someone.
bent bAcks of people
lookIng for
Dinner.
such busy hAnds.

that's his bottLe, his cup
and that fOam mattress
besIde the
fence on Seventh.
that thin mAn
he's sleepIng
Deeply long before
night Arrives.

THE KITCHEN
ALUMINUM NIGHTS:
10th Anniversary Celebration at
Bond International Casino, 1526 Broadway

SUNDAY JUNE 14	MONDAY, JUNE 15
8pm-2am	8pm-2am
GLENN BRANCA	LAURIE ANDERSON
DAVID BYRNE	ROBERT ASHLEY
DNA	BUSH TETRAS
DOUGLAS DUNN	RHYS CHATHAM
FAB FIVE FREDDY	LAURA DEAN MUSICIANS
JOHN GIORNO	GEORGE LEWIS
PHILIP GLASS ENSEMBLE	MEREDITH MONK
LEROY JENKINS	BEBE MILLER DANCERS
LOVE OF LIFE ORCHESTRA	STEVE REICH & MUSICIANS
RAYBEATS	VEDO/DEVO
ZEV	

$15 per evening in advance. $25 for both evenings.
Available through Ticketron, Bond's box office, Fiorucci,
Bleecker Bob's & Soho Music Gallery
The Festival is a benefit for Artists fees for 1981-82.
[progam subject to change]

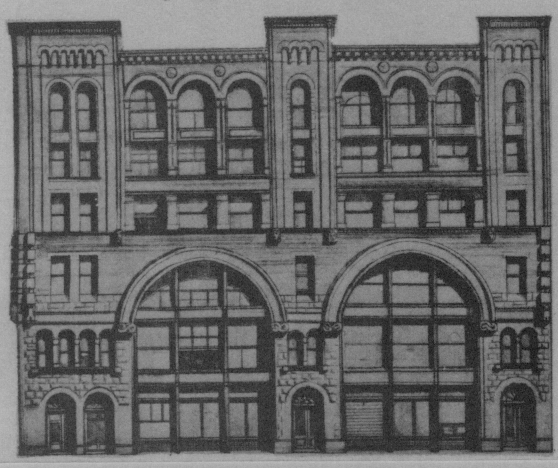

Next page left: Club 57 Schedule (1980)

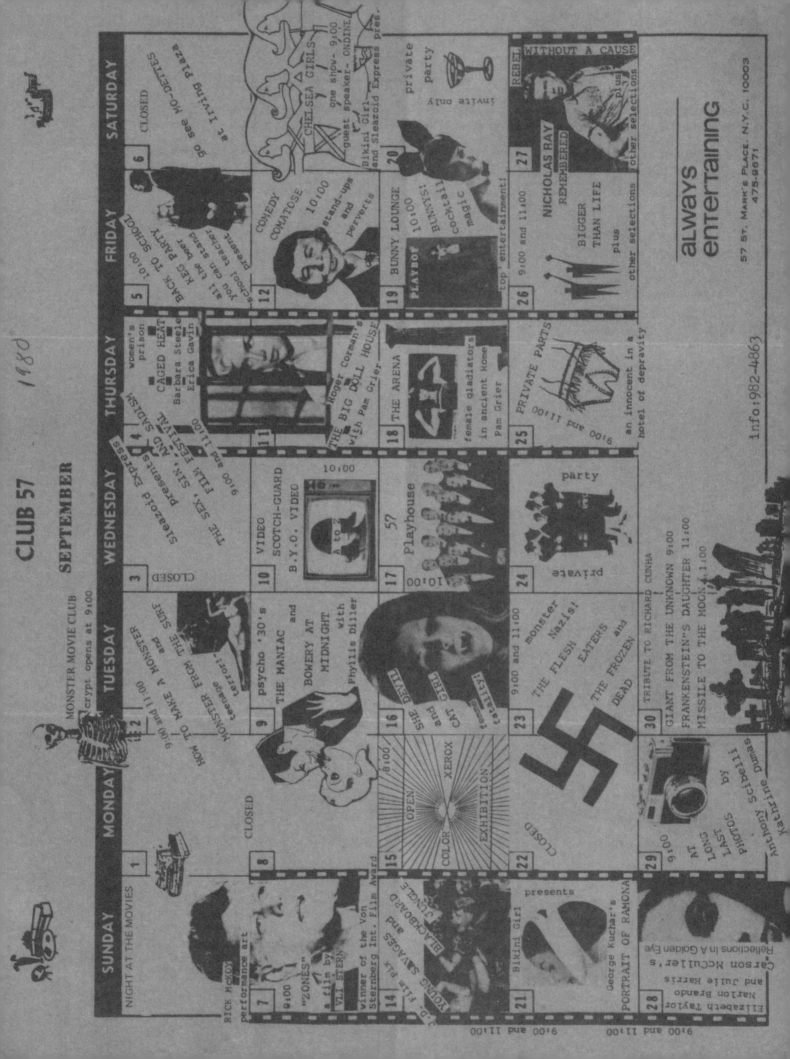

Black Story & White Story *by Holly Anderson*

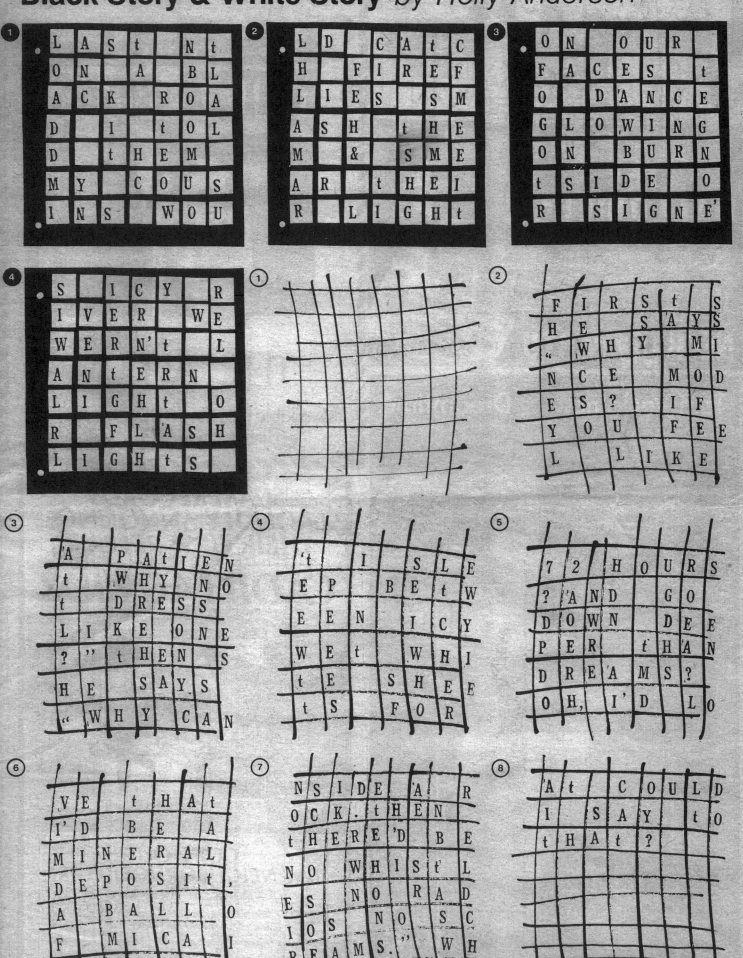

1 LAST NT ON A BL ACK ROA DD I tOL D tHE M MY COU S INS WOU

2 LD CAt C H FIRE F LIES H tHE ASH & SME M ARtHEI R LIGHt

3 ON OUR FACES t O DANCE E GLOWING ON BURN O t SIDE O R SIGNE'

4 S ICY R IVER WE L WERN'tEL ANtERN LIGHt O R FLASH LIGHtS

①

② FIRSt SS HE WHY AYMI "NCE MOD EYS? IFF YOU FE L LIKE

③ 'At PAtIE N WHY NO t DRESS S LIKE ONE S?" tHEN S HE SAYS "WHY CAN

④ 't I SLE EP BE tW EEN ICY WEt WHI tE SHER tS FOR

⑤ 72 HOURS ?'AND GO DOWN DE PER tHAN DREAMS? OH, I'D LO

⑥ VE tHA t I'D BE A MINERAL DEPOSIt, A BALLO F MICA I

⑦ NSIDE 'A R OCK.tHEN tHERE'D BE NO WHISt L ES NO RAD IOS NO S REAMS." WH

⑧ At COULD I SAY t O tHAt ?

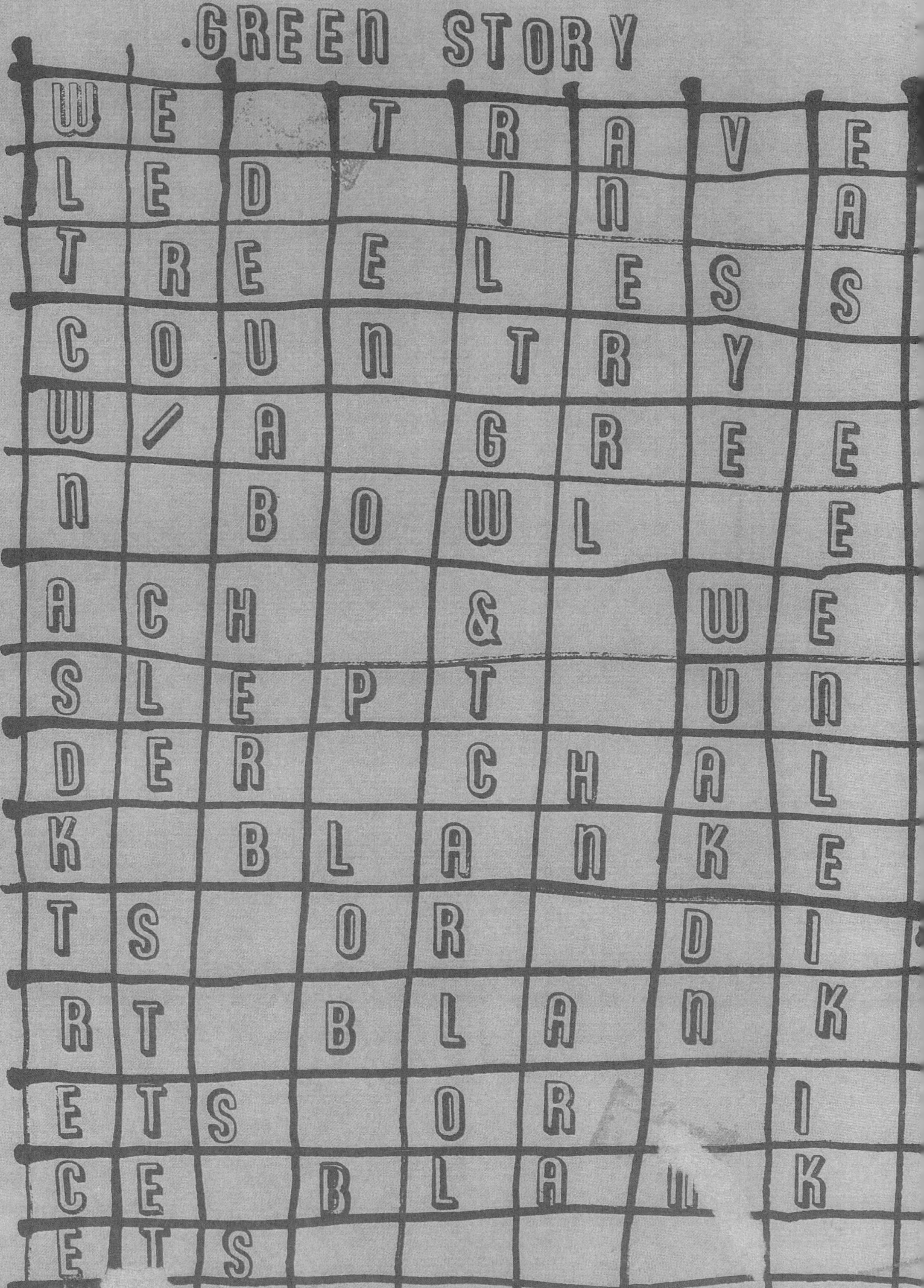

W E   T R A V E
L E D   I N   A S
T R E E L E S S
C O U N T R Y E E
W / A   G R E E E
N   B O W L E
A C H   &   W E
S L E P T   U N
D E R   C H A L
K   B L A N K E
T S   O R D I
R T   B L A N K
E T S   O R   I
C E   B L A N K
E T S

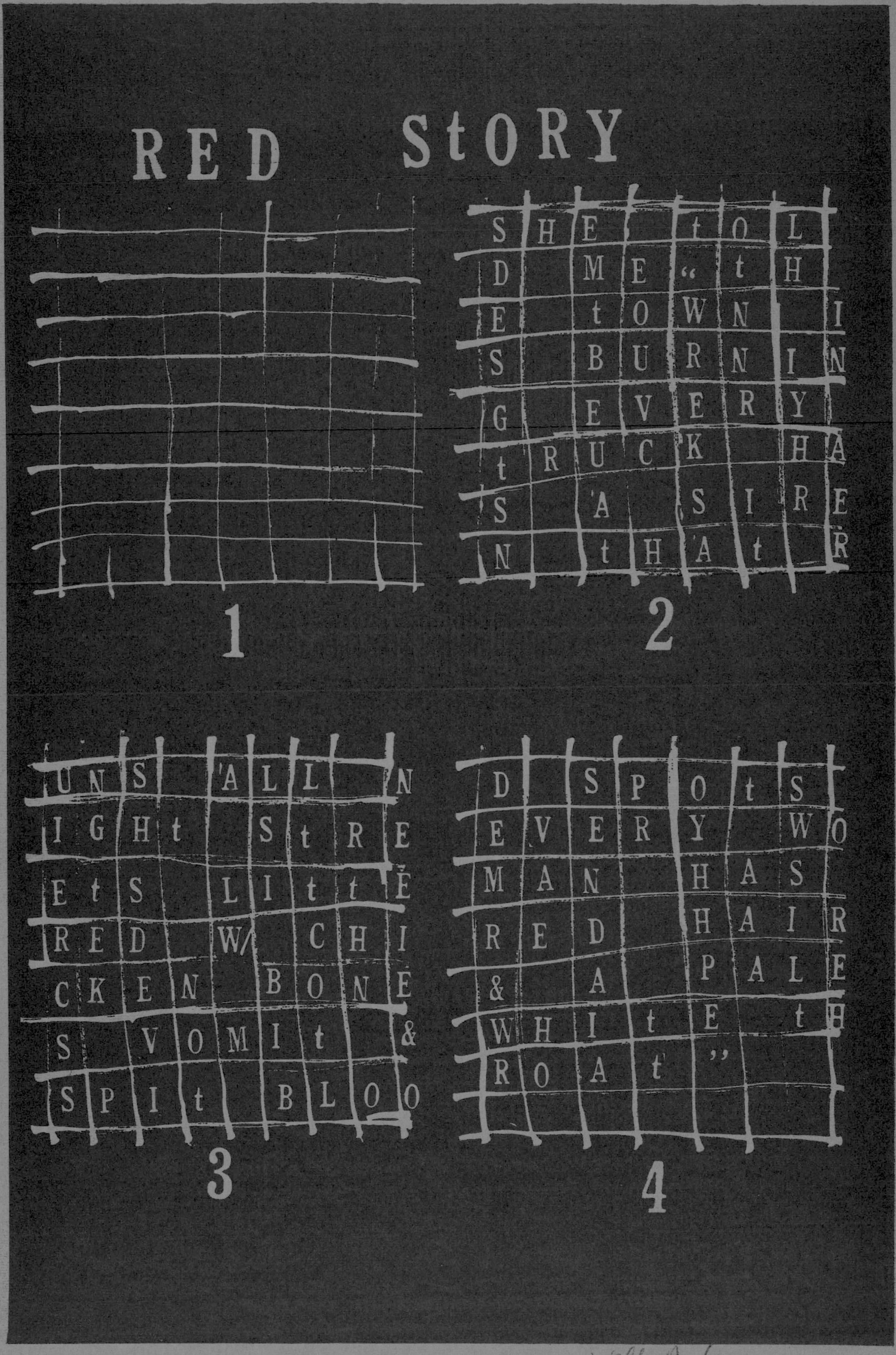

1

2

S	H	E		t	O	L
D		ME	"	t	H	
ES		t	O	W	N	I
S		B	U	R	N	I	N
G		E	V	E	R	Y
t		R	U	C	K	H	A
S		A		S	I	R	E
N		t	H	A	t		R

3

U	N	S		A	L	L		N
I	G	H	t		S	t	R	E
E	t	S		L	I	t	t	E
R	E	D		W/		C	H	I	E
C	K	E	N		B	O	N	E
S		V	O	M	I	t		&
S	P	I	t		B	L	O	O

4

D		S	P	O	t	S
E	V	E	R	Y		W	O
M	A	N		H	A	S
R	E	D		H	A	I	R
&		A		P	A	L	E
W	H	I	t	E		t
R	O	A	t		"

O N   t H E   F
A R   S I D E
O F   B R A C K
I S H   W A t E
R I N   t H E E
W R E C K A G E
Y O U   S I G N

A L E D   U S E N
W I t H   B E N
t   A R M S .
I N   t H E   W
R E C K A G E
Y O U   W A V E
D   B L U E   R

A G S .   Y O U
S A I D   'S I S
t E R S   N O W
L E A D   U S
t O   t H E   C
I S t E R N   F
O R   W E   M U

S t   W A S H
A W A Y   t H E
S E   M A R K S'
.

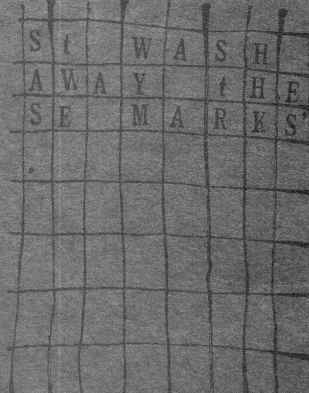

HOLLY ANDERSON

(two) Blue Story

IT WAS N'T LONG A
FTER TH IS THAT AT
HE DIAMOND FIRST TY
PPEARED ON MANY DA
SURFACES. WHO HA RE
MADE THIS MARK? WI
ALL AROUND US? N A
BEGAN T AT 2 OING H
T ON STERNA & A
NDS. ACROSS OUR F
ORE HEADS OR THRO

ATS NEEDLED BLUE E
DIAMONDS WERE ST
RUNG. GRASSES SIG
NALED GRASSES. GL
ASS DIDN'T GLINT.
METAL RUSTED IN
DRAWERS. METAL RU
STED OUTDOORS.

HOLLY ANDERSON

(two) Blue Story

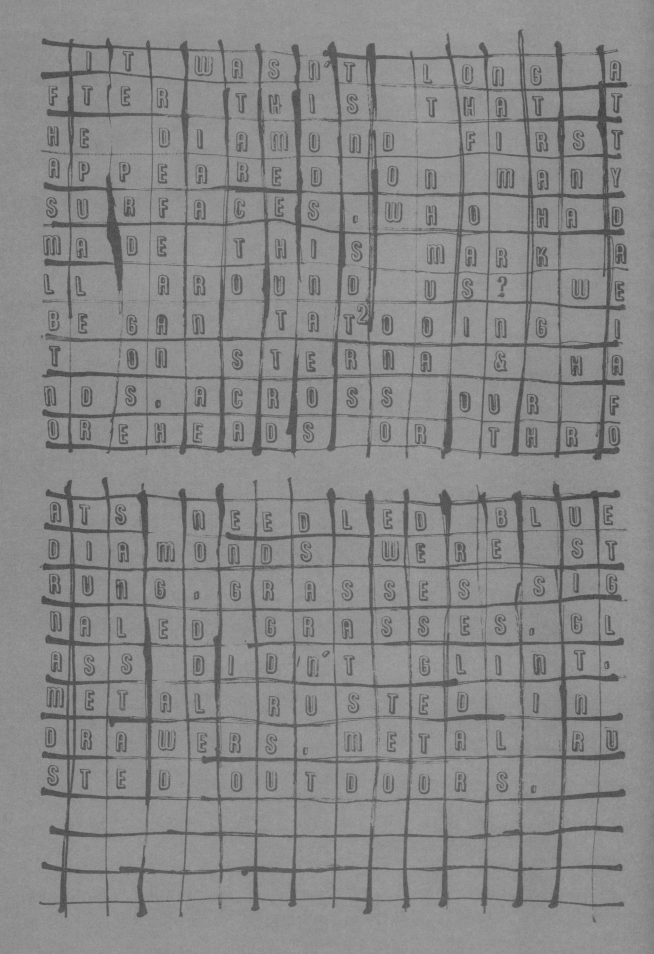

HOLLY ANDERSON

BOMB

VOLUME 1 ISSUE 1 NEW YORK SPRING 1981

$3.50

Max Blagg

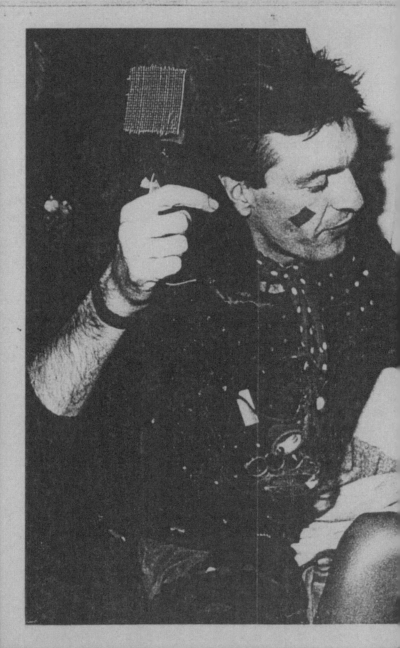

Clowns At Bay / Cadill

12000 Girlscouts Cant

Appearing in New York

Jim Farmer

ng Down on Dynamite

ng & Other Tuneful Melodies

er 1981

Counter-Clockwise:

"Grafñti": *Public Illumination Magazine* No. 13 (1981)
Art: Kip Herring

The Low-Tech Manual, Cover (1981) Art: Art Spiegelma

Eileen Myles at Attitude Art, Flyer/Postcard (1981)

Zone No. 7, Cover (1981)
Art: Michael Madore

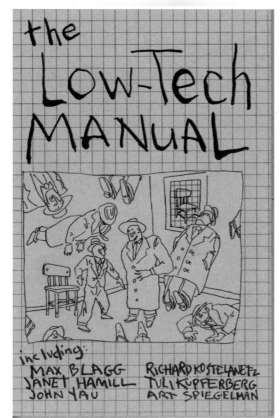

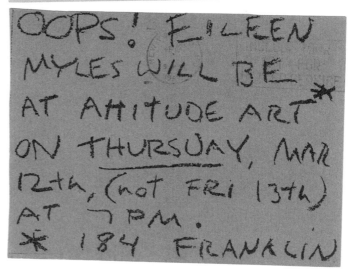

ZONE

COLLABORATIONS

Ascher/Straus
Deem & Vance
Bernstein & Silliman
Sherry & Yau
Acconci
Kostelanetz
Porter
More!

The Wooster Group: Point Judith

#7, Spring/Summer 1981

$2.50

FROM *BAGATELLES* (1981)

PETER CHERCHES

Sniffing each other was our favorite pastime. We would produce various and sundry odors for each other's benefit. Some of our odors were mutual, but certainly not all. She produced many odors which I could not duplicate, and vice-versa. We spent many pleasant hours producing odors for each other. When we became familiar with each other's repertoire of odors, we began to make requests. It was pure ecstasy. When we were sniffing each other nothing else mattered. We had each other, and as far as we were concerned, who cared how the world smelled.

* * *

You take a lot out of me, she said to me. I know, I told her in her own voice.

* * *

Where is she, I wondered, when she wasn't there. If she's not here she could be anywhere. She could be anywhere and not alone.

I began to imagine the worst. At every imagining I thought I had imagined the worst, then I imagined something even worse. It got to the point where my imaginings no longer included her. I realized that the worst did not encompass her. As my imaginings continued, as worst superceded worst, making the preceding worst only worse, I began to forget her. As worst got worse, I forgot her more. Things were getting pretty bad, and I had almost forgotten her completely, when she reappeared.

* * *

Our life together has its limits, I said.

What exactly do you mean, she said. Our life together is limited in time and space, I said. Oh, she said.

* * *

Once, while I was licking her, she disappeared. I knew she had disappeared, because my tongue was lapping at the air. I was distressed, but I kept on licking. I licked for some time, until I felt her body again on my tongue.

* * *

We had been together for some time by this time. Many years. We had stopped counting. We celebrated anniversaries, but as far as we were concerned each anniversary meant just another year. We kept records, of course, and had we wanted to know we could certainly have looked it up, but neither of us ever did. Sometimes, however, the subject did come up. This was inevitable. For instance, we would have a fight and she would say, it's been many years, hasn't it. And I, still in the spirit of combat, would say, yes, many, indeed. Or, feeling a bit nostalgic she would say, it's been many years, hasn't it. And I, caught, up in the spirit of nostalgia, would say, yes, many, indeed. And, occasionally, simply musing about time and the two of us, she would say, it's been many years, hasn't it. And I, similarly musing about the two of us and time, would say, yes, many, indeed. It's been many years.

* * *

You're a prick, she said. You're a cunt, I said.

Peter Cherches

Colorful Tales

Purgatory Pie Press

1983 New York

"Italian Food" from Colorful Tales (1983)
Text: Peter Cherches;
Design: Purgatory Pie Press

⬤⬤⬤⬤ had never seen Anna quite ⬤⬤⬤⬤
⬤⬤⬤ Of course, from her standpoint it was ⬤⬤⬤
⬤⬤⬤ explaining. That, however was ⬤⬤⬤
⬤⬤⬤ your family?" she asked. ⬤⬤⬤
⬤⬤⬤
⬤⬤⬤ the last time he had ⬤⬤⬤
⬤⬤⬤ some kind of commitment ⬤⬤⬤
⬤⬤⬤ more than one ⬤⬤⬤
⬤⬤⬤ if there were some way ⬤⬤⬤
⬤⬤⬤ safely. But no, that would be ⬤⬤⬤
⬤⬤⬤ if her husband were to find ⬤⬤⬤
⬤⬤⬤ for a few moments and then ⬤⬤⬤
⬤⬤⬤ Jonathan and the ⬤⬤⬤
⬤⬤⬤ the dog, the furniture ⬤⬤⬤
⬤⬤⬤ ugly, very ugly ⬤⬤⬤
⬤⬤⬤ perhaps lasagna," he ⬤⬤⬤
⬤⬤⬤ Italian food at a time like ⬤⬤⬤
⬤⬤⬤ picked up the knife that ⬤⬤⬤
⬤⬤⬤ grabbed her ⬤⬤⬤
⬤⬤⬤
⬤⬤⬤ ever try that again," ⬤⬤⬤
⬤⬤⬤ besides," he said, "I like Italian ⬤⬤⬤
⬤⬤⬤ and left it at that.

You're a prick, she said. You're a cunt, I said. You're a prick, she said. You're a cunt, I said. I forgot what we're arguing about, she said. Pricks and cunts, I said.

* * *

We decided to try something new.
Afterwards, I asked her what she thought.
It seemed familiar, she said. Are you sure we've never done that before.
Positive.
It seemed so familiar. I think we did something like it a long time ago.
I know what you're thinking of, I said. But it wasn't exactly the same thing.

* * *

She was lying motionless. I went over and kicked her, not too hard, just hard enough to see if she was still alive. She was, because she moved in a certain way. That's good, I thought, because if she's still alive it means that we can resume.

* * *

I sat for a while and she walked. Then she got tired and sat, so I walked. I walked for a while, then I told her I wanted to sit, so she got up and walked again. I sat there, watching her walk, remembering how we used to walk together.

* * *

We tried to put each other into words. But words weren't enough. So we put each other into sentences. No good. Paragraphs. Unsatisfactory. Chapters. Not quite right. A book. Books. Volume upon volume upon volume. It just wouldn't work. Nothing was enough, everything was too much.

from LOW TECH PRESS

FIVE+FIVE

FEATURING:

Ken Tisa
Peter Cherches
Michael La Bombarda
Michael Madore
Thomas McGonigle
Edward Jacobus
Tom Ahern
Jennifer Nostrand
Zagreus Bowery
Jörga Cardin

NEWSPAPER POEM (1981)

BOB WITZ

in bobs bigboy restaurant in sw los angeles 2 holdupmen w/

shotguns fastfood restaurant lineup 11 in meatfreezer and blast

w/ shotgun fire unknown amt from cashregister from customers

3 dead 6 wounded 2 escape fire

a stray shepherd dog was hit by a train trying to avoid taunts

and rocks of thoughtless juveniles give to associated human societies

35000 people live on the streets of nyc

have you seen these people yvonne is 4'11" and weights 100 lbs

depressed abt her marks and what she shld do faild all her courses

during the last marking period told her younger sister she was

leaving home cldnt show report card to mother

20 yr old woman prostitute real name unknown body found wooded area

near orchard beach parking lot her head had been crushd

john lennon is dead

world mourns

2 are shot at lennon tribute in apparently drugrelated dispute

saudis up oil prices $2 a barrel

cop shot in queens

after being hit w/ a blast of buckshot bossett staggered into a

bedroom and barricaded himself 2 shotguns and a rifle were found

in the bedroom of the 3room apt alone except for doberman pinscher

dog shot w/ tranquilizer drugcutting operation phony address

criminal record out on good behavior taken to booth mem hospital

being questioned

5 + 5 Announcement, Low Tech Press (1984)
Art: Jörga Cardin

vitales bulletproof vest was at the cleaners when he was wounded

investigating a burglary at florist shop flowers by pete stoppd 2

men for questioning innocuous answer men boltd officers pursued

jimmy help me im shot

winfield a yankee for 10 yrs $13 million

mug and kill without emotion or regret no ties no skills menial

jobs w/ no future illusion of superhuman strength drug habits

lost nuts loonies set them free no matter what the charge

coldeyed youths prowl the cities

its wild and its real

i really loved the guy: paul mccartney a bitter cruel blow

the 80s are still going to be beautiful john believed in it

paul wanted to play for the folks john stay in studio live family

not like elvis trappd defeated hopeless john had beaten it all

drugs fame damage loved his son and yoko life

restless outspoken creative

3 die in crash during chase in dallas 3 counts of manslaughter

possession of marijuana evading arrest and speeding

british explorers reach southpole snowmobile trek 1100 miles most

of it unchartd

stomach was hardening that meant internal bleeding i cldnt pick him

up he was too heavy i tried flaggd down a passerby other cops helpd

indian oil theft columbian jet hijackd call 221-2178 for tax relief

trees growing grass flowers grain children sunshine

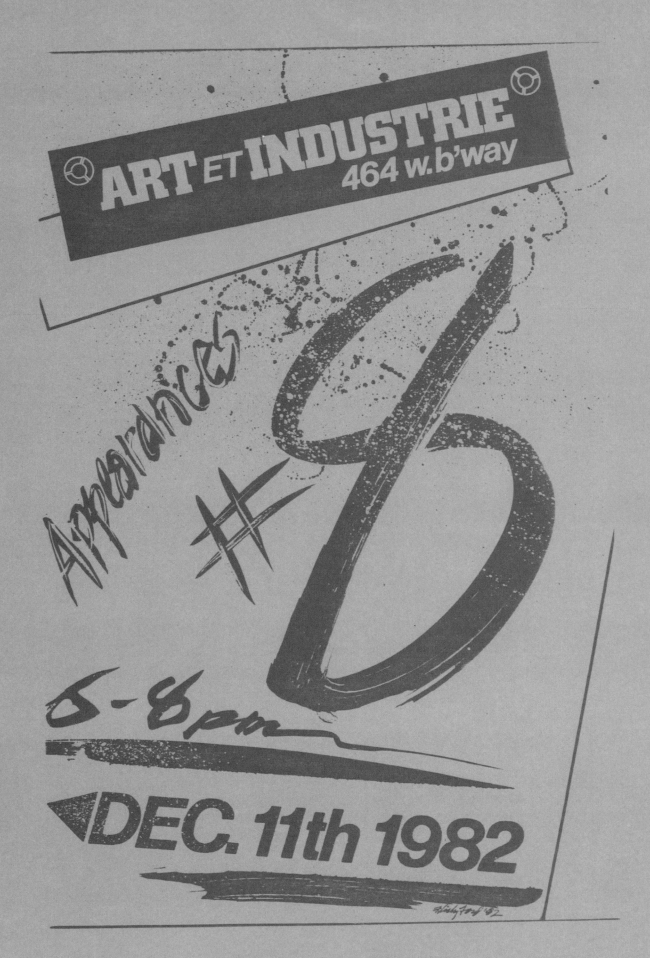

ART ET INDUSTRIE
464 w. b'way

Appearances #3

6-8 pm

DEC. 11th 1982

TO LAUNCH A
WOMAN'S HEALTH
CARE CAMPAIGN
IN EL SALVADOR

3RD
Annual

Featuring Woman
Writers of the
Lower East Side

ROBERTA ALLEN
ZOE ANGLESEY
CONSTANCE DeJONG
ANNE FORER
HARRIET MALINOWITZ
ROBBIE McAULEY
EILEEN MYLES
BERNADETTE MAYER
ANN ROWER
SARAH SCHULMAN
SUSAN SHERMAN
CATHERINE TEXIER
LYNNE TILLMAN
SUSIE TIMMONS
SARAH WILKINSON
and others

LITERARY BENEFIT
LITERARY BENEFIT

JAMES

3PM – 8PM
Sunday Sept. 28
St. Mark's Church
2nd Ave. & 10th St.

$5.00 TICKETS
AVAILABLE
St. Marks Bookshop
13 St. Marks Place &
Womanbooks 92nd &
Amsterdam CHILD
CARE PROVIDED
FOR MORE INFO.
(212) 673-8204

SPONSORED BY
WOMEN'S
ASSOCIATION OF
EL SALVADOR &
THE POETRY
PROJECT AT ST.
MARK'S CHURCH

3rd Annual AMES Literary Benefit At The Poetry Project, Flyer (1980)

HAIKU FROM *PUBLIC ILLUMINATION MAGAZINE* (1982–1989)

MR. BASHO

off the pier
in the salty brine
coney island white
  fish
float at noon.

[1982]

feeding the pigeons
in the park
one breadcrumb falls

[1982]

the black hooker in red
when business is slow
sells dope to her "friends"

[1982]

canal st.
abandoned stone saint
blesses the wall

[1985]

washing windshields
the homeless man
laughing to himself

[1989]

ANYTHING
BY
ANYBODY

COM PRESS 10/5/81

UPSTART

benefit poetry reading

Tuesday, October 6

8 pm

Harkness Theater
Butler Library

RON PADGETT

Born in Tulsa, Oklahoma. Attended Central High. Drove a red sportscar. Magazines: PARIS REVIEW, NEW YORKER, COLUMBIA REVIEW, SUN, Z, etc. Books: TRIANGLES IN THE AFTER-NOON, GREAT BALLS OF FIRE, TOUJOURS l'AMOUR, AN ANTHOLOGY OF NEW YORK POETS, etc. Columbia College '64, where he won the Boar's Head and Woodberry Poetry Prizes.

BRAD GOOCH

Is a Wilhemina model. His latest book costs $1000. Columbia '73, where he won the Acadamy of American Poets Prize. Born in Kingston, Penn. Went to school, was in the band. Played clarinet. Books: PICTURES-STORIES, THE DAILY NEWS, ANOTHER COUNTRY TUN. Magazines: LITTLE CAESAR, ZZZ, THE WORLD, COLUMBIA REVIEW, CHRISTOPHER STREET, etc.

MICHAEL LALLY

Ashbery calls him "The Francois Villon of the '70's." Born Orange NJ. Maga-zines: THE PARTISAN REVIEW, THE MASSA-CHUSETTS REVIEW, LITTLE CAESAR, etc. Books: THE SOUTH ORANGE SONNETS, DUES ROCKY DIES YELLOW, MY LIFE, JUST LET ME DO IT, etc.

PENELOPE MILFORD

Nominated for an Acadamy Award for Best Supporting Actre in "Coming Home." Featured in "Valentino," "Endless Love," etc.

TIM DLUGOS

Takes incredible risks in his poems. Ex-member of a Catholic religias order. Seriously considering re-entering one. Born in Western Mass. Newest books of poems soon-to-be-out are a big book called ENTRE NOUS, by LITTLE CAESAR PRESS, & a small one called A FAST LIFE, Sherwood Press. Last Book: JE SUIS EIN AMERICANO. Magazines: SUN & MOON, LITTLE CAESAR, ZZZ, THE WORLD,

Admission $2.50

ZOOIN' IN ALPHABET TOWN (1982)

BOB HOLMAN

For David Henderson

Black spaces
Between buildings
Hadn't been there

Ooo, a little squirming
In a zoo now
Be cool
In the center
Don't get picked off
At the end
Of the line
To be eaten

Piles of rubbish
Broken glass & cans & jewels
Shimmering rubbish
Artificial moon

Neon blink
Between A & B
CLUB round & round
Neon blink
Good times here
Put together by one or two people
It's not like they're part
Of an international chain
Except the international chain of
No cover No minimum
No maximum
To the good times

Sign says Free Public Baths

Sign says Wholesale Vegetable Distributor

Big tapestry, brilliant
Jesus. Jesus! Window
Slams down.

Sidewalk covered with acronyms
HEW, HUD. Asbestos.
The man who invented asbestos
Died a few years later
Of lung cancer
All the buildings insulated with it
Madison Square insulated with it
Until the elephants knocked it down

Nuyorican girls club
Teen Angels go
For a young boy's legs
Sweet torment, 6th St.
Well, the liquor store on Avenue C
Now there's a sight
Hard to get a bottle
Even when you got the money
Security door, bullet-proof plexiglass
Attack-train doberman shepherd
Hey, that liquor sure is priceless stuff

Roaming around food aromas
Bread baking
Ripe mangoes for a second
Did you get that
For a second strong mango

Tropical moon music

Music music music

7th between B & C
Right before dawn
Pushcart people
In the distance
Comin' up
Comin' up
Avenue C
From down below Houston St.
Settle down
Light little fires
Like a Gypsy caravan
It really was
Fruits, vegetables, candles
Mangoes? Not then

Not for long
With the Lower East Side Charcuterie
Do you accept food stamps for your pate?
Show me the way
To the next sushi bar
Cappuccino would be fine
Chevre & a nice lite wine

Hey, look over there
What used to be a Camaro
Parked where a building used to be
All the glass broken out
All the windows in the building broken out
It's the right place
No tires
Not going anywhere
It take a lot of cinder blocks
To seal up

The city cracks

Put that Camaro in a museum!

Crossing Avenue A
Feeling the DMZ
On 11th St., Paradise Alley
Kerouac wrote here
Then a shooting gallery
Now the junkies are blocked in

At one time neigh highly Jewish
Yeshiva here
The Irish controlling the waterfront
So the Jewish kids didn't go swimming

On 3rd St. some row houses
Hamilton Fish built them
Middle class, 1830's
7th St. bourgeoisie

Yo! Peace Eye Books
Kosher Dairy
Allen Ginsberg ate here
Muggers left his poems
Poems still here

Graffiti
I remember

What it said
I don't remember

A beautiful image
Street-lit

Images sustain community

Gentrification cuts out
Music music music

The garbage
Hell I wrote a letter
Three days later
Two garbagemen
Came to the door

OK OK, let's trace it
Inside the detail
Let's trace the origins of garbage
Remember Lionel Ziffrin,
Famous (Zif) comics founder
Wandering late at night
Collecting icons
Old Ukrainian ones, homemade ones
Agents of Christianity also out late at night
Out to destroy the icons
Battle of the icons

Several places, they built their own icons
Birds on sheets, crate altars
Jars of liquid amphetamine
With different colored pebbles in them
People working all the time all the time
& then somebody flipping out
& trashing the whole place

Stomping in the night! Amphetaminos!

Reality sense community
Pockets of beauty
Survival music
Get it together before it disappears

The people the buildings & whatnot

People out there, life
Goes on in its everyday
Disaster area

Up on 75th & 5th with a beer on the street
Illegal to drink there, babes
Except Perrier
In a paper bag

Down here Esquire photoed some bums
Then polished them
Before & After
Now they're rich Hollywood stars
With agents
Now they're back on the Bowery
Wined

A bag lady listening through the door salsas

Tripping on D at 2 or 3
Sinister street
But keep it looking messed up
Maybe the gentry can't set up shop

In the apartments it's cozy
Outside, the garbage is camouflage
When the streets get cleaned up
The people who've been living here
Won't be able to afford to anymore

Painted walls
Empty buildings
Darkness at twilight

BENZENE

4

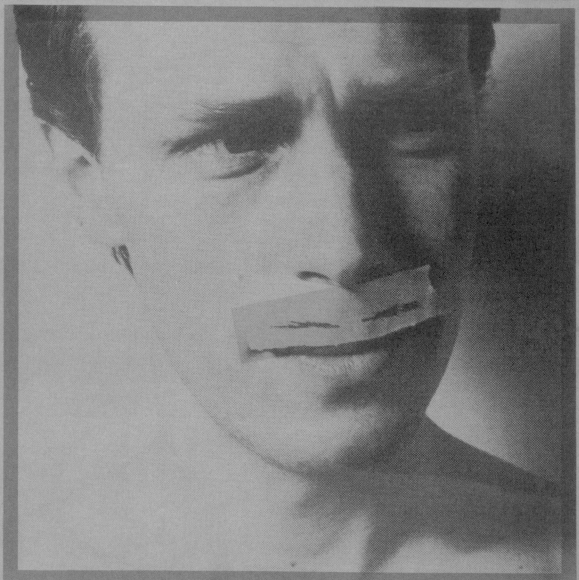

WINTER 1982 $2

Benzene No. 4, Cover (1982)
Art: Robert Younger; Design: Allan Bealy

BENZENE EDITIONS $4

THE
NOTHING
ISSUE
PART ONE

ZONE 10

 Benzene/Zone No. 10, the Nothing Isue
(Part One), Cover (1981-5)
Art/Design: Allan Bealy

BOMB

Painters and Writers   1982

P U B L I S H I N G   P A R T Y

TUESDAY, NOVEMBER 30
9–11pm
(4th floor)

Danceteria

30 W 21st NYC   THIS INVITATION ADMITS TWO

Bomb, Publishing Party at Danceteria,
Invitation (1982)
Art: Mary Heilman; Design: Mark Magill

3 Teens Kill 4 at the Underground
Flyer (1982)

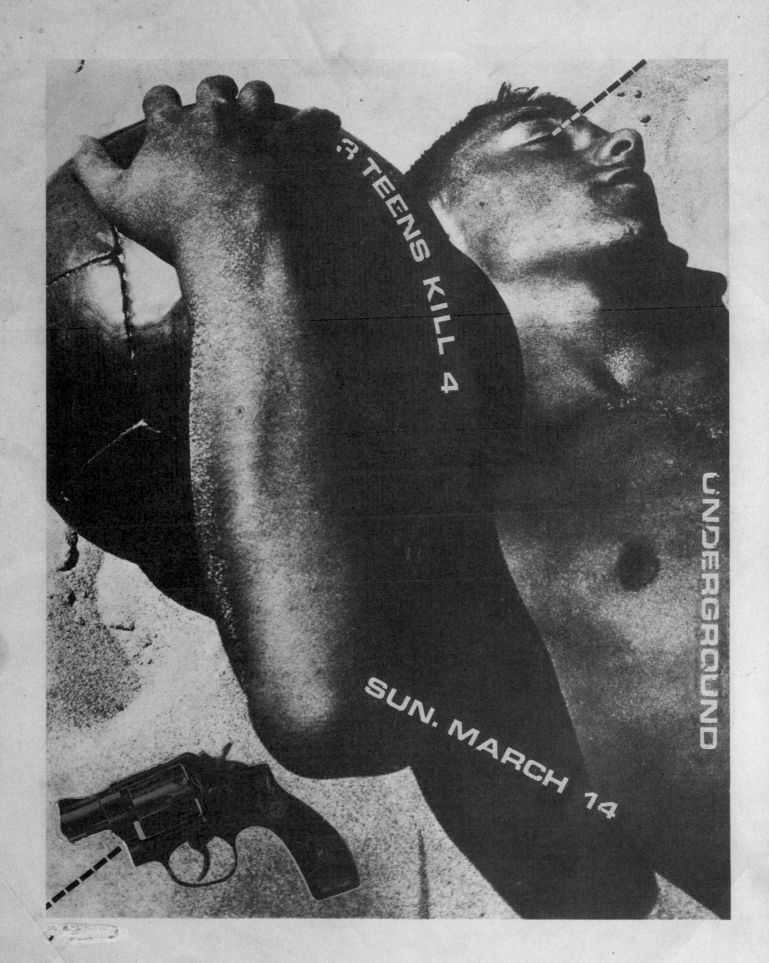

Adulterers Anonymous

by Lydia Lunch and Exene Cervenka

Adulterers Anonymous by Lydia Lunch and Exene Cervenka. Cover (1982) Photo: David Arnoff

E-826

WHILE YOU WERE OUT (1982)

PENNY ARCADE

Hello, darling! It's show time, darling! And everything is coming up roses! Is everybody happy?

Andy Warhol was my husband! Candy Darling was my wife and you are all my beautiful children!

You're beautiful because you understand how beautiful the world is, how beautiful I am and I told the world, "you're not paying Andrea Whips because she's beautiful but because the world is beautiful and the world must pay!"

You may not realize who I am. This generation is the slow group.

Sesame Street caused brain damage! Skippy peanut butter makes the brain cells stick together!

Yesterday, I ran through the subway, whispering, "Who will fill me full of jelly, custard and cream?" People ran out shrieking!

When I shriek in public, people take notice! I'm a first, I'm a second, I'm a ding dong baby and I'm on my way up there! Up there with James Dean and Marilyn Monroe! Marilyn's been dead so many years. You better love me while you can darling!

Last night, I rode down in my elevator 108 times to make sure that the doorman was staying awake for the other tenants. He called me a stupid cunt! But I told him darling, "A cunt is a useful thing!"

It's getting dull out there darling! Dangerously dull. Haven't you noticed? It's turning into a mall out there!

Have you seen the downtown art scene lately? Who are those young Republicans with purple hair and multiple piercings? You know, the ones who keep telling us how fab everything is.

Couldn't they afford a longer adjective?

It's like the made for tv movie of the 60's and 70's and it isn't even in living color! Thank god I'm an acid freak!

Thank god I'm a country girl!

I'm a real acid freak darling, I've got some very freaky things in my bag! I'm a real blonde darling! Look at these grapefruits! I'm a real woman! I'm gonna be on top tonight!

Oh! I just had a vicious acid flashback! I was completely surrounded by colored rats but I knew that no one would believe me darling! So I brought them back with me! Look at these fabulous colors! Don't worry darling! This is not performance art darling!

Performance art is the vinyl miniskirt of the 80's.

I am going to call Andy Warhol and tell him all about you. You can do this too darling, if you take LSD cut with speed.

When alchemy fails I turn to chemistry!

Hello Andy, darling. This is Andrea, darling.
Hello Andy . . . I love you darling, do you love me?
I love you darling!

I loved you when you were hated and I hated you
when you were loved!

Listen, darling. I just met these fabulous people
and I just know that you could make them into
fairly big stars darling.

I can't take them to Max's darling!

Because they hate me there! Because that blonde
boy, he spread salad dressing all over his chest and
then he wouldn't pay for it!

Did I really sign Candy Darling's name on the check?

How fabulous ESP is!

I love you darling! Do you love me? I love you.

I'm going to throw an I Ching for all of you!

You look like you could use it. See! A circle of
psychedelic rats! Thats very, very good. And see?
There are three red rats in a row! That's very
auspicious darling. Oh, and a changing rat!

If you were real homosexuals, you would know that
this color was chartreuse! Have you noticed how they
keep maligning homosexuals? Why? Homosexuals are
so fabulous and they give flawless dinner parties. It's
the romosexuals that they should worry about, darling.

The ones who roam the streets. Not the homosexuals
who stay home! Look at your social ecology! It's like
the sinking of Atlantis!

I come from a long line that doesn't have many
people left standing in it. 15 years from now people
will be standing around at cocktail parties saying,
"I remember when there were faggots, freaks and
queens darling! And it was fabulous!"

See darling, sometimes less is more but a lot of times
darling, less is less. It's a small world darling, but not
if you have to clean it!

People of the future! When you dig this film up in my
time capsule archives, I'll be downtown darling, home
of the real stars.

But when you dig up a downtown superstar darling . . .
she just dries up and blows away.

See there's a difference between a big piece of art
with a little bit of shit in it . . . and a big piece of shit
with a little bit of art in it!

It's a small world darling! But not if you have
to clean it.

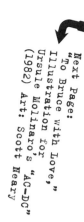
Next Page:
"To Bruce with Love,"
Illustration for
Ursule Molinaro's "AC-DC"
(1982) Art: Scott Neary

AC-DC (1982)

URSULE MOLINARO

For Bruce Benderson, With Love

She isn't sure if it's a shot she hears, or the backfiring of a truck.

Before she sees two bare bony legs groping down the fire escape outside her bedroom window. In freezing April drizzle. Followed by tight buttocks clad in leopard undershorts. Followed by an unbuttoned white shirt, & a tight white face under a punk hair cut: a crest of orange bristles sticking up from an otherwise shaved head.

She opens her window & pulls the half-naked figure inside. Relocking her window.

He doesn't resist, except with his eyes: Why is she doing this?

He lets her shove him toward the livingroom. Like an object: she thinks: used to being picked up & put down. His naked feet slur traceless across her naked livingroom floor. She shoves him toward the fireplace. Crawl up the flue: she says to him.

Huh? He stands looking at her, his eyes searching her face: What does she want from him?

They turned the heat off a week ago: she says: Just hang in there until it's over.

Outside the livingroom window on the street side, sirens scream closer, converging on her building. He frowns at her, his eyes contracting to brilliant black dots, then hoists himself up into the sooty brick shaft. His toes push against the sides of the fireplace & out of sight.

Why is she doing this?

She walks to the livingroom window & counts: nine police cars. From which spill: sixteen policemen of varying sizes some with axes who disappear into her main entrance. One car with two policemen remains sitting at the curb.

Her bells rings. She goes to press the buzzer, wondering what she'll do if the cold-numbed object lets go & falls at their feet.

She opens her door & stands leaning against the inner frame.

The retired high school teacher in the apartment below hers is asking what type of criminal they're looking for. She doesn't hear their answer; if they give an answer. Only the retired high school teacher's retired voice, saying that: he's glad he's retired. They're living in terrible times when a teacher can't turn his back on a class to write something on the blackboard.

A sea of upturned police faces is surging up the stairs. Yes: she says truthfully: Yes, I saw somebody groping down the fire escape.

Why is she doing this?

She's a reasonable-sounding woman, dressed in reasonable clothes: clean jeans & a black turtleneck sweater. Her typewriter is still running in her bedroom, where she works. She'd obviously been typing when she saw whomever they're looking for. If whoever she saw & pulled inside is who they're looking for. For whatever reason. She doesn't tell them that whoever she saw & pulled inside is half-naked, hanging inside the flue above her fireplace in leopard undershorts.

Four policemen have followed her into her bedroom/workroom & are nudging her to open the window. Faster. It sticks sometimes: she says; but then hurriedly complies when she sees one of them raise an ax.

Two policemen start running down the fire escape. Two others start running up toward the roof. &

"TO BRUCE WITH LOVE"

almost collide with two more who are climbing out through the bedroom window of the couple upstairs.

Who aren't home at this hour   —The policemen must have broken down their door.—   Who don't come home until around 4:30–5:00 o'clock. The husband usually half an hour ahead of the wife.

Who squeaks like a mouse when they make love. Almost the instant she walks into the upstairs apartment. & the satisfied husband gurgles like a stopped-up kitchen sink.

He should be coming home just about now.

Although . . .   it now occurs to her that she heard something up there before she heard what she's now sure was a shot. She now wishes that she hadn't concentrated quite so hard on "The Infections of the Inner Ear" which she's translating for a medical publication. The deadline for the "Inner Ear" is 9:00 a.m. tomorrow. & she still has more than half to go. She now wishes that she'd listened before inviting what might be a half-naked murderer to hide in her flue.

She may of course be hiding the intended murder victim, who managed to escape half naked.

He certainly looked like a victim, out there on her fire escape. Which is why she felt prompted to pull him inside. Her philosophy   borrowed from Simone Weil, the Jewish saint of WW II   requires that she throw her weight, though it be slight, onto the lighter scale.

On which she now finds herself in the company of a punk-object on the run from authority. For want of a more original direction to his life. A half-naked faddist, who probably ignores the history behind the fashion on which he's elaborating with orange bristles & leopard underwear.

Although, even if he did know all about it, he wouldn't be the first unimaginative drop-out to be in love with images of totalitarian discipline. Nor the first victim to get a kick out of wearing the clothes of his jailers.

The rest of his aberrant imitation-Nazi costume is probably lying in the absent couple's apartment upstairs.

Where she now hears stomping & scurrying. A metal object thudding to the floor. Slow, heavy voices berating a high-pitched whine.

An ambulance has pulled up outside the main entrance. Her door is still open. As is her bedroom window.

Which the last of the four returning policemen considerately pulls down shut behind him. Telling her that: it's chilly out there. Unseasonably chilly for April. Is their landlord still giving them heat?

She shakes her head, her throat constricting, & escorts them into the hall. They tell her: not to worry. They'll be keeping an eye on the place. They press a card into her hand with an emergency number to call in case she sees somebody out there again.

The retired high school teacher's voice is coming up the stairs, talking about the terrible neighborhood they live in. His face brightens as he catches sight of her, standing in her open door.

He considers her the only other intellectual in their building, & tries to trap her into conversations every time he meets her in the hall downstairs, on her way in or on her way out. Almost every time she goes in or out. He either watches for her to come home from his livingroom window, or else he listens for her to unlock her door   after he has heard her stop typing & promptly hurries out into the hall, to dump his garbage or to check his mail.

He worries her more than the policemen. Who will eventually go away, after they find   or don't find whomever they're looking for. The way the place is built, the retired high school teacher probably knows her daily moves more intimately than she does. Just as she can't help knowing every mouse-&-gurgle detail of the lovemaking couple upstairs.

She wonders if the retired high school teacher will be able to distinguish between a radio voice & the live voice of the half-naked punk-object up her flue, who may want to say something after he slides back down.

When she'll present him with a plan of how to escape to get rid of him.

—She may never get rid of him. He may be too numb to leave, & she may not have the guts to lead him by the hand out of the watched building, past the police car at the curb. Undetected even by the retired high school teacher.

He will spend the night, & the next day, & the night after that. A week. A month. A year. Threatening to call the police & tell them that she pulled him inside every time she tries to push him out. She's stuck with him for life. Beyond her own duration, into all eternity.—

She continues to lean against her open door, not wishing to shut it in the retired high school teacher's brightened face. He is visibly expecting to be invited into her apartment. Where he has never been. She isn't working now: he heard her stop typing half an hour ago.

Fortunately for her, the policemen are shooing all tenants back behind their respective doors. She closes hers   smiling bright regret at the retiring high school teacher who turns mechanically & heads back down the stairs.

She walks to her livingroom window & takes up a watching position.

There's much commotion out in the hall & on the stairs. Topped by the incessant high-pitched whine from the absent couple's apartment. It is now whining down the stairs. & the absent couple's apartment door slams shut.

***

After a while she sees four policemen emerge from the main entrance, carrying a strung-out body in a silver jumpsuit. One side of which is soaked in blood.

She can see the carrying policemen being careful not to let the body bleed onto their uniforms; policemen pay their own cleaning bills.

After another while she disbelievingly recognizes the face of the strung-out silver body as that of the overhead husband. Who normally is home by now. At least that's what she'd always assumed. Assuming that what she normally heard at about this hour were the footsteps of the homecoming husband   & not somebody else's   soon to be followed by the homecoming footsteps of the mouse wife.

Whom she sees rounding the corner of their street.

& breaking into a run at the sight of the police cars in front of their main entrance. & of the ambulance, into which attendants & careful policemen are hoisting the husband's strung-out silver body.

With a bloody flesh-stripped bone hanging off what used to be a shoulder.

Shot off by the half-naked   half-successful murderer up her flue: she thinks with a shudder.

& starts, & almost cries out, because he's sneezing directly behind her, craning an imprudent neck to see the mouse wife being helped into the ambulance by a policeman. —With an expeditive pat on the mouse wife's up-ending bottom.

She motions for him to step back from the window —Does he want the police to spot him?— Again he obeys, his black pin-prick eyes again searching her face for the reason why she did what she did.

A reason that fully evaporated at the sight of the husband's shot-up shoulder. She pulls down the window shade & turns to face him. He's soot-streaked & shaking, asking: WHY? through chattering teeth.

Because she doesn't like to see half-naked bodies running from uniforms with axes: she says. —Truthfully. In keeping with her philosophy.— That, & the ice cold drizzle.

Huh? You like naked bodies?

There is a pointed primness to his mouth. Which becomes primmer as he grins, baring wide-spaced pointed teeth.

She shrugs. She doesn't tell him that she'd have done the same for a wet cat. She doesn't wish to offend the species of someone who may be used to settling arguments by shooting. Even if he looks too numb to do anything. & has no gun. But there are knives in her kitchen. A hammer. A small handsaw. All the necessary props for a horrorfilm scenario.

Which she quickly suppresses, lest she imprint the image on his apparently vacant & therefore all the more receptive mind.

Forcing herself to think instead that she'll get out of this situation as inadvertently & philosophically as she got into it. She's safer letting him think that she is after his slightly knock-kneed body.

A thought she visibly reinforces in his mind when she suggests that he take a hot bath.

There's a different look in his eyes no longer questioning; almost smug as he obediently follows her into the bathroom: Now he knows why she pulled him inside.

She refrains from suggesting further that he wash the orange out of his hair or cut if off, if it doesn't wash out to make himself less conspicuous for his exit from the building. He is obviously unjustifiably vain about his appearance, & might turn actively hostile if he hears her practical suggestion as disapproval. The stereotype establishment reaction to his stereotype anti-establishment looks. Which might shake his newly found trust in her concupiscence.

—Perhaps he will consent to pulling her black stocking cap down over his ears, when she presents him with her plan for getting him past the police car at the curb.—

If the police car is still sitting at the curb. She doesn't dare check, in case they see her lift the window shade which they may have seen her pull down. On orange bristles craning behind her, watching the mouse wife being patted on her butt.

He may also take offense if she shows herself too eager to be rid of him.

He has started running the water, & she turns the radio on. For the benefit of the retired highschool teacher downstairs. Who probably is still watching the street from his livingroom window.

For whose benefit she also refrains from returning to her typewriter while the bathwater is running. To "The Infections of the Inner Ear," for which her editor will send a messenger at 9:00 a.m. tomorrow. She still has seventeen pages to go.

Which she carries to the livingroom table, & tries to translate soundlessly, in long hand —with wet palms: her pencil is smudging all over the manuscript— while she waits for the bather to come out of the bathroom.

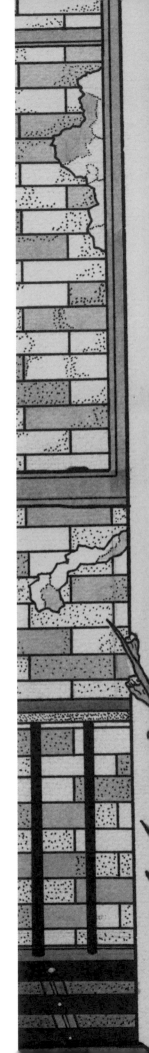

Wearing her striped terrycloth robe & slippers.

He sits down across from her in the corner of the couch, letting her robe fall open to show a   gaping leopard. He's AC-DC: he tells her: He can play any role she wants him to play.

He doesn't believe that her jeans & black turtleneck sweater which she takes off & trades him for her robe aren't implements of her own sexual fantasy: disguising him as herself, as a turn-on.

That she means for him to leave, in that disguise.

With an additional black stocking cap pulled over his telltale hair.

—Carrying a fat manila envelope, filled with copies of a previous translation, & bearing the name, & address of a publisher. To show to the two policemen at the curb   if they're still sitting in their car at the curb, questioning anyone leaving   or entering   the building.

To tell the two policemen   if they're still there, & ask   that he's a messenger, sent to pick up a manuscript in apartment 2W.

Which is something that happens routinely, as the probably still watching retired high school teacher in 1W will readily confirm. If necessary.

Especially if he has heard her buzz the messenger in.

Which she will do right now: he has 1 to 3 minutes to get out.

He doesn't believe that she means it. & is baring his wide-spaced pointed teeth in a knowing grin: he's getting the picture.

As long as she doesn't climax turning the messenger in: he grins.

Although: He's clean. They got nothing on him. They can't nail him for not sticking around when that stupid mother started playing with his rifle.

She finds it hard to believe that the upstairs husband aimed at his own shoulder. But she says nothing. Who was trying to shoot whom is none of her business. Her business is "The Infections of the Inner Ear." Which she must finish if it takes all night.

She does mean it: she says earnestly: She's got work to do.

She hopes he won't insist, but if that's the only way to get rid of him, she'll go through with it. She'll close her eyes, & concentrate on Simone Weil, hoping that he has neither herpes, nor amoebas, nor any other fashionable disease currently preying on the promiscuous.

Although: How does she know that he's promiscuous? She's committing the very sin of majority judgment she wanted to counterbalance by throwing her impetuous featherweight onto the lighter scale.

But: He thought she was hurting. He doesn't see no man around.

She shrugs. She got carried away: she says. — Truthfully again, though not in the sense she allows him to hear. She must finish all these pages by 9:00 a.m. tomorrow: she says, tapping the pages with a sweaty hand.

Okay. Okay.

He isn't as offended as she'd expected him to be. In *her* vanity. He isn't that interested; he's numb.

But not numb enough to obey her this time. He isn't going anywhere for real, dressed like this. In her clothes. When he's got his own stuff lying upstairs. His 400$ leather jacket from Spain. His 200$ boots. His 180$ black leather pants. He's going back upstairs & get them.

Maybe he'll come back down with some cocaine. If they didn't take it. If that mother didn't flush it down the toilet 16,000$ worth   after shooting himself in the shoulder.

That mother would have done better to sweep the borax up from along outside their door when the sirens started coming. The police may be stupid, but not stupid enough to think that that borax along outside their door was put there to keep out the roaches. They know what it means: That it means that a new supply has come in.

Has she ever tried cocaine sex? Nice. Real smooth.

She escorts him to her bedroom window & lets him out. Relocking it after him. Watching his feet disappear on the rainpolished iron. Hoping that she won't see them coming back down, in case the police locked the upstairs window.

She kneels beside her typewriter, muttering a prayer of relief when she hears his footsteps overhead. He has put on his 200$ boots, & is pacing.

But he isn't leaving. & may, of course, be preparing to come back down. With or without cocaine. Tomorrow she'll have gates put on the brdroom window.

She forces herself to start typing. After a while she hears the pacing stop. Perhaps he has sacked out on the absent couple's bed.

She has translated eleven of the seventeen pages when she hears the mouse wife walk into the upstairs foyer. Around 1:00 a.m. She hears his footsteps wake up & go to meet hers. Together they walk into the bedroom.

She hears a long muffled conversation   followed by silence   followed by long gusts of muffled laughter. Which eventually culminates in the familiar squeak.

Which continues on & off, off & on, paragraphing her translation. It's on   on on on: sustained by cocaine? she wonders   when she types her name after the last word: ear, at 3:38 a.m.

She's awakened by her bell at exactly 9:00 a.m. & staggers to open her door. To face an orange-bristled, black-leathered messenger. Who grins knowingly as he asks for the manila envelope.

LUNCH BREAK (1982)
HAL SIROWITZ

Father finds the porno movie a good place to eat his lunch.

He tries not to make too much noise

when he bites into his matzoh sandwich.

His wife prepared it the night before,

because she didn't like to wake up with him.

He goes to the theater which has a black cat;

she rubs up against his legs when he feeds her tuna fish.

He would rather go to the cowboy movies,

but the gunfire hurts his ears.

LECTURE ON THIRD AVENUE (AFTER V-EFFECT) (1982)

MICHAEL CARTER

terror is released in lower manhattan
and the terrorists neither carry guns
nor subvert the state
but simply buy it off with promises
with their hollow promises their mastercards
the premises of pay-as-you-come democracy
and this dont sit well with the whores down third avenue
already awake tonight and all-of-a-sudden awake unable
to afford their higher prices

this is the side effect of the v-effect
always to be followed by the alienation effect

and we who still care still desire to find the motor
that continues to run the tyranny of time
as today 1982 uptown moves downtown
where harry helmsley offers a million dollars
to buy off other peoples' dreams
to accept means that we really are all prostitutes
and that love is a commodity and art a reality for a
few good men better in business than they are in
beds where their galvanized unconscious opens
in wet dreams that flow like honey

like honey we got the neighborhood anyway and if you
dont give us an inch well take a mile and then canvass
brooklyn to the boondocks of connecticut where we'll
stop because rocks
and trees are traditional beauty
and because there are no people there
no human potential

where a spring runs clear
and no one stamps saratoga on it
nor runs after it with a real estate sign

justice is a word
and history has been unkind to it
but I have seen more hands and noses in garbage cans
on city streets this spring than I can count
than I could hitherto imagine

because misfortune can also be a great spur
to creation and instill resentment
and nowhere among the garbagepickers are there signs of
ostensible shame
and now we build a tower to be a symbol in which some
people will even live their lives
there will be men and women on the fiftieth floor
looking out on loisaida with binoculars
and easy-all-their-life intellectuals
decide if marx was right
and accountants decide how much is left
all these people with their heads in the clouds as well as
their bodies who will hear aeolian harps but its only sound
on the stereo the graffitists know who eventually post
the news they will ignore upon the basement doors with white
paint and anger that this is just the last hurrah no
more

and the subways will run underneath
the dirty filthy subways full of rats and desperate junkie
s and the noise
the noise
the noise
the noise
the noise
the noise

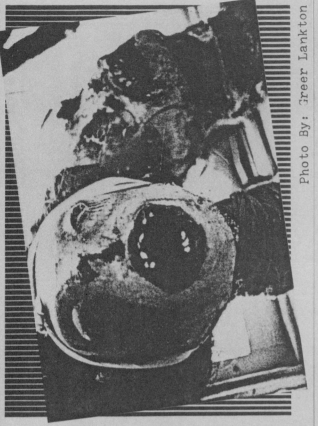

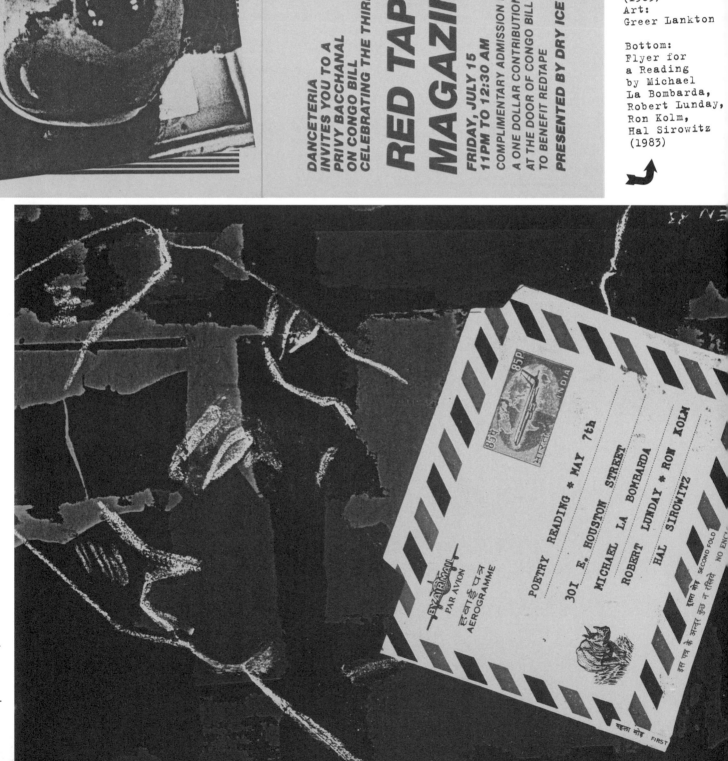

Top:
Handbill for
Redtape No.
3 Benefit at
Danceteria
(1983)
Art:
Greer Lankton

Bottom:
Flyer for
a Reading
by Michael
La Bombarda,
Robert Lunday,
Ron Kolm,
Hal Sirowitz
(1983)

APPEARANCES

Number 10

$4.00

IN THE DARK (1983)

ERIC BOGOSIAN

THE SECOND FRANK

MMMMM. MMMMM. I wait for dark. The black comes for me. Some people are afraid when the sun goes down. MMMMMM. MMMMMMM. But for me . . . me . . . for me it's good in the deep dark. Warm and dark and close. Some people are afraid of small places. Tight spots. Restrictive. MMMMM. MMMMMM. Not me. Not me. I'm right at home, I'm in the right place. The good dark place. Like a baby in its womb. Like a rat in its hole, I'm *okay*.

Ever see the black skid marks on the highway? Ever wonder what happened? I don't. I think about the tires. The rubber. The black rubber. Burning. Melting. Pouring down in ropes. In sheets. In long black ribbons all around me. Twisting all around me. Around and around. Black and tight. Close and dark. Holding me. Hiding me in the darkness.

Don't you love the smell of black rubber? Maybe not. It's an acquired taste. It takes awhile. Some people never like it. Don't really understand. You can work your way up. Black leather. Black plastic. Then black rubber. Tight. Black. Rubber. Up against you. Holding. Pressing. Keeping. Resilient but firm. When you're inside, you're outside. The legs. The arms. The chest. The groin. The head. All smooth. All black. In control. Everything is held in place. Like a machine. Like a god. Like a perfect machine I stand before the mirror in my uniform. A million miles inside, in the dark. In the hiding place where none can find me.

Don't get me wrong. I enjoy it. I know just what I'm doing. So tight. Holding me. Holding me hard. Better not let go. No one could hold me like that. Perfect. Every muscle. Encased in pure

black. So that nothing's lost. Everything is held onto. Every flinch. Every drop. All mine. For me.

THE SHINING STAR

Okay, yeh, yeh, I got something to say, alright? I got a few last words. This is what I got to say: You don't know. You don't know anything about me, and you don't know nothing about the world. About reality. Got it? It's like, who the hell are you people? Who are you to say: He dies? What gives you that right? My peers. Huh. Bullshit. You're not my peers because I look down on you. You and your fat-ass existence. You and your TV brains. You've never been anywhere, you've never seen nothing, all you know is what some idiot on the boob tube tells you. Hah.

So maybe I killed those girls. So what? I didn't, but what if I did? Insignificant people die every day. You don't seem to be too upset when there's war going on or children are starving in Africa. What do you think about that? You're responsible for that and you're responsible for putting me away. You understand what that means? First of all, I'm innocent. But second of all, I'm somebody, 'cause I've seen the world. I have been in the desert, man, and I have seen the shining star. I have been with the Kings, man, and we rode the wind. I know what the truth is and the truth is that I count and you don't. It's like when you're a little kid and you step on an ant on the sidewalk. You know they don't count. Well, it's the same with me. You're just a bunch of ants. You're not even alive as far as I know. You could just be a bunch of robots. You might be robots filled with blood and guts but you're still robots. I understand that because I have seen the shining star in the desert, man. I have seen it. I have been in the desert riding a hog at 150 miles per hour and I have seen reality go by. I have been "through" it. I have tripped in places you don't even know exist. Places you couldn't even dream about if you tried. I've been in Nam, man, I have looked death right in the eyes and I saw stars and stripes. You dig what I'm saying? I'm not *an* American, I'm *the* American.

And no one can dispute me. Those who have tried are very sorry now. 'Cause I'm always ready. There's a war coming and this is only the beginning, see. Only the strong will survive. Hand to hand. Mind to mind. I don't pump iron for nothing, see? Kung fu, meditation. I'm ready for anything. I passed every test. I know I'm being tested all the time. Sometimes when I catch someone testing me they say they don't know what I'm talking about. But that's part of the test too. I know. It's all part of the test. You're part of the test. You can't fool me.

See, I've got to survive, because it all passes through me. It's up to me to hold it together. You've got to be able to give up, go all the way and come all the way back. It's like if there was a candle right here, I could put my hand over it and I wouldn't get burnt. I wouldn't. 'Cause I can take it. Like, some people think I'm a drug addict 'cause I stick a needle in my arm, but I'm just testing myself, see, making myself harder. Harder and harder.

And you people, you people, you're just living out your little safe lives. You think you know about stuff, you think you can tell me about stuff. You can't tell me about anything 'cause I have seen it all, man.

I have shook hands with the devil. And you wanna come here and fight with me about it and you will lose, man, because I'm the stronger one, the stronger one always wins. It's the law of the jungle, survival of the fittest. And I am stronger physically, mentally, and spiritually. That's the big joke, see. You're just here 'cause I'm here. You just came here tonight to see me, 'cause *I'm* the one. *I'm* up here and you're just sitting there, scared. You want to kill me. Like Jesus. 'Cause you're afraid. So you think you can just put me away and that's the end of it. But that's where you're wrong, see. 'Cause I'm everywhere. I'm in the air. You can't put me away. I'm inside you. That's what it is, the law, the shining star, it doesn't go away. It's always there. When everything's gone, I'll still be here.

OUR GANG

What? I said we were just standing around. Nothing. I dunno, don't get yourself all excited, wait a minute, let me think. Uh, we were looking at Art's new engine. He had a new engine put into his Camaro. We were just talking. Just drinking beers. We weren't bothering anybody, we were in our part of the parking lot. Uh uh, we weren't fighting. Uh, wait, yeh, that's Billy. Billy had blood on his shirt because . . . because of something with his girlfriend, I dunno, she punched him or something. We were just minding our own business, that's all. Wolf was fucking around with his car, 'cause some guys were playing cards in his headlights, you know, and so Wolf was doing that thing where you hold your foot on the brakes and gun the engine at the same time. You know, the tires burn

BLACK MARKET PRESS

the 2nd annual

presents

FEAST OF UNBRAINING

monday
MAY 24
8:00

ST.
CLEMENTS
CHURCH

423
W. 46th

admission

limited
seating

reservations
suggested
856-3643

POETRY - MIME - MUSIC - TAP DANCING - TURTLE RACES - SNIPE HUNTS - the always revolting REVOLTING THEATRE - GREENPOINT ARTISTS JAM - GEEK LIBERATION TROUPE - ALFRED JARRY MEMORIAL TABERNACLE CHOIR - THOMAS PYNCHON LOOKALIKE CONTEST - PRIZES - SURPRISES - CLONES -

POST FREAK, MUTANT LIT CELEBRATION for the benefit of

 SMOKE SIGNALS

and maybe there's a chance that he'll let go the brakes and run over the guys playing the cards. You know, that kind of shit. We weren't causing trouble. Nobody had any weapons or anything. We don't go in for that bullshit . . . So then that chick comes over. Nobody asked her to come over, you know. She'd been to the parking lot before. Not when I was there, but they said that, I dunno, Larry, I guess, they said that you know she blew guys if they wanted. Why should they lie? There's girls like that. They just want attention, or they're upset because they broke up with their boyfriends. I dunno. Sometimes they're just crazy chicks. They come from other towns, like poorer towns or something and we're easy to find, you know. We're always here . . . I'm getting to that. So the next thing I knew, everyone was crowded around Wolf's car. The guys playing cards just kept playing. I think maybe one of them, Chub, mighta got up because he never gets any, you know. He's one of those guys who collects every *Playboy* and still lives with his mother. I mean, for him it was a dream come true. His big chance to score. I don't think he got it up though . . . Yeh, I guess I did, I dunno, I was drunk. I just remember somebody pushing me over to the car and she was lying back . . . What? Yeh, I guess someone was holding her, but they said she was a whore. She looked like she was enjoying it, she was moving all over the place. I just kinda fell on top a her and everyone was shouting. I just remember she smelled kinda funny and she had a shitload of eye makeup on. Boy, she was cheap . . . Then somebody, I guess Larry, pulled me off and then everyone was moving for the cars real fast, they said there was an open house in the North End, so we all took off for there and I don't remember what happened to her. I was too drunk. I musta passed out . . . What? Yeh, of course I'm sorry. I wished I wasn't there in the first place.

HE'S NEVER GONNA TALK

We, we, uh, we had this young guy. He came in and, uh, well he was brought in, and, uh, we knew all about him. We knew already. But he was being very uncooperative so, this is only an example, so in this guy's case we, uh, well look: The first thing you got to do is you make him understand some things, you know, so it's important to hit him alot of times and let him see who's hitting him. That's important. I hit him a few times. So then, um . . . Where? Oh, I hit him in the face. It's not really important, 'cause usually if you're kind of careful you're not going to hit him so hard that it's anything that has to be taken care of right away, you know, he just gets a little puffy in the face, or sometimes some teeth crack or something, but that's not important. Then it's important to frighten him a little bit, so what we do is we've got this big bucket in the middle of the room filled with water. Dirty water. And you just bring the guy over, with his hands tied. And then you grab him right behind the neck. Just push him right down into the water. You know, keep his head under for a couple of minutes, just to panic him a little. They buck a little, you gotta hold tight. Then you pull 'em back up. You don't want to drown 'em. 'Cause they get real worn out that way. You see what I mean? Then they're ready. So, uh, well then we get down to the regular stuff. Which is just you get a table, a regular table, plain metal table. You strip him and he's wet and cold and you put him on the cold metal table. Just tie him down, arms, legs, torso. So he can't move. Then you can do whatever you want. I usually start with cigarettes. Because, um, again it's important to get the psychological intention across. And he sees you smoking the cigarette. And everybody is afraid of fire. And then you just burn him. Just push the cigarette, it goes right in the skin. Just like soft, like wax. Sometimes you just leave the cigarette. While it lies there it hurts. And, um, there's clamps. Clamp around the head. Or clamp around the thumb. That hurts alot. It's good, 'cause you can twist it to just the right degree. You know, precise. The one around the head is a good one, 'cause that hurts. And, um, sometimes we, then we'll get some tape, duct tape, you put that over the eyes, over the mouth. They can still breathe, but you can control him really quickly. Pinch the nostrils, you got 'em. And then when you're ready to get down to business, really that is basically very intense pain. Spread the hand out on a wooden block. Smash the fingers gets the desired results. But I really don't like that, I used to like it alot, when I was younger I used to enjoy breaking bones and stuff. But now it's more, um, like I like the electricity stuff. It's clean, it's fast. And it's very . . . no, no, you don't do it that way. You just put it on the balls. Just tie the wire around the balls. And that's what hurts alot. Yeh, we got a doctor who's there 'cause he can tell us where to put it exactly. And there's some other spots that are good. Um, around the lips is good, and there's the fingers, especially if you've smashed the fingers, that's good, too. Armpits are good. The asshole, the bottoms of the feet and the palms of the hands, the nipples are very good. Those are all good spots. And if you've been doing everything right, then by the time you get to all that—well, they get kind of exhausted. In the case of this one guy, by the time we got to the electrical stuff, and everything, we sort of realized that he wasn't going to say anything. He was kind of useless. So, uh, I don't know, there was this one guy there who had this rope. So we, uh, we just hung him. It was part of it. While we did the stuff. Yeh, we hung him. I mean, if he isn't going to talk while you're hanging him, he's never gonna talk.

THE THROAT

I am constantly amazed, almost frightened, by the sensitive complexity of the human physical plant. The human body that is. Consider the throat. Normally used for transmitting air, food, and speech, it is the body's most vital highway. It is nothing less than the path between heart and mind. And it must be kept in perfect working order, clean of debris, lubricated, warm, and nourished.

It is aesthetically pleasing as well. For the neck is one of the most graceful and erotic parts of the body. The slightest touch on the throat brings feelings of titillation and pleasure.

The throat is such a sensitive thing. A small disorder can cause a sore throat, or worse, a diseased throat. Fever and pain set in and, if they persist, the throat becomes a source of intense irritation. It becomes the sole center of conscious attention. Imagine for a moment a canker in the throat. Sore and open. Deep inside. Burning. Or many cankers, inflamed and bleeding. The throat becomes dry as the pain increases. It is impossible to swallow.

Then the discovery that the cankers are malignant. Cancer of the throat. Life-threatening, it must be removed. Perhaps the vocal chords are destroyed in the process; a hole is left. A new voice is created. The whole personality changes. Crippled . . . perhaps no voice at all. Mute.

The throat is very vulnerable. It must be protected at all costs. Imagine being punched in the throat. Or strangulation. Asphyxiation. Tighter and tighter, then blackout. A piece of wire is all that's needed. But perhaps the worst of all is the most spectacular: the slitting of the throat with a straight razor. One deft move, deep and quick. The wound is fatal, yet consciousness persists.

IN THE DARK

ERIC BOGOSIAN

Eric Bogosian,
In the Dark,
Cover (1983)
Photo:
Paula Court

$4.95

JUST ANOTHER ASSHOLE

THIS IS IT? (1983)

BARBARA ESS

So this is it? It's not what I expected at all. Maybe the seeds of my bloated expectations were sown that hot summer night lying in the back seat of the Buick convertible half asleep. They carried me gently from my bed and tucked me into the car, put the top down and then we were moving. The radio was on and I could hear them talking and laughing in the front seat. Everything seemed as it should be. Above, the shimmering undersides of trees lit by headlights flew by, while the sultry air washed over me, breathing a wind of false promise for the future.

What connects that summer night to a day standing on a cliff on the west coast of England looking down at my hands as they age before me—fingers all bony, skin becoming shriveled? I part a bush and watch a hummingbird frantically flap its wings and suck the juices from a flower. I pick sharks teeth and petrified wood millions of years old from the cliff while down there on the beach a boy and girl cling to each other on a blanket—all emotion and sensation. I watch calmly, objectively: their emotion, the light in spirals of tiny violet and blue particles bouncing off the ocean, the sated hummingbird, the sharks teeth, the heavy sticks of petrified wood, my bony hands—all equal.

What I didn't know that night in the back seat of the convertible was that preceding this ride by some years, an atom bomb had been dropped on a city, scorching thousands, skin hanging off bodies. And that some people thought that such family outings were made possible by that suffering. But I didn't know about it. And I still don't except for TV and the movies. I didn't know what lust

or longing was either. Except I had this book, *Peyton Place*, that I read secretly in bed at night. I was especially thrilled at the section where the couple was on the beach and he was touching her breasts and the headlights of a car surprised them, as I clutched a pillow between my legs.

That night in the convertible certainly didn't prepare me for the icy NYC morning when I woke up and realized I had no money at all. There was snow on the streets and I walked in my sneakers to the waitressing agency on Fulton Street. I had gone there once before. If you get there early there's more of a chance to be sent out on a lunch job. The last time in a similarly desperate situation, I had arrived broke and by three o'clock I had a full stomach and twelve dollars. Cash. It isn't exactly on a first-come-first-serve basis. So when I got there it looked good. The competition wasn't too keen. An elderly white haired lady and a middle-aged woman who was clearly a little drunk. I thought my relative youth would triumph. But they had the uniforms and even white waitress shoes and I had my sneakers. So by noon I gave up and walked back. Passed a restaurant where in the window I could see a fat couple brazenly eating big plates of spaghetti.

I went back to the place I was staying—a small room in this artist's studio that reeked of the polyurethane casts of men's penises that were manufactured there. I was thinking of the first penis I had ever seen. It was when I was a member of The Meatballs and Spaghetti Club which met behind the garage down the hill from where I lived. There were three members: me, Richie R., and Kenny.

We would make our genitals available for perusal until the club was busted and we all got punished.

The Buddhists say that we are born into suffering; when we inherit a body at birth we also inherit suffering. Until we get off the Wheel of Birth and Death. Until we no longer need to have a body.

I remember one time in Fez in a sort of camping ground, there was a blue VW van, an olive tree, a concrete structure with toilets and showers, a blonde American couple, some pots and pans, a Moroccan guy with his jalaba, a blanket, a dark night sky with millions of stars, and my own body. I was sort of floating around, lost, confused. There was all this stuff, but I didn't know where "I" belonged. I felt elated, but lonely.

In high school I wasn't very popular, but I got good grades. That didn't keep me from being miserable. I longed for that all caring, loving person, who would solve all my problems, but I was prepared to rage against that person. For fun, Charlotte W. and I used to peg our skirts, stuff our brassieres with socks, put the collars of our jackets up and go out on Route #6 and hitch hike rides with guys in cars who were going anywhere.

At the San Diego zoo they did a survey to find out what animals and exhibits the public wanted most to see. Snakes came in very low on the poll. Yet, the snake house had the highest attendance record of any exhibit in the zoo.

I had this dream. I am in a shallow pool of water. Then I want to go out. But surrounding me on the edges of the pool are snakes in the water all different sizes and shapes. I move to one part, there's a snake so I go to another part to climb out. There's another snake so I dare not pass. I'm not frantic and I don't feel trapped. There's probably a place I can slip through. But everywhere I go where there seems to be only water and rocks, there's a snake. I am encircled but I still don't feel desperate. I am confident there is some way out, but at each effort I am surprised by a snake barring the way.

What does it mean? Perhaps it is necessary to embrace the snake. I used to be afraid to get on the toilet (I didn't *really* believe this, but my body was afraid) because if there were snakes down there in the water they might crawl up and go inside of me. In Mexico, though, the Indians say that stroking the skin of a live snake confers wisdom to that which strokes it.

What is it that's so fascinating about snakes and Nazis? The big flags with swastikas. The duped Hitler youth in endless parades. The huge pavilions with ranks of orderly people doing gymnastics and raising their arms at exact 45° angles. And that little ugly man shouting and getting red in the face. The tales of ultimate depravity. Those tons of bodies being pushed into troughs with bull dozers. And the lamp shades made out of the skin of Jews as delicate as the crust of my Grandma's apple strudel.

My grandmother was deaf. She and my grandfather didn't speak to each other for fifteen years. She used to go on visiting rounds of her children's homes and stay for a few weeks, play with the grandchildren and bake up a storm. Challeh breads, blintzes, prune humintosh, apple cakes and apple strudel. My mother would carefully wrap them up and put them in this huge overstuffed freezer we had in the basement. Then once my grandmother died. About five years later, my mother decided to clean out the freezer and found one of Grandma's apple strudels in the bottom. She brought it upstairs and heated it in the oven. We ate in reverent silence, like taking the Eucharist.

Joseph Papp presents

SEDUCTION OF CHAOS

MON
MAY 24
8 PM
$5

UNS (a.k.a. ZEV)
BARBARA ESS
& LISTEN TO THE ANIMAL
THE NIHILISTICS

READING from Jonathan Schell's
THE FATE OF THE EARTH:

Jim Fouratt   Merle Ginsberg
Lynn Holst   Tim Sommers
Glenn Branca   Kiki Smith
Barbara Barg   Eric Mitchell

THE PUBLIC THEATER   425 LAFAYETTE ST.

FILM: PETER WATKINS, THE WAR GAME, 6:45 PM ($1)

INSTALLATION: JOSEPH NECHVATAL

CARDIAC (1983)

MAX BLAGG

I want a car that I can ride in
a powerpack cadillac a coked-up cadillac
a rustproof dustproof chrome roof cadillac
a gimcrack cadillac a come-stained cadillac
whacked out cadillac
smokestack cadillac shockstop cadillac
cadillac cadillac lac lac lactose
pure rose cream and shiny
skin tight cadillac fishtit cadillac
switch hit cadillac
fleshtone cadillac shinbone cadillac
assassinated cadillac (that's the JFK
Dallas version of Cadillac)
a poontang cadillac! El Dorado! Coup de Ville!
Fleetwood Custom brand new whitewalls
a dismantled cadillac a D-cup cadillac
Jayne Mansfield's head
in the back of her big pink cadillac
and the chihuahuas lying dead on the highway
by the roofless cadillac that bloody caddy
o caddy, o daddy
Cos this ain't no Honda no Buick Skylark,
es no Toyota, no Yamahaha
Forget Ford Fairlane and Chevrolaylay
they ain't our speedo oh no no no no
This is America and we drive Cadillacs
cadillacs all kinda cadillacs
Yo, swell fins on this here Caddy
Hey flag down that big black caddy
that black black black cadillac
and come on over here
and step inside your daddy's caddy
it's got green leather seats
and folding ashtrays

brand new FM all the options
So we take a drive into the night
and then we park it in the darkness
under a werewolf moon
and come on over here
climb into the back of your daddy's caddy
your slow smile surrounds me
and as you crawl over
that green leather seat
your skirt rides up and I can see
I can see oh say can you see
by that green dashboard light
the sudden flash of shiny thigh
we are coiled like hibernating snakes
in the back of your daddy's caddy
your creamy skin laid on green leather
and isn't that the whitest skin
the whitest skin I've ever seen?
and the radio reminds us
Don't forget the Motor city
oh don't forget the Motor City!
and your left leg is hooked over the front
seat and I've got fluid drive
klik klik your legs are locking
klik klik this caddy's rocking
I can feel the blood beneath
the surface of your seamless skin
I can trace the specific contours
of your skull as surely as
that topographer tracing the contours
of the skin of the planet
and is this not America beneath my hands?
Its mountains and rivers and the missile silos
six miles beneath the cornfields of Kansas?

No, that is not this
this is purely human
stroking you in the back
of your daddy's caddy
stoking you in the back
of your daddy's caddy
Listen to my blood humming
listen to my heart coming
and the tumblers fall into place
and the padlock pops and
you slide wide open
and we're wrapped in
this perfect envelope of flesh
in the back of your daddy's caddy
and your private parts are more perfect
than the grillwork on an El Dorado
O caddy, o daddy!
O sweet god of motor cars
there is no cadillac
Cadillac is just one of the
alltime great American words
and I wish I wish I wish—
I wish your daddy was here to see it.

PRACTICING WITHOUT A LICENSE (1983)

RICHARD PRINCE

From limo, to V. I. P. lounge, to first class cabin. It sounds great but like any other isolation or prescribed modification, getting first class treatment is just another form of humiliation.

She never liked being singled out or doted over, and did as much as she could to do her part, ("my fair share") to rally against, what would have otherwise been a completely and provided for existence.

Most of her friends thought she was crazy for rejecting privileged treatment, but she knew too that these were outsiders, ones on the other side of the fence, looking over . . . smacking their lips and panting, making wishes and projecting impressions on what to them looked to be the good ship lollypop.

They could never imagine that being part of the aristocracy measured out to little more than being the result of a wedding contract, a contract prearranged on the basis of a merging of two pieces of real estate. A child that had to do more with blood than love.

"We're like recidivists," she would say. "Mental patients. In for the third time. We'll never be granted re-evaluation. It's almost as if our lot is medical . . . a plan where medicine has somehow collaborated secretly with the everyday functions of government, and come up with some kind of national health act . . . and with any criticism of our background, the relatives start mumbling and signing commitment papers, trying to absolve themselves by patting you on the hand and wiping the drool from your mouth."

"What? You don't want the ranch? Impossible. Dear, you must get a bit more rest."

Just the accusation of not being quite thankful and she could find herself suddenly on arbitrary and subjective ground. One foot here and one there. It wasn't exactly borderline, but her refusal to inherit could be made into a case.

She wanted to try it on her own, herself, leaving her name and history behind.

"Here, take it. You can have it. It's all yours."

The more she tried to convince them, the more they felt even her need to convince a symptom rather than a delinquency or rebellion.

"Look Ma, no hands."

The stepping out was an admission, a declaration of what was simply next. And one way or another, even if it meant destroying the nest, she was prepared to get out, cut out, get kicked out.

"Most of my life has been planned and I've had little to say about it. As far as I can tell my routines are ones that guarantee a certain amount of applause. The days run together, one into the next. Quiet and semi-alcoholic. Credible and polite notices. I'm winding up an uninvolved woman."

"What to wear and who will sit next to whom at my next dinner party is my only expected suspense."

He didn't know why people tried to put a tag on him just because he liked to drink alone. In fact he'd always felt that the proper time to start drinking was right around two in the morning, after the house-hold had shut down and everybody was fast asleep.

It seemed a proper time to belt back a few, to toast the ghosts of the manor ("to just us ghosts"), beckoning the transparencies till about five or five-thirty.

The paramount concern was of course, the definition, and although it was somewhat ungraceful,

the privation at least was isolated and contained, and the knowing of where you would be from beginning to end, he felt, was, an intelligent advantage.

Getting pissed in public is unattractive, (most of it being accidental anyway) and unless you're William Powell in *The Thin Man*, it's advisable to stop at two shots and remain pleasant. The immobility one may receive from a private tipping is not only socially allowed, but is a recommended form of relaxation, (kissing it off as they say) and in some circles a highly respected accessory for late-nite cinema viewing.

The practice of polishing off a bit of scotch when the majority of the population is asleep is not so much an auto-enlightener . . . a substitute for a good cry, or even a hyper-reductive exchange where the lifting of the glass reads as comma or pause, (a formal kind of prop that's traditionally necessary in conversation that's essentially chit-chat) but rather something simple, plain, purposeful . . . a beastly little hanging that becomes quite satisfying, as say . . . the ability to con with a convincingly appropriated charm.

She says sometimes if you don't know a person particularly well, one of the ways to check them out quickly, say like a once-over, is to take a fast look in their medicine cabinet and see what kinds of prescriptions or drugs they use.

She says she does this at parties or anytime she's invited to someone's place she's just met.

He was always surprised how these tests, (she always called this business "tests") didn't sound like a kind of obnoxious backstabbing. He didn't know, maybe it was just knowing what she was like. She never seemed to hesitate or think about the inappropriateness of what she did, or how poking her nose into someone else's business could become an unpleasant scene if stumbled upon.

She always sounded so up when she'd talk about her discoveries, as if what she was doing was reading tea leaves or uncovering hidden machinery.

She would say, "sometimes you can tell more about someone by opening their medicine chest than looking at the books on their shelves, or the things they collect and put up on their walls. You can actually tell a lot about a stranger, what they do and how they do it, by what their doctor tells them to take four or five times a day."

Maybe it was just because she was a rich little precocious snot . . . twenty-one, looking sixteen, harmless and coquettish . . . getting away with a lot more than that luke-warm brain of hers let on about.

"It's her rich family I know," he said, "it's probably because I wish I could've had the same thing so I could maybe think like her. I mean I wouldn't mind bailing out on that type of thinking."

Anyway she says all this "lowdown" was especially good because you could get a take on how someone's day to day routine was tempered, and how much "gravity" their moving about needed.

She said she needed to know these things. She said it saved her time.

"It's nosy but nothing personal. It's like carrying someone's picture around in your wallet, right in the side where you put the money."

She never paid much attention to the proper requirements of turning a routine into gold and any flirtation with a well-synched groove made her skip about like a blind bird flying backwards. She used to refer to her target, her goal . . . as something close to the final destination of a U-2 rocket. The kind the Germans use to lob over London. The kind when the engines ran out of gas over a city, any place would do.

***

X was her real name but most of her friends didn't know that, they knew her as Connie A. Connie. Her reason for the change was for a little bit of melodrama, and the kind of privacy that could only be had by lying through your teeth. The safety thing was a lot about her insecurity, about losing what she had just got.

She had become successful fronting a no-wave band and had just signed a recording contract and got a nice advance, enough to buy a place in Tribeca, but the whole thing happened so fast she figured she was going to lose it just as quickly as it had come.

The privacy and the fake name was something to hide behind and a way to push a personality that had to do with what she thought was expected of her. It wasn't any kind of genuine fascination with character, or role model or even hero worship. Connie A. Connie was about how things worked and was as calculated as it was fictive.

The calculation was about business, the desire to project the right image, an image that would sell . . . the bad girl, the sympathetic slut, the girl from the wrong side of the tracks. The trouble was the fiction was always about five seconds away from coming apart and X thought that at any moment, Connie A. Connie would be found out for what she was . . . a basically serious funny woman with about as much chance for a "rep" as a spayed puppy.

"It's always difficult, especially at first, to disbelieve in what you do."

Things like that were easy for her to say because she was never frank. That's why she was at the head of the line. She had the ability to reject intimacy without impairing affection. Her standards and values were willful reactions to his. She was smart. She would say things like, "I'm not a genius . . . but I do have unusual feelings . . ."

Her routines were clever and sometimes silly and full of sounds spoken with a voice other than her own. Her words were meant to eliminate competition and help. She had said repeatedly, if she ever married, it would be for the name change first and the honeymoon second.

She turned the camera on. She was lying on the bed looking straight up at the ceiling. She wanted to make a videotape and have it sound and look like it was sent away for. Like the things they have in the back of the magazines and on cereal boxes.

"There was nothing there that seemed to be us. He was sitting in a chair at the foot of the bed, looking at me, just sitting there in a trance, still, not moving at all. His feet were propped up on the end of the bed. I don't know if he was listening or not . . . seeing anything or what. I turned the radio up as far as it could go.

He didn't have anything on. He was comfortable. He *looked* comfortable. My head was on the pillow propped up so my chin was on my chest. I could see down myself and him at the end there. I couldn't hear anything except the noise from the radio. I was touching myself and I know that doesn't make it happen for me, but I thought, well, maybe this time . . . maybe with a little more determination.

He wasn't sitting anymore. He was in a position. His skin was red, very bright. The color was sinking in and out when he breathed. It looked like there was a candle in him that made him sweat and glow. The sweat would sit on top of his skin, then run off from getting too big.

The sweat beaded up and moved off faster because he had his cock on his own. He had it in his hand and he wasn't really moving it . . . he was just holding it as if it was going to take off and leave. Straight out in that position, his body was like the long side of a triangle . . . irontailed, and against the chair with none of his butt on the seat.

I brought my legs up and he was right through the center. I put a blanket over my head and it was like looking through a viewfinder. It was dark and I was in there and everything was incredibly focused . . . very sharp, and my attention was concentrated in a way that my touching myself made my stomach contract and push out like something inside me was misfiring. The little pouts got quicker together and lost any spacing they had. The pace got mixed up and there was no more starts and stops, just my body locking up into a smooth, huge charlie-horse. I couldn't tell where the horse was. It felt like it was all over. It had gotten away from me and everything turned real bright for a second or two. I snapped like a filament in a lightbulb just before the light goes out. I kept swinging after the bell like a bum fighter in his last fight.

I kept playing it back. Only half of us were in it. The camera had been pointed at me. I was going to show it to him, the tape . . . I was thinking about showing it to him, that part of it, but I thought writing it out like this would make my voice and thoughts seem a lot more memorized. This way it was kind of like having a dummy on my knee. The sound of my voice could sound like it was coming out from over there instead of here. I thought this way it was better for him too. He didn't want to see the tape. He doesn't like the real thing . . . just something close to it. And this was the closest thing I could think of that could come anywhere close to the unreal real of the real thing."

He met a girl recently who said she liked to listen to Abba. She said one of their songs, "S.O.S." made her feel pretty good. She said when she listened to it, it reminded her of a large room, with lots of people in it, all facing towards her, and watching her up close as she received the final inches of Secretariat's penis.

At the time he didn't think this thought particularly abnormal. He said he was thoroughly aware of the rise in demand for pictures exhibiting individuals having sex with animals. Bestiality had become increasingly popular in 1981 and had displaced many of the more standardized groupings shown in peep show arcades. What did surprise him was the pedigree of the horse, its specificness, a particular horse, a famous and successful horse.

He was also aware of the international reputation of Abba and the fact that they had sold more records than any other pop group in 1980.

The combination or he supposed the association between the two successes, probably had an infinite number of explanations, but what he couldn't help thinking about was the apparent pleasure with which the episode was told to him by his new friend. He had always associated unrestricted sex with people smiling and the pleasure in her retelling seemed funny and her funniness sounded frightening.

He saw Karen tonight. She came into where he was having dinner. One of those coincidences. An X-ing of a place on a map. Something that happens occasionally to people who have parted ways even in a city the size of New York.

He was eating with a friend and when he saw her, his look became excessive but necessary, almost redundant, as if his daydream could this time be assuredly described as a waking one.

His friend grabbed him back and wondered what was behind them.

Karen had bleached her hair a bright blonde, an almost buff white. He had seen her with it in other colors. When they lived together it was black. He runs into her now it seems about once a year. She either acts like he's not there, or comes up to him and kisses him on the mouth before he can get out of the way. Tonight she committed herself first by laughing, letting him know at least, she knew who he was.

He was sitting in a booth and felt protected. One up on her. His look was really just right because by the time he realized who she was, he was already looking at his friend and any expression of surprise was directed at him, instead of given away to her.

He kept talking to his friend as if nothing special was happening. Karen walked by the booth with her own friend and sat a couple of booths away with her back to both of them. He said to his friend that the woman behind them, with her back to them, was an old girlfriend, a girlfriend who he was never in love with, but nevertheless someone he cared for and someone who at one time was part of his life.

They talked about how this could happen. How two people could share a certain amount of time together, most of it being close, some of it being intense, and then meet after it's long over and never even say hello.

It was as if his seeing her there was an illusion, or at least an impression of one, like she was a transparency, an image carried to a wall by light. His friend asked him what had happened to make it break up. He started to tell but hesitated once he began, knowing it was too complicated and involved, and that if these things became clear, he might want them back. Playing it down only interested his friend more, and he began to give in, almost finding it necessary to say something. Of course he wanted to tell him straight away, but he knew if he did, it would be more about telling himself and not his friend . . . and telling himself, about her, for about the one-hundredth time.

"Karen had met a girl who waited tables at the Local on Waverly Place. The Local was a restaurant and bar, a place where people read poetry and artists exchanged the things they did for a tab, for some money to eat. Karen and this girl made it together, but I didn't find out right away and when I did, I felt left out and jealous . . . feeling foolish and ignorant, like how could I be so stupid about not seeing what was happening. The hard thing was, I liked the girl, so being shut off from both of them, knowing they preferred each other, was a new and strange way to be shattered.

I wanted in, and either I wanted Karen back or this new girl now, and for a while the only thing I could do was pretend to be big about the whole thing, and act like their affair was fine, and everything was okay . . . like go ahead, I'm busy, don't worry about me, you know . . . all the stupid excuses that didn't make a bit of difference because you knew they were going to be together no matter how you faced it.

I tried to talk to her about it, to Karen, but she said she didn't understand what the problem was. She said it wasn't like it was another guy, and if it really was screwing me up, maybe we could be together, the three of us . . . that she'd talk to the girl about it, that maybe it wouldn't be such a problem if I felt part of her new friend.

Being with both of them was something I was always thinking about, but I figured if anything like that was going to happen it was probably best if it was brought up by one of them first. Karen, I think, knew that this is what I wanted right from the start, right from the first time I saw the girl, and even more, after I had seen them together. It was unfair. It was like Karen won the toss of a coin and knew I would have chosen the girl for my team too.

Karen was two inches taller and two inches thicker than the girl, but to me they looked the same. Their looks were so close that if you didn't stop them and line them up next to each other and go over them like you would a family portrait, you might think they were sisters.

I don't want to describe how they looked. It was more about when I looked at them . . . what happened to me, what I felt they were doing by knowing how their 'look' affected me.

They were the ones who knew what they looked like and this creature type of physicality, the kind only a certain 'type' of bi-sexual woman can have ruined the shit out of me. I mean when both of them were in the same room, letting me stare, it absolutely drove me into a fit, and I had to leave as soon as I could get what was there to be seen, memorized.

They were a pair of Amazons, a couple of tribal white Hollywood natives, right out of central casting, lookers who had long enough legs to make the arch in their backs curve out in the front, making it real enough so if they had wanted to, they could have been part of a sacrificial ceremony, two frenzied brides to be . . . figures in a line, dancing up and down with the people of Kau.

They enjoyed making it, like being permanent kids until it was over. I used to walk into the bedroom and they'd be on the bed, naked, going over each other, like apes, grooming each other, not really doing anything fast, just stretching and yawning, rubbing the backs of their necks, scratching each other's heads, taking their time . . . knowing that when they got around to getting each other off, it'd be for so many times, they'd be dead for hours after. They were handsome when they made it. Sometimes I thought I loved them. Luckily for my own sanity, it was just envy.

When it finally happened, we made the bed bigger. The three of us were walking home and it was late and just about a block away from the apartment we found a mattress, one that someone had thrown out, a single one, pretty decent . . . we picked it up and said let's do it.

Karen was using the girl to get me to stay on. That's one way I thought about it. It sounds bad, but it made sense. The only thing that Karen and I had between us was sex, and when we didn't have that, nothing worked and the whole thing stopped. We lived together for about a year and a half and separated twice. When we came back we did it willingly, not even talking about what we wanted, just knowing that when it worked, it made up for all the rest.

We got out of our clothes as if we were changing to go somewhere. We put a sheet over the new mattress and used a throw from the ottoman for a pillow. We walked around naked like we were getting a physical, and the only thing that looked in place was my cock, pointing straight out . . . coming up slowly, slapping against my belly when I walked to go to the bathroom.

It was strange. Any expected or anticipated extra charges were not, as I had imagined, being or becoming exactly accelerated, and there certainly seemed to be a kind of awkwardness, maybe a tension that put a reserve on the craziness and fun that I was betting on. What I had hoped to be a night with a couple of strangers was somehow turning into nothing particular and started to resemble something disarmingly flat and familiar.

I got to the bathroom and sat and waited to go soft so I could take a piss. I tried to think about the image I had looked forward to and it stayed hard. It felt like whatever blood was there expected more, and if there was a place for the blood to go I didn't know about it.

wedge

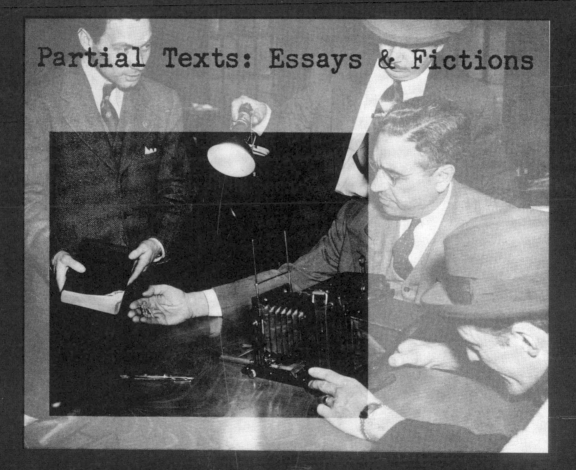

Partial Texts: Essays & Fictions

NUMBERS 3/4/5   1983   FIFTEEN DOLLARS

Wedge, Partial Texts: Essays and Fictions,
Issues 3/4/5 Winter/Summer/Spring
Cover, (1983)

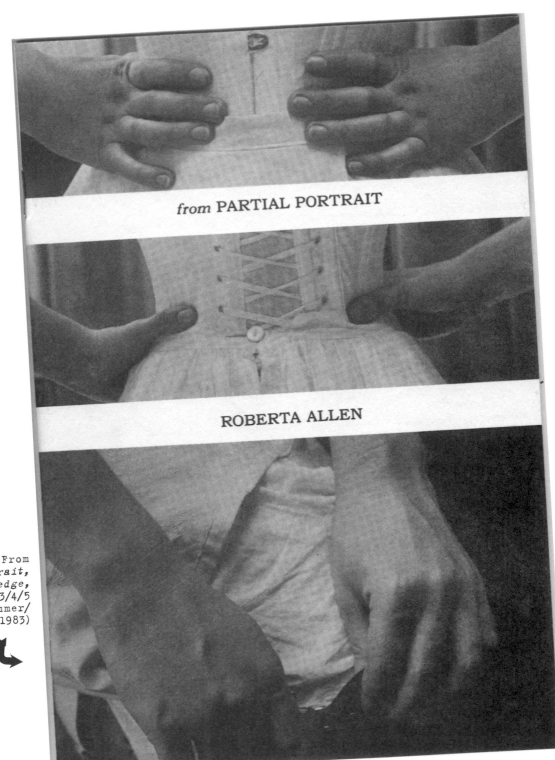

from *PARTIAL PORTRAIT*

ROBERTA ALLEN

Roberta Allen, From
Partial Portrait,
Cover, from *Wedge*,
Issues 3/4/5
Winter/Summer/
Spring (1983)

The piss burned inside and I squeezed it hard, trying to force the fucker to obey. This was not the way to start. Everything was becoming too hardboiled. I stuck my cock in the sink and ran the cold water. I heard Karen yell. She said, 'where are you' and she said it like she sounded upset. I was ready but I felt what was outside didn't have any color. I was standing in the wings. The whole thing began to feel a little like showtime.

When I came into the room the girl was spread out on the bed, belly down, looking at a magazine, glancing at the pages, turning each one with a snap, waiting it seemed for things to begin. The girl had a habit and I had seen her do it before, of striking a pose . . . and even though it didn't look to be comfortable or a natural way to relax, her position, however made up, invited one to wonder how something like that could ever change or move, and why, in a world where only something classic could be frozen and still, how could this little number pull it off with such tease and delinquency.

Karen came out of the kitchen and shut out the light. I heard the girl's magazine fly past my legs and skip along the floor and settle and close. Karen climbed in with the girl and I got in the original bed. What happened next was one of the things that I've told myself over and over, and wished, that maybe I could roll it back, back at least to the point where I could get another chance, a chance so everything could go another way, maybe the way I so wanted it to be.

I couldn't wait and I couldn't believe being there. It was like I really wanted it to happen so I only paid attention to what I was thinking. I didn't think about the fact that this was the first time, and I was new . . . and it should have been me just lying there, staying back and letting them get used to me, next to them .

. . letting it come around on its own, and not pressing or forcing them with my fear of having them know I was afraid that I'd hear one of them say, 'get out.'

Karen and the girl should have done what they'd always done, but I got between them with Karen on one side and the girl on the other, falling for the picture that I had set in my head. I get really pissed at myself when I think about it because Karen thought I was making a play, just for the girl and it wasn't that at all . . . I was just so on edge and excited that I was, if anything, *half-thinking*, and because I didn't know who was who, I tried to hold up the play for a second, to get an idea of how who felt. I shouldn't have asked and I know it sounded dumb, but I couldn't believe how great the girl moved and I wanted to make sure I knew it was her.

I mean it's hard to see and talk about it again, but I made a mistake and thought we were children."

His friend asked him if that was it, and he said basically yes. His friend asked him if anything happened after and he told him a few things, things he kept finding out about Karen. Like she had another boyfriend and she had a pill doctor and the girl and her were starting to try physical drugs.

"I was a fucking idiot thinking the three of us could be close and pretend at keeping everything outside. Thinking what was ours would be between us and everything else would be for the rest of the world."

"The thing that hurts me the most is seeing her now and having to fake like I don't know it's her. It hasn't changed. It's still stupid. It's still like I'm acting it out, instead of acting on it. It's like a rehearsal. I keep moving through the scene as if I knew what it was suppose to be. I still have the same stupid sense about how it should be instead of how it is . . ."

Hal Sirowitz,
"Crumbs" (1984)
Text:
Hal Sirowitz;
Design:
Purgatory Pie Press

Crumbs
by Hal Sirowitz

Dikko Faust: design, lino-cut & printing.
Folio & Optima types, Vandercook letterpress,
Tumba paper.

© 1984 Hal Sirowitz & Purgatory Pie Press 338 Mott 4B NYC NY 10012

23 of 150. PC III No. 8

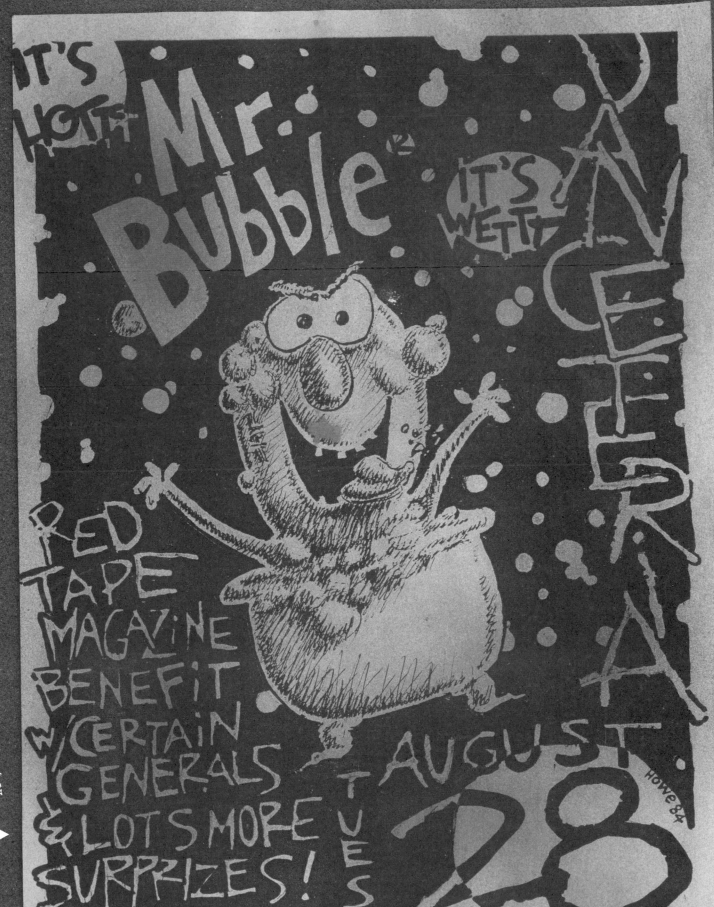

Poetry Reading

2nd Ave & 10th St.

**DENNIS
COOPER
&
ALICE
NOTLEY**
at
*The Poetry
Project*
St. Mark's Church

*Oct. 3
8 PM
Wednesday*

a.n.

THE UNDERGROUND FILM BULLETIN

50¢

eth & scott b.

nick zedd

lydia lunch

jack smith

m. henry jones

george kuchar

Summer 1984   Volume 1 Number 2

Featuring stories by:
David Wojnarowicz, Catherine Texier, Patrick McGrath, Miguel Pinero,
Raul–Santiago Sebazco, Joel Rose, Lisa Blaushild, Lynne Tillman,
William Barbari, Mike Topp, Reinaldo Arana, Bina Sharif,
and the tragic end to a photo romance by Hektor Munoz and Mario Sostre.
Free stamps and postcards inside!

BETWEEN C AND D

Post–Modern Lower East Side Fiction Magazine

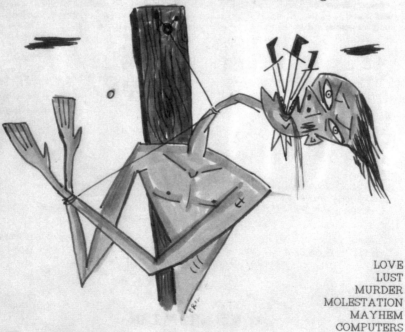

LOVE
LUST
MURDER
MOLESTATION
MAYHEM
COMPUTERS

$4.00 $5.00 OUTSIDE NEW YORK CITY

FIVE STORIES (1984)

MIKE TOPP

1 A woman ran an employment agency for girls. The girls were supposed to be going to jobs, but they just disappeared. A man in an automobile spoke to the woman and told her he'd found the girls' trunks at some place, but no girls. He was a night doctor and was going to take the woman to the hospital.

2 A sixty-year-old man one morning went from his home into the fields. The people of his village had subsisted without water for centuries. He decided to live on flowers like a bee. When his money was gone, he would go out to the fields and gather some more flowers. One evening when he was out gathering poppies he found a yellow spring that furnished enough water for many villages. Everyone was happy. Now if you try to talk to him he won't even answer you, but only give a drunken smile.

3 A young man became a soldier and was killed by a bomb. Locusts laid their eggs in his corpse. When the worms were mature, they took wing and flew North. When the wife of the soldier saw them, she turned pale, and she knew her husband was dead. She thought of his corpse rotting in the desert. That night she dreamed she rode a white horse that was so fast it left no hoofprints. She found her dead husband and looked at his face eaten by the locusts and she began to cry. Afterward she never let her children harm any insects. That same winter a swarm of locusts nested in her heart.

4 A woman made a pornographic movie in which she sucked on men's penises for four hours and thirty-one minutes. She made many more movies after that. Near the end of her life she told a newspaper reporter she'd been drugged by the director in her first movie. The story of her adventure spread far and wide, and soon made her famous.

5 A man found himself in a strange country many miles from home. He was taken there at night by a large black pig. While traveling they passed a beach full of crabs that had human faces on their backs. He walked around a little, stepped, and slipped on something clammy, and began to scream; his face was tense and pale. When he awoke, cedars laughed in the sunlight, oaks beckoned, and the birches bent far down and waved . . .

3 STORIES (1984)

LISA BLAUSHILD

COMPETITION

My boyfriend and my mother are sleeping together. I told you I see other women, he said. Stop acting so surprised.

I see them around town. They sit in front of me at the movies and make out. In restaurants they sit at the next table and play footsies. At parties my mother sits in my boyfriend's lap, her arms wrapped around his neck, her head on his shoulder. When his hand disappears underneath her skirt she gives me a wink.

My mother sits on the edge of my bed and tells me she has had better. We are in our nightgowns. We sip hot chocolate. I'm not complaining, she says, but I've had better.

They want to use my room. I stand in front of the door, blocking their path. Not again, I say. My mother forms her hands into a prayer gesture. Please? she says. My boyfriend opens his wallet and waves money in my face. What's wrong with your room? I ask. My boyfriend shrugs. I can't get it up in there.

Photographs of my boyfriend and my mother fucking were exhibited at the Neikrug Gallery. I was invited to the opening. I held a drink and stood around. I'm basically very shy, I overheard my mother telling an interviewer. My boyfriend pulled me close and pointed to a photograph. I'm going to make this one next year's Christmas card, he said. What do you think about that?

My boyfriend slaps my mother across the face and calls her a cunt. She collapses in tears. What do you possibly see in him? she asks me. I wipe her nose with a Kleenex. We're through, she shouts at my boyfriend. My boyfriend breaks a chair. I mop his brow and whisper to him that she probably doesn't mean it. My mother spits in my boyfriend's face. He wags his finger at her. I'm going to have to spank you for that, he says. He chases her upstairs.

They spend weekends in bed. When they're hungry they pound their fists on the wall. I bring them their meals on a tray. When I enter my mother covers herself with a sheet. My boyfriend smiles at me and says, I hope you're happy with this arrangement.

For my birthday my mother gave me a cassette of my boyfriend talking dirty to her over the telephone. This is for your own good, she said. I want you to know exactly the kind of man you're crazy enough to be involved with, she said, pressing the PLAY button. I stared out the window. She held the tape recorder against her ear, her other hand in her lap. Now honestly, she said to me later, there are plenty of men out there. Don't you think you can do better.

We flipped a coin and my mother got him New Year's Eve. The two of them decided to have a quiet celebration at home. They snuggled together on the couch in the living room, drinking champagne. I stood on a chair and counted down out loud. At midnight I tooted a little horn and threw confetti into the air. My boyfriend kissed me at five past. Don't forget, he said, you get me Thanksgiving.

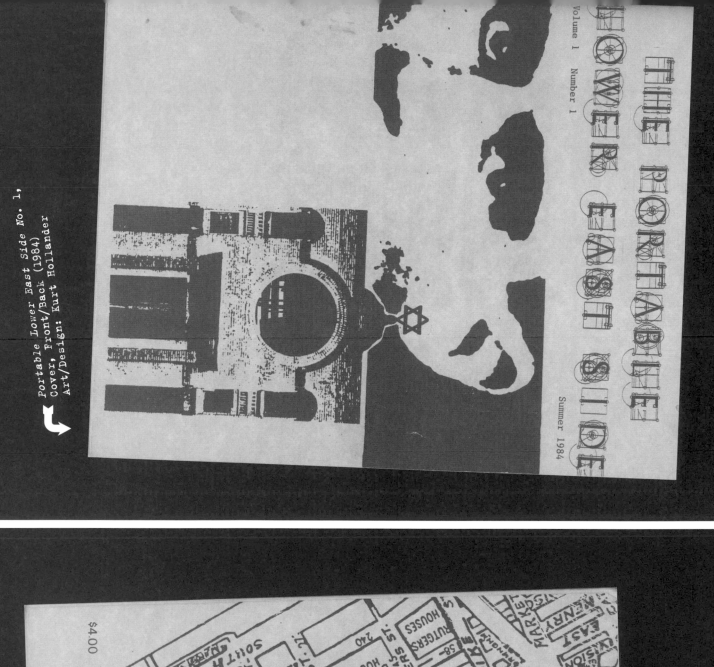

THE PORTABLE LOWER EAST SIDE

Volume 1 Number 1

Summer 1984

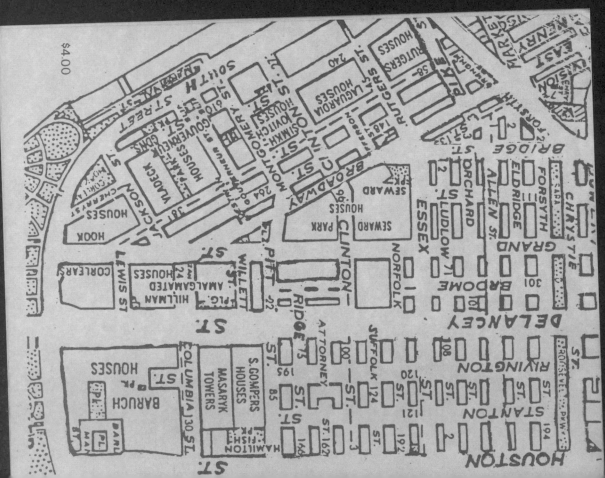

$4.00

Portable Lower East Side No. 1,
Cover, Front/Back (1984)
Art/Design: Kurt Hollander

When my boyfriend is asleep my mother and I go through his wallet. We are worried he is seeing another woman. We examine restaurant receipts and phone numbers written on scraps of paper. Sometimes my mother calls one of the numbers and hangs up. I reassure her. Don't worry, I say, he's just seeing us.

My mother asked my boyfriend not to see me anymore. She's no good, she said. She's a loser. And she's so skinny. I can introduce you to some nice girls, she said, showing him photographs of some of my friends.

My mother and I mud wrestle. We roll in the dirt and pull each other's hair. My boyfriend drinks beer and cheers us on. Loser goes home alone.

HOW TO PICK UP IMPOTENT MEN

Go to that famous bar in the Village for men who can't get it up.

Sit next to the man who looks the most depressed. Whisper in his ear that fucking isn't everything. Tell him you like walking in the rain and holding hands just as much. Tell him your favorite part of sex is the hugging and kissing. Tell him he probably just hasn't met the right woman. Ask him to come home with you.

Later in bed tell him what you really want is to get laid. Order him to try or get out. When it's over ask him if he started yet. Accuse him of liking boys. Tell him you'd see him again but you think he's too old to change. Have him leave without carfare in the middle of the night.

THE COUPLE

I'm in the mood.

I make a special dinner: filet mignon, salad with bacon bits, red wine. The table is set with the plates we save for company and tall white candles. I am wearing a sheer negligee with nothing underneath. Our favorite Sinatra album is playing on the stereo. I take the phone off the hook and wait for him to come home.

"Hey, what's all this?" he asks, looking around the living room, staring me up and down. "Am I in the right house?" he asks, giving me a wink.

"I missed you," I say.

"I missed you, too," he says, kissing me.

We eat in silence. Occasionally our eyes meet and we smile. We are thinking about later.

"Are you sure you're not too tired?" I ask.

"When have I ever been too tired?" he asks.

I clear the table. He follows me into the kitchen and tells me the dishes can wait. He takes my hand and we go into the bedroom.

We take off our clothes and do it to ourselves. I do it to myself and he watches, then he does it to himself and I watch.

Afterwards, we share a cigarette.

"How was it?" he asks.

"Nice," I say. "I thought about Howard, that kid who works behind the counter at the 7-Eleven."

"It was good for me, too," he says, stretching his fingers. "I thought about Sheri Miller, the new receptionist at the office." He turns over in the bed and faces the wall. "Good night, honey," he says. "Sweet dreams."

"Good night," I say, and get up and do the dishes.

THE ST. MARK'S BATHS (1984)

TOM SAVAGE

Naked bodies trellised by time
Watch to open to it.
Old men with big bellies, sad eyes,
dark, unmanageable pricks. Hopeless.
Go away. It's time for the monastery
for you, old men. You've had your fun
or if you haven't, it's too late.
Cruel, young men with soft, perfect forms
who beckon to you but are then too tired,
open up to it. I offer you my love.
If you cannot give me your love,
what are you doing here?
The life of a shadow is unrewarding
even though the hot moments offer
themselves, thick and thin.
Then there are the others with whom
contact is possible. Not too old
to be repulsive; not too young
to be conceited. These have often
built up their muscles as recompense
for the crime of having aged.
But they know the simple pain of rejection,
fear want, know that to be cruel is
to bring cruelty one's way.
With these some fucking is possible.
There may even be one or two open
to conversation.

Ground Zero 1-4, 1984, from the East Village Eye Art/Words: James Romberger and Marguerite Van Cook

TV (1984)

BRAD GOOCH

The only light on in the room is the green lit-up dial of the stereo radio/record-player. Click as the record goes off. Doug gets up off the couch in one section of a big loft in Tribeca. He turns off the record player and puts on a black/white portable Japanese TV set. It's Sunday night. A movie comes on the little screen. He keeps the sound off. You can see a toothpaste commercial that interrupts the movie. It is a hot night in August. Doug goes back and sits in the dark watching the screen, lights a cigarette, takes a sip of water with ice. At the end of the room is a line of three big windows that are filled with a dull yellow light from outside. Not many street noises. Doug gets up and walks over to the window. The apartment is air-conditioned, though not very well. The air is cool but canned. Doug looks at the empty European brick streets in his part of town. All around are big old warehouses that are being converted into lofts. Across the street he can see a Japanese guy and his girlfriend making out on a mattress on the floor of their empty loft. He watches them a lot at night.

Phone rings. Doug turns on the lights, big overhead office fluorescent lights, and goes over to a desk in another part of the loft to answer the phone. It is a guy named Jeff who lives a few floors down in the same building. They had met that afternoon at the diner down the street. Jeff used to be a lawyer but had stopped practice after saving up money for a few years and now he is painting realistic houses. Asks Doug if he wants to come down for a drink.

Doug does and does not. He is interested by Jeff but was also having a good time sitting by himself. He knows he has to go to work tomorrow at the travel agency and doesn't know if he wants to get involved in talking and smoking and drinking. Doesn't know if he wants to get carried away. Tells Jeff that he's busy right now but might call him a little later. Goes back to the light switch and turns the lights off. Turns the sound up on the TV. It is Spencer Tracy and Katharine Hepburn arguing in a duplex apartment. She is standing next to a big rubber plant. Her voice makes Doug's stomach crawl in a good way. He decides to go out for a walk. Does want to meet someone or at least have a drink but not Jeff, not right now. Goes to a local bar. Has a beer. No one very interesting and no one talks to him so he leaves. Out on the street is starting to feel jumpy. Sort of wants an adventure but isn't committed yet. He walks down the long street. Starts heading back to his house. Then gets the idea that he wants to visit those two Japanese people who are always fucking in the building across from him. Tries to figure out how to pull it off. Goes to the building, sees the name Yuki on one of the bells on the floor number, 5, across from his. He rings the bell. Voice asks who is it through the metal box. He answers "Jeff, I live in the building across the street." Now he feels sort of nervous but not as nervous as an outsider, knowing the story, might think. He also feels confident. Goes up the stairs fast, a couple at a time, knocks on grey wood door.

Yuki answers the door. He has black hair, wears a silk black polo shirt, black corduroys, white socks and white sneakers. Doug has on blue jeans and a cottony green shirt and penny loafers with paint specks on them; no socks.

Doug: This I know sounds crazy but I live across the street and am not a creep and just got this impulse to come up here and talk to you. I've seen you through the window, and saw you once by yourself at the diner. And I'm not following you around. And if you're busy I'll just leave since even if I get inside I don't have anything to say and feel embarrassed now. But I'm not drunk or stoned.

Yuki: So come in. (Makes a quizzical half-yes half-no face.) Let's give it a try.

Doug goes in. Yuki's girlfriend, who isn't Japanese after all, is sitting in a folding director's chair. She has blond hair and is dressed more like Doug, with blue jeans and a pink cotton shirt tied above the belly button; no shoes. Her name is Sally.

Sally: No, don't go through it again, I heard what you said at the door. I'm not feeling suspicious and I'm not drunk or stoned either, so come on in. Maybe it has something to do with the I Ching or the moon.

Yuki: Were you just lonely? Is that why you came over?

Doug: No.

Yuki: Do you want a beer? Or vodka?

Doug: A vodka on the rocks would be good. I guess I should have brought you a present or something, to pay my way in.

Sally: Well, it's over now, so let's just pretend we've known each other for years and you just

stopped by. You and I went to the same high school in Illinois. I recognized you on the street yesterday and asked you to come over and meet my Japanese boyfriend. So that's a good reason to be here. Agree?

Doug: Yes. Is tonight the full moon?

Yuki: Tomorrow, I think. But then it's sort of full for about three days.

Doug: I think it's really true about the moon. I can't count the number of times I've been speeding down some strange street on the Upper East Side or somewhere on some dumb mission and looked up and saw a full moon. That seems to explain it.

Sally: Maybe you're just feeling your own personal tides.

Doug: I could argue either side. Now, since I took up the lunatic position it's only right that you give the other side, that it's in yourself and not in the moon.

Sally: You're right. Bergman said that people spend their lives trying on masks, and they usually pick the masks that are least like themselves.

Doug: So you continued your education after our days in high school? I thought you cheerleaders just got married and settled down with the local factory owner's son. What was his name, in our case, Richard? Yeah, that's it, a Polish name. Richard Yastremski, or something like that.

Yuki walks over with the vodka. He and Sally already have beers.

Yuki: Don't be nervous. Relax.

So the three of them sit around a little uncomfortably for awhile. Doug gets up and goes to the window and looks at his own loft, lit-up, then down at Jeff's, lit-up, then up and down the street again. Expects to see a horse, but doesn't. Then he goes back and sits in a chair. There is next to nothing in the loft.

Doug: So what do you do?

Yuki: I work for a guy who makes rugs and tapestries. But I never bring any of my work home with me.

Sally: I waitress at that diner where you said you saw Yuki by himself. I'm insulted you didn't notice me. Are you a gay blade?

Doug looks annoyed for a minute, but it is a minor annoyance, like bedbugs.

Doug: The simplest answer is yes.

Sally: Well that explains it.

Doug: I don't think it does.

Sally: So are you interested in Yuki? Which one of us do you concentrate on when you stare-in from across the street?

Doug feels rotten for a minute. He had somehow expected that the brashness of his act, after he found out they were nice people, not psychotics, would lead to a nice evening. Maybe that there was even some mystic reason for his being here. Now it was getting rough. He didn't like Sally. He didn't think that she liked him.

Yuki: (in fake English accent) Why, darling, you're going to make our guest uncomfortable.

Doug: I hope this incident doesn't make you go out and buy shades.

Sally: I'm really a nice person, honest, but I don't think this unusual meeting is working anymore.

Doug: Oh is that what it is? I just thought I was catching jungle rot.

Yuki: I'd like to get together with you sometime, Doug, maybe for dinner. But this three-way is not working out too well. Did you notice?

Doug: I think I better go now.

Doug is getting angry and red and is trying to hide it and wishes he hadn't come over. He is also feeling lonely and wishes he had a family to go home to, just right now, because if he wasn't lonely when he walked in, he is now, or more precisely, feeling isolated. He is also jealous of Sally. And is getting an electrical attachment to Yuki.

Sally: Why don't you two go out for a walk. It's no big deal. I just want to get to bed early. Yuki, instead of having dinner with our mysterious visitor, why not strike while the iron is hot, and go for a walk.

Yuki: No. (to Doug) Let me show you downstairs.

Yuki goes down the stairs first. He turns around every so often to say things to Doug. The steps are wooden and narrow but there is a light on each landing so it's not dark.

Doug: What kind of tapestries do you do? Do you do your own or just work on your boss's?

Yuki: I do my own. I like to represent a few things that don't go together, like a grey tenement building, a dragon, a green olive tree and some wild bird, and try to get them to make sense by the colors, to trick them into a whole. It's like setting up some kind of riddle for myself and then trying to solve it.

Doug is looking a lot at Yuki's hands. They are both rough and soft at the same time. Doug definitely has a little crush on Yuki and now that they're going down the steps the visit seems OK again. Doug reminds himself that he gets crushes on artists a lot.

They get to the landing. Yuki doesn't open the door yet but just stands there. Doug stands there too.

Doug: I'd apologize or something but I don't want to.

Yuki: Here's my number.

He hands Doug a card that is black and white and has his number at work written on it.

Doug looks at Yuki. Vice versa.

Doug: Do you know what time it is?

Yuki: Two o'clock.

Doug: Hmmm.

Doug is out on the street again. He blinks around for awhile. A cab goes by. Unusual in this neighborhood. He heads down to the river. Past the tile entrance to a subway. Under the old West Side Highway. Gets reasonably close to the water, though still separated by some big sanitation enclosure. The sanitation guys are just getting off work. They come out of the compound still in their green trousers and work shirts with red writing on them. Doug wonders if they have to wash their own uniforms. He then sees them pile into different big white sanitation trucks and rumble off. They must be getting to work, not getting off work. Next a woman smoking a cigarette, middle-aged, tough looking but interesting comes out of the compound. She looks pointedly at Doug. At first he thinks about getting involved but then realizes he's had enough. His idea was somehow a soothing session with the river but that doesn't seem possible from here and he doesn't want to walk and doesn't want to meet anybody else. This will have to be a night that can't be laid out in a story. She gets in a blue Dodge and leaves. Doug heads home.

Then he gets one last bright idea. Walks over a few blocks to a TV repairman's shop he knows. This guy always works all night, never in the day, and leaves his place open so anyone can walk in. Doug had had to get his TV fixed a few times and got to know the repairman's schedule. Now he drops in sometimes, especially if he's a little drunk, and visits. The shop is right below street level, but the door is wide open, and through the display window of rabbit antennas you can see some TVs and tables and a general mess. The anti-burglary gate is pushed back from the door. Doug goes down the steps and in.

Doug: Hiya Richard.

Richard looks up, no twitch. He's about thirty-five. Has slicked-back black hair, is dressed in coveralls, and covered with dirt.

Richard: Hi. Just getting home from a bar or something?

Doug: No, I was wondering if I could watch a little TV.

Richard: Why not? But this isn't the neighborhood barbershop you know. (He smiles: one tooth missing; reserved, but heartwarming.) Sometimes I think I'm running like a small town barbershop for night people and other perverts. (Laughs)

Doug wonders what he means by perverts. One brush with that is enough for one night. What Doug wants now is definitely TV. He put in his time with people. He feels mixed. TV helps straighten him out.

Doug: Can I change the stations?

Richard: Sure. Look I'm real busy tonight. Can't talk too much but you do what you want. I like you. I'm sure you'll be a mayor of New York someday, so right now learn what you can from that TV, you may be able to use it in one of your speeches, and shut up, OK?

Doug: (winks)

Doug thinks it's odd that Richard took that older guy tone with him when they're practically the same age, give or take five years, but he doesn't care much since he's getting what he wants. He sits down on a yellow vinyl kitchen chair with steel tube legs that is patched with adhesive tape. The light comes straight down, hard, from the ceiling. He bends over in toilet position to fiddle with the switches. Settles on a Johnny Carson talk show.

Johnny is interviewing a lady all dressed in a fake-jewel dress with a slit up the side. She keeps getting up out of her chair and making jerky motions and sitting down again. She smokes and leans against Johnny's desk. Gives him a kiss every so often. Ed McMahon picks up a package of some detergent and shows it to the camera. Johnny looks annoyed at this lady but that could just be his manner. Maybe it's a way to get her to talk. Maybe he figures out psychological quirks in all his guests and then plays off them. Maybe he's a genius. Maybe the show is all masks. Maybe it is like a Balinese masked play and if we weren't so inside our own culture we would be able to see that.

Doug's mind works this way for awhile. Pretty soon he gets up. His head feels more emptied-out.

Doug: Good-night Richard.

Richard: Good-night kid. What did you learn?

Doug feels embarrassed not to have anything bright to answer that might make Richard like him

more. Doug smiles. He's in bed by four o'clock. Up by eight. It turns out to be a long Monday because he's so tired. Feels fuzzy around his heart. So he gets home pretty early and makes spaghetti. Calls Jeff. They make a date to have dinner on Tuesday night. Doug is in bed by 9 o'clock to make up for the night before and is up at 8 the next day, Tuesday, which gives him eleven hours. He feels better all Tuesday, has some color.

Next Page Left: Hi Tech Low life Discourse, and Dance," at Darinka, "Film, 1984, Flyer (1984) August, 1984, Flyer (1984)

Next Page Right: New Observations (edited by Lynn Tillman), No. 26 (1984) Critical Love: Edited by Lynn Tillman) Art/Design:ugism:il) (Critical Love: Edited Mark Magill

CRITICAL LOVE

Edited by Lynne Tillman

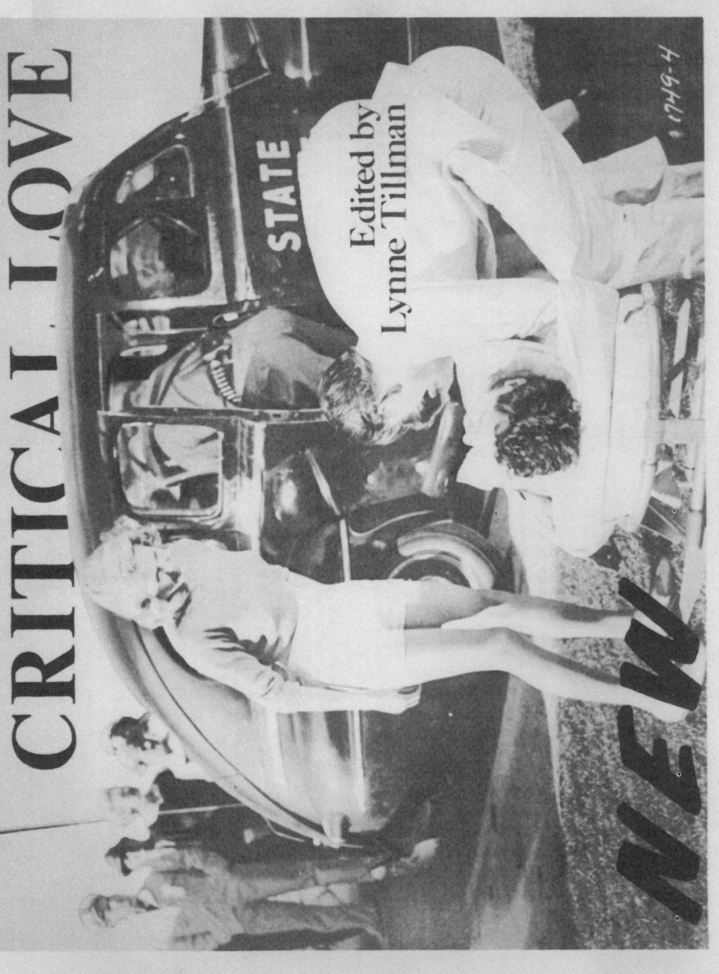

STATE

new

OBSERVATIONS

Lynn Tillman with Kiki Smith:
From "Madame Realism" (1984)
Text: Lynne Tillman; Art: Kiki Smith

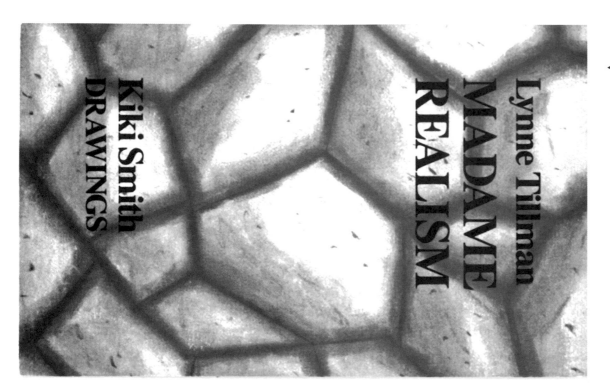

Lynne Tillman

MADAME
REALISM

Kiki Smith
DRAWINGS

Madame Realism read from *The New
York Times:* "The Soviet Ambassador
to Portugal had formally apologized
for a statement issued by his embassy
that called Mario Soares, the Socialist
leader, a lunatic in need of prolonged
psychiatric treatment. The embassy
said the sentence should have read
'these kinds of lies can only come
from persons with a sick imagination,
and these lies need prolonged analysis
and adequate treatment.'" Clever
people plot their lives with strategies
not unlike those used by governments.
We all do business. And our lies are in
need of prolonged analysis and adequate treatment.

Soho Arts Weekly, No. 1,
September 25, 1985, Cover (1985)
Art: Art Spiegelman

John Cage
Ron Padgett
John Giorno
Mabou Mines
Spalding Gray
The Wooster Group
The Hi Sheriffs of Blue
Bradley Wester & Diane Torr
Butch Morris & Jessica Hagedorn
Pedro Pietri & Cyn. Zarco
Jonathan Baumbach
Kenward Elmslie
Laura Foreman
Jonas Mekas
Bob Holman
Jon Gibson
John Watts
Sonorexia
Ism

ZONE
MAGAZINE

PRESENTS

A BENEFIT FOR
NOTHING
ZONE's NOTHING ISSUE out in March

SYMPHONY SPACE
BROADWAY & 95 ST NYC
Monday 25 January
7:30pm
864-5400

N
THING

tickets in advance $7.50   at door $8.00   poster © Dikko Faust 238 Mott 4B NYC 925-3462

Buy tickets now at BLEECKER BOB'S 179 MacDougal off W8 & SOHO MUSIC GALLERY 26 Wooster near Grand
Tickets on sale 18 January at SYMPHONY SPACE box office

Poster for Benefit for Nothing (1982)
Design: Dikko Faust/
Purgatory Pie Press

Avenue E

featuring

Gary Indiana
Cookie Mueller

with

Steve Cee
Tony Clay
Ann Craig
Kate Dillon
Frank Green
Robert Kaplan
Anele Rubin

music by

Stephanie Crawford

at

703 East Sixth Street
just east of Avenue C
475–5758

Benefit Party $5.

Sunday, March 17th 9:00 PM

Fall 1985   Volume 2 Number 2

Featuring stories by:
Yolande Villemaire, Reinaldo Povod, Normandi Ellis, Darius James,
Catherine Texier, Gary Indiana, Mike Topp, Peter Cherches,
Joan Harvey, Lee Eiferman, Eileen Myles, Nina Zivancevic
included with every issue:
Your very own set of elegant Salvadorian Cocktail Napkins
Cover art by Barbara Kruger. Back cover by Jeffrey Danneman.

BETWEEN C AND D
Post–Literate Lower East Side Fiction Magazine

You are the perfect crime

BIRTH
REBIRTH
AFTER BIRTH
STILL BIRTH
COMPUTERS

$4.00 $5.00 OUTSIDE NEW YORK CITY

Clockwise from Bottom Left:

Blatant Artifice No. 1, Cover (1986)
Art: Paul Kalinowski

Anarcadium Pan by Carl Watson,
Cover (1985) Art: Matt Straub

The Right Side of My Brain,
Pyramid Club, Flyer (1986)

Between C & D Reading at
Darinka/ABC No Rio,
Flyer (1985)

ANARCADIUM PAN

Carl Watson

BA
BLATANT ARTIFICE

HALLWALLS

FICTION ANTHOLOGY, VOL. II

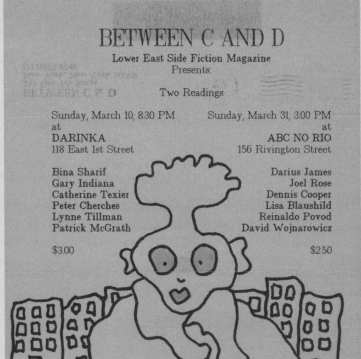

BETWEEN C AND D
Lower East Side Fiction Magazine
Presents:

Two Readings

Sunday, March 10, 8:30 PM   Sunday, March 31, 3:00 PM
at   at
DARINKA   ABC NO RIO
118 East 1st Street   156 Rivington Street

Bina Sharif   Darius James
Gary Indiana   Joel Rose
Catherine Texier   Dennis Cooper
Peter Cherches   Lisa Blaushild
Lynne Tillman   Reinaldo Povod
Patrick McGrath   David Wojnarowicz

$3.00 $2.50

THE RIGHT SIDE OF MY BRAIN

film by R. KERN   **starring LYDIA LUNCH**

PYRAMID CLUB   **FEB 18 1986 11 PM**   **Rated X**

A counter-void weekly, and a new voice for the culturally deprived

saw

SOHO ARTS WEEKLY

VOL. 1 NO. 9 DEC. 4, 1985
$1.00

Photo By Jenkinson/Palwonsky

Baby Birds (1985) Karen Finley

1

Baby Birds by Karen Finley

She dreams. She dreams of strangling baby birds. Blubirds, wrens and robins. With her thumbs she pushes back on their beak, against soft, small, feathered neck til it snaps like a breaking twig.

She dreams. She dreams of being locked in a cage and singing loudly and off key with her loved ones standing behind her whispering very loudly "She has an ugly voice. Doesn't she? She has an ugly voice." Oh. leave it to the loved ones to judge us like they do. It's always the loved ones who interferes with our dreams.

She dreams. She dreams of falling out of a fifth story window. As she falls she catches herself by holding on to the window ledge. It's January and the ledge is made of stone. Icy cold. Her hands are stuck to the icy ledge like a frosted fudgesicle to a wet tongue. The cold, the sharp edges of the ice & stone cuts through her fingers, her flesh, her bone. It doesn't matter though for she has ugly fingers. She sees the blood gush out of her limbs the harder she holds

K. Finley

on to the ledge. She can hear her blood leave her body. The blood flows down her limbs. She can hear her own death. Her husband walks below the building as she hangs. Her shadow is cast on the concrete before him. ~~but~~ but he hadn't memorized her shadow and she didn't know how to wear perfume. She wasn't that kind of a girl. So she called out for help. "Help! HELP! "she cried. But the wind was in a mean mood and took her cries half way around the world to a child's crib. so it's mother could hear her own child cry.

This dream was considered very important to the doctors. For in the past she had dreams of tortures, rapes and beatings where no sounds would come out at all. She'd open up her mouth and move her lips but no sounds would come out at all.

But she knew that these ~~doctors~~ were wrong. For these were the same doctors who anaesthized her during the birth of her children. These were the same doctors that gave her episiotomies.

Baby Birds

K. FINLEY

No more sexual feelings for her after childbirth.

But she knew that it really wasn't the doctors fault. No, she knew that it really was her problem. The problem was the way she projected her feminity. She felt if she wasn't passive, well, she jisst didn't feel desireable. And if she wasn't desireable she JUST DIDN'T FEEL FEMALE. And, if she WASN'T FEMALE, well, THE WHOLE WORLD WOULD CAVE IN.

Like when Martin died. Like when Desi Arnaz, Liberace, Danny Kaye died. All of my heroes are dyeing on me. And Desi will never get back together with Lucy. And your little girl will never grow up. All of my boys are dyeing on me. All of my babies are dyeing on me. Oh, I wish I could relieve you of your pain. I wish I could relieve you of your suffering.

Like when my father finally

<u>'Baby Birds</u>   4
Karen Finley

Told me he loved me after 40
years then went into the
bathroom, locked the door,
put up pictures of children
from the Sears Catalogue,
arranged mirrors, black stockings,
and garters to look at while he
masterbated as he hung himself
from the shower stall. Whatever
turns you on, girl. It's that
ultimate erection. It's that
ultimate orgasm. Whatever turns
you on, woman. Whatever, Whatever,
Whatever turns you on.

   And when he died — Volcanoes
erupted. Cyclones appeared. Coyotes
came out of their caves. Old
people were struck by lightning.
Don't you know that I don't
want anymore deaths on my
conscience? For I already
have a ~~abortion~~ on my conscience
from when a member of my
own family RAPED me.
Don't worry, I won't mention
your name. Don't worry, I won't
mention your name.

And the season

And the reason why my father committed suicide is that he no longer found me attractive.

And by now, you can tell that I prefer talking about the fear of living as opposed to the fear of dying.

FROM "IDIOGLOSSIA"* (1985)

ANNE TURYN

* **idioglossia—1.** a private form of speech invented by one child or by children who are in close contact, as twins. Twin language. **2.** a pathological condition characterized by speech so distorted as to be unintelligible.

selections from the diaries:

The studier: It's been arranged that I will pick up the guide when I arrive on the continent and we will travel to the interior. With a lot of luck the guide's native language will be related to the one the people (if there are any) speak—or even that he is as gifted in languages as they claim.

The studied: This record will be kept in the same spirit we track time and record goods, fortunes good and bad—to note the stories of each day. Until the time the marking system is perfected, it is my secret.

The studier: The span of time between this moment and my departure is narrowing rapidly, too swiftly to complete the lists of all I must include in my preparations, let alone complete the packing. It seems I can never be thorough enough. I am so agitated about my journey I cannot comply with sleep. When I finally do sleep, I think of what lies ahead—strange peoples, lacking circumstances, the unknown. (Oh, that the eventual includes fame and then fortune!)

The studied: Fresh sun, on my way home today, with my arms loaded down with foods, neglecting to look about me, but rather looking inward, then speaking suddenly to myself in my own manner about other possible places and other probable creatures—tripped, dropping everything! As

my parent says, with your thoughts in the sky it is difficult to place all feet on the ground.

The studier: If there are people, ~~and they have a language~~ and they are illiterate, how can I know how quickly the language changes. How to recapture slang which existed in earlier times. . . . Will there be a way to identify slang. The more a language is spoken, the faster it changes. . . .

The studied: So much giddiness intoxicates us these last few days! We've played "Deeper Meaning" every night until so late it seems that it will be tomorrow by the time the sounds arrive from our toes. The coveted sounds are those we discover right before tomorrow, in the crevice between this night and that day, when everything but our thoughts are suspended. Tonight sleep seduces me as these marks are made. . . .

The studier: The faster a language is spoken, the greater the change?

The studied: If this method of marking can be completed, perhaps it can be applied to some of the other ways we talk. My other way of talking has been congesting my dreams, day and night for the past weeks. Perhaps the marking is poisoning my talk, but it seems not. . . .

The studier: (The only reason leaving is sad is that there is no one I leave behind. . .). In a few days time I will be halfway there. Everything is ready to be loaded—the cameras, the tape recorders, the typewriters, the guns.

The studied: This other way of talking is straining my thoughts so . . . in a way it had never done before. Fearsome thoughts, doubtful ones, creep into me that something is happening to me, or my time is nearly up . . . the marking system perhaps has disjointed my thoughts. This scratching is not the same as thinking, maybe the time to stop doing it has traveled to me. Every detail has always been remembered, recalled, recognized. . . maybe this system is not necessary at all. My thoughts dictate: fine for numbers, money, time, but never for such clouds as wishes, thoughts, stories.

The studier: I hope I can master their language not unquickly myself. I can't fathom how it will be to communicate with no one but myself. Of course the radio is no converser at that distance, with those mountains. (Neither will those barbarians be (if any exist). . . their speech will mimic the word itself—ba . . bar . . . . It's too late to change my mind. Besides I need to write up my findings and publish.)

The studied: Days have hobbled by. . . no mark-making in this system. . . .

The studier: (I'll need to rework this journal no doubt.)

The studied: My dreams are drenched with different beasts and other places. . . and my other way of talking.

The studied: Conversations multiply about mortals that are approaching. It is said they look almost like we do. To perfect a system of thoughts—as pleasant as standing still in the rain that arrives between the seasons.

The studier: I'm not sure if I will make it. It

is so hot, then so cold and blustery at night. Perhaps the reports I invested in were merely rumors. We have enough provisions to turn back now. ~~I could always invent~~

——ied: None of us could play "Deeper Meaning" tonight. Everyone is alive with talk of other beings. Too tiresome. . . .

——ier: (If the guide does not desist from addressing me as "chief" my patience will vanish.)

——ied: The misty season is leaving and the blustery one is welcomed.

——ier: It is too late to turn back. We must go ahead, unless we are indeed traveling in circles as it feels we are.

——ied: The accounts are circling us, that beings are venturing to us. They have been seen, dressed in strange colors and hauling much.

——ier: Smoke means fire. We are within sight of the site. We are camping at some distance tonight and will make our approach in the morning. I hope it is peaceful. . . .

——ied: This system of marking may be able to be applied to all the ways of talking. It captures sound, and through sound only, meaning.

——ier: The guide has gone ahead. I am alone, waiting.

——ied: Creatures! Here!

——ier: We are at the outskirts of the community, waiting.

——*ied:* Almost everyone of us has taken a stare at these creatures—so much like and not like us. Some of us have gotten close enough to hear them conversing—a way not ours it is said. Some of us went to them—not me—but were unable to exchange thoughts.

——*ier:* We are still on the outskirts.

——*ied:* We stayed up all night talking excitedly about these fellows. Finally the stories are substantiated. No one can remember first hand, not even the parents' parents' parents, the oldest ones, can remember their parents' parents' experience with others. It is only the stories that tell us this. We still do not know if these creatures are indeed people—just because their vocal chords vibrate does not mean they are people. If actions can "mean" the way words can. . . .

——*ier:* They certainly jabber away.

——*ied:* Perhaps my marking device will be to me the way the stories are to all of us. . . the stories exist in more than one place at a time, so these thoughts can exist in these marks as well.

——*ier:* The people have been approaching us singly and many have attempted verbal communication. (I have never been so alone).

——*ied:* Most of us have taken a look or approached these people-like beings. Staring is still enough for me.

——*ier:* The guide has not made sense of their language. He continues to try. I wait.

——*ied:* Not one of us who tries can talk with these beings. . . there is more to harvest talking with the birds.

——*ier:* The guide is growing increasingly frustrated. He ~~claims~~ hypothesizes that the people all speak different languages. (I knew I should have taken an expert from the university, I am becoming irritated.)

——*ied:* These other beings entered our home today slowly, with their hands in front of them.

——*ier:* I could swear I heard a few English phrases today. This hot wind is affecting me.

——*ier:* I have spent days listening to these people speak separately, I think they ARE speaking different languages; the sounds they make differ from person to person most radically, How could this be dialect or free variation in a community this small and insular?

——*ied:* The beings speak louder and louder, especially the strange one, but none of us can talk with them. Still my desire has been not to go near them. They were talking so brashly the screeching was heard as murmuring across the vista.

——*ier:* They do speak a language to each other that the guide is mastering, while they speak differently to us. They appear amiable, yet could they be purposely undermining us with gibberish? Is it a language game like pig latin? (Is it a hoax?)

——*ied:* Everyone but a few of the shy ones has tried their private way of talking with the others. My turn is soon.

FROM *SWIMMING TO CAMBODIA* (1985)

SPALDING GRAY

Whenever I travel, if I have the time, I go by train. Because I like to hang out in the lounge car. I hear such great stories there—fantastic! Perhaps it's because they think they'll never see me again. It's like a big, rolling confessional.

I was on my way to Chicago from New York City when this guy came up to me and said, "Hi, I'm Jim Bean. Mind if I sit down?"

"No, I'm Spalding Gray, have a seat. What's up Jim?"

"Oh, nothing much. I'm in the Navy."

"Really? Where are you stationed?"

"Guantanamo Bay."

"Where's that?"

"Cuba."

"Really? What's it like?"

"Oh, we don't get into Cuba, man. It's totally illegal. We go down to the Virgin Islands whenever we want R & R. We get free flights down there."

"What do you do there?"

"Get laid."

"Go to whores?"

"No. I never paid for sex in my life. I get picked up by couples. I like to swing, I mean, I'm into that, you know? Threesomes, triangles, pyramids—there's power in that."

And I could see how he would be picked up. He was cute enough—insidious, but still cute. The only kind of demented thing about him was that his ears hadn't grown. They were like those little pasta shells. It was as if his body had grown but his ears hadn't caught up yet.

So I said, "Where are you off to?"

"Pittsburgh."

"Pittsburgh, my god. What's up there?"

"My wife."

"Really? How long has it been since you saw her?"

"Oh, about a year."

"I bet she's been doing some swinging herself."

"No, man, I know her. She's got fucking cobwebs growing between her legs. I wouldn't mind watching her get fucked by a guy once, no, I wouldn't mind that at all."

"Well that's quite a trip, coming from Cuba to Pittsburgh."

"No, no. I'm not stationed in Cuba anymore, man. I'm in Philly."

"Oh, well what's going on in Philly?"

"Can't tell you. No way. Top secret."

"Oh, come on, Jim. Top secret in Philadelphia? You can tell me."

"No way."

And he proceeded to have five more rum cokes and tell me that in Philadelphia he is on a battleship in a waterproof chamber; chained one arm to the wall for five hours a day, next to a green button, with earphones on. I could just see those little ears waiting for orders to fire his rockets from their waterproof silos onto the Russians. He sits there waiting with those earphones on, high on blue-flake cocaine, a new breed from Peru that he loves, with a lot of coffee because the Navy can't test for cocaine. They can test for marijuana five days after you smoke a joint, but not the cocaine. He sits there high on cocaine, chained to the wall, next to the green button, in a waterproof chamber.

"Why waterproof?" I asked. I thought I'd just start with the details and work out. I know I could have said, "Why a green button?" but it didn't matter at that point.

"Waterproof, man, because when the ship sinks and I go down to the bottom of the ocean, any ocean, anywhere, I'm still there in my waterproof chamber and I can push that green button, activate my rocket and it fires out of the waterproof silo and up, up, up it goes. I get a fucking erection every time I think of firing a rocket on those Russians. We're going to win! We're going to win this fucking war. I like the Navy, though. I fucking *like* the Navy. I get to travel everywhere. I've been to Africa, Sweden, India. I fucking didn't like Africa, though. I don't know why, but black women just don't turn me on."

Now here's a guy, if the women in the country don't turn him on, he misses the entire landscape. It's just one big fuzzball, a big black outline and he steps through to the other side of the world and comes out in Sweden.

"I fucking love Sweden, man. You get to see real Russkies in Sweden. They're marched in at gunpoint and they're only allowed two beers. We're drinking all the fucking beer we want. We're drunk on our asses, saying, 'Hey, Russkies, what's it like in Moscow this time of year?' And then we pay a couple of Swedish whores to go over and put their heads in the Russkies' laps. You should see those fuckers sweat, man. They are so stupid. We're going to win. We're going to win the fuckin' war. I mean, they are really *dumb*. They've got liquid fuel in their rockets, they're rusty and they're going to sputter, they're going to pop, they're going to land in our cornfields."

"Wait a minute, Jim. Cornfields? I mean, haven't you read the literature? It's bad enough if they land in the cornfields. We're all doomed."

"No, they're stupid. You won't believe this. The Russians don't even have electro intercoms in their ships. They still speak through tubes!"

Suddenly I had this enormous fondness for the Russian Navy. The whole of Mother Russia. The thought of these men speaking, like innocent children, through empty toilet paper rolls, where you could

still hear compassion, doubt, envy, brotherly love, ambivalence, all those human tones coming through the tube.

Jim was very patriotic. I thought it only existed on the covers of *Newsweek* and *Time*. But no, if you take the train from New York to Chicago, there it is against a pumpkin-orange sunset, Three Mile Island. Jim stood up and saluted those three big towers, then sat back down.

Meanwhile I was trying to make a mild stand. I was trying to talk him out of his ideas. I don't know what my platform was—I mean, he was standing for all of America and I was just concerned for myself at that point. I really felt as if I were looking my death in the face. I'm not making up any of these stories, I'm really not. And if *he* was making up the story he was telling me, I figure he's white, and if he wants it bad enough and he's in the Navy, if he wasn't down in that waterproof chamber then, he must be down there now.

"Jim, Jim," I said, "you don't want to do it. Remember what happened to the guy who dropped the bomb on Hiroshima? He went crazy!"

"That asshole? He was not properly brainwashed. I," he said with great pride, "have been properly brainwashed. Also there is the nuclear destruct club. Do you think I'm the only one who's going to be pressing that green button? There's a whole bunch of us going to do it."

"Wait, wait, wait. You, all of you, don't want to die, do you? You're going to die if you push that button. Think of all you have to live for." I had to think hard about this one. "The blue-flake cocaine, for instance. Getting picked up by couples. The Swedish whores. Blowing away the cobwebs between your wife's legs. I mean, really."

"No, I'm not going to die. We get 'pubs.'"

Everything was abbreviated, and "pubs" meant Navy publications that tell them where to go to avoid radiation. And I could see him down there, after the rest of us have all been vaporized. He'll be down there in Tasmania or New Zealand starting this new red-faced, pea-brained, small-eared humanoid race. And I thought, the Mother needs a rest, Mother Earth needs a long, long rest.

If we're lucky he'll end up in Africa.

Anyway, he was beginning to realize that I wasn't totally on his side. It was hard to see that because I didn't have as detailed a platform as he had. Finally, he turned to me and said, "Listen Mr. Spalding," (I think by then he was calling me Gary Spalding) "you would not be doing that thing you do, writing, talking, whatever it is you do in the theatre, if it were not for me and the United States Navy stopping the Russians from taking over the world."

And I thought, wait a minute, maybe he's right. Maybe the Russians *are* trying to take over the world. Maybe *I'm* the one who's brainwashed. Maybe I've been hanging out with liberals too long. I mean, after all this time I thought I was a conscientious pacifist but maybe I've been deluding myself. Maybe I'm just a passive-aggressive unconscious coward, and like any good liberal, I should question everything. For instance, when did I last make a stand, any kind of stand, about anything? When did I just stand up for something right? Let alone America. What is America? Every time I try to think of America as a unit I get anxious. I think that's part of the reason I moved to Manhattan; I wanted to live on "an island off the coast of America." I wanted to live somewhere between America and Europe, a piece of land with very defined boundaries and only eight million people.

So I had no concept of America or of making a stand. I hated contact sports when I was a kid—I really

didn't like the bumps. When I moved to New York City I wanted to be able to make a stand, so I took karate. But I had that horrid feeling of bone bouncing on bone whenever I hit my instructor or he hit me.

When I was in the seventh grade I fell in love with Judy Dorci. Butchy Coca was in love with her too. He lived on the other side of the tracks. He had a black leather motorcycle jacket and I had a camel's hair coat. I was careful never to go into his territory—I stayed in mine, Barrington, Rhode Island—but they didn't have a five-and-dime in Barrington and I had to buy Christmas presents. I went over to Warren, Rhode Island, Butchy's territory, to the five-and-dime, and one of Butchy's gang saw me—put the finger on me. I stepped outside and there they were, eight of them, like in *High Noon*, one foot up against the brick wall, smoking Chesterfield Regulars. I thought, this is it. I'm going to know what it's like to make a stand—but why rush it?

I ducked into the Warren Gazette just to look at Christmas cards, take my time, and there was Mr. Walker from Barrington. I said, "Hi, Mr. Walker, are you going my way?"

"I am. My car is out back. Do you mind going out the back door?"

"Nope. Let's go."

When I arrived in London for the first time, I was jet-lagging and I had to rent a car to go up to Edinburgh so I felt a little out of it. All right, I was driving on the wrong side of the road—easily done—you know, no big deal. I cut a guy off first thing, and when I rolled down the window to apologize, he said, "Take off those glasses, mate, I'm going to punch you out." Just like a British redcoat announcing his intentions ahead of time.

I just rolled up the window. Why rush it?

***

Last year I cut a man off on Hudson Street in Manhattan. I cut off a man from New Jersey, which is one of the worst things you can do. A man from New Jersey! And I rolled down the window—why I do this, I don't know—to apologize again. This time I saw the fist coming toward me and I thought, now I'll know what it's like to have my jaw broken in five places. At the last minute, just seconds before making contact with my face, he pulled the punch and hit the side of the van instead. He walked off with his knuckles bleeding, cursing. I rolled up the window and pulled out. Why rush it?

I had a friend who wanted to rush it, because he was going into the Army and he'd never been punched out. So he went to his friend Paul and said, "Paul, I've never been punched out. But I'm drafted, I'm going into the Army. Please punch me out Paul, quick." And Paul knocked him out.

I didn't want to go into the Army. I didn't want to get punched out. So I checked all the boxes. I admit it. I did it. I checked "homosexual" and "has trouble sleeping." Where it asked "What do you do when you can't sleep?" I put that I drank.

My mother was at home at the time having an incurable nervous breakdown and I was studying acting. I thought that if worse came to worse I would just act the way she was acting and I'd get out of the Army. But there was a guy in front of me who looked very much like me; we both had beards. They touched him first, on the shoulder, and he just went bananas. He flipped out and they took him away screaming.

Now how was I going to follow that? I was depressed on two counts. One, it looked like I was going to be drafted, and two, it looked like I was a bad actor.

Recently in Manhattan, I was up early on a Sunday for some reason. It's rare. If you're up early in New York City on a Sunday, there's a strange overlap between those who are up early and those who haven't gone to bed yet. I was down in the Canal Street subway station—concrete no man's land. There were no subways coming, no law and order down there. There was just this one other guy and he was coming toward me. I knew he wanted something—I could feel the vibes. He needed something from me, wanted something. He was about to demand something.

"Hey man, you got change for a quarter?"

"Uh, yeah, I think I do. Here—wait a minute, I got two dimes here and one, two, three, four pennies. How's that?"

"Nope."

"Well, what are we going to do?"

"I got a quarter and a nickel. Got three dimes?"

"Yep, I do. Here." And I counted them out carefully in his hand.

He turned, walked away, then turned back to me and said, "You only gave me two dimes, man."

"Wait a minute. I'm very careful about money matters."

Now, was this where I was going to make my stand?

"Very well. If you feel you need another dime, here."

Renée has this upstairs neighbor who is a member of the Art Mafia. She has her own gallery in Soho, along with a drinking problem, and she is unbearable. She plays her quadrophonic machine at all hours, full blast, Bob Dylan's "Sarah," over and over again. Something must have happened to her way back when that song was popular and she can't get it out of her head. She comes in drunk, puts it on at 1:30 in the morning. Now if it was 1:30 every morning, it would be great. It would be like feeding time, you know. You could get through it. You'd get used to it. But it's 1:35 or it's 2:10 or it's 4:14.

You call the police but it does no good. She turns it down, they leave, she turns it up. You call the police again, they come, she turns it down, they leave, she turns it up. What can you do? You can't go to the landlord—he's Italian Mafia and lives in New Jersey.

I don't know which Mafia I dislike the most. I'm leaning toward liking the Italian Mafia because they are just immoral and still believe in mother and child. But the Art Mafia is immoral and, from what I can tell, they've stopped procreating.

So we're in Renée's apartment and I call up, "Please stop persecuting us." And she sends down these young, new artists who have gotten rich and famous in New York, but are now camping out in sleeping bags until they find their niches. And they say, "Hey man. MAN. You know New York is Party City. That's why we moved here. So we could have parties on weekday nights. If you don't like it, move to the country—OLD MAN."

I try to practice my Buddhist Tolerance—I am turning all my cheeks to the wall at this point. I mean, really, Buddhist Tolerance in New York is just one big pacifist-escapist rationalization. Renée is not practicing it. She is pacing while steam comes screaming out of her navel.

Now there are some people who say that this woman should be killed. And I find that I'm not saying no. I don't protest it. They are talking about vigilantes.

I don't know the language. I knew the language when I was with my people in Boston in 1962, in whitebread homogeneous Boston, brick-wall Boston. In the old days, when I spoke a common language with my people, they had what was called the "hi-fi." And when the hi-fi was too loud, all I had to do was call up and say, "Hi, Puffy. Spuddy Gray, down here. Yeah. You guessed it. The hi-fi is a little loud. Yeah. I wouldn't say anything but I've got an early dance class in the morning. Great. Thanks

a lot. Yeah, Merry Christmas to you too, Puff." Down it would go. You see I knew the language.

Now Renée knows the language because her father was in the Jewish Mafia. So she calls up, "Bet you want to die, right? Bitch! Bitch! Cunt! I'll beat your fucking face in with a baseball bat. Bitch!" And she slams down the phone. The music gets louder.

One day I was walking out the door carrying an empty bottle of Molson Golden. I guess I was going to get my nickel back. And I heard this party noise coming from upstairs and I was seized with gut rage. Maybe I'd had a few drinks and the rage finally made it to my gut. Not that my intellect wasn't still working—it was going like a ticker tape, repeating that old adage, "All weakness tends to corrupt, and impotence corrupts absolutely." I just took the bottle and *hurled* it—my arm practically came out of its socket. It went up the flight of stairs, hit the door and exploded like a hand grenade. They charged out with their bats and guns. I ran. Because it was an act of passion, I had forgotten to tell Renée I was going to do it and she was behind me, picking up some plastic garbage bags or something. She was way behind me so when they got to her door they met up with her. But she was innocent and they recognized that. They recognized that she was truly innocent and they didn't kill her. So there's hope.

But I wonder, how do we begin to approach the so-called Cold War (or Now-Heating-Up War) between Russia and America if I can't even begin to resolve the Hot War down on Northmoor and Greenwich in lower Manhattan?

Soho Arts Weekly, Vol. 1 No. 8,
November 27, 1985, Cover (1985)
Photo: Elaine Ellman

A Counter-Void Weekly, And A New Voice For The Culturally Deprived

VOL. 1 NO. 8 NOV. 27, 1985 $1.00

SOHO ARTS WEEKLY

"Couple." **PHOTOS BY ELAINE ELLMAN** *SEE INTERVIEW INSIDE.*

Winter 1985   Volume 1 Number 4

Featuring stories by:
Dennis Cooper, Reinaldo Povod, Lisa Blaushild,
Gary Indiana, Darius James, Peter Conte, Mark Leyner, Peter Cherches,
Mike Topp, Lois Elaine Griffith, and Lenora Champagne
included with every issue:
David Wojnarowicz/ Marion S. collaborative wall–size poster
Ready for Hanging

BETWEEN C AND D

Neo–Expressionist Lower East Side Fiction Magazine

DEATH
DISEASE
HEARTACHE
SUBWAY CRIME
COMPUTERS

$4.00 $5.00 OUTSIDE NEW YORK CITY

How to Get Rid of Pimples

by Cookie Mueller

GO-GOING—NEW YORK & NEW JERSEY—1978–79 (1985)

COOKIE MUELLER

In the beginning I just couldn't bring myself to do floor work. Bumping and grinding while laying on the floor looked completely ludicrous to me.

I would have made more tips if I had; the girls who did floor work always had stacks of one dollar bills in their G-strings. They wore the money like a tiny green fringe tu-tu flapping around their hips.

Those girls brought their own personal floor mats on stage with them for their half-hour sets. They'd just unroll their fake fur bathroom rugs on the stage floor and lay down and start undulating.

It seemed so inane. . . convulsing there on a dirty dynel shag pad on a "stage," which was usually nothing but a flimsy fly-by-night platform the size of a dinner table, while stone-faced male loners sat in a circle around it, clutching their overpriced drinks, watching intently this twitching female flesh parcel.

No, that wasn't for me. I just danced. On two feet.

I had decided to topless go-go dance when I first moved to New York from Provincetown. It wasn't something I especially wanted on my resume but I had been casting around, looking for work. . . something to pay the bills while I was making a start at designing clothes, searching film parts and writing. I was down to thirty-seven dollars. That kind of money doesn't go far in New York, especially when you have a kid.

I'd tried waitressing when I was sixteen and found out fast it wasn't my calling in life. I always screwed up. People were always bitching about the missing side orders. I spilled everything, had a lot of walk-outs. It's a horrible job, demanding, demeaning. I started hating people. I wound up throwing food.

I'd worked in offices when I was eighteen, and that always turned into a fiasco; anyway the pay was so low and it took all day, five days a week. I needed some kind of job that didn't have such long hours and paid really well.

A go-go friend suggested dancing. She gave me her agent's name. I got the job.

The agent was straight out of a cheesy '50s gangster B movie, second generation Italian, the good-looking-twenty-years-ago type, flare collared polyester Nik-Nik shirt, pasta belly, lots of big rings on the pinkies.

He sat in a greasy office filled with cigar smoke, pictures of broads on the walls, the telephone ringing.

Every Monday the place was packed with girls getting the next week's bookings and picking up their checks. He called everybody sweetheart or honey. He was close: all the girls had phoney names like Jujubee, ChiChi, CoCo, Sugarplum, Dumpling, BonBon, Sweetie Pie.

Most topless bars in the city had eight hour work shifts, noon to eight or eight to four a.m. The bars in New Jersey had five hour shifts.

I liked working in Jersey more, where topless was against the law; the dancers had to wear a little something on top. That eliminated my stretch marks and sag problem that came with the pregnancy and breast feeding package. It was less sleazy in Jersey; the bars were local hangouts for regulars; the customers didn't feel like they were getting ripped off because drinks were cheap. Dancers made more money in Jersey anyway, and there, no one would ever recognize me from John Waters movies, not that they did in Manhattan go-go bars, but I always had this horror. People in Jersey didn't go to those kind of movies.

Actually it wasn't a horrible job, when I thought about it I was just there exercising and getting paid for it. I was never in better shape: tight buns, strong legs, flat stomach. Working in Jersey, I began to wonder why every woman didn't want to go-go.

But then, every time I worked in a bar in Manhattan, I discovered why all over again.

Manhattan go-go bars are really sleazy. The owners sometimes want you to go in the back rooms to do hand jobs on the creeps. They made customers buy outrageously priced little bottles of champagne; some managers demanded that you "flash" . . . show your puss, when they knew you could get busted for that.

Of course, right over on the next block a guy could walk into a strip joint and get a bird's eye view deep into the internal structure of a vagina for a dollar; in fact, he could stick his nose right in if he wanted, but in topless places, because they served liquor, nothing like this was supposed to go on.

I was working the day shift at the Pretty Purple Pussy Cat, doing my half-an-hour-on, half-an-hour-off. I was working the same half-hour as Taffy, on stages facing each other. The other two girls, Marshmallow and Lollipop, went on after us. With those names, the place could have been a candy store.

Taffy was wallowing on her bathroom rug, with all the customers at her stage, ogling. She had piles of bills tucked in everywhere, mostly ones, but when somebody wanted her to flash, she'd do it for a five.

I was on the other stage, knocking myself out doing flips, splits, high kicks, triple spot turns, with nobody watching me, thinking that somebody with respect for a real dancer would soon toss me some fifty dollar bills. Nobody did.

I watched Taffy. She was laying there pumping her hips and looking right into the eyes of the men. She was turning them on, obviously.

I was exhausted. I'd been up since seven-thirty getting Max to school; then I had this early interview at Macy's to show some buyer a couple of silk blouses I'd designed. After that, I'd gone for a cold reading for some low budget independent cable TV movie.

All I wanted to do was lie down.

When the half-hour was over, I put my little mini-dress over the pink sequined G-string and got off the stage. In Manhattan the dancers are required to hustle drinks from the customers. . . or at least try. Nobody was buying drinks for me, but Taffy called me over to sit next to her and a customer.

"Buy her a drink," Taffy told the guy and he ordered me vodka soda.

Taffy pulled her chair next to mine.

"Sweetheart, I've been watching you bust your ass over there and you ought to give it a rest, girl. You ain't making no tips. Look here," she looked down at her G-string, "I got a mess of money here," she flipped through the bills hanging on her hips, "and I got more in my pockets here." She put her hands in her mini-dress pockets and pulled out handfuls of ones and fives, even a lot of tens and twenties. "And I didn't make this working too hard."

"For some reason," I told her, "I just can't bring myself to lie down up there. It looks so stupid. . . I mean, you don't look stupid, the idea is so stupid."

"I know just what you mean," she said. "I used to feel the same way when I started working these bars, but you get over it."

She lit a cigarette and put her Revlon Cherries in the Snow lips to my ear.

"Look," she whispered, "these guys just want to look at something they can fantasize about. They like to feel horny, it makes them happy."

"I think I'd feel like an asshole," I said.

"Oh shit, forget it. You want to make money or not? Just try it next set. Lay there and look right into their eyes. Remember to do that part, otherwise it doesn't work. You have to make it personal."

The next set I took my scarf on stage with me and I laid it on the floor. Nobody would want to lay on the slimy platform without something under them.

Feeling dumb, I got on the scarf and put my head back and looked at the ceiling while I did some sort of cold Jane Fonda–type floor workouts. There was a customer sitting there in front of me but he didn't look very interested.

"That ain't it," Taffy yelled to me from across the room. She pointed at her eyes.

So I made myself look into this guy's eyes. It worked immediately. He started peeling off the ones and handing them to me. This made me start putting some sex into the workout. I undulated all over the place, just like an eel in heat.

Other customers started moving over to my stage looking for something hot, I guess. They loved it hot.

By the end of the set I had twenty or thirty dollars and it was so easy on the heel bunions and the toe corns, so relaxing for the calf muscles. Wow! What a job!

"I should'nta told you nothin'," Taffy said, "you took all my paying customers."

So I had graduated. Every working day I'd dance the first half of the set and when I got tired I'd just lie down and stare into eyes and pump the hips, do leg lifts, things like that.

I worked this job for a year or so, two or three days a week, saved some money. I worked in Jersey mostly, taking the Path train to Newark, and then taking a cab. There weren't too many problems except for having too much to drink during the day. It would be an ideal job for an alcoholic, I often thought.

One day I was working in a Manhattan bar where sometimes the owner would try to act like a pimp. I hated working there, but it was the only place the agent had left on a Wednesday, since I forgot to see him on Monday booking day.

I was doing floor work in front of a customer and he was handing me dollars. He asked me to sit and drink with him when I came off the stage. So I did.

He was a young guy from Brooklyn, a blond meathead who wasn't unlike all the other meatheads who hung around go-go bars everyday. He was buying vodkas, and he was getting drunk and I was getting drunk. He was telling me his life, his astrological sign, the standard rap.

"Ya read about dem tree peoples killed in Brooklyn yestaday?" he asked. "Was inna Post and da News. Sawr it onna tube too, late night news."

"Yeah, I saw it. Terrible," I said. I had seen it. Pretty grisly, it was too. Torsos in green garbage bags, with treasure hunt notes leading to the heads, which were in black garbage bags.

"I did dat," he smiled. "I killed dem. Cut 'em up. Waddn't too easy eitha."

I turned and looked at him very closely. He was proudly smiling but he looked really serious, although he didn't look like a killer, except maybe for his eyes. . . but then I don't know if I'd ever looked in the eyes of a killer before.

"You didn't do that," I laughed.

"Oh yeah, I did. It kinda bodda me a lill, but dey was assholes. Ya don know. When dey died der was no human lives lost. Dey was animals. Deserved it. Fugging animals." He looked into his sixth vodka and drained it.

When he started to cry, I half believed his story.

What could I say? Could I say something like: "Oh, don't feel so bad. Tomorrow's another day. Forget all

about these heads and bodies. You're just depressed."
That wasn't really appropriate under the circumstances.

"Ya know, I have dis gun, heer, in ma coat," he
looked around to see if anybody was watching, then
withdrew it quickly and showed it to me.

I was beginning to believe him.

"I have dis index finga too from onna dem animal."
He pulled out a plastic ziplock bag with a human
finger in it. The blood was caked around the stump.
He put it away fast.

I think I just sat there staring at his pocket for
a while.

"Well . . . . . ." I just didn't know what to say.
What could I say? What would be the right thing to
say when something like this happens?

Maybe I could say, "Oh. Isn't that interesting
looking!"

I thought that maybe I should say something to
the bouncer though, but this guy would figure it out
if I told him I was going to the bathroom and instead
started whispering to the tough guy in the corner. He
might go on some wild shooting spree. No, I couldn't
say anything. I just drank the rest of my vodka and
tried not to stare at him aghast.

The other dancer, Pepper, got off the stage and
it was my turn.

"I need to talk ta ya sommoor," he said. "Comon
back afta. I'll be real pissed if ya don't."

I certainly didn't want to piss him off.

"Don't worry, I'll be right here in front of you
and I'll sit with you again after my set," I said and
he smiled.

If I hadn't been slightly drunk I think I might not
have been able to dance, maybe not even able to
undulate on the floor. Considering the circumstances, I
was very nonchalant, but I decided not to do any floor
work in front of him now. I didn't want to get this guy

aroused or anything. I just stepped around on
the stage while he smiled at me.

Pepper started to sit down with him to ask
him for the drink.

"Gedda fug outta heer," he pushed her away. Then
he felt bad. "Hey look, girlie, I'm sorry, ba I'm savin' my
dough fa dis chick heer," he pointed to me. "I like er."

Great. Just great, I thought.

While I was dancing and trying to smile at him,
thinking about garbage bags and heads, a bunch of
men came in the bar talking to each other.

One of the guys stopped to look at me and he
handed me a fifty dollar bill.

"Come have a drink with me after your set," he said
and winked. Then he walked to the end of the bar and
sat down with his buddies. They were all talking to the
owner and looking at the girls, nodding and laughing.

The gesture wasn't unusual, but the fifty was.

I loved the fifty but the killer didn't.

"Ya ain't gonna sit wit im. Are ya?"

"No. Never."

"Yall havta give im bak dat fifty," he looked
over at the guys.

"Yeah," I said, "I was going to do that anyway."

Then the bar owner, one of those Grade D bad
eggs, walked over to me and whispered in my ear,
"This group of guys back there are friends of mine.
They want to party with you, Venus and Fever. In the
back room. Go there after the set. They got lots of
money. We can both make a little."

He walked off before I could tell him I wasn't
interested. First of all I didn't go to backrooms
and then of course there was this angry young man
sitting here. . . .

He was getting angrier by the minute. He'd heard
what the owner asked me to do so he kept looking at
the guy who gave me the fifty. He clenched his fists,

ground his teeth, bit his lip. His face was getting all red. There was going to be trouble.

What could I do? Getting shot or beheaded wasn't the way I had planned to go out. I didn't have many options: (1) I could sit the rest of the evening with the killer, but at closing time he'd probably follow me home. (2) I could maybe call the police, but the killer might see me at the phone, get paranoid, and shoot me. (3) I could go to the bathroom and climb out the window, if only the bathroom had a window. (4) I could quit the job, and walk out while the killer was in the bathroom, but he looked like he had a good bladder.

"Hey, ya name again?" the Brooklyn Butcher yelled up at me over the music. I told him.

"Dat ain't ya reel name," he sneered. "Tell me ya reel name."

"That is my real name."

"It ain't," he barked.

"Okay," I said, "you're right. My real name is Charlene Moore." Any name would do. The kid swallowed his next vodka and started on another one, then another. His eyes were very green and the whites were very red after those twelve vodkas.

"I'm gonna tell dat fugging asshole bak dere dat ya sittin wit me afta ya dance." He got up and stumbled to the back of the room. I froze.

When he got there he started poking his finger at this fifty dollar guy. The guy stood there taking all this abuse and then he just hit the kid killer in the face, really hard. The kid butcher fell on the floor, and his gun fell out of his pocket and slid across the carpet, and disappeared under a huge stationary space heater radiator thing.

He saw it when it slid, and they saw it, and everybody pounced on the space heater and started wailing in pain because the heater was so hot.

Then the kid just scrambled for the door and left the bar, fast.

The bouncer and the owner let him run. They all started bending around the heater, but they couldn't find the gun because, first of all, the bar was so dark, and the heater was so wide and hot.

Finally somebody got a broom and pushed it out.

I got off the stage and walked up to them while were all huddled around the gun. I told them all about the kid, the whole story. Nobody believed me.

The owner took the gun and disappeared into his office; the rest of the guys just started drinking again; the girls started dancing again, so I went back to the stage.

All the party boys forgot about their party even before I finished my set. They left, all fired up, talking about how "they were going to find that little motherfucker."

I made a phone call to the police. I described the kid, told them everything he told me about himself. They weren't too interested until I told them about the finger. I didn't mention the bar or the gun, I just said I met this kid in some restaurant. I told them my name was Charlene Moore. They thanked me and hung up.

That was the last day I worked as a go-go dancer; I never wanted to see any of those sleazy joints again. I didn't want to writhe on another floor in my life. I didn't want to be forced to talk to any more creepy dummies in dark smelly dives; I was perfectly capable of finding creepy dummies on my own time. I didn't want to be in the same room with murderers or birdbrains or desperate people anymore.

After all, I'd made my first fifty dollar bill that day. Not a bad way to finish up.

When I got home I hung up my pink sequined G-string, and there it hangs to this day; gathering dust. It still sparkles just a little when the sun hits it.

BENEFIT PARTY FOR:
THE PORTABLE LOWER EAST SIDE

WITH KANDOMBE
AT NEITHER/NOR 8pm
703 E. 6th JULY 23 $3.00

WILD HISTORY

THREE STORIES FROM *THE TRAVELING WOMAN* (1986)

ROBERTA ALLEN

THE WOUND

When she finds her husband with the woman, they are only sitting speaking softly to one another—but instantly she knows. She feels a lightning-like stab; an old wound splits open, and the pain sinks so deep she staggers. She tells herself she feels nothing. And without a sound she moves into the light where they can see her.

When the woman with downcast eyes slides past her out the door, the husband tells his wife he loves that woman, and he cries. And he makes love to his wife as she lies numb in the darkness; hardly aware he is inside her body, she digs her fingernails deep into his flesh.

IMPOSTER

She knows the man sitting across the room in her apartment pretending to read the newspaper is jacking off. She knows it because of the way the newspaper almost imperceptibly flutters with an unmistakable rhythm; a small wind blown by the action of the hand hidden. The man waits for her roommate who is working late. From the start she told her roommate there is something peculiar about that man, even before they did it in the motel, even before she knew what he made her say, made her do, made her wear. Didn't she find this odd she asked her, but her roommate is infatuated: he's a doctor, she's going to be a doctor's wife, this woman wearing purple tights. Later, she will look for proof to show her roommate that the man is an imposter: brave or reckless enough to call his bluff, she will let him pierce her ears; watch him nervously sterilize the needle. Cautiously, he will penetrate each lobe;

careful to avoid infection. Later, a court will convict him after her testimony that he pretended to be a doctor, but they will not recover her roommate's life savings. Later still, after serving his prison term, her roommate will meet him by accident in a restaurant where he will work as dishwasher; she will still be infatuated. Right now she prays for her roommate's immediate return as she hears his breaths quicken.

THE PACT

Without ever seeing each other they understood how they would never meet and it was agreed that this would be their secret. And each one would remain a fantasy; a creation and invention, a daydream of the other.

That was until everything started getting out of hand, and each one gradually got carried away, and what started as an innocent exploit, became rife with accusations, innuendoes, brutal outbursts, and endless emotional upheavals. This was not part of the agreement.

They had assumed that lack of physical contact would prevent outrageous incidents and painful pronouncements. Instead, however, hours spent in prolonged fantasies, produced futile and frustrating desires to really have it out with each other.

It became clear they could no longer keep this up without serious consequences. Therefore, secretly they decided to separate, though they had never met. But in truth, each one only fabricated new falsehoods, imagined new injuries, and created new circumstances for the other. And so it continues.

Retailed by MAX BLAGG. At MADAME ROSA'S/ St. John's Lane (Beach St. betw. West B'Way & Varick
NYC. Tuesday Nov.25/86. 10 p.m. Adm: $5.00. Tel. 219-2207. Girlscouts admitted free.

POEM WITH A TITLE AT THE END (1986)

JIM FEAST

—the Statue of Liberty
       broken, shattered
       covered with shit
lying somewhere sweeping, back
swept up like hair

befuddled, muddled, muddy
armless, harpless, helpless, harmless

Soon we will have a new Statue of Liberty with B. Dylan's
"I Pity the Poor Immigrant" blaring from loudspeakers in her jaw.
a new Venus de Milo
—this time without a torso

She asks, tentatively, questioningly, "A tired loop in yr walk."
     Then consolingly, beside me in bed, her brass arms a kind of
Mottled, sickle pear color
     like Nhi's
whispering, "How many times have you counted on something
that can't return."

Poem with a Title at the End

Max Blagg, Chocolate Daydreams at Madame Rosa's,
Flyer (1986)

ISSUE NO. 34 DEC. 31, 1986 FREE!

music, theater, art, movies from New York's cultural core.

DOWNTOWN

second coming

A Screenplay
By Mike Golden

MICKEY YO AND THE ALPHABET TOWN
BOOGIE BAND *TELL IT LIKE IT IS.*

MODERN SAINT #271 (1986)

TAMA JANOWITZ

After I became a prostitute, I had to deal with penises of every imaginable shape and size. Some large, others quite shriveled and pendulous of testicle. Some blue-veined and reeking of Stilton, some miserly. Some crabbed, enchanted, dusted with pearls like the great minarets of the Taj Mahal, jesting penises, ringed as the tail of a raccoon, fervent, crested, impossible to live with, marigold-scented. More and more I became grateful I didn't have to own one of these appendages.

Of course I had a pimp; he wasn't an ordinary sort of person but had been a double Ph.D. candidate in philosophy and American literature at the University of Massachusetts. When we first became friends he was driving a taxicab, but soon found this left him little time for his own work, which was to write.

When my job as script girl for a German-produced movie to be filmed in Venezuela fell through, it became obvious we were going to have to figure out a different way to make money fast. For a pimp and a prostitute, Bob and I had a very unusual relationship. As far as his role went, he could have cared less. But I didn't mind; I paid the bills, bought his ribbons, and then if I felt like handing over any extra money to him, it was up to me. At night I would come in for a rest and find him lying on the bed reading Kant, or Heidegger's "What Is a Thing?"

Often our discussions would be so lengthy and intense I would have to gently interrupt him to say that if I didn't get back out to work the evening would be over and I wouldn't have filled my self-imposed nightly quota.

I was like a social worker for lepers. My clients had a chunk of their body they wanted to give away; for a price I was there to receive it. Crimes, sins, nightmares, hunks of hair: it was surprising how many of them had something to dispose of. The more I charged, the easier it was for them to breathe freely once more.

As a child my favorite books had been about women who entered the convent. They were giving themselves up to a higher cause. But there are no convents for Jewish girls.

For myself, I had to choose the most difficult profession available to me; at night I often couldn't sleep, feeling myself adrift in a sea of seminal fluid. It was on these evenings that Bob and I took drugs. He would softly tie up my arm and inject me with a little heroin, or, if none was available, a little something else. For himself there was nothing he liked better, though he was careful not to shoot up too frequently.

Neither of us was a very good housekeeper. Months would go by, during which time the floor of our Avenue A walk-up would become littered with empty syringes, cartons of fried rice, douche bags, black lace brassieres, whips, garrotes, harnesses, bootlaces, busted snaps, Cracker Jacks, torn Kleenexes, and packages of half-eaten Ring Dings and nacho corn chips. The elements of our respective trades.

I was always surprised to realize how intelligent the cockroaches in our neighborhood were. Bob was reluctant to poison them or step on them. He would turn the light off and whip it back on again to demonstrate his point.

It's obvious they're running for their lives, he said. To kill something that wants to live so desperately is in direct contradiction to any kind of philosophy, religion, belief system that I hold. Long after the bomb falls and you and your good deeds are gone, cockroaches will still be here, prowling the streets like armored cars.

Sometimes I wished Bob was more aggressive as a pimp. There were moments on the street when I felt frightened; there were a lot of terminal cases out there, and often I was in situations that could have become dangerous. Bob felt it was important that I accept anyone who wanted me.

From each according to his ability, to each according to his need.

Still, I could have used more help from him than I got.

But then Bob would arrive at the hospital, bringing me flowers and pastrami on rye and I realized that for me to change pimps and choose a more aggressive one, one who would be out there hustling for me and carrying a knife, would be to embrace a lifestyle that was genuinely alien to me, despite my middle-class upbringing.

When I was near Bob, with his long graceful hands, his silky mustache, his interesting theories of life and death, I felt that for the first time in my life I had arrived at a place where I was growing intellectually as well as emotionally. Bob was both sadist and masochist to me; for him I was madonna and whore. Life with him was never dull.

In any case, I liked having the things that money could buy. Originally I hailed from a wealthy suburb of Chattanooga, Tennessee, from one of the few Jewish families in the area. My great-grandfather had come from Lithuania at the turn of the century, peddling needles, threads, elixirs, yarmulkes, violin strings, and small condiments able to cure the incurable. All carried on a pack on his back; his burden was a heavy one, eight children raised in the Jewish persuasion. Two generations later my father owned the only Cadillac car dealership in town. I suppose part of my genetic makeup has given me this love of material objects. Or maybe it's just a phase I will outgrow

as soon as I get everything I want. Even saints have human flaws; it is overcoming their own frailties that makes them greater than the sum of their parts.

I went to college at an exclusive women's seminary in Virginia. Until my big falling-out with Daddy, when I sent home F's for two successive semesters, and got expelled after being suspended twice, I had my own BMW and a Morgan mare, Chatty Cathy, boarded in the stables at school.

But I could never accept the role life had assigned to me; I fell in love with Jimmy Dee Williams, the fat boy who pumped gas at the 7-Eleven, and though the marriage only lasted six months, Daddy never felt the same about me. Well, he said, there are treatment programs for people like you. I didn't mind the time I spent in the institution. Fond recollections can be found in all walks of life. Yet if I had been allowed to go to a co-ed school I know things would have turned out differently for me.

Back in college the other girls would spend long evenings drinking beer and sitting on the rocking chairs that ringed the great plantation hall—the school had taken over many of the original buildings on a tobacco estate, and the new buildings were built in a Georgian style in a great semicircle facing the old mansion—gossiping about boys and worrying if they would pass French. But meanwhile I had to show them that I was wild and daring; I would pick Jimmy Dee up when he got off work and the two of us would smoke grass and drive around, bored and restless in the heat. One evening I drove right up onto the lawn and Jimmy Dee pulled down his pants to press his great buttocks, gleaming white, against the cool air-conditioned glass window of the car. That was the second time I was suspended from school; the first was when I had an affair with one of the black cafeteria workers in my dorm room, a man with only one arm who tasted of bacon and hair oil. . . . The only reason I was allowed to stay after that was that Daddy donated money to the school to build a new swimming pool. He never understood that no matter what he did, they were always going to think of him only as a rich Jew. . . .

I was finally asked to leave for good when Jimmy Dee and I were caught sneaking into the school pond, which was closed for swimming after dark. Both stark naked, dripping with mud and algae. . . . I tried to explain to Miss Ferguson, the dean, that I always got wild when there was a full moon, but, prim and proper in her mahogany office, smelling of verbena and more faintly of shit, she said she could see no future for a girl like me, that never in the course of all her years. . . . I had to laugh.

Before Daddy could find out about my marriage and divorce and take the car back from me (and have me locked up again? But there are no convents for Jewish girls), I had driven north to New York, sold the car for $2,000, found an apartment, and bought some new clothes. I landed a job in an internship program at a major advertising agency, even though I didn't have a college degree. . . . Once more Daddy spoke to me on the telephone; Mother and Mopsy even came up for a visit. . . .

I might never have found my vocation if I hadn't been evicted from my apartment, and after finding a new place in the East Village, met Bruno (ah, Bruno, that Aryan German, pinched, brittle in his leather trenchcoat, rigid as a crustacean—even a saint has her failures), who offered me the job of script girl on the film he was making in Venezuela, which in the end didn't work out at all.

But one thing leads to the next (doesn't it always?) and it was through Bruno I met Bob, and now at night, cruising the great long avenues of the city, dust and grit tossed feverishly in the massive canyons between the skyscrapers, it often occurs to me that I am no more and no less, a thought that I hadn't realized until my days as a prostitute began. (True, I have my bad days, when I cannot rise from bed, but who can claim he does not? Who?) I could have written a book about my experiences out on the street, but all my thoughts are handed over to Bob, who lies on the bed dreamily eating whatever I bring him—a hamburger from McDonald's, crab soufflé from a French restaurant in the theater district, a platter of rumaki with hot peanut sauce in an easy carry-out container from an Indonesian restaurant open until 1:00 A.M., plates of macaroni tender and creamy as the sauce that oozes out from between the legs of my clientele.

As in the convent, life is not easy . . . crouched in dark alleys, giggling in hotel rooms or the back seat of limousines, I have to be a constant actress, on my guard and yet fitting into every situation. Always the wedge of moon above, reminding me of my destiny and holy water.

FREE FLEXIDISC INSIDE!

BENZENE

$3.50

WINTER 1983

URSULE MOLINARO
JUDY LOPATIN
BRUCE BENDERSON

JOHN GIORNO
JAMES SHERRY
LOU HORVATH
REESE WILLIAMS
ANNE TURYN
+ MORE

PLUS SPECIAL MAGAZINE SUPPLEMENT   MC:3

Benzene No. 7, Photo of Judy Lopatin, Cover (1983)
Photo: Anne Turyn

MODERN ROMANCES (1986)

JUDY LOPATIN

NEW WAVE MOVIE: LOVE SCENE

LUCIE ET GUY walking along the street. Guy
stopping and pushing her against the gate
of a storefront.

—I love you, don't you realize that.

I've refused princesses. Don't you know what
that means, you jerk, when I say I love you—

(Shaking her, grabbing her by her hair, yanking it)

—I love you, I love you.

(Then:)

—I know what it is. You have something that I've
never seen in another woman.

Lucie (lightly): But I'm not a woman. I'm just
a girl . . .

Guy: I realize what it is now. It's . . . that cross
between FEAR and VIOLENCE.

Lucie gives him a look that means: please be
careful with me.

NEW WAVE MOVIE: SEX SCENE

At Guy's place. Under the covers naked. Rubbing
against each other. Lucie urging him: Finger me,
Guy. Harder.

Guy protesting: These are not just any fingers.

Lucie: I'll do it myself then.

He won't let her. Holding her down he murmurs:

—You look like a little demented Cleopatra.

CHARACTER OF OUR HEROINE

Lucie is a New Wave singer and guitarist. Who
(never) reveals herself in her actions and the stories
she tells about herself.

PASSION

Lucie met Guy (for example) at Village Oldies.
They talked about music. They had the same tastes,
only he knew everything about every record ever
made. He told her he played guitar, she told him
she wrote songs.

Idyll in Washington Square Park: she played
for him, he read her poetry aloud to her.

The first day (it was day) she went to Guy's
apartment, he told her he didn't like women and
hadn't liked them in 4 years. Women, he thought,
and told her so, were stupid. Lucie shocked him
because she wasn't (stupid). Also, he didn't like
sex. Lucie agreed: I can see how it bores you. But
anyway, somehow, they did fuck that night. She
says it was pretty good. There was blood on the
wall. She doesn't know how it got there. He must've
wiped his hand on the wall after fingering her.

That was the only time they ever fucked,
though since then they've slept together.

That was not the first time Lucie saw the
blood on the wall. At a rock club, she met a lead
vocalist who stood at the back of the stage, yelling
in a raincoat. Between sets they ducked into the
ladies' room and he fucked her with a beer bottle.
She didn't feel a thing, but out came the blood.

Together they smeared it on the wall.

FIDELITY

Guy used to live with another guy, called Roger.
That was the summer Lucie met them. Then the
arrangements changed: Roger moved out to live with
a girl, and another girl (Laura) moved in with Guy,

on a more or less platonic basis ("Guy didn't want to fuck her"). Lucie likes one story that was told to her:

One time Laura came home after Lucie had been over. Lucie and Guy had been lying on the couch (daybed). Laura wanted to know how come there was gum on the sheets. Guy said he'd bought some gum that day. Laura said: Oh yeah? What brand?

Then she said: What's that new cologne you have that smells like orange blossoms? Come here and smell these sheets.

And all Guy (caught) could say was Uh-oh.

TEEN IDOL

Fear and violence, continued.

Quoting Guy, Lucie is reminded of The Man She Knew in Buffalo.

When she was 15 and waiting for the bus near a pornohouse, a man offered her a ride home. He asked her if she wanted to make some money. Lucie said yes, if it wouldn't involve sex.

He agreed. He only liked sex if it was imaginative. He liked stories. Lucie said she could tell him stories. He said he'd pay her $50 if she could tell him a good story.

Over a period of two or three months, in three or four or five storytelling sessions, Lucie told him stories about ripping little girls' thighs apart with pliers until they bled. About him fucking her mother in the ass. Him killing her sisters. (This because she was supposed to hate them and be jealous of them. Just a story.)

Things The Man wanted Lucie to do for him: Eat cigarette butts. Lick car tires. Play with pliers on her tits and lick them. Things he wanted to do to Lucie: Spit in her face. Things Lucie refused to do: Eat out ashtrays, piss on him.

The Man would call at her house to arrange their meetings. Lucie told her mother he was a filmmaker. He was. He made porn movies. He had fliers he sold to soldiers at Fort Dix for $10 each. He wanted to make up a flier featuring Lucie alone, a whole portfolio of pictures. In addition wanted her to pose for a magazine he had—the kind with American girls' pictures in the magazines distributed in Europe, and European girls in the American issues. So no one would recognize them.

Lucie hated it when he spit on her. Thick, gobby spit. Doing stuff for him wouldn't bother her so much when she was doing it, but the next day she would feel disgusted with herself.

When he spit on her he would say: That's a blockage I have to get out. You have to overcome these blockages.

He also said he hated his mother and he hated women—generally, not personally. He wouldn't hurt Lucie, personally. He told her: I think you're a real nice kid.

He looked like Frankie Valli with pockmarks.

CHEMISTRY

Why Lucie Likes Roger: He appreciates her, puts her on a pedestal. Notices her and compliments her on her lipstick, her nail polish, things other guys take for granted. Likes her sleazy image. Thinks she's sexy. Adores her. Most of all, wants her.

Why People Don't Like Lucie (According to Lucie): She's Too Competitive . . . Has Too Much Energy.

What Roger Must Like: Butyl acetate, toluene, nitro-cellulose, ethyl acetate, isopropryl alcohol, formaldehyde resin, dibutyl phthalate, camphor, stearalkonium hectorite, quarternium-18, benzophenone-1, silica, D&C reds #6, #34, #7, iron oxides (ingredients of Lucie's nail polish).

ELECTRA COMPLEX

Lucie reminisces: My father has the nicest cock I ever saw. . . . But he always had this hangnail.

"It was sick—you don't know what it did to me"

"I hated my father for so long"

"Disgusting"

"Somebody has their hands where they're not supposed to"

It started when she was six. She would sleep with her father because she was wetting the bed. Her mother worked nights (a nurse). When he started doing it she would wake up and be too scared to do anything but pretend to be asleep. She stopped sleeping with him. He'd come in to her room and try to do it. When she was about 10 she wouldn't let him.

"Stop, leave your piggish hands off me"

It runs in his family, she says. His brother does it. His brother tried to do it to her (that's how she knows).

POPULARITY

Before: Lucie was precocious, spending one pubescent summer in a black-lit basement room with a nervous breakdown. . . .

After: Lucie has dyed her hair black, because it is fashionable, and/or to cover the gray. Living up to the underground tends to ruin one's bloom of youth.

Everyone, sooner or later, needs Loving Care.

Now Lucie has a steady boyfriend, Spencer, who spanks her.

Lucie's figure before & after: She never eats, but she never loses weight. Before she was

popular, somebody called her The Goodyear Blimp (behind her back). Then she bought a pair of sadomasochistic boots with heels high enough to make her look taller and thus thinner.

It is difficult to go out walking much, in such boots, so Spencer brings her her food. If he doesn't, she doesn't eat, but usually he does, and she does, or so at least it seems, since she doesn't lose weight, and thus must not miss many meals.

One advantage of having a steady boyfriend (Lucie admits) is You've Got Someone To Depend On.

GOING STEADY

Steady sex is another such advantage. Besides:

It is oh so suspenseful to sleep with Spencer, because when he wakes up screaming and shaking her in the middle of the night she's sure he's going to kill her. . . .

But it's only a thrill and a chill. Only a delicious taste of death. Because Lucie can depend on her steady.

SIN SUFFER AND REPENT

I break the rules, announces Lucie to all her new boyfriends, it is just as easy to suffer and repent without going to the trouble of sinning.

That is the fun of modern romance, nothing can ever be a terrible mistake, so over and over again you can look over your shoulder and see the arms of your past, see them encircle your waist with comfort so cold you don't feel a thing—

FROM *GIRLS, VISIONS AND EVERYTHING* (1986)

SARAH SCHULMAN

Friday morning Lila woke up with Emily at six o'clock and found a small gift box lying on her stomach.

"What's this?"

"A good luck present for the Worst Performance Festival tonight."

Lila opened the box. Inside was a lace brassiere with an underwire and a little pink flower stitched in between the cups. Next to it sat black lace underpants with another stitched pink rose. She shut the box quickly, and opened it again, slowly, to look more closely.

"Are you embarrassed?" Emily asked.

No. It was intimate, so involved with Lila's life that she was thrilled to the teeth.

"The right size and everything."

Lila imagined Emily standing thoughtfully at the counter, fingering the bras, deciding which one she would buy.

"I know my baby's breasts."

"I know you do."

The house was packed that night for the Worst, which was the third act on a bill at AVANT-GARDE-ARAMA, a former Ukrainian restaurant turned performance club. Fortunately for Lila, Isabel and Company, the opening piece was a woman eating a grapefruit and the following was a man walking around in a circle with a paper bag over his head talking about how much he liked to pee before going on stage. All the girls were there, except for Muriel, who was sunning herself somewhere on the Costa del Sol.

The lights came up on Helen Hayes and Mike Miller, the administrative heavy of the ARAMA. They were sitting at a panel-like table with official looking nameplates. Suddenly Lila rushed out into the crowd in tight black pants and a tight black t-shirt that said "Soon To Be A Major Homosexual."

"Good evening ladies and friends. I will be your emcee for this evening and I am pleased to be with this special audience. Who else but you, people who pay five dollars to come see this kind of work, could be better qualified to pick the worst performer of 1984? But first, before we begin, I want to remind you that all of us here tonight, well, we are a community, a community of enemies. And we have to stay close to each other so we can watch out and protect ourselves. To give you an idea for the criteria by which to judge the participants, we have an excerpt from last year's winner, Amy Cohen. I will now read to you from her prize-winning text, *Artificial Turtle*:

> *Inside out. Empty Box as silence.*
> *Empty box as monument to . . . emptiness*

"Isn't that just awful?"

The audience, getting into the groove, booed wildly, then, pleased with themselves, applauded and cheered. Isabel had promised Lila that they would. She understood the simple fact that people like to be insulted in public because they think it means they're important.

"Tonight we are proud to introduce our panel of minor celebrity judges from competing cliques to vote down each other's friends. First, representing the girls from the Kitsch-Inn, the Platinum Angel Herself, Helen Hayes."

Helen was dressed to her divaish teeth.

"It's simply terrible to be here tonight."

"Thank you, tell us Helen, how was your show at Dance-a-teria last night?"

"Pretty bad, pretty bad. I think it would have been competitive in this festival."

"That's great Helen, isn't she swell ladies and gentlemen? Thanks doll. And now, representing the boys, the Avant-Garde's head cheerleader, Mike Miller. Hey Mike, I love your beard. Thank you and enjoy the show."

Lila and Isabel had agreed before hand that Mike would have no lines and no microphone. Those boys talked too much anyway. As he sat there looking stupid, Helen announced the first entry.

"Our opening act tonight will be East Village Performance Artist Isabel Schwartz with her piece, *My Brilliant Career,* improvisational ruminations on nothing."

Isabel entered in her pink baseball pants, yellow sneakers and black sunglasses.

"Look, I don't have anything to say to you and you don't have anything to say to me," she sighed, looked as bored as possible, like she was too big for Carnegie Hall. "I don't even like you. I thought about coming here with the slides of my lesbian honeymoon at Grossinger's, but we're only getting ten dollars

for this performance, so why waste a good idea for ten dollars? Instead, I'd like to read to you from my reviews. *Isabel Schwartz is a Genius, Isabel Schwartz is a whiz on stage, Isabel Schwartz is witty and exuberant.* That's all you deserve. Good-bye."

"Well," said Helen. "That was pretty terrible. Very annoying at times. It's going to be tough to beat. *Dance Magazine* called our next performer, *an actor with the wit, personal style and glamour of a young Dustin Hoffman.* Will you please welcome Ratso Tootsie."

Roberta walked calmly onto the stage, scratching her head, dragging her robes and drinking a beer. She took a cassette tape out of her pocket and dropped it on the floor. Then she took out a box of slides and tossed them uncaringly in the air. Finally she unraveled a film all over the stage. She finished the beer, spit on the floor and left.

"Thank you Ratso," said Helen, with a impeccable display of dishonest politeness.

"The slides were very experimental but I found the film slightly opaque. Our next performer Patty Dyke uses time and space to interpret the self, herself, in all its post-modern incarnations. Patty's influences include Artaud, Rimbaud, Van Gogh, The Go-Go's and Uncle Ho."

It was Isabel again. This time she was dressed in a pink and green bath towel. She was plugged into a walkman and danced to the music that no one else could hear. But when the chorus came on, she scream out, "Beat it, just beat it," and hit herself on the head with a stick. Helen, looking properly upset, tried to ease her off the stage, but Isabel, being the prototype horrible performer, started making a scene.

"I've given you everything," she shouted, running up to a stunned and silent Mike and pulling his beard, "everything and you just fucked me in the ass you dumb prick," and then she threw off the towel.

After intermission, when the audience had calmed down, the lights came up slowly on the final segment of the show, "The Lesbian Nuns and Their Dirty Habits: The Real True Story (With Carlos)." There were Lila, Isabel and Roberta dressed as nuns with incense and chanting and holy water and Bach organ music played in slow motion in the background. The three of them were mumbling "Domini, Domini" and spraying holy water on everyone. When they finished their procession, each one assumed a pose in a different shadow and put on their name plates. Lila was "Sister Roger," Roberta, "Sister Fresnel," and Isabel, "Sister Bruce Weber."

Helen announced "The Flying Nun" and Lila pouted, slapped her thigh and said, "Come on Carlos, we've got to think of a way to save the convent. I know, a bake sale!" To which Helen, chomping on a cigar replied, "But seester." Lila held on to her habit and made a few Gidget type moves to get ready for the take-off.

Reading from her index cards Helen announced sister number two, Julie Andrews.

Roberta plastered a big smile on her face and began to teach the audience to sing Do-Re-Mi, until, right in the middle of *Me, a name I call myself*, she yelled out "Stop, stop. This is a sham. When I was a kid I was in love with Julie Andrews. I had her picture on my mirror. I dressed like her, I had a Julie Andrews wallet. My mother took me to all her movies. One day I got the address of her fan club and I wrote her a long letter. Julie, I said, Julie I love you, I love you. And do you know what she did, that bitch? She sent me back an autographed picture. I cried for days, my mother tried to console me with a Julie Andrews coloring book. Then Halloween came, and she took me to Woolworth's tempting me with a Mary Poppins costume but I said no. You know why? Do you know why? Because I didn't want to be Julie Andrews. I wanted to have Julie Andrews."

"And now," announced the lovely Helen Hayes, "Sister number three, The Singing Nun." At which point Isabel whipped out an electric guitar and started singing "Dominique." The others joined in. Unfortunately, they hadn't rehearsed this part of the show and none of them knew the lyrics so they just kept singing "Dominique-ah, nique-ah, nique-ah" over and over again until The Flying Nun took off, the Singing Nun switched to Hound Dog and Julie Andrews started making out with a woman in the first row.

Finally Helen had the foresight to turn out the lights. So went the Worst Performance Festival. Oh, well, that's show biz.

THE CRACKED MIRROR
Redtape No.6 1986

FROM "PHIL SPECTOR A PERFORMANCE POEM FOR THREE GROUPS OF VOICES" (1986)

EMILY XYZ

Single-spaced lines read simultaneously. Underlines overlap. All lines pick up without pause.

A He wasn't all there I can tell you for sure

B genius-genius. genius-genius. genius-genius. genius-genius.

C well it was just—well it was just—well it was just—well it was just—

A The first time I heard him I thought: My God! This man is crazy, he'll kill us all.

B I went along with it—we all did! I went along with it—we all did!
C It was just his idea   of how things should be
                 A You could say no   but why would you?

B It was a great opportunity

C He knew what people wanted to hear. Everybody believed in him.
  <u>Everybody believed in him</u>.

A <u>it wasn't like you had a choice</u> It wasn't like you had a choice
It wasn't like you had a choice It wasn't like you had a choice

B he heard voices and he listened to them, he heard the noise in the street and he listened

C the people in the street heard their own voices and they followed the noise to its source

A they made a noise I will never forget as long as I live they made a noise I will never forget as long as I live

B It was the chance of a lifetime, of course I went along with it—we all did!

C I would've done just about anything he wanted at that point

A You don't say NO to someone like that, you don't say NO to someone like that, you don't say NO

B not if you want to live to see not if you want to live to see not if you want to live

C he hears voices he hears voices he hears voices he hears voices
A So do I, so do I, so do I, so do I, so do I

B of course if I had known then, of course if I had known then, of course if I had known
C how were we to know that? nobody knew back then how were we to know that? nobody

A things just happened, why ask why, things just happened, why ask why?

B no one knew it would end like that, no one knew no one knew no one knew

C damned if I can remember how it started. damn if I can remember how it started.

A wé were victims too wé were all trapped, wé were victims too wé were all fooled
B I'd do it all again I'd do it all again I'd do it all again

C look you'll go along with anybody
                                A in that situation
                                      B who says he can help you get

C and back then nobody knew anything. and back then nobody knew anything.

A at the time it seemed like the safest
                            B it was the way things were and you went along with it

C well it was just
                    A nobody knew

B you don't say NO to someone like that you don't say NO to someone like that
C chance of a lifetime. chance of a lifetime. chance of a lifetime. chance of a lifetime.

A you would'a been killed

B do it all again

C he came on the radio and cars started and I heard glass breaking in the street, he came on the radio and girls started dancing, he came on the radio and the stars cascaded, news of the world, and he comes on and on on the radio a sound I've never heard, a thousand voices all at once and the glass glass in the street street, crazy with stars, WOR WOR WOR—

A (*rhumba rhythm*) testing, testing—one, two—testing, testing—one, two testing testing—one, two
B they made a noise I will never forget as long as I love
C I still hear in my head

B and we thought he was kidding

C QUIET EVERYBODY!—Okay, take one:

ALL THE IRONY OF THE BERLIN WALL, AS RELATED BY SURVIVORS OF THE WARSAW GHETTO

C Ready—click—rolling:

A We got on the train at Kochstrasse, Checkpoint Charlie, heading towards Tegel. We found we could not get off

B Berlin wall Berlin wall Berlin wall Berlin wall Berlin wall
C kennedy kennedy kennedy kennedy kennedy
A stadtmitte stadtmitte stadtmitte stadtmitte
                                 C Make all the noise you want,
                                     no one can hear

A Not till Reinickindorfer strasse/ Slowly through East Berlin stations/ That were used by everybody/ But now used by nobody/ and soldiers stand on platforms/ sometimes armed with rifles

B [*under, starting at "East Berlin stations"*] stadtmitte, stadtmitte, stadtmitte Heinrich Heine strasse. Jannowitz Brucke. Alexanderplatz. Rosenthaler platz. Bernauer strasse. Nord bahn hof. Oranienburger strasse. stadtmitte, stadtmitte
                 C Testing, testing—check one two!

B They are soldiers, they don't talk and they don't listen
                 C We're rolling, tape is rolling
                       A under the Berlin wall. over the Berlin wall

C Quiet please!

A we found we could not get out

B Crowd in, everybody crowd in, get closer to the mikes
        C checkpoint checkpoint one two three

A I never saw anything like it
        B I remember thinking, Good! See how they like it
                A we just stood there staring

C All right, come on, I need everybody in here now—Please come in and stand as close to the microphones as you can possibly get—yes, good, OK, CROWD IN, I need as many people in here as the room will hold

B more people more people more people more people my people my people my people

A all of a sudden we realized

C I want this sound to be—not loud, but HUGE

A between us and the rest of the world, between us and the rest of the world
B this city is going to fall this city is going to fall this city is going

A On the 19th day of November 1940 I saw the gates of the Warsaw ghetto sealed, shut for ever
        B shut for ever
              C Nobody in, nobody out

A we stood there staring we stood there
              C There were so many people crowded in there you could hardly breath, let alone sing

B let alone play the drums
A let alone tell right from wrong

B then in Warsaw bad to worse bad to worse bad to worse bad to worse
A I saw Warsaw's doors close and close forever, nineteen November 1940
              C nineteen 1940

B we were there for hours, over and over again

    A we were there for hours, over and over again

        C a parody of artistic expression, 6 7 8—

[*pause*]

A I was walking to work that day, I recall / I got to the gate at Gesia Street / <u>It was shut</u>.

B <u>IT WAS SHUT</u>

C what?

A I turned back / I walked to **each** of the other gates / All of them were shut / That was the end of that / I went back home and waited / to see what would happen. That was the 19th day of November / nineteen-forty.

C then came more people forced in forced into the oldest poorest most run-down section of town

      B Forced to find housing for themselves they wandered

door to door, over and under they stood all night no room no food no water

A Is there any room / Is there any room /

B Everybody IN! Move move move move!

      C TESTING testing one two three

          A More people more people my people

B trains came and the soldiers marched them herd them

        A GO

B slaughter platform herd them

        A GO

B train comes run for cover hold up uprising some won't go, train comes turn ragged back <u>and run for life</u>

A <u>ghost of hope</u> chance march to slaughter, train comes, march smoke still uprising

C screaming for days screaming

    B they brought the walls down

C screaming for days screaming

B they brought the walls down they brought them down

C He's a creepy guy, I've seen him fly high in the hills, he's got a gun he's got ALOTTA guns—

A He held us at gunpoint and he ordered us to sing, just like that, he said SING he said
SING and don't stop until I tell ya to stop—

B train came to the northern gate

C walk forward walk forward walk forward to where the streets end

A and stand forever, now walk forward forward to where the tracks begin

B and past where the past ends and stand forever and closer, closer

A closer and pack them in, faster, faster far to go no food no water

C I swear I thought I would die in that little room, no room to move, all you could do
was sing and sing and sing—
                                 B There was never a noise like this made, never

A I did it because I wanted to I did it because I had to

B he called out our names and he raised his rifle

C they creep from east to west from east to west
                          B remembering nothing, trying to escape trying to escape

A try to leave you find, all the lines are drawn, and you
                                   B and you belong to someone else now
C and you live by the wall and you die by the wall, and when Phil went to the well to the wall he saw
        B held them at gunpoint and ordered them to pray
                                           C people live above our heads with rifles raised, rifles raised

A the doors start closing, the landscape changes, you live by the wall you die by the wall
        B and Phil he don't smile he just says Follow and they follow him, a
controlled collection that sings aloud, when allowed, and they end up in a crowded room
unable to breathe, they faint

C Phil raises a rifle and they stand, they stand there and they sing, they sing and they tear the roof off—

        A & B Mother I sing I sing I sing I sing mother I sing I mother

C Phil, a blank expression on his face

B Phil his black hair his shades his eyes incandescent

A food water no

B fling myself against the doors a bruising flying face flying face into the wall, falling down a world of color

C Phil you love me don't you don't you don't you don't you don't you click ROLLING!

A you live by the wall you die

[*pause*]

ALL PHIL BUILDS THE AMERICAN WALL

B I think it out first. I think things out. I think. I think things. I think. I think. things. it out. think:

C Is this what you really want?

A sacrifice sacrifice sacrifice sacrifice
B trade-off trade-off trade-off trade-off

C It's not what anyone wants, but

A You're in a mess now, excuse the expression
B Just try and make the best of it

C you gotta bend you gotta bend you gotta bend you gotta bend
A you gotta be yourself you gotta be yourself you gotta be yourself

B Bad timing bad judgment bad advice bad move—

C It's business, you understand

A Bullshit, bullshit

B It's not what anyone wants

C Bend or break—take your pick Bend or break—take your pick
A Hey, it's your funeral Hey, it's your funeral Hey, it's your funeral

B That's it, take it or leave it

                                     C Look, you started it

A You got it

B Did I not warn you?

C Do you want this or don't you?

A That's what you *think* you would do

B Just be sure to get it in writing
C Just so we understand each other

A You got it

B Now think:

C Just do it and see what happens. Just do it and see what happens.
A Is this what I want? Will I be sorry? Is this the right thing? Will I be happy?

B See what happens? See what happens?
C Just do it and see what happens.
A Some dream dreams, some hear voices—Some dream dreams, some hear voices

Chatter: YOOOO-HOOOO! / The land of the free—The land of the freeee / giggling / Then what? Then what? / drunken singing of "Be My Baby" or other Spector hit; any other miscellaneous deranged-sounding vocalizing. *Individual voices continue this, quietly at first, then becoming more intense under the following lines, which are spoken by any two or more voices at once:*

1) *(Slow, like Nico, and a little slurry):*
Phil's built himself a fortress in the hills. If it falls on anyone it'll kill 'em. A piece fell on Lenny Bruce. He holds people hostage there, he surrounds them, he imprisons them. Phil can't face life because he is schizophrenic. I wish we could see him.

2) YOO-HOO! PHIL! You fuckin psychotic

3) Take two and ready—Go! Phil's built himself a fortress in the hills. If it falls on anyone it'll kill 'em. A piece fell on Lenny Bruce. He holds people hostage there, he surrounds them, he imprisons them. Phil can't face life because he is schizophrenic. I wish we could see him.

4) YOO-HOO! PHIL! You fuckin psychotic

5) he surrounds them, they surrender,

ALL: HE'S A GENIUS

FIVE

Constance DeJong Joe Gibbons Tama Janowitz
Richard Prince Leslie Thornton

PERFORMANCE / READING

MONDAY MARCH 17th
8:00 PM

ADMISSION $4.00

WITH:

RICHARD BANDANZA

CARMELITA TROPICANA AND

RON KOLM

1986

AT: ST. MARK'S CHURCH, 10th ST. & 2nd AVENUE

KOSTABI

Summer 1986   Volume 2 Number 4

Featuring stories by:
Barry Yourgrau, Reina Fondreli, Gary Indiana, Catherine Texier,
Marnie Mueller, Jeffrey DeShell, Bruce Benderson,
Blake Walmsley, Mitchell Kriegman, Peter Wortsman, Kenneth Bernard,
Craig Gholson, Nicole Brossard, and Lynne Tillman
Included free with every issue: Cherches/Feldman Flexi–Disk!
Front Cover art by Kiki Smith. Back Cover by Jolie Stahl.

BETWEEN C AND D

Post–Patriotic Lower East Side Fiction Magazine

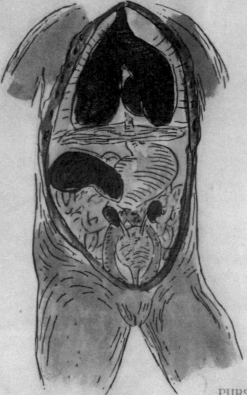

LIFE
LIBERTY
PURSUIT OF HAPPINESS
COMPUTERS

$4.00 $5.00 OUTSIDE NEW YORK CITY

86
'86

NEW YEARS DAY
MARATHON
BENEFIT

HELP CELEBRATE
POETRY PROJECT'S
TWENTIETH YEAR

ST MARK'S CHURCH
BEGINNING AT 7PM
CONTRIBUTION $10

THE POETRY PROJECT AT ST MARK'S 2 AVE. & 10 ST. NEW YORK NEW YORK CITY 10003 212.674.0910 CHURCH

Celebrate with
Special MC Haoui Montaug and
Miguel Algarin
William Allen
Bruce Andrews
Zoe Anglesey
Penny Arcade
John Ash
Richard Bandanza
Barbara Barg
Will Bennett
John Bernd
Charles Bernstein
Tone Blevins
Jim Brodey
John Cage
Jim Carroll
Susan Cataldo
Lenora Champagne
Peter Cherches and Jane Goldberg
Yoshiko Chuma
Jim Cohn
Gregory Corso
Thulani Davis
Jane Delynn
Tim Dlugos
Kevin Duffy
Johnny Eagle
Richard Elovich
Kenward Elmslie
Karen Finley
Ellen Fisher
Terry Fox
Cliff Fyman
Allen Ginsberg
Merle Ginsberg
John Giorno
John Godfrey
Brad Gooch
Lois Elaine Griffith
Jessica Hagedorn
Kimiko Hahn
Bob Holman
Holly Hughes
Gary Indiana
Tama Janowitz
Joseph Jarman
Patricia Jones
Vincent Katz
Ron Kolm
Daniel Krakauer
Chris Kraus
Rochelle Kraut
Bill Kushner
Michael Lally
Phoebe Legere and the Guillotine
Roland Legiardi-Laura
Rose Lesniach
Steve Levine
Mabou Mines
Maria Mancini
Patrick McGrath
Jackson MacLow/Anne Tardoes
Frank Maya
Yvonne Meier
Shelley Miller
Cookie Mueller
Eileen Myles
Marc Nasdor
Jim Neu and Roberta Levine
Michael O'Donoghue
Maureen Owen
Pat Olezko
Nicky Paraiso
Everett Quinton
David Rattray
Rene Ricard
Vito Ricci and Ann Rower
Randy Rollison
Bob Rosenthal
Frank Rubino
James Ruggia
Tom Savage
Harris Schiff
Paul Schmidt
Michael Scholnick
James Sherry
Claudia Siege
James Siena /Chaza Dean
Sally Silvers and Jon Zorn
Ram Singh
Split Britches
Elizabeth Swados
Greg "Ironman" Tate
Steven Taylor
Fiona Templeton
Catherine Texier
Lynne Tillman
Susie Timmons
Paul Violi
Diane Ward
The Washington Squares
Hannah Weiner
R. Weiss
Jeff Weiss
Jeff Wright
Emily XYZ
Don Yorty
Barry Yourgrau
Bill Zavatsky
Nina Zivancevic

THE POETRY PROJECT

2nd Ave & l0th St. NYC 10003

(212) 674-09l0

October

5 Open Reading

7 Kenneth Koch

12 David Wojnarowicz & Bill Rice

14 Peter Schjeldahl & Ann Lauterbach

19 Nina Zivancevic & Lizzie Mercier-Decloux

21 Carla Harryman & John Yau

25 Ed Sanders: Book Party for Thirsting for Peace in a Raging Country
    7PM   Admission FREE

26 Elliot Katz & Vicki Stanbury

28 Shuntaro Tanikawa, William I. Elliott &
    Kazuo Kawamura

November

1 6 Poets, 16 min.: On Sources, Solutions and Inspirations

2 Open Reading

4 Jayne Cortez & Barbara Barg

9 Rikki Ducornet & John Godfrey

11 Jack Collom & Marjorie Welish

16 Rene Ricard & Eileen Myles

18 John Ashbery & John Ash

23 Nick Zedd & Michael Osterhau

30 Greg Masters & Kurt Hollander

All events begin at 8 PM, admission by contribution of $5, except where noted. Programs subject to change.

WORKSHOPS:
Tuesdays at 7PM "Poetry and Prose" taught by Bernadette Mayer
Fridays at 7 PM "Fiction, Prose and Poetry" taught by Charlotte Carter
Saturdays at 12 PM "Poetry, Journals and Romanticism" taught by Jeff Wright

The Poetry Project receives generous financial support from these public and private agencies: The New York State Council on the Arts, The National Endowment for the Arts, The Jerome Foundation, Morgan Guaranty & Trust Company , Mobil Foundation, New York City's Dept. of Cultural Affairs, Con Edison, The New Hope Foundation, Kulchur Foundation, New York Community Trust, Film Video Arts, Inc., Poets and Writers, The Foundation for Contemporary Performing arts, The Aaron Diamond Foundation, Gramercy Park Foundation and Apple Computers, Inc. Also, the membership of the Poetry Project and individuals.

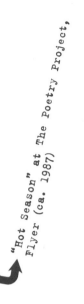

"Hot Season" at The Poetry Project,
Flyer (ca. 1987)

International Eye, Vol. 8 No. 72, Cover (1987)
Photo: Isabel Snyder;
Art Director: Donald Schneider

ON BOHOMELESSNESS: A CONVOLUTED GUIDE TO THE OTHER SIDE (1987)

DARIUS JAMES

I. Who are the Bohomeless?

You've bought them drinks at Vazac's, picked them up at Save the Robots, let them smoke all your cigarettes, and given them food money on the pretext of subway fare home. They are one of New York City's most misunderstood social groups: the homeless bohemian, or the Bohomeless. But who are they exactly? Hellspawn of mucus-secreting sewer people and poststructuralist art critics with coke nasal-drip? Or boho hobos living on the outskirts of Soho? Are the Bohomelessness suburban teens with cancer fuzz-cuts and woeful, Keane-like eyes seated on the stoops of Saint Mark's Place, accosting you for loose change? Or subway-dwelling frottage freaks who rasp, with fetid breath disjointed passages from *High Performance* and *Re/Search* magazines on how the use of video monitors in open-air performance spaces has brought the homeless shambling, like blue-hued ghouls, into the mainstream of mall-mad consumer culture? They are all of these things and more.

And how is it that the sex lives of Bohomeless are not any more exciting than your own but charged to your Diners Club card? What trick of Crowleyan subterfuge allows the Bohomeless to evade accounting for their actions by insisting *David Lettermen isn't funny*? Why do the Bohomeless display a marked inability to match a pair of socks? And most importantly, (considering your most likely encounter with the Bohomeless will occur at 4:30 in the morning when he appears at your door with a pin-eyed slattern on his arm, reeking of cheap booze and stale cigarette smoke, eyes red and askew, lips flapping rapidly, with a convoluted tale of how he was tossed through the doors of an after-hours dive by a steroid-swollen *He Beast* because of, uh, *constipation,* and, uh, well, besides, he's never even *seen* a set of *works*) do you really want one sleeping on your floor? Well, do you? Maybe not. . . .

II. What is the history of the Bohomeless, or, who is on the floor of Gillis Groceries and what did he mean by the "Big D"?

To understand the Bohomeless, we must begin with an understanding of the Bohemian. For those born in the first litter of TV babies, initial introduction to bohemianism was not Herbert Huncke and his dealings with the upstarts at Columbia, Kerouac's amphetamine agitations on toilet paper rolls, or even Ted Joans renting himself out in Scarsdale, but television's original "Not Ready For Prime Time" *Dobie Gillis* dope fiend—*Maynard G. Krebs.*

Maynard wore threadbare threads. His main vocation was talking to negros in Sweden on the Gillis' phone: "Get me Diz, dig? (PAUSE) Yo, Diz, what it is? You go down on yo' horn, baby! Like, I dig yo' blow, you know? (PAUSE) Not on yo' axe! YOUR BLOW! (PAUSE) Wow, No need to get *chilly*, I'm already *cool*! (CLICK) . . . *Diz?* . . . *Diz* . . ." Maynard holed up in his crib, listening to jazz, hookah hose hanging from his mouth, reading *The Village Voice*, a weekly muckraker partly conceived by Norman Mailer (who thought hip was a French

Ron Kolm/Public Illumination Magazine
Parody (1986)
Art: Tom Zimmer

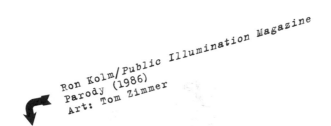

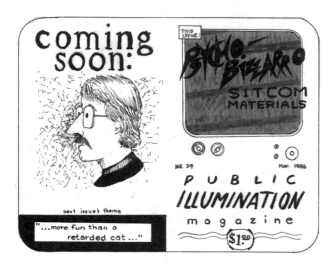

spade flavored with postwar funk) as a *Weekly World News* for beatniks ("SQUARE DIGS POT. HEAD BLOWS UP. WRITES BAD POETRY.")

Maynard's most memorable characteristic was his reaction to work. If asked to assist in any activity requiring the slightest physical exertion, Maynard's body froze, his eyeballs popped in distension and he squawked like a parrot with a cracker up his ass. The differences between Maynard and today's Bohomeless are: (1) Sillier haircuts; (2) The poststructuralist presence; (3) *Fangoria* ("the only mag that matters") is required reading; and (4) Rick Rubin has replaced Haile Selassie as God.

III. What is the Bohomeless term of endearment for their lovers?

RENT! The Bohomeless are an unusually bright and creative class of people with all the comforts of home and no place to put them. They have all of their faculties and, if they take their medication, are capable of intelligent decision-making (except in bars: beer and bad lighting are their two worst enemies). They are well dressed (even if their clothes do come from your closet), and are, perversely, self-sufficient.

The Bohomeless are not wholly victims of circumstance; they are homeless, in part, by choice. They are a group with an uncompromising commitment to their art *by any means necessary*, and, like Brooke and her Calvins, *nothing gets between them and Their Muse* (especially, as my father has suggested I get for years, A *J-O-B*). Furthermore many are involved in disciplines that require mobility: addled aspirants either in search of (fill in the blank), or fleeing from (you figure it out); self-involved Artaudian actors; European heroin-addicts on extended holiday; dull-witted noise rockers who forget where they parked their van; performance artists who *defy* rational description; jazz musicians who tell you they're in for the night and end up on your couch for six months. The nomadic nature of their existence precludes any possibility of "roots" beyond a P.O. Box and an answering machine, if that. Even serious romantic commitments are viewed as vampires to the Muse. The outlook of the Bohomeless is a result of the shattered idealism of the young artist's revolutionary fervor wedded to the night vision of the after-hours dive. With the street-seasoned jazzman as his mentor, the struggling artist learns new skills to insure his continued survival. And with ex-'60s rads turned slumlords schmoozing it up with the unlikely likes of Jerry Rubin and buying up the Lower East Side with the brain-damaged notion it's going to be the next suburb of Westchester, with the Lower East Side's Puerto Rican populous relocated to a housing project at the bottom of the East River, the radically aware Bohomeless must ask themselves, WHY THE FUCK PAY RENT?!! (The message is tagged in bold black splatter on E. Ville walls: "Better no rent than igno-rent!!!") Or as the opposition to Rubin's born-again booshiehood has said: "America is the land of the *free*, right? And free means *you don't pay, DON'T IT?*"

IV. How do the Bohomeless live?

The Bohomeless lifestyle disproves the notion that there is no such thing as a free lunch. Or dinner, for that matter (though, occasionally, the Bohomeless have been known to fork over the necessary $1.25 for that platter of congealed *hog's sweat* advertised as "The Breakfast Special." Unlike Allen Ginsberg, who once asked: "Where can I buy groceries with my good looks?" the Bohomeless can and do survive on the strength of good looks alone. ("We live on charm, charity, and *MasterCard*!" shouted one beer-crazed boho without home from the podium of a downtown poets' den. "As Jack Kerouac said, striking a Karl Malden pose, *'I don't sleep in the street without it!'*")

You won't find the Bohomeless sleeping over steaming sewer grates, in the Tompkins Square bandshell, or inside an abandoned packing crate parked at the intersection of First and Houston—coughing wads of phlegm and smearing it on your windshield is not the Bohomeless *style*. Where you will find the Bohomeless is near the drink table at gallery openings or celeb-studded Lit parties, anywhere with free drinks and a buffet, cultivating friends among the real charge-card carrying. Bohomelessness is not the stuff third-rate reporters, undercover in the ninth circle of hell, build their careers on. No. The lives of the Bohomeless are as random as a throw of the bones. One night might find them cuddled with a runaway teen, all

CRACK!!!ed up, under the silky covers of a futon on the top floor of a duplex with exposed brick walls and oak floors, cooled by the twirling of an overhead fan; and the next in a painter's studio, wrapped in discarded canvassing, on a floor littered with lumps of cat shit, dreaming of the night before.

V. Should You Take a Bohomeless to Lunch?

Bohomelessness isn't a problem. It's a solution, an alternative to spreading cheek 9 to 5 for the sole profit of real-estate greedheads. It's sorta like homesteading without the grunt work. The Bohomeless live according to a private *Tao*, bending like bamboo reeds in the wind. And springing back with the reed's resilience. Or some such mystical mumbo-jumbo. For myself, the idea of the Bohomelessness is a social fiction, like any of the other fictions we create and exploit. I don't have anything useful to say about the very real problem of homelessness. I do have *one* suggestion, though. For every bag person found dead on the street, abduct a landlord. Tie him to the *Venus of Rivington Street* in front of a bank of gigantic Marshall Amps. Let Demo Moe, the only living band in NYC, thrash and blaspheme against God, nature, and humankind for 24 nonstop hours. With the bag person's corpse blue and bloated before him, maggots writhing in its eyeholes, offer a choice: either you eat it or we eat you.

Anything for a free lunch, right?

THE PORTABLE LOWER EAST SIDE

Volume 4   Number 1

Spring 1987

SONGS OF THE CITY

FROM *HAUNTED HOUSES* (1987)

LYNNE TILLMAN

Mark said he had nothing to hide because he wasn't afraid of being called unnatural. Grace and he were sitting at the bar and were talking about the play Mark wanted to base on Wilde's "The Birthday of the Infanta." He'd changed his mind; no hospital setting, no nurse. He especially wanted to end with the fairy tale's last line, "For the future let those who come to play with me have no heart." "You've got to have something to hide," Grace said, finishing her beer and lighting a cigarette. They agreed that Wilde was as cruel if not crueler than Poe, because of how the fairy tale begins with the preparations for the Infanta's birthday, and how her birth killed her mother, the beautiful queen, whom the king is still mourning twelve years later. He keeps her embalmed body on display so that he can visit her once a month. "He visits her once a month like his period," Grace laughed.

The cast of characters would include the King, the little Dwarf, who doesn't know how ugly he is, and who is brought to the palace to entertain the Infanta, the Infanta, who is the image of her mother, and as cruel as she is beautiful, the flowers who speak and the Infanta's entourage. They can be whoever's in the bar that night, Mark figured, wanting to give the play a kind of lived-in feeling. "Truth, beauty, beauty, truth," he declaimed in the nearly empty bar. It was late afternoon or happy hour. Mark felt there was something really rotten at the bottom of it, and Grace agreed, feeling pretty rotten herself.

You only attack the things that give you trouble, he went on. "Trouble," the woman three barstools from them yelled. "What do you know about trouble? Trouble is my middle name." Mark peered down the bar, past this woman, to a new face, one covered by a four-day beard that gave it, this nearly ugly face, a handsome aspect, or, at least, character. Men can get away with anything, Grace thought, watching Mark continuing to look, and then at last walking over to him and pulling up a barstool. Up close his face was both rugged and motherly, or so it seemed to Mark, who forced himself to speak and was answered indifferently by the stranger who didn't look up, as if he couldn't be bothered. "I'm not interested," he said, "I'm into pussy." Mark excused himself, nearly falling off his seat, returning fast to Grace, wondering how he could use that in the play.

Grace told Mark her latest cat dream in which a mother cat has five kittens, very fast, in a big, messy house. The toilet has been pulled out of the bathroom and there's nowhere to piss. A child is sleeping or dead under piles of wet clothes. There's water everywhere and from nowhere to piss they go to "Nowhere to Run," which was arguably the second-best Martha and the Vandellas song, after "Heat Wave." Nowhere to run nowhere to hide and back to hiding and Mark's definition of himself and Grace as demonstration models that would never get bought. Grace said she didn't want to get bought, but wouldn't mind being rented. Mark said he wanted to get married someday and so did she, because deep down there had to be that urge, waiting there like her maternal self, repressed, but ready at any moment to wear white. "Babies," Grace snapped. "You'd be a much better mother than I would." The way Mark saw it, the King would approach the coffin and cry out, as he did in Wilde's story, *"Mi reina, mi reina,"* then drop to his knees weeping, after covering her embalmed face with kisses, Grace added. That would be the beginning of the play, especially since the King nearly ruined his kingdom on account of his love for her, when she was alive, and perhaps even drove him crazy, his obsession was so great. She died of his excessive demands on her, or so Mark figured, but Grace stressed that the birth of the Infanta killed her, and that's why the King couldn't stand the sight of his beautiful daughter. "Passion brings a terrible blindness upon its servants," Mark quoted, and of course there's the little Dwarf, who has never seen himself at all. And who will die of a broken heart when he does, realizing that the Infanta was only laughing at him.

Mark would've liked to have taken his love and locked him in a room, kept him there, thrown away the key. He would put a line into the King's mouth: "I have set myself in agony upon your strangeness." "Was the Queen strange?" Grace asked. "I don't know," Mark answered, "but it's a play on your highness." "Oh," Grace said, "very funny." Possession is nine-tenths of the law, but would the law cover Mark's keeping his love locked away in a room in Providence. "The law doesn't cover what you want it to cover," he said sullenly.

Grace would be the Infanta and Mark the little Dwarf, although he toyed with playing both the King and the Dwarf. What constituted the most hideous costume and overall design for the Dwarf was under discussion. Something has to be missing. Something has to be hanging from his chin. One of his eyes must be out of the socket or blinded. He would have to have tiny hairy hands without fingernails. Dirty matted hair. Sores, running ones. An enormous nose. Or a face with no nose at all. A head much too large for its pathetic body. No proportion. Mark would play the Dwarf on his knees, like Jose Ferrer as Toulouse-Lautrec.

The woman who said trouble was her middle name was raging down the end of the bar. "You have a beautiful face, a man loves you. You have a face like a monkey, you only get screwed. Screwed. It's better to be old. You don't care about that. None of that. Can't be fooled anymore." Mark studied Grace's face. "You're pretty, but your nose is a little too big. You're not perfect, there's something just a little bit off about you." He kept studying, and Grace said only Christ was perfect, and she didn't mind. She also didn't mind being called pretty, if she could use it to her advantage, although the advantages were weird. Take the Infanta. Her beauty is almost a trick. And connected to evil. "And your lower lip should be fuller," Mark continued, "the better to beguile." "And you've got too much lip," Grace said, "it makes you lopsided. That's what makes you perfect to play the Dwarf. But imagine if you were really ugly, with a face only a mother could love."

The Infanta never really had a mother, unless you count a woman dying for six months as your mother. Grace thought of Ellen in the mental hospital, and how she didn't really have a mother, either. It was when Ellen called Grace mother that Grace decided to quit that job because, as she told Mark, I'd only end up hurting her. They said goodbye when Ellen was lucid, but Ellen couldn't understand that it was goodbye forever. She touched Grace's hair and for the first time in Grace's life she was moved to sadness for someone else. It made her feel impotent, then angry, that big empty feeling. No one loved her, Ellen, or the Infanta. And it's your right to be mean or crazy. "The King didn't even stay with the Infanta on her birthday," Grace complained. "He was busy taking care of the state," Mark teased. Even though he'd said she wouldn't have to memorize anything, the Infanta's role was growing and Grace was beginning to think that Mark should play it. "I'll never learn it all." "Ah, you're a natural," he said. And she said, "When I hear that word, I want to dye my hair black."

Late at night Grace couldn't memorize her lines and stared into space and then out the space through the window. The empty streets had a ghostliness that was part of night, and there wasn't anything necessarily worse about the night than the day, except for the darkness, which was only natural. The day dyes its hair, too, she thought, that's why it's weird and why I like it, even if it's scary. Under cover of night. The dark. The guy at the bar talking about those murders in Providence. A man stalking women, one after another. Mark and she had been arguing about the end of the Dwarf, his death, and whether or not he had to die, or if it could end differently. Grace said he had to die, and Mark thought maybe he could be put on a respirator and the Infanta forced to confront the consequences of her actions before he died. But then you couldn't use the last line, Grace argued, and that's when the guy at the bar yelled at them about just talking about death like that when real people were being killed, not storybook dwarfs, and who cares anyway, and Mark talked about wanting to give people hope and the guy said he was hopeless, just another artist. "Real murders take place in the real world," he yelled. "What's real?" Mark yelled back. Later in her room Grace wasn't convinced about anything. He said real murder in a menacing way. Real murder committed by real people out there. Out there. "Or even in here," the guy added. Mark was sure he was a cop, undercover, bent on scaring the demimonde. There's épater le bourgeois and there's épater la scum. Dying of a broken heart is different from being murdered, and she doubted that anyone really died because of love. It seemed so stupid.

After the Dwarf and the Infanta, the flowers had the biggest parts. Carmen, a transsexual, wanted to be either a violet or a tulip, but because of expediency, she would play all the flowers, in one. She can make her own costume, Mark said, anything she wants. "The flowers are vicious little snobs," Carmen said, preparing to recite her lines: "He really is too ugly to be allowed to play anywhere we are." "He should drink poppy juice and go to sleep for a thousand years." "He is a perfect horror, and if he comes near me, I will sting him with my thorns." In Wilde's story the violets don't actually speak but reflect that the Dwarf's ugliness is ostentatious and he would have shown much better taste if he had just looked sad. Carmen said Wilde was right, ugliness does look like misery, and Grace said he wasn't saying that. And Mark said he was saying that the reason the Dwarf was despised was because his imperfections made him stand out, and given his lowly origins, he's supposed to be invisible.

It adds up, it doesn't add up. The flowers are snobs, and they're part of nature, but then so is the Dwarf, whom they disdain. Ugliness is kind, beauty is cruel, yet the Dwarf also succumbs to the beauty of the Infanta, because beauty is always beyond reproach, innocent. "Can beauty be innocent and cruel at the same time," Grace wondered aloud to Mark. "Maybe," Mark said, "beauty is as ambiguous as evil and ugliness and innocence." Grace told Mark that she had the feeling that getting old means that you're taken over and forced to forget your innocence. Mark couldn't believe that Grace thought of herself as innocent. She said she wasn't talking about sex, and what had that got to do with innocence anyway. To Grace, innocence meant the time before time counted, when days were long, when summer stretched ahead of you as a real long time and you could do nothing and that was all right. The time she went to summer camp and it seemed like forever. Innocence meant not seeing how ugly things were. Innocence meant that you think of yourself as doing the right thing, even if it looked wrong. Innocence meant you were never going to die and no one you loved would either. Innocence meant you'd never grow old because you could not really be touched. Maybe she meant damaged, she couldn't get damaged. You could still leave, turn away.

"Turn to me," the guy at the bar said. It was the guy who told Mark he was into pussy. He was back, holding racing gloves in one hand, a drink in another. He had all his fingers and he looked dangerous, like the evil hero in a grade B movie. Grace smiled to herself. More like a character actor than a star, and he thought she was smiling at him. Mark had said if she was so into her innocence, maybe she should play the Dwarf. She kept on smiling and talking drunkenly to the stranger. Mark watched them leave. Carmen said that real girls had it much too easy. He took her to a seedy hotel next to the Greyhound Bus Station, and it was all perfect as far as Grace was concerned, except that there was something about him that she couldn't put into words. He stayed here from time to time, he said, when he was in town. His leather jacket was worn, his black pants tight, his hands were large and rough, and he had books on the floor, the kind she wouldn't have expected. Like Nietzsche.

The room was small, with a single electric light bulb hanging from the ceiling, a draft shaking it every once and a while. He had some Jack in the Black in his bag, and they kept on drinking. He didn't seem to notice the place, and Grace supposed he'd seen worse. Maybe everything. When they made love his large hands moved her body around, positioning it finally on a diagonal across the bed. Her body fit into the old mattress as if into a mold. He hardly kissed her and kept repositioning her body into that same spot. Any excitement she had had fled and she went through the motions with him. Neon lights flashed on and off. The glare from crummy signs made it hard to sleep, and Grace woke, dressed fast, and left his room. He called himself Hunter, his last name, he said. She didn't wake him.

Grace repeated this story to Lisa, the singer who worked with the band every other week. "Sounds like a pervert," Lisa said. "A pervert," Mark exclaimed. "Did you ever see *The Naked Kiss*? 'He gave me the naked kiss, the kiss of a pervert.'" "Women are much sweeter," Lisa continued. "Then," Mark went on, "there's that line when he asks her to marry him and he says, 'Our life will be paradise because we are both abnormal.'" Grace ignored Mark as best she could to concentrate on Lisa and the idea of sex with women, at least trying it, and not being able to shake the feeling that being with Hunter was like being with a ghost. She didn't think he came either, not that it really mattered.

Time, actually the sundial, is taken aback by the Dwarf. But the birds like him because he used to feed them in the forest. The flowers think the birds are awful because well-bred people always stay in the same place, like themselves, they say. And the lizards are tolerant of him. Mark called them humanists. Mark wanted to make the scene in which the Dwarf remembers the forest as paradisaical as possible, given the restrictions of the bar, of course. The forest is his Eden, before his fall, his look into the mirror. That's everyone's fall, Grace thought. Grace and Mark couldn't remember the first time they'd looked into mirrors, and wondered what they'd thought. Little kids see themselves for the first time and somehow figure out that that creature is themselves. The Dwarf's long walk through the palace seeking the Infanta leads

him to find himself in the mirror. He finally realizes it's himself because he's carrying the rose she gave him after he had performed for her. But the Dwarf is too horrified by his image, just like the flowers. Was his image of himself perfect? Then he sees it's not true. Grace said she was reminded of when her mother thought she was old enough to be left alone at night and told her that now she was her own baby-sitter. "What's that got to do with this?" Mark asked. Grace said she didn't know, it just came to mind.

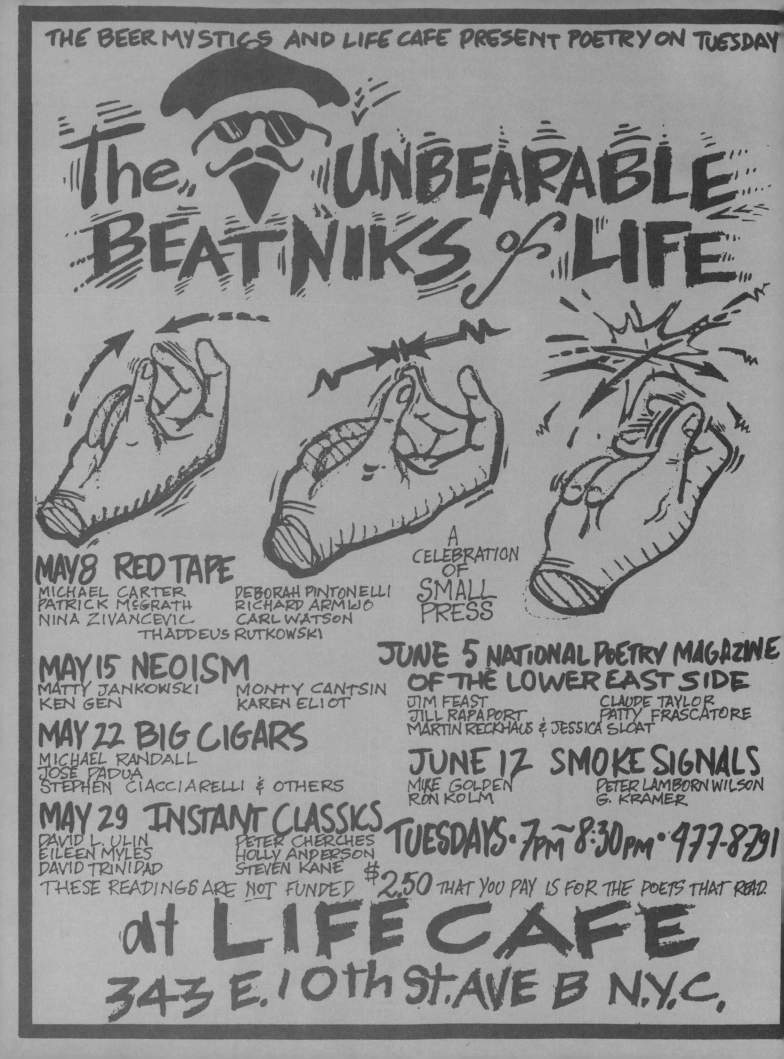

THE BEER MYSTICS AND LIFE CAFE PRESENT POETRY ON TUESDAY

The UNBEARABLE BEATNIKS of LIFE

A CELEBRATION OF SMALL PRESS

MAY 8 RED TAPE
MICHAEL CARTER   DEBORAH PINTONELLI
PATRICK McGRATH   RICHARD ARMIJO
NINA ZIVANCEVIC   CARL WATSON
        THADDEUS RUTKOWSKI

MAY 15 NEOISM
MATTY JANKOWSKI   MONTY CANTSIN
KEN GEN   KAREN ELIOT

MAY 22 BIG CIGARS
MICHAEL RANDALL
JOSE PADUA
STEPHEN CIACCIARELLI & OTHERS

MAY 29 INSTANT CLASSICS
DAVID L. ULIN   PETER CHERCHES
EILEEN MYLES   HOLLY ANDERSON
DAVID TRINIDAD   STEVEN KANE

JUNE 5 NATIONAL POETRY MAGAZINE OF THE LOWER EAST SIDE
JIM FEAST   CLAUDE TAYLOR
JILL RAPAPORT   PATTY FRASCATORE
MARTIN RECKHAUS & JESSICA SLOAT

JUNE 17 SMOKE SIGNALS
MIKE GOLDEN   PETER LAMBORN WILSON
RON KOLM   G. KRAMER

TUESDAYS • 7PM ~ 8:30 PM • 977-8791

THESE READINGS ARE NOT FUNDED $2.50 THAT YOU PAY IS FOR THE POETS THAT READ.

at LIFE CAFE
343 E. 10th St. AVE B N.Y.C.

THE REPLACEMENTS

SEPTEMBER 1987 $1

COVER

ARTS NEW YORK

GOING
APE OVER
GUERRILLA
GIRLS

INTERVIEWS
Barbara Kruger
Washington Squares
Lenny Kaye

NMS '87

COMPUTERS IN
THE ARTS

JUDD TULLY ON
HUNT SLONEM

72 PLAYS BY
KENNETH KOCH

Cover, Vol. 1 No. 7, September 1987, Cover (1987)

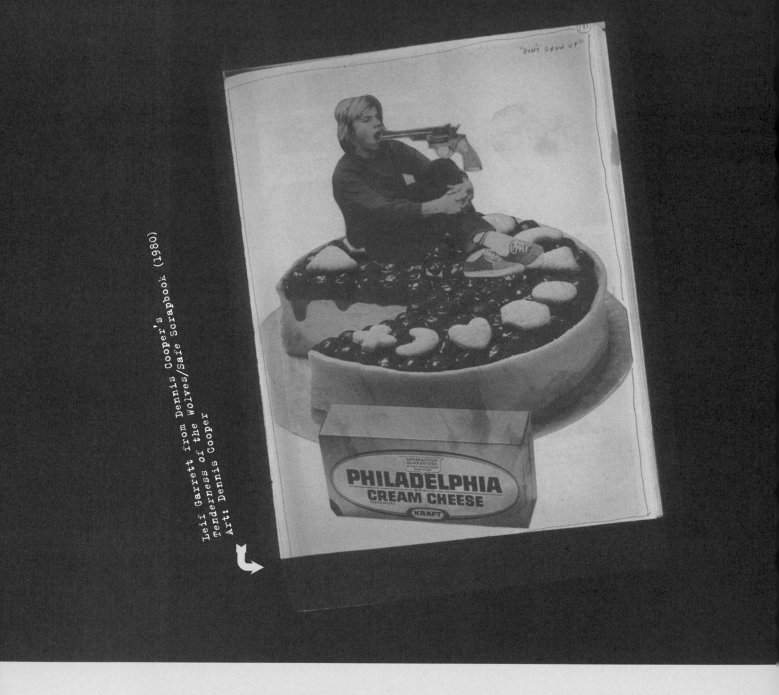

"DON'T GROW UP"

Leif Garrett from Dennis Cooper's
Tenderness of the Wolves/Safe Scrapbook (1980)
Art: Dennis Cooper

PHILADELPHIA
BRAND
CREAM CHEESE
PASTEURIZED
KRAFT

SATISFACTION
GUARANTEED
or your money back
from Kraft

GEORGE: WEDNESDAY, THURSDAY, FRIDAY (1987)

DENNIS COOPER

GEORGE STREAKED toward his room. "I'm home." He passed the kitchen door. His dad was drinking espresso. "George, wait . . ." He double-bolted his door. "I know it's here." He pawed through a desk drawer. At the bottom were two crinkled, typewritten pages.

They contained detailed descriptions, in French, of how he looked, smelled and tasted.

Philippe had presented them to him a few weeks ago, with the words, "This is you in a—how you say—nutshell." "He should know," George thought. "Now if I buy a French dictionary . . ."

"George?" He dropped the pages and kicked them under his bed. "Just a second." He let his dad in. "Son, I thought we might go for a drive to the ridge and look down at the pretty lights. How about it?" That was the last thing George wanted to do. "I'm busy." "I just thought . . ." "*Really*, dad."

Mr. Miles wandered back to the kitchen. George lifted his Mickey Mouse cap, grabbed a tab of the acid he'd stashed there, and slipped it under his tongue. He set The Cramps' "Garbage Man" fortyfive on his turntable . . . *Do you understand? / Do you understand?* . . . By its end he was seeing things.

There was a huge map of Disneyland over his bed. He liked to stare at it, picture his favorite Lands or imagine new areas stocked with rides. Acid helped. He closed his eyes and, in ten seconds flat, he was tiptoeing through an attraction.

Room after room after room of incredible holograms. Over his head, a Milky Way of skulls snapping like turtles. He was knee-deep in a lime-green fog, scattered through which were see-through ghosts, skimpy as kleenexes. A booming, vaguely familiar voice wafted out of the camouflaged speakers. "Georges?"

"Shit, what time is it?" He opened his eyes. For a couple of seconds the ride and his bedroom were double-exposed like a photograph. The Goofy clock on his night table read six-thirty-seven. "I'm late," he gasped, shooting up to his feet. "Bye, dad." He slammed the front door.

He stood on the sidewalk and stuck out his thumb. A trucker chose him. The guy seemed friendly enough, but he kept asking personal questions. "Do you have a girlfriend?" he leered at one point. "Look, I'm on acid, so leave me alone, all right?" That shut him up. George hallucinated in peace.

He knocked. Philippe let him in. "Georges, uh: my friend Tom is here and I thought . . ." "Phil, he's a spectacle." It was an older man. He sort of looked like a stork wearing glasses. "Thanks," George said quickly. "Uh, Tom," Philippe said, "Georges and I will be very alone for a minute."

"I thought a change would be good," he continued, once Tom left the room. George was pissed off, but the acid made anger seem corny to him at that moment. More than anything, he was amazed by Philippe's eyes. They were unusually warm, but he felt even less warmth than ever from them.

"Be prepared and I will see you back here." George walked to the bathroom, stripped. He stared at the mirror while all sorts of scattered thoughts raced through his mind. None stayed long enough to complete themselves. "Later," he said aloud, popping a zit on his upper back.

He lay face down on the living room rug. Philippe's friend said some nice things about him. One of the two guys caressed his ass, then used some fingers to open its hole so wide George felt cold air rush in. "Maybe," Tom said, to which Philippe answered, "Good."

How had Philippe put it? "Your asshole looks like a child's pout . . ." George couldn't remember the rest. "Shit, baby." That was Philippe's voice, so George pushed a couple of turds out. "What does he normally eat?" Tom asked. "Hamburgers, french fries, candy bars . . ." "I could have guessed," Tom mumbled.

Two fingers slid up his ass. Since he'd met Philippe, George had learned how to count them. Two more joined in. He hadn't taken that many before. "Not bad," he thought. Someone felt for his lips, pried them open and four fingers slid down his throat. "He's got a big mouth," Tom whispered. "I love that."

George gagged a few times. "Let it loose," Philippe said in a soothing voice. George didn't want to, then he was vomiting. When that ran out he noticed most of Tom's hand was inside his hole. The other was fiddling around in his throat like it had dropped something.

Someone was spanking him. Picturing how his ass looked usually helped him relax. He knew the thing was bright red, but he couldn't imagine an arm sticking out of it. Maybe it looked like an elephant. If that was so, Tom's continual praise made more sense. "Really," George thought, "that *would* be great."

"Oh, God, I . . . take this child . . . beyond the . . . shit!" Some of the words were Tom's, some Philippe's. Come splattered over his ass, back and legs. Then the hands withdrew. "Is there anything else you want to understand?" That was Philippe's voice. "No, got it." Tom.

George sat up. He couldn't see very well, but he picked out Tom's glasses. "Do you have any idea how soft you are inside?" Tom asked. George felt incredibly stoned. He managed to say, "I guess." Philippe laughed. "You must have been fisted before." That was Tom again. "No." George shook his head.

Once George had showered and dressed, Tom gave him a lift. All the way home Tom kept asking if he had enjoyed himself, then if he liked playing dead, then if he'd thought about killing himself. "I'm not sure. Maybe. Not really." "Just between us," he said, "if you decide to go all the way, call me. I'm in the book."

George lay in bed wondering what the guy meant by "all the way." Did that mean Tom would dissuade him, or did that imply he'd assist? George decided to jot down the guy's number, just in case. He tiptoed into the hall, scanned the phone book and crept back to safety.

He looked around at his room. There was the Disneyland map; there the poster of Pluto, his ears flying up in the air; there the Mickey and Minnie desk lamp; there the oval-shaped mirror with Donald Duck chasing his nephews around the frame. He struggled up, took the mirror from its nail.

He laid it out on the floor. He pulled his ass open, hoping to see what the men were so wild about. He could have guessed it'd resemble a

cave, but, with the swelling and stuff, it looked exactly like Injun Joe's Cave, his eighth or ninth favorite Disneyland ride at the moment.

He'd stumbled on it five years ago. Even though, once inside, it was a slight disappointment—too narrow and crowded—he still made a beeline for it at least once every visit and spent a while outside its painted mouth, squinting into the dark, covered with goose bumps.

He climbed into bed and was almost asleep when he thought of his diary. He hadn't written in it for weeks. Once he'd thought it would empty him out. But those writings were no help. They just kept his feelings from getting lost. "Still, why not?"

"**D**RUGS ARE finally getting to me. I'm going through things I guess I shouldn't because it seems fun, but it isn't. Does that make sense? I don't know anymore, and I don't really care. Life's sort of out of control, though I guess that's my own stupid fault.

"I think the last time I wrote Cliff and I were best friends. He changed a lot. We wave to each other at school, but that's it. I shouldn't have let him have sex with me. He told me we would be friends for eternity. He said a lot of things. All shit.

"This is so boring. I guess that's why I stopped writing. I'm fucked up. I don't know what to do. I don't even think I'm alive anymore. I'm walking around but I'm not really there. If I didn't have sex with Philippe I'd go nuts.

"School's nothing. I hate my friends. Nobody's interested in me anymore. They think I'm cute then they get really bored. If I don't sleep with people they hate me. But when I do they think they know me or something. I hope not.

"I don't know what I should call Philippe. He doesn't love me, I guess. It's weird he's not getting bored, but that's because he pretends I'm dead. I can't understand what that stuff's all about. But I don't mind. It doesn't matter.

"I've been trying to make myself great for a long time. I know I'm too closed around people, but when I talk, like with Cliff, it doesn't make any difference. I can still be amusing sometimes, except it's more like just weird lately.

"I keep saying I'll change and I want to. But all I do is get tense. That's okay for a while. Acid's great but I think stupid things while I'm on it. I still dream of living in Disneyland. I don't know how long I've been saying that.

"I guess I hope something fantastic is going to happen. I don't think it's up to me. I'll try but it's hard to say stuff like that without getting bored. Like right now I'm totally bored. I don't understand that."

GEORGE FELT like shit. The clock focused. Seven-twelve. He dressed and ran to the bus stop. His shirt was on inside out. "Shit." He climbed in and sat behind Jerry Cox. George liked to look at the back of his head. His hair was blond, wavy, thick. It made George think of a crystal ball. He planned the day ahead.

At school he hit the head, took some acid. He was hallucinating all morning. Algebra, Woodshop and History drifted past, like puffy clouds when he laid on his back. At noon he dumped his textbooks in his locker and filled up a tray in the lunch room. Paul was waiting for him at their usual table.

After a few minutes Sally and Max, her new boyfriend, joined in. Max told some racist jokes. Sally constructed a tower of Pepsi cans and dubbed it "George Miles Nude." They shared an angry look. Paul pointed out a drug dealer who sold "the best grass in the universe." George made a mental note.

George was taking his last bite of spice cake when Fred, a dumb jock, wandered by. The guy always made fun of him, so George ignored the creep. "Hey, fag," Fred said as he sauntered by, "I hear you're lousy in bed." George pretended he hadn't quite heard that.

"George, what . . ." "Forget it, Paul." Sally piped in: "What's this about? Something wrong, George?" He tried to play it cool. "No, nothing. It's just some bullshit a former best friend of mine's spreading around." Sally's face whitened. "Gee, I thought I was your former best friend." "Jesus," George thought.

Ten minutes later George saw liar David sit down at the next table. He leaned over and yelled, "I hear you're Cliff's latest fuck." David blushed, spilled some milk down his shirt. "Oh, hi. I didn't think you would mind. I admire you a lot." George scowled and left him in peace. "Anyway, Sally . . ."

The bell rang. George waved goodbye. He was heading for Chemistry class when he thought he heard, "Hey, Miles." Mr. McGough pinned his head in a vice grip, dragging him into an empty classroom. "Got any grass, addict?" "No, fucking let me go!" "Oh, such a tough kid," the teacher laughed.

George drew up his courage. "When are we going to hang out?" "Ahem," McGough grinned, "I like you, George. You know that. If I were gay . . ." But George knew he was gay. He'd propositioned Paul recently, then thrown a fit when it didn't work out. Next thing Paul knew, there was a giant red F on his book report.

There was no point in confronting McGough. He'd never drop his guard. "See ya," George said. "Fuck it," is what he meant. He was a few minutes late for class, but no problem. He poured the blue liquid in with the yellow stuff and brought the goo to a boil. Blub, blub, blub.

$CO_2 + NO$ = nitrogen oxide or some such shit. He'd never made sense of any of it. He watched the second hand spinning around and around and around. On his way to the bus, he took the rest of his acid. The trip home was better than usual. They almost hit an old man in a crosswalk.

He slammed the front door and stopped in the kitchen. "I want your ass here, now, this second!" It was his dad's voice. George strolled to the den, threw himself on the couch. Puff, their Siamese cat, got confused and leapt off. "What's this?" his dad bellowed, holding some paper up. It was Philippe's list.

George thought, "If I tell him the truth I'll have to sneak out from now on. But if say it's a joke he'll think I'm crazy and then what?" He had to say something. "Someone I slept with once gave that to me. I thought it was weird, but she wants to be a biology teacher."

"What's the girl's name?" "Forget it! I'm not going to tell you that. She's just a strange girl. Besides, it's been months. Let's drop it." "No, this is serious, George," his dad shouted, "I know a little French. I've never seen such filth!" Phlegm flew out of his mouth when he got to the *f*.

George saw his chance to escape. "How dare you spit on me!" He rose to his feet. His dad shoved him back on the couch. "I'm taking you to see someone," he said. "Maybe she can do something. I give up. Get your coat." George trotted into his room, swearing under his breath.

Drawers had been yanked out and dumped on the bed, posters ripped up, books thrown about. George was amazed by how flimsy his kingdom had been. One person brought the thing tumbling down. Then he remembered his diary. He shoved his arm under the mattress. It was there, locked tight. "Phew!"

GEORGE WAS surprised when their car stopped in front of a hospital. "I thought you meant a psychiatrist," he

moaned. His dad shook his head. "Just go in. She's in room thirty-nine, on the top floor. I'll be back in an hour." George entered the place thinking, "I'm not nearly stoned enough."

A nurse saw him traipsing around the halls. "You look like you're lost," she smiled. George admitted that he was. The address plate for room thirty-nine had apparently fallen off. She gave the door a push. "You're on your own." Inside, his mom was asleep. It looked permanent.

There was a video monitor near his head. A little light was drawing mountains across it. George watched for a while. It wasn't interesting. It was like one of those odd things that came on a tv screen after a station went off for the night. Was it trying to say something?

He listened to the mechanical whirr of the monitor. Once he thought he heard a scratchy voice say, "This is it." "Oh!" Some nurse, a new one, had walked in. "You must be this woman's son. Just a minute, I'll wake her up." Before George could say, "Don't," she'd rustled her way to the bed.

She squeezed his mom's shoulder. Her eyes flipped open. She glanced around. "Your child's here," the nurse chirped. She left. George and his mother looked blankly at each other. "Hi. Dad dropped me off." She didn't say anything, so George peeked at the monitor. It held the same boring image.

By the time he got back to her face she was opening and closing her mouth. Finally sounds came out. "George," she sighed, then, after several more jaw movements, "yes." This was what George had expected. She'd become scary. He wanted some acid.

She was trying to talk again. "Your father," she wheezed, "told me . . . something." Her face scrambled in an attempt to remember. George couldn't think how to distract her. He smiled, hoping she'd tell him how cute he was. Eventually she did, not in so many words, but her eyes said it. Or he assumed they had.

He glanced out the window. All he could see was the wall of another wing. One of its windows was open and, though the insides were dark, he heard a tv set. That's where that voice must have come from. He couldn't tell what was on, maybe news or a soap opera. Something too serious.

"Nice day," he said. His mom appeared to agree. "So, school's going fine. You know me, I try . . ." He talked about every uninteresting thing he could think of. She watched him. At least her eyes were pointed his way. They could have been saying, *"You're cute,* or, *It's a nice day,* or, *Go on."*

He looked at the monitor. Its puny mountains were gone. There was a light jetting over the screen, a straight line being started again and again. It made him think of John, pencil to paper, erasing, redrawing, until he had gotten George right. When that thought disappeared, he saw the light.

He'd seen that happen in movies. He knew what it meant. He stared at his mom for a while. Then he stood up, walked into the hall and stopped the first nurse he saw. "Mom's . . . shit . . . dead." She yelled to another nurse, who came running. "Where?" they asked, kind of angrily. "The room with no number," George said.

He sat on a low brick wall near the hospital entrance. He watched people go in and out. As they approached the door it sensed their presence and swung open. There were doors like that everywhere, but he'd never thought about them before. He stood and inched toward it. When he was five feet away it opened.

The car drove up. George climbed in. They'd already gone a few blocks when his dad asked,

"How is she?" George thought a second. "Dead." He was glad when his dad didn't say anything. They made a U-turn, parked, locked up and walked toward the entrance. When they were five feet away from the door it opened.

"WELL, IT'S over. She's dead. I don't know what I'm supposed to think. I just wish I wasn't there when it happened. Dad thinks it's my fault. He didn't say so, but I can tell. Shit, he's the one who upset her. He did it, not me. I was just there.

"I'm going to use this to make myself change, like a starting point. I think that's the best thing to do. I won't buy any more drugs. I'll try not to do what I always do. I never do anything other than school and Philippe.

"Tomorrow I'll clean up my room and make it look like a normal place. I think I'll burn all my Disneyland stuff so I can't change my mind. Nobody else was ever interested in the stuff anyway, and all my feelings for it are destroyed by the drugs now.

"I called Cliff tonight, just to talk. He doesn't care anymore. He kept saying how cute David was. I guess they're in love. He said that David is sort of obsessed or whatever with me. I don't know why, but it pisses him off. I hung up.

"It's strange I'm not sad about mom. I guess it took such a long time I felt everything I could feel already. I wish I hadn't been there, but I'm glad the last person she looked at was me. She really loved me once. Likewise, I guess.

"I think I'm afraid of stuff. Maybe that's it. I was afraid mom would die, but now she has and it's okay. I can't let it stop me from doing things. I'm going to keep that in mind from now on. I mean it.

"I'm not ready to sleep. I have one hit of acid left. I've decided to take it and go visit Tom, Philippe's friend. It's like a party or something to say my goodbye to the person I am. I'll let you know what happens. I'm off."

GEORGE SAT on a couch, sipping gin from a tumbler. Tom was building a fire in the fireplace. George was sufficiently high, but the way Tom was watching the flames made him jumpy. "So, whatcha been up to?" Tom jabbed a log with an iron bar. George tried again. "Nice place." He meant the paintings.

"A friend did them." Tom set down the bar. "My friend believes corpses dream," he said. "Try to imagine each work is the dream of a murdered child." George couldn't. "Poor baby. School hasn't done you a lick of good, has it?" George could relate to that. "Nope."

"But you don't need to know anything, do you? Your beauty is far more profound than the works of our fine intellectuals, don't you think?" "I don't know," George chortled nervously. "What a bizarre thing to say." Tom wandered over and kissed, or rather, sucked George's mouth as if it were a snakebite.

George laughed so hard he spilled his drink on his shirt. Tom ripped it open. "Hey," George said, "I need to wear this tomorrow." "Don't kid me," Tom snapped. "You know you won't need a shirt." George didn't know what that meant, but he was too stoned to fight. "Okay, I'm sorry. Go on. Really."

George's new jeans got the same treatment. Next thing he knew everything he'd had on was turning black in the fireplace. Tom dragged him onto the rug, did the vacuuming bit on his ass. George tried to shit, but he just hadn't eaten enough. "That's okay," Tom said, and wiped his mouth. "I get the idea."

"Wait here." Tom left the room. George stretched his legs. He'd begun to hallucinate slightly. He kept confusing the windows and paintings. "It's about time," he thought. Tom was a creep but now things wouldn't matter so much. He was about to go over and refill his tumbler when Tom came back.

"Lie on your stomach," he barked. George did. He heard a clinking noise, and felt a tiny sharp pain in his ass. "It's just some novocain," Tom muttered, "so I can take you apart, sans your pointless emotions." "That's considerate," George thought. Just then his ass grew so numb he felt sliced in half.

"Let's go." George, walking unsteadily, followed the man down a steep flight of stairs. Maybe it was the numbness but he couldn't see very well. There was something on one of the walls, a shelf? Things piled all over it? Tom took a piece of the blur in his hand. It looked fun. No, it looked kind of dangerous.

Tom raised the blur to the level of George's chest. "Do you know what's inside that cute body of yours?" George didn't have any idea, but he couldn't risk sounding naive. "I think I do." "Really?" Tom said. "You might be surprised. Would you like to know?" George shrugged. That seemed the safest response.

George was about to cry. He was right on the edge. He had to hand it to Tom. He couldn't remember the last time he'd been so upset. When Tom indicated the floor, George went flat. He heard a series of sounds. The only thing they remotely resembled was somebody chopping a tree down.

Tom didn't talk for a while. The sounds continued. George listened attentively. He realized he was being chopped down. He sort of wished he could know how it felt, but Tom was right. He'd be crying his eyes out and miss the good parts. It was enough to see his blood covering the floor like a magic rug.

The strange-sounding music stopped. George heard a soft voice. "Any last words?" it asked. George was surprised by the question. If he

Cuz Poets', Banquet, Photo of Richard Hell, (1988)
Dennis Cooper, Ishmael Houston-Jones   Photo: Chris Stein

was supposed to be dead, how could he talk? Still, why not? "Dead . . . men . . . tell . . . no . . . tales," he said in his best spooky voice.

When Tom didn't laugh George bit his lip. That's all it took. He burst into tears. He felt a couple of slashes across his back. "I said no fucking emotions!" Tom yelled. "Do you want me to kill you or not?" "No," George sobbed. "Well, then what are you doing here?" "I don't know," George blubbered, "I don't know."

He was rolled onto his back. Through his tears he saw Tom's glasses. "Get out of here!" They came flying off. "Now! Stand!" George struggled up to his feet. "I don't have anything to wear," he choked. Tom stormed out of the room, then came back with a blanket and threw it at George's head.

George made his way to the door. "No, this way," Tom said, forcing open a small window near the ceiling. "You'll drip all over my house!" George dragged himself through the dusty rectangle. A hand grabbed his ankle. "Don't tell anyone how this

happened," Tom hissed. "You're dead if you do."

George stumbled home, crumpling to the sidewalk occasionally. When headlights appeared in the distance he hid in the closest bush. The walk took hours. The blanket was no help at all. It got soaked with blood and grew very cold. He'd cry a while, then shiver, which made him cry again.

The house was dark. He climbed through his window. When he saw the ruins of his room it made him cry again. He found a note from his dad on the foot of the bed. *David called. Who's he?* "Good question," George thought, "and I've got a better one." He scrounged around in the rubble and found his mirror.

His ass wasn't really an ass anymore. He couldn't look at it. He dropped the mirror. It shattered. He walked down the hall and knocked twice on his dad's door. After a minute it opened. George looked in the man's puffy eyes. "Umm," he whispered, "I think you should call for an ambulance."

FEAR ON 11TH STREET AND AVENUE A, NEW YORK CITY (1987)

DENISE DUHAMEL

Now the papers are saying pesticides will kill us

rather than preservatives. I pass the school yard

where the Catholic girls snack. Cheeze Doodles and apples.

No parent today knows what to pack in a lunch box

and the plaid little uniforms

hold each girl in: lines in the weave cross

like directions, blurry decisions.

A supervising nun sinks in her wimple. All the things she can't do,

she thinks, to save them, her face growing smaller.

She dodges their basketball.

Who said the Catholic church has you for life

if it had you when you were five? I remember my prayers at odd times

and these girls already look afraid.

But it's not just the church. It's America.

I fear the children I know will become missing children,

that I will lose everyone I need to some hideous cancer.

I fear automobiles, all kinds of relationships.

I fear that the IRS will find out the deductions I claimed this year

I made up, that an agent will find a crumpled draft of this poem

even if fear edits this line out . . . I have no privacy,

no protection, yet I am anonymous. I sometimes think

the sidewalk will swallow me up. So I know when the girls

line up to go inside and one screams to her friend

"If you step on a crack, you'll break your mother's back . . ."

she means it. She feels all that responsibility, that guilt.

There's only one brown girl who doesn't do what she should.

She's dancing by herself to a song on her Walkman.

One of her red knee socks bunches at her ankle and slips into her sneaker.

And the shoulder strap of her jumper has unbuckled so her bib flaps.

Maybe she can save us. I clutch the school yard's chain link fence.

Please, little girl, grow up to be pope or president.

James Strahs and Peter Cherches, Book Party at La Mama La Galleria, Flyer (1987)

La Mama La Galleria PRESENTS

JAMES STRAHS
author of Queer + Alone (PAJ)

+

PETER CHERCHES
author of Between a Dream and a Cup of Coffee (Red Dust)

Reading / Book Party

FRIDAY, DECEMBER 11, 8PM

6 EAST FIRST STREET (Between Bowery & 2nd Ave.)

THE ANGEL (1987)

PATRICK McGRATH

YOU KNOW the Bowery, I presume? It was on the Bowery that I first caught a glimpse of Harry Talboys. I was a writer in those days, and I lived in a five-story walk-up by the men's shelter. I didn't realize at the time that Harry Talboys lived in the same building, though of course I was familiar with the powerful smell of incense that contaminated the lower floors. It was high summer when I met him, high summer in Manhattan, when liquid heat settles on the body of the city like an incubus, and one's whole activity devolves to a languid commerce of flesh and fluids, the ingestion and excretion of the one by the other, and all sane organisms quite simply estivate. I was certainly estivating; I rose late in the day, and after certain minimal ritualistic gestures of the writerly kind made my way to the liquor store. It was on one of these errands, on a garbage-strewn and urine-pungent sidewalk, beneath a blazing sun, and slimed in my own sweat, that I first encountered Harry Talboys.

He was making stately progress down the Bowery with a cane. Let me describe him: a tall, thin figure in a seersucker suit the grubbiness of which, the fraying cuffs, the cigarette burns and faded reddish wine stain on the crotch could not altogether disguise the quality of the fabric and the elegance of the cut. Very erect, very tall, very slow, on his head a Panama hat; and his face a veritable atlas of human experience, the nose a great hooked bone of a thing projecting like the prow of a ship, and the mouth—well, the mouth had foundered somewhat, but the old man animated it with lipstick! He must have been at least eighty. His shirt collar was not clean, and he wore a silk tie of some pastel shade—pale lilac or mauve, I seem to remember; and in his buttonhole

a fresh white lily. (I never saw Harry Talboys without a fresh flower in his buttonhole.) And as I say, he was making his way down the Bowery, and the men from the men's shelter drinking at the corner of Third Street greeted him warmly. "Hey, Harry!" they called; "Yo, Harry!" and he moved through them with all the graceful condescension of royalty, briefly lifting his Panama to reveal a liver-spotted skull devoid of all but a last few wisps of snow-white hair. Watching this performance I was much taken with the dignity of the old fellow, and with his lipstick. Was there, I asked myself, a story here?

OUR FRIENDSHIP began well: he asked me into his apartment for a drink. Such a hot day, he said, hanging up his Panama in the hallway and leaning his stick in the corner; productive activity, he said, was quite out of the question. His accent, to my surprise, was old Boston. (I'm from the North End myself.) The odor of incense was strong, and so was the perfume he wore. He was very liberally scented and smelled, in fact, like an old lady, but there was, I detected it even then, something unpleasant about it, a nuance, a suggestion of overripeness in the bouquet.

Are you familiar with the apartments of the Lower East Side? Designed essentially as holding tanks for wage laborers, they do not err on the side of expansiveness. We entered Harry's living room. Crowded bookshelves, a pair of deep seedy armchairs that faced windows with a clear prospect north to the Chrysler Building, and between the windows, on a rounded, slender-stemmed table of varnished black wood, a vase full of lilies. Directly above the lilies, and between the windows, hung a large crucifix, the body of the Saviour pinned to a cross of white ivory with nailheads of mother-of-pearl. Hanging from the ceiling in the far corner of the room, on a length of copper chain, was the censer whence the fumes emanated. No air conditioner, no fan. There was, however, ice in the kitchen, and Harry made us each a large gin-and-tonic. Then he lowered himself stiffly toward an armchair, the final stage of this operation being a sort of abandoned plunge followed by a long sigh. "Cigarettes," he murmured, rummaging through the pockets of his jacket.

"You have no cats," I said.

"Dreadful creatures," he said. "Can't abide them. Your very good health, Bernard Finnegan!"

We drank. He asked me about my writing. I began to explain, but he quickly lost interest. His gaze shifted to the window, to the glittering blade that the Chrysler Building becomes in the shimmering blue heat of certain summer days. His books impressed me. A good many classical authors—Petronius was represented, Apuleius and Lactantius, and certain of the early Christian writers, Bede and Augustine among others. When I rose to leave, he asked me for my telephone number. Would I, he wondered, have a drink with him again? Yes, I said, with pleasure.

"GIN?"

The censer was, as before, smoldering gently on its chain. It reminded me of my childhood, of chapels and churches in which I had fidgeted through innumerable interminable Masses. Harry's perfume, slightly rotten though it was, one grew accustomed to; not the incense. The stink of it was apparent as soon as one entered the building. I asked him why he burned it.

"Does it disturb you?" he said. He was slicing a lemon on the kitchen counter, very slowly. I was in the other room. The Chrysler Building was glowing

in the dusk, and there were red streaks to the west, over the Hudson.

"It makes me feel like a schoolboy."

He looked at me carefully then, those watery blue eyes of his fixing me like a pair of headlights. "Are you a Catholic?" he said.

"Lapsed."

"I too."

He sighed. He became preoccupied. He appeared to be pondering our common connection to the Roman faith. "When I was a young man," he said, when we were settled in our armchairs, "I called myself a Catholic but I lived like a pagan. Oh, I could drink in those days, Bernard! I could drink till dawn. Today, as you see, after one gin I become"—here he smiled with gentle irony—"desperately befuddled. But then! I was happy with my gods, like the ancients. Do you know what we thought the body was, Bernard, back in the Twenties? A temple in which there was nothing unclean. A shrine, to be adorned for the ritual of love! We lived for the moment, Bernard—the purpose of life was to express yourself, and if you were unhappy that was because you were maladjusted, and if you were maladjusted it was because you were repressed. We were excitable, you see, and if there was one thing we would not tolerate"—he turned toward me in his armchair—"it was boredom! Dullness! Anathema!" He gazed off into the night. There was a silence.

"Go on," I said.

"It didn't last. I remember coming back to New York in 1929 . . . My friends all seemed to be dead, or married, or alcoholic . . ." Another pause. "I don't suppose you know the *Rhapsody in Blue*? He hummed the opening bars, and there was suddenly a tone, in the thickening and aromatic dusk, of intense melancholy, rendered all the more poignant by the slow, faltering cadence of the old man's melody.

He said little more that evening, and when I rose to leave he was distant and abstracted. He did apologize, though, for being "such a wretched host."

THE SUMMER progressed. In a gin-blurred heat haze we slipped into August. I spent two or three hours a day at my table and told myself I was working. In fact I made several verbal sketches of Harry Talboys; to what use I would put them I had no clear idea at the time.

The thunderstorms began—brief showers of intense rain, with lightning and thunder, which did nothing to disturb the pall of stale heat that clung to the stinking city. They ended as suddenly as they began, and left the streets still steaming and fetid. It occurred to me that I should more actively prompt Harry to reminisce. I wondered if, between us, we might not produce a memoir of the Twenties? We would call it *An Old Man Remembers the Jazz Age*, or something of the sort; lavishly illustrated with photographs from the period, it would stand as an expressive personal document of modern America in the innocent exuberance of its golden youth. The more I thought about it, the surer I felt that such a book was needed. I mentioned the idea to Harry when next I saw him. "I knew an angel once," he murmured. "That was in the Twenties."

IT WAS, they said, the hottest summer in thirty years, and there was a distinct possibility that the garbage men would go on strike. A rather grisly murder occurred in an abandoned building over on Avenue C; the body was mutilated and drained of all its blood. The *New York Post* suggested that a vampire was on the loose. My own habits became increasingly nocturnal, and my productivity declined still further. I did manage to spend one afternoon in the public library looking at material from the Twenties, and made up a list of questions to put to Harry, questions which I hoped would release a rich flow of anecdotes. I felt like a prospector: if only, I thought, I could sink my probe with enough precision, up would gush the stuff to make us both some real money. The times were right, I became more certain than ever, for *An Old Man Remembers the Jazz Age*.

But Harry was harder to draw out than I'd anticipated. When next I broached the topic—it was a Friday evening, and the sunset was gorgeous—he spoke again of his angel. He was relaxed and affable, I remember, and I humored him. "You mean metaphorically he was an angel, Harry," I said. "You mean he was a very good man."

"Oh, no," said Harry, turning toward me. "No, he was not a good man at all!" The armchairs were, as usual, facing the windows, angled only slightly toward each other, so we sat as if piloting some great craft into the darkling sky. "But he was a real angel, absolutely authentic."

"Who was he, Harry?"

"His name," said Harry, "was Anson Havershaw." He sat forward and peered at me. "You do want to hear the story?" he said. "I should hate to bore you."

WHEN WAS it, precisely, that I began to take Harry's angel seriously? I suppose there was something in the tale that caught my imagination immediately. He described to me how, as a very young man, and fresh from Harvard, he had glimpsed across the floor of an elegant New York speakeasy a man who bore a striking resemblance to himself. "An uncanny physical likeness," said Harry. "Perfectly extraordinary." He had lost sight of the man, and spent an hour looking for him, without success. He returned to the speakeasy night after night; a week later he saw him again. He introduced himself. The other was Anson Havershaw, a wealthy and sophisticated young dandy, "a much more polished character than I," said Harry, "and he recognized the similarity between us at once; it amused him. He asked me to lunch with him the following day at the Biltmore, and said that we should become friends."

All light had faded from the sky by this point. There was a long pause. "Well, we did become friends," said Harry at last, "very good friends indeed. Oh, enough, Bernard!" He was sitting with one long leg crossed over the other, ankles sockless, his left hand clutching his right shoulder and his gaze fixed on the distant spire, which glittered in the darkness like a dagger. All the tension, all the vitality seemed suddenly to drain out of him. He sat there deflated and exhausted. The room was by this time full of shadows, and Harry was slumped in his armchair like a corpse. The exertion involved in his flight of memory seemed to have sharpened the foul smell that clung to him, for the perfume could no longer mask it at all. I moved quietly to the door. "Call me," I said, "when you want to continue." A hand flapped wearily from the arm of the chair. I left him there, alone in the shadows.

"IT WAS some weeks later, when we were on terms of intimacy," said Harry, when next we met, "that Anson first invited me to his house. The front door was opened by his valet, an Englishman called Allardice. He showed me into Anson's dressing room and left me there.

"I settled myself to wait. After a few minutes Anson entered in a silk dressing gown of Chinese design, followed by Allardice. He greeted me warmly and asked if Allardice could get me anything; then he told me to talk to him while he dressed—or rather, while Allardice dressed him."

A long pause here; Harry's fingers were kneading the arm of the chair. Then he began to speak quickly and warmly. "Anson stepped up to the glass and slipped the gown from his shoulders; he stood there quite naked, with one foot advanced and turned very slightly outwards, and his fingers caught lightly on his hips. How tall and slender, and hairless he was! And white, Bernard, white as milk!"

Harry at this point sat up quite erect in his armchair and lifted a hand to sketch Anson's figure in the air before him. "He had a neck like the stem of a flower," he said softly, "and narrow shoulders; and his chest was very flat, and very finely nippled, and merged imperceptibly into a belly punctuated by the merest suggestion of a navel. He stood before the glass and gazed at himself with all the impersonal admiration he might have expended on a piece of fine porcelain or a Ming vase, as though he knew he was quite beautiful, and suffered no impulse to humility on the point. . . ."

Harry turned to me and held out his glass. There were pearls of perspiration on his forehead, and his smell was very bad. I gave him more gin. "Then," he went on, "he had me come close and examine his body. There was a slight flap of skin midway between his hipbones, and believe me, Bernard, a flap is all it was; there was no knot to it. It was"—Harry groped for words—"vestigial! It was . . . decorative!"

Silence in that gloom-laden and incense-reeking room.

"I asked him what he was. 'I have not your nature; he said quite simply. 'I am of the angels.'"

Harry's gaze shifted back to the open window. "The dressing proceeded," he whispered, "and when Anson looked upon his final perfection, Allardice came forward with a flower for his buttonhole—an orchid, I think it was; and then at last the hush and reverence were banished. 'Come, Harry,' he cried, and together we glided down the stairs, with Allardice, close behind, intent upon the flurry of instructions Anson was giving him with regard to the evening. I was, I suppose, utterly mystified, and utterly intoxicated by this time, for I followed him; I followed him like a shadow. . . ."

Harry fell silent again. His hand was still lifted in the air, and trembling, as he stared out of the window. As for myself, I felt suddenly impatient of this talk. These, I said to myself, are nothing but the gin-fired fantasies of a maudlin old queen. I muttered some excuse and left; Harry barely noticed.

THERE COMES a day, in the ripe maturity of late summer, when you first detect a suggestion of the season to come; often as subtle as a play of evening light against familiar bricks, or the drift of a few brown leaves descending, it signals imminent release from savage heat and intemperate growth. You anticipate cool, misty days, and a slow, comely decadence in the order of the natural. Such a day now dawned; and my pale northern soul, in its pale northern breast, quietly exulted as the earth slowly turned its face from the sun. This quickening of the spirit was accompanied, in my relationship with Harry, by disillusion and withdrawal. Oddly enough, though, I spoke of his angel to no one; it was as though I'd tucked it into some dark grotto of my brain, there to hold it secret and inviolate.

The murder victim of Avenue C, ran the prevailing theory, was a double-crosser involved in a major drug deal. The nastiness was presumed to be a warning to others not to make the same mistake. The garbage men went out on strike for three days, but a settlement was reached before things really began to go bad, and the trucks were soon rolling

again—stinking ripely and clouded with insects, noxious monsters trumpeting and wheezing through the midnight streets. The one that serviced my block was called *The Pioneer*, and on the side of it was painted a covered wagon rumbling across some western prairie. When I found myself downwind of *The Pioneer*, I thought, unkindly, of Harry.

It was at around this time that I began to toy with the notion of a historical novel about heretics. I'd chanced upon a gnostic tale in which Satan, a great god, creates a human body and persuades a spirit called Arbal-Jesus to project his being into it for a few moments. Arbal-Jesus complies with Satan's seemingly innocent request, but once inside the body he finds himself trapped, and cannot escape. He screams in agony, but Satan only laughs; and then mocks his captive by sexually violating him. Arbal-Jesus' only consolation is that another spirit accompanies him in the body, and guarantees his release. That spirit is Death.

But then the brief taste of fall vanished, and the heat returned with greater ferocity than ever. On my way out one morning I met Harry. "Bernard," he said, "why do I never see you now?" I felt guilty. He looked rather more seedy than usual; his jaw was stubbled with fine white hairs, and traces of dried blood adhered to his nostrils. His bony fingers clutched my arm. "Come down this evening," he said. "I have gin." Poor old man, I thought, lonely and shabby, scraping about in two rooms after all these years . . . why does he still cling to the raft?

I knocked on Harry's door around seven. All was as usual—the smells, the gin, the Chrysler Building rising like a jeweled spearhead against the sky, and upon Harry's wall the crucifix shining in the shadows of the fading day. Poor old Harry; I sensed immediately he wanted to continue with his story, but was holding back out of deference to me. I felt compelled to reopen the subject, though not simply out of courtesy to an old man's obsession. I had been thinking some more about this shadowy figure, the beautiful, decadent Anson Havershaw, he of the milk-white flesh and the nonexistent navel, and about Harry's cryptic but no doubt carnal relationship with him. It was, I felt, a most bizarre fiction he had begun to weave about a man who, I presumed, had in fact actually existed, and indeed might still be alive.

So Harry began to talk. He described how Anson swept him into a summer of hectic and dazzling pleasures, of long nights, riotous and frenzied, when all of America seemed to be convulsed in a spasm of fevered gaiety, and the two of them had moved through the revels like a pair of gods, languid, elegant, twin souls presiding with heavy-lidded eyes over the nation's binge. That summer, the summer of 1925, Harry often found himself leaving Anson's house in the first light of dawn, still in evening clothes, and slipping into the welcome gloom of St. Ignatius Loyola on Park Avenue. "You wouldn't know it, Bernard," he said; "they tore it down in 1947. A lovely church, Gothic Revival; I miss it . . . at the early Mass it would be lit only by the dim, blood-red glow from the stained-glass windows, and by a pair of white candles that rose from gilded holders on either side of the altar and threw out a gorgeous, shimmering halo. . . . The priest I knew well, an ascetic young Jesuit; I remember how his pale face caught the candlelight as he turned to the congregation—the whole effect was so strangely beautiful, Bernard, if you had seen it you would understand the attraction Catholicism held for so many of us . . . it was the emotional appeal, really; disciplined Christianity we found more difficult to embrace. . . ."

Harry rambled on in this vein for some minutes, his eyes on the spire and his fingers curled about his glass. My own thoughts drifted off down parallel tracks, lulled comfortably by his voice. As a raconteur Harry was slow and fastidious; he composed his sentences with scrupulous care and lingered indulgently over his more graceful phrases. "I doubt I would have done well in business," he was saying, inconsequentially; "I just haven't the kidney for it. One needs strong nerves, and I was always much too effete. Anson used to say that the world was a brothel, and he was right, of course. So where is one to turn? I can tell you where I turned: straight into the arms of Mother Church!" He swallowed the rest of his gin. "But that's another story, and forgive me, Bernard, I seem to be digressing again. All this happened so very long ago, you see, that I tend to confuse the order in which things occurred. . . .

"There are two questions, Bernard, that have to be addressed to an angel. One concerns his origins; the other, his purpose."

AT THESE words I began to pay active attention once more. This angel business was, of course, nonsense; but I had come to suspect that something rather fantastic, or even perverse, might lie behind it.

"About his origins I could learn almost nothing," Harry continued. "People said he arrived in New York during the last year of the first war; he had apparently been raised in Ireland by his mother, who was from Boston and had married into an obscure branch of the Havershaws of Cork, an eccentric family, so they said; but then, you see, well-born Europeans with cloudy origins have always been drifting into New York, and so long as their manners and their money are adequate—particularly the latter—they're admitted to society and no one's very bothered about where they've come from. We are, after all, a republic."

Boston! At the mention of Boston an idea suddenly

occurred to me. Harry was old Boston, this I knew, and I wondered whether this angel of his might be nothing more than an elaborate sexual disguise. Anson Havershaw, by this theory, was simply an alter ego, a detached figment of Harry's neurotic imagination, a double or other constructed as a sort of libidinal escape valve. In other words, Harry transcended his own guilty carnality by assuming at one remove the identity of an angel—this would explain the physical resemblance between the two, and the contradictory themes of hedonism and spirituality; what Catholic, after all, lapsed or otherwise, could ever believe the body was a temple in which nothing was unclean? I watched Harry smiling to himself, and his expression, in the twilight, and despite the patrician dignity of the nose, seemed suddenly silly, pathetic.

"And his purpose?" I said drily.

"Ah." The pleasure slowly ebbed from his face, and he began to make an unpleasant sucking noise with his dentures. "Who knows?" he said at last. "Who knows what an angel would be doing in a century like this one? Maybe he was just meant to be an angel for our times." There was a long pause. "Immortal spirit burned in him, you see. . . . Sin meant nothing to him; he was pure soul. This was his tragedy."

"His tragedy?"

Harry nodded. "To be pure soul in an age that would not believe its existence." He asked me to give him more gin. I was feeling very irritable as I poured his gin.

WE SAT there, Harry and I, in silence, he no doubt contemplating these spurious memories of his, while I wondered how soon I could decently escape. Harry had taken from his pocket a small jade compact and was powdering his face with rapid, jerky movements, his eyes averted from me so I had only the beaky profile. "Pure soul," he

repeated, in a murmur, "in an age that would not believe its existence."

"What happened to him?" I said wearily.

"Oh," he replied, snapping shut the compact, "I lost sight of him. I believe he came to a bad end; I believe he was sent to prison."

"No he wasn't."

Harry looked at me sharply. There was, for the first time in our relationship, a genuinely honest contact between us. All the rest had been indulgence on his part and acquiescence on mine. "Am I so transparent?" he said. "I suppose I must be. Dear Bernard, you're angry with me."

I rose to my feet and moved to the window and stared into the night. "I don't think Anson Havershaw ever existed," I said. "There was instead a man consumed with guilt who created a fairy story about angels and spirits in order to conceal certain truths from himself." Why, I thought, do old drunks always choose me to tell their stories to?

"I haven't told you the complete truth," said Harry.

"There was no Anson Havershaw," I said.

"Oh there was, there was. There is," said Harry. A pause. Then: "There was no Harry Talboys."

I turned. This I was not prepared for.

"I am Anson Havershaw."

I laughed.

He nodded. "I shall show you," he said, and rising to his feet, he began laboriously to remove his jacket, and then to unbutton his shirt.

IN THE middle of Harry's ceiling was a fixture into which three light bulbs were screwed. A short length of chain hung from it; Harry pulled the chain, and the room was flooded with a harsh raw light. Beneath his shirt, it now became apparent, he wore a garment of some sort of off-white surgical plastic.

Slowly he removed his shirt. The plastic, which was quite grubby, encased him like a sleeveless tunic from his upper chest to a line somewhere below the belt of his trousers. It was fastened down the side by a series of little buckles, and a very narrow fringe of dirty gauze peeped from the upper edge, where the skin was rubbed to an angry rash. Harry's arms were the arms of a very old man, the flesh hanging from the bone in loose white withered flaps. He smiled slightly, for I suppose I must have been gazing with horrified curiosity at this bizarre corset of his. I was standing close to the incense, and as Harry fumbled with the buckles I brought the censer up under my nose; for the smell rapidly became very bad indeed. He dropped his trousers and underpants. The corset extended to his lower belly, forming a line just above a hairless pubis and a tiny, uncircumcised penis all puckered up and wrinkled in upon itself. He loosed the final straps; holding the corset to his body with his fingers, he told me gently that I must not be shocked. And then he revealed himself to me.

There was, first of all, the smell; a wave of unspeakable foulness was released with the removal of the corset, and to defend my senses I was forced to clamp my nostrils and inhale the incense with my mouth. Harry's flesh had rotted off his lower ribs and belly, and the clotted skin still clinging to the ribs and hipbones that bordered the hole was in a state of gelatinous putrescence. In the hole I caught the faint gleam of his spine, and amid an indistinct bundle of piping the forms of shadowy organs. I saw sutures on his intestines, and the marks of neat stitching, and a cluster of discolored organic vessels bound with a thin strip of translucent plastic. He should have been dead, and I suppose I must have whispered as much, for I heard him say that he could not die. How long I stood there gazing into his decaying torso I do not know; at some point I seemed to become detached from my own body and saw as if from high up and far away the two figures standing in the room, the flowers and the crucifix between them, myself clutching the censer and Harry standing with his opened body and his trousers at his ankles. It took long enough, I suppose, for the full horror of his condition to be borne home to me. This is what it means to be an angel, I remember thinking, in our times at least: eternal life burned in him while his body, his temple, crumbled about the flame. Out there in the hot night the city trembled with a febrile life of its own, and somewhere a siren leaped into sudden desolate pain. All I saw then was a young man standing in the corner of a shabby room watching an old man pull up his trousers.

AS I write this it is late January, and very cold outside. Snow lies heaped in filthy piles along the edge of the sidewalk, and the Chrysler Building is a bleak gray needle against a thickening winter afternoon sky. The men from the men's shelter huddle in the doorways in the Bowery, selling cigarettes from off the tops of plastic milk crates, and the smell of incense still pervades the lower floors of the building. I can't help thinking of him as Harry—it seems somehow to suit him better. He asked me to write an account of our friendship, I wouldn't otherwise have done it; writing seems futile now. Everything seems futile, for some reason I don't fully understand, and I keep wondering why any of us cling to the raft. The one consolation I can find is the presence of that other spirit traveling with us in the body—a consolation denied my rotting friend downstairs, whoever, whatever, he is.

NEIGHBOR (1987)
THURSTON MOORE

the fellowship of the buried lives

walks by the window of the

laundromat on 13th + A

i'm hanging out with old puerto

rican women sitting on the

bench staring at the spinning

wash like staring at tv

eating a candy bar, drinking coffee, smoking cigs.

a tall freak fantastic is pulling out frayed black frill

from the drier

what can/did/do i do—19, new in town

so . . .

i don't do nothing

please,

don't ever leaf me

BOMB

New Art, Writing, Theatre and Film

DIANE MICHALS
CHRISTOPHER DURANG
STEVE ERICKSON
MONA SIMPSON

Summer 1987 $5.00

"THE RED HIGH HEELS" FROM *LOVE ME TENDER* (1987)
CATHERINE TEXIER

HOT SUMMER night. Nipples erect, hard, hard, under palms, then fingertips working, intense. Moist down there where. . . . The ass is taut, small and round, pushed out, thighs opened, buttocks spread out. Her breasts swell. He is a tongue. He is saliva, movement, spiraling inside her mouth tasting of sex. The tips of their tongues meet, two magnets. Two insects throwing their antennae forward in a deadly seduction dance. The tips of their tongues. They move together like fingers pressed against a mirror.

They've met at a costume party in Williamsburg, Brooklyn, where somebody dressed as a spider kept extending six black arms and legs—their long shadows played against the white brick wall like *ombres chinoises*. He had carrot hair, cropped short, and a mouth like a ripe plum. He was not in costume. He was grave, with an ironical flutter in his eyes. She, on the other hand, was in costume. An eighteenth-century French marquise with her breasts propped up, having a hard time competing with the boys sporting fake breasts in outrageous *décolletés*.

Put on your red high heels, your silk bra, your garters and your smoke stockings, Julian whispers. Get dressed for me.

Jet-black in the room. Three o'clock in the morning in a Lower East Side tenement with Puerto Rican voices yelling mothafucka followed by a cascade of broken glass, and vanishing

women's laughter mixed with the lingering smell of a long-dead barbecue fire.

Go ahead. Slut!

Lulu turns around slowly. Poses on one hip. Now he can vaguely make out her short blond hair pushed back to one side. Her face, white as a moon. A pink neon heart hanging from the fire escape throbs through the shades, on one of her legs.

What?

Even for fun, even for sex, she won't let him call her that.

He laughs softly.

Slut. Go get dressed for me.

WALKING ACROSS the Williamsburg Bridge on a moonless night, blinded by the lights lacing downtown Manhattan. His hips moved like a dancer's, like a street boy's. His hand fumbled on the layers of taffeta and satin to grab her ass.

I'd like to fuck you right here.

She got wet in the crotch.

The wide skirts made it easy. She was not wearing underpants. When they were finished he pissed over the railing down toward the dark river on which the lights were running an oily dance.

We have to do it again, he said. And in a whisper: I will make you come next time.

That did it for her. First time a man even noticed. She was not going to let this one slip away easily.

I SAW you with him! yells the man in the street.

Saw what! You were drunk. A drunken son-of-a-bitch! I told you. *Hijo de puta.*

Liar! You fucking liar.

Maricón!

HE TURNS on the fan. His cock limp from the interruption. She shuffles through her clothes in the dark. Close to the window, he lifts up the shade. Even on tiptoes he can't see the sidewalk on their side of the street because of the fire escape. He hears someone running.

She walks back from the bathroom. Strong, confident steps of sexy high heels clapping on the bare wood floor.

I can't even see you. She laughs a throaty laugh. No, don't turn on the light.

In the dark she is on him, her hands on his shoulders, down his smooth chest, the cold, cool leather of her shoes against his thighs. He pulls a breast slowly out of the bra, feels the bulge, reaches for the nipple with his lips.

She moans. He moves his mouth down, down the loose silk of her pants, loose enough to provide a space in which he inserts a tongue, probes with a finger. In Luang Prabang, Laos, he had fucked a prostitute with red high heels which made her swing, a tight miniskirt, and a length of black lace stockings in between.

She had laughed and giggled when he had gone down on her.

MOTHAFUCKA! GODDAM mothafucka!

THEN THERE was this picture from the Vietnam war he had recently seen in a pulp magazine. Vietnamese girls making it with American soldiers. All crew cut, clean-cut—as much as you could make out from the picture, because one couldn't really see their faces—their cocks erect, three or four of them in one room, the girls naked, straddling them, breasts high and full. The girls laughing together, patiently waiting to be finished off, making themselves comfortable on the mouths sucking them.

She moans. Legs spread out. Moving her ass up and down.

I love it.

YOU'RE A fucking junkie! screams the woman. Where is the money? Did you give him the money?

***

SWEET BUTTOCKS clad in silk. Ass all over his mouth. He bites. He licks. The fabric is an instant stimulant/irritant. Her breasts hang heavy in his hands. His hands maddeningly light, soft, refusing to squeeze, to tear apart.

Oh boy!

Wiggling her breasts, wiggling her ass. His cock, hard, looking for flesh, anything, to bury itself. He slaps her. His nails bite into her back.

Ouch!

Outside a flurry of words in Spanish erupts, rousing screams from the street.

Have you ever been whipped?

Jesus Christ!

Have you?

Ouch! Stop it! You're hurting me!

I want to tie you up and give it to you real good.

Are you crazy? Let me go!

FUCKING BASTARD!

And then. . . . Was it a gun? Usually it's a busted muffler. Or a firecracker.

HE HAS freckles on his hands. Just a few. Very light. She noticed them the second time. His skin is pale and creamy, even on his chest. His touch causes her flesh to tremble, lines of sweat to ooze where his fingers have been.

He appears in the middle of the night, slim figure on the doorstep, and vanishes at dawn. Sometimes for days. Weeks once.

His hands—you can't see the freckles in the dark, he doesn't like to have the light on when they make love at her place, other than the neon heart throbbing across the floor—his hands slam down hard on her backside.

You little. . . .

He's got her tight between his knees. His nails run quick lines of pain down her shoulder blades.

Stop it! This isn't funny!

Don't you love it?

The sneer he has sometimes. His lips curling up on very white, narrow teeth.

IT'S A gun. A gun has gone off. A scream. Intense. Isolated. People running, somebody tripping on a garbage can. The shrill of a woman's voice.

Let go of me. Didn't you hear?

What?

The nails stop digging. But he keeps a tight grip on her arms.

Wasn't it a gun?

A gun? You're crazy!

Didn't you hear?

Yeah. Must've been a firecracker.

No. Let me go.

Dead silence in the street. They get up, stand by the window, lift up the shade a tiny bit.

A small crowd has gathered. A body lying across the sidewalk has been half-covered with a shirt. Blood trickles down into the gutter. An ambulance howls down the block. Eight police cars block the corner, their lights throwing angry flashes of red on nearby buildings.

Is it . . . the man?

What man?

You know . . . the couple fighting. . . .

Who knows, he says, a hand cupping a breast, free over the thin bra strap, pulling her toward the rumpled sheets.

Fucking junkies!

"MONEY" FROM *KILL THE POOR* (1988)

JOEL ROSE

Money makes the world go round!
The world go round!
The world go round!
Money makes the world go round
with such a happy sound!
Money, money, money, money . . .

GET THIS! This is gonna make your hair stand on end: Every day of Annabelle's life, since day one, she has a picture taken of herself. Including today, a Polaroid, before we come over here to see this apartment on Avenue E. Eleven thousand, three hundred and sixty-eight, so far, all laid out in front of her. "Look, Zho, this day one thousand eighty-two. I am thirteen days short of *trois ans*."

"Gorgeous," I say.

This was all her mother's idea to begin with. Third kid, but the first born alive; two stillborn in the maquis during the war. Then it was a long time coming, the conception of delicate Annabelle. Now to make sure, record every day of her precious daughter's life from the day Annabelle hotfoots it out of the womb up there in Normandy. Every change, every nuance. Annabelle says it just struck the old lady, came to her out of a dream or hallucination, camera ready:

Annabelle? Annabelle? Look at me, sweet thing. There, there, Pittou. Say *fromage*. . . .

LET ME tell you how we can afford to buy a place on the Lower East Side, no matter how cheap:

We got some money from an incident that went down at the Gotham, where Annabelle worked as an exotic dancer.

"Say what, Zho?"

Ahem . . . Bite my tongue. Rather, *Annabelle* got some money from an incident that occurred at the Gotham dime-a-dance strip joint where she worked just to pay the rent. She didn't really like it.

Stay with me here. There's a certain mentality today—moneywise. Do you agree or what? Every fat fuck on the make. Not that Annabelle didn't deserve the money Leonardo wound up paying her. Not to mention, otherwise, we'd still be living over all those blind people, hearing the squeal of brakes, those horrific screams. . . .

Right after I was born my old man used to sell his papers off a standpipe sticking out of a building on Seventh Avenue and Forty-seventh Street. Right outside the hottest strip joint in New York City. That's how I remember it when I was a kid. Me and my sister. My father in earmuffs, his nose red.

One night, nothing personal, Leonardo, the Gotham floor manager, who has the same basic shape and size as a mirror armoire, cut Annabelle's face with a bottle opener. He claimed he lost control.

Didn't know what it was about, didn't know why he did it. High on something. Smoking crack. Cut her one hell of a slice right across the cheek, hooked her lip and tore it pretty good. When I go inside people are backed up, looking. I push some away, step in front of him. Blood running down her face, but no tears. I tell him, "Leonardo, put it down, bro," and he laughs at me, and says, "Listen, you little Jew! . . ."

Later he apologizes, repeats that he didn't know what came over him, this mindless violence. He smiles, pays her thirty thousand bucks to keep her mouth shut, no cops, no authorities, keep his business open, keep his liquor license. He arranges to have the cut stitched up by a customer he claims is an "A number one" Park Avenue plastic surgeon. Later, I swear, I see the guy advertising on tv, looking at me through the void, the voidoid, "A number one," saying that you too can be all you ever dreamed and more, me thinking, looking back at him, watching him at his table, drooling over the girls, the spittle running down his chin, pulling his six-dollar Beck's that much closer across the table, my folks calling me in the bedroom, six months after my sister died, saying, Jo-Jo, we been talking, you seem depressed, would you like a nose job, the guy looking at me out of the screen, his eyes saying, we can do a number on you too, sir, me thinking, man, you can kiss my skinny white ass. . . .

Annabelle looks at me, blank, no comprehension, and asks me what kind of doctor advertises on television. "I'm not an American. I never heard of such a thing. In France doctors don't advertise. . . ."

I say that's exactly the point.

Fucking Leonardo. She fingers the scar, says she'll hold a grudge till the day she dies, longer.

She'll get him back, no matter when it is. This man, the size of a deep freeze, with a heart like a pint of Haagen-Dazs deep in its cavity.

So, listen, I'm telling her, my gal, all is not lost, you got me out of this deal, right, your Zho-Zho, your baa-by, your American, girl, remember me? I run to your aid when you're in danger, my own physical welfare be damned, not to mention the long green that comes to bear, the thirty thousand to the better we're going to make work for us.

In the end, I got the dame to boot, so who says justice is not mine? Me, just a regular guy, the star of no novel or motion picture, I got her, a sexy beautiful girl, French like I say, *mon mec*. That's America, right? Land of opportunity.

Annabelle laughs, unimpressed. "Zho, you sick."

I ask myself, has anyone ever said my name better?

Yesterday I showed her this story I tore out of the paper and brought home from work, some woman in Harlem wins sixty-five million bucks because a hospital refused to treat her after she ate—get this—a bad chicken wing and got food poisoning. Then we saw her on the six o'clock news. Crying, says she lost her husband because of what had happened, her health was a mess, some kind of terrible infection spread to her spine. Her life was over, she said, but now the hospital was gonna pay, she'd teach those people a lesson! Annabelle says, "What lesson?" Nothing's gonna change. Those people don't care. They won't remember. They see another poor black woman come in, they gonna run to her, grovel, say, "Yes, ma'am, what can we do for you today?" Or even provide decent health care?

Annabelle shakes her head. No way. She says this country is fucked! Racially, classically, economically, politically. Fucked.

We're sitting on the stoop outside the building on Avenue E.

I wouldn't mind having sixty-five million dollars. Even half that, sis.

"What are these people asking for the apartment?" I ask her.

"I don't know."

"Well, we'll talk 'em down, no matter what. . . ."

"Let's see it first, okay, Zho?"

Sure, sure, okay, understood.

"Don't fuck it up."

She looks at me. How?—beseechingly. The neighborhood makes her nervous, scares her to death. Rightfully so. The pushers barking, C & D, coke and dope, coke and dope. The addicts is about. Shifty, skinny, gaunt, cruising the street in their low-riding Chevys, slouch hats down over their eyes, lining up for the buy.

Behind us the door opens.

BUILDING, I'D say, built somewhere between 1870 and 1890. Old-law tenement, which only means it's got a little airshaft in the center for ventilation. Soiled badly on the outside, facade crumbling, cornice falling down, look up, jagged edge of torn tin, a sword dangling over our heads, but hey, dude, I'm willing to be open-minded. That's cool! Live dangerously. Annabelle swears the lady on the phone said wait'll you see the apartment, you won't believe it, so don't prejudge.

The block I know. Did I tell you my family's from this block? The same block I sit right now stoopwise, my grandmother came to in 1903 when she arrived in America from Hungary. The block my mother was born on. Always a good block. "A good block, Joe." I remember it from when I was a kid, when we came to the temple, came to the doctor, came to the nurse, came to see the lady with the alligator purse. To visit my mama's friend, still there, ensconced, long after my mama and her family got out. And now I see the little skinny soldiers of chaos and anarchy creeping about in those low riders and beat autos, you see them in the street, they look you right in the eye, sitting on the stoop, and their gaze is cold, b, their gaze is fucking freezing.

I follow a white broad inside, says her name is Betty, just call her Beneficia. Got a gut on her. She looking at me like I'm from a different planet, but I'm not, I'm from the Earth. Just like you. It's only my eyes, they're from Mars.

"Are you all right?"

"Sure, sure."

"He's always like that," Annabelle says pleasantly, and they go inside, chatting like they've known each other for the last hundred and fifty years.

Down the hall I trail, little boy lost, see the building crying, crying, save me, save me, Joe, ragged around the edges, but coming back, no question. Annabelle looks back down the long hallway at me, her eyes asking what do I want, please behave.

Hey, this ragged-ass building don't bother me. I'm used to it. I've lived in worse than this. The world's ragged around the edges and I don't condemn it for decrepitude. I notice the stairwell is marble, still square. Run this by you real quick, carpenter lingo: *The stairs is plumb.* See? None of them is at an angle or falling down. None of the kickers gone. They's all there, no treads missing, though worn smooth, concave like a bowl, a million feet having trudged up and down these stairs, hiking to some promised land, high in the heavens. Probably five hundred thousand of those feet belong to junkies, prodding and jabbing needles, even between their toes, taking that long hike, all within the last ten or fifteen years. And I see all the old plaster is knocked off the walls, and the bricks is clean and the glass is all neat and trim in the hall windows, not a shard showing, nothing knocked out or busted. No graffiti. No filth. Surprising for this neighborhood. Pretty nice deal. People do a job like this, people like this Betty, this big white Betty, this Beneficia, they should be proud of themselves, the shit holes I've seen down in this neighborhood. Woman deserves a medal!

Somewhere up above, she's into her rap. "What you see is the sweat of collective labor," she says. "What you're buying into here, why it's so cheap, is the sweat of our collective brow, all the brows who live here. A decent place to live. We've done it all ourselves," she crows proudly. "Bought this building, and the one next door, from the landlord three years ago for two thousand dollars, some back oil bills, and fourteen thousand in scofflawed parking tickets. Since then we're putting it back together ourselves. Independent of all bureaucracy, all city agencies. No contractors, no city inspectors, no codes, no intervention. Only hard work, just build our houses, just build our homes." She's finished. Nothing to do but follow her on up, me huffing

and puffing, look up her skirt, see yards of cotton billowing, her white underwear covering her big butt. Beneficia climbing the stairs like a mountain goat.

I take a break, Annabelle and Beneficia going ahead. Directly below me, on the first floor a door opens. I see an eyeball in the crack. It opens no further, just an inch, the eyeball peering up at me. I peer back.

"Hey, how far up?" I call to Beneficia.

"Four floors."

I sing to myself, "I'm a lone cowhand, on the Rio Grande . . ."

My shape ain't so good, standing around at the job all day. La grande madame and la petite mademoiselle leave me far below in their wake. Huff, huff and climb. Huff, huff and climb. "Hey, up dere!"

"Door's open," big bad Betty calls down. "Just come on up when you're ready. Take your time."

I hear Annabelle say, "Oh, eet's beautiful," the accent grating on me. *Oh, eet's beautiful.* Huff, huff, doo-wop, catch my breath, sit down, light a cigarette. Below me, the guy who was peeking out his door steps out into the hall. He cranes his neck and looks up into the stairwell.

Hey, here I am! Hey you, monkey-face! What do you want? Mind your own business! Pleasant guy—I y'am, I y'am. But I don't say this. What you think I am? One got to know how to live in the big city, though you shouldn't believe everything you read. Things are changing in this country. Used to be, you know, you could trust everybody, everybody's normal, everybody's like us, you and me, your neighbor and your pal. Nowadays who's gonna argue about convention, it's all up for debate, ain't that right? This guy looking up into my puss. Me breathing hard trying to catch a second wind. None of his business. "Hey, buddy, you live here?"

He says nothing, pallor of gray face, slinks away ratlike under the stairs. I hear a door slam.

Above me a man's waiting, dark skin, dark hair, dark eyes, looks like an American Indian—*How, keemosabee . . .*—and takes my hand when I say, "I'm Jo-Jo Peltz."

"Proud to make your acquaintance," he says. "Beneficio Gomez." Half the size of his wife.

Annabelle's sitting on a couch in the living room. She says, "Eet's lovely, Zho. Eet's beautiful, no?"

Sure, sure, the place is a veritable wonderland. A palace. Versailles. What can I say? Beneficia gushes, jumps right in, tells me how once, before the Flood, it was six apartments, now incorporated into one stately, majestic, phenomenal space. She tells me how their group of homesteaders took the building over from the landlord. "There'd been a fire, it was on the verge of being abandoned." The place was being overrun by junksters. A group of people from other buildings on the block got together to try to rescue the building. In a way these two buildings, situated in the exact middle, anchor the entire block. "Stability was essential. The only legitimate tenant here was a guy named Ike, who lived in the basement. He's still there."

"I think I saw him," I says.

"He can't be missed," Beneficio quickly ventures, sitting up straight. "But he's harmless."

"I wouldn't say that," interjects his wife, her voice acidic and I look up, hmmm.

Beneficio gives me the Cook's tour of the premises, shows me how they opened up the apartments. Originally, there were three apartments on each floor. A small, square four-room unit in the front and another in the rear connected by a narrow three-room railroad apartment in the center. At one point, when plumbing came indoors, there was a shared water closet at the center rear on each floor. He shows me where the hall was and the side-by-side front doors that opened into either kitchen.

"The apartment's not quite finished yet," he apologizes, "but all the heavy demolition is complete," and if there's no sink in the bathroom and the sheetrock's up but not taped, so be it. There's a monstrous wooden scaffolding over the stairwell leading upstairs, no railing on the rudimentary staircase, the dirty, splintery floors covered by a hideous mustard-colored rug, but there's no describing the charm, the space, the expanse, the pink brick walls, the warm light. This is the Lower East Side. This is the neighborhood where twenty million immigrants settled when they first arrived in America. Nothing has changed. On the streets outside the open window, we hear jabbering, and a car alarm going off, the waves of electronic noise sounding to me like: CAR-TOY CAR-TOY CAR-TOY CAR-TOY CAR-TOY CAR-TOY. . . .

"Somebody turn that off!"

Beneficio leans out the window. "It's that damn Dagmar's car again."

He says the guy's got one of these cheap alarms goes off every time the garbage truck goes by or somebody breathes too hard.

Annabelle is sitting quietly, breathing deeply, trying to suss the place out, gather her impressions. Conversation dies, the siren finally stops, Beneficia sighs, "Thank God."

Annabelle forces a smile, says she loves it, but, frankly, she has some concern. Not the apartment, the apartment's a stunner, *incroyable*, but the neighborhood, says if it were just *her*. . . .

Beneficio and Beneficia look at me like it's me holding her back, my fault. I got to explain, Hey, I'm a street dude, born and bred, my family's from this neighborhood, I can take care of myself. It's not me she's worried about, no way. I walk the streets of any neighborhood in this city. I tell them Annabelle's pregnant. She's worried about navigating the highways and byways of urban America with our little helpless offspring, you understand? Their faces light up.

"A baby!"

"The neighborhood?" Annabelle pleads. "Is it a danger?" Did they ever have any problems?

They jump on it. "Oh no." This isn't a bad neighborhood. It looks so much worse than it really is. They've got two kids. This is a *family* neighborhood. Sure, the drugs are on the street, but nobody likes drugs, most of all the people who live here, the Puerto Ricans are just as worried about their kids as any of us, drugs proliferating. . . . But the violence, that's between the junkies. Beneficia says she comes home late at night, never had an incident. They call upstairs and their son comes down to prove a point.

He's fifteen or sixteen, face like a tomahawk, wearing army fatigues. "This is Benny," Beneficio says.

We shake hands. The kid's got one of these vise grips, crunch up your bones. I say, "Hey, watch that! I'm a concert violinist."

Beneficia says, "Are you really?"

Then the sister comes down. Her name's Gloria. She's maybe fourteen, with a little baby fat, but she's gonna be a beauty when she grows up, almond eyes, dark skin. Slinking down the stairs, watching.

I ask Beneficia what an apartment like this one costs, what are they asking?

She says to tell the truth, they already had it sold. Beneficio works for IBM, who's transferring him down to Boca Raton, Florida—do I know it?—growth capital of the world, gateway to the new Southern Kingdom. "Lovely," she says. "We bought a house down there and sold this one, to an Italian fashion designer. But the designer went home to get some details straightened out in her factory, and left power of attorney with her lawyer, and he came down here, took one look, and said, 'Sorry, in good conscience I can't.'"

"Say what? Good what? Can't what?" I ask.

"He's doing his job. Frankly, we're not entirely legal. But slowly we're working on it."

"Meaning what?"

"There's no two ways about it, you're taking a gamble. There's no denying that. The building's not exactly kosher. This can be your home, but it's not just sitting here all perfect, you're going to have to work at it. Hard. The building has a vacate order. The city claims it's unsafe. There's been a fire here. No one was living here except for Ike downstairs. There were no systems, no water, no gas, no electricity. No roof. Slowly we've restored what was here, but officially the building's still classified U.B., unsafe building, and there's no C of O—that's your certificate of occupancy—so no one can legally live here, even though we do, of course, that's because after we bought it. . . ."

She says a lot of buildings on the block are done the same way. Almost all of them. Some have had a dispensation from the state attorney general's office, but that's because Louie Lefkowitz was from this block and made a special case.

She says when people started the corporation— that's what she called it, *The Corporation*, EAT CO, E Avenue Tenants' Corp.—it was five hundred a unit to buy in, a unit being one original apartment. "We have six," cost three thousand dollars. "But the building's not what it was when we started. It's come a long way. It's a little rough in the wintertime, but by and large. . . .

"And we put in seventeen in materials, not to mention our own labor, and we contracted an electrician and a plumber. . . ."

Somebody appears at the top of the stairs. "Oh, Mewie," Beneficia exclaims, like it's her long-lost cousin, back from the Amazon after a lifetime living with the Yanomami.

Meanwhile, Benny's lost interest and split. Went upstairs, came down with a plastic machine gun and left. Now this skinny bird's standing up there, bearded, his Mansoneyes gleaming down on us.

"Who's this?"

"Our next-door neighbor, Mewie Cotton."

How'd he get there? Beneficio gave me the tour of the house, didn't see *him* up there. Spooky. Unless he'd been hiding in the closet.

"That's one thing we haven't gotten round to," Beneficio says sheepishly. "Closets."

Beneficia says this Mewie character climbs over from his apartment in the adjacent building. She shows us the well window, overlooking the air shaft, five stories up, between buildings. "Climb over?" I say. "That's dangerous. He could fall."

"Nah, it's easy. No problem." He sits down, smiles. "Don't mind me!"

Suddenly Beneficia jumps up with a brilliant idea. Maybe Annabelle would feel better if she talked to another woman who lives here, someone more her age and inclination. She throws open the window and knocks on the fourth-floor window across the well. "Don't let her appearance distract you. She's very nice, a very smart girl."

The girl arrives at the window sporting a red mohawk with black tips. Beneficia takes Annabelle's arm, steers her over and makes the introductions: Scarlet B, Annabelle Peltz.

But Annabelle says, "No, not Peltz. I use my own name, not Zho's."

They lean toward each other. Annabelle and Scarlet. This is the old neighborhood. I see it now. Strong. It freezes me. Annabelle pregnant, holding her belly, standing by an open window in a tenement on Avenue E, the block my mother was born, chatting with a red-and-black-headed punkette named Scarlet.

The skinny bird, this Mewie, leans closer, says something to me.

"What's that?" I says, turn to him, look into those red eyes.

He's grinning at me, pats my knee, says, "Hey, I hear you're pregnant. Congratulations!"

FULCRUM OF DISASTER (1988)

SUSIE TIMMONS

leaning against the gate on st. marks place I realized its from
the viewpoint of the sky
the yonder
storm sign with elevation omitted

good kissing or making out is the same as condensed rockabilly
drummer ghost or a hypnotized wolf with two x's for eyes swallowing
shifting.
[initial flaw]

distance is the same as time, emptiness is a kind of speed moving
slowly with extreme consciousness. the distance
belongs to somebody else, secondary concern was dictated
to the weaver, intact but invisible

I felt like a piece of lace made from ice
or I felt like three blue stars
streetlight in the yellow leaves of a ginkgo tree, I felt the cold
dark iron of the fence, I felt compressed energized, sparkling.
[but I was mistaken, and so we arrive at the fulcrum of disaster]

one week ago
enormous conglomerate snowflakes
tumbled and careened down the brick wall
whirling around in bare branches
embraced by dead grapevines

[I wish you didn't love me so much]
[I never had a choice]

futile rejoinder

snow is so interior, preoccupied, oblivious, more interior than
my own internal self, I mean it never can snow inside us
inside me I thought about what you might be doing, you're in
my heart now [shrivel] no question, frost beads along my hair
sliding, half skating past the silent abandon in Tompkins Sq. Park

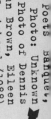

FROM *TOTEM OF THE DEPRAVED* (1988)

NICK ZEDD

At noon, a thirty-five year old man stepped out onto Eighth Street between First and Second Avenues buck naked. Couples out for a stroll looked the other way as a thick brown goo oozed out of his anal cavity onto the pavement. The naked man, his cracked skin a charcoal color of built up dirt, was oblivious to the people walking around him as he shit on the sidewalk.

On a park bench on Fourth Street, a black guy with a beard sat motionless. His eyes were closed. Long tendrils of snot, long since solidified, hung from both nostrils, waving in the breeze. The strings of solidified slime were an inch thick and emerged from the two orifices planted in his face. They hung over his blubbery lips, rooting themselves in his greasy thatch of beard. The man appeared to be dead, but I didn't want to get close enough to find out.

A block away, an old bum thrust a paper cup into the faces of people walking down First Avenue, mumbling something about spare change while his cock hung out of the hole in his pants. While walking across Thirteenth Street with Sue, I saw a guy with a mustache pissing next to a cop car. When Sue looked at him, the guy said, "C'mere baby," and smiled. He then put his dick in his pants, opened the front door of the cop car and got in. I noticed his badge as they drove away.

The junkie lies on my bed doing nothing.
She is worthless.
Our apartment is filled with garbage.
I write the word "bad" on her ass.
She does nothing.
She will not do the dishes.
She will not throw out the garbage.
She will not do the laundry.

She will ignore the roaches.
She will die.
Who am I to judge?
I am worthless too.
Because I am with her.
And I will do nothing too.
I am so full of hate it makes me want to explode.

I have tried to accept the monumental triviality of this life. I have tried to reconcile myself to the lunatics, liars and mediocritons who have surrounded me in this world of shit, but it doesn't work. The only thing that can keep me from killing myself is to kill you. I know I'm no better than you or the next creep. It's just that deep down, I can't bring myself to believe it. I'm sorry, but you maggots really are beneath me and I hate you beyond words. I've tried to be indifferent but I just can't. It must be a chemical imbalance. I can't help hating the WHOLE HUMAN RACE.

I had to go somewhere quick after my pig roommate with the fake French accent married an art fag with a beat-up guitar and told me to get out. I stuck her with a two hundred dollar phone bill and skipped town for a month. When I returned, Sue and I moved into a basement on 17th Street with the dwarf super whose demise I immediately set to work planning.

Sadly, my plans were sidetracked by the presence of Andrea, a red haired crackhead who decided to move in next door in order to be closer to me and Sue. The first thing she did was convince Sue to quit her job as a bartender in order to become a go-go dancer on Times Square. She then got her hooked on dope and seduced her into a lesbian relationship. I killed time jerking off to Glow reruns while Sue and Andrea kept busy licking each other's cunts next door.

One night, after driving a cab, I came home to discover three girls in my bed. As I looked at the zonked out Sue lying with Andrea and her scraggly girlfriend, all I wanted was some peace and quiet. After giving Andrea and her scrawny friend the boot, I proceeded to administer a severe tongue lashing to Sue's dolphin-like clit. The more I plunged my undulating tongue into her trembling twat, the louder her squeals became as I slurped away at her quivering clit, oozing fuckjuice and sweat. Sue's thighs shuddered in ecstasy as my fingers slid up and down and my tongue thrust deeper into her gaping cunt, wrenching squeals of delight from her throat. I was slurping for my life. Sue paid half the rent and I couldn't afford to have her run off with a pair of dykes from New Jersey. My tongue burrowed deep into the soft pink crevice of her clit and my right middle finger slowly penetrated her anus, going all the way in, as she shuddered and twisted in a violent paroxysm, emitting squeals of pain I'd never heard. For two full hours, I shoved my penis down her throat and got her to come repeatedly by sucking and licking her clit. When it came time for me to take a piss, she opened her mouth and a hot stream splashed down her throat. She inhaled lines of dope as I crouched over her and allowed my bowels to empty a load of shit onto her back. I then smeared the soft brown excrement over and around and onto her two big breasts as she pulled me down onto my back and straddled my head with her legs. A shower of shit blasted out of her rectum onto my face as I opened my mouth to taste the warm oozing substance. I then violently vomited onto her face and licked the puke and shit up in order to gag and vomit again.

I felt totally clean. My insides were empty and covering the woman I loved. We rolled around and covered ourselves in vomit and shit and continued to lick each other's assholes until our tongues were sore. I snorted two bags of coke and puked all over a copy of the Good News Bible before passing out. When I awoke the next morning, the color TV and both VCRs were gone. Sue left a note saying she wouldn't be coming back.

So now I was sitting alone in this wreck, filled with vomit and shit, wondering what to do next. Why did she leave? Who did she leave me for? I didn't really care, but it gave me something to do with my mind as I lay there covered in shit. What a fool I am. A brainless fucking retard in a room alone. I just can't get along with anyone, I guess. Nobody's up to my standards. I made up this story by the way.

I don't know . . . I'm attracted to their beauty . . . elevated. . . . It transcends the dullness in my life, but after a month of looking at them, I'm bored out of my mind. I don't want to know about their fingernail polish. I don't want to hear about what food they ate or what perfume they just bought. I don't need to see what clothes this girl just bought or what recipe she just found. I need to have my brain stimulated and all I can get is drivel. A useless stream of nothing perpetually for hours on end; the utter, unending boredom of living with a fool. There must be someone out there—a being with a functional brain who's half worth fucking. But who'd put up with an asshole like me? Forget it.

I'm trying to think of what I'm going to do next and I'm failing miserably. I don't give a shit. My whole world is falling apart and I just don't give a shit. Isn't that a laugh? How many years have I been trying to live in this stupid city, and for what? All my friends gave up and left like rats off a sinking ship and here I am alone in a room covered in shit, wondering what to do next. The world is in chaos outside my door. I'll try to forget the present. Remember the past.

BOMB
LEMANN
MARDEN
MAPPLETHORPE

New Art, Writing, Theatre and Film   Winter 1988 $6.00

FICTION: INDIANA   McGRATH   MORROW   KONDOLEON

Bomb No. 22, Cover (1988)
Bomb Photo: Jimmy DeSana
Cover Design: Stanley Moss

At times like these, my mind wanders, pondering the misfortunes of even bigger fuckups than myself. It makes me feel better to think of how Tommy ruined his life.

Like the time he got so drunk in that bar uptown he didn't know what he was saying and three guys took a dislike to his presence. When one of them called him a fuckhead, he called the fat one a faggot. Out on the sidewalk, Tommy had his face beaten to a pulp by three drunken college students, landing

him in the emergency ward of the very same hospital where he worked during the day, doing cancer research. The boot heels and pounding fists of the three drunk fucks fractured the cheekbones and split his right eyelid, necessitating reconstructive surgery.

In the process, doctors discovered four abscessed wisdom teeth, pulled them out and left the entire right side of his face numb for six months, a drooping eyelid and a few stitches the only visible evidence of his encounter with the academic community.

MORE OR LESS URGENT (1988)

NINA ZIVANCEVIC

Walt Whitman said, "breath oxygen
and trees,"
     Brooklyn breathes salsa and chicken broth
and geraniums of buildings
        tremble erect over the East River
—magnified shadows below Wall Street agencies
tourists stockings are on sale!
Russian churches dream a thousand bells
and the blood wedding of Torquemada
takes place inside the Rockefeller Center fountain,
and if I were Allen Ginsberg I would say "Oh!"
And if I were a child of gluttonous labels I would
add an "Ach! Guten achtung meine liebe Traumerei!"
I'll fly a plane to Canada!
I'll stop eating raw peanuts inside this Donald Duck dream . . .
And I don't want   no, I don't want to
repeat   to repeat myself
as I   as I am not
as I am not John Giorno and I am
   not I   as I am not
an astral body either
as we all breathe liquid

and swallow down bubbles of air
as we are the air itself
    as we also try to become liquid
as we are already heavy
as we see ourselves as the painted fractured icons
of an oppressive age
        at our age! this stage! of development!
and as I am not my friend Jeff
I do not perceive us as apes . . . and through
some veiled kindness I let my mistakes
   take their shape
under this immense sky
    so different at different hours
genuinely relative to match Einstein's brain
inside the whole circus the whole circuit
the whole hole holy spirit, oh!
Country ruled by Walt Disney's acid characters, oh!
A doughnut for breakfast and a fix for supper, oh!
And the woman behind me says loudly:
"It ain't your stuff, buddy,"
and then she adds: "Take it easy."

BIG CIGARS

#3 WINTER 1988 $2.50

ABILENE

ABILENE. IT'S SNOWING IN ABILENE. STOP.

STOP.
—ROLLO WHITEHEAD

STATEN ISLAND AND NEW YORK

STATEN ISLAND FERRY POETRY FESTIVAL 1988

FRIDAY, SEPTEMBER 23rd, 7:00 PM

*BOAT LEAVING ST. GEORGE

FRONT DECK
CROSS CULTURAL COMMUNICATIONS (LONG ISLAND)
STANLEY H. BARKAN
LAURA BOSS
ENID DAME
SANG HEE KWAK
DONALD LEV
LISA FLUEGEL
SANDRA HOCHMAN
MINDY RINKENICH

BACK DECK
HARBOR POETS (STATEN ISLAND)
HELEN DECKER
GARY GULLO
JIM LYNCH
C.F. BORGMAN
GERARD RIZZA
BERNADETTE GOLDMAN

UPPER DECK – FRONT
HARBOR POETS (STATEN ISLAND)
NANCY LINDY
STEVEN KHINOY

SUB ROSA (BROOKLYN/MANHATTAN)
NICO VASSILAKIS
NOEMIE MAXWELL

POTATO BUGS (STATEN ISLAND)
TOMY TOLEDO
RICHARD SHIELDS

UPPER DECK – BACK
[CAREN ALKALAY–HEISEN
READ BY LISA FLUEGEL]
PHIL GOOD
SILVIA HALL
DEVREY YARBROUGH
ERIC SELVIN SMITH
ZORAN VRAGOLOV

*BOAT LEAVING WHITEHALL

FRONT DECK
NATIONAL POETRY MAGAZINE OF THE LOWER EAST SIDE (MANHATTAN)
STEPHAN PAUL MILLER
JAMES FEAST
KATHRINE KOCH
MARK STATMAN
CHRIS CANTWELL
BERNADETTE MAYER

BACK DECK
DOWNTOWN (MANHATTAN)
DOROTHY FRIEDMAN
GARY AZON
LEHMAN WEICHSELBAUM

CULTURE SHOCK (BROOKLYN)
FRED CALERO

CAROL WIERZBICKI
BOB BAGNELL

UPPER DECK – FRONT
BIG CIGARS (WASHINGTON, DC/BROOKLYN)
MICHAEL RANDALL
STEPHEN CIACCIARELLI

COVER (MANHATTAN)
JEFF WRIGHT
SHELLEY MILLER
ANELE RUBIN
BETTY WILLIAMS

UPPER DECK – BACK
APPEARANCES (MANHATTAN)
RON KOLM

BASEBALL DIGEST (CALIFORNIA/MANHATTAN)
MARY LEARY
KATHERINE ARNOLDI
MARGUERITE
TERRY QUINN
LYNDA CRAWFORD

*DIRECTIONS:

WHITEHALL–SOUTH FERRY TERMINAL, SUBWAY #1, #4, OR #5
ST. GEORGE–STATEN ISLAND FERRY TERMINAL, ANY PUBLIC TRANSPORTATION

WE WOULD LIKE TO GIVE THANKS TO THE DEPARTMENT OF TRANSPORTATION, BUREAU OF TRANSIT,
OPERATIONS AND TO THE CAPTAINS AND FERRY PERSONAL WHO HAVE MADE THIS EVENT POSSIBLE.
ALSO THANKS TO ALL THE PARTICIPATING MAGAZINES AND READERS, AND ALSO SPECIAL THANKS
TO CROSS CULTURAL COMMUNICATIONS AND MR. S.H. BARKAN FOR THE PUBLICATION OF THE
SHORT ANTOLOGY WHICH WILL INCLUDE ALL THE POETS OF THIS FESTIVAL.

FOR MORE INFORMATION PLEASE CONTACT FERRY POETRY FESTIVAL COORDINATORS
ZORAN VRAGOLOV OR JIM FEAST AT (718) 720-5123
RECEPTION FOLLING FESTIVAL

NEWS ★ CLUBS ★ MUSIC ★ STYLE ★ MOVIES ★ PEOPLE

NEW YORK CITY ★ OCTOBER 1988 ★ $1.95

Style: Design in fashion

PAPER

culture vulture

In touch with the Feelies

Why vote?

Robert Longo's new direction

Elvira and her bosom buddy

Elton John's dirty pictures

ART FILM DANCE MUSIC

Karen Finley
the arts on up

Opposite Page: *Big Cigars, no. 3*, Cover (1988)
Artist/Designer: Michael Randall
This Page Top:
Staten Island Poetry Festival, Poster (1988)
Bottom: *Paper Magazine*, Photo of Karen Finley,
October 1988 Photo: Richard Pandiscio

MEXICO CITY BLUES

by Jack Kerouac

a reading with live music

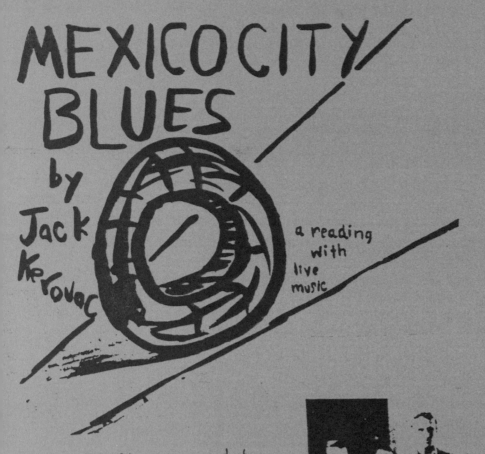

92 Choruses read by

Allen Ginsberg — 88,89,90,91

Tom Savage — 3,51

Jim Brodey — 6,17

Lita Hornick — 12,30,53

Susie Timmons — 16,19

Vicki Hudspith — 42,43,74,76

Charles Bernstein — 49,59,111,122

Elio Schneeman — 52,54

Bob Rosenthal — 55,56,57

Simon Pettet — 63,65,68

Barbara Barg — 79,80,81,82

Lee Ann Brown/
　Steven Taylor — 89

Jeff Wright — 94,95,96

Maggie Dubris — 100,103,64

Steve Carey — 104, 216A, 216B

Lewis Warsh — 108, 109, 110

(pause)

Gerard Malanga — 113

Allen Ginsberg — 97,98,99

David Trinidad — 91, 121, 144

Rochelle Kraut — 13

David Shapiro — 127

Judith Malina — 128,129,130

Hanon Reznikov — 131,132,133

Nina Zivancevic — 143,145

Eileen Myles — 146

Bob Holman — 156,157,158,159

Jerome Rothenberg — 162,163,164,165

Carl Solomon — 27, 190

Michael Scholnick — 181,195,196,202

John Yau — 208,209,210

Richard Meyers — 211, 214, 227

Vincent Katz — 228,230,231,171

Allen Ginsberg — 242

lil Ti Pousse — 239,240,241

plus surprise Guests
improvised music going with it
proved by
Cyro Batista, Charlie Morrow,
Steven Taylor, Samir Safwat,
Mark Ettinger
and a host of others

MCs : Myles and Katz

Conceived by Vincent Katz

Knitting Factory, N
December 4, 1988
"an afternoon jam sess
on Sunday"

Previous Spread:
Left: Mexico City Blues by Kack Kerouac,
Knitting Factory, Flyer (1988)
Right: Living Theater, Flyer (1984)
Art/Design: David Sandlin

GATHERING BRUISES (1989)

MAX BLAGG

For Cookie Mueller

October light triggers an avalanche of sighs
each sunset full of small regrets
this thin world stripped
of another spiritcatcher,
luminous creature whose tattooed hands
and silver bangles lit up the rat race,
whose feral eyes spelled "Danger"
despite her great sweet heart.
Shaman's gaze cracking the lens
as she leans against a doorjamb
a deep blonde shining
illuminated from the inside
and if you look at her eyes
they are green green green green.
She glows in the dark.

and now Im dreaming of the past
I am conjuring you Cookie
as you step out of a cab
into the pouring rain
with that diamond smile
and your golden hair piled high
Who could ever say "No" to you, hon?
We all spread our raincoats in the mud
and guided you in
you knew where you were going
it was '79 or thereabouts
everybody had a massive appetite
and a tiny purse
and we were gunning it, no mercy,
no navigator,
wired to the sky
kicking the doors off their hinges

dancing with broken bottles
biting down hard
on anything that moved.
There were some gorgeous moments
and everybody and you
looked so incredibly lovely—
like you would live forever.

BEAUTIES WHO LIVE ONLY FOR AN AFTERNOON (1989)

DENISE DUHAMEL

(In Memory of Cookie Mueller)

Your rib cage lives on as a tree house for adolescent swallows
who, if they've never had a chance to rebel, do now.
A KEEP OUT sign tacked to your sternum—
that is how I like to think of you.
The swallows who make you their hideout
pick up your essence so later this winter
they'll crisscross out of their flying formation
gathering enough angry swallows
to do gray skywriting:
"Bush, eat shit." Or "Find a cure, you bastards."
"Cookie shouldn't have had to die."
You read your stories in the dankness
of the Lower East Side's ABC No Rio
and I talked about you for weeks.
"She's kind of skinny," I told everyone.
"She's got the coolest leather jacket I've ever seen."
You said, "Send me your chapbook,"
but I think you were too sick
to ever write back. I didn't know then you had AIDS.
You read instead of motorcycles,
your guys. You read of what you did in Turkey.
The way you had sex with men
in chairs. The car has become a symbol
for freedom in contemporary women's fiction,
but you wrote of more—your bike, the wind.
You were in John Water's movies,
one in which you had sex with a chicken.
And Cookie, if you ask me, that right there
makes you a star. You were the bad girl
everyone wants to be.
And your sweet husband, Vittorio, a sailor like Popeye,
a jagged lid of a tin can
wrenched open to pour spinach through an IV

into his arm. He said he wanted to be a dolphin
next time around. Known to flirt with them in barrooms,
he sometimes saw these swimming mammals
rising from shipwrecks to greet the angels.
You lain, side by side, in the same hospital room.
He to go first, you not much after.
I wondered if you whispered about other romantic
couples—Romeo and Juliet, Sid and Nancy.
You wrote, "The wall eyed butcher
cleaves to his heart the butterflies,
the fleeting and elusive beauties
who live only for an afternoon."
In Vittorio's companion drawing, the meat seller is cross-eyed
as though the yellow and orange Monarchs
are bees, driving him crazy.
The butcher's expression is mean and manly,
but his apron is clean, and his mouth
wears the color of red lipstick.
I say small prayers for your son Max who survives,
ten and confused, and I think I meet him
whenever I see a boy light a tiny cherry bomb
and stick it in the coin slot
of a New York City public telephone.

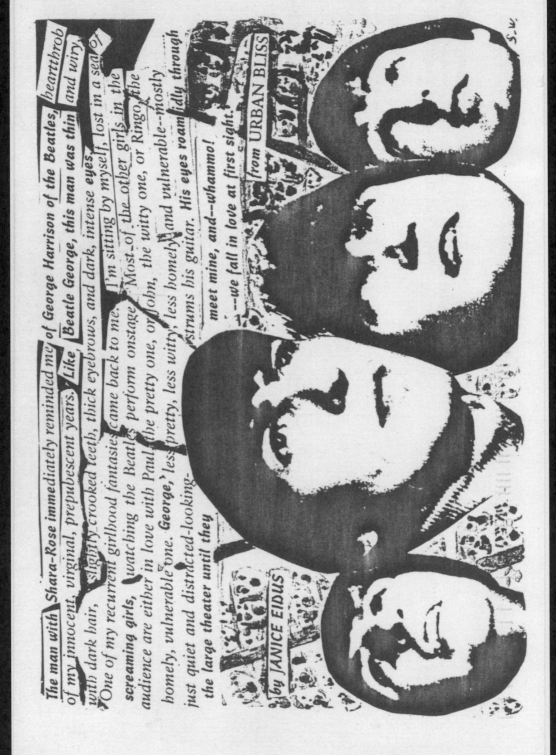

The man with Shara-Rose immediately reminded me of George Harrison of the Beatles, *heartthrob* of my innocent, virginal, prepubescent years. Like *Beatle George*, this man was thin and wiry, with dark hair, slightly crooked teeth, thick eyebrows, and dark, intense eyes.

One of my recurrent girlhood fantasies came back to me. I'm sitting by myself, lost in a sea of screaming girls, watching the Beatles perform onstage. Most of the other girls in the audience are either in love with Paul, the pretty one, or John, the witty one, or Ringo, the homely, vulnerable one. George, less pretty, less witty, less homely and vulnerable—mostly just quiet and distracted-looking—strums his guitar. His eyes roam idly through the large theater until they meet mine, and—whammo!
—we fall in love at first sight.

from URBAN BLISS

by JANICE EIDUS

S.W.

Advertisement for Janice Eidus's *Urban Bliss* (ca. early '90s) Art/Design: Susan Weinstein

ON THE SIDE OF THE ROAD (1989)

JANICE EIDUS

MARGERIE STOOD, throwing up, bending down, on the side of the road. This had been going on for a long time: driving, hardly eating, throwing up, hating the driving. But the alternative—remaining inside the apartment in her town—only occasionally seemed any better. The apartment, when last she'd seen it, had an unopened box of Rice Krispies on the table and a can of Mr. Pibb's in the refrigerator.

She drove. Panicking each time she had to pass yet one more car (checking her blind spot three and four times) or worse, a truck; wincing at sudden, sharp turns. This is my lane, or this is my way, or this is my life, she thought in rhythm with Tanya Tucker on the radio. Lately the winds had been so fierce that she'd felt engaged in a match, as though another pair of hands on the steering wheel were insistently turning in the opposite direction.

One night she drove into a town with three movie theaters and seven bars, and chose, randomly, to enter the fourth bar she came upon. The jukebox was playing a song about a couple very happy in their love until the woman became obsessed with the idea of striking it big in Southern California and left the man back in Tennessee; but, five years later, at the song's conclusion, she's a barmaid in Southern California, while he's living in a mansion in Tennessee.

Margerie sat down at the bar and ordered a Hamm's, wondering if she'd turned out the car lights. What if she hadn't, and the battery ran down, and she had to stay here, in this town, while an unknown mechanic probed and possibly abused parts of her car? She was nauseated immediately, because this was not the town she had chosen to come to, and therefore, she couldn't stay here. Her finger had not landed here; this would merely be absurd.

A man—he was from this town, she guessed, but he might just as well have been plucked from the town she had chosen to live in—sat down beside her at the bar, shifting the weight of his thin, angular body, touching the silver buckle on his leather belt with the finger where the ring usually was. "Cold out there," he said.

"I smell of vomit," she replied. "I've been puking on and off for a few weeks."

He stood up, didn't look back, and walked out of the bar. A few moments later she heard a car start. What if it was her car? What if he had broken in and started it up with a bobby pin, the way the tough boys used to? Once, in the staircase of their building, Tommy Gaglione, his hand beneath her bra, had said, "I took a Mustang clear out to Queens the other night! Queens, man. Doin' 90."

Tommy Gaglione had grown up to become a junkie. One day on the subway she'd spotted him and noted the giveaway sallow skin and decaying teeth, the short-sleeved muscle shirt (exactly the same style, or perhaps exactly the same shirt, from the old days) revealing needle tracks down both arms, lacing onto his hands. Margerie had supposed she ought to feel embarrassed, but she hadn't. She'd been on her way to meet her husband for lunch. Tommy had seen her, too, and grinned in the old way so that she'd know, then nodded out, a contraband cigarette dangling from his lips. She had whispered, almost to him, but not quite to him, as she stood before the opening subway doors, "Your brother didn't . . ." and then she was out the doors, inside the station, heading—with all the others—for an exit. Billy Gaglione, Tommy's brother, had become a cop. Or so Margerie was certain she remembered having heard.

Margerie's own brother, who'd been Tommy's friend, had been killed in a wreck when he was nineteen, in a stolen Ford, his body prone and twisted on the highway, though the brown paper bags and tubes of airplane glue remained upright on the back seat.

The advertising man Margerie later married had grown bored, after the first six months, of hearing about the old Brooklyn neighborhood and her family's hardships, her father's business failures and his untimely death; of Margerie's own decision, at seventeen, to free herself from that Brooklyn world with its women in hair rollers, its hold-ups, rapes, beatings, and streetcorner singing groups composed of inarticulate budding gangsters; of how she had then flirted, instead, with the bohemian East Village life: clap and crabs by the time she was eighteen, pot and LSD, mysticism, and an abortion. Just one month, in fact, before Margerie's decision to leave her husband and to come to the town she had chosen, she'd threatened—only slightly not seriously—to murder him with one of their kitchen knives, if he didn't listen one more time to her story of the painful abortion in a New Jersey motel by a doctor without a license who blew his nose and drooled.

She'd first met her husband at a party. He was thirty-three, and she was twenty-three and polished, by then, at being an articulate, vivacious, slightly mysterious hip young girl with a past, impressing him by what he was pleased to label "vampish innocence," and by the abandoned fluency with which she spoke to men of all ages and professions at the party, revealing intimate details of her life in a chatty voice while sipping a constantly refilled glass of bourbon. Even Tommy Gaglione, back in the staircase, had often been forced to mutter, "Shut up!" impatient to get his tongue inside her mouth.

Now, without saying a word—she rarely spoke any longer—Margerie stood up and walked out of the bar, hoping that her car was still in the lot. She had hardly touched her beer; all this time she'd been surviving on Dairy Queen and MacDonald milkshakes, unable even to look at the oozing burgers that the other customers devoured. The chill had fogged up her car's windows with spiderwebs of icy moisture, and Margerie worried that the battery would die, but the car started immediately, and she maneuvered out of the parking lot, back and forth from reverse to drive, without getting stuck on any snow, all of which she felt meant it was time to head back to the apartment in the town she had chosen, two years ago, as the place in which she would live and die. The Interstate was the same whichever direction she drove, and the men still said, "Foxy Beaver," over their CB radios in the southern accents they affected, out here so far from the South, in this part of the country with no distinctive accent and intonation of its own.

Finally she was back at the apartment. Her old and near-deaf neighbor lady had somehow gotten inside her mailbox (probably she'd known the mailman for forty years and had simply said, "Jack, can I have the mail for that quiet lady in number four while she's on her trip?") and had stacked the mail outside Margerie's door, tying it neatly with a pink wool bow. The mail consisted of five letters from her husband.

He had been writing letters for the entire two years, without pause, still attempting, at times, to seduce her back with anecdotes about singing waitresses and rollerskating waiters in new bistros in the West Village, and up-to-date news of his latest accounts; at other times he merely vented his rage. He could not understand that she would stick to this decision, made two years ago on a Sunday, because she had to.

Margerie had gone to visit her mother that Sunday, via the subway into Brooklyn; although her husband wouldn't have viewed a cab ride as an extravagance, she was uncomfortable allowing strange men, seen only as broad backs and half-profiles, to chauffeur her, while the crowded, noisy, subterranean IND seemed hardly a vehicle at all. She was carrying a thick cut of steak and a package of sticky buns from a new bakery. For a solid moment, Margerie's mother had peered through the peekhole, before opening the door in her baggy print housedress. They seated themselves side by side at the kitchen table, elbows upon the scrubbed vinyl tablecloth, beneath the two photographs—one of Margerie's father, who had been killed, along with three other passengers, including a fifteen-year-old girl, on a crowded Manhattan bus by a soft-spoken junior high school social studies teacher who declared no memory of the act—and the other, a slightly blurred photograph of Margerie's brother in a torn T-shirt, with lidded eyes, during the James Dean/Marlon Brando days he'd never grown out of. Her mother spoke of a new, tasty low-calorie pudding, of a novel by Joyce Carol Oates she'd taken out of the branch library, of bursitis of the shoulder. As always, the Venetian blinds remained shut, so that the men out on the streets could not take advantage of the view a ground floor apartment might offer.

Tragedies, Margerie's mother believed, were not hers alone: a next-door neighbor had both forehead and neck scarred forever by an eighteen year old with a jagged tin can that had once held chick peas; the Puerto Rican child down the hall had lost an arm while being dangled between subway cars by the fourth cousin everyone had always called El Loco, El Bobo. Margerie's mother proudly called herself a "liberal" if asked, and swore she harbored no resentment against the two dead men who had left her in such a neighborhood (where she was now too settled to leave) supporting herself by secretarial work in her middle years.

Margerie left early, afraid to walk to the station in the dark, not staying to share the steak.

Her husband was eating a defrosted blueberry pie and playing "Jeopardy" with their son in the living room, with the TV on. "I'm moving," she announced, before her coat was off. "I'm moving," she repeated, entering the living room, lifting the large atlas from the bookcase, opening to a map of the United States on page twenty-nine, closing her eyes, flinging her finger down, "here."

And he was still writing her letters, after two years. In one letter he'd said, "You have broken all the rules, my dear, and so I see no reason why I should follow any. Besides, who would I ask for the etiquette involved? Emily Post? Joyce Brothers?"

Margerie looked around the apartment, then at the five letters and their pink bow, and then walked over to the sink and threw up, scaring a tiny spider. Maybe she should brush her teeth, if there was any toothpaste. On the bathroom floor lay a wrinkled tube of something called "Proud," a new brand from one of the old corporations—one of her husband's most important clients, in fact, if she could remember any longer which were the clients and which were the crucial potential clients.

Afterward, she splashed cold water on her face and lay down on the unmade bed, which was surrounded by two years worth of letters. Flicking the radio switch to On, she heard a voice estimating the number of hogs and cows to be slaughtered in the town's stockyards the next day. She flicked the switch to Off and coughed a thin, pale saliva into an aluminum ashtray, then heaved and shuddered, head hanging over the side of the bed.

One of the newly-arrived letters was ripped, slightly, in the corner, and bore what looked like a catsup stain beside the stamp. She would open that one. The apartment was cold and she buttoned her sweater.

Margie, I ran into your old friend Laurie, from your "group." She wanted me to be sure to tell you she's been promoted to a "well-paying managerial position" and that your support back in those days was a "true and valid" part of her learning to become "more assertive."

This was, then, one of the "rational" letters, one of the sarcastic, mocking ones. She read on.

But Margie, I still miss you in bed. Don't you miss me, miss my touch at night, miss the things we did? Or are you actually managing to have affairs out there in that godforsaken crap town in which you've chosen to rot, for whatever personal, pathological reasons?

No, it was not a rational one, after all. Perhaps he had had a drink, or two drinks, between paragraphs. Perhaps he'd gone out to a cocktail party, perhaps spent the night with a woman much younger than himself, and returned to the letter, hungover, the following morning. Ignoring the rest of the letter, she noted, despite herself, the postscript.

P.S. Maybe you no longer exist for me. Maybe each of these letters is an end in itself.

Margerie dropped the letter onto the floor with all the others. She needed no sleep, she decided, and stood, draping her coat across her shoulders, opening the door and walking to the car, parked across the street. The battery didn't catch, and then it caught and died. Finally it started, but the back right tire spun uselessly, until she went outside and placed a ripped grocery sack beneath it, on top of the ice. There was a hole on the thumb of her left glove, and the wind hurt the exposed flesh. The sun was not out yet.

Margerie had driven a full six blocks, had made it to the dry cleaners and the post office, before needing to pull over.

Standing in front of the post office, ears and nose reddened by the wind, waiting for his morning ride to school or work, was a boy of about nineteen. He approached her. "Ma'am, are you okay?"

"Pregnant," she lied.

Blushing, he walked back to his place, but he had stepped in some of her mess, and she saw that it remained, clinging, to his maroon, pointed cowboy boots. She saw, too, that the stance and pose he affected were so similar to those of Tommy Gaglione and Whitey Lenehan and her own brother, although they hadn't wanted to appear the hardened cowboy-trucker that this boy did, but as cool, inner-city toughs, untouchable.

She drove with the radio on—she nearly always did—and sang, tunelessly, along with the woman who wished to go back to the Blue Bayou to watch the sun rise with her lost lover. The announcer came on, predicting more snow for the evening, making a wisecrack about poor old Nellie who would never able to see the sun shine again, and Margerie suddenly remembered one letter from her husband which had arrived about four months before; one which she'd opened because it had come in an off-yellow envelope.

Why *do* you stay out there? What thrill are you deriving? I stay awake at night, seriously I do, pondering your deviant pleasures. (Incidentally, I took your mother out to dinner the other night, to an Italian restaurant "without a bar" at her request.) Are you spending your days volunteering for the local 4-H? Reading Sartre and Camus to town geriatrics? Honestly, had you rehearsed

for weeks with Johnny Carson, you couldn't
have chosen a more ludicrous town. You
once said—during the "group" days—that
you were near to exorcising all the irrational
resentments and hostilities. And then you go
and pull this looney tune. Before I forget, I
did the campaign for the new health cereal,
Granette: *you* were the big health food
nut, not me; thought you'd like to know.

To that letter she'd actually mailed back a
reply, something she occasionally did, because she
did not think she hated her husband in any way
at all. She assumed he was doing an adequate
job of raising Philip: making certain that he didn't
ride his bike in the park along any but the most
populated paths, that the private school he attended
emphasized both creative and pragmatic learning,
that Father and Son still met for their weekly lunches
in the Kozy Kitchen. Her letter had been brief.

I stay only because I need to pare
things down. There is no pleasure involved.
There never has been.

He'd replied in a thick red ink with ferocious
blots and loops.

Oh, so now you fancy yourself a pear?
Well, you just come on back to the big
apple and I'll sink my sharp teeth into your
juicy skin. Let me have one more bite, my
lawful wedded fruitcake, my pear lady,
and I'll teach you the pleasures of fruit
punch, jello mold, and fruit cocktail.

On the day she'd received that letter, she'd driven
through three towns, pulling over to the side of the
road at twenty-minute intervals, seeing bits of pear,
undigested, floating in the bilious liquid, at each stop.

And now, months later, Margerie found herself
pulling into a bar in one of those same towns. Left
hand in her pocket to avoid the wind, she carefully
stepped through the icy parking lot, past the few cars
and one van already parked. Inside, standing at the
bar and ordering another Hamm's, she felt ill almost
immediately. "Not too many *ladies* come in here,"
the bartender joked by rote, answering her question
and pointing his finger in the general direction.

At the juke box, her way was blocked by a
woman with teased blonde hair, wearing a tight
white jersey turtleneck, tight black skirt, and 1955-
style Bunny Hug black shoes, bending over the
machine, reading song titles. The woman sniffed
and looked up. "Hey, what have *you* been doing?"

Margerie felt sicker than before. The woman had
spoken in a voice which might have been Tommy
Gaglione's sister's.

"I'd like to get by to wash. I don't feel . . ."

The woman straightened herself. "Come on
up to my room. This filthy outhouse won't get you
no cleaner—yeah, there are rooms upstairs—not
to mention that certain sights and odors will make
you sicker."

Margerie followed the blonde woman up narrow
stairs to a dusty second floor, and inside to her room,
in which there was a poster on one wall that read,
"Scorpio . . . Cancer" above a drawing of a nude male
and female embracing, and another that read, "Keep
On Truckin." Margerie splashed cold water on her
face, then placed her head beneath the faucet, so that
her long hair was separated into disagreeable, clinging
strands down her neck and onto her shoulders.

The blonde woman sat on the bed, watching.
"You're from the city."

Margerie nodded.

"I'm from the Bronx," the woman grinned, "around where Dion came from. But there's one thing I want to get straight, and that is that I'm not getting into some kind of friend-thing with you. I don't even like women very much, generally. I drink with men. I party with men. Nine years ago I followed my ex-husband out here, because I was one of those suckers who married for *love*. What I'm saying is that you and I aren't going to be girlfriends."

Margerie spotted, for the first time, the now-faded tracks along the woman's arms: "I hadn't thought so." Obviously they were old, though, from the days of Dion and the Belmonts and her ex-husband. There was also a prominent, fresh bruise. The water ran and Margerie stood, foolishly, until the blonde woman walked to the sink and turned off the faucet. "Okay, baby," she laughed, "you're as clean as you're going to be until you get home."

Downstairs, the woman stopped before the jukebox again. "Help me pick out a song. Should I play one about how helpless she feels loving a no-good man, or one about screw you, buddy, Mama didn't raise me to live with a bum like you."

"It doesn't matter." Margerie feared she might throw up again. "Any. None."

The woman laughed slightly. "Press E-13." Margerie's fingers shook.

The blonde woman leaned against the Wurlitzer sign.

"Okay. Catch you later."

And Margerie heard her brother affectionately calling out to his kid sister as he left the house for one of his adventures: "Take it light, bimbo. Catch you later, bitch . . ."

Margerie left the bar and began to drive, skidding sharply at the very first turn she had to make. She wondered, a few minutes later, as she waited for a traffic light to change, if she should reply to her husband's last letter. The next town had a lit-up Dairy Queen, and she ordered a vanilla shake. Inside her car, in the parking lot, she sat, sipping and writing, her pen mimicking the rhythm of the announcer's voice on the radio, warning motorists of extremely hazardous road conditions.

You ask why I'm here, you imply that there is something unconscious driving me. You use the word "pathology." Yes. Something with no name at all. If you can think of a label for it, I'm sure you'll copyright it, find the perfect designer and the most fetching TV model. You'll celebrate with whiskey sours. But until you name it, it is all mine.

Slowly driving back to her apartment, back to the town she had chosen, she mailed the letter en route, dropping it into the snow-covered slot of a mailbox on the side of the road. Much later that night she lay in bed, listening to winds raging and howling, which she was nearly convinced were not winds at all, but hundreds of car engines being revved-up and stopped, starting and dying, all night long.

HANUMAN BOOKS PRESENTS

A Reading of Poetry and Prose

GREGORY CORSO	VINCENT KATZ
ELAINE EQUI	TAYLOR MEAD
AMY GERSTLER	COOKIE MUELLER
ALLEN GINSBERG	EILEEN MYLES
RICHARD HELL	RENE RICARD
HERBERT HUNCKE	DAVID TRINIDAD
GARY INDIANA	JOHN WIENERS

St. Mark's Church   Second Avenue at 10th Street
Thursday, May 18th, 1989
8:00 pm $10. donation

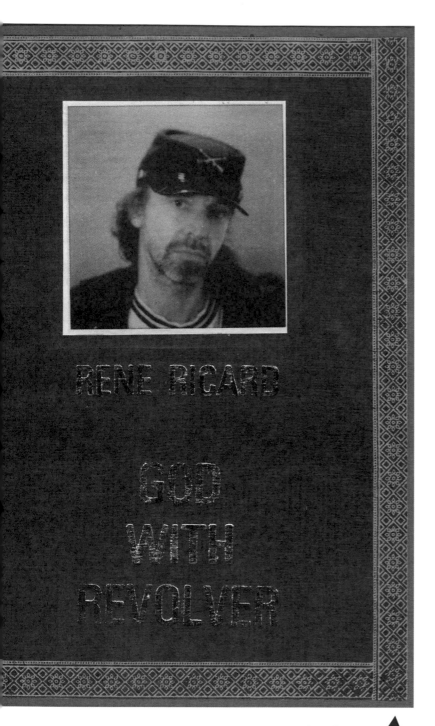

Rene Ricard, *God with Revolver*,
Cover (1989)
Cover design: C. T. Nachiappan

BREAD AND WATER (1989)
EILEEN MYLES

A roll from the bakery at sixth street with flecks of
garlic on the top and a giant glass of ice cold water. A
batch of broken merits which Claudia left on the table
in the bar last night. Two knives on the table—one
for slicing one for buttering. Ever since Christmas
we've had a lot of butter around here. Christine buys
the lightly salted sticks and I like breakstone's sweet
whipped butter better in the tub. I like the fact that
the tubs are waxy. Chris comes in and we talk about
our delirious days. She forgot to ask for the money
for the pills last night so she had to pay Elinor twelve
dollars for everybody. She had a hot dog for lunch
because she saw all these people walking around
with briefcases eating hot dogs so she thought that's
what I need! She said her hot dog was so good
she wants to keep eating them all day. That's what
her eyes look like. Jim woke me up and invited me
Sunday to Staten Island for dinner. 115 Stuyvesant
Place. I put on my jeans and kept lying in my bed
laughing about last night—drinking lots of coffee
and smoking lots of cigarettes. I went out on the fire
escape and took pictures of the virgin and the mop
and the trees behind the fire escape black and then
I held out the camera and took a picture of myself.
I went to St. Mark's Place and tried to get the film
processed. That'll be two dollars deposit. Um. Joe she
doesn't have two bucks can we forego it. He looks
up and down at me and my coat and says no. I ask
the guy for a little bag so I won't screw up my film.
He looks at me like I'm crazy and I stick the little bag
in my pocket and I go out the door. Even at the xerox
place I was told they couldn't do two-sided copying.
Then he said come back at four. Maybe I can. Chris
goes out and comes in with some campbell's tomato

soup and marlboros. You can do them both at the same time. I keep thinking in my mind for about a half hour *Merchard, Merchard*. Finally I call her that. We lick each other's navels, I smell her crotch and smell blood. She tells me she's got a crammer in herself. That's what the girls in Libertyville high school called tampons. I call the xerox place and he tells me he just did it. Chris I don't want to go out at all. Do you want to come walk around with me. My mind does but my body doesn't. Staple stuff go to the post office—is she a lesbian—she says she'll put the stuff in their PO box. She says don't make such a big deal out of it with her eyes when I thank you too hard. It's cold I'm walking over there. He's painting the place and she's in Brooklyn has a workshop tonight. I say Eileen was here and the guy painting the kitchen looks curious. A relative I think. Cutting into the village MacDougal street no Sullivan. Missed kettle of fish maybe googies no Village Corner on the way home. Dark becks ale. I guess I am too tired to do anything now. But cigarettes will go and thirst will come and I'm hungry could go to workshop and ask Barbara for some money but she always loans me money. Easy. I hate to be so legal but. We decide to move to California and become Froggi and Carrot-Face. Wimminsong—some lesbian culture identity who knows. I live in a commune in San Diego and my name is Froggi Wimminsong. Nah. Stuck dried tomato soup in an old bowl and I'm hungry. A glass piggy sitting on the desk and totally empty. Eileen Froggi Wimminsong. Look it's twenty-five past seven. This night. I want a teevee and a pizza. A six-pack. Everyone's sitting down at their seats at the workshop now. Mostly people I know. Me and Merchard have

stayed home because we are weary and Merchard is reading seth material in a pink and black ski sweater and an afghan surrounds her. It is gold rust and plastic turquoise. On the wall is a funny polka-dot umbrella hat. I want a rich visitor. Please me. I do a little fart and Merchard seems to like it. It's one of those nights where I've got to be strange and gross rather than pizza and television. I've already laid on top of Merchard for a while but then she couldn't cough. Across first avenue a red burning liquor sign cuts through the blackness of my black window and the wavering trees. Merchard clears her throat. Heat's coming up in the building a big bang goes outside and sets off a dog barking which sets off something I can't hear. For extrinsic reasons I should've gone to this reading—to get six dollars to give Bob a book. Last night I went to a reading and gave Barbara twelve forks and Chris four pills and Michael gave me a magazine and Kate who I missed gave Christine books for both of us. If these things aren't moving around I hardly see the point in going anywhere. I called Kate at two A.M. to tell her how much I liked the book but she was asleep and not ready to re-adjust. Merchard is still clearing her throat. Though the heat's coming up it feels that my upper legs are getting cold. I need some paper anyway so walking into the kitchen I decide to move. I start heating up some coffee and eye the brownulated sugar to put that in too. Hurry hurry I'm hungry and cold. The thing wrong with the night if you stay in is all you have is sounds and changing temperatures—for instance I just put a reddish orange plaid flannel shirt on which I stole from Jimmy Schuyler because it was getting chilly out by the window and now I'm hearing a police car wheeeoo

wheeeoo but that's all you get at night if you stay in. Puff a hiss of heat is coming in the room, footsteps over my head voices coughing—now that's not much. Or I could mention Merchard softly turning her pages.

Thing is I want to go neither outside nor inside tonight. Talk about how *I* feel or all that. Today I was thinking that though I felt pretty fried from last night and making everyone who saw me suspicious I still felt good—in my body and frisky, I liked my ideas—watching things as they go. I thought it would keep being that way but here it is night and everything's different. I just started doing this thing between remembering and imagining. Last night I'm taking what happened and unspooling each look into a conversation or really playing each conversation as they really were. I saw him chugging down something that looked like pills and I had already downed two but wanted more so I came over. He only had one lousy one he said but I said I'll take that. He didn't like giving it to me either it was out of shortage of pills or how he was feeling towards me that I think. But I'm going on to a more genial conversation with him now where he's saying Eileen who could say no to you. Yeah, that's how I feel—smiling. I never say no to anybody—Susan told me in the bar last week that that was a fault. Directionless. I tried to tell her that I just never care and once in a while I do and then I change places and start saying yes to everything over there. That's all it's like. But I plan to get him something so I can keep asking him for stuff. It's like people who want to "get" sex. Is that possible. In periods of normally perverse and abundant sexuality I never think of getting sex. It's nice too since nobody knows where your strings are. I don't actually think money is a string. You just want it need it.

Please. Cats do not walk on the pink table. After I've cleaned it. I can eat my hot dogs on a dirty table but once it's clean no cat shall walk upon it. A mug of cold water a steaming yellow mug of dark brown coffee a smoking cigarette. I'd like to talk about the hot dog. There were two. This is the third day I've started off with a couple of dogs in a roll. Tuesday a gigantic roll, mustard and onions. And Merchard was there of course eating her own two. Wednesday I sliced mine and put them in a roll along with mayonnaise, onions, tomatoes and tabasco sauce. Delicious. And Merchard was eating her own two and quite disgusted by mine. Yesterday we left the bag of rolls out on the table all afternoon and in early evening I place them in the fridge. This morning I eat my hot dogs simple: sliced in a round stale roll with simply mustard. Merchard is out applying for a job and anyway there were only two dogs left in the pack. A stale roll is terrible. I ate it dutifully mostly in spite of the milky and painful state I'm in. Got roaring drunk last night. Maybe roaring is too loud. I was quietly stinking—was somewhat making out with a guy and a woman in the bar and otherwise it was pretty silent. With my mouth drooping. Merchard told me of it. It's funny—my evening began after the meeting. Alice and I had a couple of quick bourbons in the bar and she told me about bisexual personal ads she read in the voice while looking for an apartment. As she left the bar she told me she was drunk. I think I went on to take those as clues as to how my evening should go. Now I'm kind of torn—should I go on the wagon or something? I rub my hand across my face and it feels slimy and bumpy. But I've been through revulsion before. I should clean this place but I haven't the energy. Coffee grounds and cat litter on the floor. Plaster from the ceiling white falling on this table. I think what money there is left is with Merchard. In the pocket of the jacket she's wearing now I wore last night. I've got this new teal blue maine jacket with grey knit cuffs and collar which Merchard wore last night. I tell her she doesn't look that great in it. I think she knows it's not out of possessiveness I say that but how I see things. Susan loaned me the jacket for four months. I had always admired it on her. I went over to her new apartment one evening and we drank cranberry juice and vodka and she showed me her clothes and I told her which ones I liked. Somehow she was determined that I should come away with a jacket. Her mother wore the jacket in her youth. Really it's the kind of jacket you wear in photographs building a snowman in your backyard with your brother in 1954. And even then it was a handmedown. I tend to wear a lot of clothes like that. Also clothes I see my father wearing in photographs from the forties. Or even the thirties. Chinos white teeshirts. It's funny last night I had nightmares about my dad. Haven't had those for years. I think I will go on the wagon for a while. At least till Tuesday when we have dinner with Michael. Now I wonder if the mailman came. Bringing me money from a poor artist fund. Started by a rich artist. The joke is I'm not an artist but you can't get money without a category. Merchard puts the blue jacket on and asks me how it looks and I say not for those people. Wear the suede. I meant not for any people. She looks too much like she's building a snowman. Merchard either looks very classic or very young. Hasn't the mail come yet? She looks great in black shirts and she wears lipstick easily and looks dramatic. I love Merchard and think she's beautiful. It's funny the night before last she got quite bombed. We take turns. For months Merchard did not get her period. I got two. Now I'm late as hell and Merchard keeps perfect time. Yesterday we put ten dollars down on a teevee. A massive black RCA from the fifties. Another old family photograph. One night last week we sat in bed and I showed her every one. She liked

the one with some Alan Shepherd rocket blasting off on an old-fashioned teevee with a glazed madonna planter on the top. It was such a serious picture when it was taken—historical and all but now it looks funny and quaint. Camp's aunt. Merchard comes in. She got the job. It's on Pearl Street. The mailman did come and nothing in our box. Perhaps they know I'm not an artist. Merchard has to wear black pants white shirt and a black bow tie. She was introduced to one of the waiters there—Christine this is peter pan. They're going to be friends. What if they know I'm not an artist. Shit. Yesterday at the meeting the vote was neck and neck—I hold this final vote in my hand—we drew our breaths—and he won. Groan I did out loud I may not be an artist but I am a poor sport. I want to see us win. I mean I like him too but she should win. Oh well. I like drinking bourbon in the bar with Alice. I asked her for a pill and she gave me one of those speckled oblongs. Later on I was taking two thousand milligrams of vitamin C and I noticed how similar the pills were. C is white but equally oblong. And I get to take two and get to take them whenever I want saying that I do have some or I do have some money. Usually I steal vitamins. I tuck them inside my suede jacket or I slip them in the pocket of my dirty white jacket. Once I had a bag of grapes and stood there munching them in the drugstore and dropped in a bottle of Es when the woman at the cosmetic counter turned. Thievery is a split second art and that's why I love it. It's like being a comedian to be a thief. And also it's being able to turn any situation to advantage. I had a lousy time at George Plimpton's party so I stole a brown hat and a green and yellow preppy scarf. I jumped in a cab and headed down to the Duchess to meet Rose. I know I made a great entrance in that getup and the brown hat wound up on Rose's head. I think she's lost it. Months later I learned from Rae that the hat belonged to Michael Braziller. It was pretty expensive and he was quite pissed. Luckily he knows neither me nor Rose and probably never will unless we become South American or Yugoslavian male poets. It always comes around but nobody knows about it. Last night we left the bar and went across the street to get a pizza. The place was packed and we turned to leave and as she stepped out the door Chris said grab the ten. Right off a check. I did and we got our pizza take out and brought it to a bar. Christine said a couple of guys were making weird lustful remarks about our pizza. How they wanted some. Now I call that pretty fucking strange. I just asked Merchard if she'd like to split that beer in the fridge. She said no go ahead you have it. But I can't. It would make me an alcoholic. You've got to fight fire with fire. That's why I will never really go on the wagon. Then I'd be an alcoholic. Or an ex-alcoholic. Ugly Ugly Ugly. I would like to be an ex-smoker. They just look cleaner and their skin's so nice and they seem so happy. So what if they can't think anymore. I can't talk when I stop smoking. My sentences come out screwed up and gasping and I'm always breathing heavy and spitting. What a beast.

The mailman came today when we were asleep. Yesterday we sat around with the door a crack open and he never arrived. The day before Philip gave me a pink slip that he found in his mailbox. A new mailman and a real fuckup. It said I should go to Cooper Square Station to pick it up. No box was checked on the slip to say what it was. I knew what it was and it would solve Merchard and I's financial crisis immediately. No one could find anything addressed to "Eileen Myles" at the inquiry window. I understood. Undoubtedly it was what I was waiting for. Merchard got dressed early this morning, around noon, and trotted down to our box. Thousands of things but not what we needed. We lay in bed weeping and mock weeping and groaning and then harmonizing our groans. We get very funny on the verge of I don't know what. The other evening outside the post office Merchard suggested we cash in our chips. I agreed. We proceeded to El Centro. We had a dollar thirty five and four cigarettes. We sat in a booth in the back where there was no possibility of anyone offering us a friendly drink. Three guys lay sleeping in their own booths. The short fat tough bartender said things to them like fungoo hell will freeze over before you've spent ten bucks in here and they snarled at her and got up reeling towards the front. We had our two little watery drafts had tipped her the rest of the money except for a nickel. We would quit everything after this beer. Become glowing entities Merchard suggested. We sipped and discussed Sanpaku. Merchard's brother had told her about it years ago in Illinois. He spent a week drawing down his eyes and saying what do you think Chris? Do you think I look Sanpaku? Then we walked slow as hell to 27th Street. Rose and Andy were eating things out of bowls and swallowing pills to help them digest. Andy went out and bought a six of becks and Chris and I drank and smoked Barbara's kents all through the meeting. A fruitful one. Chassler drove us home and I told him I liked his haircut when I got out. We slept deeply once we realized there was no one who would give us credit or loan us money.

Yesterday was the day we waited and waited and the mailman never came. I guess they know I'm not an artist. The phone company called and said we'd be turned off Monday. I put on a grey hooded smock and pencilled some whiskers and a moustache on my face and curled up on the bed. Every time Merchard spoke and elicited a response I felt pained. The sound of my own voice broke my haze each time. The phone rang and a woman told me to come take a test Monday for a job. I looked at myself in the mirror

Panic DJ! Cooper Union, Flyer (1990)
Photo: Michael Wakefield;
Design: Jonathan Andrews

In the Tradition of Lincoln, Twain & Roosevelt

Panic DJ! at The Cooper Union

Think the Other Thought!
The Impossible Rap is ready to appear/ Is it possible that you are ready to hear?/ It has something to do with what you just said/ It's the thought you can't remember/ In the back of your head/ It's the dream you can't surrender/ When you get out of bed/ Just Return to Sender/ Think the Other Thought instead!
B. Holman, "Impossible Rap"

Bob Holman, the Panic DJ!, and his Main Motor Scooter, Vito Ricci in a performance of poetry, rap and song at the Great Hall at the Cooper Union, Astor Place, New York, NY.
212 353 4196

"Panic DJ explodes with jounce and pounce!"
Gwendolyn Brooks, 1989

**New Poems
The Great Hall, Cooper Union
Tuesday, 20 March 8 PM
Free**

and washed my face and started thinking. Merchard and I threw ourselves down on the bed and raised our arms in the air harmonizing our animal sounds directing them to the goddess's ears. I realized I could get back our ten dollar deposit on the giant black RCA we really wanted. We bombed down to St. Mark's Place and I showed the guy my slip and asked for our ten dollars back. He tried to throw us out of the store—five people have tried to buy that teevee but I was saving it for you so you can't get your money back—Get out of here! I pleaded, tried to reason called him a bastard and he awkwardly called me a bastard back. Somehow only males are called bastards. He was a large black guy who was really getting fed up. Get out of my store, now. *No.* I want my money back. I jumped in anger in this weird characteristic way I have since a child. I look like an angry frog. You can jump your ass off but you're not going to get your money back. You've got to give it to me. We're hungry. We won't have any dinner tonight. Nothing. You've got this store with all these teevees. You don't need my ten dollars. You're just doing it for spite. I didn't do it on purpose to you. I'd rather have that teevee. I love that teevee. But tonight I'm so broke I can't eat. Everytime he said get out I said no. I've never used this tactic before. Finally he peeled a wrinkly ten off a small wad of bills—Here, now get out. I was so worked up as we headed down St. Mark's Place. Merchard was patting me on the back and we turned into the deli on first ave and sixth street and bought two six packs of tuborg gold in bottles and a pack of marlboros. We felt so much better drinking and smoking and seeing a future and then the buzzer rang and it was Tim and we gave him a beer and the three of us looked at the cameras and the film and the way this apartment is laid out and wondered what kind of movie we were going to make.

By nine o'clock we had finished filming and Christine had blood all over her shirt and thousands of beer bottles sat on the table and cigarette butts and wires and lights were looping in and out of everything. The scene with the hand going toward the phone and then the cleaver and the squirt of blood was great. Or when I fell back from being stabbed I think and really hit Tim's nose so both of us looked pretty pained and Merchard thought it shot well. We were gleaming and pleased but no cigarettes were left so we went out in the rain and bought some and headed to the St. Mark's Bar and Grille to show Tim what a great place it was but it was a drag. I called Tom and Richard to borrow money but they weren't home. We thought it over a while. Chris came back from the bathroom excited that it was a quarter of eleven and Alice's workshop would be out and all drinking at El Centro. Tim was looking for pills and Chris and I just wanted someone to buy us drinks. The place was empty. So was the Ukrainian place. Actually it was packed but with wrong people. We wound up standing inside the 5th street deli trying to think of someone to call. Or we had one idea but no one had the nerve to call her. I asked Tim for a dollar and went to the deli and bought a box of lorna doones. They made us sick and we decided to spend the rest of the weekend starving not smoking not drinking and taking advantage of our situation by cleaning out. She fell asleep pretty quickly—I started to but as I was falling heard her voice go Eileen are you in there? It scared the shit out of me. I was either out of my body or Chris was talking to me from inside her dream. I touched her to reassure us and she barely woke and I told her I had a nightmare and she put her arm around me and fell back to sleep. I felt safer now so I could explore the situation. Every time I closed my eyes lights started flashing colors were reeling and I could almost make pictures out of them. One window was too bright and the closed one was full of ominous shadows. I felt I was flipping out. Then I remembered about a year ago when Joe and Tom were making a movie here and the place felt spooked afterwards. Like movies leave ghosts or spirits plus the sensation of watching or being watched doesn't stop when the film runs out.

First I shut the door across the window. It's cold. I'm shivering. But then I open it. I don't like to lose the light. The windows are so dirty and spotted. Outside looks like an old-fashioned painting. I don't like paintings but this one. The christmas interview is sitting on the table. Carter Calls To Arms. To Russia With Hate. He asked me if I'd be home at one so I called him collect at twenty past. Said we'd meet at 5th and second ave. Walked into the vicious bodega. Two women from there beat Christine up. Two months I'd walk in there drunk buy some marlboros say you hate women. You do. Once the ugly one raised a baseball bat from behind the counter. Go ahead. All these guys were standing around. We stared at each other for a moment. Then I left.

We walked into the bodega last night at one thirty and he went for the freezer pulled out two red and white sixes of bud in cans. I love men. If we're going to *drink*, we're going to *drink*. Big solid hand going for two sixes putting them down on the counter picking up the bag and going out the door. Stayed up till about five. We've got Susan's teevee for a week. Talking watching Joe Franklin move termite celebrities around seats asking asshole questions never wondering what the answer might be. Still a dream of mine to be on a talk show. Couldn't you be on because you always wanted to be a guest. Still I'd need an agent to do my explaining. So nice to see them yesterday. Big floppy house all their paintings like messy Gertrude Stein. Smoking his chesterfields drinking her beers we go

out & get more of everything. A conversation always unfinished. The Truman Capote piece I was telling you about is in this red and green interview. We were watching teevee some old movie we didn't see but kept flickering while we talked. How everything's equal since I've been fucked over worse by women than men almost more because it hurts more. A woman uses you because you let her in so naturally never expected it's just chess. I've learned so much. Women per se. Men per se. Everything feels equal. Trust per se. You walk away thinking what a great man what a great woman. How really nice they are. In or by itself; intrinsically. No such thing. You make a hole in the weave if you expect anything to be something through and through. There. I've gotten to explain it. You look at people. They look at you. Sure. It's like have you been a catholic. Someone wants you to be a machine or else they think its just a passing phase. Lesbian per se. For their benefit I should be a mannequin—no, I never think of fucking men—they're never cute I think they smell, etc. Then you don't talk to them and it gets worse like nobody's real. I mean I am a dyke per se but unless I squelch all my ambiguities—be like a guy who won't admit another guy is cute or he'd be a faggot—Oh, no. Well I don't care. I just intend to carry on. I'm not going to worry about my persuasions or everyone's intentions—I know *just how* real I am. Honestly. Money in the bank.

The phone's half off, the power's going off tomorrow. I am unemployed. So is Merchard. I owe the woman in the bakery 4.65. I'll have to be flirty when I come back. I owe Mario across the street 3.59. I owe Vince upstairs two bucks. I owe Bruce next door 10. Philip downstairs 5. Greg 5. Rose 25. Andy 5. Richard 5. Ted Greenwald 5. Vicki 15. Helene 100. Gertie 150. Susan 110. Didi a dollar. Lots of dollars, so many dollars I can't remember.

New Observations (Edited by Mike Topp),
No. 66 (1989)
Art: Ida Applebroog

So many dentists (2) and of course the Harvard Coop—thirty dollars. I woke up with no tampax—blood streaming through my jeans so I took them off and I'm walking around like a giant thirty year old baby woman with an olive green towel between my legs. Fell back to sleep that way with my diaper on. Merchard goes down and gets the mail. A rebate check from the Harvard Coop for 2.41. Breakfast! Tampax! I pack my jeans with toilet paper and the two of us stroll to the check cashing place. The guy shakes his head at my teeny endowment. Deducts his and I get 2.01. I shake my head. Merchard suggests we go to the "Certified" on second avenue where we can get everything and probably steal. It turns out to be "Associated" but what the fuck's the difference so I don't point it out. Cram tampax down my jeans. Buy some eggs. Merchard's got a taste for ham she says so we try schacht's. Too dear. Spanish place on sixth and first has cheap ham. Two rolls at the bakery. Forty cents. We've got sixteen cents left. Heat up the rest of the coffee. I do the eggs, she does the ham. Everything's great, sun streaming onto our roaring breakfast, butter salt pepper everything being wolfed down by two lesbians per se while the cat countlessly assaults the trash bag and Merchard hurls her across the room. Once or twice. We let the cat—Little Andy—lick our dishes on the floor. The coffee's all gone. We'd love another pot. And also I suggest a big tall glass of good orange juice. She agrees. Would you like a glass of ice water. OK, I'm washing the glasses, setting them up. Dropping cubes into the tall ice tea glass and the shorter broader beer mug. I set them out. We're sitting in the sun, drinking our water. I'm smoking, Merchard's talking about really quitting today. I should too I proffer since I have no idea where the next pack is coming from. But I love to smoke. She'll probably quit—at least for a while.

Ulle hasn't called yet. Merchard's going to do it today since I'm gushing blood and want to stay home and be cozy and warm. If Ulle hasn't called by now—it's quarter to three. So we lose $15. Start planning the other afternoon. She goes to the refrigerator and pulls out a couple of beers. A six wound up left from last night. Our future. The phone rings. Merchard's chugging her beer—I'm going to be late, I'm going to be late. Do you think I should have another beer. Maybe she should bring a couple—Ulle'd like one. Would that be cool? No, don't do it. So I go to get one right now. There. Pop. That's all times falling into each other. Merchard's still putting on her brown leather gloves, I mean Chris. She's looking English French American *lesbian*, not dyke. There's a difference, at least right now. I'm looking at her standing there, looking at her in her orange construction boots and everything else dark. I'm really adoring her as she's leaving and by the second she's getting more and more beautiful look at her eyes all green and golden brown and gigantic and these unreal lashes. Two are caught between her nose and her eyes are just sitting there and you know how people who really love you or who you irritate are always coming over and picking something off you. Well I can't even tell her I like those two lashes just where they are. Her entirety goes out the door. Eileen's entirety is lying on the couch watching teevee, waiting for them to turn us off.

BITTEN BY A MONKEY

Satie's Sports & Divertissements

Guest Editor:
Mike Topp

Contributors:
**John Cage
Ida Applebroog
Claudia Hart
Patrick McGrath
Eileen Myles
William Wegman
Michael Smith
Tom Ahern
Richard Ledes
Karen Fredericks
Peter Cherches
Allan Bealy
John Baldessari
Ron Kolm
Ron Padgett
Steve Levine**

FROM *BEER MYSTIC* (1989)

BART PLANTENGA

The world grows bigger as the light leaves it.
　　　—Beryl Markham, Aviatrix, *West with the Night*

As I grew older I became a drunk. Why?
Because I like ecstasy of the mind.
　　　　　　　—Jack Kerouac

The vigilant light trails my transient shadow here, eats away at it like vermin gnawing through drywall. And I can hear my voice being mocked by its own echo and vice versa. And when you think thoughts they feel like the thoughts of someone else. And they probably are. When I say something, what I hear is something different. I hear the baffling defiance of our surroundings to conform to prescribed parameters of bliss. And I am *this* small. (I show you my pinkie.)

I sometimes hung with Jude along the Tropic of Mirth and Mire. 40°42' latitude, 74° longitude around 103rd Street. . . . Jude's severe look kept bugs and guys out of her face. It's amazing how makeup can do so much of the work of esteem and attitude. Her brows were like crossed scimitars. Her eyes fixed, going nowhere except right through you. Until you get to know her. And then all is candy. Including her eyes. She is beautiful even when she's frowning like a Sherman Tank.

But I really liked her. The way she'd lean over the bar with her skirt hiked up to reveal the sacral segments of her tailbone, ordering drinks based solely on the sensuous shape of the bottle and the aesthetic quality of the exotic labels, which was her ever-ready remedy for writer's constipation. I watched her squint to read one: "Jameson, established since 1780, sine metu. . . . From the rich countryside of Ireland come nature's finest barley and crystal clear water."

"You can read that? I don't even see the label."

"My eyes get better the more I drink."

"Me too. But I gotta have *lots*." Then reaching, one knee up on the bar, she pointed to just short of touching the actual bottles. "I mean, you drink much more you'll be seein' that I am as erect as a hollyhock."

She could, even with the dead weight of me in tow, pry multiple drinks out of any bartender, armed only with her insouciant smile, clingy dresses, the sighs that emerged from her décolletage, and her witty repartee. This surgically precise extraction of drinks was a sight to behold. Every gesture calculated and allusive, culled from the repertoires of Dietrich, Hayworth, and Dorothy Parker. Her actions seldom (but then more and more) involved a compromise of any someone's character, at least back when Jude still benefited from that magical psychotropic state of liquor + hormones = enhanced vision.

I find bars that offer respite from the cumulative insanity outside. Taverns with Coltrane and candles. Cafés with Goa jazz, pubs with music that is played on long, long wet strings. Bowers of timelessness, quiet temples, Amsterdam's "brown cafes," Prague's rowdy *pivnices* (Old One Eye), the neon-lineamented zinc bars of Paris (Bar Iguan), NYC's outpost dives (Sally's, Downtown Beirut, The Cool Mine) where clocks are all a mess (at Eike & Linde's in Amsterdam, the clocks run backwards!); where play time doesn't pass so much as nourish; where one doesn't age so much as beam.

It is the mouth-to-mouth, the intimacy, spittle entering the glass as beer enters you, clocks losing their tick, hearts losing their beat, a hum, the hum inside the humerus, that long bone in a human arm which extends from thirst to shoulder, to elbow, is linked to the ulna, radius, carpus, metacarpus, phalanx, and around the circumference of the beer glass. Palm, the Belgian beer, is properly poured into a glass seemingly cast from the perfect breast. This is where the ruddy-cheeked smile embodies essential theories of ecstasy's architecture. Where eyes sit in the smile's crescent like warm eggs, oblivious to the idio-tautological, er, ideological tricks of the time-managers.

Convivial bars where barkeeps intuit your desires, where you can stare at a wall and they can sense you are watching the filmstrip that is already inside yourself and they don't ask "what's up buddy?" Where you manufacture your own fanfare, lean back into your own character, where you cannot depend on a logothematic backdrop (Harley Davidson Café, the DKNY Inseam), festive psycho-diorama (TGIF at 12th and Second), or some simulacrum saloon (Hard Rock Café or Slim Jerkey's) where MTV-enhanced waitpersons memorize jokes to "entertain" tips out of you and your wallet. Or offer you pithy correctives like "smile and the whole world smiles back."

Jude's Sang Froid Bar was *not* one of these cloisters. It had all the atmosphere of an outpatient clinic dressed up as a pinball arcade and was filled with hunched-over chunky MBAs contemplating the killings they were about to make on a market ergonomically designed to accommodate their kind.

This is where *she* taught *me* how to "kill" a beer. Open can. Tip head back. Can on lips until back of head touches backbone. Now punch hole in bottom of can with a church key. Beer floods down the gullet, her lovely neck fully exposed to over-watted tracklights.

"Ten seconds or less. Killed. Cheap shotgun drunk. Courtesy of cruel gravity and some '60s noir film I saw with a rowdy boy I once dated outa Detroit." Not that she deigned to ever drink beer for beer's sake. This was performance. "It's pure white trash." She liked white trashisms without having to be associated with it demographically. "It's one of the only good things about gravity. Otherwise gravity just causes jowls, causes your breasts to sag."

"Not mine. Maybe yours."

Jude had splendid legs; slender and dramatic, aromatic, aerodynamic like a letter opener in Place Pigalle. Much of her wardrobe seemed to enhance the linear drama of her limbs or her breasts in excelsis (I'm reminded of Gauguin paintings where breadfruit and breasts get confused for one another) served up so that elegies could more easily be written about them. I have sketched them and used a thesaurus to get at their . . . *numinosity.*

But when I rhapsodized onward and drooly about the firm and delirious cudgel lumps of her gastrocnemius muscles in her calves in the Sang Froid she reacted quite peculiarly; commenced to whistle, pound her fists, leap into the thick air, let the imaginary egg timer ring. Mocked my less-than-original observation with game-show hysteria. I'd been the 10,000th man to tell her that—in fact. And of those 10,000 only one hundred had gotten any further (or so she claimed). Figure it out; I had a 1% chance with her. But really, I had a much better chance when I realized that I had not factored in her own (disguised) despair.

"You like my haircut, you like me. It's as simple as that," she said. But it wasn't. The simpler people say things are the more difficult you can expect them to be.

"How do you do it? I mean how does muscle make us dream? I mean your calves, just by lookin' at them makes me hard . . ."

"I do a lot of reaching for top-shelf liquor." I couldn't take my eyes off her legs.

"Furman, you're subtle as a chainsaw staring down a birthday cake."

Be careful, even basic human gestures, a smile, or unscrewing the cap off her rum bottle could be enough semiotic signal to send her into reveries of swooning. She was always hoping the swooning itself would hurtle her, hurtling you or me along with her ever further afield.

First came her hoping, then wishing, then begging as the night of drinking collapses into her slinky gelatinous swoon (like a studied movie still) to render her more pliable, more palatable. . . .

Back at her place I sat on my hands on the arm of her sofabed. Jude had no real lamps in her place except for the one over her word processor. Just some candles and about twenty two-watt night lights that made her place look like a forest full of giant fireflies or a small town planetarium. And as my prize for being the 10,000th flatterer she had decided to read me one of her very own short stories. It had won an award, she assured me, of some prestige.

In the 1980s she was the Edna St. Vincent Millay of her milieu—fascinating, sharp, ebullient, red hair, flairful fashions, and a book with the ballast of much acclaim. This by her own reckoning but corroborated by others whom I trusted. But her plunge from bon vivant to bonbon, from devil-may-care to devil-may-snare was a dramatic if avoidable denouement. The rightful compliments and lusts that used to leap into her very midst suddenly had to be fished for, cajoled, and pried from the mouths of men.

In her day her kiss was a devastating testament to ruthless abandonment and unrequited priapic throbs. But now her kiss might seem more akin to supplication, with the sucking action of a Dust Buster. Of a simple embrace, a kiss goodnight, she created Peyton Places in the cold chambers of her heart. And the men she could not have whom she desired so much?—well, she began to marvel at her ulcers. They emerged as gastro-intestinal proofs of the profundity of her sufferings. Because, after all, she was no ordinary romantic. She was epic, post-Victorian. She chose guys already in relationships so that her fate was comfortably sealed and so that her sadness would manifest itself in fiction that then subsequently corresponded to her basic philosophy of hope deferred.

I needed ale but she is a scotch tippler and that spells trouble. In her fridge . . . one LITE beer (whose brand I will not even dignify by ridiculing!). Which guy was that designed to keep overnight? And this, even its mitigating alcohol potential, did not derail me from my long spiral out of glorious priapism and into utter flaccidness. I am suddenly no longer taken by her, or rather, the part she has written for me to play—my erection as her spiritual prosthesis.

Our dynamic forced from me inane niceties, compliments on choice of earrings, socks, rum adjectives to protect her fragile composition, that tenuous matrix of beliefs, hopes, and misconceptions. The kinds of accolades that would undo blouse buttons.

She could stare at one word on her screen all day, agonizing over whether that word was the perfect one. And the next day whether that perfect word was preceded by the perfect adjective. In 10 years she'd have another short story. A perfect story that would mean nothing in a stylish and admirably obsolete way. The words all attached to the proper emotions. And there the short story would lie like a cow heart on a piece of wax paper in a butcher shop.

Her parents had purchased a computer for her, but because the screen was so bright and upset the dusky aspect of her room she had unplugged it. She did not want to conquer its manuals and its disdainful illumination for fear it would conquer her. It had been a week since she'd unplugged it. She had heard about viruses that rewrite your writing so that the writer loses control of what s/he has written. She had almost decided to dump it.

"I dunno, its blank stare is a kind of contempt, I dunno, with all its substantial memory and all." What'd I think? Well, I guess that all depended on how far I needed to flatter her (and convince myself how lucky I was to be here with her) to be able to negotiate my mindless fingers up the smooth flanks of !eg.

She confined herself, for the most part, to this garret that had been decorated to harass/torment her. Overwrought wallpaper, gruesome gnarly fixtures, dark olive-green office furniture that had been rescued from an old accounting firm filled with Burroughs adding machines. Overrun by a kind of neglect that baffled pride of place. Or accommodation to the scrivener's muse. The weight of sorrow in this place plowed right into her face. Living here would mean having to constantly apologize to appliances or things for moving them around.

And she sat there, puffed out in her old heavy swivel chair, pretty as a worried bird on a broken twig, reams of tortuously rewritten words on her lap (red arrows and blue lines at crazy crisscrosses all over the pages), stories that "came from somewhere but went nowhere."

I sipped the LITE without dirtying my lips on the can itself. This required a steady hand. . . . And after a long kissing and body-rummaging session, I offered to demonstrate (a proper how-to—had no man ever done this for her?) the correct piston action of how the fist caresses and skins the prick of all its shine and spit. I could almost hear her manufacturing the appropriate phrases to properly convey her disgust at being forced to partake of the mechanics of auto-gratification and dovetailing this scene into some other locale. Can I say, at this point, in all fairness, that to her sex meant the alleviation of all responsibility, concern, and attention to the other?

"I'm a romantic not a mechanic." Is how I remember her putting it after I had made a deal out of her being less than attentive to the finer tunings of amour. Like I was just a tree she needed to rub up against for long enough. Or something.

With all this *self-consciousness* came its own moral tapeworm: the fact that we would accentuate our *selves* to elaborate into high drama every gesture to assure that each of us would figure heavily in one another's *roman à clefs*. And so writing was allowed to devour the very love we claimed to covet. The writing would precede us, set up the lighting, create the backdrop, seal the destiny of the scenario. And then we'd arrive. In fact, everything was subservient and nothing until put into words. The action resembling a carnivorous plant that devours the very bee that will ensure the species' survival.

My visits to her garret could be likened to the way a priest solemnly enters the cell of a death-row inmate. At one point she held up a manuscript she claimed she'd been working on for months, ripped up this story that had never worked, and tossed the snippets up into the dead air. And watched from the sagging hollow of her couch as the confetti rained down on us. . . .

I got down on my hands and knees and started to rewrite the story in a new way. She laughed and then as quickly stopped. That I wasn't mocking her wasn't clear enough for her to NOT throw me out.

In her elevator I looked in the mirror, repeated the line I never got to use, "Jude, you can bait the hook but you cannot catch the fish."

And when I leave Jude's I have to walk. And when I walk I see her legs. I make words sing of her legs and words act like the dreams of legs.

They are Parisian dreams. Pale Greek statuary in the Tuilleries. They walk toward me, and what is the name of that drug of insinuation?

When I walk I think, and when I think I become a genius, and when I walk in the lucent light, a Bedouin celestial navigation—type of starlight, I feel like an alchemist approaching the knowledge of perfection. I have discovered the knowledge of perfection like an alchemist might with a six-pak coursing through alimentary canal—colon and rectum—ancient phantom stops along the Rockaway-bound A train. Brew is the sextant of elixir, an alchemy that transforms sharp objects, projectiles of control, architectures of neglect, and belligerent light strategies into a soft contoured womb, spinning everything of mind and blur, of environ and reverie, into its non-spatial and non-temporal delirious core. This state (migration inside stasis, daydreams of the stoneface) is attained, some say, as we move from light beer to dark, where the blood becomes aqua vitae and the conscious will becomes flooded with personal lumen naturae or psycho-magnetic bio-luminescence.

With that I uncap a Lambic, something special (from Belgium, where Lembeek or Lime Creek refers to the limey character of the soil)—from the clandestine confines of a paper sack! A paper sack because they who own the city and supply the uniforms for the police, they want to contain vision so they can tinker it into the shapes that will flatter themselves.

Don't guzzle your Lambic because it aligns itself with anarchist thought by inviting *wild* microflora to *spontaneously* ferment. Sip and swish and let this most unusual beer linger on your taste buds. This is what I do—I walk, I sip, I swish, I swallow, I smile and the longer I walk, the more adept I become at synthesizing knowing and being.

FROM *HORSE CRAZY* (1989)

GARY INDIANA

WHO KNOWS what hearts and souls have in them? On the answering machine a message from Victor, who tells me when I call him that Paul, long ago my lover for two years, is sick. People use a special tone of voice, now, for illness, that marks the difference between sick and dying.

I've heard he's sick.

And so this body whose secret parts were my main pleasure in life for longer than anyone else's transforms itself into a fount of contagion. Paul passes over into the territory of no-longer-quite-alive, and I calculate that if he got it five years ago, the general incubation period, he must have been infectious on each of the fifty or sixty occasions when we slept together, giving me a much better than average chance of being infected.

He wants to see you. He's asked for you.

I haven't seen Paul in over a year. One day I saw him on the street with the man he's been living with, a tall, gangly man, whereas Paul has a rugged, packed look about him and that face, the map of Macedonia. We said hello goodbye very pleasantly and I considered that if he hadn't had a continual need to fuck all over town we might've moved in together and had a normal relationship, if there is such a thing. He liked having someone at home, waiting for him. I never could wait for people. Victor says, he came back from abroad and his roommate found him the next morning bleeding from the mouth.

Maybe it's because we didn't love each other that we broke off without any rancor, without even really breaking off. We met every three or four nights in the corner bar, the one near my house where I still sometimes drink with Victor. Paul and I never made dates or anything, and some nights we saw each other there but went home with other people, if Paul didn't feel like doing it with me he would say: Let's get together real soon.

How long has he been sick.

We stopped sleeping together when people still referred to "gay cancer" and thought it came from using poppers. For a long time I moved back and forth from Europe, each time I returned the thing had become more of a subject, I heard of this one that one getting pneumonia and fading out. Paul said once: It's getting scary, it's getting close. He'd met Jason years ago and they had made it once in a while, Paul told me, when it wasn't you it usually was him, and then he and Jason moved into a place on Cornelia Street, signing a joint lease, which was practically marriage.

They've had him in the hospital for two weeks.

At first the people who died were people I barely knew, or people from earlier lives who'd been in a lot of the same rooms, their deaths were disconcerting but seemed to happen on a distant planet. At first people would say: Well, he must have been leading a secret life, taking all kinds of drugs and going to the Mineshaft. Because at first, most people who got ill did seem the same ones who never finished an evening at four A.M., piled into taxis together when the regular bars closed. And then of course there was this other thing with needles, if it spread by blood and sperm, people who used needles would naturally get it.

The worst thing is, I can't feel anything for Paul. I'm too scared for myself.

But you'll go see him, I hope.

Of course I will.

Except that I am, in this particular business, a bigger coward than I'd like to be. Victor and I used to drink with Perkins when Perkins turned up in the bar, and when Perkins got ill, I didn't go to the hospital, he had one bout of pneumonia and the now-familiar remission, and Chas, who lives in a building behind my building, called raising money to get Perkins a color TV, since he had to stay in all the time, and I never gave any, I promised to, in the early autumn, and one mild afternoon I saw Perkins at Astor Place, looking all of his fifty-four years which he never had previously, he said, Call me sometime, and the next I heard it went into his brain and they brought him into St. Vincent's raving, Victor went four or five times, I said, My God, Victor, what do you say?

The thing is, Victor said, when he feels all right he doesn't feel as if he's dying, the worst thing is acting morbid and stricken about it. You just go have a normal conversation with him. But it's too late now because he isn't lucid for more than a few minutes during any given visit. At first he's his old self and then he babbles.

I never thought I'd be so chickenshit about anything.

But this new situation, with Paul, what does it mean? And with Gregory? Another thing about Perkins: he had, for a time, a comely Irish lover named Mike, a slender boy with soft brown eyes and a small wisp of a mustache, they were together for a while and then they weren't. Mike fucked everything that walked, one night we found ourselves using the toilet in Nightbirds when it was still an after-hours joint and I let him piss in my mouth, then we screwed at my place the whole next day in every conceivable position. He called a few days later and warned me his doctor thought he had hepatitis B, as it happened I'd just had a typhoid shot for my visa to Thailand and got a bad reaction, my pee turned red, then it passed on and Mike phoned just before I left to say his results turned out negative.

Mike moved to California and then Hawaii for several months and when he came back he lived with Perkins again but soon after that he started looking spectral and then stopped going out and then everyone heard that he had it and a few months later everyone heard that he died. That was four years before Perkins came down with it and when Perkins came down with it he told everyone he was sure he got it from Mike, though how Perkins could be sure, since Perkins took it up the can as often as possible from anyone available, was a mystery. Yet he insisted that Mike had been the source.

Until now Mike has been the only person I know I've slept with who later died from it and I used to think that because I recovered from the typhoid shot, which I got after I slept with him, that meant I hadn't caught it from him, and I also rationalized that maybe Mike caught it in California or Hawaii and then gave it to Perkins when he moved back to New York, in which case Perkins' incubation period may have only been a year or two, or rather four years, I keep getting dates mixed up, I went to Thailand in '81 and I think I'd already stopped sleeping with Paul, so if I didn't get it from Mike possibly I didn't get it from Paul either. But with Mike I could only have been exposed once, and some people think repeated exposure is necessary for the virus to take hold, so if it had only been Mike I could now feel fairly confident though how can anyone who ever did anything with anybody feel at all confident, and with Paul, of course, the case is quite different, his dong has been in every hole in my body hundreds of times squirting away like the Trevi Fountain, I've rimmed him too, and once when he cut his finger chopping up some terrible cocaine he bought in the Spike I even sucked his blood.

Now, of course, everyone's conscious about the problem, but as somebody said in the paper the horses are out of the barn, how can you possibly know if, back in the days of sexual pot luck, someone you met by chance and screwed and never saw again wasn't a carrier? Not that I've had so many in the last few years, but they don't really know if numbers are important, even if I don't have it I probably have the antibodies and if I have the antibodies I'm probably a carrier. So if I do it with Gregory I risk infecting him. And then, I don't know about Gregory, either. He says he hasn't taken heroin in five years, but junkies who do manage to kick usually fuck up several times before they get off it, maybe five years isn't so precise either, in addition to that Gregory looks like a magazine cover and I can't imagine he hasn't satisfied all his sexual appetites regularly, in fact he's alluded to dark periods of the past, hinted that when he used heroin he did some hustling here and there, he's so well-spoken and smart it's hard to imagine him peddling his dick on the sidewalk but who knows what people will do. Anyway, I threw myself at him in less than a second after seeing that face and I'm shy, there must have been hundreds of opportunities. Thousands.

Victor says he'll go with me to see Paul.

I realize that I really am in love with Gregory.

These have to be peculiar times.

IT WOULDN'T be strange to get it and then to decide as Perkins did that this one particular person gave it to you, one out of ten or fifty or a hundred, maybe because that person made you feel something special, had done wonderful things in bed or gotten you to trust him physically and mentally as no one else ever had. Mike for example had miraculous talents because his sexual demands were flagrant and overpowering, he was socially rather genteel but I remember in the bathroom at Nightbirds and later too he talked dirty and tough, Kneel down, bitch, suck that dick, he actually said things like, Yeah, you want that big dick, sure, you wanna get fucked with that big prick, and of course the pissing, which had introduced itself as a specially filthy surprise, but the way he insisted on it made it seem like an ordinary thing people really ought to do. Mike was an incredibly complete fuck, he exhausted your imagination and wiped out your memory of other fucks, when Perkins remembered making love perhaps he only thought of Mike and things Mike did to him. You would naturally connect your most vivid memory of pleasure to infection and death because the others weren't remotely worth getting sick from, just pale skimpy traces of sex crossed with thin trickles of "bodily fluids," if the two things had to be linked, better for a cherished memory of sex to connect with transmission of the microbe.

In any case, if you had sex now it was a matter of deciding, even if you took elaborate precautions, whether the degree of risk involved (and who could calculate that?) was "worth it," whether your need for that kind of experience with another person outweighed, in a sense, your desire for survival.

When I think about Perkins in that fifth-floor walk-up watching the color TV his friends gave him, I imagine him measuring out his life in half-hour segments, telling time by the flow of images and the chatter of voices, his thoughts melting into the TV. As he wasted away the set continued entertaining him, keeping his mind off things. It showed him funny pictures that weren't really funny and brought him news of catastrophes that were somehow beside the point. The TV made his death feel vicarious and filled his bedroom with another world he could enter when this one ran its course. A quilt covered the bed, the same bed he'd slept in with Mike, the room was big and chilly with a thin musty carpet covering the wood floor, brown velour drapes hiding the arched windows. His bedside lamp had a pink shade, the square table near his pillows had pill bottles and a water glass on it, he didn't feel as though he were dying, Victor said, he just knew, intellectually, that his death was coming sooner rather than later. Sooner than expected. But does anybody expect to die? Even when one is quite old, it must seem a fantastic event, if you're ninety you can still imagine living, say, till ninety-five.

M. IS lying in the darkness of his own bedroom, a plywood cubicle within his vast loft, near the southern tip of the island. He's talking into his cordless telephone, which gives local calls the scratchy echo of long distance.

We live in large and small boxes in buildings on regularly shaped streets. We see each other seldom because we are busy. Nothing happens to us except dinner parties and visits to the dentist and work, our lives have the generic flavor of deferred pleasure and sublimation until we fall in love or die.

M. is thirty-six, rich, successful. He's a closer friend to me than Victor but I haven't been in his apartment in years. When you're busy you use the telephone.

Contamination, he says, through the telephone crackle.

Like water, I tell him.

Water, blood, sputum, spit, urine, semen, any kind of fluid. It's all in the food chain, M. declares. You have to imagine particles, like from Chernobyl, settling into the water table like—like little dissolving snowflakes. They sink into the ground when it rains, go into the water, everybody drinks it. Some people get a little bit, some people get a lot. Or maybe it gets eaten by a cow or a pig, it grows into grass and some *swines* store it up in their tissues, and then you pop into the local deli for a ham sandwich with a little mustard, on some nice rye bread, presto you've got AIDS.

AND WHAT if I die, right away instead of later on, if for instance I take the blood test, it's positive, I'll never finish anything important, I won't leave anything behind. Or just a few things, of no historical interest. On the immortality front I will fail, ashes to ashes, and no health insurance either, I'll become a ward of the city and be put in one of those wards where the doctors and nurses shun you for fear of catching it, and none of your friends comes to the hospital. Libby would come, M. would come, Victor would come, my friend Jane would definitely come, but how would I die, what would I be like, and how lugubrious for them, if it's a big ward there's bound to be others dying in the same room, dying with the television on, perhaps they make them wear headphones but when the ward got deathly quiet at night I'd hear the little bug noises in their earpieces. Is that the point, to leave something behind, it's really a silly ambition, if you're dead what difference does it make. Of course they say it's why people have children, they can remember you for a time, though mainly they remember pain, pain from their terrible childhoods, even if their parents loved them, it's usually so twisted it's as bad as hate, and even when it isn't, the other children torture you and make fun of all your little quirks and debilities, you try to escape into fantasies but those are poisoned from the very outset, while you're still in first grade they've already turned you into a monster, you spend your whole adult life trying to wipe out all the things they've taught you to do, trying not to hate yourself.

I never talk about my childhood because I only remember pain. And then I keep meeting people like Gregory who think they're as they are because of the father or because of the mother, he seems so clear about it, my father did this to me and my mother did that, therefore I am. I don't know what either of my parents did. My mother says she regrets slapping me too often and I can't remember ever being slapped. Maybe she remembers wrong. When you go into psychotherapy they teach you to invent false memories of childhood beatings and sexual abuse, people become addicted to these simple explanations of why they're monsters.

And now everyone is going to die before they figure anything out, I'm going to die before I can be truly loved, I'll die with every sort of bitter memory of my last lover's coldness and Paul's faithlessness, though really that didn't matter with him, I'm not bitter against him, but why couldn't I have what I had with him with someone who loved me, and I'll die before I can make Gregory love me, I can see I'm fated to cash it in without a single memory of real happiness. What is real happiness. Is it this business of living with another person, I never really lived with anybody, I thought no one could stand it. You think you'll have a long life, so you do everything at a snail's pace, before I tried to write *Burma* I started a book about a family, one sister was a socialite, another was crippled in a wheelchair, the brother was a fag actor in Off-Broadway, the parents had been murdered in their townhouse, I only wrote two scenes of that book,

the sister in bed with her boyfriend and the brother getting drunk on the set of a soap opera, not bad, oh yes and one scene with the sister racing through the townhouse in her wheelchair, she'd had special ramps built so she could get around. Before that I tried something like a love story based on me and that California surfer type I fucked a few times when I lived in Boston, a shoplifter. Nobody shoplifts any more, I remember when everyone did it, it showed your contempt for the capitalist system. Everyone worships capitalism today. Look at this obscene medical system. If Paul doesn't have insurance he's probably in a room full of other people's contagion, they say the patients with AIDS go into Sloan-Kettering perfectly healthy and pick up diseases in the waiting room, it's how Michael got pneumonia, I almost forgot about Michael, his apartment windows used to be right there, the windows still are there but he's dead.

Maybe I'm dying anyway, faster than others because I smoke so many cigarettes. I try and try quitting and nothing works. I can lay awake at night telling myself, You will not smoke a cigarette tomorrow, your body doesn't want you to smoke, when you go to the hypnotist he makes you close your eyes and tells you your brain is going down a steep flight of steps, that you're on an elevator going down, deep down into the hypnotic state, it sounds like a car salesman, and when you emerge from hypnosis, he says, You will have no desire for a cigarette, all cravings for a cigarette will have left your body, and whenever you feel a temporary urge for a cigarette you will tell yourself, "I need my body to live." The impulse only lasts for ninety seconds, he says, after ninety seconds you will no longer crave a cigarette. I ought to go back because I did stop for six hours, thinking the whole time, I'm a nonsmoker now, since telling myself I'm a nonsmoker now was one of the hypnotic suggestions, and even while I smoked the first ten cigarettes the same night, I still thought: I'm a nonsmoker now.

They say if you're infected and have the antibodies you might not come down with the fatal syndrome, therefore you should build up your immune system, which I'm tearing down with cigarettes and alcohol, sometimes I drink nothing for weeks and then for reasons I've never figured out I'll get drunk at a party and then drunk again the following night, sometimes for as many as six or seven nights running, then stop again, though I never stop smoking, I wake up wanting a cigarette, it's crazy, but then again, Perkins went into AA two full years before getting ill, he stopped smoking at the same time, he began looking wonderful, his skin all clear, the bags around his eyes vanished, he'd always been youthful anyway but then he became spectacular again, young again, and immediately got sick. And Michael the same story exactly: he gave up drugs and alcohol and cigarettes, toned himself up at the gym, etherealized himself like some ideal sexual object, but without screwing around because even then he was frightened of catching it, and perhaps a year passed before Michael's glands mysteriously swelled up, he woke one day in a high fever, they treated him at St. Vincent's for pneumonia, he recovered, then I saw him out and around, he said he felt normal and the only difference was you suddenly know that anything can kill you. I despised Michael but near the end he wrote a hilarious story about assholes, assholes taking over the world, assholes that turn into mouths that breathe and talk and kiss, it wasn't original with him but so what, he laughed right to the grave about the whole thing, which I can't help respecting, really, he died his own particular death without any pietistic nonsense or feelings of solidarity with anything, least of all the social contract, he'd had a good time while he was here, lots of laughs, plenty of weird scenes, his one full-length film which somebody somewhere has, Michael didn't want much in life besides kicks, I don't think death found him with a lot of plans pending for the future. Whereas Paul, this can't possibly feel natural to him, something further, quite a few things further were supposed to happen, he's always gotten acting work, always a play, a movie, something, never a starring part but it would've happened eventually, Michael had had plans once upon a time, but then his wife went through the windshield on the Ventura Freeway, after that Michael wanted a good time and eons of forgetfulness, but at the very least, he must have wanted to live. Life doesn't care about what anybody wants.

I SEE Gregory again, for five minutes, on his way into work. I'm walking along lower Broadway, deciding about shoes.

I've got to see you real soon, he tells me. I really want you to see my work.

When he speaks I fall into a terrified ecstasy. I'm losing my will to this man, who embraces me on the corner of Prince and Broadway and purrs: But mainly, I want us to become very close. I feel as if we are already. I've been walking along here thinking it might be the route he will take to the restaurant today. I'm not saying anything about Paul, though I want to tell Gregory everything I'm feeling and thinking. Not yet. If ever.

HE HAS a beautiful smell, a faint nicotine funk mixed with some essential oil, opopanax or civet, in his fur-flapped hat he looks like an expensively bred animal, the thick nose a sexual warning, a carnal threat. And he looks as if he might dart away from me, slip out of my grip, jump to someone else like a fickle cat. He's interested in everything that doesn't interest me when I'm with him, little events in the street, what other people wear, how other people look, window displays, marquees, he dates everything, clocks everything, he's obsessed with defining this minute, this period, this era, he savors details and tiny nuances, he knows about what's on television and all the new movies and every song that's played on the radio, his fixation with the inessential, the passing moment, also makes me feel he'll slink off to someone else, almost unconsciously, to whatever offers him momentary pleasure without obligations. I pretend an interest in his interests, wanting to seem modern and up-to-date, and in fact all this junk he likes bores me silly. But I try seeing it through his eyes, I begin learning what something will look like to Gregory. Magazine pictures start falling apart when I study them, break down into sex messages, sales points, prescriptions of what people are supposed to be in this time, this place. He has more energy, more appetite than I do. As if the world were still offering him unlimited possibilities, endless options. As if he'd been born yesterday and still had a whole lifetime to make choices. His face lights up like a child's when he sees, for example, a stunningly well-dressed Puerto Rican girl.

I NEED him and I need money. The editor who hired me at the magazine offers an advance of $400, which I take. We've been friends for a long while before this, long enough for him to say: Just imagine, this time you know you can pay me back.

I call Gregory at home, on a day he doesn't work: Let me take you out to dinner. His voice is withdrawn, not exactly irritated but not expansively friendly, as it's always been. I'm dead, he tells me. I need to be alone, I'm so fucking wired from working. I didn't mean to bother you, I say, coolly, and he says: Please don't be like that, don't get an attitude just because I'm exhausted.

His voice sounds like it's wrapped in flannel, but it suddenly turns genial and clear. I really can't see you tonight, he says, then he tells me stories of the job, what happened last night, which customers insulted him, Philippe's latest outrages, all with eager irony, as if to say: Look how well I put up with such insanity.

We talk for an hour, about everything and nothing. Something keeps getting shunted aside. He throws himself into amusing me as if this will compensate for not seeing me. I wonder if he's seeing someone else. He reads my thoughts. If I could be with anybody right now, he says, I'd be with you. Try to understand, I always need a day or two completely alone, just to stop my nerves jumping all over my skin.

I don't dare say: I could help you. After all, Gloria thought she could calm him down by opening her body to him, and she was obviously wrong. I don't want to blow it with him. But why has it always got to be me who's worried about blowing it. Days and days go by without seeing him, I know he's thinking about me but he doesn't want to come closer. Maybe there's something about me he's afraid of.

I WAKE up with tears running down my face but I can't tell if I'm crying. Nerves. Plastic coating on the parts that feel.

Nationalistic Poetry Magazine on the Lower East Side, Vol. 4 No. 1, Cover (1989)

THE
NATIONALISTIC POETRY MAGAZINE
OF THE LOWER EAST SIDE $2

**WINTER1989
VOL. 4, NO. 1,
ISSUE 14**

special liberal mandate issue

Crypto-Fascist issue

Top: Poets and Painters at
Blue Mountain, Flyer
(1989–90)

Bottom: Photo of Dennis
Cooper, Tim Dlugos, Bob
Flanagan, NYC Subway
(ca. 1981)
Photo: Sheree Rose

CARL WATSON + SHARON MESMER
St. mark's church–the poetry project–2nd ave. & 10th street
MON., 8 MAY, 8PM, $3.00

~ POETRY ~

Carl Watson and Sharon Mesmer,
St. Mark's Church, Flyer (1989)
Art: Sharon Mesmer

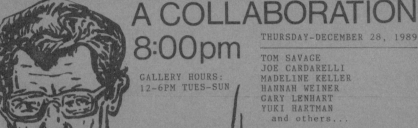

BLUE MOUNTAIN
121 WOOSTER STREET
NEW YORK, N.Y. 10012
226-9402

presents
POETRY READINGS
in conjunction with the exhibition
POETS & PAINTERS:
A COLLABORATION
8:00pm

GALLERY HOURS:
12–6PM TUES–SUN

THURSDAY–DECEMBER 28, 1989

TOM SAVAGE
JOE CARDARELLI
MADELINE KELLER
HANNAH WEINER
GARY LENHART
YUKI HARTMAN
 and others...

THURSDAY–JANUARY 4, 1990

RON KOLM
JIM BRODY
HAL SIROWITZ
CORINNE ROBBINS
DAVID LEVESON
 and others...

THURSDAY–JANUARY 11, 1990

JOAN NICHOLSON
SPARROW
ELLEN CARTER
VYT BAKAITIS
ELIZABETH FOX
JOANNA GUNDERSON
GRAYSON DANTZIC
SUSAN KINSOLVING
GAIL FAIRBANK
JEPTHA EVANS

FOR FURTHER INFORMATION: 212-533-3893 or 718-643-3395

Top: Lisa Blaushild: "The Other Woman" (1985-86)
Text: Lisa Blaushild; Design: Purgatory Pie Press

Bottom: Instant Classics Reading at Nosmo King,
Flyer (1990)

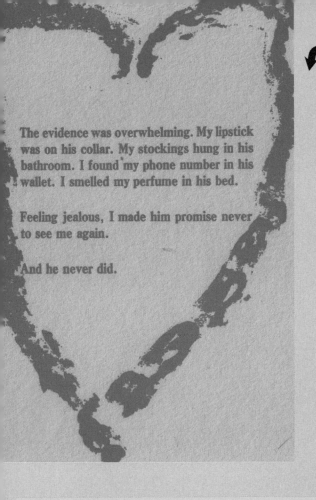

The evidence was overwhelming. My lipstick was on his collar. My stockings hung in his bathroom. I found my phone number in his wallet. I smelled my perfume in his bed.

Feeling jealous, I made him promise never to see me again.

And he never did.

The Other Woman
by Lisa Blaushild

Heart & mouth by Esther K Smith
Letterpress by Dikko on Rosaspina rag

©1985 Lisa Blaushild & Purgatory Pie Press 238 Mott 4B NY10012

1986 2nd edition: 5(

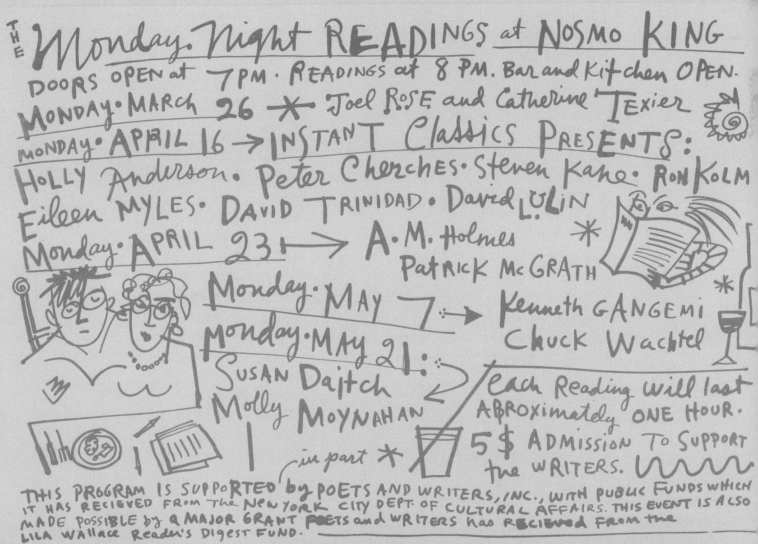

THE Monday. Night READINGS at NOSMO KING
DOORS OPEN at 7 PM. READINGS at 8 PM. Bar and Kitchen OPEN.
MONDAY. MARCH 26 ✳ Joel Rose and Catherine Texier
MONDAY. APRIL 16 → INSTANT Classics PRESENTS:
HOLLY Anderson. Peter Cherches. Steven Kane. RonKolm
Eileen MYLES. DAVID TRINIDAD. David L. ULIN
Monday. APRIL 23 → A.M. Holmes ✳
Patrick McGRATH
Monday. MAY 7 → Kenneth GANGEMI
Chuck Wachtel
Monday. MAY 21: Each Reading will last
SUSAN Daitch → ABROXIMATELY ONE HOUR.
Molly MOYNAHAN
in part ✳ 5$ ADMISSION TO SUPPORT
the WRITERS.

THIS PROGRAM IS SUPPORTED by POETS AND WRITERS, INC., WITH PUBLIC FUNDS WHICH
IT HAS RECIEVED FROM THE NEW YORK CITY DEPT. OF CULTURAL AFFAIRS. THIS EVENT IS ALSO
MADE POSSIBLE by a MAJOR GRANT POETS and WRITERS has RECIEVED FROM THE
LILA WALLACE Reader's DIGEST FUND.

G-9 (1989)

TIM DLUGOS

I'm at a double wake
in Springfield, for a childhood
friend and his father
who died years ago. I join
my aunt in the queue of mourners
and walk into a brown study,
a sepia room with books
and magazines. The father's
in a coffin; he looks exhumed,
the worse for wear. But where
my friend's remains should be
there's just the empty base
of an urn. Where are his ashes?
His mother hands me
a paper cup with pills:
leucovorin, Zovirax,
and AZT. "Henry
wanted you to have these,"
she sneers. "Take all
you want, for all the good
they'll do." "Dlugos.
Meester Dlugos." A lamp
snaps on. Raquel,
not Welch, the chubby
nurse, is standing by my bed.
It's 6 a.m., time to flush
the heplock and hook up
the I.V. line. False dawn
is changing into day, infusing
the sky above the Hudson
with a flush of light.
My roommate stirs
beyond the pinstriped curtain.
My first time here on G-9,
the AIDS ward, the cheery
D & D Building intentionality
of the decor made me feel

like jumping out a window.
I'd been lying on a gurney
in an E.R. corridor
for nineteen hours, next to
a psychotic druggie
with a voice like Abbie
Hoffman's. He was tied
up, or down, with strips
of cloth (he'd tried to slug
a nurse) and sent up
a grating adenoidal whine
all night. "Nurse . . . nurse . . .
untie me, *please* . . . these
rags have strange powers."
By the time they found
a bed for me, I was in
no mood to appreciate the clever
curtains in my room,
the same fabric exactly
as the drapes and sheets
of a P-town guest house
in which I once—partied? stayed?
All I can remember is
the pattern. Nor did it
help to have the biggest queen
on the nursing staff
clap his hands delightedly
and welcome me to AIDS-land.
I wanted to drop
dead immediately. That
was the low point. Today
these people are my friends,
in the process of restoring
me to life a second time.
I can walk and talk
and breathe simultaneously
now. I draw a breath
and sing "Happy Birthday"
to my roommate Joe.
He's 51 today. I didn't think

he'd make it. Three weeks
ago they told him that he had
aplastic anemia, and nothing
could be done. Joe had been
a rotten patient, moaning
operatically, throwing chairs
at nurses. When he got
the bad news, there was
a big change. He called
the relatives with whom
he had been disaffected,
was anointed and communicated
for the first time since the age
of eight when he was raped
by a priest, and made a will.
As death drew nearer, Joe
grew nicer, almost serene.
Then the anemia
began to disappear, not
because of medicines, but
on its own. Ready to die,
it looks like Joe has more
of life to go. He'll go
home soon. "When will *you*
get out of here?" he asks me.
I don't know; when the X-ray
shows no more pneumonia.
I've been here three weeks
this time. What have I
accomplished? Read some
Balzac, spent "quality
time" with friends, come back
from death's door, and
prayed, prayed a lot.
Barry Bragg, a former
lover of a former
lover and a new
Episcopalian, has AIDS too,
and gave me a leatherbound
and gold-trimmed copy of the Office,

the one with all the antiphons.
My list of daily intercessions
is as long as a Russian
novel. I pray about AIDS
last. Last week I made a list
of all my friends who've died
or who are living and infected.
Every day since, I've remembered
someone I forgot to list.
This morning it was Chasen
Gaver, the performance poet
from DC. I don't know
if he's still around. I liked
him and could never stand
his poetry, which made it
difficult to be a friend,
although I wanted to defend
him one excruciating night
at a Folio reading, where
Chasen snapped his fingers
and danced around spouting
frothy nonsense about Andy
Warhol to the rolling eyes
of self-important "language-
centered" poets, whose dismissive
attitude and ugly manners
were worse by far than anything
that Chasen ever wrote.
Charles was his real name;
a classmate at Antioch
dubbed him "Chasen," after
the restaurant, I guess.
Once I start remembering,
so much comes back.
There are forty-nine names
on my list of the dead,
thirty-two names of the sick.
Cookie Mueller changed
lists Saturday. They all
will, I guess, the living,

I mean, unless I go
before them, in which case
I may be on somebody's
list myself. It's hard
to imagine so many people
I love dying, but no harder
than to comprehend so many
already gone. My beloved
Bobby, maniac and boyfriend.
Barry reminded me that he
had sex with Bobby
on the coat pile at his Christmas
party, two years in a row.
That's the way our life
together used to be, a lot
of great adventures. Who'll
remember Bobby's stories
about driving in his debutante
date's father's white Mercedes
from hole to hole of the golf course
at the poshest country club
in Birmingham at 3 a.m.,
or taking off his clothes
in the redneck bar on a dare,
or working on *Stay Hungry*
as the dresser of a then-
unknown named Schwarzenegger.
Who will be around to anthologize
his purple cracker similes:
"Sweatin' like a nigger
on Election Day," "Hotter
than a half-fucked fox
in a forest fire." The ones
that I remember have to do
with heat, Bobby shirtless,
sweating on the dance floor
of the tiny bar in what is now
a shelter for the indigent
with AIDS on the dockstrip,
stripping shirts off Chuck Shaw,

Barry Bragg and me, rolling
up the tom rags, using them
as pom-poms, then bolting
off down West Street, gracefully
(despite the overwhelming
weight of his inebriation)
vaulting over trash cans
as he sang, "I like to be
in America" in a Puerto Rican
accent. When I pass,
who'll remember, who will care
about these joys and wonders?
I'm haunted by that more
than by the faces
of the dead and dying.
A speaker crackles near
my bed and nurses
streak down the corridor.
The black guy on the respirator
next door bought the farm,
Maria tells me later, but
only when I ask. She has tears
in her eyes. She'd known him
since his first day on G-9
a long time ago. Will I also
become a fond, fondly regarded
regular, back for stays
the way retired retiring
widowers return to the hotel
in Nova Scotia or Provence
where they vacationed with
their wives? I expect so, although
that's down the road; today's
enough to fill my plate. A bell
rings, like the gong that marks
the start of a fight. It's 10
and Derek's here to make
the bed, Derek who at 16
saw Bob Marley's funeral
in the football stadium

in Kingston, hot tears
pouring down his face.
He sings as he folds
linens, "You can fool
some of the people some
of the time," dancing
a little softshoe as he works.
There's a reason he came in
just now; *Divorce Court*
drones on Joe's TV, and
Derek is hooked. I can't
believe the script is plausible
to him, Jamaican hipster
that he is, but he stands
transfixed by the parade
of faithless wives and screwed-up
husbands. The judge is testy;
so am I, unwilling
auditor of drivel. Phone
my friends to block it out:
David, Jane and Eileen. I missed
the bash for David's magazine
on Monday and Eileen's reading
last night. Jane says that
Marie-Christine flew off
to Marseilles where her mother
has cancer of the brain,
reminding me that AIDS
is just a tiny fragment
of life's pain. Eileen has
been thinking about Bobby, too,
the dinner that we threw
when he returned to New York
after getting sick. Pencil-thin,
disfigured by KS, he held forth
with as much kinetic charm
as ever. What we have
to cherish is not only
what we can recall of how
things were before the plague,

but how we each responded
once it started. People
have been great to me.
An avalanche of love
has come my way
since I got sick, and not
just moral support.
Jaime's on the board
of PEN's new fund
for AIDS; he's helping out.
Don Windham slipped a check
inside a note, and Brad
Gooch got me something
from the Howard Brookner Fund.
Who'd have thought when we
dressed up in ladies'
clothes for a night for a hoot
in Brad ("June Buntt") and
Howard ("Lili La Lean")'s suite
at the Chelsea that things
would have turned out this way:
Howard dead at 35, Chris Cox
("Kay Sera Sera")'s friend Bill
gone too, "Bernadette of Lourdes"
(guess who) with AIDS,
God knows how many positive.
Those 14th Street wigs and enormous
stingers and Martinis don't
provoke nostalgia for a time
when love and death were less
inextricably linked, but
for the stories we would tell
the morning after, best
when they involved our friends,
second-best, our heroes.
J.J. Mitchell was a master
of the genre. When he learned
he had AIDS, I told him
he should write them down.
His mind went first. I'll tell you

one of his best. J.J. was
Jerome Robbins' houseguest
at Bridgehampton. Every morning
they would have a contest
to see who could finish
the *Times* crossword first.
Robbins always won, until
a day when he was clearly
baffled. Grumbling, scratching
over letters, he finally
threw his pen down. "J.J.,
tell me what I'm doing wrong."
One clue was "Great 20th-c.
choreographer." The solution
was "Massine," but Robbins
had placed his own name
in the space. Every word
around it had been changed
to try to make the puzzle
work, except that answer.
At this point there'd be
a horsey laugh from JJ.
—"Isn't that *great?*"
he'd say through clenched
teeth ("Locust Valley lockjaw").
It was, and there were lots
more where that one came from,
only you can't get there anymore.
He's dropped into the maw
waiting for the G-9
denizens and for all flesh,
as silent as the hearts
that beat upon the beds
up here: the heart of the drop-
dead beautiful East Village
kid who came in yesterday,
Charles Frost's heart nine inches
from the spleen they're taking
out tomorrow, the heart of
the demented girl whose screams

roll down the hallways
late at night, hearts that long
for lovers, for reprieve,
for old lives, for another chance.
My heart, so calm most days,
sinks like a brick
to think of all that heartache.
I've been staying sane with
program tools, turning everything
over to God "as I understand
him." I don't understand him.
Thank God I read so much
Calvin last spring; the absolute
necessity of blind obedience
to a sometimes comforting,
sometimes repellent, always
incomprehensible Source
of light and life stayed
with me. God can seem
so foreign, a parent
from another country,
like my Dad and his own
father speaking Polish
in the kitchen. I wouldn't
trust a father or a God
too much like me, though.
That is why I pack up all
my cares and woes, and load them
on the conveyor belt, the speed
of which I can't control, like
Chaplin on the assembly line
in *Modern Times* or Lucy on TV.
I don't need to run
machines today. I'm standing
on a moving sidewalk
headed for the dark
or light, whatever's there.
Duncan Hannah visits, and
we talk of out-of-body
experiences. His was

amazing. Bingeing on vodka
in his dorm at Bard, he woke
to see a naked boy
in fetal posture on the floor.
Was it a corpse, a classmate,
a pickup from the blackout
of the previous night? Duncan
didn't know. He struggled
out of bed, walked over
to the youth, and touched
his shoulder. The boy turned;
it was Duncan himself.
My own experience was
milder, don't make me flee
screaming from the room
as Duncan did. It happened
on a Tibetan meditation
weekend at the Cowley Fathers'
house in Cambridge.
Michael Koonsman led it,
healer whose enormous paws
directed energy. He touched
my spine to straighten up
my posture, and I gasped
at the rush. We were chanting
to Tara, goddess of compassion
and peace, in the basement chapel
late at night. I felt myself
drawn upward, not levitating
physically, but still somehow
above my body. A sense
of bliss surrounded me.
It lasted ten or fifteen
minutes. When I came down,
my forehead hurt. The spot
where the "third eye" appears
in Buddhist art felt
as though someone had pushed
a pencil through it.
The soreness lasted for a week.

Michael wasn't surprised.
He did a lot of work
with people with AIDS
in the epidemic's early days,
but when he started losing
weight and having trouble
with a cough, he was filled
with denial. By the time
he checked into St. Luke's,
he was in dreadful shape.
The respirator down his throat
squelched the contagious
enthusiasm of his voice,
but he could still spell out
what he wanted to say
on a plastic Ouija board
beside his bed. When
the doctor who came in
to tell him the results
of his bronchoscopy said,
"Father, I'm afraid I have
bad news," Michael grabbed
the board and spelled,
"The truth is always
Good News." After he died,
I had a dream in which
I was a student in a class
that he was posthumously
teaching. With mock annoyance
he exclaimed, "Oh, Tim!
I can't believe you really think
that AIDS is a disease!"
There's evidence in that
direction, I'll tell him
if the dream recurs: the shiny
hamburger-in-lucite look
of the big lesion on my face;
the smaller ones I daub
with makeup; the loss
of forty pounds in a year;

the fatigue that comes on
at the least convenient times.
The symptoms float like algae
on the surface of the grace
that buoys me up today.
Arthur comes in with
the Sacrament, and we have
to leave the room (Joe's
Italian family has arrived
for birthday cheer) to find
some quiet. Walk out
to the breezeway, where
it might as well be
August for the stifling
heat. On Amsterdam,
pedestrians and drivers are
oblivious to our small aerie,
as we peer through the grille
like cloistered nuns. Since
leaving G-9 the first time,
I always slow my car down
on this block, and stare up
at this window, to the unit
where my life was saved.
It's strange how quickly
hospitals feel foreign
when you leave, and how normal
their conventions seem as soon
as you check in. From below,
it's like checking out the windows
of the West Street Jail; hard
to imagine what goes on there,
even if you know firsthand.
The sun is going down as I
receive communion. I wish
the rite's familiar magic
didn't dull my gratitude
for this enormous gift.
I wish I had a closer personal
relationship with Christ,

which I know sounds corny
and alarming. Janet Campbell
gave me a remarkable ikon
the last time I was here;
Christ is in a chair, a throne,
and St. John the Divine,
an androgyne who looks a bit
like Janet, rests his head
upon the Savior's shoulder.
James Madden, priest of Cowley,
dead of cancer earlier
this year at 39, gave her
the image, telling her not to
be afraid to imitate St. John.
There may come a time when
I'm unable to respond with words,
or works, or gratitude to AIDS;
a time when my attitude
caves in, when I'm as weak
as the men who lie across
the dayroom couches hour
after hour, watching sitcoms,
drawing blanks. Maybe
my head will be shaved
and scarred from surgery;
maybe I'll be pencil-
thin and paler than
a ghost, pale as the vesper
light outside my window now.
It would be good to know
that I could close my eyes
and lean my head back
on his shoulder then,
as natural and trusting
as I'd be with a cherished
love. At this moment,
Chris walks in, Christopher
Earl Wiss of Kansas City
and New York, my lover,
my last lover, my first

healthy and enduring relationship
in sobriety, the man
with whom I choose
to share what I have
left of life and time.
This is the hardest
and happiest moment
of the day. G-9
is no place to affirm
a relationship. Two hours
in a chair beside my bed
after eight hours of work
night after night for weeks
. . . it's been a long haul,
and Chris gets tired.
Last week he exploded,
"I hate this, I hate your
being sick and having AIDS
and lying in a hospital
where I can only see you
with a visitor's pass. I hate
that this is going to
get worse." I hate it,
too. We kiss, embrace,
and Chris climbs into bed
beside me, to air-mattress
squeaks. Hold on. We hold on
to each other, to a hope
of how we'll be when I get out.
Let him hold on, please
don't let him lose his
willingness to stick with me,
to make love and to make
love work, to extend
the happiness we've shared.
Please don't let AIDS
make me a monster
or a burden is my prayer.
Too soon, Chris has to leave.
I walk him to the elevator

bank, then totter back
so Raquel can open my I.V.
again. It's not even
mid-evening, but I'm nodding
off. My life's so full, even
(especially?) when I'm here
on G-9. When it's time
to move on to the next step,
that will be a great adventure,
too. Helena Hughes, Tibetan
Buddhist, tells me that
there are three stages in death.
The first is white, like passing
through a thick but porous wall.
The second stage is red;
the third is black, and then
you're finished, ready
for the next event. I'm glad
she has a road map, but I don't
feel the need for one myself.
I've trust enough in all
that's happened in my life,
the unexpected love
and gentleness that rushes in
to fill the arid spaces
in my heart, the way the city
glow fills up the sky
above the river, making it
seem less than night. When
Joe O'Hare flew in last week,
he asked what were the best
times of my New York years;
I said "Today," and meant it.
I hope that death will lift me
by the hair like an angel
in a Hebrew myth, snatch me with
the strength of sleep's embrace,
and gently set me down
where I'm supposed to be,
in just the right place.

PART THREE
THE 1990S

INTRODUCTION TO THE 1990S

. . . Tourists bringing pictures to sell
    to artists in their annual disposition
Civilians telling cops to move on
Coffeehouses that sell brandy
    in their coffee cups
Eugene O'Neill insisting on coffee
John Barrymore in offbroadway Hamlet
Walt Whitman cruising on MacDougal
Ike & Mamie drunk in Minettas
Khrushchev singing peat bog soldiers
    in the circle (with a balalaika)
Everybody kissing & hugging squeezing
Khrushchev & Eisenhower a big fat kiss
The world an art
Life a joy
The village comes to life again . . .
        —Tuli Kupferberg, from "Greenwich Village
            of My Dreams," 1960

ITS DEMISE has been announced countless times, and the Downtown scene will continue to be reborn and to gasp for final breaths. Yes, Downtown writing still exists, but not in as concentrated a scene as in the heyday years represented in this book.

In fact, in the early '90s seasoned writers began to show a new tendency toward reminiscence and memoir—sure signs of a changing of the guard. At the same time, voices emerged or came of age, including those of Susan Daitch, Maggie Dubris, Thaddeus Rutkowski, and Mary Gaitskill. The period also signaled the ascendancy of Sonic Youth, who debuted in 1981 and by the early '90s were hugely successful, with myriad offshoots and business ventures (including a record label, zine, and fashion label). By 1992, Nirvana's Seattle version of the Downtown aesthetic had spread through the malls and suburbs of America.

It was also the year quintessential East Village (then SoHo) Renaissance man David Wojnarowicz died of AIDS and was memorialized via mourning and demonstrations. A precursor to Moore and other multitasking visionaries, Wojnarowicz has received more credit for his 1978–79 "Arthur Rimbaud in New York" photo series, map works, later installations, film works, and AIDS activism than for his visionary prose. Hopefully this anthology's republication of his powerful "Self-Portrait in Twenty-Three Rounds" will help bring attention to his brilliant prose work.

It is interesting to note that many Downtown writers haven't kept writing. Often, they are no longer in contact and have no idea of their brethren's whereabouts. This dispersal is due to countless factors. For starters, the stock market crashed and aesthetic forefather Andy Warhol died in 1987. Rent went up and became a cloying musical. Gentrification forced artists out of the spaces they'd helped pioneer, leading to a physical separation of the community. A leveled tent city caused a riot in Tompkins Square Park in 1988.

Through it all, the Downtown spirit kept kicking. In fact, in 1992 two Downtown poets, Eileen Myles and Sparrow, ran for president. The amply bearded Sparrow has run every four years since, even moving to the Republican ticket in 1996 and publishing *Republican Like Me*, a book about this experience; but Eileen Myles ran her sometimes humorous, often profound, "openly female" and "openly lesbian" "Write in Myles" campaign just one time, focusing on freedom of choice and speech and affordable health care. (One of her campaign flyers is reproduced on page 420 of this section.)

In a letter from October 12, 1992, Myles addresses her potential voters:

When you step in the booth on election day, do a write in vote. I think it's like this big blank wall on the border. How do you do it—you illuminate it, your write in vote. Not Clinton, not Bush, not Perot, maybe me. You'll be alone in that booth & it's so dirty like a peephole or a dressing room or a confession. But you're really not so free—until, pen in hand, you pull the lever, you push the button, I believe it's red and then on the upper left face of the voting booth you spread the metal wings above the title, "President," and an empty white space appears, empty as poetry and this is your freedom of speech.[1]

Still, it can't be denied that by the early '90s the prime period of the scene had dissolved under the weight of its own successes and failures. Hype and bad press created a backlash. (When the poet Max Blagg read his work for a Gap commercial in 1993, the animosity toward him was palpable. For her part, Denise Duhamel wrote a rather humorous rejoinder, "Why the Gap Should Have Picked Me Instead of Max Blagg for Its Television Poetry Commercial," pleading her case to the khaki-wearing powers that be.) Some misplaced a sense of their own relevance, never equaling the power and insurgency of their earlier work. Others became such a part of the pop culture fabric that they could no longer shock or, in some cases, engage. As writers graduated from small presses to the more tangled webs of the big leagues, the do-it-yourself spirit evaporated and the torch was passed. Less dramatically, people took academic jobs. Some had children and left the city. The early '90s saw writers pushing in different directions, often jumping off into separate quarters for the next phase of their careers.

Interestingly, while the majority of the books excerpted in *Up Is Up, but So Is Down* are out of print (or suffering from a publisher's inattention), the focus on music and the repackaging of the more challenging sounds of New York City's recent past continues: in 2004, long-time label ZE records reissued James Chance's studio albums along with discs by Downtown chanteuse (and ex–*Village Voice* theater critic) Cristina. A Washington, D.C., label, Acute, reissued discs by Glenn Branca, New York City's Audika has reestablished Arthur Russell's reputation, and Table of the Elements produced a box set of Rhys Chatham's major works from the early '70s to late '80s (ditto for the earlier work of Tony Conrad). New York City's DFA Records has successfully updated disco punk. Rhino released the career-spanning *Spurts: The Richard Hell Story* in 2005. Even casual alternative music fans know Pussy Galore, G. G. Allin, and the Ramones.

But this book is an attempt to allow the voices of the participants themselves to tell their own story. Because this is very much *not* the product of an academic or other outsider, the best description of this transition comes from within the poignant and wonderfully biting eulogy at the end of Mike Golden's "War Stars":

In retrospect, it was a glorious time. A stupid, wonderful party none of us will probably ever be invited to again. For most of us it wasn't about celebrities preening for photo-ops and snorting their brains out at Studio 54, but it was about the quest for fame, and it was about the party, the never ending boogie of the downtown party. It was about misdirected energy looking for meaning, and about deadening the senses to fill whatever loss you were trying to recover from, and it was definitely about sex. Real live sex acts, boys & girls, and the surreal sexual fantasies that grew out of that same garden of trying to fill up the hole of ever lasting loss. It was about all the bad art that drugs and the hunger for fame could create, it was about an almost Renaissance that almost happened before AIDS became a full blown epidemic, and the party either ended, or became co-opted as the lifestyle of choice in a grunge theme park once upon a time known as the Lower East Side.[2]

Before it faded, though, the early '90s produced some excellent examples of the best of the Downtown scene, planting the seeds for future bifurcations.

NOTES

1. Eileen Myles, "Letter to Citizens" from Write in Myles, October 12, 1992, 3.
2. From "War Stars," an excerpt from the unpublished fictional memoir "Giving Up the Ghost" by Mike Golden, n.p.

"Letter Bomb" (1992)
Walter Sipser

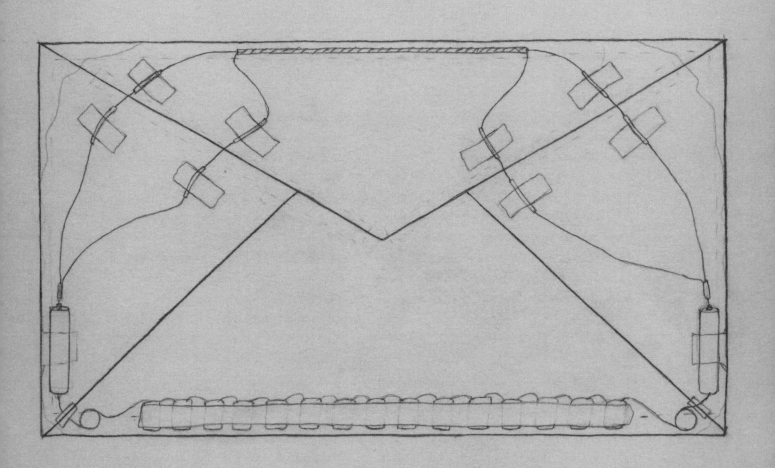

FROM "NORTH OF ABYSSINIA" (1990)

MAGGIE DUBRIS

BUT IT'S 1990. Women lean against the cars on 45th Street, nylon stretched across their bruised thighs. We like to call this block, "The Boulevard of Broken Dreams," because when they were paving it they ground up a bunch of glass and mixed it in with the blacktop, so now the whole street twinkles, soft and sparkling in the fallen night. When we get a job there, we look at each other and say, "Check it out. Someone must have had too much to drink and is throwing up all over the Boulevard of Broken Dreams again. We'd better turn on the siren!" On the corner of Ninth Avenue, Ice the skel is sitting on his milk crate, his head in his hands. In the middle of the block is a park where he climbs the fence and sleeps, far away from the whores and the delis.

WE ARE on our way to 36th Street, to an all night Korean restaurant. It's the only place in the city where you can get eel rolls at four in the morning. A cop told us about it, a cop who's dead now, kicked off the roof by a perp one night when we weren't working. Sometimes I can still see him walking up and down 42nd Street, with his hands jammed into his pockets. But then he turns and it's not him. It's a different cop, walking down the same street, in the same uniform, with that same walk they all have, bulky and stiff from the bulletproof vest.

I USED to think that working on an ambulance would be like being in a war. I thought that I would go up against death, face to face, and that I would

win, because I wanted to so much. But that's not how it is. Really, the coin is twirling in the air by the time we get called. And we walk in, and do the same things over and over, and sometimes the people live, and sometimes they die. We might as well sit around them in a circle, crossing our fingers and whispering, "Heads, heads, heads," for all the effect we have. It's as if we still dance beneath a primitive moon, the laws of action and reaction yet unformed, waiting to fall into place under some apple tree where Isaac Newton daydreams, a thousand years away.

MOSTLY, IT doesn't affect me. I just put a sheet over them and drive off. Sometimes I drive down Memory Lane. This corner was where we found a man frozen to death, the first one of 1986. That restaurant was where we had a woman and her daughter killed by a car that took the turn too fast, crashing through the window so hard that it drove venetian blinds under the skin of the daughter's legs. But it's only moments. Moments that have passed.

SO WE drive and we drive, back across the summer, heat rolling in waves off the hood of the ambulance. Her neighbor called because no one had seen her since the Fourth of July. He was banging on the door with a bat when we got there. "I know she's home," he told us, "because she never goes out." We stood around for awhile and watched him hit the door. He was making comments in between whaps. "She's got no place to go." Whap. "Big old lady like her." Whap. "Just stays home and eats all the time." He was making lots of noise, but having no effect on the door. There were a bunch of kids hanging around with baseball caps on. They were afraid to talk to us because we were so official and had all this equipment. So they whispered to each other very loudly, with their hands cupped around their mouths. "She probably got *murdered*," one boy was saying, "They should just go in the window. I bet she's lying there *dead*." I was starting to feel stupid. "Hey," I said very loudly, "let's go through the window." My partner looked at me like I had gone nuts. A wave of agreement came at us from the crowd, which had grown to include most of the neighbors who had been out in the courtyard drinking beer, and were now clustered around seeing if maybe this would prove more interesting. We went back out and the man who had been banging on the door boosted me up. The apartment was totally dark. In the light that came from under the door I could see the woman, a black shadow lying on the floor. She didn't move at all. My partner by this time had been swept up in all this and was going, "Do you want me to break the window?" All thoughts of waiting for the cops to get there had fallen away. We were emergency workers doing emergency type things. He broke the window and I wiggled through. It smelled terrible, like something was rotting. The woman was lying face down on the wooden floor, and I figured she was dead. But as my eyes adjusted to the light I saw that she was breathing. She was a

huge woman, lying there completely naked. I went over and touched her arm. She was burning up. Her hand was wedged underneath her, and when I pulled it out so I could take a pulse it was wrinkled and cool, as if all the blood had been squeezed out days ago. She must have lain on top of it, not moving, for a week at least. I could see something bubbling in the folds of her skin around her thighs and buttocks. Shit, I thought, somebody threw lye on her. I got some bottles of sterile water out of my bag and started rinsing her off. I heard my partner yelling through the door so I let him in. A few of the neighbors followed. But most of them stopped at the edge of the doorway and just looked in, momentarily stunned by the smell. My partner shined his flashlight on the woman as I rinsed, and we saw that it wasn't lye. It was hundreds of maggots squirming against each other. The neighbors began to melt away.

ON SOME island, in some deep blue sea, reptiles follow the sun with their eyes. Their blood is clear, and grows hot through the long afternoons. In the red dawn, or purple dusk, they crawl towards a beach, seeking the heat that rises from white sand. Their black eyes move, and as the steam begins to spread, reveal a strange yearning, born of steam that rises, and heat that disappears into cool air. If one takes warning from the shade of the sky, it is only the vague premonition of change. To flee when the ocean approaches, and return when the ocean retreats.

WE DRIVE across 54th Street. The Grateful Dead are playing at Roseland, and the block is filled with hippies. There seem to be hundreds of them, sitting cross-legged in the parking lot or leaning against cars in their tie-dyed shirts, drinking out of paper bags. It smells like 1970. Pot and sweat and beer, the summer nearly over and music drowning it all. Nine months earlier, the street silent and buried in snow, we picked up a French tourist who was killed by a bunch of boys, his wife leaning against a car with her fist jammed into her mouth, snow melting on her glove as she watched us carry him into the bus.

ON FIRST Avenue, next to the river, there is a building made of blue tile, and that building is the morgue. In the basement the dead are laid out on aluminum tables, with gutters around them to drain away the blood. Facing the Avenue is the Medical Examiner's Office, where the families are taken to identify the bodies. On the second floor is the Milton Halperin Museum of Pathology. It's a huge dusty place full of glass display cases. Some of it seem sort of arranged, but nothing is labeled. There is a case filled with these tumors that have somehow grown teeth, each one sliced in half and put into a bottle of formaldehyde. Another case is empty except for what looks like an aquarium. Inside the aquarium is a piece of skin from someone's back, with a baby's leg growing out of it. There are rows of fetuses in old pickle jars, a pile of bones with manila tags tied to them, pairs of shoes that people have apparently been knocked out of, the laces still knotted in neat bows. Along the walls are hundreds of photos and newspaper clippings, each one framed in black plastic. The strangest section is an aisle that contains nothing but objects: An old tin bathtub, a pair of roller skates

with wooden wheels, a silk dress on a dressmaker's form, a sled with all the finish worn off . . .

A NORMAN Rockwell nightmare. The mother on the bed, exhausted but happy. The father beaming, with one arm around her and the other outstretched, waiting for us to congratulate him on the new arrival. "It's a boy," he said. I looked down at the object of their affection, who was lying on a sheet between the mother's legs. It was a tiny blue baby, so premature his skin was almost transparent. His head was the size of a lemon, and every so often he would try to breathe, his chest collapsing with the effort. The father was rattling on about how there was no time to call the ambulance so he just delivered the baby himself. There were bic lighters lying all around and some empty crack vials on the end table. They must have been too high to get rid of them before we got there. It was the woman's ninth baby. "They all came early, but they all lived," she told us. But there were no kids in the apartment. No toys, no clothes. Just the lighters and the blood and this dying baby boy. I picked him up and began to breathe into his mouth, little puffs of air that didn't even fill my cheeks. I was holding him in my hand, my fingers curled around his head and his hands dangling along my wrist. We left the mother with the police, calling for another unit to come get her, and took the baby over to the hospital. No one thought that he would live, but a week later I called up and they said that he was doing well. After a few months we were down there with another patient, and we decided to go up and visit the baby. He was lying in his crib next to a stuffed Big Bird, hardly moving but looking like he'd gotten a lot fatter at least. The nurse came over to us. "He's in kidney failure," she said, "that's why he's all swollen up like that." I asked her if the parents had given him the toy.

She said no, she'd never seen his parents up there. Some other baby's father was so happy when his child got out of the unit that he had bought Big Birds for all the babies, and put them into all the cribs.

THE AFTERNOON shadows are starting to lean. My grandfather loved to drive. If he was feeling lonesome he would go out to his car, silver and blue and shining in the town where he lived in southern Michigan, where soot from the foundries made the curtains look dirty no matter how many times my grandma threw them in the wash. He would drive out past the Black River, past rows of houses peeling in the summer heat, the women with their white trash arms hanging up clothes, he would roll down the window and drive, driving into whatever lay yonder.

YOU SEE, we could just get in a car and go somewhere. We could head for the hills and none of this would happen. Me with my red high heels and my skirt rolled up above my knees. You with your walking stick, and a big old Stetson hat. After supper you could fill the kitchen with gray clouds of cigar smoke, and I could open the windows and shoo you outside. Then I'd leave the dishes dripping in the sink, and come sit on the porch combing out my hair. The shells of cars and washing machines would rust in our yard. We would have two dogs tied up out there, and when they heard the engines revving up out on the highway they would bark and pull at their ropes. And we would kick off our shoes and laugh, knowing that this was the only place we had ever wanted to be.

EVEN IN that soft light he looked pretty sick. He coughed, and this amazing amount of blood shot out of his mouth onto my shoes. I never saw anything like it. When I get surprised by something, I try not to show it. I make myself look important and bored, so that the patients don't know there's anything wrong. He looked down at the blood covered sidewalk and put his hand over his mouth, backing away. "Oh my God," he said, "oh my God, what's happening to me." I didn't know, so I lied. "Oh, we see this all the time. If you cough too hard you can rupture a little artery in your lungs. It's easy to fix, they just sew it right up." I have this theory that certain lies become facts at the moment they leave my mouth. I was hoping that this was going to be one of them. I was hoping that he wouldn't die before we got him to the hospital. He was trying to smile at me. He had blood between all his teeth so he looked kind of horrible and brave at the same time. We put him on the stretcher and I got some Clorox from the back of the bus and poured it on the blood. Some man who was washing his car came over and started spraying water on it. "Is he okay?" he asked me. "Oh, yeah," I said, "he's fine." On the way in he kept coughing up more blood, filling basin after basin until I finally gave him the trash can to spit into. He was talking the whole time, but not about what was happening. Just talking and picking balls of lint off his cuffs. We rolled him into the emergency room and he started crying. "I hate this," he said, "I hate feeling so helpless. I hate it when I came in here and no one knows me. They just put on their gloves and go, 'another guy with AIDS.'"

DRY LEAVES cover the hill. I watch your shadow take on my profile, your eyes the curious flatness that used to be mine. In this world that used to be mine. We lay on a mattress. If it was day or night, I never knew. Someone stirred in a blue dream, slipping on a jacket, and headed out, into the cold.

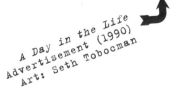

A Day in the Life
Advertisement (1990)
Art: Seth Tobocman

THE NEW SCHOOL 1990 (1990)
RICHARD ARMIJO

the moire silk screen booth eight teen nine tea nine
watch the escape of semen; the relaxation of a mental knot
itch of the indexing digit
seem to go in somersault
curiously through the window pane

where are you off to my sweet Sweetheart
going to view the patterns at the big adult book shop?

wishing on edison state highway nos. twenty-seven
upon a star wishing
927 5309
422 8582
525 9543
all the way to New Brunswick
liquor beading on my eye lashes
wanting it to be rain

white men mud men adobe men
they say eight inches long and two in diameter
lets go someplace we saw in a picture show

niggardly rectangle what have you?
a pile of paper
a mournful Black edge
oh come along why don't you come along
lets go someplace we saw . . .

tea-room like, reduced grocery specials
wheatpaste and sketch manilla paper
aluminum stoppages bolted over the glory-holes
by the normal Gestapo
yes,
that is what became of the third floor
of the Frankfurt School

FOLK (1990)

JOHN FARRIS

(For Sienna)

The ex-cane cutter, at dusk
on Broadway, tunes his *quatro*,
its tones swathed with dusk, a romance
with dark eyes, the luminosity

of the moon reflected in them, full as two breasts
much later; for now, the sun sets
in his quick fingers: Broadway
is red, La Salle is red,

Tieman is red, the girls
skipping rope, laughing in Spanish,
calling out to friends in Spanish. The friends,
calling back in Spanish, are red too.

The *quatrero*, the ex-cane
cutter, laments having left his hometown,
Mayagüez, very difficult in D# minor,
                         very folk,

                    the scrape
of steel wheels against steel
rails, the carriages of the Interboro
swaying in slow ascent

from 116th Street to these tropics, to this
redness, in accompaniment
to this redness, reflecting the sun's red
eye going down in its glass windows;

a neighborhood *maraquero*
joining in, the *quatrero* imitates
the thin piping of the *coqui*, the soft coo-
coo-roo-coo of the dove, the

soft eyes of the little girls, laughing, skipping.

FROM *THE COLORIST* (1990)

SUSAN DAITCH

PHANTOM STUDIOS was located in an office block which looked like an imitation of an early Louis Sullivan building, Orientalist and grimy: cast iron window mullions and lobby mosaics of Egyptian lotus blossoms were rarely cleaned. On the ninth floor the reception area and corridors of Phantom Comics were gray and austere in comparison, but individual art rooms, cluttered with mock-ups, props, and storyboards took on the character of whatever serial was being produced in them. The first door on the left was the studio, which produced a Camelot sort of knock-off, it was full of crenellated shapes, pictures of knights and chess monsters. The prehistoric serial, down the hall, typically had winged pterodactyls and other dinosaurs suspended from the ceiling, someone had copied a bit of a cave painting along one wall. The detective and police procedural studios were in badly lit adjoining rooms with scrappy yellow walls. Stacks of law enforcement paraphernalia and movie stills lay in corners. These serials were scripted by a tired-looking man who wore a trench coat. The Gothic studio was run mainly by women with inky hair and black-rimmed eyes who could be overheard talking about Poe and Victorian sexuality; they were intensely disliked by the scripter of the spy serial because they refused to lend him a back issue or a bottle of red ink, no one remembered the source of their particular cold war. I could never find the door to his studio.

The Electra story where I worked as a colorist was the only Phantom serial left which took place in outer space, so the studio inherited some of the models from previous, phased-out comics. Space ships which had been new during the McCarthy era lay in a lumpy row along the windows facing Thirty-ninth Street. Nobody knew what to do with them. The room was divided by low partitions, separating the drawing tables of the artists from the desks of the writers. Although he worked in an alcove, the activities of the *Electra* room revolved around the serial's scripter, Mr. Loonan. Tacked above his desk were a few wrappers from hollow chocolate robots he had given out last Christmas. He had eaten some of them himself and saved the gold papers with their green and rose geometric patterns. They flattened into symmetrical abstractions. Each one was different. Propped beside one of the windows he kept a magnetic toy called a Wooly Willy composed of a man's blank face painted on a sheet of pink cardboard, covered by a shallow plastic box. Inside the box were powdered iron filings. By waving a magnetized stick over the box, eyebrows, hair, or a beard would appear on the magnetic man's bare features. The clumps of iron filings stuck to the wand like wads of spinach Popeye might squeeze from a can. Loonan claimed the Wooly Willy was over twenty years old. He played with the toy when he had trouble with what he called plot points. At first Laurel Quan Liu, the inker and I thought the toy was amusing but the number of changes which could be made to the magnetic face were so limited, we soon found its presence annoying, and tried to look away when Mr. Loonan played with it. Nearby on the floor were boxes of movie stills which were used as references for difficult compositions, and camera angles. Once in a while an artist might look through them for an image of a cockpit or a body twisted in an unnatural position. Scattered across Mr. Loonan's desk were pages which looked like scripts with camera directions written between blocks of dialogue.

Over the shoulder shot, past the fat man in shadow. Highlight of Electra's face.

Dr. K.
She came out of your image duplicator. That's all I can tell you because that's all I know, and that's all anyone will ever know about her.

Electra
What do you mean?

Dr. K.
I mean the cipher for yesterday's duplications has been lost, perhaps deliberately obscured.

Electra
That's not possible.

High angle shot reveals another figure, the duplicant, in the shadow. On the top of the frame, Dr. K.'s words: *But I'm afraid it is.*

I filled lifeless pages of frames, leaving only speech balloons blank. My colors gave the drawings the illusion of spatial depth and could imply dramatic content, while the stories themselves were very conventional. After writer, inker, and letterer had done their jobs, the colorist's territory was mood. A kitchen could be bright and cheerful (chrome yellow and cadmium), signifying security and good news, or it could be dark and ominous (sepia, Hooker's green), signifying an absent mother figure or household appliances discovered to have a life of their own.

I filled in colors of my choice but didn't write the stories themselves. That was the job of scripter, Mr. Loonan. If the obvious twist in plot lay right before him, he was consistently blind to it. In spite of his occasional ingenuity, I often grew bored with Electra, Mr. Loonan's dream warrior. Her bravado scarcely covered what was really conventional femininity. There were more male power figures in the serial than you could shake a stick at. Sometimes they bailed her out, if not, they were there just in case. A story of restricted themes: adventure, rescue, jailing, malevolent stepmothers who looked like post–Industrial Revolution Cyclopses while Neo-Nazi scientists with Russian names planned construction of the Ultimate Parent Entity. Over the years Electra hadn't changed much, on the premise that the audience grew up and was replaced by another. She was not phototropic. She thrived on dark space which seemed abstractly ironic for a champion of good causes, but Mr. Loonan liked drawn blinds and often told me that he wrote best at night.

Jane without Tarzan, Lois without Clark, Maggie without Jiggs, Spiderwoman, Batgirl, Modesty Blaise. When I read cartoons after school, they were all my characters. I didn't see teachers or classmates in villainous roles or as victims of comic treachery. I identified with no character or situation. I read the stories in spite of the fact that I found them disturbing. Most, except for the shrewish Maggie and beanpole Olive Oyl, looked like pin-ups, and it seemed to me the artists in charge didn't care a fig for verisimilitude. I didn't know anyone who looked like Ms. Marvel or Claire Voyant but real lessons could be culled from Red Sonja or Dazzler. A drop of reality took the form of advice. In the comics I found a cautionary tale or two. When Spiderwoman was surprised by a Japanese spy or Batgirl was recognized at her librarian's job, these scenes posed a definition of the idea of risk, and those circumstances were a model which seemed, if not realistic, to present a definite possibility. Those possibilities were not all that far-fetched. Even at Phantom, when Mr. Regozin insisted that anything might happen, I knew he was right. The man on the roof might find me again. Coloring might be taken over by computer and I would be destitute. All kinds of fears were given a voice and in each solution lay superhuman strength and heroism, and at the core of that heroism lay the heroine's solitary existence. The scripters would use words like "hook" and potential or denied romance colleagues were more like sidekicks than complicated equals. Each woman had to be unattached for the serial to continue; and I kept this in mind at all times. You can have 2 identities, (Why not 100?) the comics seemed to say, go ahead, do it, but watch out. One might peek around the edges of the other, and it's just those hints that give you away: the monogrammed cuff links you forgot to change, the accent that slips out on certain words, the telephone number written on a newspaper left on a train.

It was September and Phantom Comics, Ltd. was busy producing the Christmas issues. Mr. Loonan needed new angles on catastrophe. The director, Mr. Regozin, said the Electra story was becoming too predictable, too repetitious and they were losing readers. Readers always knew the end of the story, even if the end was nowhere in sight for the next ten issues. Each comic had to be set up as if the predictable end might be imperiled at every other frame. Two fates, happy marriage and death, could be approached but must never actually be met. For anyone or anything in space to fall, even superficially, in love with Electra was useless. Love for Electra was doomed, and death a subject of close brushes, but never the big end. If ingeniously devised delays, or obstacles in space ever turned fatal to Electra, they would be fatal for everyone else in the office.

Both Loonan and Regozin were short men but where the scripter's features were angular, Mr. Regozin's were round. Neither office intrigue nor comic flap would deter Mr. Regozin. He moved products out of the shop and never missed a deadline. Loonan might marshal us like a comic martinet but he was timid in the face of Mr. Regozin. Electra's scripter looked saurian in green or black turtleneck sweaters. Sometimes there were science fiction books stuffed into his pockets. He had dark hair and the pale skin of someone who, like Electra, rarely saw the sun. Regozin, flushed and unsmiling, wore red-rimmed glasses, loud ties and lapel pins of cartoon characters. Krazy Kat days were usually bad. Mighty Mouse days were good. Felix the Cat, Mickey Mouse, and Nancy were subject to interpretation.

I often felt like an intimidated prisoner of Phantom. The target of Regozin's anger might be ridiculously trivial (a misspelled word had gotten too far along in the various stages of the printing process to be corrected) or the target of his rantings might be what I considered a case of misjudgment: Electra, he thought, was out of frame too often, but I still felt crushed by his weekly performances.

Regozin continually called Loonan into his office, then Loonan would repeat the director's injustices to his staff. Too much emphasis on Electra's skills. Loonan didn't take enough risks. Retire the Orion character. Introduce a new threat. All kinds of things are terrifying in space. Write down your nightmares. About once a week Mr. Loonan might wake feeling vaguely depressed or frightened, aware he'd had a nightmare but its images were elusive. He did say that. He had never made a practice of remembering his dreams and deliberately tried to forget them. Even if they didn't evaporate immediately, even if he remembered them during the day, I don't think he would have repeated the contents to his staff. Pursuit through unfinished rooms, corners occupied by ambiguous specters, the fleeting return of dead family and friends, whatever happened in dreams, these were not subjects for the Electra story. Mr. Regozin, however, believed all kinds of sources, once sorted, moulded, and edited, were entirely suitable. Content was endless. He found what he called original material in mundane places. He was, at all times, all ears. The previous week Regozin had overheard two fourteen-year-old boys talking about jet packs, a space station, something about interlocking parts, reconnaissance probes, rotating hexagonal joints. "I should have hired them on the spot," he said. The director hinted that Loonan's imagination had grown plodding and pedestrian. Electra had lost all sense of intrigue. She never fell in love with the wrong man or woman, never underwent a personality change, or had a treasonous crew member aboard her ship. Mr. Loonan's fascination with the Electra story was the adoration of the creator. Mr. Loonan lived alone.

I suggested to him that it was difficult to maintain intrigue in a story when people rarely went outside. Why don't you have them land on a planet? Laurel proposed that he plant a fifth columnist on Electra's ship.

Mr. Loonan rubbed his eyes under his glasses as if to say: fifth columnist, this isn't Catalonia in 1937, this is 32nd Street, forget about the Unificacion Marxista and the Spanish Civil War. He returned to his desk, ignoring us.

There were rumors Phantom was going to phase out Electra, and Loonan began to plot each book with the resignation of a man who sensed he would soon be rejected. Phantom might place him on another comic; *Red Sonja, She-Devil with a Sword* or *Dazzler* were weak substitutes, the inventions of other men. It was Electra Mr. Loonan loved, with her superhuman strength, and micro-quick reflexes. She occupied a whole Loonan day and part of his nights as well. He had no other obsessions or interests, drank black coffee, thrived under fluorescent lights, and passionately thought out loud. Bits of Electra episodes floated past us, the try-out audience whose opinions didn't really matter. Laurel turned up her radio. Loonan looked hurt. She got a Walkman. As if close proximity to comic book heros lent him the tyrannical authority, he would hover around my desk, checking my colors constantly. He never seemed to understand, yet he surely must have known, that however saturated my colors appeared on the layouts, they always printed down to the same hue when cheap ink and paper faded almost immediately. It was inevitable, yet he wanted to have Electra last. Even if we could have drawn her on archival paper, I don't think that was the kind of preservation he had in mind. Loonan was after the mythic.

Blue stands for black and white in frames which have no colors—a long shot of Electra at the controls of her spaceship, almost pensive; there is no text. A close-up shot, the misregistration of color and ink make her eyes look even bigger. Eyebrows like Elizabeth Taylor's, like apostrophes. Tears are simple, Laurel does the outlines. When Electra demonstrates her test tube generated strength, her powers are signified by rays, sometimes arcing out of the frame. She's nearly naked in every caper, occasionally Mr. Loonan will suggest boots and gloves. Shock is simulated in their faces. *Ah*, *Blam*, and *whap* aren't part of Electra's style. Expletives are suggested without being used too often. She isn't a borderline parody like *Superwoman*, not a parasite like *Spiderwoman*. No one at Phantom would have used the word ideology but Laurel said they made Electra into a comic book version of the Holy Virgin Mary, even if she didn't wear much clothing.

Loonan explained a frame split into eight sections as if divided by spokes of a wheel, Electra's head in the middle. In each section she tried to land on a random planet or comet and was continually turned away. Orion had spread rumors in the galaxy that she wasn't a heroine but one of the following: a scout for pirates, a cast off counter-spy, a psychobiotic polluter with minimal free will. The power and momentum of spreading tales intrigued Mr. Loonan. Orion's tales were easily launched and each time one was repeated, it was altered a little, and the implications for Electra appeared uglier. I colored a planet governed by a creature who looked like the wicked stepmother in Disney's Snow White. Blonds are usually good and gentle like Betty. Dark Veronicas are greedy and possessive. Loonan was a stickler on the symbolic and he considered his directives on questions of color to be a reinforcement of classical thinking on aesthetics.

In the middle of his explanation a man walked in, asked to use the bathroom, then came back a few minutes later. He was wearing a wrinkled black jacket. When I looked closer I could see faintly that it was plaid and I stared hard at his back as if picking out the blocks in an Ad Reinhart painting. He had very long arms. He was reading Goethe's *Theory of Colors*. Loonan introduced him as Martin Chatfield, the temporary letterer, and told him that he noticed he was late. He was the tallest man ever seen at Phantom Comics. Curly hair fell over his forehead like a bunch of black grapes. Mr. Loonan showed him to his desk and told him he was trying to run a business, not a toy shop, and to get to work.

He smiled nervously at the scripter, said something about lost keys and sorry. He didn't yet know that no one in the studio took Mr. Loonan's threats very seriously. He looked at the pens Loonan gave him as if they were Loonan's own laundry. They did need to be cleaned, but Martin insisted he had brought his own. Loonan, at his desk, muttered about authority figures and their problems in two-dimensional space. Laurel put on her Walkman.

Martin turned closer to me, saying he no longer read what he wrote. As a child he was told he had a lovely hand, but it's the twentieth century, kings' and bishops' scribes have long been out of work so he ended up in the funnies. Martin moved slowly, and seemed out of place in the little office where everyone suspected we might all be canned any minute. After his last job, he said, he had gone to Berlin to stay with an American woman who translated subtitles for films and lived near the wall. I watched him letter.

YOU THINK SHE'LL BE A PROBLEM? WE'LL ARRANGE A SHORT CIRCUIT.

ARIADNE LIFTED THE DECODER FROM THE DEAD MAN'S JACKET.

SHE HEARD THE SOUND OF A WINDOW BEING OPENED.

Listening to Martin talk about lettering, its history, and his own influences was like having a radio on in the background. I listened because I didn't have to think while coloring. He lined up his Ames guide on a T-square. Not all comic lettering is the same. Some letterers can be identified by their style, but Martin was freelance and temporary. His interest in comic lettering was transient. It was a skill which required precision and the precision lent professionalism to a man who felt amateurish about most things. I would later learn that Martin had enough interests and occupations, each held for a brief period of time, to sound authoritative if the listener didn't know any better. He knew enough about being an actor, and enough about writing scripts to convince someone that with the donation of a large sum of money he could complete a project undoubtedly destined for commercial success. He collected all kinds of unusual junk in his apartment, but could describe the objects as if they were rare antiquities, each unique in a special way and worth small fortunes. If he could concentrate and be consistent long enough he would have been a great con artist but he didn't go after serious quarry. In the studio, from the moment just after we had been introduced, he pretended to be an expert of sorts, not a scavenging dilettante.

In the fifties, he explained, letterers were always men who began in the comics and hoped to move on to magazines like *The Saturday Evening Post*. He spoke with a sentimentality I found annoying, as if he were some sort of noble relic no one really valued anymore. He told me lettering was a better job than coloring, and, in the past, colorists had always been women because it was thought they had more patience. Hundreds of them worked in rows in large halls doing color separations on acetate sheets. That was before the morality crackdown on horror in the comics, before the Kefauver Commission swept away the severed limbs and sales of Dr. Martin's red ink (carmine #26, scarlet #35) plummeted.

I looked up a minor character, a duplicant named Hermes, in my comic index. The character index includes such details as height, weight, and eye color: a strange alliance of factual statistics applied to creatures which exist mainly in boys' imaginations. Hermes appeared so many issues ago I could no longer remember his colors. He was a thief on a grand scale who wore a low crowned hat. Rows of Dr. Martin's inks in their little glass bottles glowed fuchsia, orange, malachite, violet, and Yves Klein blue on my desk. I picked up Nile green, #20, for Hermes' hat, added a few drops of water to the ink.

Electra wore Prussian blue #17. The interior of her spaceship was bluish black #38 except where she sat under a cone of light, chrome yellow #3, diluted 50%. It was always night in space. Under the yellow light Electra held a Payne's gray #10 gun and a Van dyke brown #9 square which represented a photograph. Each subsequent frame was a close-up shot which brought the square nearer. It was a sepia print of a man dressed as a World War II soldier and he was tied to a chair. Something about a time warp beyond Mars and going steadily backwards, I wasn't paying close attention.

By the windows, near a corner, Mr. Loonan spoke to himself, in varying voices.

"'You're my kind of girl, sweetie.' 'That's what you think.' Door slam. Stupid thing to say. Orion causes everyone on Electra's ship to fall asleep. Even the image duplicator has Z's tracking across its video display terminal. No, the image duplicator is a machine and can't. That's what stopped O."

Beside me Martin read quietly out loud from his book.

221. Primary objects may be considered firstly as *original*, as images which are impressed on the eye by things before it, and which assure us of their validity. To these secondary images may be opposed as *derived* images, which remain in the organ when the object itself is taken away; those apparent after-images, which have been circumstantially treated in the doctrine of physiological colours.

At 5:30 Loonan left for a meeting with Mr. Regozin. He took things out of his pockets so the objects wouldn't stick out: a black notebook, his glasses case, small change. He combed his hair, straightened his tie, put the styrofoam cups he'd been punching his thumbs through all day into the trash as if he were going to the electric chair. All those gestures that I never thought about twice seemed supportive of a hopeless case. Laurel was still humming along with her Walkman. Martin screwed the caps on all his pens.

We walked down the hall and I motioned to Laurel to walk very quietly past Mr. Regozin's door. Through the bumpy glass, we saw the smear of his long desk and the two men were only gray blurs. We stopped on either side of the door so we couldn't be seen through the window. I thought I heard Mr. Loonan plead that Electra kept Phantom Comics solidly in the black, and Mr. Regozin said that was no longer true. One quick glance through the dappled glass: Loonan's nose looked increasingly beaky and Mr. Regozin's more bulbous, his glasses frighteningly large.

The elevator was packed and as we waited for the next one, Martin caught up with us. He said he'd just seen Mr. Loonan walking quickly into the men's room. Martin had wanted to go in himself, but Loonan had seemed very upset and Martin wanted to avoid him. Laurel told him that if he took the stairs he would find another men's room one flight up or down.

LOVE IS A MANY SPLENDORED THING IN BROOKLYN (1990)

SHARON MESMER

She's a white girl dancing braless in his teenage basement bedroom.
He's a whey-faced Polack with his tonsils in a bottle.
She's planning to seduce him on the Staten Island Ferry.
He's marrow-close and loaded with his first true kiss.

She thinks, "You're nobody till you remind somebody of their mother."
He just wants to go to Bombay and be alone.
She just wants a few near death experiences.
He's hungry for passion bitter and damp as a last cigarette.

She first saw him masturbating off the Brooklyn Bridge on Easter.
He first saw her face down on Christmas day, repeating,
   "Don't I know you from Kuwait?"
She imagined him blonde and bovine between the stale sheets of a
   Times Square Hotel.
He imagined his next confession.

He invited her over for some chicken pot pie.
He lived on Dyre Avenue, the Bronx.
A plastic St. Anthony stood on the lawn.
His mother was on the phone with her sister Rosetta.

He had a low I.Q. but figured he could hide it.
His parents being cousins was what caused it.
Someone once told him his dull look was sexy.
He thought he'd be smart to talk about religion.

Her cheap cologne was intoxicating.
His slow tongue was shaking:
   words frequent and forgettable as waves.
She was imagining a cocktail party diamond-high above Manhattan.
He was imagining excitement like a Biblical epic.

Her heart was breaking like an Arctic ice floe.
He put on his blond armor.

She felt numb as needles.
He felt like Longinus on the subway.

They went down to his basement and closed the door.
She spotted "Victoria's Secret" catalogues under back issues of
Intellectual American.
He said, "I only buy them for the articles."
They watched Star Trek videos with the sound turned off.
They played old James Taylor records.

He said, "I'd like to explore the erotic aspects of this relationship."
She said, "Can it wait till the commercial?"
He said, "Have you ever read 'The Wasteland'?"
She said, "My last boyfriend took me to Hoboken for the weekend."

He drove her home on the Belt Parkway.
They stopped in the shadow of the Verrazano Bridge.
They felt like tourists in a phantom America.

He put his hand inside her blouse.
He smiled and said, "You like that, don't you?"
She felt hot and monotonous like a country of no seasons.
She fantasized a bath and baby powder.

He had the sensation of running hard on a dark suburban street,
feeling skinless and full of eyes.
He said, "Be my Ariadne."
Ten minutes passed big and slow like clouds.
She said, "What's an Ariadne?"

He recalled a book by Aldous Huxley:
"The Genius and the Goddess."
He began eagerly to anticipate
the terror in the morning,
the terror in the evening,
the terror at suppertime,
an abuse so true he would touch the stars.

Now she's a white girl dancing braless in his teenage basement bedroom.
Now he's a whey-faced Polack flying crosstown towards Arabia.

The Unbearables Group Photo (ca. 1992)
Notations: Ron Kolm

MIKE TOPP

CARL WATSON

MICHAEL RANDALL

BOB WITZ

bart plantenga's FAREWELL PARTY AT THE OLD KNITTING FACTORY ON HOUSTON ST.

RON KOLM

SHARON MESMER

RUSTY HOOVER

JUDY NYLON

MEARY FORTUNE

NANCY KOAN

JOE MAYNARD

CHRIS POTT

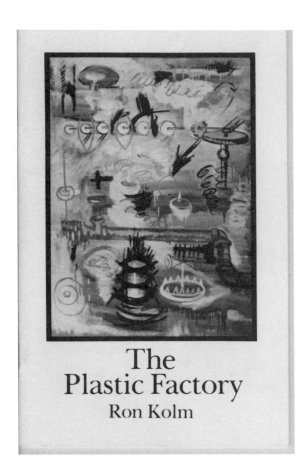

The Plastic Factory
by Ron Kolm, Cover (1989)
Art: Michael Randall

INTO THE SUNSET (1990)

MICHAEL RANDALL

Real estate, appliances,
things to eat—
that's all she can talk about.
But I'm not listening,
all I can think about tonight
is the sky.

It's twilight
and autumn
and I'm twenty-nine years old today.

A woman I can't seem to get along with
is taking me out to dinner.
Thirty years, almost,
and I've never made a major purchase.
But to her, I think,
this seems like cowardice,

and not bravery.

And yet we attain this small perfection
in the back of a cab going west on Houston.

We ride, in silence,
into a beautiful, fiery
sunset.

Image Brilliance at the
Knitting Factory,
Flyer (1990)

Image brilliance

BYARD   LANCASTER   ALTOSAX,REEDS

VITO   RICCI   GUITAR,ELECTRONICS

ANN   ROWER   WORDS

STEVE   DALACHINSKY   WORDS

IN AN EVENING OF PRECONCEIVED AND IMPROVISED

MUSIC   SONG   AND   POETRY

JUNE   15 ,   1990   FRIDAY   7:30 P.M

IN THE KNOT ROOM

PART ONE OF
THE OTHER DOWNTOWN   AT THE
DOWNTOWN SCENE   KNITTING FACTORY
                                      47 E.HOUSTON STREET
                                              N.Y. N.Y.

                          ADMISSION $5.00

                              FUNDED BY
                                 YOU
                          THE AUDIENCE

FOR INFORMATION CALL
1-212-925-5256
1-212-219-3055

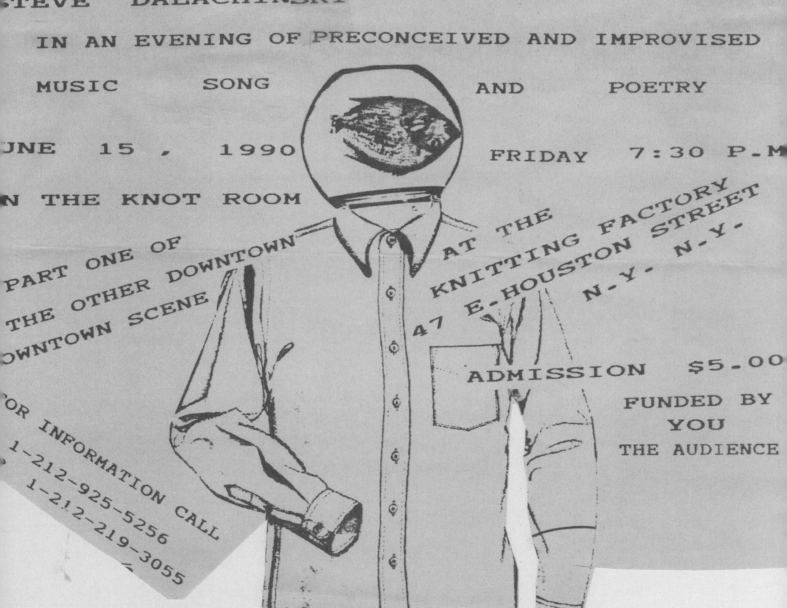

FROM "LOVERS SLASH FRIENDS" (1990)

ANN ROWER

I

We were lovers/friends but I'm afraid that writing about him will make him come back into my life again if he isn't dead. Every time the phone rings I imagine it's him. But then I'm easily spooked. It's only been a couple of days since they sewed me back up and sent me home from the hospital. No sewing really. I have stainless steel staples, fifteen of them. I'm on two every four hours painkillers. Really floating by this time, floating and scared. Soon to be scarred, home alone. V.'s out of town. I start to work on my story about that time in July 84 that Russell came to town and lost it—and suddenly I'm losing it too. I scare myself and take two more but all the time I'm nervous that he will come here, that by writing about him, he'll appear. I'll have made him come here, all my fault, like that other day, four years ago. . . . Flashback: Vito screams, "Of course he'll come here. You never know what people like that will do" . . . crystal knob, defective Paralyzer canister scene. No—start with the old "July 7th, was a disaster" bit. No. Start with "it starts with phone calls."

II

When you interview show biz types and ask how did it start they always say: with a phone call. It starts with phone calls. Life/death. It started with Russell's first phone call. But really it started with Rose's. The fourth of July. Excitement. Anxiety. So close. Both have an x in them. Ted's dead Rose said.

Oh no! Oh shit. I can't go on. I haven't heart. I just typed this whole story onto the word processor I just rented. The first thing I wrote, then tried to save it and pushed the wrong key and had my first wipe out. I was tired and wanted to watch TV. I don't really know yet how to stop working in the middle of something. I do know if you just shut it off, you lose everything. So I tried to save it and instead the machine started emitting these sharp loud beeps and at the same time little exclamation points coming on the screen in time to the beeps and I freaked. I shut the machine off and when I tried to start it again there was nothing.

III

July 7th was a disaster. It went from bad to worse, the way bad seems to generate bad, like somehow news of Ted's death led to my getting caught at school, which resulted in Russell's first phone call, which started the whole terrible episode. When Rose called, it was Monday morning, I was going out the door, looking crisp and feeling on target, heading for my last class of the summer. According to Rose, Ted Berrigan died on the fourth. The great poet exploded. I'd always joked with Ted that he was the only person older than me so I couldn't help feeling I would be next. I picked up Ted's *Sonnets* and a tape I had of him reading at the Ear Inn with Greg Masters and took it to school. I put it on in class, real cool, or thinking to be until I broke down, my voice broke anyway, leaving me feeling crazy the way it does when anything breaks in an institutional setting like school.

SVA no longer allows drinking at school functions since the law was changed to twenty-one, but then, especially since it was traditional to have wine at art openings and SVA is one student art opening after another, it was not uncommon for drinking, usually moderate, to occur at school but moderation was not the theme of the day. So we, Jane and I, got caught, each doing something different but something we had done a zillion times before without incident, by the worst school guard: Nick. Jane and I hated Nick to begin with. He kept *Playboy* centerfolds and sometimes photos of female SVA models on his wall. It made the female students of his office mate, who ran the literary magazine, very nervous. Jane and I had plotted multi-revenge but never done it. But maybe he knew how we felt. Moreover, Nick looked like the only reason he left the Latin American country he came from was because they wouldn't let him be dictator. Plus this time across the hall were three middle-eastern students, I remember Jane said her students brought rum in juice jars, which is why she got in trouble along with me. They had, in their drunkenness, balled up a huge roll of plastic wrap, lit it, and dropped it out the window. Probably, Jane, always the smart one, said, they were reenacting the raid on Entebbe. The flaming ball of bubblewrap fell and landed right on the head of some guy who lived on 21st Street and he went nuts. Though unharmed, he came roaring upstairs to the 8th floor where he surmised, correctly, the flaming missile had come from, and Nick the guard and they came looking for the culprits. Of course, ultimately Nick was responsible for security and discipline, so he was in trouble too, scared for his job at this point and just as enraged the other guy. They opened all the doors. Most of the classrooms were empty, until they came to one on the end which was empty, except for three big innocent looking students wearing yarmulkes and hanging out the window. My door was the last they opened. Thank God Jane

walked in when she did, a minute or two before.

"Sarah, let's take a walk," she said sternly, sweetly, slightly slurred. Slurred but firm. So I was in the bathroom being yelled at by her—are you crazy, etc.—when Nick the guard walked in on my students. They were so zoned at that moment that they were actually sitting quietly—a little too quietly—and listening to someone reading aloud but something gave them away so when I returned, Jane and I found Nick and this strange man with the almost burned head screaming at them. They suddenly all looked very young and pale and upset, even Paul and Anthony the ex-marine and also Jane's three Israeli students. Nick then screamed at me and Jane and said we'd better clean up, the party's over and he was going to call the President of the School David Rhodes and tell him that we had been derelict (my word) in supervising our students and we should be fired so we were only charged with neglect (being absent from the classroom) and not intent, which in my case involved a felony but still, getting caught is always a terrible shock.

Needing more alcohol like a hole in the head, or anywhere, actually, where there never was a hole before, Jane and I then went to Caramba, to have frozen margaritas. We had planned it the day before and we wanted to act normal, like nothing had really happened, like though Nick said he was going to tell the president, and have us fired—I could see the *Post* headlines already—see my mother seeing them—the six o'clock news—he really wouldn't tell, a typical tequila dream. David Barr was a waiter there then, so Paul and Laura came too. After two margaritas, I moved from Jane's table to Paul's.

I remember Jane said, "Go ahead, that boy seems to have a calming effect on you." But after four margaritas I wasn't calm. I was drunk. I staggered home, hysterical, miserable, ashamed. The phone was ringing as I came up the stairs. I figured it was the president of the school already calling to say you're fired and I'm reporting you to the police. But I was wrong.

Hello.
Hello. It's me.
Russell?
Yes.
How you been?
I been fine. Perfect.
I'm so glad.
Guess where I am?
Sacramento.
No.
At your cousin's house in Santa Barbara.
No, guess again.
I have no idea.
Sixth Street.
You're here?
Sixth Street and 2nd Avenue.
I can't believe it.
I'm in a restaurant with my boss and two other people. The two are going back tomorrow and me and my boss are staying here to hook up the computers at Time/Life into this international network. The program's called W.H.I.S.P.E.R. but I'm not allowed to tell you what the letters stand for. I've been here for five hours.
When can I see you.
It's 10:26. You know I can't.
You mean you don't want to.
How long are you gonna be in town.

As long as it takes. Tomorrow?
I'm busy till 5. You can call me after 5.
(Silence). It's not that important.
Click

Hotel Warwick.
Russell Parker please.
Ringing 404.
That's all right, I'll call back.
Click

Hello.
Hi.
Why are we having so much trouble?
You sound angry.
I am angry.
Why are you angry.
Cause you're angry.
I'm not angry.
You know you are.
I was angry but now I'm not. I got home late Friday and I tried you Saturday.
You didn't try hard enough and now I'm angry.
Are you alright?
I'm flying.
I thought so.
It started to happen just as soon as I landed in New York.
It's funny. I can hear it in your voice.
It's not funny.
Are you gonna be ok?
Are you coming up here?
Now?
It's 10:04. It's impossible. I'll come tomorrow for lunch.
Let me think. You can't just walk in here you know. You have to work at Time/Life. I can't sign you

in because I'm working for someone else. And M.'s
not here tomorrow.

M.?

Would you believe, she works here, as a temp.
I walked by her desk, she didn't even recognize
me at first, then she did a take, and twisted around,
like she'd seen a fuckin' ghost, man.

Unbelievable. How is M.? Is she still married to Bill?

M. hasn't got a kind bone in her body. That's
why I left her.

Maybe I should wait to come on a day when
she's there though.

You sure are trying to put this off.

Click

Hotel Warwick.

Russell Parker please, room 404.

Hello?

Hi. How are you feeling.

Fine. Fine.

You getting ready to go to work?

I'm making my way over there.

Listen. I can't come today. I forgot I have to go to
unemployment. Today's the first time and I have to go
to Section C and sometimes they keep you all day.

Come here. They have unemployment in the
basement of Time/Life.

They do?

Yes. Junk unemployment.

Click

Hello?

Hi. Where were you?

Know what time it is? Vito'll kill me.

Where were you today?

I was at unemployment all day. I couldn't come.
Come now.

It's 2 a.m. Russell. You shouldn't call so late.

You shouldn't hang me up.

I'm sorry. I'll come tomorrow. Where can I meet you?

Don't bother. I don't trust you anymore. You still
live at 65 Greene?

Please don't.

I'll see you tomorrow.

Don't come here.

At your house.

Click

So the next day at breakfast I decide I must tell Vito
that Russell is in town. It was a matter of his safety.

Vito . . .

What?

You remember Russell Parker? . . . More coffee?

Eh.

Do you?

That fuckin' maniac from Sacramento?

He's in New York.

What's he doing in New York?

Muffin?

Tell me.

Interfacing some international computer network
up at Time/Life.

I thought he was crazy. He got better?

That's just it. He did. He learned about computers
in six months. He's a genius. He called me a few
days ago and said he was in New York. He sounded
fine and I was going to have lunch with him—

You were going to have lunch with him?

Yes, and then I didn't talk to him for a few days
and I called him last night—

You called him?

Yes, and he sounded totally crazy. It seemed
to happen in just a few days. He said it was from
being in New York, the excitement I guess, you know

like on that program about herpes and how it said sometimes a very good fuck will bring on an attack, an outbreak of herpes, the concept of stress includes something the doctors call happy stress. I mean, I'm sure nothing will happen, I mean, I know he won't come here but maybe you shouldn't answer the door if the bell rings and you're not expecting anyone, okay?

This is not the time to break off with people like this.

I'm sure he won't come here.

Of course he'll come here. You never know what people like that will do. I'm leaving.

Please, don't.

I'm going to the library to look at *Billboard*. Wanna take a walk to the Village?

I wanna stay home and work on this story. I mean, I guess it would be nice to take a walk.

Sarah! You're driving me crazy. I'm leaving.

Get me a book.

Don't answer the door.

Bye . . .

Vito is gone less than a minute when the doorbell rings and I lose it completely. Why didn't I go with him. It's Russell coming to get me. I run in all directions away from and then back to the door. I can't stand it. My insides are coming out. I feel trapped inside. It rings again. I have to see. I tiptoe downstairs and peek around the window. I see a long tall shadow and the shadow of eyeglasses' frames. Russell is a long tall man who wears glasses. I lose it some more and tiptoe back upstairs and lock the door. Something's ticking. I check the door to make sure it's locked. The phone rings. I hit the ceiling. He must have gone to the corner to call. It rings ten times. I'm climbing the walls.

I thought I had heard my landlord shouting before at someone. It must have been at Russell for ringing my bell so much. I have to see. I run down fast and open the door cautiously.

A bolt of light and heat hits me, a blast of empty street. I dash across and knock on the landlord's door. No answer. I'm frantic. Who will help me if Russell comes back? If he's calling me from the corner. If he's watching me from the phone booth. I knock again. No answer. I try the old crystal doorknob. Nothing. I give it a turn. Still nothing. I give it a little tug and the knob comes off in my hand. I panic some more and run back up the stairs holding this ancient cool crystal doorknob for dear life and lock the door again. I wish I had a paralyzer. The buzzsaw across the way buzzes. I think it's my bell. I run back to the door and check it. I'm not sure which way it goes. How can I defend myself. Try to find the paralyzer. Black wet fear dripping down the stairs, a dead boy, a stain, running away, mad images. The bell rings. Then I hear the door open. I scream Don't. But it was too late.

The doorknob started to turn. In my terror and confusion I had turned the police lock the wrong way. The door had been wide open all the time. I heard the sound of his foot kicking against the bottom of the door. It sounded like he was wearing boots. In an instant I flashed on our whole erotic life together, the boots, the bruises, the power he had over us, the wild feeling we had for him, so deep it could be shared. In the summer, season of sleevelessness and shorts, it got so you could tell by the freshest bluest bruises who he'd been with the night before. Until that night. The first blackout. Strange, I remembered it was strange. No subways but lots of busses. No lights but the phones worked. Is M. there? He wouldn't answer. Just come over. Streets black—doubt. Unfamiliar. Sinister. Russell thought the blackout was Manson's Helter Skelter.

You been living in California too long, I said sarcastically. I think Bloomingdale's blew the power.

You been living in New York too long, he sneered.

We didn't know till much later that the whole Eastern Seaboard had been on a four-stage alert.

I laughed nervously.

Let's go to bed, he said.

In a flash I knew you must be up there. I remember the flash of white, him stepping out of his clothes. Sharing a cigarette, three on a match. You looking away involuntarily from both of us. By weaving his fingers in between yours and mine he moved yours down. He slid my hand in between his and yours and he took his away and I took yours.

You're so soft, you said.

I remember the way he had of taking my arm and (Ow!) twisting it behind my back so I had to flip over on my stomach. . . . (Ouch!) Then he did me in the ass and I liked your hearing me. It was exciting watching you and not nearly as threatening as I would have thought. Not threatening at all. Being there beside you was like we were neither rivals nor lovers. We were one. Afterwards we lay on our backs, him in the middle. He still had his boots on. You and I stared at the cracks in the ceiling, looking very solemn and somewhat blown away, maybe wondering how it would be without him. He looked from one to the other, from you to me and said,

It looks like Mt. Rushmore.

Always did like a guy with a snappy comeback.

That was years ago but he was still wearing those same boots, though it was July. The door opened all the way and I saw that he did have a knife. A kitchen knife. My favorite kind. It's called a boner.

I raised the paralyzer. He raised the knife. Our eyes widened more then narrowed down. I pushed the button. Nothing happened. He twitched, then froze. I pushed again. Nothing was happening. How come it always works for Veronica Hamel on *Hill Street Blues*? Canal Street fucking junk. I threw it away and pushed past him, past the knife and ran downstairs. At the bottom lay V., my beloved, hacked to pieces, his library books spotted with blood. One had been for me. Oh what a sweet man. Now he was dead and it was my fault for courting disaster. In shame, I let myself fall over his body, the blood already thickening, the body stiffening and cold. I heard the heavy boots on the stairs coming to get me, as I was lying on the corpse of my mate. I caught a glimpse of Russell's dick, big and hard flopping up to his stomach only it was big and kind of gray, like it was covered with sticky cobwebs and then it was hard and cold and looked like steel. At last, the threesome of my dreams, a Sarah sandwich, only V. was lying beneath me bleeding to death and Russell was sticking it to me from behind, in a place where there never was a hole before. The phone is still ringing. It's him.

Guess where I am.

Downstairs?

No.

On the corner.

No.

Where?

Bellevue.

Oh no! What happened?

My boss brought me here. I just hope nothing happens. I don't want to lose my job.

Are you alright?

I'm fine. It's over.

It's amazing. I can hear it going out of your voice.

They put me in a straight jacket last night.

I'll come tomorrow.

Visiting hours are 2–4 and 7–9.

I'll be there.

I mean, you're the first person I called when I came to New York. You are the only person who ever writes to me. It's just that you bring out the worst in me and that's *bad*. And that's the best.

Click

Hello?

Hello. Is this Russell Parker?

What happened. Why didn't you come?

I did come. I was there. They said there was no one there by that name. They said they had a Harold Parker and a Howard Parker but no Russell Parker.

I forgot to tell you they signed me in under Howard.

I forgot your real name is Howard.

So you went home?

No. Then I went over to the psycho ward on 29th Street. It's from another century. There wasn't anyone around to even ask. I think the morgue is in that building, isn't it? There are no lights. I couldn't see. I even went up to the third floor, to your ward. No one even asked me where I was going. There was a big sign that said: "Visitors, beware. There are patients on elopement precautions on this floor. Open all doors carefully." (I kept thinking how my horoscope for today was avoid confrontation—how Vito would be so mad if I got killed, or if he did.) I'll come tomorrow.

Hello?

Hello. May I speak to Russell Parker, I mean Howard please.

Wait a minute.

Hi.

Is this Russell?

No.

I want to speak to Howard Parker please.

Wait.

Yes, I'll wait.

Hello?

Hi, Russell.

This isn't Russell. This is Harold.

Harold Parker?

Yes.

Oh, I'm sorry Harold, I have got the wrong Parker. Could you get Howard for me? Bye.

Hello?

Hello.

I'm coming now.

I can't have visitors today.

Why not?

I have to be observed. I spent hours with this shrink yesterday. He likes me. He's the one that can release me.

Your boss seems like an understanding guy.

He's a good guy.

You think your job is safe?

I have absolutely no idea what is going to happen to me.

Click

Hello?

Russell.

I want you to speak to a friend of mine. His name is John. Wait I'll get him.

Russell—

Hello?

Hi, John. How are you?

I'm in trouble.

Trouble?

Yeah. I'm in trouble. Next time you call just ask for Led Zeppelin.

OK John, I will. John, can I talk to Russell?

Hi.

Russell?

I'm famous around here.

Are you okay?

Yeah. I've been okay since yesterday morning. I'll be out of here soon.

Great. I'm coming to see you.

M. came to see me.

How is she?

Things with M. are absolutely perfect. She thought she had lost me.

I'm glad. This has been crazy—oops—I mean not seeing you yet, but I don't want to see you when you're, when you're . . . not . . . making sense.

I always make sense.

Does it make sense to say I'm the first one you called, I am the only one that writes, and that I bring out the worst in you and that's the best. Does that make sense?

Did I say that?

Don't you remember?

No.

I thought you remembered everything.

What makes you think that?

You always say it.

I do?

It scares me.

Well, you must feel safe now, with me locked up.

Click

Hello?

Hi.

Russell?

I was waiting to hear from you.

Really? Listen, I can't come tomorrow at visiting hours. I'll see you Saturday.

By Saturday I hope I might even be out of here.

Where will you go?

Back to the Warwick, unless my boss decides he wants to keep me in his custody. They're trying to reach him today. But I hope they don't, cause I know they'll release me by Saturday and I could go back to the Warwick. You could come there. My boss is very busy. They probably won't be able to reach him and I'm sure I'll be out Saturday. But call here first.

I can't wait.

This time put the birthmark on your tit.

What?

Last time I saw you visited me you had this little black spot of ink on your nose. This time put it on your tit.

Click

Hello.

John?

Don't call me John. Call me Led Zeppelin.

I meant Led Zeppelin. Can I speak to Russell?

He's not here.

Did they release him?

Nope. His boss took him back to California this morning.

Are you sure?

His boss came in a limo and took him to Newark Airport and they flew back in his private jet.

But it's only Saturday. Are you sure he didn't say the Hotel Warwick? Please, it's very important, John—

I told you never to call me that.

I meant Led Zeppelin.

Now I'm really in trouble.

Click

BEAUTIFUL YOUTH (1990)

THADDEUS RUTKOWSKI

I "bag raced" whenever I could. To compete, another bag racer and I would find an open area. There, we would put paper bags over our heads, lean toward each other and set the bags on fire. Then we would turn and run in opposite directions. Whoever got farther before tearing the bag from his head won.

Each time I took off, I would see a sheet of flame that quickly became a fire-edged square. Through it, I had a narrow-angle view of ground and sky. Soon, I could smell burnt hair. Usually, by the time I pulled off my bag, the other racer already would have extinguished his headgear.

*

When my scalp began to peel, my parents took me to a doctor who prescribed a sulfur medication for the outside of my entire body.

At home, I stood in the bathtub while my father sponged the orange liquid onto my skin. He started at my head and worked down. When he got below my waist, he said, "Soon, you'll have so much hair on your balls I won't even know you."

Then he retreated to his studio, where he had books filled with photographs of "beautiful youths."

*

My mother collected a sample of my blood and took me to the hospital where she worked. In the laboratory, I saw some organs in jars. One jar held an enlarged heart, another a diminished brain. I also saw an exhibit of objects dug from people's bodies. Among the hooks and splinters was a handgun labeled "Smuggling attempt."

My mother told me I was okay. Then she took a bag of old blood out of a cooler. When we got home, she sprinkled the blood onto plants in the yard.

*

Alone, I conducted a chemistry experiment. I poured alcohol onto a metal table and threw a lit match at the clear puddle. There was a concussion of air as the alcohol ignited.

When the fire died down, I was not satisfied, so I found a grocery bag, put it over my head, and lit it. I stood for a moment, looking at the up-close sheet of flame; then I started to run. No one was watching, which was too bad. I spread fire with my head.

*

When my parents came home, my father went to investigate.

"What happened?" my mother asked.

"He torched his bedroom," my father said.

My father called me a fuckster. Then he went into his studio and shut the door, presumably so he could look privately at his photographs of budding youths.

My mother tried to talk to me. "All I want is for you to be happy," she said. "But I can't tell if you are unless you let me know. It's very simple. You let me know, and then I can tell. So will you let me know?"

*

I walked to a farm field and screamed obscenities at the grazing cows. They were a good audience. I picked some Queen Anne's lace, rolled it in paper, and smoked it. A fire caught inside my head. Soon I had to fight to make a sound.

Later, I looked out a window and saw waves of smoke rising from the field where I had been. A siren went off as the smoke turned from white to yellow to brown. After dark, a glowing red line snaked up the nearest mountain.

IN THE ABBEY OF ARCANE SYNTHESIS: RANDOM THOUGHTS POSING AS ANALYSIS IN THE GLOBAL PAN-ASSASSINATION CRISIS (1990)

CARL WATSON

I was supposed to be going to a movie, but I went to a bar instead. Impulse sometimes rules my life; much like a prosthetic device, or a high price tag on a piece of damaged goods, it lends the illusion of wholeness or value. I may lumber toward my Bethlehem on a plastic limb, but am always just that much further away from whatever I intend. Call it prophylaxis—the need prevents conception. And it shields me from confusion. One doctor called it a subjective form of Premonition Psychosis. Another called it Panophobia, Fear-of-Everything. But then doctors will say anything to pad the bill.

But let me explain. I went to a bar; I think it's just because I was on 8th avenue and there's a Blarney Stone there. I could have been anywhere else, but I'm attracted to this particular bar like a theologist to a bright light at the end of a tunnel or a moth to its own death scenario of frying on a lightbulb and liking it. The Blarney Stone gives the gift of gab so I thought I'd talk to myself a spell, buy myself a couple drinks from the "hospital bottle of ha-ha-ha" as it's sometimes called. I was looking for heaven on earth and at that point I would have made anything fit the description. It's never really hard to do. The place was chaotic like heaven should be too—steamy and noisy with clatter. And like most any other afterlife experience I ever imagined, people were selling heroin inside, pastrami hot plates and low cost casual sex.

I wasn't feeling all that casual at the time, so I ordered a beer and sat down. I often substitute memories for experience and since I had to be satisfied with remembering a movie instead of actually

seeing one, I *remembered* "Prince of Darkness"—that John Carpenter film about how the devil lives as a jar of anti-matter in the basement of a church and all these physicists come to check him out. The devil was a big enough thing to them, probably cause they don't actually live with him. The water in that jar was a greenish yellow color, like the light in the bar as reflected in the glasses of beer I was drinking, one after another. I was drinking a lot because something was getting under my skin and it wasn't a healthy glow either, but more like a pall or a sucking tick.

It was the week that Abbie Hoffman died which is why I bought the paper. (I'm a big spender in times of mourning. Ask any of my dead girlfriends.) Anyway I was reading an article in section four about some scientists who claimed to have committed fusion in a glass jar. I didn't know what fusion was. (I thought it was a kind of music.) The scientists said all they had to do was pass certain psychotic currents through heavy water, which they described as being "troubled"—that is water where the "rational" atoms are replaced by "delirium" atoms. Matter will then be overcome by raw tension when the pressures inside the jar are equal to that of the sun. I didn't understand, but it did seem like an appropriate description of a headache to me.

On the same page of the paper was another article about an ancient sister city of Babylon. Surveillance helicopters and cartographic airplanes were flying over the region investigating satellite images of geological patterns and faint discolorations of the landscape which were taken for clues to a past civilization. I wasn't sure why this mattered so I decided their obsession had something to do with justifying the Law. After all, the more discoveries archeologists make, the endless empires they uncover—the more us conscientious voters are compelled to admit there has always been a state. And if we have never lived without law (law and death that is)—why change things now? It's the typical passive/aggressive reaction of science to the arcane. And just for a minute it can seem there's nowhere else to go.

In fact this impasse itself is brought to you by science. And since science is a pack of laws like dogs, society and science can thus be related by their communal hunger, a self-consumption, a dream that devours its purported function. The empire of the senseless remains intact to the last—in fact, one author wrote a book about it, entitled "Back to Babylon." But back to my analysis, which like that of the scientists', gets even more complex and introverted as it descends like a circling vulture on the urban corpse they called evidence. Think of the decaying orbit of a comicbook moon arriving (not coincidentally) upon a temple in that ancient city, where, carved above a temple door was an image of the original Grim Reaper—the Babylonian God of Death and Pestilence. It was as if the moon was looking in a mirror. The reflection laughed and combed its hair. In the basement of the temple dead people were buried in huge clay jars. They would like to remember a day when they too combed their hair in flattering mirrors.

In any case, people started writing anthropological equations connecting the past to the present, which seemed like a lot of trouble to go through to validate the histrionics of death, but people will go to any lengths to fill a void—just check out your television set if you don't believe it. Then look around your living room. The mantelpieces of us mortals are covered with placebos—jars of preserved death, jars of anti-matter, jars of skin spackle. In psychoanalytic terms our lives could be called one huge Denial Fest.

But just because you put something in a jar doesn't mean you're protected. The prophylactic qualities of mummification are only 90% effective. Case in point: there was a TV show (Alfred Hitchcock, Twilight Zone) I don't remember, but many of my generation do remember, in which a man cuts up his wife and keeps her head in a jar. He buries her body in a swamp out back, but he keeps the jar on his nightstand. The eyes of his wife look like two pickled eggs. Her hair is a smashed seaweed-esque bouffant. The image stuck in my mind. These days I go to Twilight Zone Encounter Groups. The fact that this scene haunts other people I know just shows how media has replaced myth as our primal memory—the collective unconscious being physically tapped, translated into digital or binary transmissions.

Now it is integral to the concept of a jar that you're supposed to use what's in it later. Remember the jars in your grandma's pantry (if she had any), or the jars of the deformed fetuses in backrooms of medical schools where all the potential carny workers who wouldn't find work because they were never born are kept. If we're saving them for some future circus society it seems kind of fruitless. But for now they're safe in jars and they can't get to us, can't sell us a scam or parade their eccentricities before us. Like so many past modes of oppression, it seemed like a safe thing to do at the time—jar them up. But it bred a new archetype which eventually manifest itself as just another threat in our godless human pantheon—the Jarhead.

In bubblegum lingo a "jarhead" is one of many funny terms for a dummy or a marine. But in metempsychotic terminology it means someone who carries the dead in his head, that tortured wanderer with a humid brain full of relics that may constitute all knowledge. Some schools of psychoanalytic thought believe that pickled men, mutant babies and murder victims soaked in formaldehyde fill the heads of the best and brightest as they walk the open air mental hospitals of our streets. It may seem obscene to worship them, but then polytheism *is* sexy. In lieu of an appropriate segue, I let the plurality of spiritual prurience be my guide and bought a ticket to a burlesque show. I didn't know the definition of burlesque had changed. One of the women there kept a fetus in a jar of formaldehyde—a sweet little aborted fetus with a tattooed heart. People gazed upon it with a great deal of ceremony. Indeed, I learned that slinky women in black dresses would carry this fetus down runways in different cities across the nation while bright footlights accentuated their curves and made the jaded masses crave them. And all the time that little tattooed heart would be beating like a fire engine in its jar of discolored liquor—a little heart like a siren song, like an anarchist's scarlet bomb.

Now I don't mean to imply that anarchists are bomb throwing radicals or even embryo coveters, but the point is, and this is what the lady said—she said "The heart is the anarchist's secret bomb." She was perhaps referring to the a-rhythmic disease which scrambles the dominant beat or code of power, as if the dangerous fluttering of one man's weakness could function as society's demise—sort of a domino theory of sickness as strength. That's why some anarchists are decadent, others are Dadaists. Some plant viruses in corporate computer networks and some (like myself) don't do anything but drink and wise off to the blank walls of our cages. There are many ways to bring the system down, many ways to affect disorder

after all. I figure if I can move things just a little bit, maybe by thought alone—maybe that will be enough.

Problem is—sometimes we're just not too sure what thought is. We receive radio or video programs in our heads and we don't know where they came from. We only might think we are thinking. That's how we receive premonitions and prophetic dreams and instructions, as if they were being broadcast from the future back through time via high-speed, super-spun, hyper sub-subparticles moving faster than the velocity of light. They say if you travel fast enough forward you go back, back to the punctuation point separating possibility from destiny. This leads me to wonder: if I purchase enough stone-washed, antiqued, pre-aged consumer goods will I see myself coming back from a distant decayed state to warn myself not to make a particular mistake which might seem insignificant to me now. I imagine myself stepping out of a mirror or jumping off an uptown bus, and I have to say to myself without laughing, "Hey, don't take that train trip to Baltimore, pal, because somehow it will cause World War Three." Or "Don't drink that jar of kool-aid buster, no matter how much you trust Jesus or Reverend Jim or whoever. It may well act exactly like that innocent pre-biotic fluid you desire, but it's not really potable, it's not winding down to disorder at all—it's becoming something. It's becoming the infection of information that will grow and plague you as the state of your indoctrination becomes better known to you."

That's how it goes. The message is always something you don't want to know—the smallest act you do affects the future. And that makes you nervous as hell. So you drink up on the dare, be it whisky, green beer or the honeyed words of the local corporate whore. Not to get all prohibitionist about it, but that's how the devil gets in your soul. It not only leaves you envious of the past, but the present and the future and the pluperfect too. In fact all tenses cheat you fair. It seems sometimes like you don't cohabit anywhere with yourself. I mean—did you ever wish you could wake up from this life you *seem* to lead to discover you lived in Paradise after all? Sometimes I sit around wondering what timeline I'm in—whether this history is as valid as any other history, like if maybe someone had spit a different direction twenty years ago or called out another man's name at the climax of a sex act, I might right now be depressed for a nobler cause than cable TV rights or Caller Identification Phone Service Blockage Access. But then again, maybe not.

There are different forms of explanation, many of which don't even use words. There is the verbless essay our eyes see, that takes us from object to insight. Then there is the one which is all verbs, the modern one which is nothing but insensed motion. This is the one that scares us (meaning me) most. Because motion needs a map—either a machine, a system of roads on a piece of paper or an electron-spectro- radio- cardio- micrograph to define it. Lacking such a map, we have the human body. We can let the body generate language or vice versa. Either way is risky—there's always an aspect to it we don't control. For instance, perhaps I say something to you. If you misinterpret the hidden vectors within my sentence you may get punished. You may never reach me or my meaning. You may end up in a place where you despise me, or love me for false reasons. In that same manner I may follow the momentum of my own conversation toward something I never meant to say. There are two or more things going on inside every one thing—a deception in each intention and hidden agendas underlie every notion we believe we believe. There must be a way to make it mean, a roman road

connecting the barbaric city to its sophisticated territories. But to find it we must use it.

Recently, by monitoring neuronal electric fields, scientists have discovered that the so-called isthmus of the brain—a thin strip of tissue between islands—connects the spatial and verbal centers of the left and right halves, as in individual/communal, flagrant excess/conservative restraint. A communist/capitalist bicamerality you might say. But history marches on. For now that particular psycho-Berlin wall has fallen, the iron curtain is lifted and East meets West in the department store checkout line as Capitalism runs rampant through both hemispheres and the human mind wrestles with the notion that logic and emotion are the same thing after all. But that shouldn't surprise anybody. It had to pull together at some point. We need a Unified Field Theory of Behavior just to get through the day.

It is said the characters who cross this land bridge of the brain, resemble in their foraging patterns, migrating animals of prelinguistic times, searching for food and/or evolutionary mutations to sustain themselves before the vacuum outside—an abyss we've learned to call the "Indifference of Phenomenon." This essential vacuity suggests why the brain's hieroglyphics, the heart's pyrotechnics, the cuneiform inscriptions on clay urns of the ancient dead or even the delirium atoms in the jars of Troubled Water all have a similar binding clause—they are the alphabets of yet inconsummate energies looking for events to explain them. We might call them empty symbols searching for muscles in human tongues and hearts. But humans do wired things in their subservience to signs and signs do weird things to humans.

Someone crucifies a pigeon in the alley. There's a thimbleful of blood and a candle made from bone marrow. A man with a crowned crescent moon tattoo on his left bicep idles by. It makes a frightening pastiche from which one might extrapolate with rambunctious uncertainty a scenario in which Christ is an extra terrestrial and Satan is a cowboy from Saturn with a lisp. We can change their costumes and time slots but they're still messing with our minds. Kinetic emissions fuck us boldly over. Inanimate objects reach out and touch someone with telepsychotic phone calls. No thing changes something. Outside the halls of our skulls insane murderers walk the earth and the moon is full every night. We must reconstruct only to deconstruct. The wheel rolls on.

We turn to media for answers. Differential equations ramifying *ad infinitum* on a computer screen both assemble from pure nothingness then expose to impure profusion a plot to assassinate the pandemic god Pan. Since an infection this broad must by definition be lawless, the field becomes one of nonconstraint. The death threat implies that once again Mere Inhibition wants to be loosed upon the world. Enough becomes enough. The need to contain all rogue energies (as inhibition demands) not only justifies various burial rituals throughout the universe but also partly describes the bizarre events in Mexico that transpired the same week the Babylonian temple was unearthed and Abbie Hoffman died.

A coffin was discovered by authorities in a maize field. Inside were human brains and a dead turtle. There were also bowls of burned goats heads and a mutilated rooster. The papers blamed the scene on Satan worshipping drug runners, but some thought the perpetrators may have been government agents, paid to bring about the death of Abbie Hoffman through black magic. Hoffman as we all know was the '60s anarchist who was caricatured *in memoriam* by a liberal NY tabloid as a satyrical Pan-like personage. No one wanted to say he was assassinated, though government authorities generally do want to assassinate whatever is sensual, radical and anarchistic. And Pan was a man of the people. But worse, in his scope, he was moral (if morality is thought of as Progressive Energy). Therefore moral men and women of the people must be destroyed. Scapegoats are craved to this end. Then there are those, including myself, who see a new cult of Pan developing in many American cities today. People are wearing cloven-hoof shoes in the privacy of their homes. Hirsute trousers and ram-horn hats are selling faster than hotcakes at pagan party supply stores. Formerly stoic midwesterners are playing pipes and dancing at wild Baccanalian ceremonies around small town fountains late at night. It just has to mean something.

The official story of course is that Abbie Hoffman committed suicide—but even if that's true, we can still assume he was *murdered by indifference*, greed and despair—diseases the government encourages—because Negative Energies once loosed upon the world are hard to arrest. They make us seek Authority and Guidance. And we must give up something for this insurance. We give ourselves up to magic. Talismanic curios and fetishes are recruited to the protection of those who participate in the psycho-chemical warfare. The Mexican Sacrifice Cult, for instance wore necklaces of human vertebrae, because they symbolized the channel through which Progressive Energies could pass from the earth to the brain. In Kundalini yoga this energy is often pictured as a serpent, which is also the symbol of Satan. The ambiguity ramifies when we remember that the Gnostics saw the serpent as the bearer of true knowledge and thus related to

Christ—a revolutionary who sought to destroy the oppressive order of a tyrannical legislative god.

Furthermore we must understand why the classic image of Pan was bastardized to stand-in for the Christian Devil. Both are agents of disorder, which becomes evil when the objective is control. One controls best by threat. And threat is first or best perceived as something physical. So the church brahmins decided to make evil visible, physical, connected to pleasure and pain somehow. Through the Pan-Devil image merger Christ befriends his green brother via the serpent as a common symbol. Sensual and anarchistic—here is the schizophrenic hero who tramples order for the sake of love. Jesus and Lucifer, back to arrogant back, meet at the spine, this slithering s-curve sign of the times. God sees the devil in the mirror after all. The cross turned upside down is Satan's sign. The bullet going in is always the bullet coming back. The shooter is also the target. We could laugh it off as Zen bullshit. We could call it a masochistic relationship. We could then say the relationship is strained. But it doesn't matter. All relationships are strained to the breaking point in this world. No one gets along or agrees on anything really, except that we all agree on that one thing. Cults grow up as a form of bonding.

To relate the Human Sacrifice Cult to the Pan Cult would be a mistake probably, and could breed a cult in itself—a cult of Obsessive Relaters—tinkers, bricoleurs finding connections where there aren't any, even if there ought to be. To relate the Human Sacrifice Cult to the Heavy Water Chemists does not necessarily prove the theory of parallel development of ways of knowing either. But we know love is parallel to lust and dreams often die in the dust of excess ambition. In any case to be disgusted or frightened by the sight of a human head yawning

in its frustration or laughing at absurdity is to relate to the stoic skull underneath the emotional skin that disguises it. Which is just one more way of relating to death. And death never ends.

Events just keep happening, regardless of everything. That same prophetic week, workmen digging in the basement of an old synagogue in Williamsburg, Brooklyn, unearthed a skeleton. A shovel struck a mound of ash and a skull rolled out. Rumors had it that the skull made kissing noises which frightened the workers. Fear of proliferating meanings however made for a truncated investigation and the future was not changed except that the rabbis announced publicly how it had always been a strange enchanted building, and that announcement in turn brought on a flush of tourists whose flashbulbs began to affect the radioactive half-life of the unstable masonry. The effects were subtle and sometimes perceived as dreams by people in the neighborhood. In fact my friend who lived nearby had a dream the very next night: first there was soft music, he said, then still water, then two skulls kissed in a mirror—one rose from the leaden depths of the spirit like a fish; the other tore itself free from the bondage of human flesh—they seemed to bridge time in an act of uncompromised if clinical love.

Exactly one year later (the UPI wire would report) a human skull was hollowed out with a spoon and packed with radiation detectors. It was then covered with a make-believe skin-like substance and fired into space. The idea was to suck data from the void in the name of higher representation, but the effect was less mimetic than messianic. The thing was called a Phantom Head and the scientists who cared for it said it was not a "passenger" or a "pilgrim" but rather a free-roaming amulet in which the generic confusion of the spiritual realm could be rarified by technology. Upon retrieval, scientists would slice the Phantom Head into thin sections. They would look at it under a microscope and examine the worms that bred on its decomposed sensations. However, the skull raced so fast through space, it tweaked on the overload and never returned.

But back to the dream. My friend woke up changed in his spiritual and political inclinations. He began to see the beauty of opposition. He began to understand his own divided intuitions as the two brain halves facing each other down like clowns, mocking each other's abilities, colliding on opinions of what they think is right. A situation is born in the center of the fight, a pancreatic embittered disposition, which may just be a solution to the fascism of either wing's extreme. It is as if the anarchist tendency, like a hologram held together by multiple violent perspectives, cannot hold its own for however long it's needed to bring resolution to the world unless differences of opinion continue to exist. When debate dies so does faith. And faithlessness breeds inattention, or "wandering" thinking.

I myself am one of those wanderers, and therefore inattentive to many things—rhetorical sense and logical development not least among them. One friend tells me I make the world worse through my inattention—as if I should have any affect at all— but that's the point; if you're not part of the solution you're part of the cause. Another friend tells me I have to get on stage sometime or I'm just a pawn, a lumpen fan, an audience *in perpetea*. I felt I was being accused, so in defense I changed that noun to a passive verb—I claimed a state of being "audienced"—meaning we were all victims of an omnipotent albeit aggressive stage. I have spent my life, it's true, passively being an audience to others' phobias, such as this free-association-

conspiracy theory, this jerry-masonry, this reckless methodology of searching for the seed to discontent and emptiness and building on it. Some people call Pessimism what I call Optimism, which just goes to show how pessimistic *they* are. Disorder the senses, destroy logic. It's an old battle cry. And it's true it can be suicidal to advocate such a sacrificial thought process—the nail in the tree of knowledge, the optimism that bleeds the mind and occasionally achieves an unrelenting clarity of purpose. Purpose without peer pressure. Why there's something positively beatific about it.

But then the long history of mystic trade guilds proves to us that a spirituality can be created from pragmatics. The way I see it is—if I have to think, it better accomplish something. Perhaps this can only be brought about through decay, and resistance to decay, and resistance to resistance and so on and on until conviction collapses and the orbit of the oppressive idea degenerates as the satellite approaches its progenitor (in imitation of scientific analysis). And unlike the falcon who cannot hear the cry of the falconer, this tether is tightened by despair as the dream homes onto the black eye hole of entropy. Somehow we all became the enemy by simply not understanding. Such misinterpretations manifest themselves as writhing wormholes between people, or between people and things. The event horizon of that wormhole approaches and recedes like an invisible fabulous animal, a birth channel wagging its glorious gate before our terrified eyes. We can't depend on anything to hold true at the other end. Conception *is* so elusive after all. We've got a rat by the tail and we don't know if we're dead or alive or even if we're doing what we think we're doing most of the time. Anarchists believe that given the chance people will rule themselves just fine. A literal pig's head passing for a god on a stick sees how even a soupcon of government corrupts.

It's hard to decide what to do in the face of the roller-coaster reality we seem to be riding. We know that something is happening, phenomena sometimes seem to exist. The grid looks like a matter/event blanket full of dips and valleys. The gravitational waves from hip happenings millions of light years away move the atoms on our planet ever so slightly. A crab nebula or a box office disaster in the galaxy of Xenophobe can make your coffee taste just a little bitter today. In fact everything is in motion constantly from all the events that ever happened or ever will. The largest event is made minuscule in transmission. That we are puppets of miniaturized time and space is not an easy bullet to bite. Even the future is cast back before the present, affecting us in retrospect. It's hard to believe we have any will, much less that we know where we are going even after we get there.

My friend who dreamed of flying skulls left town several days after Hoffman's death. As time passed, I heard things through the grapevine—he was doing this, doing that. He wanted to be an artist and a politician. He wanted to be an anarchist. He said he had something to show the world. But somewhere along the way things went bad—he discovered he had no place to sleep and no inclination either. Actually he was just trying to resolve the ambivalence that was destroying him. He was stuck in the in-between, on the road, screaming like a demented cherub shot through an umbilical cord that seemed to have no end. On one side of this great vein was death; the other side was madness. He was fighting for control—for control of his effectiveness, the very concept he would destroy if he could. It was a double bind of the worst kind. I remember how he used to say, "Buddy," he

said, "you're never more than one irrational second away from changing the universe permanently in a simple spasm of your nervous fingers." It didn't make much sense then, but it did later—because the last I heard, he'd bought a gun and was living in his car, drinking corn whisky out of a glass jar and waiting for someone to fuck with him. And somebody probably did. That narrative path might explain a lot of things. It can also serve as a closing theme or motif: Way out there in America, on a white hot highway, one drunk bullet could shatter the hapless face of a possible savior, or another dictator, another cult leader, or simply another innocent inquisitor, and without choice or spiritual gain, the dream of grace must rebegin.

 Photo of Bruce Benderson (1985)
Photo: Scott Neary

A VISIT FROM MOM (1990)

BRUCE BENDERSON

Last night, when I had sex with a suspected murderer. It was in the Carter Hotel, or maybe the Rio or the Fulton. About six this morning, actually.

Was it in the Carter, or was it the Fulton? I forget which one. It's the one that lets you pay with a credit card. After which you must convince the second party to leave when you do. Or else the signed credit slip at the desk will have the time added to it until he decides to check out. This is a situation that might be called awkward—isn't it?—when the second party is homeless and when, if you stay, you won't get any sleep yourself . . . no . . . you probably wouldn't.

I had come from Port Authority where I had taken Mom to make sure she got on the airport bus safely. I wanted to make certain. There are a lot of troublemakers hanging around Port Authority. Mom was in New York for a regional conference of the United Jewish Appeal. Since her conference was near the Algonquin, I had told her to meet me there for a drink. From there I knew it would be easy to get a cab to Port Authority, a few blocks away. Mom is beginning to have a little trouble getting around, and the streets were icy.

Everyone knows Port Authority is an unofficial shelter for the homeless. The terminal is not far from the *Times* building on Forty-third Street, opposite which is a place where drag queens wearing gowns

and pants suits go to use the bathroom or perfume themselves at the bar. But today, as it was barely six P.M., only a poor queen named Missy was sitting at the bar. Missy was dressed down in a muddy old turtleneck. The bar was stifling, but I kept my coat on. It was the one I'd bought on sale at Barney's that I knew Mom would approve of. I was also wearing the sweater that she had sent me for Hanukkah.

I remember thinking how pretty Mom still looks with her soft white hair, sparkling blue eyes, and lots of rouge. Yet what a relief it is to get her safely onto the airport bus and know that she's on her way home. I guess it's a relief, although after she's gone, I always miss seeing her. Over sherry and peanuts, Mom had told me about her work with the less fortunate aged, the Meals on Wheels program she helps organize in our hometown, the parties for senior citizens, the craft afternoons at the center. Mom had also been to Lord & Taylor that day to look for knitwear for Aunt Heidi. I chided her for sallying out over the icy sidewalks, but I didn't make a big deal out of it, because I figure Mom's sense of independence is the most important thing she has left.

I must have been in the bar at least an hour when the Bouncer came in with his brother. The brother looked like he had been in jail. He had a jail body. It's a thickness of certain parts coming from constant, unsupervised exercise of those parts, I suppose. Nor was his goatee, or the tattoos that said AVENGER and BABY LOVE, any evidence to the contrary, especially since the tattoos looked like they'd been drawn with a razor blade, after which shoe polish is carefully rubbed in the wound. The bouncer took his seat by the door, while his brother went to sit on a stool by the bathroom. It was the brother's job to keep an eye on the head.

Mom is having a little trouble getting around these days. I guess it's osteoporosis. But otherwise she is clear as a bell and just as energetic as ever. She and I have always been as close as anyone could be. Whenever I had a secret, an adolescent worry about not being popular or sports-minded enough—when I thought I would die if I didn't tell somebody—there was Mom, eager to lend an ear. I always told her. And I still do, almost always. Yet there are now certain things I just would not say to Mom, because I figure that being close to the end—her own mortality—is enough for her to worry about. It's time I took care of my problems myself.

Yet by the second sherry, Mom's irrepressible concern rose to the surface. She said that she had had enough of talking about herself and wanted to know all about what was going on in my life. What about the job in school production at the textbook company? Was I happy there and did I think there was some kind of future?

Although I myself have never been in prison, I feel that my great sociability, cheerful openness, and keen, observant behavior have informed me about the experience. Having been in jail must be, I've always thought, a powerful psychic marker. I will admit that there is something about a person who has been in jail that attracts me. Which is not to say I take the experience at all lightly—I doubt that I would survive it. But how does someone who has been in jail speak to his wife or child when he is pleased or displeased by her or his behavior? How does somebody who has been in jail make love with somebody else? What would he be thinking about to get excited? Having been in prison leaves its imprint on a person's body, which becomes vigilant and tense like a coil. Yet a person who has been in jail seems somewhat resigned; his body speaks of great patience. Take the bouncer's brother, with his strong-looking wrists, stubby, scarred hands, sullen face, and tattoos reading ON THE EDGE, AVENGER, etc., running up one bulging arm. As he perched on the stool, he held a wooden club, one eye constantly on the bathroom door, though there was still no one in the bar except myself and Missy. No, he could wait all night for somebody to try to use the bathroom for the wrong purpose, the hand was waiting on the club.

Exactly what did I do between this time and six in the morning? What could I have been doing in all that time? I keep wondering. I put Mom on the bus for her plane, which was supposed to leave at eight-thirty . . . so I must have put her on the bus near seven; I must have sat with her in Port Authority until a little after seven. Which means I didn't get to the bar until after seven. I guess it is a relief that she's gone, though I do kind of miss her. But there are so many things that could happen to her in this dangerous city. Also, I start to resent her prying too much into my business. I now remember that as we sat waiting for the bus, she brought up the job business again. She said she knew from experience, from the days when she and Dad were both working to make enough money to give the children a nice home and a good education, that by a certain age— my age, she added pointedly, looking at me with her piercing, uncompromising blue eyes—a person has to make a real commitment to a job, instead of just camping out there, if he wants to get somewhere.

I decided that there was no sense in complaining to Mom about the job. No sense in trying to explain that mechanically shifting papers from one desk to another, keeping logs and making lists, writing memos, was far from anything a real human could make a commitment to. I didn't want Mom to know that I hated working there, even felt humiliated by it sometimes. What sense would it have made to tell her that? To make her worry about my future as she sat in the dismal departures area of Newark airport waiting for a plane that would take her back to desolate upstate? So all I said was that the job was just a way of making money. Clear and simple. I didn't like it or dislike it and that was good enough for me.

Now I remember. I didn't stay in the bar the whole time. Instead I left to go eat—hadn't the bartender said it was nine-thirty shortly before?—across the street to get some lamb from the Greek. It was surprisingly good lamb, and I ate a very gelatinous rice pudding. As I ate, through the window I could see a few queens making their way across the ice to the bar. Their heels looked so skinny and high that I was afraid one of them would slip and fall. It was so cold out, but even so, a lot of them were dressed to the nines. Why not go back to the bar? I thought.

Why not go back to the bar?

As we sat in Port Authority, the conversation had somehow turned to Mom's will and her worries that I would not handle the money she had "slaved for" in any reasonable way. It is my opinion that Mom should really think about enjoying the money herself while she still can. Instead of worrying about how I am going to use it. In the first place, she has nothing to worry about, and in the next place, if she wants to put restrictions on it from beyond the grave, then she shouldn't be leaving her precious money to me at all.

"Who knows? Your father and I could use it all up in a nursing home if we got sick," Mom suggested.

Seeing the queens slide across the ice to the bar had made me want to go back in. If Mom wanted to put restrictions on me from beyond the grave, that was fine, but tonight I didn't want to think about it. Inside the bar I recognized another queen, a very tall Latin in a leopard-print sheath, pantomiming the song that was playing to a tubby businessman. Missy was propped in a corner. Her face looked anesthetized into a Mona Lisa smile. The very strong wrists of the bouncer's brother were still resting on the club in his lap as he sat perched near the head. It was as if the wrists were on display; I remember that I kept looking at them. Finally I spoke to him. "What's up?"

"I'm working, man," he answered.

The bouncer's brother started to talk. He was from the Bronx, but he was trying to get a place to stay in Manhattan. And yes, he had been in jail, a year and a half, or maybe six months, ago—but it was a strange story that he guessed most people wouldn't believe. It seems that he had been arrested on suspicion of killing his twin brother. They had been smoking crack all day (something he used to do but didn't do anymore, he added)—and when one of the "rocks" from one of the vials seemed to have disappeared, he began thinking that his twin was holding out on him, after which he started to turn the room upside down. (In fact, it had happened at the Carter, or was it the Fulton?) He turned over the mattress and looked under tables, crawled on his hands and knees across the carpet looking for the rock, until he was overcome with anger at his twin, whom he thought he had caught a glimpse of in the mirror laughing at him; so he went to his brother's clothes—both of them were naked at the time because it was summer and there was no air-conditioning—he went to the clothes and looked in all the pockets, he even tore the cuffs of the pants apart, but still didn't find the rock, so he decided to send his brother out to get more. Neither of them had any money. "That don't matter to me," he growled, feeling as if he were about to snap, "You go out there and you find another bottle 'cause you been holding out on me." And since he was four minutes older than his brother, the brother obeyed.

The rest is somewhat unclear, but the gist of it seems to be that his twin happened to go to a bodega on Ninth Avenue looking for crack just when there was a drug war going on; supposedly mistaken for a backup man, he was shot. After which somebody—who is now in hiding, but at the time was staying in a room next door at the hotel—testified that he had heard the twins arguing shortly before the murder. . . .

I feel really bad about the way Mom said good-bye. With the talk about the will the last topic we spoke of. I didn't want Mom to know how much I hated that job, or that I was planning on leaving it. So I held it in. Mom must have been out for blood, though, because the more I would try to shift the subject to something uncontroversial, the more adamantly she returned to what she surmised might be my problems. Then suddenly she said, "You drink too much."

To be perfectly honest, I had been to an AA meeting just the night before. I have never had a blackout or hurt myself or anything like that, but I was worried about the amount of time I was wasting getting drunk. The AA meeting only seemed to increase my anxiety. Their never fully acknowledged portrayal of drinking as a world entered by excess, a world that was ruled tyrannically by drink, in which you could never hope for any control except by self-exile; the idea that you had to go through a door to another world that was just as uncontrollable as the first, but that was more conventional, and structured in a way that made your survival more likely; the idea that you had to endure life knowing that this door between the two worlds was always there, yet never opening it again . . . seemed to transform living into a continual struggle against the temptation for self-annihilation.

I wanted to live as if there were one world, not two.

It was time for Mom to get on the bus. I assured her that I wasn't drinking too much, but this did not seem to allay her fears entirely. Instead she began to talk about diaper days. There was a startling contrast between me and my older brother, she said, who had suffered greatly because of hyperactivity and its effect on the nerves of others, while I had been a practically troubleless toddler who never complained and always smiled and laughed, who spoke in complete sentences by the age of one and a half; these sentences often incorporated the word *please*. But then, by adolescence, the two brothers seemed mysteriously to change places: The older brother abruptly settles down and starts doing what he is supposed to. He enters medical school. Now the younger brother begins ". . . sowing wild oats. I guess your brother had already gotten it out of his system."

I actually didn't go to the bar right after I left Port Authority. It occurs to me that I went to the peep show at Show World. There was a film in my booth called *Bigger the Better* with a scene in a classroom in which the teacher asks one student to stay after class because his marks are not up to par. They end up making it, during which the student, who has an inhumanly large cock, fucks the teacher in the ass on top of a desk.

As I kissed Mom good-bye at the bus, I took a good look at what she was wearing. She was wearing a lovely suit of pink wool, and her shoes were cream, very fashionable. Mom refused to wear "old-lady" shoes even if they might be more practical at this point. She was holding a cream-colored purse and her suede briefcase that I assumed was full of papers having to do with the United Jewish Appeal. "Take care of yourself, honey," she said.

It wasn't the strenuousness of Mom's occasional visits to New York that worried me, but her life-style in the wintry land of upstate New York with my aging father. Both of them still drove despite his considerable loss of eyesight and her hearing problem. Her reflexes were obviously much slower than they had been in her prime, and although the area was far from congested, compared to this city, I was constantly picturing the sudden swerve of a car at a lonely intersection, literally feeling the brittle fragility of their old bones at the impact of the accident. What, the thought had sometimes occurred to me, despite my efforts to repress it, would I do if one of them were injured and totally incapacitated, yet lingered for years? How would I manage to care for them? How much, I thought with a guilty swallow, was I depending on the security of my inheritance? Anyway, neither of them understood or approved of what they thought of as my life-style. Something told me that any inheritance would have severe restrictions placed on it in an effort to control my life—after their death—according to a plan of their choosing.

During the recitation of the bouncer's brother, who had been arrested for the murder of his twin brother, his broad wrists stayed displayed on the club, unmoving. He told me that, in actuality, he was working two jobs this evening. He had to watch the bathroom to keep the crack-heads from going

in and to keep the drag queens from turning tricks in there. But if I was looking for a good time, he would be glad to get somebody else to take over for him. I went into the john and counted the bills in my pocket, realizing that—not counting whatever might be in the envelope Mom had slipped into my hand as her lips brushed mine before stepping onto the bus—I had only thirty dollars. Taking Mom's envelope out of my pocket, I opened it, glancing at the front of the card on which were written the words *To My Son*. Inside it was fifty dollars. The bouncer's brother had said he wanted sixty, and I was planning to use my credit card for the hotel room. I left the bathroom and nodded to the bouncer's brother, who went to speak to the bartender.

The bouncer's brother is called Mike. I was disturbed by the fact that Mike left the bar wearing only his T-shirt. "I'll pick up my coat in a minute," he assured me cryptically. Then, as soon as I had paid for the room, he took a long mumbling look at the number on the key and handed it back to me. "Wait for me up there and I'll be back."

How, I wondered, as I stood in the room still wearing my coat, had I ended up waiting on the fourteenth floor of a hotel—it was the Rio, I think—for someone who had been accused of murdering his brother? The setup was beginning to seem more and more obvious to me. He knew the room number. After he went back, supposedly to get his coat, he would return with a friend, who would wait somewhere on this floor. At the right moment, perhaps with the aid of a weapon to keep me still, Mike would leap up and let his friend in. The two of them would roll me.

Mom and Dad's golden, or fiftieth, anniversary a couple of years ago was our most successful family affair in years. My brother Joe and I had planned it, though it had begun as his idea. For our celebration, we chose an inn by the lake where the whole family had spent countless summers when we were children. "Don't get us anything extravagant," Mom had cautioned. "We won't live long enough to enjoy it." Joe and I hadn't listened. Together we bought Mom a gold watchband and Dad a high-tech snowblower for the driveway. Unfortunately, I had been short of money at the time and had to work out an agreement with Joe where I paid for only a quarter of it. Dinner at the inn had taken on the form of a joyous tribute to the longevity of my parents' relationship. And all of Mom's and Dad's oldest friends were there. Our cousins even came all the way from California. It occurred to me that Mom and Dad had always acted on their concern for me by being intensely practical on my birthdays, Bar Mitzvah, and graduation, never getting me anything that was likely to be damaged by childish carelessness—no matter how much I begged for it.

There was a knock on the door of the hotel room, but I stood rooted. Finally Mike began calling me through a crack in the door. "Hey, will you open up, it's me."

Trembling, I moved to the door and opened it slightly. Mike pushed it against me so that I stumbled backwards, and he walked in. Then he closed the door and locked it.

"What's a matter with you?" he asked, staring at my still-coated figure. "You hiding a gun there or something?"

Mike started to undress until he was down to his underwear. His body was an unstable column of muscles beginning at his shoulders and lats and tapering only at his shins and feet. One nipple was sliced diagonally by a six-inch scar. The name Mickey had been hand-tattooed above his waist. "Well, go ahead," he said. "Peel down."

Only because I noticed that Mike placed all of his clothes on a table, out of reach of the bed, did I hesitantly begin to remove my coat. For I knew that if he had been hiding a weapon, he would have kept the clothes within reach of the bed. I took off my shoes. Mike, in his black briefs, stood watching. Was I imagining that one ear seemed to be cocked toward the door?

Mike got onto the bed and motioned me to him. In my white briefs, I padded to the edge of the bed and sat down. "Relax, man, would you," he muttered. I lay down next to him and he raised one hand and tweaked my nipple. Then he said, "This may have to cost you."

In fact, the aforementioned lake at which our family had summered often returned in dreams. For my birthday, which is in July, Mom would bake the kind of layered butter-frosting cake you rarely see anymore, and Dad would make hot dogs and hamburgers on the grill. Aunt Heidi always came out for the day on Greyhound, and in her bag was a present for me. Two rules were waived for the day: I was allowed to take the boat as far away as I wanted, and I could stay up as long as I liked. Understandably, my memories of those days have the scent of adventure, sun-spangled water followed by endless nights shot with stars.

"Relax, man, would you. I mean, you got to pay more depending on what you want to do." Mike leapt to a standing position on the bed and pulled down the black briefs. With his back to me, and legs straddling mine, he bent forward and spread his cheeks. "How's this? Look at that hole. Isn't it something?" He began to gyrate.

As soon as I had slipped on the rubber that I got out of my wallet, Mike began to twist his ass onto my cock. He straddled me and began to rock back and forth so that the bed shook and my cock slid in and out. Clenching his teeth, he mumbled, "That's right, man, it belongs to you. Treat it right and you'll own it." Then, having soon been directed to "shoot that cream deep inside," I hastened toward an orgasm, after which Mike raised himself deftly from my phallus.

"I'm hungry," Mike said.

"What's this you said about it costing me?"

Mike's body stiffened as his eyes got that look of someone about to begin a complicated tale. "You don't know who you're with," he began. "You don't know who you've got right here in this room." Mike went on to detail his identity. According to him, he was closely connected to the bar owners—too closely for comfort, he added. As a matter of fact, one of them, after whom the bar took its name, had been watching our every move and had instructed Mike to leave his jacket as collateral before we walked together to the hotel. Mike had been very hesitant to go with me at all, "seeing that these guys tend to think they own somebody and I am kind of their boy." But they had generously given their permission. Go with the guy and give him a good time, they had counseled when he came back for the coat. But make sure he makes it worth your while. Now what would Mike do, he wanted me to tell him, if he came back to the bar with his ass full of grease and didn't have all the money—the one hundred and fifty dollars—they were expecting? What is more, it would be foolish for me to suppose that they couldn't find out where anybody lived.

Dipping my hand into my pants pocket, I pulled out all the cash I had. Mom's card flipped out, too, and floated down to the floor. "Hey!" Mike said, bending toward the card, "is it your birthday?"

I knelt quickly and snatched the card away, bending it in half as I stuffed it back in my pocket.

"Don't touch that!" I snapped.

Mike and I began to get dressed, but he was stewing. "There's only eighty dollars here," he hissed. "What the fuck do you expect me to say when I get back?"

"I told you, that's all I have."

But Mike was not to be daunted. Crawling around the carpet, he began cursing, accusing me of taking his socks. When he stood up, his face was livid and his entire muscular body was trembling. "All right, keep the damn socks," he spat, "if you're that kind of pervert, but you gotta pay for 'em!" He pulled his Adidases on over bare feet, grabbed me roughly by the Hanukkah sweater, and forced me toward the door. "C'mon, man, you must have a bankcard in that wallet. We're going to a cash machine!" As we left the room, I noticed dirty white socks sticking out from under the bed.

Planes move so incredibly faster than real time, and by now, six A.M., Mom would have gotten home long ago and been asleep, with Dad, her husband, for several hours. I do hope she got home safely and that there was no trouble at the airport.

There was a place called HUBERTS MUSEUM on 42nd st. It was a basement place hardly anyone went to. I'd get sucked off by a deaf mute for ten dollars. Sometimes his friends would watch. Outside the bathroom were magnifying machines. If you looked into them you could see portraits of American presidents painted on the heads of pins.

FROM *TWO GIRLS, FAT AND THIN* (1991)

MARY GAITSKILL

Justine Shade was a neurotic, antisocial twenty-eight-year-old. She had few friends, and as she saw them infrequently, her main source of entertainment was an erratic series of boyfriends who wandered through her small apartment, often making snide comments about her décor. She was serious about her career as a journalist, but she sold very few articles. This was because she got ideas at the rate of about one a year, and once she had one, she went through a lengthy process of mentally sniffing, poking, and pinching it before she decided what to do with it.

To support herself, she worked part time as an assistant secretary for a doctor of internal medicine. The job was lulling and comfortingly dull. Dr. Winkgard was an energetic, square, bad-tempered, good-hearted man, and his wife Glenda was a beautiful forty-year-old whose bright, erotic spirit, in combination with the stubborn way she held her mouth, made Justine think of a pungent, freshly cut lemon. The living room–like office was furnished with proud armchairs, a fiercely thin-cushioned sofa, a drawing of a geometric cat, and a radio that perpetually leaked a thin stream of classical music. The black-and-white striped walls and the purple carpet haughtily complemented each other. This office was the last place Justine would have expected to get an idea. But the fateful article on Anna Granite, which would, in an entirely unforeseen

fashion, alter the course of her life, was born as she sat behind her desk, peacefully sorting papers.

She spent much of the day behind this desk with Glenda, welcoming the patients as they teetered in on their canes, hats listing on their heads. She wrote down their names, addresses, and birth dates on large index cards and guided them down the treacherously rumple-rugged hall to the electrocardiogram room, where she got them to take off their clothes and lie on the table so she could wire them to the machine. The EKG was a uniquely intimate process. The old, often odorous and clammy body lay spread out before her, affable and trusting, willing to let her squeeze blobs of white conducting glue on its ankles and wrists. Women lay docile as she lifted their limp breasts for the little red suction cups, even if there were lumpy brown sores beneath them. She saw eczema and swollen ankles and fragile chests bearing terrible scars. A lady with one eye blinded by milky fluid showed her the dainty bag of protective talismans she kept safety-pinned to her dirty bra.

One day she asked a fat, sweating woman how she was, and the lady burst into tears. "My husband, he is beating me," she said. "I am bruised, see?" Justine was alarmed to see brown and purple splotches on her chest and stomach. Her alarm flustered her, and she didn't know what to say. "Why don't you hit him back?" she asked idiotically. "You're pretty big."

"Oh, he would kill me, he would crush me! He was in the army, he is strong, he knows how to kill!"

"Can't you leave?"

"Where would I go? I have no children. I have no one. He is going to kill me!" The weeping little eyes were finely shot with yellow veins.

Justine handed her a box of Kleenex. She took the EKG printout into Dr. Winkgard's office. "I think something terrible is happening," she said. "Mrs. Rabinowitz says her husband is beating her."

"Mrs. Rabinowitz is crazy," he said. "It's a very tragic case. She has a brain disease."

"But I saw bruises."

"Well, he does beat her sometimes, but she exaggerates. Sometimes she thinks the pills I give her are poison and she won't take them. It is a tragedy."

He went into the cardiogram room, and Justine heard him ask in his vibrant red ball of a voice, "How are we today, Mrs. Rabinowitz?" She took the manila folders of patients already seen and went back to the reception area. Mrs. Winkgard was picking the wilting blossoms from orchids in a vase, her head tilted slightly in appraisal.

"Glenda, Mrs. Rabinowitz just told me something terrible. She says her husband beats her. I told the doctor and he—"

"Yes, yes," said Glenda. "I know the situation. It is very sad. Both Jonathan and I have spoken to Mr. Rabinowitz. It seems to help for a while, but then he reverts. We've spoken to her as well. The problem is, she is as disturbed as he is."

"But it seems that something—"

The buzzer rang, and Glenda put a finger to her lips. It was Mrs. Wolfen, Mrs. Rabinowitz's sister. Her entrance, a dour presentation of ragged gray overcoat, folded hands, and disapproving jowls, effectively ended the conversation.

Sometimes a young person with a delicate heart would come into the office. If that person was a young woman, Dr. Winkgard would poke his smiling head out of his office to watch her advance towards him, his grin-wrinkled face set in the gloating, indulgent expression of a client just introduced to a teenaged prostitute. If it was a young man, the doctor would grin a more robust, less languid grin and swing his hand through the air until it violently connected with the patient in a handshake of health and camaraderie that would have floored an oldster.

"It is good for him to look at a young body for a change," said Glenda.

It was from one of these diversionary young bodies that Justine got her idea.

He was a small nervous boy with a large round forehead, a saucy jawline, palpitations, and shortness of breath. Justine took him into the EKG room and closed the door. He took off his shirt and lay down; the little room became their private planet, with Dr. and Mrs. Winkgard hovering in the distance like friendly stars.

"What do you do?" asked Justine.

"I'm a writer," he said, "although I've never been published." He lifted his pretty head and looked at the painless clamps on his wrists and ankles.

"It'll only take a minute," she said.

He dropped his head back on the institutional pillow. "The thing is, I find it so hard to concentrate. I haven't written anything for a while."

"I write too," she said.

"Oh, then you understand."

The machine began to whirr; the thin needles jerkily sketched their abstract of the boy's heart.

"What do you think of Anna Granite?" he asked.

"I've never read her."

"Really? Oh, you've got to read her. She's the most unique writer. Of course, I don't believe in what she says politically, but still she's so powerful. Especially now, when people are so into whining and abdicating responsibility, it's good to read somebody advocating strength and power, and doing things. She had a lot of influence on me. I even thought of joining a Definitist organization."

"A what?"

"You know, the groups they used to have in the sixties where they got around and studied Granite's work. They're still around."

"You're kidding." She cut the printout on the tiny teeth of the machine and stuck it on the mounting paper. "I mean I knew she was popular, but—"

Dr. Winkgard entered with a broad flap of the door, shoulders squared in his white coat. "Come, Justine, what is taking so long?"

She returned to the stack of papers at her desk and brooded excitedly. It is hard to say why the Anna Granite story had impressed her, but almost immediately upon hearing it she formed the tiny damp mushroom of an idea. Justine was morbidly attracted to obsessions, particularly the useless, embarrassing obsessions of the thwarted. She could not help but be drawn to the spectacle of flesh-and-blood humans forming their lives in conjunction with the shadows invented by a mediocre novelist.

"Glenda, have you ever read anything by Anna Granite?"

"Ah yes." Mrs. Winkgard nodded, her stubborn mouth set in admiration. "Very good writing, very dramatic. The clarity, the way she states her case. I read *The Bulwark* at a time when I was undergoing a crisis, and it gave me such moral support to read about those strong characters doing great things."

When Justine left work she bought a bag of cookies and rode home on the subway eating them with queenly elation, impervious to the crumpled bags and bad smells, the empty soda cans rattling about her feet. When she entered her apartment, she stripped off her pantyhose and called an editor she knew at *Urban Vision*.

The next day, she placed brief ads in *Manhattan Thing*, a monthly, and the weekly *Urban Vision*. To be sure she reached the serious nut population, she made up several index cards bearing a neutral statement which she placed on bulletin boards in rightwing bookstores, cafés, and an NYU building. She serendipitously stuck one on the wall of a laundromat in Queens where she had gone to argue with an ex-boyfriend before loaning him some money. Then she bought all of Granite's books, and started reading *The Last Woman Alive*, the story of a young woman caught in the grip of a socialist revolution in an imaginary society.

On Thursdays she went to the library with her notebook under her arm and did research. Granite had cut a colorful path through the media, starting with a few mild reviews of her early short-story collection, building in the seventies into lengthy, incredulous, outraged reviews as well as full-blown features about the "Stern Young Cult of Anna Granite," eventually culminating in sarcastic editorial denunciations by Austin Heller, Shepard Shale, and Michael Brindle, the foremost magazine intellectuals of the left and right wings. The last little noise was a long obituary in *Opinion* by Heller in which he told the story of their tentative friendship and eventual violent feud, after which Granite refused to be in the same room with him. He gloatingly referred to a time Granite "bawled" at a party after being insulted by a professor.

Justine left the library feeling as though she had been reading one of Granite's novels—the proud declarations, the dedicated followers, the triumphant public appearances, the controversy, the feuds, the denunciations, the main character storming from the room with her cape streaming from her shoulders after a violent confrontation with archenemy Austin Heller.

She began getting answers to her ads. The voices sounded like young, cramp-shouldered people taking their lunch breaks in cafeterias lit by humming fluorescent lights. She pictured women with sad hair in flower-print dresses and men with fleshy chests and hands. They all described what Granite had done for them, how she had made them value their lives, how she had inspired them to strive for the best they were capable of, whether as secretaries or as engineers. She made appointments to interview some of them, including one fellow who claimed to be a "Definitist intellectual."

Meanwhile, Katya, the heroine of *The Last Woman Alone*, had refused to join the Collectivist party, and had subsequently been thrown out of the academy, where she had been studying higher mathematics. She had been forced into an affair with the philosophically wrong Captain Dagmarov in order to save the life of her lover, Rex.

A week after the dissemination of the cards, she received a call from someone with a high-pitched voice that reminded her of a thin stalk with a rash of fleshy bumps. His name was Bernard, and, in addition to giving her the address of a study group that he attended in Brooklyn, he supplied her with the phone number of Dr. Wilson Bean, Granite's "intellectual protégé."

Bean's voice sounded as if it were being dragged along the bottom of an old tin tub. He didn't want to be interviewed; he spent minutes castigating the press, which he said had "crucified" him in the past, yet he continued talking. She pursued him down the center of his defense with the laser of her cold, clear voice, and she could feel herself contacting him. Grudgingly, with a lot of rasping around the bottom of the old tub, he agreed to talk to her again after she'd read *The Bulwark* and *The Gods Disdained*. He also advised her to attend the annual Definitist conference in Philadelphia, which would take place in a few weeks.

She hung up elated; the phone rang immediately. It was another Granite fan, a woman with a voice that, although riddled with peculiarity and tension, stroked Justine along the inside of her skull in a way that both repelled and attracted her. She said her name was Dorothy Never and she sounded like a nut. She'd been calling for days, she said, and she was so glad to have finally gotten through. Justine, trying to infuse her voice with seriousness and authority, was genuinely excited to hear that she had been a member of the original Definitist movement and had personally known Anna Granite, Beau Bradley, and Wilson Bean. She seemed not only willing but pathetically eager to be interviewed. They arranged a time, and Justine hung up full of amazement at the desire some people have for attention and publicity.

In the meantime, Katya had perished on the ice floe in an effort to escape to America, Captain Dagmarov had killed himself on realizing that he was philosophically in error, and Rex, having been broken by the collectivist society around him, was writing pornography for a living.

DIVINE COMEDY (1991)

RON KOLM

I.

Let's take a walk
You said.
Okay, I said
And here we are
High above the East River
On a pedestrian walkway
On the Triboro Bridge
Hiking from Astoria
To Randall's Island
As rush-hour traffic
Streams by.
I hate my life
You say
And I know
You're not joking.
I wonder if you're
Thinking of jumping
And what I would do
If you did.
It's a long way down
To the tug
Pushing a barge
On fiery waters
As it disappears
Beneath the bridge.
Should I grab
For your arm
And probably die too
Or simply admit
I want to live
And let you fall.
It's late afternoon

When we finally reach
Our destination
Descending a cement
Stairway that deposits us
Onto a parking lot
Near the Manhattan
Psychiatric Center.

II.

We're both too tired
To turn around
And walk back
Over the bridge.
The only other exit
Off this island
Is a narrow
Pedestrian overpass
That connects it
With Manhattan
But to get there
We have to cross
The grounds of the
Mental institution
And blocking our way
Is a guard in a booth.
You're reporters!
He shouts at us,
Trying to do
Another fucking expose!
No, we protest,
We just want to get back
To the city so we can
Take a subway home.

He pats us down
And searches our bags
Then grudgingly waves us on.
It's early evening now
And large bright lights
Come on, illuminating
Everything surreally.
We can clearly see inmates
Through plate-glass windows
In low, ranch-style buildings
Watching TV.
If it weren't
For the barbed-wire
You'd almost think
We were in suburbia.

III.

Beyond the last building
The underbrush thickens
And the asphalt path
Is cracked and broken.
It's pitch black—
A hot, humid night.
Indistinct shapes
Dart into the bushes
In front of us—
I take out
My Swiss Army Knife
All two inches of it
And flick it open
Just in case
And, like that
We come upon
The other guard booth
Burnt out
And abandoned long ago.

I'm not feeling too good
But you grab my arm
And motion
To a string of lights
Rising above the trees
And I realize
It's the foot bridge.
As we step onto it
We're almost swept away
By a wave of humanity
Swarming from Manhattan
Onto Randall's Island—
A never ending procession
Of shopping bag ladies
Sneaker kids, junkies
And soda can collectors—
And we the only two leaving
Tired and relieved
And even perhaps vaguely
In love with each other.

IN BROOKLYN (1991)

DEBORAH PINTONELLI

I'm in the backyard with Aunt June pinning up the laundry on a summer morning. She's complaining about Liza's awful pound cake and how Liza didn't bring enough cash to Bingo last night. We're doing this quickly, though, as soon it will get very hot and we want to be back inside watching the late morning soaps before that happens.

The yard is beautiful at this time of year. Large, luscious peonies with tiny black ants roaming their velvety petals lift up their fuchsia, pale pink, and white faces to the sun. Grapevines that my grandfather planted when he first bought the house in 1942 twist thickly around a network of pipes built up over the walk. Fat, bloody tomatoes and tall, thin stalks of corn and gigantic yellow squash burst out of the vegetable patch. The grass is a deliciously soft blanket of iridescent green.

As we pin the last of the laundry up I inhale the thick, sweet air and become slightly intoxicated in the process. Unfortunately, at this moment I also let my eyes rest briefly on the darkened, greasy stain under the stairway that is Mr. Pantozza's kitchen window.

What I see beyond that stain are Mr. Pantozza's green eyes staring at me from within. I shudder though it is by now very, very hot.

Aunt June says, "Did you remember to call Uncle Frank and wish him a happy birthday?" I almost don't hear her because I'm disturbed by Mr. Pantozza, by knowing that he's watching. He's been our tenant for almost twenty years. For as long as I can remember I've been in charge of making sure he has everything he needs. He has all sorts of things wrong with him and can't get around too easily.

He keeps his first floor apartment totally dark, with the only fresh air coming in from a small window fan near the back door. So, what with the four dogs and the fact that he never really bathes, the smell of the place is unreal. He is usually sitting at the kitchen table drinking coffee and smoking cigarettes—this is what he does all day, and almost all night long.

I'm not extremely pretty, but I know I have a great shape, which saves me. Well, I *am* pretty, but you see, I've got the family nose in all its glory sitting smack in the middle of my face. The long, beak-like, bumpy Genovese nose. But I've got Grandma's tits, which compete with the nose and win every time. And I've got Dad's creamy, dark skin. I go out with Michael Sullivan, who's so white he looks like an albino with his platinum hair and pale blue eyes. We look good together.

Mr. Pantozza has never cared a bit about my nose or the color of my skin. You see, he's been in love with me ever since the day that I came down with the plate of fresh scagliatelle and asked him if he needed anything from the store. "No," he said that day, "but take this five dollars and buy yourself something." From that point on I went down to see him at least a few times a week during the school year, and daily during the summer. We'd play Monopoly, Parcheezi, gin rummy. He'd buy me all sorts of sodas, desserts, toys, dresses, shoes. I'd sit on his lap and call him Uncle.

Back then, I didn't notice the smell in his rooms. I didn't pay any attention to the collection of guns in his top bureau drawer, or to the fact that though he had a telephone, it never rang, and that he never had any visitors except for my family.

Even for them to come down was rare, and now it seems kind of odd that they would leave it to me to look after him all of these years. But I guess they saw no harm in it. I guess they saw an old man being entertained by a child, and nothing more.

We'd sit at his kitchen table (he never used the other five rooms) under a dusty bulb and he'd talk and roll cigarettes and drink coffee and talk and talk. One by one, as he told his stories, the dogs would come up to be petted or fed bits of beef jerky from the pocket of his shirt. Though he didn't bathe often, he always wore a clean shirt and undershirt, and kept a fresh white handkerchief in his pocket into which he blew his long, shiny nose.

If he got me to sit on his lap after giving me a particularly longed-for gift, he'd have to run his hand over me for a minute before I squirmed away. He always got this awful look on his face when he did that; a look which fascinated and frightened me and I kick myself now for having felt that way, for having let things get to the point where now all that has to happen is that I see (or think I see) his eyes in the window and I get the severe creeps.

But I liked having his undivided attention. My family is so big, I get lost in it sometimes. It's always like, "Oh, Marisa do this, do that, you're a cutie, get outta here"—stuff like that. Everything's hustle and bustle and work, work, work. After all the cooking, cleaning and homework, I'm off with my friends. So it made me feel all-powerful to have this old man do whatever I wanted.

Mama, when she was alive, encouraged it. She'd see my new pair of shoes or my dress, and say, "Ah, Sammy's little favorite! There's a good girl, now I don't have to buy you anything for awhile!" And Papa'd say, "Pantozza's a little weird, but he's good people underneath."

I know he watches me when Michael comes over and we sit at the picnic table under the grapevines. I have no choice, Papa doesn't want me to go out on dates. He wants me here at home, where he can keep track of me. He imagines that I can't get pregnant in my own backyard. Michael likes to make out under the stairs where it's dark and private but it's also way too close to Mr. Pantozza's back door. But there really isn't anywhere else for us to go that's out of Papa's sight, so we do it there, but I have to hold back the part of me that's revolted, that feels the green eyes on my skin.

I still have to go into his apartment once in awhile to bring him some groceries and the paper, and that's when he tells me what he thinks of me and Michael. "I saw you with that boy last night," he'll say, puffing at his cigarette, almost letting the burning end of it touch the tip of his nose as he inhales, "I saw him with his hands all over you. I bet he was hard and wanted to put it inside of you. You wanted him to do that, didn't you?"

I do my best to ignore him. I don't look at his face, which I know will still have that awful look on it after all these years. I listen to him wheeze with his one good lung as he puffs on yet another cigarette. He sounds like he is going to die and sometimes I wish he would. Then I feel guilty for feeling that way, so I say, "Oh, you're just imagining things, we were just talking."

And then I notice that the spot where his penis is in his pants is still worn, dry-looking. Sometimes I can't help looking at that spot for a second, and then at his eyes, which are always amazingly calm, but which flash for a minute if he notices me looking. "Come here for a minute," he'll say innocently.

When I was eleven-almost-twelve Mr. Pantozza gave me a stack of books to read. "Here," he said, "these will help improve your reading skills." The stories were about men who liked to be spanked and put to bed with diapers on. They liked to have the diapers changed by pretty, busty young women named "Daisy" or "Candy." One was about an old man who liked to drink warm pee provided by black women with hefty buttocks. They would squat over his mouth and piss while he fondled their butts.

I would get excited while reading these books, sitting in Mr. Pantozza's empty living room on rainy Saturdays. I would scrunch down on the sofa so that the seam of my jeans dug into my crotch. I did this for many hours at a time, not worrying about whether or not he was watching me.

Simpler, and easier to understand were the magazines in his bathroom. The usual collection of *Playboy, Penthouse* and *Hustler* provided me with my first glimpses of naked bodies: extremely young women with tiny, shaved snatches adorned each shiny page. My only problem was that I didn't look like the girls in the photos. I was dark. Everything about me was dark, dark, dark, and everything about them was luridly pink. And by the time I turned twelve I weighed 110 lbs., and I was very strong. I could outrun most of my class and was a pretty good athlete in general. None of the girls pictured in *Playboy* weighed more than that, and they were all inches taller than me.

But as I've said, Mr. Pantozza has never had any problem with my looks. "There might be some coon in you," he'd say when I complained, "but it hasn't done you any harm." This would set him off laughing, for any kind of racial slur was almost as titillating to him as the stuff in the magazines.

Once, during this same summer, I was in the washroom with a *Hustler* magazine. Mr. Pantozza opened the door. I froze as he stood over me, afraid that he was finally going to do something

bad. "Mari," he said sweetly, "let uncle Sammy see you for a minute, just a minute." I didn't know what he meant. "This," he said, putting his hand on my knee and pushing it aside. He brushed my hands away and pushed my legs open even farther. "If you only knew how beautiful you are, how like a lovely flower you are there in the middle, past those brown thighs." Then he smiled.

"I could kiss the flower, if you'd like me to," he said, nodding his head and wetting his lips with his tongue. I didn't know what to say. He wasn't being harsh or mean; he was, in fact, being much kinder than usual. I wondered if it would be like in the books when the man and the woman or the two women put their mouths on each other. "Or I could kiss your mouth, which is also like a tender rose, a frail blossom." A what? I noticed he didn't have his teeth in, which was good, I guessed, because then he couldn't all of a sudden decide to get mean again and bite me like a dog.

All of the air in the room seemed to vanish. I was hot, and felt like I had to pee more. And I wanted some water, too.

He leaned over and put his mouth on mine, driving his smoky tongue inside, running it all over my tongue, my teeth, my tonsils, practically. I said into his mouth that I had to pee and he shook his head yes, like it was okay so I peed and then he put his hand down there to cup me while I peed and it got all over the fuzzy red toilet seat that I hated so much and I was glad, thinking then for some stupid reason that he would now have to throw it away because it was ruined.

For a minute I pushed down on his hand, liking the way it felt. We stayed like this for awhile, with him moaning and shivering like he was cold. When he finally pulled his mouth off of mine his palm held a little puddle of pee.

Then suddenly I didn't like it anymore. It was getting all messy and stupid and I was hot and thirsty. I struggled and pushed him away. He seemed to sense that this was going to be his one and only opportunity to be so close to me and mumbled something about not being done, but I said that I was and I pulled up my jeans and ran out of the room fast.

It seemed to be okay soon after that, though. I was young and I forgot things quickly. Soon he and I were the same as always, playing games, eating too much watermelon, reading comic books and watching tv. My father said, "Yeah, Pantozza's okay. Look at how good he treats Marisa."

Aunt June and I are watching "As The World Turns" and eating chicken salad sandwiches. She looks at me and asks, "What's wrong, Mar? Something the matter?" She thinks I'm bored spending my summer at home while most of my friends are away on vacation somewhere. I shake my head. Then I decide to tell her something of what I am feeling. "I just wish that old man downstairs would finally die." She is appalled. "Why, Mari? Why? He's been so good to you all of these years!" She couldn't even begin to understand. "He just gets on my nerves, that's all. I'm tired of being his godammned nursemaid."

She decides she understands. "Honey, look, you'll feel better when Mikey comes back from his vacation," she says knowingly. "He'll take you out somewhere nice. You'll get all dolled up, then you'll feel better." She turns back to the soap opera with satisfaction.

It's one of those oppressive summer days when it wants to rain but can't so I can't even go sit on the porch with a book. I can call my friend Barb, but I've already done that. I pace the apartment, going to the fridge to look at the veal roast for dinner, taking out a coke and drinking half of it, turning on the radio in my bedroom for a minute. Nothing to do. I feel like the whole building is rotten, stinking with that beast down there in his lair. My father should throw him out, I think, the apartment is overrun by mice and bugs and we could get a lot more rent from a new tenant. I think about this all afternoon long, not really knowing why I'm suddenly so obsessed with the subject.

Then I'm in the yard cutting some flowers. Through the darkened, greasy stain that is Mr. Pantozza's kitchen window I can see his hands in the light of the dusty bulb as they move to roll and light a cigarette. The oversized mug of coffee is lifted to his lips and put down again. Through the whirl of the window fan's blades, I can hear the strains of Lite FM and one of his dogs yapping for a snack. He sees me looking at him and snaps off the light.

JANINE, OR HOW MY GRANDMOTHER DIED AND LEFT ME HOLDING THE BANANA (1991)

JOE MAYNARD

She walked into Max's, the ultra-cool lower east side bar every night after her day-gig at an established mid-town gallery. To me, I was cooler than her, cuz I couldn't afford a beer. But to her, well, she sometimes bought me one—her way of connecting with the little people.

I hated how she dressed down in three hundred dollar work boots, and ripped jeans imported from Luxembourg. She was a rich, perfect looking cunt. I wanted to smack her in the mouth so that at least her teeth were crooked, but I never even asked her on a date.

I fantasized, though. I fantasized about laying her out over the hood of a primer grey '67 Chevelle, but when it got down to it, she was so fucking rich and untouchable, it wouldn't phase her. She'd wear rape the same way she wore everything else. While I hammered down, pistons roaring under the hood, hot metal frying the fat off her ass, she'd say, "I'm so down and out and there's nothing I can do but take it like a fallen angel. Also, this whole rape and violence thing looks great with my leather corset."

That's Janine.

Alex was another story. She was smart. She was a staunch feminist She was no looker.

Her last year in college, she'd curated an exhibition of prints from the seventeenth century portraying women as objects of abuse. The imagery included Saint Katherine whose breasts were cut off in a public square, Joan of Arc, and a bunch of others. It received rave reviews. But despite the fact that the world was her oyster, she was determined to persuade herself that she was suffering the utmost persecution from the male dominant system. Virtually any ritual in the world looked like rape to her, and she wrote volumes of essays with titles like "Fingernail Polish: The Eclipse of Female Identity," "Setting the Table for Genocide," and "High-heeled Shackles."

For years we shared an apartment. Though her career didn't sky-rocket the way she had anticipated after her early success, she worked at a prestigious arts organization, not so far from where Janine worked, while I painted in a back room most of the day and worked 4–10 in a bookstore downtown.

At work, I advised over-educated girls like Alex what books they should buy to be one up on their peers, or better yet, make their professors look like fools. Jack's Bookmark, where I worked, had a reputation for being a well kept secret. I was congratulated amply by the young comp lit coeds for my book-savant efforts, usually after a mid-term "A," but often the excitement of an unkempt man, like myself, exposing them to new authors that would change their lives completely, drove them to near orgasm, and they made it seem as if my professional reputation was on the line if I did not copulate with them in a private corner, perhaps over a pile of rejected paperbacks, or a firm sloppy slam over a push-cart of literary quarterlies, something, anything that would allow them to stain a page at Jack's Bookmark, show us they'd arrived. The job was good for that kind of instant fuck that everyone needs. That renewed vigor for life you get watching butterflies burst from cocoons.

At home, well, Alex and I were too used to each other to fuck that much, but every night she sucked my dick before we fell asleep. You might think it was an indication of some bottomless well of love she had for me. Well, it wasn't. When she gave head, she was in control. My dick was her toy. She knew exactly what to do to make me hard, or make me come, or to keep me hard or keep me from coming. She was a genuine manipulator who constantly fought for domination and was no different in bed.

She didn't talk to her sister Elise for a year once, because one Christmas they got in an argument over mashed potatoes. Alex leaves the skins in the mashed potatoes. She claims it's healthier. Elise's husband complained to Elise because he preferred them without the skin. When Elise made a case for mashed potatoes without skins to Alex, Alex knew it was because of her brother-in-law, and suggested that Elise mash the potatoes herself, since she was an obvious professional. The way Alex told the story made me hate Elise. Elise was painted as an insipid bimbo, and I was a jerk through association if I didn't zealously condemn her as well. When Elise called to make up, I told her that Alex didn't need a Stepford Wife for a sister and hung up. They didn't speak until the next Christmas.

When Alex and I split up, she told my friends that I had maliciously driven her to alcohol, that I was unfeeling, only cared about my cock, and couldn't love someone with a mind of their own. Her rants had little truth, but I knew that the same way I was convinced that her sister was a second class human because of the potato incident, my friends must have been equally convinced that I was a complete jerk for splitting up.

After we split-up, I roamed the streets of the city alone and—well—depressed. I sat in Max's for hours scribbling page after page of complete nonsense into a diary, complaining to Corky the skinhead bartender about how much I hated yuppies, while hoards of them walked in and out ordering spritzers, Rolling Rocks, and Cardhu, desperately trying to be part of a scene.

In this scene, Janine was queen.

"Feminism is for weak women," she told me one day, "Women who can't dominate men through nature need a mechanism to . . ." she sipped her scotch and gave a pensive look while I let my eyes flutter to the heaven below her neck, "do it with." She sipped her Scotch again, this time a good, proper swig, then concluded, "Feminism is one, a dildo is another." I was grateful she shared this with me. It made me feel "not so bad"—like it was O.K. to be just a horny loser. But it also made me resent her. She made it clear that she was more powerful than I was. She knew I wanted her, like everybody else did, and that no matter how bad I wanted her, she didn't want me. But worse, it implied that action begat thought, and that people like me, who she considered to be intellectual, only existed because they couldn't make a genuine impact on movers and shakers like herself.

So you can imagine my excitement when she asked if I wanted to split a loft space with her. Mind you I didn't even like her, but just the thought of her made my dick rock hard. Around her I was glad to be the horny prick that I was deep inside, under the layers of feminist indoctrinations that suffocated my libido. I could fawn over her, visually devour her cleavage from across the table, and rather than tell me I'm a pig, she'd flirt. Flirt, but at the same time let me know I could only look.

She showed the space to me. It was long and narrow. Four walls with windows on one side. Plumbing fixtures projected from a three foot square in the middle of the floor like surgically exposed industrial ganglia. Though the windows looked into an alley with broken glass, and abandoned, rusty machinery, they filled the lengthy space with white ambient light. Janine suggested I pay one-third of the rent for half the space, and in exchange for the cheap rent, install dry-wall, a bathroom, and new kitchen cabinets for which she would supply money for materials. I agreed.

I spent a week emptying garbage, spraying for vermin, and refinishing the floors. I crashed, rent free, in a sleeping bag in the cleanest corner of the loft, saving myself a few bucks, while I diligently completed the project. Then I built a bathroom, and kitchen twice, since the first time she didn't like the fixtures I'd chosen. In other words, she took me shopping for fucking shower heads, taking great care to point out the finer subtleties of her chosen accoutrements to me, and the various Home Improvement Center sales people. Within a month though, the space was ready, and she moved in.

Well, she didn't exactly move in. She had a nice apartment on Park Avenue South that her parents bought for her. But she used the space to paint realistic paintings of stuffed animals, on badly patterned fabrics for which she spent hours shopping. I thought her work was awful. I couldn't imagine that anyone would find the subject matter interesting enough to continue for months. I couldn't imagine staying awake while cranking out hundreds and hundreds of paintings that were essentially the same one-liner repeated.

She put them up in bars around town like Max's. She had lots of parties in the loft to which she invited fancy uptown collectors for private

viewings of her latest works. On these occasions, she would slip me a twenty to get lost for three or four hours. Full of resentment, but grateful for a little drinking money, I would go down to Max's and play pinball till the twenty ran out.

As time went by collectors began showing up at the loft at all hours. My space was in the back, so one day I decided to hang one of my paintings in the kitchen hoping someone who mattered would see it. I had just hung it on the only blank wall in the apartment, and though I regretted losing the last refuge from our collective bric-a-brac, I felt proud of the piece. Janine walked in with her latest shopping coup. "Look," she said, "Pink vinyl, isn't it great? Hey, what are you doing?"

"I'm putting up a painting, what does it look like?"

"It doesn't look like anything I want to look at every time I walk in the door."

I argued that it was communal space, space that I'd built that she used as a showroom, and that none of the collectors ever saw my work because it was kept in back. But she countered my protests, saying that my artwork was my business and her artwork was her business. "At any rate," she said, "I don't think my collectors would be interested in your paintings." So of course, I resigned myself to taking it down, realizing the mistake I made moving in with her.

"You're a mover and a shaker," I said, not being able to repress the point of contention.

"I'm a mover and shaker, that's right," she scolded as if she were my appointed social worker, "But it's better than what you are."

"What's that?"

"You're a . . . ," she paused and looked at me with both pity and contempt, "You're like this zombie condemned to roam the earth rationalizing your failures." It was probably the most articulate thing

I ever heard her say, so I wondered who told her, while she proceeded with a less than intelligent diatribe that concluded with her saying, "I'm just too sick of you to even look at one of your stupid paintings. What do you do back there anyway?"

"Maybe I read," I said realizing that reading was something that I'd never seen her do.

"You think your smart just cuz you read," she said, "Me, I don't have to read, I just do it."

"You don't read?"

"I read magazines, but books . . ." She paused, examined the finish of her fingernails, and proceeded with a softer, more pensive tone, "It's not like I'm proud of it, but I haven't actually finished a book, cover to cover. But at least I get it. My point is that you read all the time, but you just don't get it."

"Get what?" I sighed. She was right, whatever she was talking about I didn't get, but I had a feeling she didn't either.

I went down to Max's where Corky the skinhead bartender greeted me with a big toothy smile, and asked me about my lovely roommate.

"She's fine," I said, "Just fine. One day you and I are going to be drinking Thunderbird in a gutter, and she's gonna bounce a quarter off our heads."

"Speak for yourself, Jose." He was slapping pinball change on the counter. "I don't want to say anything that might upset my future bride." And he meant Janine.

My resentment increased when one day I saw her picture in *Art Star*. It was a glossy full-color photo of her holding a stuffed elephant, in front of a fluorescent green backdrop. Interspersed throughout the article were black and white reproductions of perhaps a half dozen of her paintings. The article attached all sorts

of deconstructivist meaning to her work, quoting passages from Baudrillard and Umberto Eco. The intellectual praise, especially after she more or less confessed to being illiterate, infuriated me. I avoided contact with her, eating and drinking my coffee in the back instead of around the kitchen table, waiting for the day I had enough money to find a new place.

So she beat me to the punch and asked me to leave. I didn't argue, but the timing wasn't exactly ideal on my financial time clock. I packed my belongings into a stockroom at the bookstore—mostly paintings and art supplies—and got a cheap room in a hotel for men on 105th Street.

After I moved out of the loft, I often saw her at Max's, but she acted as if we didn't know each other. She and Corky started screwing. They made a point of feverishly kissing in my presence, as if saying, "You aren't happening, we are." They were stupid happy, and I just sat there watching Corky prime himself for the day she'd dump him, feverishly hoping he'd beat the shit out of her the day it happened. But I knew better. The only thing Corky had going for him was that he looked cool behind the bar, after all, Janine was the dream-fuck of the century. If she dumped him, he'd probably be licking her toes like a dog, while she kicked him out of the door, then whine on the stoop until she got the cops to drag him away, or worse, he'd just be thankful for the once in a lifetime opportunity and shake her hand on his way out.

One day they came into the bookstore. I was stacking books by the register, no more than ten feet away, but they didn't acknowledge me. I stood watching as they asked Harry, the manager on duty, for a book. Harry, a reformed heroin addict who used to sell books on the sidewalk in the old days with Jack the owner, was a wonderfully humble, soft spoken person, virtues completely wasted on people like Janine, and even though they asked for something along the lines of Rod McKuen, he didn't become snide or uppity about it. What he did do though when she leaned over the counter with her push up bra, and sweet smile, orthodontically aligned to perfection, is sort of gasp, lose his bearings for a second. When he snapped out of it he politely said that he didn't carry that sort of book as a rule, and suggested Barnes and Noble. "That was just what we expected from a geeky place like this!" She turned to make her exit, each step landing her corked heels hard against the floor creating a deep, feminine resonance in the floorboards. Her powerful ass wiggled away, leaving the store with our dicks stuck to it like medals on a general's chest, then her head re-appeared through the door and lackadaisically said, "Come on, Corky, let's go to Barnes and Noble."

Days later, I ran into Alex on a subway platform. The train was delayed and we were forced to talk to each other. She was cataloguing an exhibit of contemporary paintings. She said during installation, she and Janine had a nice conversation, and Janine had mentioned we'd been roommates. I asked how Janine was doing, couldn't help asking what she said about me. Alex said Janine extended no wishes good or bad to me, only mentioned we'd been roommates.

The thought of the two women meeting behind my back enraged me. I always figured if they ever met, Alex would instantly hate Janine, but it sounded like they had something in common, and I was sure that it was me—what else could they have "a nice conversation" about? The conversation that must have taken place unfolded hundreds of times in a matter of a few seconds, each time exposing a nuance I had not previously thought of. "He's a nice guy," perhaps said with accidental condescension. "I met him at

Max's." "Oh, you go there, too?" Even these scenarios were more than what must have happened. I was afraid of an even more subtle degradation: Perhaps I didn't strike any chord what so ever in Janine.

Alex must have found great satisfaction trying to convey the lack of regard Janine had for me. Surely, it was satisfying to know that any innuendo was the right innuendo. God made moments like this for lesser women like Alex to savor. She seemed to say, "See, I am not attractive, but neither am I a pathetic reptile like you." That is the pleasure of moments like that one, on the platform, with an ex-boyfriend and the delayed train nowhere in sight.

But the train finally arrived. I asked Alex if perhaps she wanted dinner. She lived in Hell's Kitchen, and I had to go there for some guitar parts, anyway, but mainly I wanted any news on Janine I could get.

We ate at a diner that looked like it used to be a Howard Johnson's. Alex talked about her career, and I talked about which books I'd been meaning to read. She had gained weight. I could see it in her jowls. I remembered how well she gave head. The neighborhood was making me horny. I found myself with an erection, while eating a cheeseburger, staring at an A-frame sign of a woman fondling her breasts, hoping to hear something about Janine, but having to settle for a verbal resume from a woman I no longer cared for, but never the less a woman who gave really good head. I should have walked out to jerk-off in one of those booths across the street, but couldn't leave the table. I was stuck. Alex went on and on: ". . . and even though I have a Masters, it just doesn't matter there. I'm just out-secretaried by the little bitch." She let out her famous sigh that was meant to reveal the degree of persecution she was enduring. We talked over an hour. It became dark.

"Hey," I said noticing a neon sign of an erection, "doesn't that look like that Bruce Nauman piece?"

"No, listen," she said angrily, "I was telling you something important." She talked for hours, and still no mention of Janine. No new erotic image to conjure. No girlie little thing to hate. Just talk.

She paid the bill. We walked west across 48th Street towards her block. She seemed to be inviting me over by not saying good-bye. I was rock-hard, and I couldn't wait for her parted lips to slide over the rim of my cock. The memory of Alex's oral proficiency overtook the obsessive images of Janine.

She had stopped talking. I started to feel her gaze. I looked her way, and she returned my look with a resigned smile. It was nearly one in the morning and the streets were empty except for a few prostitutes. It was quiet enough to hear her breathing. I listened to my own breath and tried to control it, but our heavy breath and heavy footsteps made me breathe harder and step harder and my dick started to scream for her lips.

A few doors from her apartment, under the steps of a Greek Orthodox Church, a prostitute knelt, her eyes illuminated by street ambiance. She was on a level lower than the sidewalk, where the church kept their garbage cans. As we passed, she leaned forward, resting most of her weight on her arms, and looked up. She was dressed in black leather, low cut. I looked her in the eye, taking in the milky white cleavage that spilled over her leather corset. She ran her tongue over her lip. She looked vaguely like Janine, except tonight she could be bought.

We got to the door of Alex's building. "I know you'll think I'm a tease," she said. "but I really don't feel good about it now. In fact, I don't think it would be healthy for me to see you again." I watched her lips as she talked, mesmerized by

imagined suction over the rim of my penis, but before I knew it the door was closed and she was ascending the staircase of her building with heavy, end of a hard-day's steps, and then she was out of sight. The traffic on eleventh avenue replaced the void of her absence. I walked back to where the prostitute knelt in the shadow. She had been vomiting, which was why she bad been kneeling in the shadows. If she touched my dick, I'd come.

"Are you O.K.?" I asked walking towards her.

"Leave me alone," she answered, coughing up a string of phlegm. The smell of patchouli, puked alcohol and garbage hit me. I walked up the block to 10th Avenue, listening to her body heave behind me. Her wretched smell stayed in my nostrils the whole walk home—53 blocks—to 105th, where I went to bed, jerking off under the sheets with my mind's eye concentrating on a woman who had Janine's face, clothes and body, Alex's mouth, and I was being sucked in the shadows of the Greek Orthodox church, the fleshy white girl on all fours in tight black leather, and I came with my toes in her warm puke, and her painted fingernail up my ass. She was moaning even though my dick was all the way down her phlegm coated throat.

"EIGHTEEN TO TWENTY-ONE" (1991)

DAVID TRINIDAD

I

He said his name was Nick; later I learned
he'd crossed the country on stolen credit
cards—I found the receipts in the guest house
I rented for only three months. Over
a period of two weeks, he threatened
to tell my parents I was gay, blackmailed
me, tied me up, crawled through a window and
waited under my bed, and raped me at
knifepoint without lubricant. A neighbor
heard screams and called my parents, who arrived
with a loaded gun in my mother's purse.
But Nick was gone. I moved back home, began
therapy, and learned that the burning in
my rectum was gonorrhea, not nerves.

II

Our first date, Dick bought me dinner and played
"Moon River" (at my request) on his grand
piano. Soon after that, he moved to
San Diego, but drove up every weekend to see me. We'd sleep at his "uncles"'s
quaint cottage in Benedict Canyon—part
of Jean Harlow's old estate. One night, Dick
spit out my cum in the bathroom sink; I
didn't ask why. The next morning, over
steak and eggs at Du-Par's, Dick asked me to
think about San Diego, said he'd put
me through school. I liked him because he looked
like Sonny Bono, but sipped my coffee
and glanced away. Still, Dick picked up the bill.

III

More than anything, I wanted Charlie
to notice me. I spent one summer in
and around his swimming pool, talking to
his roommates, Rudy and Ned. All three of
them were from New York; I loved their stories
about the bars and baths, Fire Island, docks
after dark. I watched for Charlie, played board
games with Rudy and Ned, crashed on the couch.
Occasionally, Charlie came home without a trick and I slipped into his bed
and slept next to him. Once, he rolled over
and kissed me—bourbon on his breath—and we
had sex at last. I was disappointed,
though: his dick was so small it didn't hurt.

IV

I made a list in my blue notebook: *Nick,
Dick, Charlie, Kevin, Howard, Tom* . . . . Kevin
had been the boyfriend of an overweight
girl I knew in high school. I spotted him
at a birthday bash—on a yacht—for an
eccentric blond "starlet" who called herself
Countess Kerushka. Kevin and I left
together, ended up thrashing around
on his waterbed while his mother, who'd
just had a breakdown, slept in the next room.
Howard was Kevin's best friend. We went for
a drive one night, ended up parking. His
lips felt like sandpaper, and I couldn't
cum—but I added his name to the list.

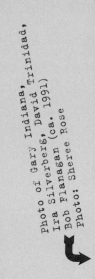

Photo of Gary Indiana,
Ira Silverberg (ca. 1991)
Bob Flanagan
Photo: Sheree Rose
David Trinidad,

V

Tom used spit for lubricant and fucked me
on the floor of his Volkswagen van while
his ex-lover (also named Tom) drove and
watched (I was sure) in the rearview mirror.
Another of his exes, Geraldo,
once cornered me in Tom's bathroom, kissed me
and asked: "What does he see in you?" At a
gay students' potluck, I refilled my wine
glass and watched Tom flirt with several other
men in the room. Outside, I paced, chain-smoked,
kicked a dent in his van and, when he came
looking for me, slugged him as hard as I
could. It was the end of the affair, but
only the beginning of my drinking.

VI

I ordered another wine cooler and
stared at his tight white pants—the outline of
his cock hung halfway down his thigh. After
a few more drinks, I asked him to dance to
"The First Time Ever I Saw Your Face." He
pressed himself against me and wrapped his arms
around my neck. I followed him to his

apartment but, once in bed, lost interest.
I told him I was hung up on someone.
As I got dressed, he said: "If you love him,
you should go to him." Instead, I drove back
to the bar, drank more, and picked up a blond
bodybuilder who, once we were in bed,
whispered "Give me your tongue"—which turned me off.

VII

As one young guy screwed another young guy
on the screen, the man sitting a couple
seats to my right—who'd been staring at me
for the longest time—slid over. He stared
a little longer, then leaned against me
and held a bottle of poppers to my
nose. When it wore off, he was rubbing my
crotch. Slowly, he unzipped my pants, pulled back
my underwear, lowered his head, licked some
pre-cum from the tip of my dick, and then
went down on it. As he sucked, he held the
bottle up. I took it, twisted the cap
off and sniffed, then looked up at the two guys
on the screen, then up at the black ceiling.

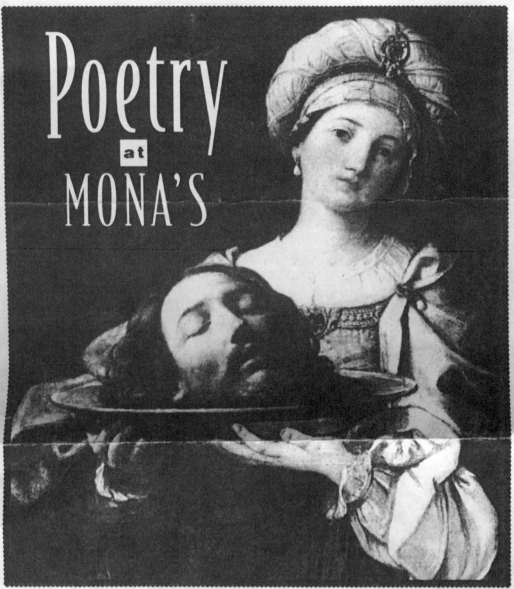

Poetry at MONA'S

Poetry at Mona's, 224 Avenue B, between 13th and 14th
All Shows Saturdays 4:00 PM, Admission FREE

February 26	Don Yorty	Raymond Metrulis
March 5	Michael Carter	Carl Watson
March 12	Donald Jennings	Ivan Robertson
March 19	Marcella Harb	Fielding Dawson
March 26	Lee williams and Her Girl Gang	
April 2	Maggie Estep	Donna Cartelli
April 9	Eileen Myles	Kelly Cogswell
April 16	Phil Kline	Luc Sante
April 23	Linda Yablonski	Tom Carey
April 30	Merry Fortune	Sheila Alson
May 7	Elio Schneeman	Harris Schiff
May 14	Lewis Warsh	Christian X. Hunter
May 21	Suzanne Ironbiter	Charles Borkhuis
May 28	Evan McHale	Angela Graham
June 4	Donal Ward	John Hedigan

EPIPHANY ALBUMS

"THE ALBUM THAT CHANGED MY LIFE"

READINGS BY LENNY KAYE, IRWIN CHUSID, LINDA YABLONSKY, FRANK NIMS, SILVIA SANZA, ED FRIEDMAN, JOSE PADUA, J.P. OLSON, DARIUS JAMES, SHANNON KETCH & CARL WATSON

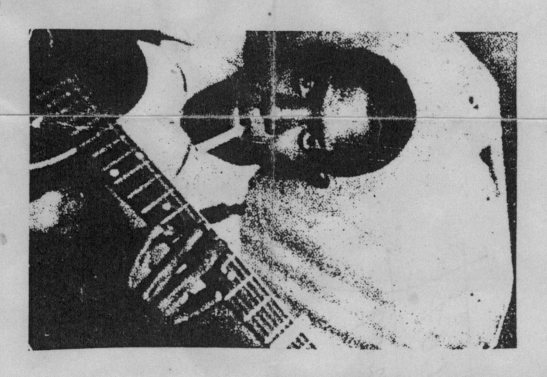

**FRIDAY, OCTOBER 9TH AT 10:30
THE POETRY PROJECT
ST. MARK'S CHURCH
SECOND AVENUE & TENTH STREET
674-0910
$5 SUGGESTED CONTRIBUTION**

A Celebration for Scarlet

Alice Notley

Douglas Oliver

Elinor Nauen

Johnny Stanton

Maureen Owen

Rudy Burckhardt

Susie Timmons

Bob Holman

Eileen Myles

Fielding Dawson

Lois Griffith

Ron Padgett

Sheila Alson

Tom Savage

+ a gala raffle & social dancing

Friday, January 18, 8 PM
Nuyorican Poets Cafe
236 East Third Street (B - C)

Contribution $5

Our Phone Flea Market Begins
See pg. 42

DOWNTOWN

ISSUE NO. 249 JUNE 19-26, 1991 **FREE**

Politics, Poetry, Philosophy, Art, Theater, Film, Media, Music And Hidden Agendas

Shawn Eichman outside the Federal Court. PHOTO BY PAUL KHEISEL.

Freedom Fighter Wins Battle (Sorta)
See pg. 9

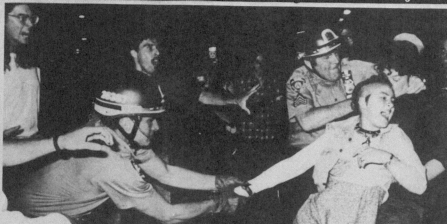

By all appearances: cops brutalizing protestor. PHOTO BY DAVID SORCHER.

'Justice' At Tompkins Square

"Both the Borough President and I are absolutely outraged that there was no effort to respond to our repeated efforts to find out what was planned for the park. The Mayor's action was *anticommunity!* When you know you are going to do something drastic, bring in police, *tell* the community—not *consult with*, but *tell*—that their park is off-limits—that's anticommunity."

See Green, pg. 10

Tompkins says that the park renovation is "all politics. The bandshell is acoustically sound—I've worked as a stagehand and I know. This has happened before—after the riots in the Civil War, the park was razed and was a pit of rubble for several years. If there's trouble in the park, there's something wrong in the city, even the nation, which needs to be addressed. The riot in '67 was a reflection of the strife over Vietnam."

Robert Dornhelm.

Romanian Nightmare
See pg. 22

The Bayonne Nipple Company

The Bayonne Nipple Company lies on a pleasant, tree-lined street in New Jersey.
Everyone in Bayonne is happy to have it there.
When people awake in Bayonne they have pork chops for breakfast. They loosen their belts, open up their umbrellas and walk

to their 9 to 5 jobs at the Bayonne Nipple Company. They are clerks, keeping track of nipples. There's nothing else they'd rather do, and nowhere else they'd rather be. than in Bayonne, a town where it's OK to be a chubby little geezer walking to work in the rain.

See pgs. 16-17

Nightingale's: So Hot!
See pg. 27

PLEASE RECYCLE THIS NEWSPAPER

Previous 4 pages in order:
Epiphany Blues at the Poetry Project, Flyer (1992)

Scarlet Benefit at Nuyorican Poets Cafe, Flyer (1991)

Downtown Magazine, No. 249, June 19-26, 1991, Cover (1991)

"Dope Brands 1981-1991" (1992) Art: Walter Sipser

A SHORT HISTORY OF EVERYONE IN THE WORLD (1992)

JOSE PADUA

On the train going
back to my home town
people are laughing at the
drunk who's making fun
of the bald spot on a guy
a few rows up.
Across the aisle from me
a deaf man is making garbled passes
at all the women walking by
on the way to the club car.
Next to me a girl
with a silly haircut
is drinking a beer and
talking to everyone in sight
between drags of her cigarette.
It's one of those
holiday weekend party trains
where everyone's celebrating
and ready to tell their life story.

The drunk guy is going
to Richmond where he'll find a bar
and drink some more.
The haircut girl is going
to Philadelphia—she plans
on becoming a hairdresser.
The guy with the bald spot
has just gotten out of prison
and he's trying to stay
calm and out of trouble.
The deaf guy is just horny
and doesn't bother to read
the lips of the women
who tell him to fuck off.

When the haircut girl
asks me for my story
I tell her,
"I saved up my money
to buy this train ticket
so I could visit home
and get there comfortably.
I cut my spending in half
by eating my own shit.
Why I've been living off
the same macaroni and cheese
dinner for two months now."

"Oh," she says, startled, grimacing.

"Excuse me," I say. "I have
to go to the bathroom now."

When I stand up
everyone's quiet,
and I know that when
I get back to my seat
I'll be able to just relax
and sleep.
No stories, no loud laughter,
no more rude comments,
snide remarks or subtle innuendoes.
I'd put an end to that
because I'd just said all
there was in the world
to be said.

Gathering of the Tribes, No. 2, Cover (1992)
Photo: Ari Marcopoulos

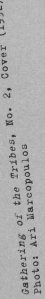

TRIBES

$5.00

A Gathering of the TRIBES:
A Multicultural Literary Magazine
of the Arts

**FEATURING: WOMEN & PERFORMANCE,
OUTTARA, EMILY CARTER, DAVID MURRAY,
LORENZO THOMAS & MORE...**

Tonight!

500 YEARS OFF THE EDGE OF THE WORLD

dia de Colón, MOn. 10/12/92

REDTAPE TRAGIC COMIX ISSUE #7

KaThe BurkhArt
◇
Norman DouGLaS
◇
joHn FarrIS
◇
deBOrah PinTONelli
◇
shArOn mESMEr
◇
baRT plAnteNGA
◇
jiLL RAPaporT
◇
juLiuS KLein
◇
ERic DRookER
◇
mikE RandaLL
◇
jiM FEasT
◇
miKE GolDen

Holly ANDERSON

Baron VON BLUMENZACK

VINDALOO

& nOt tOO mAny OThErS

"History of Amerika", ERIC DROOKER

CB's 313 GALLERY 313 bowery

8pm $3

TRAGICOMIX GALA #2

---

8 Reasons
Why You Should Write In Eileen Myles For President In '92

- She will abolish income tax! (It's invasive. Tax assets instead.)

- She will reduce defense spending by 75%. Twist our priorities back towards domestic spending.

- Under Myles we will pay our U.N. dues and stop vetoing peace keeping initiatives around the world.

- She refuses to live in the White House while there are homeless in America.

- Her vision for America is inclusive. Everyone can come. All classes, races, sexes & sexualities count.

- As an openly female & queer candidate she has primary reasons for promoting these groups.

- A poet, Myles writes her own speeches. Once elected she will continue to communicate with the American people. She will create a Department of Culture.

- She guarantees healthcare for all Americans within 90 days of her election. She needs it too!

**Veto the mainstream! Stay outside!
Vote for Eileen Myles**

Paid for by The Committee to Elect Eileen Myles

*Top: Redtape Tragicomix Gala
at CBGB's, Flyer (1992)
Art: Eric Drooker*

*Left: 8 Reasons You Should Write
in Eileen Myles for President in '92,
Flyer (1992)
Eileen Myles*

*Right: National Poetry Magazine of
the Lower East Side, Vol. 7 No. 24,
Cover (1992)
Artist/Designer: Catherine Sand*

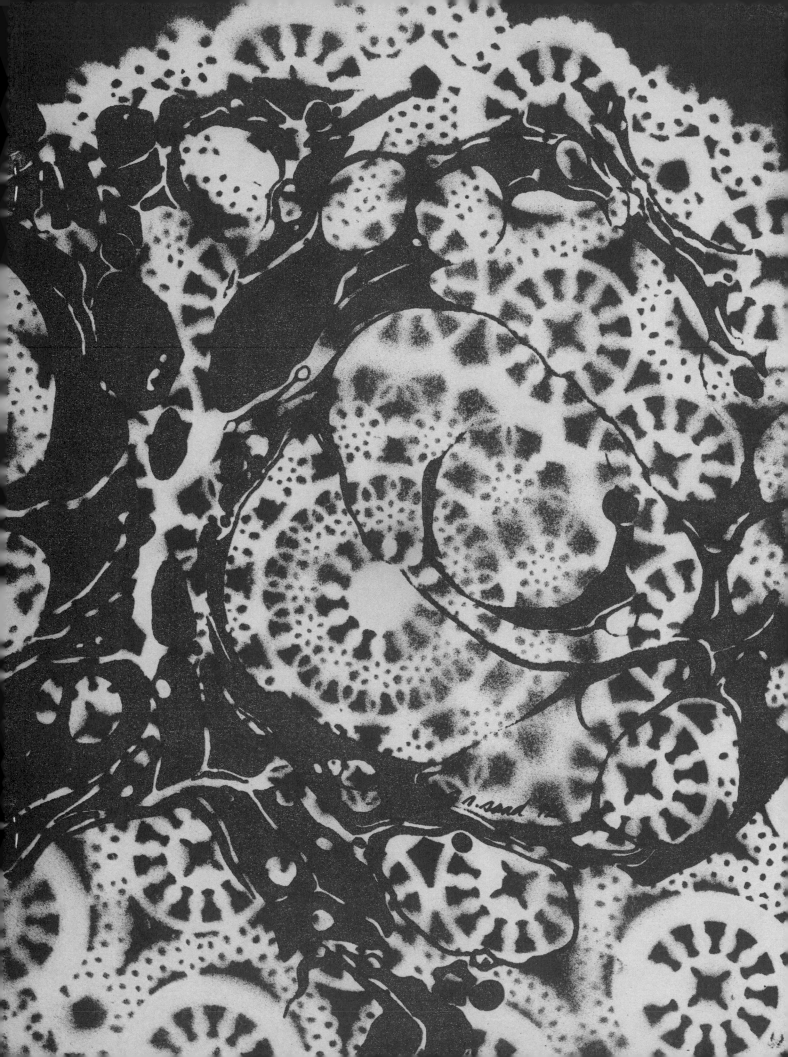

THE SHOWER (1992)

TSAURAH LITZKY

The new shower is so white and clean I think I am in a motel.
It was put in two days ago by an artist carpenter, Cliff
       Gerstenhaber.
The new landlord hired him. Gerstenhaber was cute, so I said
       smiling, "What kind of name is Gerstenhaber?"
"A long name," he said, not smiling.
You win some you lose some, I thought.

It took Gerstenhaber one day to do the job,
the old shower was put in by my old boyfriend, Louis Krim.
It took Louis two weeks to put it in.
The first time I used that shower it leaked on Bob and Betty
       downstairs.
Bob doesn't like me because he once made a play for me
and I squashed him.
Betty doesn't like me because she knows something happened,
but not what.
They think I am promiscuous and will never amount to anything,
they are wrong on both counts.
The old landlord would not put out any more money to fix
the shower, he said he had fulfilled his obligations.
They said I should shower in the public bathroom on the second
       floor.

I said I was paying for the shower and would use the shower,
they should fight the landlord.
One time when I was in the shower with Abraham, the shower
leaked so much they called 911. They said maybe someone was
having a heart attack in the shower.
The police broke down the door with an axe, ha, ha, ha.

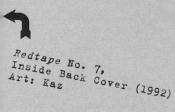

Redtape No. 7,
Inside Back Cover (1992)
Art: Kaz

I take a lot of showers, my mother told me it was an ancient Jewish
beauty secret and she was so beautiful, although I wondered where
the ancient Jews took showers when they wandered around
in the desert with Moses.

Yesterday I took a shower and the shower doesn't leak.
Time magazine says the freedom the future promises women
can be frightening, but the effect of feminism has been positive.
Today Betty said, "Hi ya, how ya doing?" when we passed in the hall.

FROM "BETWEEN THE HAMMER AND THE ANVIL" (1992)

LYDIA LUNCH

I WAS CREATED BY FORCES I CANNOT COMPETE WITH . . .
I'M CONFUSED BY RELIGIOUS HALLUCINATIONS, DELUSIONS
OF GRANDEUR, CONVULSIONS OF SELF-DESTRUCTION . . .
I'M MANIACALLY DEPRESSED, I'M TERMINALLY FUCKED-UP . . .
I'M PERMANENTLY INCOHERENT . . . I HATE MYSELF AND
I HATE EVERYTHING ELSE TOO. . . .

ENSLAVED IN A VAST WAREHOUSE OF MENTALLY ILL PEOPLES . . .
A GIANT PRISON WITH PRISONERS ENSLAVED IN CELLBLOCKS,
LOCKED UP & BOTTLED TIGHT, DETONATING THE PALACE OF
FALSE HOPE . . . TRAPT IN A TISSUE OF LIES & ILLOGIC WHERE
EVERY SOUND UTTERED CONTAINS THE LONGING FOR CRIME . . .
THE LONGING FOR CRIMES AGAINST NATURE . . . CRIMES
AGAINST REASON. . . .

EARTH PLANET OF BIRTH AND DEATH RELEASE ME FROM THIS
MENACE OF MEMORY, FROM THIS PSYCHOLOGICAL LOCKJAW
WHERE YOUTH IS THE MORTGAGED LIFE OF TIME GONE PAST . . .
WAITING ON THE LIBERATION OF RELIEF FROM THE HUMAN RACE,
THE RAT RACE . . . EXILED FROM TRUTH LIKE A MILLION OTHER
POMPOUS CORPSES GATHERED TOGETHER IN AN EMPTY EXISTENCE
WHERE MULTITUDES OF DEVIANTS INVADE THE CITY CENTERS
LIKE WARRING AND SULLEN ZOMBIES SPOUTING BILE FROM THE
BOWELS OF BAD NEIGHBORHOODS.

CEMETERIES BLOATED WITH DEMENTED CARAVANS PEOPLED
WITH THE CORRUPT, THE DECREPIT, THE MORALLY &
SPIRITUALLY BANKRUPT. . . .

THE LONELY WAIT FOR DEATH BEHIND THE THIN AND
FADING WALLS . . . THEY FINALLY RELEASED THE LAST
REMAINING PRISONERS OF THE NAZI DEATHCAMP INVASION
WHICH IS CELEBRATED LIKE A CARNIVAL SKYROCKETING
OFF INTO OBLIVION. . . .

IT'S NEVER TOO LATE TO PICK AT THE BLISTERING SCABS OF
RUSTY OLD WAR WOUNDS . . . IT'S NEVER TOO LATE TO
LEARN FROM OUR MISTAKES . . . ONLY WE NEVER LEARN
FROM OUR MISTAKES... BECAUSE IT'S ALREADY TOO LATE
TO LEARN FROM DACHAU, AUSCHWITZ, HIROSHIMA, NAGASAKI,
CAMBODIA, PHNOM PENH. . . .

LIKE AN ACROBAT IN THE DARK MUTILATING CORPSES . . .
MORE MEANINGLESS MARINES WERE BATTERED INTO MAN
MADE MEAT PADDIES AND LEFT TO ROT IN HOLY HELL BUT WHO
CARES??? IT'S THIS WAY TO THE GAS CHAMBERS LADIES &
GENTLEMEN . . . THE THEATER OF THE WHITE MAN'S REVOLUTION
IS JUST ABOUT OVER . . . REMEMBER . . . ONE DEATH IS A
TRAGEDY, BUT ONE MILLION IS ONLY A STATISTIC. . . .

SO DON'T JUST STAND THERE . . . SHOOT SOMETHING . . .
ANNIE GET YOUR GUN . . . ANNIE GET YOUR GUN . . .
THERE'S A RUMOR GOING ON THAT THE WAR HAS JUST
BEGUN . . . THAT THE WAR IS NEVER ENDING . . .
THAT THE WAR IS NEVER OVER . . . THAT THE WAR IS
JUST AN ARMY OF DRUNKEN HOOLIGANS WHO IN ORDER
TO PUMP UP THEIR LAST FADING TRICKLE OF THEIR

WANING SEXUALITY IN AN ORGY OF SENSELESS VIOLENCE . . .
PICK UP BRICKS AND BULLETS AND BOMBS IN ORDER TO
PENETRATE THE FLESH OF THE ENEMY . . . THE FLESH
OF MY FLESH . . . THE BLOOD OF MY BLOOD. . . .

OH THIS IS THE END BEAUTIFUL FRIEND . . . THE END,
NO LAUGHTER, NO SURPRISE THE END. . . .

THE END OF THE WHITE MAN'S REVOLUTION
THE END TO THE HYPOCRISY OF THE REPUBLIC OF DEMOCRACY
THE END OF COMMUNISM, FASCISM, MARXISM, CAPITALISM,
HUMANISM. . . .

IN THIS PUNY & PATHETIC LANDSCAPE OF INHUMANE WASTE
I WANDER . . . WONDERING WHY . . . WHY . . . WHY WAS
I BORN AN AMERICAN AND NOT A PALESTINIAN, PAKISTANI,
IRANIAN, PUERTO RICAN, FILIPINO, CUBAN-AFRO-AMERICAN,
DOMINICAN, AN ISRAELI, SYRIAN, TURKISH, LEBANESE OR
A COLOMBIAN . . . A COLOMBIAN WITH BIG BIG BALLS & A
QUARTER KILO OF COKE, SO THAT I COULD BETTER UNDERSTAND
THE NEED TO TRAMPLE, PILFER, PILLAGE, PLUNDER, RAPE,
RAPE, RAPE, LIKE WILD INDIANS ON SNOW COVERED MOUNTAINS
HUNDREDS OF FEET HIGH, HIGH, HIGH, UP IN THE HIMALAYAS
WHERE HANDSOME YOUNG SOLDIERS DRESSED IN IMMACULATE
CAMOUFLAGE POSE WITH MIRRORED SHADES & SUBMACHINE
GUNS ON TRIPODS, KNEELING ON PRAYER RUGS & OFFERING
PRAISE TO THE GODS WHO GAVE THEM WAR . . . THE GODS
OF WAR . . . WHO GAVE THEM SOMETHING TO BELIEVE IN . . .
SOMETHING TO DO, SOMEWHERE TO GO, SOMETHING TO DO ON
THE WEEKENDS . . . SOMETHING TO LIVE AND DIE FOR. . . .

AND MAN PLAYING GOD WILL DO AS GOD HAS DONE . . .
DESTROY, MUTILATE, TERRORIZE, PENALIZE AND PUNISH . . .
PUNISH THE EARTH . . . AND JUST LIKE HIS ANCESTOR
THE DINOSAUR WHO ONCE ROAMED SO MIGHTY . . .
MAN WILL ALSO FALL . . . MAN WILL ALSO FALL . . . FALL
INTO OBLIVION, EXTINCTION . . . BECAUSE MAN IS EXTINCT

. . . MAN IS EXTINCT . . . MAN IS MAKING HIMSELF
AND HIS USELESS CORRUPT INVENTIONS EXTINCT.

POOR RECKLESS FANATICS . . . LOST IN A LIMBO OF TIME WITHOUT
LIMITS . . . IN THE EMPTY VOID OF A NOTHINGNESS THEY
INHABIT SO WELL . . . AND NIGHT AFTER NIGHT I STILL PRAY.

I PRAY FOR BOYS THAT DON'T KNOW ANY BETTER WITH 18
BULLET HOLES BLOWN IN THEIR BELLIES . . . RUNNING IN
SQUADS OF 15–20 YEAR OLDS WHOSE SOLE JOB IS TO
KILL THE KILLERS . . . TO ANNIHILATE THE JUDGES, TERRIFY
THE JURIES, EXTERMINATE THE EXECUTIONERS, TO KILL
THE COPS, THE QUEENS, THE CHIEF AND THE KING . . .
THE KING IS DEAD . . . LONG LIVE THE QUEEN. . . .

A SINISTER NUISANCE BECOMES A NATIONAL OBSESSION .
. . NIGHT OF DEATH ON BLOOD BOULEVARD . . . A FISH
ROTS FROM THE HEAD FIRST, OH MANUEL, OH MARGARET,
OH MARCOS, OH OLLIE, OH RONNIE, BY GEORGE . . .
BOGOTA, BOLIVIA, SAN SALVADOR, SANDINISTA, BEIRUT,
BEIJING, BROOKLYN, BRIGHTON, BELFAST. . . .

THE PRICE THEY PUT ON HUMAN LIFE IS DEATH
THE PRICE THEY PUT ON HUMAN LIFE IS DEATH

THE COST OF LIVING IS HAND TO HAND COMBAT FOUGHT TOOTH
& NAIL AND ALL THE WAILING IN THE WORLD AIN'T GUNNA
SAVE YOU. . . .

LIFE IS CHEAP BUT DEATH IS FREE
LIFE IS CHEAP BUT DEATH IS FREEDOM

BAPTISMAL IN BLOOD
DEATH WEARS THE PROOF OF A CROWN FROM THE KING

THE ILLUSION OF FREEDOM HAS FINALLY DISAPPEARED
THE HORIZON HAS BEEN ABOLISHED

SLAVERY IS FREEDOM . . . . WAR IS PEACE BUT PEACE IS NOT PROFITABLE AND WAR IS BIG BUSINESS . . . SO IN ORDER TO RE-ADDRESS THE IMBALANCE OF POWER, I PLEAD WITH YOU NOW . . . ANNIE GET YOUR GUN . . . ANNIE GET YOUR GUN . . . THERE'S A RUMOR GOING ROUND THAT THE WAR HAS JUST BEGUN . . . THAT THE WAR IS NEVER ENDING . . . THAT THE WAR IS NEVER OVER . . . THAT THE WAR IS JUST AN ORGY OF SENSELESS VIOLENCE KICKED OFF BY AN ARMY OF DRUNKEN HOOLIGANS WHO IN ORDER TO PUMP UP THE LAST FADING TRICKLE OF THEIR WANING SEXUALITY PICK UP BULLETS AND BRICKS AND BOMBS IN ORDER TO BETTER PENETRATE THE FLESH OF THE ENEMY . . . THE FLESH OF THE ENEMY . . . THE FLESH OF MY FLESH, BREATH OF MY BREATH, BREAST OF MY BREAST.

THE DEATH OF ANOTHER LIVING CREATURE MEANS NOTHING
TO MEN. . . .
THE DEATH OF ANOTHER LIVING CREATURE MEANS NOTHING
TO MEN. . . .
MEANS NOTHING TO MEN. . . .
MEN ARE SO AFRAID TO DIE THAT THEY HAVE TO KILL EVERYTHING
IN SIGHT
MEN ARE SO AFRAID TO DIE THAT THEY HAVE TO KILL EVERYTHING
IN SIGHT

IF YOU CAN'T BEAT 'EM . . . KILL 'EM . . . IF YOU CAN'T KILL
'EM . . . FUCK 'EM.

IF YOU CAN'T FUCK 'EM . . . KILL 'EM. IF YOU CAN'T DO IT
GOOD, DO IT HARD.

BUT IT'S SO EASY NOT TO GIVE A SHIT . . . AND WHY SHOULD YOU . . . YOU DIDN'T ASK TO BE BORN . . . YOU DIDN'T CONTRIBUTE TO THE CONDITION THAT THE WORLD IS IN . . . TO THE CORRUPTION . . . THE CALAMITY . . . CATASTROPHE, THE CHAOS OR CONFUSION . . . WHAT THE HELL DID YOU DO . . . YOU WERE BORN INTO A WORLD THAT SET YOU UP AS A DUPE TO CONSUME, PAY TAXES, TO EAT, TO SHIT AND TO DIE . . . WHY

THE HELL SHOULD YOU WORRY ABOUT WHAT'S ALREADY GONE WRONG . . . ABOUT WHO'S DEAD AND WHO'S DYING . . . SHIT YOU'RE DYING TOO, EVERY MINUTE OF THE DYING DAY . . . LEAVE THE RAINFORESTS & THE ENVIRONMENT TO THE HIPPIE FREAKS . . . SHIT YOU'RE NOT SPAWNING ANY LITTER, SO WHY SHOULD YOU WORRY ABOUT SOMETHING YOU HAVE NO PERSONAL CONTROL OVER ANYWAY . . . YOU'RE NOT PART OF THE PROBLEM, WHY THE HELL SHOULD YOU BE PART OF THE SOLUTION. . . .

YOU SHOULD WORRY . . . BECAUSE YOU BOUGHT THE LIE ALL THE WAY DOWN THE MUTHERFUCKING LINE . . . YOU'RE ACTING EXACTLY LIKE THEY WANT YOU TO ACT . . . LIKE A FAT COMPLACENT BABY SUCKING SUGAR-TITTIE THROUGH A GLASS STRAW . . . A VEGETATING NONENTITY HAPPY AS LONG AS THE SYRUP SUPPLY DOESN'T RUN DRY . . . . YOU'RE THE GENERATION WHO MADE APATHY A MARKETABLE COMMODITY . . . AFTER ALL YOU'VE GOT ALL THE PETTY DIVERSIONS THAT THEY'LL ALLOW YOU . . . LIKE YOUR MENIAL JOB, YOUR LOUSY ART, YOUR ROTTEN ROCK BAND . . . AND ALL THE MOVIES YOU'VE YET TO SEE, ALL THE RECORDS YOU'VE YET TO BUY . . . AND OF COURSE YOUR BEST FRIEND . . . T.V. . . . THAT FIEND, THE MYOPIC CRADLER, THE JAILER, THAT HYPNOTIC NARCOTIC THAT BRAINWASHES YOU EVEN STUPIDER THAN YOU WERE TO BEGIN WITH BY RADIATING HALF A MILLION BRAIN CELLS EVERY 4–6 HOURS, MEANING TO YOU EVERY SINGLE DAY THAT YOU AREN'T INVOLVED WITH STUPID ARGUMENTS OVER ASSININE SPORTS HEROES, AGING MOVIE STARS OR HALF ASSED ROCK BANDS, WHO EARN MORE IN ONE SEASON THAN YOU WILL IN YOUR ENTIRE LIFETIME BUT THEY'RE WORTH IT, AREN'T THEY . . . I MEAN THAT'S ENTERTAINMENT AFTER ALL, AND THAT'S WHAT YOU SPEND MOST OF YOUR MONEY ON ANYWAY . . . AVERSION, DIVERSION, ANYTHING TO TAKE YOUR MIND OFF THE REAL PROBLEMS, YOUR REAL PROBLEMS. . . .

YOU FOOLED YOURSELF INTO THINKING YOU WERE REBELLIOUS JUST BECAUSE YOU DIDN'T BUY INTO THE 2.5 KIDS, THE

HOUSE, THE CAT, THE DOG & THE CAR . . . THE TRUTH IS YOU PROBABLY COULDN'T AFFORD THOSE THINGS EVEN IF YOU WANTED THEM . . . IT'S IMPOSSIBLE ENOUGH TO SUPPORT YOURSELF ON WHAT YOU BRING IN IN A WEEK, MUCH LESS TRYING TO FEED A SQUADRON OF SCREAMING KIDS, A FAT WIFE AND AN ALCOHOL OR COKE HABIT. . . .

YOU LOOK DOWN YOUR NOSE AT BORING MIDDLE AGED YUPPIES WHO YOU MISTAKE AS SINGLE MINDED MONEY-GRUBBERS WHO LIVE BY A SET OF STANDARDS THAT DON'T MEAN DIDDLY-SQUAT TO YOU . . . THE WORLD'S GREATEST EXPERT IN ARM-CHAIR AFFAIRS . . . THE TRUTH IS YOU'RE PROBABLY JUST JEALOUS BECAUSE ALTHOUGH MONEY CAN'T BUY HAPPINESS & YOU'D NEVER WANT TO ADMIT TO HAPPINESS . . . IT CAN BUY YOU ALL THE EXPENDABLES YOU MISTAKE FOR SUCH . . . MORE RECORDS . . . MORE CLOTHES . . . MORE VIDEOS . . . MORE CIGARETTES MORE HAIRSPRAY . . . MORE DRINKS & DRUGS MORE DIVERSION . . . MORE . . . MORE . . . MORE AND THAT'S ONE THING THIS COUNTRY CAN NEVER HAVE TOO MUCH OF . . . MORE. . . .

THE RIGHT TO EXCESS IS A GOD GIVEN RIGHT . . . IT'S THE

AMERICAN DREAM . . . THE WHITE MAN'S BURDEN . . . IT'S HOPE & GLORY . . . IT'S A PACK OF PUKING LIES THAT YOU BOUGHT ALL THE WAY DOWN THE LINE . . . BECAUSE THEY SET YOU UP AS A DUPE TO CONSUME . . . SO THAT THE MORE YOU HAVE . . . THE MORE YOU'RE GUNNA WANT & THE MORE YOU'RE GUNNA NEED . . . BECAUSE NEED & GREED ARE CONTAGIOUS AND YOU LIKE ME WILL NEVER BE SATISFIED . . . WILL NEVER FEEL SATISFIED, WILL NEVER FEEL LIKE WE HAVE ENOUGH, THAT ANYTHING'S EVER GOOD ENOUGH, OR FAST ENOUGH OR HARD ENOUGH OR TOUGH ENOUGH OR REAL ENOUGH . . . UNTIL YOU REALIZE THAT THE ENDLESS VOID WILL FOREVER REMAIN JUST THAT . . . THE ENDLESS VOID . . . THE ENDLESS VOID WHICH I WILL FOREVER CONTINUE TO SCREAM INTO BECAUSE MY LANGUAGE IS NOT SILENCE, MY SONG IS THE SCREAM . . . TERROR DWELLS IN THE SHADOW OF MY WINGS . . . MY HOPE IS MY FIRST BATTLE AND MY LAST GASP . . . I AM THE KNIFE WITH WHICH THE DEAD CRACK OPEN THE CASKET.

THREE POEMS FROM *I ALWAYS VOTE FOR SPARROW FOR PRESIDENT* (1992)

SPARROW

EURIPIDES

When I am President
subways will be quieter. I'll hire the
unemployed to wax the rails, and trains will
sound like ice moving over ice. And
conductors will no longer blare "Watch the
closing doors!", because no one *ever* watches
the closing doors. There's nothing to *see*
about closing doors. Instead, conductors
will read from Euripides. If you travel the
whole length of the E train, you'll hear
the whole *Medea*. Euripides is the
best guide to human life, because
he is sad, yet brave.
The same sad bravery I will bring to
the Presidency—a stance dormant since Lincoln.
"We are doomed, perhaps," I will announce. "The
sun is breaking through the sky to slay us with
cancer, because we were
foolishly indulgent with whipped cream.
But we must set our course aright."
And all the women in the nation
will weep, and the men will have a tear in their
eye that can't quite descend,
and the people will cry to repentance:
"Repentance! Repentance!"
And I will blind myself with a
canopener and wander the
streets and prophesy
and plant an oak tree, and beneath this tree
a woman will sit 7 years, and then she'll rise and
save us from the sun
and the cancer will leave our faces
and we'll sing a new song

which will resemble the music of Euripides
that has been lost for centuries. And the
conductors will sing
that, as we ride on waxed rails, like
ice over ice.

WALKING THE DOG

I will walk my
own dog
when I am
President.
I'll buy a
deep blue leash
and walk
Emile, my pooch
up and down
Pennsylvania Avenue,
stopping to speak
to Nebraskans
and Turks.
I'll carry a
map of the
earth
to look up
everyone's
town
and
a notebook to
write them down,
so that future
historians may
study my walks
forever.

AIDS

AIDS, AIDS, AIDS, AIDS, AIDS, AIDS, AIDS,
Who shall cure thee? I shall cure thee. When
I am President of the United States of America,
I shall erect a laboratory in the basement of the
White House, and, wearing a white coat, I shall raise
Beakers to the light, filled with
Blood, and expose them to gamma rays, all night.
As dawn climbs manfully over the
City of Washington, I'll throw myself into a cot,
My hair in disarray, and sleep.
Each night I shall labor thus, and each day I shall
Return to the humdrum life of President. Then,
In my third year, as I am
Delivering my State of the Union message,
The answer will come. I
Will thrust down my speech
And run from the Halls of Congress, in the middle
Of a sentence. The next day, a stunned nation will see
Me, on nationwide TV, unshaven, circles under my
Eyes, holding a test tube. "Eureka!" I will shout,
AIDS will end, and men and women that night
Will have loud, groaning sex, all over America.

Counter Clockwise from Top Left:
Public Illumination Magazine:
No. 17, 1981, Excess;
Art/Design: Prof., Dr., Dr. Zagreus Bowery
No. 21, 1982, Contraception;
Art/Design: Prof., Dr., Dr. Zagreus Bowery
No. 24, 1983, Vermin;
Art/Design: Prof., Dr., Dr. Zagreus Bowery
No. 40, 1992, Hallucinations
Art/Design: Prof., Dr., Dr. Zagreus Bowery
No. 19, "National Reflexology";
Art/Text: Pedula Clark as told to Dr. Bowery

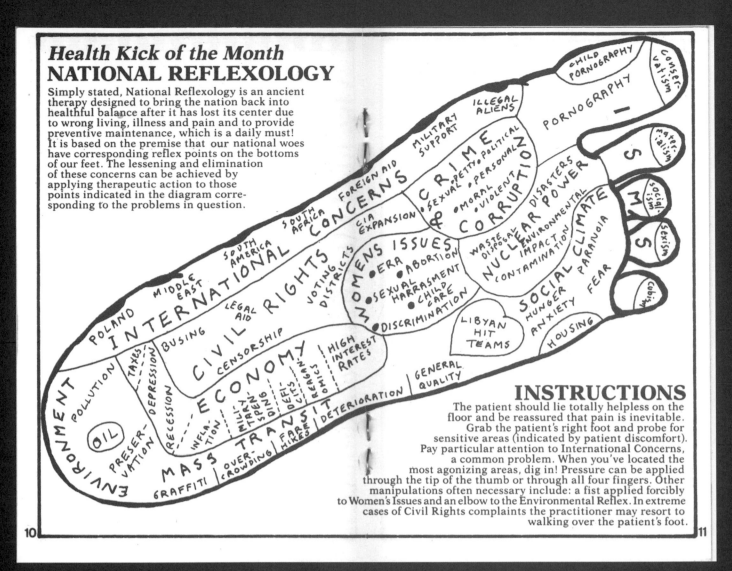

Health Kick of the Month
NATIONAL REFLEXOLOGY

Simply stated, National Reflexology is an ancient therapy designed to bring the nation back into healthful balance after it has lost its center due to wrong living, illness and pain and to provide preventive maintenance, which is a daily must! It is based on the premise that our national woes have corresponding reflex points on the bottoms of our feet. The lessening and elimination of these concerns can be achieved by applying therapeutic action to those points indicated in the diagram corresponding to the problems in question.

INSTRUCTIONS

The patient should lie totally helpless on the floor and be reassured that pain is inevitable. Grab the patient's right foot and probe for sensitive areas (indicated by patient discomfort). Pay particular attention to International Concerns, a common problem. When you've located the most agonizing areas, dig in! Pressure can be applied through the tip of the thumb or through all four fingers. Other manipulations often necessary include: a fist applied forcibly to Women's Issues and an elbow to the Environmental Reflex. In extreme cases of Civil Rights complaints the practitioner may resort to walking over the patient's foot.

10   11

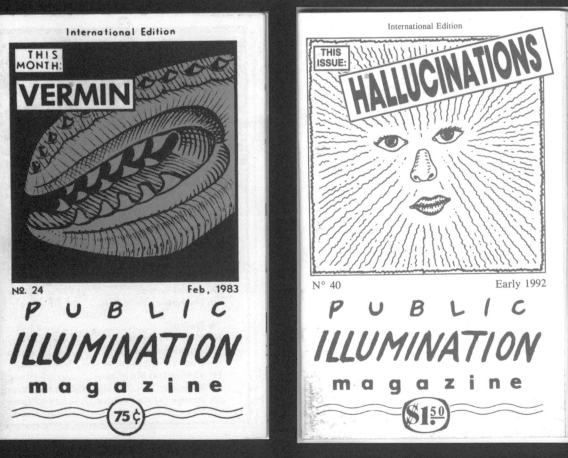

International Edition

THIS MONTH:
VERMIN

Nº. 24 — Feb, 1983

PUBLIC ILLUMINATION magazine

75¢

International Edition

THIS ISSUE:
HALLUCINATIONS

N° 40 — Early 1992

PUBLIC ILLUMINATION magazine

$1.50

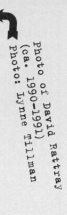

A DIVISION OF WATER (1992)

DAVID RATTRAY

FOR LIN

The Shmura Hand-Matzoh Bakery
bake their famous round matzohs
for Passover only, the baker,
a man with a long white beard,
told me at the door.
They're at 427 Broadway, Brooklyn, an
eleven-minute walk from the
bridge exit at Driggs Avenue.
Last week they closed the Williamsburg
to cars and trains.
A student is making a film
about a trainee bank teller and his
crack addict brother in which the
Williamsburg Bridge is a link between
universes where one brother makes it across
and the other doesn't.
At the point where the bridge takes off
over the river it's fifteen storeys high.
The Hebrew word *araphel* means
"thick darkness secret or high place"
But there is no such thing as obscure
poetry. The objects of a poem
are as bright and clear as can be.
The boast that its
words come from the heart
is true of each real poem, each
word written in blood.
Who wants to look at a color
so bright it hurts the eyes?
With an elevated serum nitrogen level
at about 12 thousand feet,
Tibet favors a mix of
bright reds and yellows.
Red stands for raging energy,
yellow for light.
A Sanskrit treatise on poetics
asks if a given disease were
curable by means of a certain bitter herb
but also by means of sugar candy,
who wouldn't prefer the sugar candy treatment?
The clarity of the received classics

is the bitter cure, the
golden seal, as it were,
whereas the palatable
familiarities of dailiness
offer a spun-sugar route
from darkness unto darkness.
They say action is demonic and
illumination god-like, yet
from the standpoint of reality
there's no distinction
between gods and demons,
the darkness and the light are both alike.
On the Williamsburg
at 1:15 in the afternoon on Sunday,
April 17th, a sunny day,
60 degrees with a light breeze,
I counted fourteen flattened
Prince's Plastic Weld glue tubes;
two syringes, one with
and the other without a point;
countless broken pints, Smirnoff, Ron Rico, etc.;
plus an intact Wild Irish Rose empty.
The Eleusinian mysteries saw the passage
from this life to the next
as a union of lovers over a division of water.
Some warm evening we'll picnic here,
you and I, conversing as ever about
the relativity of all
motions and watching many a boat
with their lights pass
far beneath like a star riding in space.

THE WEIRDNESS OF THE TEXT (1992)

JILL S. RAPAPORT

I tried forty times in one night to read one page of a story by the notoriously simple Anatole France and simply could not crack through because one part of my brain, having become uncoupled from the lamely proceeding train of the rest of my mind, fixed on the central insult to logic that observance of the rule of behavioral coherency had always before caused me to skip over, and undoubtedly many others before me, and this was the fact that contrary to what schoolteachers and writers would have one believe there is no reason to read printed words on a piece of paper. The words did not on this occasion jump out at me and create a world. The words lay dead and ugly on their page. Exposition and development did not occur for me. Who the hell is, or was, Anatole France?

I remember reading somewhere with greater comprehension that the surrealists went to his funeral to scoff. Reading his words I went brain-dead after successive attempts to cure the jarring death of sensation taking place in my cerebrum as I almost literally banged my head time after time against the unrelenting opacity of his yellowing page, in an old hardcover I must have picked up from a streetvendor or at the Strand on the dollar book table. The first impulse was to blame myself for the new and troubling problem of having lost the ability to read. My goal of detachment and indifference had resulted in a condition that rendered me illiterate and embarrassed. I'll tell you how it happened.

I was one of those pathetic last gasps who had once been a beautiful, intelligent, sensitive child. For years I repeated the deathless epithets of surrounding adults: "Lovely, brilliant, beloved," listening to how they clashed with the actuality of what I had become: Sullen, awkward, perverse; neurotic, catatonic, brutal.

Till the age of nine I loved to read, run, and play in the woods and the sun. Then we moved, from one state to another, vastly different state, and the character of the country changed. What had been green and yellow was now gray and black. Wild Indians no longer dominated the landscape, and if I was jarred, my parents seemed more profoundly thrown, to the point where I guess my father had no choice but to insist that I stop playing with dolls, walk, not run, and once and for all lose my depraved habit of copying Beetle Bailey cartoons in my mom's expensive drawing tablets.

Maybe he couldn't afford me anymore. In lieu of a tangible paternal love I had for years extorted daily presents from him, and jumped on him the moment he came home from work demanding to see what he had brought for me. He never dared to arrive empty-handed.

The last doll I played with was a Spanish dancer from a mail-order ad in the back of a comic book, and I'm still not sure what damage it did to my as-yet unformed sense of physical identity to take that doll out of the package she arrived in and find that underneath the ruffled skirt she had no legs. I know that at around the age of ten I wanted to cut my legs off and go places in a wheelchair.

I invented an escalator for wheelchairs and spent considerable concentration on that and other elements of legless policy, which I was still smart enough to conceal from my parents, aware that they would inevitably seek to rectify my thought by reminding me that there were people without legs who would have envied me for mine and by urging me to look with less frivolous disregard upon my natural endowments.

Some girl said that big eyes were ugly and I started scheming about ways to procure for myself a pair of narrow, long, shallow eyes, without eyeballs.

I cultivated a natural tendency to aloofness among peers that might have started with being tall and speedy, and I drew pictures underneath my desk of my teachers severed at the waist, all the while accepting with a passionate sangfroid their praise for being "lovely," and "well behaved."

Fundaments of character were shifting rapidly and my parents' pronouncements came into question: Could I really have been lovely with my hair swinging across my face and my features twisted in a rebellious rage, or brilliant when I refused to do homework or learn division, history, or sewing? Could they really have loved me when I screamed at them, calling them stupid, accusing them of first kidnapping and then hating me?

I knew what I was: A spoiled, tantrum-throwing problem, who ruined their dinners out and their peace of mind at home.

Saw a movie of "The Snow Queen," and was enchanted with a new vision of the way to be.

I was well into adulthood before I exemplified better than I could ever have wished the low-key, supremely indifferent creature of idiosyncratic legend, unfazed by anything less dramatic than the atomic leveling of her city.

Intelligence is knowing how to save yourself and in those days I was, if nothing else, a little Einstein of self-salvation.

I saw the places set aside for me in society: Criminal, reclusive, destructive, rejecting. Anyone of them had to be preferable to the cramped quarters of goodness or the terrible realism of those brought up to understand that there is no longer any such thing as direct contact with reality.

Insensibility, as of objects like a text, comes naturally to someone whose sensibility refused to flourish in the icy climate where adult beings dwelled, terminal and blue, extinguishing every invader posing threats to their stoic, unsmiling existences, including their own obstreperous progeny.

The doltishly linear narrative of an Anatole France was as grotesquely beside the point as late nineteenth-century brutes had announced it to be, and furthermore, its fundamental elements were even more disjointed in their pristine progression than the scattered limbs of the last doll before the Spanish dancer, torn from her in a rage in the late, golden period of my childhood, when dolls were possessed in order to be set upon with an aggressive vengeance, and destroyed for the crime of simulating a wholeness insupportably insulting to human children with fragmented existences.

Word Up at the Knitting Factory, Flyer (1990)

THE KNITTING FACTORY & NYPRESS PRESENT

5 NIGHTS

WORD UP

TUESDAY, JUNE 5
QUINCY TROUPE
PAUL BEATTY

SPOKEN WORD

WEDNESDAY, JUNE 6
LYDIA LUNCH
GARY LUCAS
BRIAN MORAN

THURSDAY, JUNE 7
KATHY ACKER
JOSE PADUA
KEN DiMAGGIO

JUNE 5-9

FRIDAY, JUNE 8
RICHARD HELL
GAIL SCHILKE
PAUL BEATTY

9PM

SATURDAY, JUNE 9
DARK STAR CREW
PEDRO PIETRI
BOB HOLMAN

$8 INCLUDES 1 DRINK

STAIRS

THE KNITTING FACTORY
47. E. HOUSTON
NYC
219-3055

CURATED BY: GAIL SCHILKE

SPONSORED BY

"GO AHEAD" AND "MISTAKEN IDENTITY" (1992)

BRUCE WEBER

GO AHEAD

strike that pipe

against my face

and

squish my pimples

twist that rake

inside my mouth

and

pull out my teeth

take advantage

of my achilles heel

talk me out of my dignity

hit me with your best shot

and break every vertebra

you have first amendment rights

to hit me with the plague

have some fun on my behalf

yeah

show no mercy

i'm a junkie

i'm a pimp

i'm a prostitute

i'm a crack head

i'm a cockroach

i'm a spic

i'm a jew

i'm black

i'm queer

i'm sick

i'm starving

i'm weak

i'm cold

i'm an open wound

knock me

till my senses

short circuit

till i'm immobile

till i'm useless

till i just stare

strike me again

with that 2 x 4

crush my bones

make my blood ooze

come on

you can do better

than

that

MISTAKEN IDENTITY

i wasn't there, i wasn't there, i was providing pleasure to a plastic love doll, i was conveying my regret to a broken idol, i was writing a letter to my ex-wife about the sudden emergence of my courage, i was changing the diapers of my sister's 12 year old, i was staring hard at the sun to see if it would truly blind me, i was sticking a line in the east river to see if i could catch a new wristwatch, i was humming the words to the theme song from e.t. and watching the sky for extraterrestrials, you see i was nowhere near the crime scene judge, the way i see it life's full of unbelievable things that need figuring out, that's why i have no eyewitnesses to my whereabouts at 3:30 in the morning, because i was wrestling with my own state of consciousness, i was meditating on the meaning of man's flight from a state of grace, i was studying the color, texture, shape and taste of a macintosh on a bench in tompkins square park, judge it's just a case of mistaken identity, it's just a case of mistaken identity, fuck your twenty random witnesses who picked me out on t.v. in the crowded stands of yankee stadium, it's just a case of mistaken identity

WE SHALL LIVE AGAIN

· A BENEFIT FOR ·

AIDS TREATMENT PROJECT

A NON-PROFIT TAX-EXEMPT FOUNDATION

With Penny Arcade!

And Featuring:

Legs McNeil!

Taylor Mead!   John Giorno!

Sylvere Lotringer!

Eileen Myles!   Bob Holman!

Kembra Pfahler!

Christian X. Hunter!   David Huberman!

John S. Hall (*King Missile*)

Matthew Courtney!   Wanda Phipps!

Jose Padua!

David Rattray!   Mike Osterhaut!

Baron Von Blumenzak!

Carl Watson!   Emily XYZ!

Peter Lamborn Wilson!

Joe Budenholzer!   Victor Bruce Godsey!

plus SURPRISE GUESTS!

MUSIC BY:

I Love Everybody
(with Maggie Estep)
Drunken Boat
Homer Erotic
(with Barbara Barg)

$12

Thursday,
September

10 **8PM Sharp!**

MONSTER OF CEREMONIES:
Norman Conquest!

315 Bowery (at Bleecker) NYC • (212) 982-4052

SELF-PORTRAIT IN TWENTY-THREE ROUNDS (1984/1991)

DAVID WOJNAROWICZ

So my heritage is a calculated fuck on some faraway bed while the curtains are being sucked in and out of an open window by a passing breeze. I'd be lying if I were to tell you I could remember the smell of sweat as I hadn't even been born yet. Conception's just a shot in the dark. I'm supposed to be dead right now but I just woke up this dingo motherfucker having hit me across the head with a slab of marble that instead of splitting my head open laid a neat sliver of eyeglass lens through the bull's-eye center of my left eye. We were coming through this four-and-a-half-day torture of little or no sleep. That's the breaks. We were staying at this one drag queen's house but her man did her wrong by being seen by some other queen with a vicious tongue in a darkened lot on the west side fucking some cute little puerto rican boy in the face and when me and my buddy knocked on the door to try and get a mattress to lay down on she sent a

bullet through the door thinking it was her man—after three days of no sleep and maybe a couple of stolen donuts my eyes start separating: one goes left and one goes right and after four days of sitting on some stoop on a side street head cradled in my arms seeing four hours of pairs of legs walking by too much traffic noise and junkies trying to rip us off and the sunlight so hot this is a new york summer I feel my brains slowly coming to a boil in whatever red-blue liquid the brains float in and looking down the street or walking around I begin to see large rats the size of shoeboxes; ya see them just outta the corner of your eyes, in the outer sphere of sight and when ya turn sharp to look at them they've just disappeared around the corner or down subway steps and I'm so sick my gums start bleedin' everytime I breathe and after the fifth day I start seeing what looks like the limbs of small kids, arms and legs in the mouths of these rats

and no screaming mommies or daddies to lend proof to the image and late last night me and my buddy were walking around with two meat cleavers we stole from Macy's gourmet section stuck in between our belts and dry skin lookin' for someone to mug and some queer on the upper east side tried to pick us up but my buddy's meat cleaver dropped out the back of his pants just as the guy was opening the door to his building and clang clangalang the guy went apeshit his screams bouncing through the night off half a million windows of surrounding apartments we ran thirty blocks till we felt safe. Some nights we had so much hate for the world and each other all these stupid dreams of finding his foster parents who he tried poisoning with a box of rat poison when they let him out of the attic after keeping him locked in there for a month and a half after all dear it's summer vacation and no one will miss you here's a couple of jugs of springwater and cereal don't eat it all at once we're off on a holiday after all it's better this than we return you to that nasty kids home. His parents had sharp taste buds and my buddy spent eight years in some jail for the criminally insane even though he was just a minor. Somehow though he had this idea to find his folks and scam lots of cash off them so we could start a new life. Some nights we'd walk seven or eight hundred blocks practically the whole island of manhattan crisscrossing east and west north and south each on opposite sides of the streets picking up every wino bottle we found and throwing it ten feet into the air so it crash exploded a couple of inches away from the other's feet—on nights that called for it every pane of glass in every phone booth from here to south street would dissolve in a shower of light. We slept good after a night of this in some abandoned car boiler room rooftop or lonely drag queen's palace.

* * *

If I were to leave this country and never come back or see it again in films or sleep I would still remember a number of different things that sift back in some kind of tidal motion. I remember when I was eight years old I would crawl out the window of my apartment seven stories above the ground and hold on to the ledge with ten scrawny fingers and lower myself out above the sea of cars burning up eighth avenue and hang there like a stupid motherfucker for five minutes at a time testing my own strength dangling I liked the rough texture of the bricks against the tips of my sneakers and when I got tired I'd haul myself back in for a few minutes' rest and then climb back out testing testing testing how do I control this how much control do I have how much strength do I have waking up with a mouthful of soot sleeping on these shitty bird-filled rooftops waking up to hard-assed sunlight burning the tops of my eyes and I ain't had much to eat in three days except for the steak we stole from the A&P and cooked in some bum kitchen down on the lower east side the workers were friendly to us that way and we looked clean compared to the others and really I had dirt scabs behind my ears I hadn't washed in months but once in a while in the men's room of a horn and hardart's on forty-second street in between standing around hustling for some red-eyed bastard with a pink face and a wallet full of singles to come up behind me and pinch my ass murmuring something about good times and good times for me was just one fucking night of solid sleep which was impossible I mean in the boiler room of some high-rise the pipes would start clanking and hissing like machine pistons putting together a tunnel under the river from here to jersey and it's only the morning 6:00 a.m. heat piping in to all those people up above our heads and I'm looking like one of them refugees in the back of life magazine only no care packages for me they give me some tickets up at the salvation army for three meals at a soup kitchen where you get a bowl of mucus water and sip rotten potatoes while some guy down the table is losing his eye into his soup he didn't move fast enough on the line and some fucked-up wino they hired as guard popped him in the eye with a bottle and I'm so lacking in those lovely vitamins they put in wonder-bread and real family meals that when I puff one drag off my cigarette blood pours out between my teeth sopping into the nonfilter and that buddy of mine complains that he won't smoke it after me and in the horn and hardart's there's a table full of deaf mutes and they're the loudest people in the joint one of them seventy years old takes me to a nearby hotel once a month when his disability check comes in and he has me lay down on my belly and he dry humps me harder and harder and his dick is soft and banging against my ass and his arm is mashing my little face up as he goes through his routine of pretending to come and starts hollering the way only a deaf mute can holler like donkeys braying when snakes come around but somehow in the midst of all that I love him maybe it's the way he returns to his table of friends in the cafeteria a smile busted across his face and I'm the one with the secret and twenty dollars in my pocket and then there's the fetishist who one time years ago picked me up and told me this story of how he used to be in the one platoon in fort dix where they shoved all the idiots and illiterates and poor bastards that thought kinda slow and the ones with speeth spitch speeeeeeech impediments that means you talk funny he said and I nodded one of my silent yes's that I'd give as conversation to anyone with a tongue in those days and every sunday morning this sadistic sonuvabitch of a sergeant would come into the barracks and make the guys come out one by one and attempt to publicly read the sunday funnies blondie and dagwood and beetle baily and dondi, with his stupid morals I was glad when some little delinquent punched his face in one sunday and he had a shiner three sundays in a row full color till the strip couldn't get any more mileage out of it and some cop busted the delinquent and put him back in the reform school he escaped from, and all the while these poor slobs are trying to read even one line the sergeant is saying lookit this stupid sonuvabitch how the fuck do you expect to serve this country of yours and you can't even read to save your ass and he'd run around the barracks smacking all the guys in the head one after the other and make them force them to laugh at this guy tryin' to read until it was the next guy's turn, and when we got to this guy's place there was three cats pissing all over the joint crusty brown cans of opened cat food littering the floor window open so they could leave by the fire escape and he had this thing for rubber he'd dress me up in this sergeant's outfit but with a pair of rubber sneakers that they made only during world war two when it was important to do that I guess canvas was a material they needed for the war effort or something and anyway so he would have me put on these pure rubber sneakers and the sergeant's outfit and then a rubber trenchcoat and then he'd grease up his dick and he would start fucking another rubber sneaker while on his belly and I'd have to shove my sneaker's sole against his face and tell him to lick the dirt off the bottom of it and all the while cursing at him telling him how stupid he was a fuckin' dingo stupid dog ain't worth catfood where'd you get your fuckin' brains surprised they even let ya past the m.p.'s on the front gate oughta call in the trucks and have you carted off to some idiot farm and where'd you get your brains and where'd you get your brains and when he came into his rubber sneaker he'd roll over all summer sweaty and say oh that was a good load musta ate some eggs today and I'm already removing my uniform and he says he loves the way my skeleton moves underneath my skin when I bend over to retrieve one of my socks.

"WAR STARS," AN EXCERPT FROM THE FICTIONAL MEMOIR "GIVING UP THE GHOST" (1991)

MIKE GOLDEN

Dutch Schultz was not his real name. I call him that because he was part the "I know nothing!" guard on *Hogan's Heroes,* and part gangster. Those images give me a brand to hang his identity on. In the land of *Future Schlock* all is marketing. In the beginning, mediocrity was a crime. Then it became a way of life. And finally, in the name of the parlay, it became our life sentence. Like any good Booster, I'm only laying out the proposition.

That may sound like a bleak pronouncement to whoever thought the East Village was a cool scene in the 1980s, but I'm just trying to subliminally infiltrate substance into the scenario. Which is the essence of what I said to Dutch about his lame newspaper, in the letter I'd written him six months before he called me that fateful day. Though I can't recall the exact words I said, they obviously infiltrated, because he said he wanted me to help him start a brand new underground newspaper in the East Village.

I was ready, willing and able to rock'n'roll. But you didn't have to be a genius to figure out you couldn't dance to it if it didn't have music. Money was the music of the '80s, and every time Dutch talked about it he whined like his dick was stuck in some sort of cosmic wringer. You had to invoke God, Jesus, Buddha and the Yaqui sorcerer don Juan Matus every time you wanted to get paid by Dutch Schultz. To his everlasting credit though, there were a lot worse scumbags out there than him, so remember when I trash the incompetent bastard, try to keep in mind that I have genuine affection for him, despite the fact I always suspected he was a CIA mole, and the

multi-titled counterculture rags he published for over 20 years were financed by the very corporations and government agencies he attacked, because the best possible way to discredit the counterculture was to put idiots in charge as their spokesmen.

I was obviously the next idiot in line. It was a beautiful plan! Completely consistent with undercover government infiltration of the Anti-War and Black Power movements, all through the '60s and '70s. The truth is, if your phone wasn't tapped, you just weren't a player. Dutch always talked that talk, but he never could walk the walk, probably because he was wearing cop shoes. Those shoes were the first thing I noticed when I met him.

I was sitting in this huge totally empty waiting room, outside his office, in the 611 Broadway Building, listening to a muffled argument going on inside. I'd been sitting there for close to an hour. But it was still only 6 a.m.. And unless I was still hallucinating from the night before, this was *Sunday morning coming down.* Which as it turned out, was the only time of the day and the only day Dutch would venture into the City, from the safety of his suburban Jersey digs. To say he was a paranoid rube from the sticks would've been true, but what Dutch really was was a genuine acid casualty who had never dropped a hit, or smoked a joint either for that matter. How he had reached basically the same damaged state as everyone else without massive ingestion of Owsley or Sunshine or intravenous injections of elephant tranquilizer was, and still is, a great mystery to me to this day. But apparently there's a whole tribe of

Woodstock denizens out there who never recovered from the contact high they got from the times. I may be getting bitterly philosophical here, but there is nothing more pathetic than the blackboard scrapping whine of an old hippie moaning about the good old days. If there is, I don't know what it is, and I'd been accused of being an old hippie myself, though without the beard most people thought I looked 15 years younger than I actually was. Despite myself I had become a testimony to my own inability to burn out. I had tried, Lord-God, I had tried. . . . And had righteously believed it was the inalienable right of every artist worth their medal to self destruct, but every time I leaped off the cliff, I bounced right back up again. I wasn't arrogant enough not to believe the day wouldn't come when I'd splatter, but I couldn't see that in my immediate future. In fact on that fateful morning I couldn't see the future at all.

I was hungover in the moment, as they say, patiently waiting for Dutch to finish his meeting, because I did want the gig. For some outmoded reason my sense of self-esteem needed hands-on interaction with the cultural gestalt in order to feel I was doing anything worthwhile. And that opportunity was ostensibly what Dutch was offering. Of course, the longer I waited, the more I started to question the setup.

I leaned up against the door to see if I could hear what was going on inside, and it opened a crack. Though I couldn't see all the way inside, I could hear a voice asking, "Is it possible to be all the same and all different and still mistake the clones for our doubles, and yes, vice versa too?"

I wasn't sure I'd heard what I thought I just heard, so I leaned closer to the door, and watched in horror as it swung completely open, revealing one lone long haired, white bearded Wizard of Oz figure talking to himself.

He looked over at me, without the slightest trace of surprise, and said, *"It has happened before, but there is nothing to compare it to now."*

Before you jump to any conclusions, Dutch Schultz was *not* Thomas Pynchon, lit buffs. At least I don't think so. I mean, I never saw Pynchon before, that I know of, unless of course, he *was* Dutch. . . . And he couldn't have been! Dutch was too fucking stupid, though he was smart enough to offer me a 30 percent partnership in the paper. That magnanimous offer came because he was so fucking cheap he swore he could only pay me $200 a week to start. Before I had a chance to laugh in his face, in the next breath he gave me the freedom to bring in my own *Seven Samurai,* and that, along with a piece of the action on the (nonexistent) back end, was enough to hook a culture junkie like me in. After that, I don't think there was a single thing Dutch did that was in the *Oracle's* best interests. Outside of the image he projected to his terrified staff in Jersey as some kind of cool, detached Wizard of Yaqui-O, he was a bumbling, cheating, spoiled, jealous, obsessed bad poet with a capital P . . . and that was probably only his act; like I said, in my opinion, Dutch was a mole. A lame-O Left wing mole who had been positioned in what was left of the Left by the Right, in order to discredit the Left with his gross incompetence.

Of course, I didn't see that the first morning. Outside of noting his shoes, I was so blinded by the opportunity to bring in my own team to start the quintessential alternative rag, I admit that I ignored my instincts. The idea that I could dig up all the old lip slingers of yonder yore out of Boot Hill was the ultimate hard-on for a Rotisserie fanatic like me. Not only was I going to get to pick my own point guard, I could have the shortstop of my dreams, and an All World tight end to protect me in the pocket as a I faded back into the oblivion of my imagination looking for an opening in the crease of the cosmic crack between the various cultures jockeying for position in the arena-void of the marketplace.

Within a week we moved from 611 Broadway to a cubbyhole on East 6th Street, between an Indian restaurant called *Good Karma,* and *Kelshitzamen,* a Polish-Indian joint that not only served ptomaine Tandoori with the worst of them, but threw in sides of borscht and pierogies too.

And it was here, over assorted Polish-Indian appetizers, that I made my first major mistake; I hired Moon Mullins for the dual job of Art Editor and Advertising Director, because he claimed to be totally plugged into the epidemic of new galleries sprouting up everywhere you looked in the East Village.

Like Dutch, Moon proudly wore the nametag of poet with a capital P, but his real art was born organically out of door-to-door selling encyclopedias outside Winston Salem, North Carolina. And in the beginning there was no doubt he was great at what he did, freely spouting bullshit to build up *The Oracle,* promote his career as a poet, and pick up as many chicks as he could, all at the same time. Looking like a cross between a pitifully shy Mr. Bill and a skin & bones Pillsbury doughboy, Moon had the bubbling personality of a speedfreak talkshow host, whose voice invariably turned into a high-squealing effeminate whine when his feverish pitch finally worked up to the point of closing the deal. He was the youngest in a family of seven, so as a salesman he had two things in his favor; he gave off the vibe of an exuberant puppy trying to get your attention, and like an exuberant puppy, he was so used to getting hit for shitting on the rug, and even for not shitting on the rug—to make sure he wouldn't shit on the rug—he always expected to get hit no matter what he did. With this kind of non-preventative built-in primal paper training, he not only shit on the rug every time he had the chance, he always ate exactly where he shit, and in his process, developed a noticeable twitch every time he talked shit to anybody on the street. Though he was always afraid of being hit, it never stopped him from doing exactly what he wanted to do, because he expected to get hit anyway. That he was no longer getting hit every time he opened his mouth, suddenly empowered him, and he developed what he mistakenly took for a heroic aura. *He was one of the Three Mouseketeers, man, and you could be one too! He was Zoro, Captain Marvel & The Green Hornet all rolled into one asshole, and this was the Renaissance we'd been waiting for our whole lives, and now was the time for us to do what had never been done before—it was our turn to win the World Series-Super Bowl-Publishers' Clearing House Sweepstakes—blah-blah-blah. . . .*

Blah-blah-blah. . . . I had learned very early selling was not poetry, man, and poetry was not selling, though at any given moment, both could be a high art form, and if you combined them, you had yourself a career, though not necessarily as a "real" artist. Not that art itself was anything holier than thou to crow about either. There was good art, and there was bad art, and there was a lot more bad than good, in the fusion soup of the East Village.

Yo, listen up, Cultural Elitists, wherever you're hiding! Most of the art may have been shit, but it *was* a g l o r i o u s time . . . I'd be lying if I said anything different. Everybody and their straight friend from back home in Topeka could see it, even if they were tooted out of their gourds most of the time. There was a special energy—like multicolored caption balloons—making WHOOPIE in the air above the party! When the balloons started exploding, all the old definitions changed, and for the first time the fear left over from the '70s paranoia disappeared, and nobody really gave a fuck about the '60s assassinations, or about the Military-Industrial Complex conspiracies to control the country, or about anything but having a fucking-4star-A+good time. Lame was cool and cool was lame. And for a brief 18 months in the bucket of cosmic time, the only booty ostensibly being sold at the core of this narcissistic brushfire was art. From that core, almost two dozen weekly new art rags sprung up to both dish and dis the Super & lesser stars who were part of the phenomena of *the scene,* and fight it out for the fashion, club and gallery advertising—thus dividing (whose-cooler-than-who cliques) up to fight it out in the pages of the Downtown Press Wars, as if the whole thing were a replay of the immortal Johnson County Range Wars of yonder yore. Which I guess it was: Cowboys and squatters and merchants and junkies and slackers and gamblers and whores from a different time all thought they were artists in Downtown New York between 1985 and 87. And in the ensuing ego wars that followed the initial ejaculation of so-called art, more than a few Billy the Kids were shot down in the dirt by their oldest and dearest friends. By the time it was over, when the smoke from the East Village's crash & burn finally cleared, it was obvious that the art had hardly been anything other than fodder for the 300-something-overnight-galleries serving as nothing more magical than laundries to wash South Florida coke money so it could legitimately be reinvested in South Beach real estate. Though it was not *my* drug of choice—I was allergic, and must have sneezed hundreds of thousands of dollars off tables from Alphabet Town galleries to Tribecca lofts to Flatiron parties to SoHo bistros. In my defense, I was champagne blind at least five out of seven nights a week that I wandered with one herd or another into one gallery or club after another to see one performer or another until the black sun of Downtown sensibility slipped out the back door of the clouds to puke out another day. Sometimes I staggered across East 6th Street, and crawled past *Good Karma* on all fours back into the office and passed out under my desk, but mostly (when I could remember where he was parked) I somehow managed to throw myself over trusty old Dan's rusty fender and had him lead me back to Brooklyn to throw the hoolihan.

Before long I was staying a week at a time without going home, and when I did, it was only to check my mail. It felt like I was living on East 6th, though I'm not sure that was a plus or a minus for editing the rag. The more visible you are, the easier it is for people to hit on you. Half-crazed writers, on-the-make photographers, pissed-off painters, tranced-out performance artists, guerilla filmmakers, bands all wanting you to see them do their thing . . . and give them a rave review to boot. If you're not careful you burn out before you know it.

Fortunately, or unfortunately, as the case may be, I had Moon as a buffer. All these years later, I'll give him credit; the asshole was everywhere, talking up our funky little rag, bad mouthing the competition as he sold ads, while getting interviews with artists in exchange for covers he'd promise but couldn't deliver, making deals for freebees and parties we were going to throw that we couldn't without getting the scratch from Dutch, who, paradoxically with each mini-success we managed to squeeze out of the depressed East Village economy, seemed to grow more paranoid we were out to steal his bacon.

Whether Dutch actually had any bacon to steal is open to debate, even today. One thing's certain, however, if he did, he'd lie about it, and if he didn't, he'd lie about it too. He always either had more in the till than he claimed, or less in the till than he claimed, depending on *who* was asking him *what, when, where* or *why.* Maybe that's the nature of all business, small or large. But on *The Oracle's* particular shaky ledge, when the paychecks were late, and they were more often than not late every week, the staff invariably freaked out. Particularly Moon.

I could sympathize with him without empathizing with him. I had my shit, he had his. We were all being squeezed one way or another. I didn't want to judge him if I could help it, at least as long as he did his job. And he *was* doing *his* job, particularly on the advertising end of the stick. With his ad commissions thrown into the pie, he was making at least three, sometimes four times as much as I was a week. And probably actually taking home more than Dutch, after the old prol robbed all the Peters he had to rob to pay Paul every week.

One night when the moon was void of course, Moon showed up in the office while I was editing the rag. "Come to a reading with me," he said. "Leslie Sue Weeber's reading at St. Mark's Books tonight. She was my girlfriend in college," he grinned.

That got my attention. "Oh yeah?" Leslie Sue had just made the cover of the *Times Book Review* the previous Sunday. Though I could take her writing or leave it, there was no denying

from the picture on the book jacket, she was one stoned fox. "She was *your* college girlfriend?"

"She worshipped the ground I walked on for four years."

If true, that destroyed what little validity the *Times* had just given her. "All very interesting," I said, "but tell me, what the fuck does *The Oracle* care about some middle-of-the-polluted-mainstream bestseller list Princess?"

He grinned again. "Not a fucking thing, man, but it'll be a hoot. Besides, there's a party with oodles of bubbly and hot art babes going on later on Rivington Street. We need to celebrate, man! We *really* need to celebrate."

I was never quite sure what we needed to celebrate, but no matter what the occasion was on any given night, it was impossible to pass up. Blue Monday, Cool Tuesday, Blah Wednesday, Almost Thursday, Friday-Friday-Friday . . . were all impossible to pass up.

The bookstore was packed. I stood in the back, while Moon moved up front and ghoulishly grinned at Leslie Sue in order to unnerve her.

"Excuse me," a tall guy with the Prince Valiant haircut tapped my shoulder. "I'm sorry, you probably don't remember me."

"Sure I do," I lied.

"I'm Dink Stover. And I was just wondering, are you still publishing *Before Its Time*?"

"You remember that?"

"It was a *great* magazine. Just a *great* magazine. We used to carry it here."

"Right, right. . . ."

"I was the one in charge of the mags—still am. Which is why I'm asking about it."

I ran my finger across my throat.

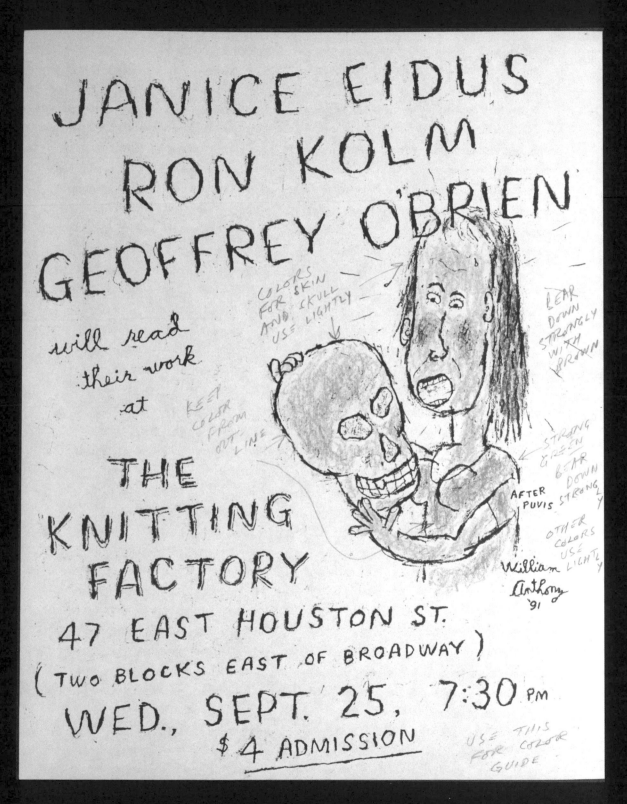

"Down for the count."

"Awwwww, that's terrible! Really terrible. What happened?"

"My partner, my best friend, my lover, my old lady. . . ." A wave of pain ran through my body as Jesse's face rose up in front of me. . . . None of those descriptions sounded very appropriate now. ". . . found a guru. . . ." When that phrase popped out of my mouth I heard a voice in my head singing, *"Found a guru, found a guru . . ."* to the tune of *Found a Peanut,* and started laughing through the pain.

People in front of us turned back towards me and glared.

Dink didn't seem to notice. "I'm really sorry about that. Really sorry. It was such a *great* magazine. In the end, copies of it will be worth a fortune."

"Thanks. Glad you liked it."

"Are there . . . do you have any . . . I'm sorry, I'm sorry, I know I shouldn't even be asking you this, but do you still have back issues left?"

There was a glaze in his eyes. I'd seen it before, but couldn't place it. It wasn't like *a true believer* glaze, or even Moon's *I'm getting away with it* glaze, it was a truly obsessive *I want it* glaze. A *J. Thadius Toad* glaze.

"Yeah, a few."

"That's *great!* That's *great!* Could I, I mean we, could the store get copies to sell to collectors?"

Two women turned around at once and let out loud "Shhhhhs."

I held my finger up over my lips, and whispered, "we'll talk about it later." Then turned my attention to Leslie Sue. She was reading from a section of the book where her main character and her friends have all been busted on spring break in Ft. Lauderdale, because her boyfriend has puked on two cops. . . . You didn't have to be an Einstein to figure out

who her boyfriend was, and even a blind man could tell by looking at the expression on Moon's face, this was a guy who couldn't be embarrassed no matter what you said to him, or about him.

I could still be embarrassed, however, so after the reading, I passed on Moon's invitation to meet his ex-girlfriend, and hung back by the door for a quick exit as he approached the table where Leslie Sue was signing copies of her book.

The first thing she said when she looked up at the grinning pumpkin standing in front of the table was, "You're going to sell it, aren't you?"

"Moi?" Mr. Innocent protested from the depths of his wounded heart.

"I don't mind if you sell it, asshole, if you read it first. But I know that's asking too much."

It truly was. Moon wasn't interested in what she thought of him, only in making a fast $25 for her signature. Perfection may be hard to find for most of us in this world, but the truly oblivious have no such problem.

NO CIE NO was another, and totally different, form of perfection. I ditched Moon at the party and ambled over through the urban blight. A small deep dank hole in the vortex of nonconformity, I'm not sure if it ever closed, much less, if it ever opened. Most of the so-called clientele hung outside on the street talking, drinking, smoking, slouching through the next pre-revolution *Tai Che* forms, exercising their inalienable right to self destruct.

I'd be less than honest if I didn't admit I felt right at home there. At least on the street. Outside the hype, desperation and ambition which ultimately trashes the hope of every scene it encounters, if you hang around long enough, NYC is just another small town waiting for something to happen. I'd lived in the perpetual state of Boho since I arrived in the late '60s, always halfway on my way from Nuevo York to Fanta Se to El-A to San Franvana, with lots of pit stops down in Memphis, before following that existential roadmap to just another nowhere. Back in the '70s, unless you were a lifer and couldn't conceive of any other way to live, the old *on the road* routine seemed to be the way to go every few years. I kept coming back because I just loved to walk-that-walk and talk-that-talk you can only do on the streets of the City. I won't to go into a litany here of all the great places that no longer exist, but something is always being born (being boring) and dying here. As for obsessions, like the best this or the next that, they always turn into something else down the line anyway. Once, believe it or not, it was fiction, it was folk music, it was *Revolution,* it was street theatre, it was Darryl & Doc, it was Szechuan, it was jazz, it was *new* journalism, it was S&M, it was blow, it was photo ops, it was disco, it was martial arts, it was punk, it was yuppies, it was performance art, it was hip hop, it was positively East 6th Street Tandoori, it was Broadway Joe, it was supermodels, screenwriters and investment bankers everywhere you looked, it was celebrity snorting, it was the personal ads, it was drag queens, it was independent films, it was New York fucking poetry, baby, before they all became generic theme parks, on *the scene today, gone tomorrow.* And during all that time, outside of consistently bumping into all the great heads and riffers hunkering down to chew the fat in the streets, the only constant I've ever seen in this City has been change.

Suddenly the instruments came out. The sweet strum of guitars out on the urban plane, under the tenements' dull glow, turned into a hootnanny, led by the High Boho of Soho himself, singing: *"Monday, nothing, Tuesday nothing, Wednesday and Thursday nothing . . ."*

"Excuse me," Dink Stover tapped me on the shoulder just as I was about to join in with Tuli. "Remember me?"

Did I remember *him*? Did I remember *me* was a better question?

"From the bookstore tonight."

"Yeah, sure."

"I was at *New Morning* before St. Mark's."

"Oh yeah, right, now I remember why I remember you!"

"I remember when you and your wife—"

He had said the Magic word! I held up my hand to stop the pain shooting straight through my arms like a bolt of lightening.

"I'm sorry, I'm sorry, but I'll never forget those ten-hour Feasts Of Unbraining you guys used to throw at The Theatre For The New City and Saint Clements Church. Jazz bands, tap dancers, standups, pie throwing contests—"

"You were there?"

"Oh yeah! They changed my life. They were, by far, the greatest happenings I ever attended. I wish you'd do 'em again now that you're doing *The Oracle.*"

"I'm not sure I've got the juice to do something like that alone."

"I know, I know. . . . You were the coolest couple I ever saw. I'm ashamed to say it now, but I was so jealous of you guys then I hated your guts." He started crying. Sat down on the curb, and started bawling. "I even hated your dog."

"Well, he's dead, if that makes you feel any better."

"I'm sorry, I'm sorry!"

"Stupid sonofabitch body blocked a Ford pickup down on AIA. About 20 miles north of Jacksonville. . . ." I sat down next to him and started crying along.

Finally, he sputtered, "He was such a cool dog, such a cool dog. . . ."

"DO YOU WANT SOMETHING?" I suddenly exploded, standing and glowering down at him.

"I'm sorry, I'm sorry, I was just hoping I could get a poem from you for the new *Pubic Chandelier*."

"I don't write poetry, man!"

"Oh yeah, sure you do. I remember!" Like a large rock just fell on his head, he stood up, and recited: *"Write a fucking poem / Every fucking time / You don't know what the fuck to do / You'll have a fucking body of work / Despite yourself."*

"That was a rant."

"A rant then! Give me a rant!"

"Lemme think about it, man."

"Sure-sure-sure-sure, the deadline's not until next month." He started talking a hundred miles a minute about the magazine then. I didn't want to hear about no *Pubic Chandelier* though. When that sort of became self evident, he started telling me about his life instead. All about his wretched life. . . . About how his ex wife tried to kill him while they were tripping on acid driving through the middle of Appalachia while working for LBJ's *War On Poverty*. I could relate to that kinda shit.

He reached over and pulled a slice of cold pizza out of the trash that someone had put their cigarette out in moments before, picked the butt out of the cheese and began chomping away on it like he'd just been handed a fresh slice of Famous Ray's.

Truthfully, I don't think I'd ever seen anything more pathetic. I sat back down on the curb next to him again. And started to say something, but couldn't find the words. He looked over at me, started to say something, then just shrugged and held the pizza out, offering me a bite. In the next moment, we were both bawling our hearts out again.

That emotionally crippled all-night-drunk wasn't what I wanted, but it sure was what I needed to put life back in perspective again. Why I'm not dead now I can't say, because there is just no way I could've driven across the Manhattan Bridge, out the BQE, across Prospect Park by myself, because once Dan pulled into the driveway, I couldn't even get out and go upstairs. It was not a pretty picture. No matter what anybody tells you, it was not a pretty picture. . . . While I was going through it, I never thought I'd miss the 1980s. To me it was all one big vapid party without a point of view. Though I was obviously right in the middle of all the downtown excess, I was also stuck carrying around the baggage of '60s-'70s ideals, and was constantly looking for meaning where there was none.

In retrospect, it was a glorious time. A stupid, wonderful party none of us will probably ever be invited to again. For most of us it wasn't about celebrities preening for photo-ops and snorting their brains out at Studio 54, but it was about the quest for fame, and it was about the party, the never ending boogie of the downtown party. It was about misdirected energy looking for meaning, and about deadening the senses to fill whatever loss you were trying to recover from, and it was definitely about sex. Real live sex acts, boys & girls, and the surreal sexual fantasies that grew out of that same garden of trying to fill up the hole of ever lasting loss. It was about all the bad art that drugs and the hunger for fame could create, it was about an almost Renaissance that almost happened before AIDS became a full blown epidemic, and the party either ended, or became co-opted as the lifestyle of choice in a grunge theme park once upon a time known as the Lower East Side.

RANT

$4.95

#3

SHALOM — ·· · 11/27/92 · ·· · ·· ·

BENEFIT FOR beet MAGAZINE

FEATURING

SPARROW master poet (sort of) & BRILLiant toiletpaper tube minstral shares his zany antics.

MALCOLM TENT — HATED BY SOME, DISPISED BY OTHERS SPEWS HIS BILE & ACCORDIAN PROWESS w/ GUITAR ACCOMPANYMENT BY JED THE HED

the ever-lovin, pie-eatin' **HAL SIROWITZ** author of "No More Birthday" & other stuff...

TZAURAH LITZKY (buddha's mistress) leads us down the path of Kali.

PAUL WIENMAN A.K.A. "White-boy" Author of zillions of chapbooks & Objets d'Art, "5th most Published Poet in amerika" says somebody, wails his rails for the FIRST TIME in NYC, or maybe the 2nd time.

& if I can get ahold of her, she's hard to find, always out of town on some Cultural exchange program or writer's colony, but I'd say a 50/50 shot that she'll show up... **SHARON MESMER**

hosted by Beet Ed. Joe Maynard

AT BIBLIOS BOOKSTORE FRI. OCT. 7 8PM

Biblios is at 317 Church St. A block below canal st.

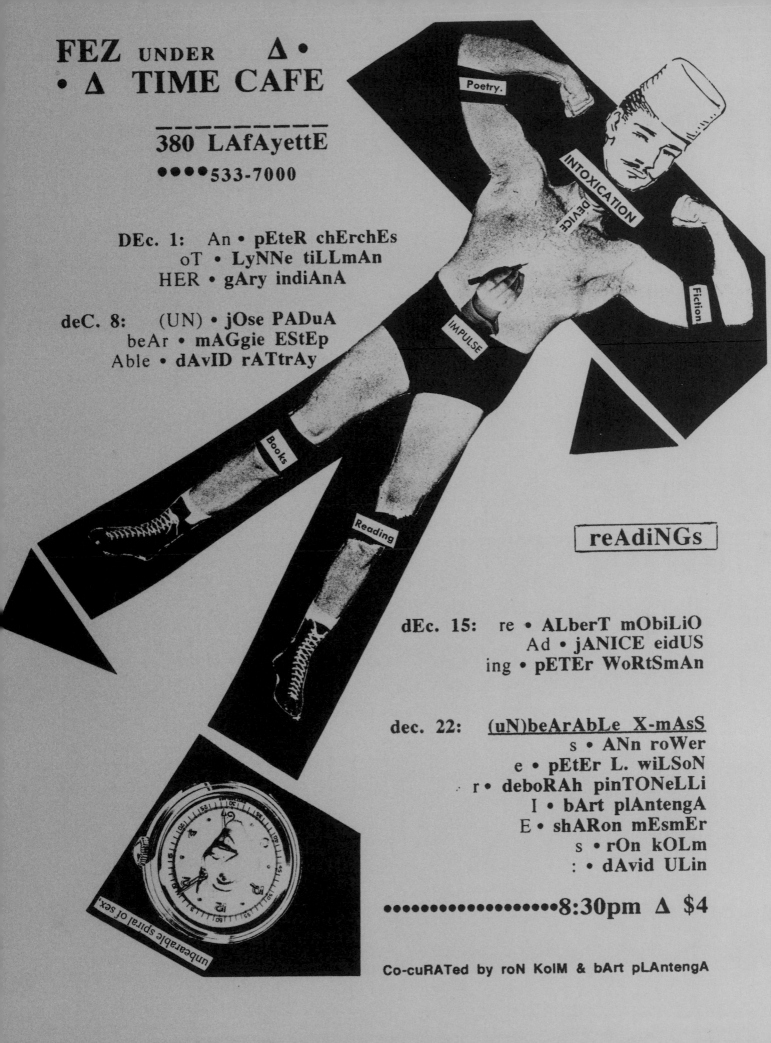

FEZ UNDER △ •
• △ TIME CAFE

----

380 LAfAyettE
●●●● 533-7000

DEc. 1: An • pEteR chErchEs
oT • LyNNe tiLLmAn
HER • gAry indiAnA

deC. 8: (UN) • jOse PADuA
beAr • mAGgie EStEp
Able • dAvID rATtrAy

Poetry.

INTOXICATION

DEVICE

Fiction

IMPULSE

Books

Reading

reAdiNGs

dEc. 15: re • ALberT mObiLiO
Ad • jANICE eidUS
ing • pETEr WoRtSmAn

dec. 22: (uN)beArAbLe X-mAsS
s • ANn roWer
e • pEtEr L. wiLSoN
r • deboRAh pinTONeLLi
I • bArt plAntengA
E • shARon mEsmEr
s • rOn kOLm
: • dAvid ULin

unbearable spiral of sex.

●●●●●●●●●●●●●●●●●●●●●●8:30pm △ $4

Co-cuRATed by roN KolM & bArt plAntengA

the unbeerable buttsteaks of boholand

present:

MADONNA / BUKOWSKI BIRTHDAY
AND
BABE RUTH DEATHDAY

MEMORIAL <u>POETRY</u>
CELEBRATION

MAX FISH * 178 LUDLOW *
fryday
AUG. 16 * 7 - 9PM

WITH:

Mike golden

deborah pintonelli

jose paDua

jennifer blOwdryer

michael raNdall

kristin armstroNg

michael cArter

Bart plantenga

david hUberman

ron KOlm

carl Watson

adam & matty jamkowSKI

jim FEAST

& OTHER SPECIAL GUESTS

YET ANOTHER UNBEARABLE BEATNIKS OF LITE EVENT:

MADONNA AND BEER

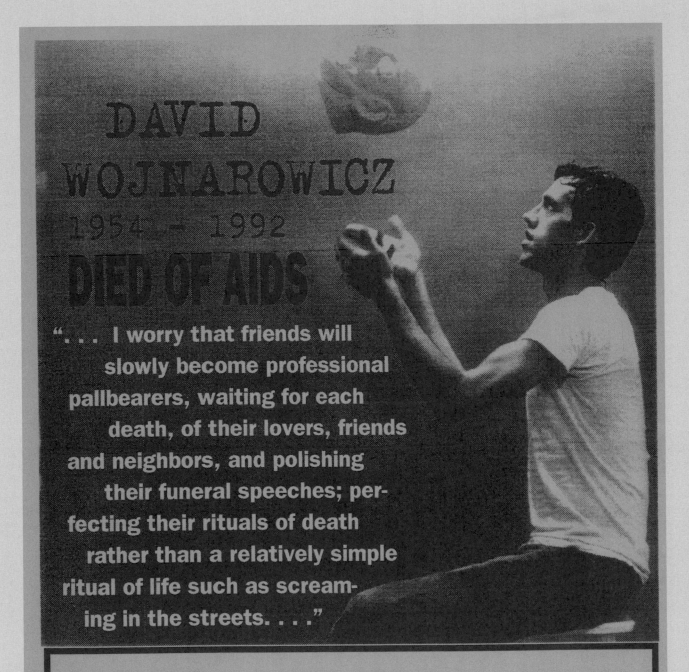

DAVID
WOJNAROWICZ
1954 - 1992
DIED OF AIDS

"... I worry that friends will
slowly become professional
pallbearers, waiting for each
death, of their lovers, friends
and neighbors, and polishing
their funeral speeches; per-
fecting their rituals of death
rather than a relatively simple
ritual of life such as screaming in the streets. ..."

Join us: MEMORIAL PROCESSION
Wednesday, July 29, 1992 @ 8 p.m.
12th Street & 2nd Avenue.

DOWN TOWN TOWN PUBLICATION ROUNDUP AN ADDENDUM

OFFERING WRITERS an opportunity to circulate their work outside mainstream publishing, Downtown magazines, zines, and journals helped save the underground from further obscurity.

In the second issue of *Gandhabba* (1984), Tom Savage encapsulated the spirit of these Downtown periodicals with his emotional discussion of the Downtown poetry community: "First, there was the general depression that surrounded the passing of Ted Berrigan and Edwin Denby. This magazine was founded as a counterpoint to that despair." Savage

remarks that outlets for poetry have "shrunken markedly" in the past decade, so he opts to make "a statement against the stunting of the poetic output" by asking poets to send him pieces longer than a page: "Only in one or two cases was I forced to do internal editing, that is, to choose an excerpt or excerpts from a work that would be too long to print in its entirety. I regret having to do so even now."[1]

Joel Rose and Catherine Texier, editors of *Between C & D*, remarked on the scene more subtly, revising slogans each issue to chart the shifting currents of the Lower East Side. Such tags included "Post-modern Lower East Side Fiction" and "Neo-Geo Post-Moribund Lower East Side Fiction Magazine."

As a testament to the strength of Rose and Texier's editorial eye, a number of works first appearing in *Between C & D* are reprinted in this book, including "The Red High Heels" from Catherine Texier's *Love Me Tender* (page 284), Lisa Blaushild's "Competition" and "The Couple" (page 178); Dennis Cooper's "George: Wednesday, Thursday, Friday" (page 264); and "A Visit from Mom" by Bruce Benderson (page 387).

Debuting in 1984, Kurt Hollander's *Portable Lower East Side* functioned as political pamphlet, multicultural literary journal, and personal fanzine. *Low Rent*, published in 1994, gathered texts from the magazine's distinguished run.

Hollander combined political writing with the writing of diverse cultures, mixing Ed Sanders with Public Enemy and compiling issues titled *Latin Americans in NYC, Assimilated Alien: New Asia*, and *New Africa*. Volume 3, numbers 1 and 2 from Winter/Summer 1986 focused on Eastern Europe. The back cover presented Eastern European countries transposed over a map of the Lower East Side. In this issue, Hollander looked at "Samizdat," the Russian word for "self-published" texts retyped by readers themselves (with carbon paper).[2]

Redtape was the manual to the darker side of the era. It was founded in 1982 by Michael Carter, and seven issues appeared over a decade, each with a different format and theme.

In the March 1984 issue of the *East Village Eye*, Carter unpacked *Redtape*'s aesthetic:

Images are immediate; they don't have to be read linearly. I began to find in the art I was collecting, the pieces that struck me the most were things that mixed a literary and artistic sensibility. . . . Another thing is people's attention span—they're so short these days, what with TV, videos, and hardcore songs that only last 60 seconds. I think it's necessary to have a visual hook. . . . I want to find a core on every page that unites the words and images, even if they're by different people."[3]

Redtape managed to outlast most of its contemporaries and went out strongly with its 1992 final *Tragicomix* issue. Dedicated to the recently deceased David Wojnarowicz, *Tragicomix* featured full-color work by Joe Coleman, KAZ, and Wojnarowicz with a beautiful front cover depicting James Romberger's pastel drawing, "The Triumph of Death (after Brueghel)," which bore a resemblance to Wojnarowicz's funeral procession, though Romberger completed the work before Wojnarowicz's death. The piece is reprinted on page 456.

The issue featured an encyclopedia of authors and visual artists of the period, with appearances by Holly Anderson, Bill Anthony, Richard Armijo, Max Blagg, Jennifer Blowdryer, Kate Burkehart, Peter Cherches, Mike Cockrill, Joe Coleman, and Gregory Corso, among others. There are also a number of collaborations such as "Faith" by Ron Kolm and David Sandlin; "Bad Karma" by Ron Kolm with accompanying drawing by Bill Anthony; and "My Name Is Eddy Paris" by Kevin Pyle and Carl Watson. Mike Golden's "Unbearable Beatniks of Light Get Real" is illustrated with a skeletal Art Spiegelman drawing.

Bringing together art and texts by Language poets, Deep Listening gurus, ABC No Rio regulars, and Lower East Side painters and graffiti archivists, *Benzene* was birthed in 1980 by Allan Bealy and printed until 1985. Bealy also published books: Peter Cherches's *Bagatelles* (1981) and *Condensed Book* (1986), Spalding Gray's *Seven Scenes from a Family Album* (1981), and Reese Williams's *Heat from the Tree* (1984), among others.

Benzene No. 8 (1983–1984) included a photo essay of David Wojnarowicz and Mike Bidlo's DIY artist space in a warehouse at the Chelsea Piers, allowing the two a venue to announce their statement of purpose:

Community: communication. Communication: word of mouth. . . . We chose the warehouse to start in by the fact that it straddled a tunnel that was a route for things arriving and departing from the city. . . . There is no rent, no electricity, no running water, no dealers, no sales, no curatorial interference. There is 24-hour access, enthusiasm, deep sudden impulse and some sense of possibility for dreaming. . . . This is something possible anywhere there are abandoned structures. This is something possible everywhere."[4]

The Nothing Issue Part One (1981–1985) combined issue 10 of *Benzene* with the final issue of Peter Cherches's *Zone,* which had debuted in 1977.

Wedge debuted in 1982, edited by Brian Wallis and Phil Mariani. Separate from *Wedge*, in 1985 Wallis published in *PARKETT* "An Absence of Vision and Drama," a series of essays on Kathy Acker, Gary Indiana, Richard Prince, and Lynne Tillman. In 1987 he edited *Blasted Allegories.*

As noted in Robert Siegle's *Suburban Ambush,* Mariani and Wallis designed the first two issues of *Wedge* to look like standard academic journals,

hoping to get it placed in as many bookstores and libraries as possible.[5] The following three issues were packaged McSweeney's-style as a collection of fourteen pamphlets, including Kathy Acker's *Implosion*, Gary Indiana's *Shanghai*, selections from Roberta Allen's *Partial Portrait*, and a section of Reese Williams's from *A Pair of Eyes.*

The editorial note opened with a quotation from William Burroughs's *Job* and went on to state that the "hybridization evident in the melding of word and image and in the blurring of distinctions between essay and fiction in these fourteen pamphlets stresses the various strategies and practices invented by the writers to conform language and writing to their specific political and social motivations," positing "a wholly different mode of textual inscription which challenges accepted sites, structures and meanings of political discourse."[6]

Dr. Zagreus Bowery's *Public Illumination* is conspicuous for its size (4 inches by 2.5 inches) as well as its sense of humor. Each issue generally focuses on a one-word theme such as "Casualties," "Underwear," "Secrets," "Foreigners," "Vermin," and "Contraception." (Two-word themes included April 1980's "Cosmetic Mutilation," July 1981's "Pain & Sorrow," and May 1983's "Flora & Fauna.") Started in 1979 by Jeffrey Isaac (an artist based in Italy who adorns each cover with his own illustrations) and published to this day, *Public Illumination* includes contributions by writers and artists using pseudonyms (for example, mr. basho's work on page 123 in this anthology). The utmost care has been taken to conceal the participants' true identities, except for Sparrow, who chose "Sparrow," and Mike Topp, who Ron Kolm claims got away with using his real name because it sounded so much like a pseudonym. Visual artists William Anthony,

Jörga Cardin, Keith Haring, Michael Madore, David Sandlin, and Tom Zummer presented styles difficult to mask. Secretive contributions have come from Steve Dalachinsky, Jim Feast, Bonny Finberg, Ron Kolm, Tuli Kupferberg, bart plantenga, and the editor of this book, among others. As Bowery put it, "the pseudonyms exist to focus attention to content rather than egos and to allow questionable taste without embarrassment."[7] Texts are kept to a maximum of 275 words and must approach the theme in one way or another. Aside from occasional centerfolds, drawings rarely spill over more than a single page.

Bob Witz began *Appearances* in 1976, focusing on contemporary art with poetry scattered throughout. The artist Hannah Wilke graced the first cover, and earlier issues included work by Eleanor Antin, Richard Armijo, John Evans, and Leon Golub, though it eventually became a balanced mix of visuals and texts. Witz treated the magazine like a work of art, often reworking each issue hundreds of times in his notebooks.

Early on, Witz released a number of single volumes of art by Keith Haring, Cara Perlman, Darrel Ellis, David N. Wells, and Candace-Hill-Montgomery, but in the 1990s his focus shifted to single-author chapbooks, by writers including Max Blagg, Ron Kolm, Hal Sirowitz with drawings by Blair Wilson, Mike Topp with drawings by William Wegman, Sparrow, Jim Feast, and Tsaurah Litzky.

Barbara Ess concocted one of the more interesting hodgepodges, *Just Another Asshole*. The first two issues were published as limited edition photocopied magazine; no. 3, edited with J. M. Sherry, was a 48-page graphic arts magazine featuring work by over one hundred artists; no. 4 appeared as four pages in the February 1980 issue of *Artforum*.

Most impressive are the final three issues edited with Glenn Branca. The no. 5 (1981) installment was a vinyl "audio magazine" (reissued on CD by Atavistic) containing seventy-seven short pieces by eighty-four people, including artists, musicians, and writers such as Phill Niblock, Rhys Chatham, Rudolph Grey, Kim Gordon, Thurston Moore, Dara Birnbuam, Carla Liss, Wharton Tiers, Jenny Holzer, Ben Bogosian, Lynne Tillman (with Dave Hofstra), Barbara Kruger, Gail Vachon, and Kiki Smith. Issue no. 6 (1983) was a 185-page book with sixty contributions by a number of the aforementioned as well as Kathy Acker, Michael Gira, Matthew Geller, Alan Moore, Cookie Mueller, Peter Nadin, Richard Prince, David Rattray, Ann Rower, Fiona Templeton, Ann Turyn, Reese Williams, and Linda Yablonsky. The final issue, *Thought Objects: Just Another Asshole no. 7* (1987), collected 122 images and nine essays based on a photography show at the Cash/Newhouse Gallery. Images included work by 120 artists.

Ann Turyn began *Top Stories* in 1978 at Hallwalls in Buffalo while working as the art center's literature curator (she took the publication with her when she relocated to New York City). *Top Stories* usually dedicated each chapbook-style issue to a single author (Laurie Anderson, Constance DeJong, Susan Daitch, Gail Vachon, Kathy Acker, Cookie Mueller, Ursule Molinaro) or a collaboration between an author and an artist (Jenny Holzer/Peter Nadin, Lynne Tillman/Jane Dickson), but there were also double issue compilations: 1986's *Five* (Constance DeJong, Joe Gibbons, Tama Janowitz, Richard Prince, and Leslie Thorton) and 1987's *Tourist Attractions*, which included fifteen authors.

Starting in 1981 and generally publishing six times a year, *New Observations* switched themes and editors each issue for two decades. Founded by Lucio Pozzi—a German with an Italian nom de plume—the magazine was eventually run by Diane Karp. The biannual editorial board included Jim Feast, Carlo McCormick, and Lynne Tillman.

Memorable issues were "Critical Love" by Lynne Tillman, "Regression" by Carlo McCormick, "Here Come the Murgatroyds" by Gary Indiana, "Responses to War" by Stephen Paul Miller and Bruce Brand, "Instant Classics" by Steven Kane and David L. Ulin, "Home Kinks" by Mike Topp, and "OULIPO" by Harry Mathews. Eventually, the magazine had funding problems and appeared less often. It stopped publication around 2000.

In 1986, Stephen Paul Miller, Jim Feast, and Carol Wierzbicki founded the *National Poetry Magazine of the Lower East Side* (years later renamed the *Unbearable Assembly Magazine*). Following the lead of Richard Kostelanetz's *Assemblage*, it included a large cast of the Unbearables as well as poets associated with the St. Mark's Poetry Project, and resembled a textual patchwork quilt. The magazine was compiled during parties at venues like CBGB's and the Cedar Tavern. It began as a monthly but eventually came out less often and moved over to theme orientation.

Lisa B. Falour produced *Bikini Girl*. Between 1978 and 1991, she published the entirety of Lynne Tillman's novel *Weird Fucks* in eight-point font, offered an S & M advice column under her alter ego, conducted enjoyably rambling interviews with anyone from Gerard Malanga (published herein) to neighborhood characters, and printed grainy photos surrounding the Mudd Club scene. *Bikini Girl* changed in size and edition with each issue, but remained pink. Some issues were photocopied in editions of fifty, whereas issue 8 had an edition of ten thousand and was a full sellout. She also did one two-hour VHS video issue in 1990. (Before *Bikini Girl* she did five issues of *Modern Girlz*.)

Another female-edited zine from the period was *Koff*. Conceived of in the Grassroots Bar on St. Mark's Place by poets Maggie Dubris and Elinor Nauen and singer-songwriter Rachel Walling (now Barker), it was the official publication of the so-called "Consumptive Poets League, Lower East Side Chapter." Three print issues were published from 1977 to 1979, and a special tee-shirt issue was produced in 1980, featuring a statement on the nature of poets and their place in the universe. One of its more entertaining and subversive aspects was a focus on naked male poets: *Koff* 1 and *Koff* 2 had cheesecake photos of Paul Violi and Lewis Warsh, and *Koff* 3 contained a foldout naked poet calendar featuring Bill Berkson, Charles Bukowski, Simon Schuchat, John Godfrey, Michael Lally, Bill Kushner, Joel Oppenheimer, Simon Pettet, Bob Holman, Tom Carey, Bob Rosenthal, and Kim Chi Ha. In addition to the nude bards, there were poems, songs, and jokes.

Still in production and glossier than most of the other publications discussed, *Bomb* started in 1981 with Betsy Sussler as editor. *Bomb* went on to publish work by Kathy Acker, Max Blagg, Joel Rose, Lisa Blaushild, Peter Cherches, Roberta Allen, Brad Gooch, Bob Holman, Susan Daitch, Gary Indiana (a serialization of *Burma* aka *Horse Crazy*), Eileen Myles, and Lynne Tillman, among others.

In the magazine, artists, writers, and filmmakers undertake the interviews. Acker made an amusing subject for artist and filmmaker Michael McClard in the first issue and again for Mark Magill in issue no. 6, e.g., "Q: Do you brush your teeth after every meal? A: Fuck you."[8] In 1982 McClard and Acker collaborated on an edition of *Hello, I'm Erica Jong*, a brief epistolary text satirizing realist, conventional feminist fiction, later recycled in Acker's *Blood & Guts in High School*.

Other periodicals included Eileen Myles's *dodgems*, Michael Freidman's *Shiny International*, Billy Miller's *Spunky International*, Steve Cannon's *Gathering of the Tribes*, Joe Maynard's *Beet* (and his later erotic zine *Pink Pages*), Mike Golden's *Smoke Signals*, *Big Cigars,* edited by Michael Randall and Jose Padua, Art Spiegelman's *Raw*, Steve Cee's *Avenue E*, Alfred Vitale's *Rant*, Richard Hell's *Cuz*, and Mike McGonigal's *Chemical Imbalance*, a key text of the punk/lit hybrid. (See also Thurston Moore's *KILLER*, *Ecstatic Peace Poetry Journal*, etc.)

Alternative newspapers were also regular sources for this writing.

Village Voice contributions to the Downtown dialogue were provided by C. Carr, Michael Musto, and especially Gary Indiana, whose regular attacks on the East Village art scene were as scathing as they were funny.

But debuting in May 1979 with James Chance on the cover, Leonard Abram's *East Village Eye* was the best chronicler of the area's rise and fall. Among others, Abrams published writing by bart plantenga, Richard Hell, Kathy Acker, Rene Ricard, Gary Indiana, and Ursule Molinaro, and Patrick McGrath's "The Erotic Potato" was serialized therein. He also gave regular columns to Richard Hell and Cookie Mueller. Mueller's "Ask Dr. Mueller," which debuted in October 1982, was an advice column. A typical dollop of wisdom could be pithy ("Q: Doc, I have some cracked lips here. What's the deal? Moe; A: Moe, Don't lick them so much in the wind. Love, Doctor Mueller"[9]) or needlessly expansive. The biggest joke of all: she wrote most of the questions herself. Mueller took the column with her to *High Times* in 1985.

Like the gentrifying landscape around it, in the mid-'80s, the *East Village Eye* cleaned up its act, covering stories on politicians as opposed to punks and raising issues in its editorials that looked outside of New York City towards a larger worldview. Fearing gentrification and watching the city shift around them, the critics also became more protective: Carlo McCormick used his "Art Seen" column to ask yuppies to stay away from Life Café, and in the next issue David Wojnarowicz's "Sidewalk Begging" raised a similar concern, memorializing "beautiful spray-painted sunsets with windows and doorways smashed through them where the rich folks moving back from the suburbs are taking over."[10]

After seven years and sixty-eight issues, the *East Village Eye* changed its name to the *Eye* in September 1986. Obviously on the economic ropes, its publishers didn't produce a November 1986 issue, and its last issue was printed in January 1987, James Chance again on its cover. This time he was doctored with an airbrush effect, and the paper was retitled the *International Eye*. This "airbrush" revision fittingly brings things up to date.

NOTES

1. Tom Savage, Introduction, *Gandhabba*, vol. 1, no. 2, 1984, i.

2. Kurt Hollander, *Portable Lower East Side,* vol. 3, nos. 1 and 2, Winter/Summer 1986, 3.

3. Michael Carter, "Editor Michael Carter Talks about *Redtape*," *East Village Eye*, vol. 5, no. 41, March 1984, 53.

4. David Wojnarowicz and Mike Bidlo, "Statement" (on the Pier), *Benzene*, no. 8, Fall/Winter 1983–1984, 13–15.

5. Brian Wallis in Robert Siegle, *Suburban Ambush: Downtown Writing and the Fiction of Insurgency* (Baltimore, Md.: Johns Hopkins University Press, 1989), 334.

6. Brian Wallis and Phil Mariani, Editorial Note, *Wedge: Partial Texts: Essays & Fictions*, Issues 3/4/5, Winter/Spring/Summer 1983, n.p.

7. Jeffrey Isaac, email to the editor, January 14, 2005.

8. Kathy Acker and Mark Magill, "Kathy Acker Answers Questions," *Bomb* no. 6, Sculpture and Fiction, 1983, 61.

9. Cookie Mueller, "Ask Dr. Mueller," *East Village Eye*, vol. 5, no. 39, December/January 1984, 51.

10. David Wojnarowicz, "Sidewalk Begging," *East Village Eye*, vol. 7, no. 59, October 1985, 14.

AFTERWORD. THE SCENE:

A CONVERSATION BETWEEN DENNIS COOPER AND EILEEN MYLES

In the following dialogue, Dennis Cooper and Eileen Myles, key figures in the Downtown scene, whose vital earlier work is included in this volume and who remain highly prolific, discuss their own New York City from the years leading up to 1974 through the 1980s and the 1990s to the recent artistic and literary developments of a younger generation. In the process they develop the idea of "Downtown" and what it means today.

Dennis Cooper: I only lived in New York for four years total, from '83 to '85, and then again from '87 to '90. For me, Downtown is as much a fantasy as a reality. Growing up in LA, and being heavily influenced by poets and musicians and performance artists associated with Downtown New York, the scene there seemed like a dream situation to me. Of course I became a member of it for a while, but my ideas and feelings about it are kind of inextricable from my early longing to be there and a certain nostalgia about my brief but key life there. You lived there a long time, so I'm sure you're much more pragmatic about Downtown than I am. But maybe the combination of a relative outsider and an insider is what Brandon's looking for.

EM: Yeah, except that so much a part of being in it was . . . a dream. I mean that a lot had to do with the fact of small films being made in the '70s and '80s in New York. I just knew they were being made right around me, and my girlfriend and I both thought, "What a great idea." You know? And that feeling led me to fiction and there was no direct exposure at all. Maybe dreaming of being inside a film.

DC: Yeah, yeah.

EM: So I'm thinking maybe we might invent, for starters, what *it* was. You know, like what . . . I mean, are we talking about literally New York or some kind of imagined scene and what was that . . . what was that to you?

DC: For me, the romance with New York really started when I was in college. The so-called second generation of the New York School poets were very hot, and their books were being published by major presses or well distributed smaller presses. So it was possible to go into my local bookstore in Pasadena and find books by Ted Berrigan and Ron Padgett and Joe Brainard and Tom Clark and Dick Gallup and Bernadette Mayer and all those guys.

The book that really sold me was this anthology edited by Ron Padgett and David Shapiro called *The New York Poets*. It covered from the Frank O'Hara generation to the youngest New York School poets at that time. That book was huge for me.

EM: Wait, what year are we in?

DC: This must have been like '72. I was going to the local city college at that time, Pasadena City College, basically taking poetry classes and workshops. I'd been pretty much exclusively interested in French poets up until then, but discovering the second generation of the New York School poets was a huge revelation. Their work was so fresh and exciting and just so relevant, and it had an interest in style and form that created a kind of bridge from the French poets I loved, who were all dead, and the world I occupied, which revolved around rock music and drugs and rebellion and poetry. It was really lucky because it was only a short time that those poets had that kind of publisher support and distribution, and that some kid in Pasadena could discover such cool poets so accidentally. Anyway, those books changed my writing and my life, and the more I found out about them and their scene of mimeo poetry magazines and St. Mark's Church and all that, the more New York became an ideal to me. I remember Kenneth Koch came to my college to do a reading, and I just cornered him and grilled him about the New York School poets, which I think he thought was kind of annoying and ridiculous, but still. So there were the poets, and then the New York Dolls and Patti Smith came along, and I discovered Robert Wilson and Richard Foreman and the Wooster Group, and this picture of an ideal, incredibly fertile scene entered my head, and that was it. I was totally in love.

EM: I remember sort of stumbling into a bookstore in Harvard Square and seeing a book called *Back in Boston Again*. With Ted Berrigan and Aram Saroyan. That was some kind of introduction for me.

DC: Oh yeah, I bought that book too.

EM: Little tiny book, and I think maybe it was Telegraph Books that published it. And I could not figure out what it was. I loved it, but I couldn't figure it out, because it was really . . . minimal. It was very close-up and sort of intimate, but there were very few details, yet it seemed like they were acting as if you already knew these guys. And it just didn't seem like writing. It felt like a screenplay. I just thought, they're acting like I'm in the same place with them and should give a shit about these people. And it *was* familiar.

There's this thing called "morphic resonance" where something gets invented all over the place, at the same time. I mean when I was in high school and would get in trouble I would do "special projects" to save my ass. And I would write these really dumb plays that resembled interviews in movie magazines with dumb stars. And you would ask them what their favorite kind of juice was and . . . just stupid kind of Andy Warhol-y kind of conversations. And there was just this level of exalted mundanity that was second nature I think to everybody at that time. I remember going into the Museum of Fine Arts in Boston and seeing this video. It was just this cute guy with black hair talking about himself. What the hell is that? And it was just the permission to be local, as if one were famous.

DC: Yeah, the Warhol thing was really a big part of my image of New York too. I forgot about that. I was already way into Warhol's films and the Velvet

Underground by the time I found the poets, and it all seemed connected to me, which I guess it was.

EM: I wonder what year *Interview* started. 'Cause I think that the first time I ever saw "um" in print was very important to me.

DC: Yeah, Gerard Malanga was the first editor of *Interview*, and that literally connected Warhol to the poetry scene.

EM: That's amazing to think that in the middle of the Warhol universe would be anything about language. But there were already all those influences, and when I picked up that Boston book, I thought, wow, this dumbness, this flatness is possible in poetry. It made poetry seem like something you could do and would do and were already doing in some way.

DC: Yeah, exactly. You mentioned Telegraph Books, and I found their books early on as well. That was a particularly exciting press because they published Berrigan and Padgett and Aram Saroyan, and then they published Patti Smith, which brought in the rock music thing, and then they published that terrific little book by the Warhol superstar Brigid Polk of her collection of ink prints of hip celebrities' scars. I thought Telegraph Books was the coolest thing going.

EM: And it suggested that there were all these relationships. People that seemed very different later, weren't, at some other point.

DC: Oh, definitely.

EM: For a while in New York when people would meet you, they'd say, "Well, when did you come on the scene?" People tried to place you. Sometimes it's gate keeping, but it's also about people's generosity, to even attribute to you things you weren't even there for. Now that they knew you they wished you were on the scene at this time or that. Morris Golde *wished* I knew O'Hara, and started to give me credit for knowing him. I remember him asking me if I knew "Frankie." And I'm thinking, Morris, I was in *high school*. But it was very . . . kind of loving. If they liked you, they saw you now and always as part of this scene. That's what I'm thinking. It was sort of utopian for a long time. Just calling it "the scene" sort of suggests there's a physical set, like a movie that we're all kind of arriving on. And . . . and you know yourself through that.

DC: Well, when I first started going to New York a lot in the mid- to late-'70s, there was still a lot of resonance from the Frank O'Hara era. Certainly there was John Ashbery and James Schuyler and the first generation poets, but there were also people like Joe Lesueur and . . . what's his name—that crazy guy who worked at the Bar on Second Avenue and had also been a lover of Frank O'Hara's. . . .

EM: Oh, J. J.

DC: Yeah, J. J. Mitchell. There was still a number of people connected to that early heyday who were completely accessible and part of the scene. So when I first came to New York, the New York School was still alive and in play, and the scene was very multigenerational and just thrilling. And I guess it was while I was living there that the whole New York School dream began to collapse or run out of gas. Your generation, my peers and good friends, was the last generation, I think, and, even then, the tag New York School didn't end up sticking to you guys. Obviously, I'm talking about you, Tim Dlugos, Brad Gooch, Steve Hamilton, Donald Britton, Cheri Fein, and so many others. But in the early '80s there was still a sense that you guys and the older New York poets were connected and involved in the same tradition, and everyone fraternized and hung out and the older poets supported the younger poets. It was really an ideal situation to me. I'd go to a party with Tim and Donald and Brad, and there would be slightly older writers like Joe Brainard and Kenward Elmslie and Ron Padgett, and then the established greats like Ashbery and Schuyler and Edwin Denby, and nonpoets too, like Donald Barthelme and Alex Katz and Roy Lichtenstein and just an incredibly multigenerational group of artists, gay and straight, who felt some kind of aesthetic and personal unity. But in retrospect, it was the end of that world, the last golden hours of the New York School, as it existed in my mind anyway.

EM: Well, it seemed like the New York School, to me, sort of collapsed out of its own sense of fatality about itself. You know? It sort of needed to do something *next*. And it seemed to me that instead it closed down on itself—I mean, like, somebody like Ashbery sort of rages on getting more famous, and Jimmy Schuyler has planted his influence everywhere. But say the next generation, like, very few of them did very much. But, *we* did okay. If we're, you know, umpteenth-generation New York School poets then our contribution was to leave it. Interestingly, the queers did. [laughing] You know?

DC: Yeah. It became increasingly straight, or dominated by heterosexuals. Even with the second generation, there was Joe Brainard and sexually ambiguous people like Anne Waldman and Bernadette Mayer. Your generation had a lot of lesbian and gay poets, but the group of writers who congregated around St. Mark's was largely hetero, and our group or the poets I felt close to were much more free floating. Maybe there was this dispersal in your generation that sped up the collapse. There wasn't a sense of St. Mark's being the center of the poetry scene the way it had been. I know that my New York poet friends felt like outsiders there. I knew the St. Mark's poets like Gary Lenhart and Michael Scholnick and Bob Holman and others, but not well. And I liked their work, but it was going off in a direction I didn't feel so connected to, and which I rightly or wrongly associated with the kind of poetry and poetics coming out of the Naropa Institute. The New York poets I was closest to weren't really part of the Naropa thing at all. Maybe that's part of why the schism happened. My friends were really clearly influenced by Ashbery and O'Hara and Schuyler, and the St. Mark's poets' work seemed more like a derivation from Ginsberg and Waldman and Berrigan. But I didn't know them well. You did, right?

EM: Yeah, they were my best friends, my buddies when I was younger. It was sort of like we were all like a bunch of guys with jean jackets passing records and books around to each other. Susie Timmons was there too, and Maggie Dubris and there was blur into bands for a lot of people that came a little later. Ann Rower was a member of the crew. She was actually making films at the time. And writing prose. It definitely was a fun scene around in the early-late '70s. But, for me, once I came out I was a black sheep and just not part of it anymore. I was hitting on the same girls the guys were and it was gross. And so, I completely lost track of what they did. And that's about the time when I met you and we all started kind of creating this other gang.

DC: Yeah, our gang of poets was a really exciting development, certainly for the LA poets who were my close friends. We had a really vital little scene in LA focused around Beyond Baroque, where I ran the reading series from '80 to '83, and the literary magazines and presses we were doing like my *Little Caesar* and Jack Skelley's *Barney* and David Trinidad's Sherwood Press. Our ventures were very influenced by New York lit magazines like *Z* and *Muzzled Ox* especially. So when the LA writers like Amy and Jack and Bob Flanagan and David Trinidad and Ed Smith and Benjamin Weissman and others became comrades with you guys, it opened up our world significantly, and the possibilities seemed endless. That cross-country gang of ours, which was completely created by Tim Dlugos, who introduced all of us and encouraged the connection, well, it was probably the single most important thing that ever happened to the LA poets in terms of our work and our careers and our lives as artists.

EM: Well, we were all moving around. It sort of defined "gang" differently. Like all the "locals" hooked up, our different scenes. I met Lynne Tillman around then too. Through David Rattray. But coming to Beyond Baroque (in LA) was maybe the second time I'd flown anywhere to do a reading—

DC: Really?

EM: —December of 1982. Yeah.

DC: I had no idea.

EM: I remember I was trying to stop drinking. But there was no way I was going to not drink in Los Angeles [laughing]. But it seemed really vital, where

there was a sense that, oh, we have friends in San Francisco and we have friends in Los Angeles—

DC: Yeah, there were the San Francisco writers like Kevin Killian, Dodie Bellamy, Robert Glück, Camille Roy. They'd come down and read at Beyond Baroque, and we'd read up north. And there were the Chicago poets too, Elaine Equi and Jerome Sala. We published each other in our magazines and eventually became passionate friends.

EM: But what preceded our scene were these magazines. I knew you through Tim, but you sent me *Little Caesar*. Then I sent you *dodgems*. The magazine was like a vehicle. It's sort of like, retrospectively then it really seemed like, in lieu of having a band, you did a magazine that got your model out there of who and what you had in mind. You know? Then you put yourself in it.

DC: Yeah, totally. Totally.

EM: 'Cause I remember when I saw *Little Caesar*, I was like, okay, he's queer, he's doing like a famous boy thing, he likes rock 'n' roll, and poetry that I like. And it was a kitschy, junky cool aesthetic that had a little push towards pornography, but it was just like a mix of things I had never seen together before, except that again it felt familiar and, like . . . mine. Like something I would be drawn to, though I never would have thought of it.

DC: Yeah. At that time the whole notion of gay literature was first appearing, and at that point it was mostly a poetry movement revolving around magazines like *Gay Sunshine* in San Francisco and *Mouth of the Dragon* in New York and *Fag*

Rag in Boston. But it was a very male-oriented scene that almost completely excluded lesbians. I was part of that movement, but I hated the total maleness of it, and *Little Caesar* was in part a kind of reaction against that pervasive attitude in the gay poetry crowd, like, "Hey women, we're masturbating in here, go away."

EM: God I think of the way lesbians were configured in the gay view of things. Even in a fag hag view of things. I remember Ann Magnuson doing this big huge character named Babe, a big dyke in a plaid flannel shirt. It was funny, but the room was all fags laughing at us and straight women then. The same old equation. I guess there were lesbian separatists off in some women's land in the Southwest called Arp. Then, there were those of us who were hanging out with gay men, you know? I'm thinking Jane DeLynn and Rose Lesniak my great love—everybody's great love. She was the connector of the pack. But the poetry world or the art world and being a dyke were like all separate things. I'd go to the Duchess and see people I still know like Elizabeth Streb, but mostly you were kind of leaving your regular culture to be a lesbian. But then that changed by the end of the eighties with WOW and a whole lesbian theater scene, but still not in poetry.

DC: Correctly or not, I had an image of the New York poetry scene as being basically bisexual or sexually experimental. Not as much among the male poets, but it wasn't a secret even out in LA that the women poets like Anne Waldman and Bernadette Mayer and others were having affairs with other women poets and women in the scene, in addition to their relationships with men. And it seemed like everyone was totally cool with that. That was definitely part of my mental image of the New York scene, that the poets' lives were wild and lyrical and open just like their poems.

EM: Hmm. Yeah. Some of my favorite poetry by both of them was about their love affair. It's funny the romance you have about other people's romances. I guess it's like movie stars. I have some picture in my head of Anne and Bernadette in the throes of their affair staying with Ted and Alice in Chicago and them having a birthday party for Ted who had just turned forty and him crying because he was old. I mean I heard this story. What a configuration. I can practically see the apartment. Rose came from Chicago. And the presence of Ted and Anne who Rose had a thing with—she was one of those conniving students who finds money to bring the poet into town that she's in love with.

DC: Sure.

EM: Part of the pattern was that poets like Ted Berrigan would leave New York and go off teaching, you know? It was like this evangelical thing. Everywhere Ted went his students would flock to New York to become poets at his behest. And likewise, just since I've been teaching in San Diego, all these students of mine have migrated to New York. And are basically even gravitating to some parts of the same scene.

DC: So there *is* still a vital poetry scene in New York? I mean tight knit, unified like it was in the early '80s.

EM: Well, the writing scene here now feels pretty straight. I just feel like—I just think in New York AIDS made all the difference. Like for instance in the "nondrinking community." When I first stopped drinking, there were loads of people who were getting off drugs and alcohol and they were straight and gay and we were all together. Obviously if you were a drug addict you would have sex with anyone, and did. But when AIDS occurred, it increasingly seemed that half the people in a given room had a tragedy in their lives and the other half of the people *did*, but not quite 'cause they didn't lose their lover or their best friend. And I just feel like it really changed—well, it changed New York. Permanently, because I just think that it was easier to be straight and not deal with AIDS. And there was no way you could do that and be gay.

DC: Yeah, *my* group of artist friends was just decimated by AIDS. I mean, Tim Dlugos tested positive and then Donald Britton and the filmmaker Howard Brookner and the performance artist John Bernd, and it was just bam, bam, bam . . . one after another in really quick succession. And then other artist friends were just drinking and drugging themselves into oblivion and hardly writing or making art anymore. Everything was just falling apart, you know? It was very heavy, and the joy and fun was gone. Like, do you remember the painter Larry Stanton? He was close with David Hockney and Henry Geldzhahler and Charles Ludlum.

EM: Yeah, I do.

DC: He was the first of my friends to die of AIDS. I saw him on the street one day, and he said he had a cold, and then literally three weeks later he was dead. That was such a shock. And then it hit my other friends very quickly. I think the fear and horror of it splintered my group of writer friends. We were almost all gay and no strangers to the baths and sex clubs like the Mine Shaft, and we got hit particularly

hard. I found myself gravitating more and more to the performance art scene in the East Village, where, for whatever reason, AIDS was a bit more of a distant concern at that time, and there was still a ton of fun and hope and vitality in the performance art crowd.

EM: Performance is exactly—when you think about poets moving on . . . you had to take the aesthetic into some other medium or it was . . . you were just going to hang out and watch it die with everybody else.

DC: Right, exactly. Yeah, so I ended up spending *much* more time at PS 122 and the Kitchen and Franklin Furnace than I did at the Poetry Project, you know? I saw the poets less and less, and my really close friends were performance artists and people associated with that scene like Anne Iobst and Lucy Sexton of Dancenoise and John Kelly and Lori Seid and Dona MacAdams and Chris Cochrane and John Walker and Jeff McMahon and especially Ishmael Houston-Jones, with whom I started collaborating on performance art pieces. I loved that scene and those people and their work, and it was really exciting to me as a writer to learn from them. But it was a strange thing to suddenly lose the world of writers. You were in the performance scene, thank God, and a couple of other writer/performers like Holly Hughes and Spalding Gray, but really very few.

EM: I had that job—working at the Poetry Project drove me out of the poetry scene quicker than anything. Every poet is a one-man band so everyone wanted something and they were all coming at your desk. It was horrible. We had an art auction then and a whole other world came tromping into the church and I wanted to tromp out with them. Actually being there too was how I started performing. PS 122 asked me to be in their benefit and I thought I'm not going to *read* in front of those people. So I memorized my poem and afterwards dancers came out and told me they liked my work. Doing something different moved me into that world. The poetry world was getting pretty homophobic too. People didn't know what to do with AIDS so they wanted to push it aside.

DC: Yeah, I remember when you started doing that. That was really a revelation, really a breakthrough.

EM: I think—well, I think it was the result of not being drunk. [Laughs] It was like . . . it was a perk or something.

DC: You were writing plays and having them performed in the scene too. I felt a real bond with you because I was doing those performance pieces with Ishmael Houston-Jones at the same time.

EM: That dance/performance scene—everyone in Doc Martens, Jo Andres, Jennifer Monson, Yvonne Meier. John Bernd. Lucy and Ann. Steve Buscemi came out of that scene. It was totally the hot scene in the '80s.

DC: It was for me. I mean, performance art was like my lifeblood. It was a little later that I got heavily involved in the contemporary art world and started writing for *Artforum* and *Art in America* and stuff. But those years hanging around PS 122 and working with Ishmael, that was definitely one of the happiest and more important times of my life. Certainly my favorite time while I was living in New York. 'Cause even when I first actually moved to New York in '83, AIDS was casting its darkness over the group of gay writers I was close with. We were doing lots of drugs and being very hedonistic, which was a blast, but it was already

dangerous at that time and had a nihilistic vibe about it. But in the performance scene, there was more of an illusion that you were immune to all of that, even though, of course, we weren't and quite a number of the performers and dancers I knew ended up dying of AIDS. Maybe it's just that the nature of performance art is inherently optimistic and geared towards pleasure and surprise. The lifestyle is just much more fun too. Instead of dragging yourself largely out of obligation to attend your friends' readings, you'd be like, "Let's go catch John Jesserun's new piece at the Kitchen, and then we can pop over to Dixon Place and see Ethyl Eichelberger, and then John Kelly's doing Dagmar Onassis at the Pyramid at midnight." It was a hugely stimulating way to spend your time.

EM: The timing of that scene was so great too. PS 122 was their space, and WOW was the girls' and it was great when everyone was living in the East Village. It would take you an hour to walk six blocks during the day you'd see so many people you knew. It was so great. And soon a lot of those people would be moving to Brooklyn and getting lofts and it still seemed that you could get "space." A lot of the dykes went there. Jennifer Monson and Jennifer Miller. So it was like another burst in New York history. It was a young scene and dancers are so comfortable in their bodies—all that circus stuff and contact improv and the dancers were all collaborating with people like John Zorn and Zeena Parkins. It was very romantic in its sense of possibility. It did remind me of when I first came to New York. It didn't seem dependent on external conditions, though it was. The money thing is always looming. In the eighties you could still work it.

In the seventies it had seemed like wealthy people actually *liked* to have pet poets and poorer people around and young people and it was very

. . . fluid. How people were willing to spend their money and who they wanted around—there wasn't a sense that poverty was a contagion. And that feeling's been gone for a long time. That's why the dance scene was so good because even though people were starting to go insane about money and real estate their thing was actually cooking.

DC: Yeah, I saw that, mostly from a distance. But yeah, people like Lita Hornick and Morris Golde were wealthy people who seemed to love the poets and supported them in different ways. Still, by the time I moved to New York,that kind of relationship between wealthy uptowners and bohemian downtowners seemed to be on the wane.

EM: Until the real estate thing really hit, there was a lot of patronage. A band would be at a rich person's party. There was food and hard liquor at book parties! But music was just there all along. . . .

DC: Well, some of the most genius punk artists like Richard Hell and Tom Verlaine and Patti Smith *were* poets too.

EM: Exactly. You went to CBGB's 'cause it was free 'cause your friends put you on the list. And all sorts of lofts still existed where . . . you know, when Thurston Moore and all those people started playing. It was just free or cheap. And so there was this constant flow to events in large spaces.

DC: Yeah, there was a lot of interest back and forth too. A lot of those musicians *were* interested in literature. I mean, I'd meet, say, Debbie Harry or David Byrne somewhere, and we'd have these long talks about literature.

EM: Debbie Harry lived in my building in Soho. There were twenty years when everyone was in the same room. That is the art now, though. The room. Art collectives, groups like LTTR (Lesbians to the Rescue) who are putting art and music and writing together in these great events. Events are starting to become the art. But I don't think that's foreign to LA is it?

DC: Yeah, well, you know, we'd had that kind of incredible, beautiful mix of different kinds of artists in Los Angeles too. There was a period in the early '80s when we were all young ambitious artists unified by the fact that very few people outside of LA took art made here seriously. My crowd was completely mixed. There were the writers and then there were the artists like Mike Kelley and Raymond Pettibon and Paul McCarthy and Steve Prina and Jim Isermann and so many others. There were musicians like John Doe and Exene of X and Tom Waits and bands like Wall of Voodoo and the Minutemen and others. The artists and musicians hung out at Beyond Baroque, and the writers and musicians hung out at LACE, which was the big alternative art space at that time, and we all went to punk clubs, and we were all collaborating with each other constantly. That mix of different kinds of artists completely constructed the work of artists of my generation. That's why the work of my writer peers is so influenced by the principles of visual art and rock music and why the work of the LA artists and musicians is unusually literary.

I'm sure your work is very influenced by the same kind of mix of artists you knew in New York. I wonder if that's why, for instance, you and I are so ambitious in our work, and why we seem to have a more global view than so many writers of our original group who've either stopped writing altogether or seem content to publish their work in such a way that it has little chance to reach beyond their immediate colleagues and friends.

EM: In New York if you wanted to connect with the art world, it seemed the only way to do it was to write about people.

DC: Yeah, of course.

EM: People's careers moved so fast and were so big. Somebody like Francesco Clemente would be my age and who he would want to collaborate with would be Allen Ginsberg. The scale was so different between writers and visual artists in New York.

DC: It's so true, and it remains true for the most part. I mean, I got to know a lot of New York artists through my friendships with Peter Schjeldahl and Raymond Foye, both of whom straddled the art and writing worlds. And it was very interesting and a great opportunity for me, but while I did get to know people like David Salle and Francesco Clemente and Eric Fischl a little, it wasn't a real back and forth or mutual interest kind of thing. It was my involvement as a critic in the art world that created whatever interest they had in me. When the East Village art scene happened, it was a little friendlier. David Wojnarowicz was a bona fide crossover artist, and some other younger artists at that time like Barbara Kruger and Richard Prince and Nan Goldin were genuinely interested in literature.

EM: At that moment.

DC: Yeah, so there was something happening in Downtown between artists of different mediums at that time. There was a certain connection between the visual artists and the writers who lived Downtown. And there were those really great magazines that worked the connection like *Between C & D* and *Redtape* and *Top Stories* and Richard Hell's *Cuz*. And then of course there was Raymond Foye's Hanuman Press, although that might have been a little later. Anyway, Hanuman was such a great press.

EM: Right, right.

DC: But even with those few years of a somewhat unified art and literary scene, it didn't feel as communal or cross-fertilizing as the scene I was describing in Los Angeles or the music/writing scene in New York during the punk era you were talking about. That's just the nature of the New York art world, I think. It's really geared toward the chic and economics, and it's pretty insular. I mean one of the main reasons I finally moved back to Los Angeles in '90 was that I had gotten deeply involved in the art world as a regular writer for *Artforum*, and I just couldn't take the ass kissing and backstabbing and careering that was going on around me. It took me about three years away from that before I could even look at art much less write about it again.

EM: New York always was utterly the marketplace. There's sort of not much else—where if you think LA, it does seem like, for instance, it seems like a lot of the art world still comes out of the art schools. And people don't have that same horror of, you know, getting there. I guess because you're up against Hollywood, so. . . .

DC: It's true.

EM: It just has a different feeling.

DC: Completely. I mean, right now the contemporary art scene in Los Angeles is as exciting and vital as any scene I've ever been a part of. It has that same beautiful, undifferentiated mixture of writers and artists of different kinds that it had in the early '80s and like it seems that New York had before the real estate boom and AIDS. It's really utopian and inspiring. It's no surprise that New York visual artists are flocking out here. It's an ideal situation in which to make art without the schmoozing and pressures to make a ton of money that you find in New York.

EM: Sounds great. So why did you move *here*?

DC: Why? Well, I came because I had so many writer friends in New York. I wanted to be around them, and . . . well, I wanted to make it as a writer, and I thought I had to be in New York for that to happen. At that time, I think that was actually true, given the dismissive attitude toward LA writers in those days. New York was just really exciting and inviting to me for the reasons I was talking about earlier. I have to say again that Tim Dlugos was just such a huge influence on me in this regard and in so many ways. He seemed to know everybody who was anybody in New York, and he introduced me to so many amazing artists, both people my age and older artists whom I'd always idolized. So I moved out there in large part to be around him and make his world my world. So from '83 when I moved to New York and lived on Twelfth Street near Second Avenue until I left New York and moved to Amsterdam in '85, that's pretty much what happened, although, like I said, AIDS curdled that world pretty quickly and I had to find my own world in the performance scene. By the time I moved back to New York after two and a half years in Amsterdam in '87, things were really

different. A lot of my friends were either sick or dead or had moved away, and I wasn't really writing poetry anymore by that point. I was pretty much a novelist, and there wasn't a community of novelists the way there was and always will be a community of poets. I was friends with Lynne Tillman and Gary Indiana and a couple of other fiction writers, but our connection had as much to do with our mutual interest in visual art as it did in our identities as fiction writers. The performance scene was still going strong and I reconnected with that and continued to make pieces with Ishmael, but what income I had came from writing about art, so I was very involved in that until I moved back to LA. I think by '90 I'd sort of had it with how difficult it was to live in New York, financially and as an artist. And I think the heavily social aspect of life in New York wore me out. I grew up in LA, which is an asocial city unless you make a big effort to be social, and I think that suits me.

EM: I remember Anne Waldman saying to me about a million years ago—I think I was debating about whether to go someplace for a period of time and worrying about whether I would miss this or that. She said, "No, the thing about New York is that it never changes." You know that no matter how many things are going on, it's sort of like so many things are going on that it also kind of stands still. You know? And you can go away for ten years and you come back and you see someone in the street and they'll say, "Oh, I haven't seen you for a while." And then they'll tell you about something and—you know, you go to one thing and then you kind of plan your whole week. 'Cause you see so many people at something and it's just like you make all these real and fake plans.

DC: [Laughing] Yeah.

EM: And you just get so completely jazzed about the encounter, which is continuous, that you just wind up on this plane—I can't sleep when I'm here, you know? I continue to love that, but it's also part of the problem, which is that it's really hard to get work done here. Even if you've got a little niche economically where you can kind of live well, people who live well also have some escape hatch, somewhere they go to work because, I guess everyone just needs it to stop. But I think when you're younger—you know, I think that's a lot of it. You can work in a maelstrom then. But really I think I feel a little fortunate to have been around for a very shaggy, messy moment when you could kind of live in that. And it seemed like there were more cracks in it than in me, and the thing was to work inside of them.

DC: So what's your New York narrative? When did you move there?

EM: I came in '74. I was coming out of some kind of know-nothing Boston. I'd heard one Frank O'Hara poem, and I went to some weird poetry group in Harvard Yard where a kind of fat girl dressed in all black with a medallion said in this kind of ponderous way that her work was influenced by the New York rock poet Patti Smith. And I just—those words seen next to each other, I'd never heard of that but it sounded so perfect. I came here, purportedly to go to graduate school, which lasted for two months and the guy who taught the poetry workshop at Queens College mentioned Frank O'Hara and then James Schuyler and gave us a Schuyler poem. And again, I'd never seen anything like this, it was someplace between children's story and, you know, new wave cinema or something. I found it incomprehensibly exciting, you know? The professor then pointed out

that these people were "so-called" New York School poets, "denizens" of St. Mark's Church. I just went there very quickly, and slowly, after going through all the poetry world's circles, I wound up in a workshop with Maggie Dubris, David Wojnarowicz, and Richard Bandanza. Just a very motley crew of kids with long hair and beards and girls with braids and it was free and St. Mark's was kind of a drop-in center that—it was really a mess, it was so great. I mean, I have a very romantic feeling about New York from, like, about '74 to '77, which was before I came out, and so I was sort of like a straight girl rambling around New York trying to figure out the scene. You know, so the result was lots of sex with men and everybody and lots of books thrust at me—"Read this"—and, you know, and just not having a clue but it being totally interesting and great and confusing. St. Mark's was the only place that really seemed to have some kind of cohesive aesthetic and seemed to be connected to larger things. People in the workshop had magazines. There was a guy named Mike Sappol who had a magazine called *Personal Injury*.

DC: Oh, yeah.

EM: It was great. He turned me on to Kathy Acker and Ronald Firbank and—these workshops were incredibly combative, because often if the person who led the workshop was a little mild then the room would be pushing back and telling them what was much more important than what they were trying to get us to read. So Sappol had a total agenda, and he was pushing fiction—he hated poetry, which in the '70s was kind of outrageous. So he was talking about the *Black Tarantula*. *Personal Injury* was my first publication, not, you know, fucking *Kayak*.

DC: [Laughing] Wow, *Kayak*, yeah. I got about a million rejection letters from them when I was first sending my poems out.

EM: *Personal Injury* was very proto-punk.

DC: Was that before the fire at St. Mark's?

EM: Yeah. Yeah, yeah, and that's a really important thing, 'cause it was such a pigsty then. You know, we'd just all go in with our beers and our cigarettes and the readings by and large sucked. Anne Waldman was the director but she wasn't there. So she was basically [laughing] kind of feathering her career, by having all of these losers from all over the world come and read. That was the way we explained it to ourselves. We were just bored out of our minds by most of them. So it was just kind of a meeting place where we would just go and get drunk and watch *any* reading. And it was kind of like *our* church. The office was a mess, it was barely being run—but, you know, there was a mimeo machine upstairs. Jim Brodey was around, so he did—you know, he was running off books upstairs, so he published my first book.

When I went to Los Angeles in '82 and saw you guys and your building and everything, it was just . . . it seemed like a new, improved version of what we used to have. We loved our mess, but the fire was great, I remember loving the fire, being really happy and just being glad St. Mark's was gone. You know, it seemed fine, and sort of fitting—you know, because at that point in your life it's just great to see things go up in flames. That was a real divider in the generations, there were all those older people—Ron Padgett—they were all like, "Oh, I'm really sad." And Ted and . . . but I loved it, "Thank God that's over." For me the crowning moment was the fire benefit at CBGB's—when the

Poetry Project was still *not.* The benefit was Richard Hell and Elvis Costello and Andre Voznesensky. And I read in it and Kathy read in it, and it was a great honor to be a poet reading in it—it was just the dream of being a poet and to be there with all the rock people. Totally seventies. It was very glamorous and great. Lita Hornick was there with, like a gold ear. You know, she just—she used to wear this fucking gold . . . piece of gold in the shape of an ear over her ear.

DC: [Laughing] Yeah, I've seen pictures of her wearing that.

EM: It was insane.

DC: *She* was insane, I mean in a sort of charming way. Anyway, I never saw St. Mark's Church before the fire, but I definitely had the feeling that after the fire destroyed the old church interior, nothing was the same again. By the time I went to a reading at St. Mark's, the church was this big, empty, sterile white space.

EM: Yeah, horrible.

DC: It wasn't intimate or pleasurable to be in there, at least for a poetry reading. I just felt like, wow, this isn't what I thought it was going to be like at all.

EM: And it wasn't. I mean, even the big room—like, they used to have most of the readings in the big room before the fire—they had pews, which made the acoustics better, and it just meant that people could be, like, lying down, making out, handing drugs over—there was a whole kind of down and dirty scene. And it just was very—it was dark and funky and fun, and the other smaller room was a mess too. After that it was the reign of Ron and Maureen, and they raised so much money and they did all these nice, good things and . . . it just was a horror. You know, you couldn't smoke in the room anymore, and the lights were all bright, and it just had this horrible antiseptic feeling. And then there was the whole fetishization of who was running the Poetry Project after that. And then there was Bernadette Mayer who kind of held the fort in a drunken stolid way. Though of course I was totally in love with her. She just stayed and stayed and it became something else. I really arrived during the decline, and the decline was great.

DC: [Laughs] I definitely got the feeling that I had missed the great period of the Poetry Project. By the time I moved there, the poets I loved and associated with the scene like Ron Padgett and Ted Berrigan and Joe Brainard and others—it didn't feel like they were a central part of the activity anymore. They were like elder statesmen who would occasionally drop by or something. It wasn't like someone new like me could just hang out with the heroes, except for Joe Brainard who I loved and was a good friend. And I knew Kenward Elmslie, who was super kind to me. But I never even really got to know Ted or Ron or Alice Notley or Anne Waldman or Bernadette Mayer or most of poets I had worshipped from afar. I mean, with the exception of Alice, who was really cool, they all were quite unfriendly [laughing], if anything. It was like, "Oh, you're that kid who did *Little Caesar*? Nice to meet you, bye." I know I was just ridiculously romantic about the New York School, but at the time it was a big letdown.

[pause]

DC: So maybe we should talk more about the visual artists. For me, like I kind of said before, my entrance into the art world was completely due to Peter Schjeldahl. We were great friends, and he took me under his wing and took me to galleries and introduced me to artists and dealers, and he got me my first real gigs writing about art for *Art in America.* He really believed in the tradition of poets writing about art that extends back to O'Hara and Ashbery and Schuyler, and he was just incredibly generous, and I owe him a ton. But the art world in the early '80s was a very different animal than the art world of the '60s where the artists and poets were big buddies. In the '80s, if you were a writer, you were a means to draw attention to the artists' work, and really nothing more. So you served a purpose, and it felt kind of like a friendship, but when you stopped serving the artists' purpose, the friendships would evaporate.

EM: Peter was, like, pivotal for me too because he was a poet observer. He knew about poetry and he knew about art. I loved his work. The art world was salvation for a poet, a new idea. When I came to New York, it seemed like there were about three ideas or about four ideas about being a poet. You could be a drug addict and kill yourself, or you could be in a band, or you could be an art writer. It was like everybody was sort of waiting to see which one you were going to be. I felt very tugged back and forth between what seemed like an utterly poet world which was Ted and Alice [Notley] and Peter's other view of things. And Peter was very much, I think, pushing me towards being an art writer. I would be part of his inner party scene sometimes just for cocktails and sometimes for dinner. And going to bars with Peter and him introducing me to people and stuff. But that only went so far and I think in those days I was much more interested in being a famous poet, so why would I want to take on this journalist identity, right? That would just interfere with, you know . . . the arc of my fame and greatness, you know? And, you know, clearly, the artists were the stars that you weren't. But you know, as soon as I saw it in action—and after being in the poetry world for ten years, with that kind of self-enforced poverty and resentment and deliberate smallness—not the people I loved, but there was sort of a cap on things. I think you wound up, you sort of unwittingly land as a younger person in the bitterness of middle-aged people's careers. By the time you're in your twenties, by the time you get to New York, your heroes are in their thirties and forties and they've sort of found their shelf on the marketplace, and they're going to speak to you from there. There was just a lot of: no kid, you're not going to get what you want. My inclination was to buck that. It just seemed like the thing was to be nothing but a poet, if there is such a thing. And it seemed most punk, to just be minimal and not do anything else. Nonetheless, it was instantly nice to get paid as an art writer. Though it was only one hundred dollars, you got a check every time you wrote something. The relationship between money and writing was just, like, luscious, you know? And in New York, if you wrote about somebody, they would come to your readings. It had, I guess, a quid pro quo feeling, but on the other hand it seemed like however you did it, you brought those people to your work. Which hopefully you also liked. And they would have you write catalog essays or something.

DC: Yeah, the catalog essays were a nice little source of money [laughing]. I'd never gotten paid that well before by any stretch, so those gigs were really seductive. One thing that's interesting to me is your and my slightly different paths through the art world. I started writing for *Art in America*, but then I moved over to *Artforum* and have written primarily for them ever since. You stuck with *Art in America*, right? And those two magazines have very different positions in the art world. *Art in America* is more . . . I don't know, traditionalist? It's always prioritized painting, for instance, even in times when painting wasn't the dominant practice. *Artforum* has been more geared toward conceptual and postconceptual art and letting the new and the trendy dictate its focus. It isn't true these days, but, in the late '80s, there was a real degree of politics involved in writing for *Artforum*. If you wrote a bad review of some art show, there'd be editorial meetings to decide if it was okay to trash a particular artist and possibly alienate the gallery where the show had been held.

EM: *Ugh.*

DC: I wrote a really bad review of this absolutely gruesome Robert Morris show that everyone in the art world was rolling their eyes about, but at *Artforum* I was brought before the editors for literally three different meetings where the possible damage of publishing the review was debated, and they finally said no, we can't risk running the review. It was surreal.

EM: Wow.

DC: It was that kind of stuff that just started to sour me on the New York art world, you know? Even though there were great exceptions. There was Artists Space where all the most radical and/or politically engaged artists exhibited and performed, both individuals and collectives like Gran Fury and bands like Swans and Sonic Youth. There was Bill Arning's White Columns, a really noble and groundbreaking alternative space. And the New Museum. And some great rebel galleries like Pat Hearn and Colin de Land's American Fine Arts and Simon Watson's old space on the Bowery and others. And, most remarkable to me, was and is the gallery Feature run by Hudson. Feature was the great shining light in the art world back then and it still is the brilliant exception to the rule. Hudson's vision as a dealer/curator puts him among the greatest artists of downtown New York. But those places were oases and oddities by default. Most of the art world was pretty soul destroying, to me anyway.

EM: I felt like I inadvertently created WAC. Remember that women's political group. WAC was the name of it, it was a big kind of women's action. . . .

DC: Yeah, yeah.

EM: Well, because I wrote a bad review of Deborah Kass. And I hadn't meant to when I saw the show, I was like, oh God, I don't really like this. And I remember Betsy Baker asking me if I felt I could write a bad review of a friend, and I took it as a challenge. What an idiot, right. Not for writing negatively, but not even understanding the question. I mean, it was a moderately bad review—but my encounter with her was hideous. "Do you realize this is *my career*?" I asked her, well, isn't your work your career? After that she decided feminist politics was. She started WAC. And it helped her career.

DC: What really cemented my decision to get out of the New York art world, as a critic, was when I wanted to review what turned out to be Jean-Michael Basquiat's last show for *Artforum*. First, it was a struggle to get them to agree. They didn't think he was worth covering at that point because

he was unfashionable. Then, it was a great show, his best in a couple of years, so I wrote a real rave, and they ran it, but they gave me incredible grief about it. They couldn't even imagine that a Basquiat show could be good because he was so over and considered such a has-been. I remember that was the point where I thought, this just totally sucks, and I don't want to be complicit in this game anymore.

EM: I mean, this is a book documenting a moment that definitely did exist, but there continues to be this thing . . . this sort of dream of this ideal space or time or place that drove people to come and be part of it. But the sense of not being there—which everyone also has—seems important to me because it's not nostalgic. It's something else. I'll talk to younger people who always feel like they came just after something and that feeling is a central piece of anyone's present-day art world—like, oops, missed it again. But you keep shooting. It's like a movie everybody's shooting inside of their heads, that you get glimpses of sometimes in reality, you know?

DC: Yeah, totally. I did feel disappointed that the real downtown New York wasn't exactly what I'd foreseen and dreamed, but that dream changed my whole life and that's what really matters. And it was an awesome and amazing scene even by the time I moved there, just kind of reconfigured from my mental image. And I really think that if AIDS hadn't happened, Downtown probably would have continued to be an amazingly fertile place that was continually evolving. I know that's naïve because the gentrification of the East Village and Lower East Side and SoHo was probably the real culprit and killer. But for me, it's impossible to think of that time in New York without the pall of the AIDS crisis, and about all my dead friends, and the incredible artists who died so fucking young. It was a hugely formative time for the artists of my generation who lived there, but it's also like remembering a war that I was really lucky to survive.

EM: And we almost can't see it from here, you know? I remember reading about some moment in the heyday of mosaic making in Venice that was entirely interrupted because of the plague. It seemed like the same kind of intervention. Blinking or falling off the cliff altogether. I think of David Wojnarowicz's painting of the buffalo being driven right over the edge.

DC: Yeah, I mean, for me and for my work, it had a real, specific effect. When I first moved there it was the beginning of the gay literary movement, and it was thrilling if tricky to be a part of that. But then AIDS snowballed, and it inspired the gay activist movement, which was great but had a real hysterical, reactionary aspect to it as well. Writing the kind of politically incorrect, confrontational novels I do, I became a bad guy and pariah to a lot of gays at that time, and I'm still paying that monster image I was tagged with back then. I was just a writer trying to do great work in my area of interest in a long-standing tradition running back through Burroughs and Genet and Sade and Rimbaud and others. If AIDS hadn't happened, my whole trajectory as a writer would have been really different on so many levels, you know?

EM: Uh huh. Yes.

DC: Your writing pushes boundaries and is confrontational in a different way than mine, so I imagine your experience as a writer during the early days of the AIDS crisis was very different.

EM: I think of Act Up, which I was never—[laughing] I just couldn't do, every time I went to those meetings, I'd just be overwhelmed by the egos. Why would I want to listen to a speech by her or him. Get me out of here. Any story about a writer's life is full of so many rifts with groups that spinned you out and the writer went elsewhere. Remember, we all started having fights around '90, '91. All sorts of people didn't speak to each other for about ten years. A lot of it was about AIDS—and careers. No one could deal—or fight, or be sad as a group. And that's just ending now, it seems to me.

You know, David Trinidad and I just started speaking again about five years ago, but with other people we're only just starting to get back in touch now. I think it's because we need to claim our history in some way. The up side of these fights for me was that I felt compelled to find women as a group for the first time, you know? Not just to be passing through the Duchess or WOW but finding a bunch for myself. I mean as the main group. One thing led to another and then it was the next great moment in New York—which continues now in some way. Again, mostly in the art world, where people like Laurie Weeks and Nicole Eisenman, Zoe Leonard, and Amy Steiner . . . Nan Goldin was sort of on the fringes or maybe the backdrop of that, the effect of her work . . . her girlfriend Siobhan Liddel was part of that scene. There was this gallery everyone started to show at, Trial Balloon. That was like the first half of the nineties. And by now it's like Le Tigre and a whole new entire girl/boy world.

I did *The New Fuck You* with Liz [Kotz] in order to recast what it meant to be a lesbian in the art world. And it was just a much decentered way of thinking about being a lesbian. What *was* lesbian? It wasn't a place but a whole world of connections. Suddenly there was a new license to be punk and kind of tranny that was written into a lesbian aesthetic. And then boom, Michelle Tea and Sister Spit, that whole crew appeared ten years ago, and now they are utterly prominent. Michelle is huge. And everyone I met then, Ali Liebegott and Anna Joy.

DC: Yeah, I was really empowered by the rise of the queer punk movement too, and by all the related zines and writers and bands. It really woke me up and reconnected me to the lesbian and gay male counterculture. It only really lasted a few years, but it was the first really positive thing to happen in the gay world in a long time, to me anyway. Like you edited *The New Fuck You* anthology, I did that kind of parallel *Discontents: New Queer Writers* anthology, and it was just such a vital, transcontinental movement. It didn't just happen in New York like so many movements do. It was spread all across the country, and New York was just one of its outposts.

EM: The gay shame moment.

DC: Yeah, it was. It was definitely a reaction against the political correctness of the gay activist movement. I think a lot of us had been feeling like the activists had their hearts in the right place, but what they were championing was basically antifun and anti-aesthetics and as rigid in its doctrine as ultraconservative creeps on the far Right. It identified itself as an anarchist movement but it was about deciding what was right and wrong and making rules. Whereas *Queer Punk* was anarchistic to its core. It helped spawn a new kind of cultural radicalism that was really pansexual.

EM: Stupidity recollected in brilliance or something. Like all our friends.

DC: I think with *Queer Punk* and the High Risk moment, maybe you and I were able to find a new kind of context or community, and it's interesting that you and I are so involved with younger writers and artists. I just feel much more comradeship with them for some reason, and I really enjoy being in the position to give them support and use whatever clout I have to help them get published and known. You feel similarly, don't you?

EM: Part of finding them is reinventing yourself. You're always losing the old scenes but new people keep arriving and it's great to put people in touch with who should know about them. Otherwise it's only your own stuff. You're in some incredible constellation for a while, so great, so exciting, what you've always wanted and then it starts to blow up. I mean, where I feel fortunate—you too, I think—is to be able to fall in with some other people. And they're always young. I've never found one that's [laughing] quite my own generation again. That's what I really am kind of hoping for at this time, because if you realize you're, like, their Burroughs, then I want to drag a few more other older people in there with me. Because we miss something by not having *this* conversation. Which is about time, you know.

DC: Yeah, well, I think that is happening—I mean, a number of our peers are finally beginning to get the respect they've always deserved. I mean Dodie Bellamy is a perfect example. And as I said before, the era when downtown New York was the font and energy source of most of what was interesting in the arts has kind of passed. If you think about the most vital artists working right now, they're scattered all over the place. That's why I guess it's a good time for this book to reassess and consolidate and celebrate Downtown, because the time when it was so singular and dominant is over, at least for the moment.

But in a lot of ways, what happened there is what gave birth to what's happening now all over. I mean both the fantasy version of Downtown that people living outside New York had, and the actual artists and their work and the personal relationships that were formed there. You and I became friends there, and I know you've always been an inspiration and source of strength for me, and we're not dissimilar figures in the sense that we're both particularly popular with younger people and artists, and are seen as writers and figures who have had a big influence on the newer generations of radical artists. So just on that personal level, our lives in the Downtown scene continue to have a real impact in some way.

EM: Yeah.

DC: It's interesting that it wound up that way, you know? [Laughs]

EM: What's that?

DC: Well, maybe it's not interesting, but I feel unbelievably lucky to have been a little part of Downtown if for no other reason than the fact that it created our particular friendship, which impacted my work and life in a big way.

EM: Well, you know, I think, even when we weren't—I've always stayed aware of what you were up to even when we lost touch. I read your work. And it always made me feel not alone. Because we came up together. To see you figuring out your next move.

DC: Yeah. Yeah. I remember when you were running for president—we weren't talking during that period, but I was like, yeah, go for it, Eileen. I could imagine all the jealousy and eye rolling and resentment that must have caused among other writers. It was so ambitious of you, and it called into question how writers are supposed to conduct themselves—you know, sit quietly at your computer and then go out in the world and kiss as many asses as you can. My ambitions play themselves out in different ways, but your boldness was something I completely related to. You know, why shouldn't writers seek the same kind of big effect that other artists seek.

EM: I think it would make sense to you, because it's kind of like your strategy in this way. To do it. A little punk grandiosity.

DC: Well, we both took full advantage of the headiness of the East Village culture, doing performance work, moving in the visual art and rock scenes, and taking ideas from our experiences there into our writing and our lives as writers.

EM: That's true. But really I'm just blowing up. Repeatedly. What I've found surprising about having a career is that so often when I've done something good, it's because I've ran with what came to me. Not the obvious things. I think I'm going to get A and instead I get B. And so, it's sort of like—to not allow B be B, but let B become A again, you know, and think, well fuck it, then I'll go there. I keep shifting my weight.

DC: Yeah, exactly.

EM: There are so many struggles and so many obstacles and also, like, so many solutions. And mostly, it seems you've got to keep being kind of playful about what a poet is, what a writer is, what a culture is, what . . . what ambition is. You know?

DC: Yeah, you just have to be totally awake and engaged and trust your instincts, and living in New York made that not only possible but kind of unavoidable.

EM: Right. It's sort of like, when people talk about, "Oh, he's in his blah period" or "She was in her this period" to not—to not attach yourself to one period or another. . . .

DC: Yeah, yeah, absolutely. There's no value to doing that to yourself at all.

ABOUT THE CONTRIBUTORS

Kathy Acker (1948–1997) was a novelist and performance artist whose books include *Pussy, King of the Pirates*; *Empire of the Senseless*; *Blood and Guts in High School*; *My Mother, Demonology*; and *Great Expectations*. (See also the Black Tarantula below.)

Roberta Allen's books include *The Dreaming Girl*, a novel; *Certain People*, stories; *The Traveling Woman*, stories; *The Daughter*, a novella-in-stories; and *Amazon Dream*, a memoir. She is also a visual artist who has exhibited worldwide.

Holly Anderson is the author of *Lily Lou* and *Sheherezade.* Her lyrics have been recorded by Mission of Burma, Consonant, Chris Brokaw, Rhys Chatham, and Lisa B. Burns.

Laurie Anderson is a performance artist, writer, director, visual artist, and vocalist best known for her multimedia presentations and innovative use of technology. Anderson was the first artist-in-residence of NASA. Her current solo performance, *The End of the Moon,* toured the United States and Europe into 2005.

Penny Arcade debuted at seventeen with John Vaccaro's Playhouse of the Ridiculous. At eighteen she became a teenage superstar for Andy Warhol's Factory and was featured in the Paul Morrissey/Warhol film *Women in Revolt.* She has collaborated with Jack Smith, Jackie Curtis, Charles Ludlam, H. M. Koutoukas, and Tom O'Horgan, among others. Her *BITCH!DYKE!FAGHAG!WHORE!* toured the world twice between 1990 and 1995. In 1999 she spearheaded the award-winning Lower East Side Biography Project, "Stemming the Tide of Cultural Amnesia." In 1989 she formed the archive of Jack Smith and in 1997, that of East Village photographer Sheyla Baykal.

Richard Armijo works as an itinerant teacher in New York City and Brooklyn. For the last decade he has continued to create and exhibit his paintings. He has writing posted on Michael Rosenthal's *legible* website.

Bruce Benderson is the author of *Pretending to Say No, User,* and *Toward the New Degeneracy.* His other works include *Sexe et Solitude, The Worst Place in New York,* and *James Bidgood.* He is a prolific translator, having rendered into English works by Robbe-Grillet, Pierre Guyotat, Virginie Despentes, and Nelly Arcan, among others. His most recent book, *The Romanian,* was awarded the Prix de Flore in France.

Kathy Acker was the **Black Tarantula** from 1973 to 1974, while living mostly in San Francisco and New York. Her work was originally published under that name, and she appeared as the Black Tarantula at public events and readings. (See also Kathy Acker above.)

Max Blagg has published three books of poetry, most recently *Pink Instrument.* His fourth book is the forthcoming *What Love Sees in the Distance.* He has performed widely in and out of New York City, is the coeditor of the art/lit magazine *Bald Ego,* and is cohost of the show *Bald Ego Online* on WPS1.org Art Radio.

Lisa Blaushild lives in New York City and writes fiction, as well as scripts for theater and film. She has just completed a novel, *Wall of Silence.*

Eric Bogosian writes plays, solos, and books. Every now and then he acts in something. His best-known plays (both of which were made into films) are *Talk Radio* (in which he starred and for which he received the Berlin Film Fest "Silver Bear") and *subUrbia*. Simon & Schuster published his second novel, *Wasted Beauty,* in 2005.

Michael Carter is the cofounder and publisher of *Redtape* and has produced hundreds of art events, readings, musical performances, and video presentations, and has staged happenings as his alter ego, "Vindaloo," at various New York clubs and cafes. He is the author of a book of poems, *Broken Noses and Metempsychoses,* and is at work on a second book of poetry, "Millennial Brushfires," and two novels, "Temporary Angels" and "Without a Net."

Peter Cherches is the author of the short fiction collections *Condensed Book* and *Between a Dream and a Cup of Coffee*. Throughout the 1980s he was active on the Downtown performance scene, both solo and in collaboration with musicians Elliott Sharp and Lee Feldman.

Dennis Cooper is the author of "The George Miles Cycle," an interconnected sequence of five novels that includes *Closer*, *Frisk*, *Try*, *Guide*, and *Period*. His most recent novels are *My Loose Thread, The Sluts,* and *God Jr.* He is a contributing editor of *Artforum* and editor-in-chief of Little House on the Bowery, a line of books by new North American fiction writers published under the auspices of Akashic Books.

Susan Daitch is the author of two novels, *L.C.* and *The Colorist*, and a collection of short stories, *Storytown*.

Steve Dalachinsky's recent books include *Trial and Error in Paris* and *Trust Fund Babies*. His CDs include *Incomplete Directions*, *Wake Up Lady Your Kid's on Fire*, and *I Thought It Was the End of the World and Then the End of the World Happened Again*.

Constance DeJong, an artist and writer, has extended her writing to a variety of forms, including books, performances, audio installations, video, and talking objects. Her first novel, *Modern Love*, was published as a serial, a series of live performances, and a one-hour radio work with original music by Philip Glass. DeJong wrote the libretto for Glass's opera *Satyagraha*. Her permanent outdoor audio installations are located in Beacon (NY), Seattle, and London. She is writing the script for *Super Vision*, a theater work of the Builder's Association that will tour in 2005–2006. *Origins Unstable*, a new novel, will be published in 2006.

Tim Dlugos was the author of several volumes of poetry. In 1996, David Trinidad edited the posthumous collection, *Powerless: Selected Poems, 1973–1990*. Dlugos died of AIDS in 1990.

Maggie Dubris is the author of *WillieWorld*, *Weep Not, My Wanton* and *Skels*. She is presently working on a novel called "Collide-O-Scope." Her website is www.maggiedubris.com.

Denise Duhamel's most recent books are *Two and Two* and *Queen for a Day: Selected and New Poems*. She has collaborated with Maureen Seaton on three volumes: *Little Novels, Oyl,* and *Exquisite Politics*. Duhamel teaches at Florida International University in Miami.

Novelist, short story writer, and essayist **Janice Eidus** is the author of four highly acclaimed books, the story collections *The Celibacy Club* and *Vito Loves Geraldine* and the novels *Urban Bliss* and *Faithful Rebecca*. She is coeditor of *It's Only Rock and Roll: An Anthology of Rock and Roll Short Stories*. Her new novel, *The War of the Rosens*, is forthcoming.

Barbara Ess began making and showing short 8-millimeter films in and around London and also performed with the Scratch Orchestra. When she returned to New York City in 1978 she became involved in the music scene and played with the bands Daily Life, the Static, and Y Pants. From 1978 to 1987 she was the editor and publisher of *Just Another Asshole #1–7*. Since 1986 her large-scale pinhole photographs and a series of videos have been exhibited widely in the United States and Europe and a monograph of this work, *I Am Not This Body*, was published by Aperture in 2001. Recently she has been collaborating with filmmaker Peggy Ahwesh on an audio project, *Radio/Guitar* (CD, Ecstatic Peace, 2001), and a vinyl release, *Thrum* (Table of the Elements, 2004). She teaches photography at Bard College.

Lisa B. Falour was a publisher, writer, artist, filmmaker, model, actress, record producer, journalist, licensed securities dealer, paralegal, legal stenographer, research assistant, radio DJ, dominatrix, call girl, bondage model, etc. She relocated to Paris, France, in 1994, where she devotes herself almost entirely to her writing.

John Farris is a poet and novelist living in New York City. He is the author of *It's Not about Time: Poems by James Farris*.

Jim Feast helped edit two of the Unbearables anthologies and has cowritten two health books. He acted as a low priest at the Unbearables' notorious No Bar initiation ceremony.

Karen Finley has written five books and has created plays, performances, installations, musical recordings, and independent videos. She performs and exhibits her work worldwide. Finley is currently a visiting professor in art and public policy at the Tisch School for the Arts at New York University.

Mary Gaitskill is the author of the novel *Two Girls, Fat and Thin* and *Veronica*, a 2005 National Book Award finalist, as well as the story collections *Bad Behavior* and *Because They Wanted To*, which was nominated for the PEN/Faulkner Award in 1998. Her story "Secretary" was the basis for the feature film of the same name. She has taught creative writing at the University of California, the University of Houston, New York University, Brown, and Syracuse.

The editor-publisher of *Smoke Signals*, **Mike Golden**'s "Unbearable Beatniks of Light Get Real" coined the moniker and inspired the formation of the infamous Downtown guerilla writers' and artists' collective, the Unbearables. His book *The Buddhist Third Class Junkmail Oracle,* which collects and studies the art and poetry of d. a. levy, is now being developed as a feature film.

Brad Gooch is the author of *God Talk: Travels in Spiritual America*; *City Poet: The Life and Times of Frank O'Hara*; *The Daily News* (poems); *Jailbait and Other Stories*; three novels—*Scary Kisses, The Golden Age of Promiscuity,* and *Zombie00*; and the books *Finding the Boyfriend Within* and *Dating the*

Greek Gods. He is Professor of English at William Paterson University of New Jersey and is currently writing a literary biography of Flannery O'Connor.

Writer, actor, and performer **Spalding Gray** (1941-2004) is the author of *Sex and Death to the Age Fourteen*; *Monster in a Box*; *It's a Slippery Slope*; *Gray's Anatomy*; and *Morning, Noon, and Night*, among other works. His appearance in *The Killing Fields* was the inspiration for his *Swimming to Cambodia*, which was also filmed by Jonathan Demme.

Richard Hell's albums include *Blank Generation*, *Destiny Street*, and *Time*. His books include the novels *Go Now* and *Godlike* and the collection of "essays poems notebooks lyrics pictures fiction" *Hot and Cold*. He writes a movie column for *Black Book* magazine.

Bob Holman's eighth book, *A Couple of Ways of Doing Something*, a collaboration with Chuck Close, was published in 2003, as was his selected poems, *The Collect Call of the Wild*. He is the editor of three anthologies, including *Aloud! Voices from the Nuyorican Poets Café,* and has released the CD *In With the Out Crowd*. He produced *Words in Your Face* and the five-part series *The United States of Poetry* for PBS, was part of MTV's *Spoken Word Unplugged,* and participated in *Def Poetry Jam* on HBO. He is chief curator of the People's Poetry Gathering, poetry guide at About.com, and proprietor of the Bowery Poetry Club (bowerypoetry.com). He is visiting professor of writing at Columbia University.

Gary Indiana is the author of six novels and five books of nonfiction and is a regular contributor to the *Los Angeles Times Book Review*, *Film Comment*, *Bookforum*, *Purple Journal*, and the *London Review of Books*. His latest book is *Schwarzenegger Syndrome*.

Before trading a life of bohemian squalor in the United States for an equally squalid life in Berlin, **Darius James** was a visible part of the most brilliant collection of alcoholics and dope fiends one could ever hope to encounter in mid-1980s New York. In addition to publishing *Negrophobia*, *That's Blaxploitation*, *Voodoo Stew I & II*, and *Froggie Chocolate's Christmas Eve*, he has also created work for gallery exhibition and the stage. "On Bohomelessness: A Convoluted Guide to the Otherside" was the first piece he wrote for the *Village Voice*.

Tama Janowitz is the author of *Slaves of New York*, *A Cannibal in Manhattan*, *American Dad*, *The Male Cross-Dressers Support Group*, and *By the Shores of Gichee Gumee*.

Passing out copies of chapbooks and zines from his ubiquitous shopping bag, **Ron Kolm** became known as "The Fuller-Brush Man of the Lower East Side." The thirty-five to forty cartons of first editions, flyers, runs of magazines, and manuscripts Ron squirreled away during three decades working in independent downtown bookstores now reside in the Fales collection in the New York University library. Ron is one of the founding fathers of the Unbearables.

Richard Kostelanetz was born in New York City in 1940. He has contributed poems, stories, articles, reviews, and experimental prose to hundreds of magazines. He has written more than fifty books of criticism, cultural history, and creative work, in addition to editing over three dozen anthologies of art and exposition. His most recent books include *SoHo: The Rise and Fall of an Artist's Colony, Three Canadian Geniuses, More Wordworks,* and second editions of *A Dictionary of the Avant-Gardes* and *Conversing with Cage.* Long active in alternative literary publishing, he cofounded Assembling Press in 1970 and alone founded Future Press in 1977 and Archae Editions in 1978.

Tuli Kupferberg is a Greenwich Village publisher, poet, and antiwar activist who got his start with the magazine *Birth* in 1958. In 1964 Kupferberg began performing and recording with Ed Sanders and Ken Weaver in the Fugs. Kupferberg's antiwar masterpiece was *1001 Way to Beat the Draft*, written in collaboration with Robert Bashlow. Tuli and Lannes Kenfield formed the Revolting Theatre in the 1970s. The Fugs were reconstituted in 1985 and continue to perform. Tuli also started cartooning in the 1980s and his latest collection of cartoons is *Teach Yourself Fucking*.

Lucy R. Lippard is a cultural critic, feminist, art critic, and political activist. She is author or editor of twenty books, most recently *On the Beaten Track: Tourism, Art, and Place.*

Tsaurah Litzky is author of the collection *Baby on the Water* as well as five earlier poetry books and a novella, *The Motion of the Ocean*. She teaches erotic writing at the New School University.

Judy Lopatin was born in Detroit and moved to New York City in 1976, in part to meet Lou Reed (which, at CBGB's, she did). "Modern Romances" is from her eponymous collection. Her stories have also appeared in numerous literary magazines.

Lydia Lunch continues her assault against complacency utilizing a wide variety of mediums ranging from the spoken and written word to music, photography, and installation. For further information consult www.lydia-lunch.org.

Joe Maynard came to New York from Tennessee to go to art school. He showed his "avant garde" art in several venues in New York and Atlanta in the 1980s. He has published fiction in dozens of zines and other periodicals and he had a column in *The Aquarian*. He now heads a country band called the Millerite Redeemers.

Patrick McGrath is the author of two story collections and six novels, including *Asylum* and *Port Mungo*. His adaptation of his novel *Spider*, directed by David Cronenberg, was produced in 2002.

Sharon Mesmer is the author of the fiction collection *The Empty Quarter* and the poetry collection *Half Angel, Half Lunch*. Her forthcoming books are *In Ordinary Time* and *Ma Vie à Yonago*. She teaches literature and writing at the New School in Manhattan and is English-language editor of *American Book Jam*, a Japanese literary magazine. She also writes a seasonal column for the French magazine *Purple Journal*.

Ursule Molinaro authored more than a dozen novels, two dozen one-act plays, three volumes of nonfiction, and over one hundred short stories. She was a self-trained artist and a founding editor of the *Chelsea Review*. She died in New York City on July 12, 2000.

As retold in "On the Loose," **Thurston Moore** moved to New York City at eighteen in 1977. He is a founder of Sonic Youth, active since 1981. Since 1983 he has involved himself with fanzine and journal publishing (*KILLER*, *Sonic Death*, *Ecstatic Peace Poetry Journal*), and archive/documentation (Ecstatic Peace records/tapes/CDs). His publications include *iron crosses and insect paranoia—poemz I wrote in a bethel, connecticut bedroom in the early/mid-'70s as an acid/glam raunchy rock creem/circus teenage punk*; *Alabama Wildman*; *WHAT I LIKE ABOUT FEMINISM*; *fuck a hippie, but be a punk*; and *total poon*.

Cookie Mueller was born in 1949 in Baltimore, Maryland. A biker chick in her youth and a teen mother, she starred in John Waters's Baltimore classics *Pink Flamingos* and *Female Trouble*. Mueller wrote the health column "Ask Dr. Mueller" for the *East Village Eye* and later served as art critic for *Details* magazine. Her writing includes the novella *Fan Mail, Frank Letters, and Crank Calls* and several collections: *Garden of Ashes*, *Walking through Clear Water in a Pool Painted Black,* and *Ask Dr. Mueller: The Writings of Cookie Mueller* (High Risk Books, 1997). She died of AIDS-related causes in 1989 at the age of forty.

Eileen Myles has written thousands of poems since she moved to New York in 1974. Her last books were *Skies, on my way* (poetry), and *Cool for You* (a novel). She teaches at the University of California, San Diego, and is working on a new novel about the hell of becoming a female poet, called *The Inferno*.

Jose Padua's poetry and fiction have appeared in *Bomb, Salon.com, Exquisite Corpse, Mondo Barbie, Another Chicago Magazine, Unbearables, Crimes of the Beats,* and many other places. He has written nonfiction for *New York Press,* *Washington City Paper*, and the *New York Times*. He was coeditor of *Big Cigars* magazine.

Nuyorican poet and playwright **Pedro Pietri**'s publications include *Illusions of a Revolving Door: Plays, The Masses Are Asses, Traffic Violations, Lost in the Museum of Natural History, Invisible Poetry,* and *Puerto Rican Obituary.* He died on March 3, 2004.

Miguel Piñero was a playwright, actor, and cofounder of the Nuyorican Poets Cafe. In 1974 his play *Short Eyes* was nominated for six Tony Awards and won the New York Drama Critics Circle Award and two Obie Awards. His life was portrayed in the film *Piñero,* directed by Leon Ichaso and starring Benjamin Bratt. He died in 1998 at the age of forty-two in New York City. As per his request in "A Lower East Side Poem," his ashes were scattered across the Lower East Side of Manhattan.

Deborah Pintonelli is the author of the collections *Meat and Memory* and *Ego Monkey,* the novel *Lies,* and a forthcoming novel titled *Robin Bell*. She has been an editor of *B City, Letter eX,* and *Ikon*.

bart plantenga is an Amsterdam-based radiomaker, sound journalist, and writer of speculative satires and metafictions: *Wiggling Wishbone: Stories of Pata-Sexual Speculation, Spermatagonia: The Isle of Man*, and the anarcho-mystical novel, *Beer Mystic*. His recent book, *Yodel-Ay-Ee-Oooo: The Secret History of Yodeling around the World,* is the first book ever to deal with this esoteric vocalization as global phenomenon.

Known primarily as a painter and photographer, **Richard Prince** edited the Tanam Press anthology *Wild History* and is the author of a collection of short stories, *Why I Go to the Movies Alone*.

Michael Randall is a guitar player, artist, writer, and director. He was coeditor of the East Village literary magazine *Big Cigars* from 1986 to 1990. He is the author of two chapbooks of poetry (*Pork and Other Poems* and *Twenty Years of Drinking*) and one of short stories (*Getting It Wrong*). He wrote and directed the semilegendary B movie *GIRLQUAKE!* His paintings have been exhibited in solo and group shows in New York and California.

Jill S. Rapaport is a writer of nonfiction and fiction prose, as well as plays, essays, poems, and songs. Her work has been published in numerous literary magazines and several anthologies and she has read and had her plays performed in venues all over New York and in other cities.

David Rattray was a poet, translator, and scholar. Living in Paris during the 1950s, Rattray retraced the steps of Antonin Artaud and became one of Artaud's first and best American translators. He went on to translate Friedrich Holderlin, Rene Crevel, and the In Nomine music of John Bull, becoming a concert-level pianist so he could better understand the logic of baroque. Chris Kraus put together and published *How I Became One of the Invisible* just before David Rattray's sudden death in 1993.

James Romberger and **Marguerite Van Cook** have been collaborating on life, comics, and art since they met each other on the Lower East Side of Manhattan in the early 1980s. Cofounders of the noted installation gallery Ground Zero, they also produced a comic strip of the same name. They collaborated with the late David Wojnarowicz on the acclaimed *Seven Miles a Second*.

Joel Rose is the author of the novels *Kill the Poor, Kill Kill Faster Faster* and *The Blackest Bird,* as well as the "urban historical" *New York Sawed in Half*. He was coeditor of *Between C & D* with Catherine Texier.

Ann Rower wrote *If You're a Girl*, a collection of stories, and two novels, *Armed Response* and *Lee and Elaine*.

Thaddeus Rutkowski is the author of *Roughhouse* and the novel *Tetched*.

Among recent books of **Edward Sanders**'s are *America: A History in Verse, Vol. 3* and *Tales of Beatnik Glory*. His most recent CD is *Thirsting for Peace*, which features the microtonal cantata of the same name.

Tom Savage has written eight published books of poetry, including, most recently *Bamiyan Poems*, *Brain Surgery Poems*, and *Political Conditions/ Physical States*.

Peter Schjeldahl is the *New Yorker*'s art critic.

Sarah Schulman is the author of nine novels: "The Child" (forthcoming), *Shimmer, Rat Bohemia*, *Empathy, People in Trouble, After Delores, Girls, Visions and Everything*, and *The Sophie Horowitz Story*, as well as "The Mere Future," which remains unpublished. Her nonfiction books include *My American History: Lesbian and Gay Life during the Reagan/Bush Years* and *Stagestruck: Theater,*

AIDS, and the Marketing of Gay America. Her recent play productions are *Manic Flight Reaction*, *Carson McCullers*, and *The Burning Deck*. She is codirector, with Jim Hubbard, of the Act Up Oral History Project (www.actuporalhistory.org).

Hal Sirowitz, the former poet laureate of Queens, has since moved to Brooklyn. He's the author of four books of poems, including *Father Said* and *Mother Said*, which has been translated into twelve languages.

Patti Smith was one of the first visionary artists of the 1970s—known for the merging of poetry and rock. She and her band released eight studio albums on Arista Records between 1975 and 2002. In 2002, *Land*, a compilation package of *Horses*, *Radio Ethiopia*, *Easter*, *Wave*, *Dream of Life*, *Gone Again*, *Peace and Noise*, and *Gung Ho,* featured album cuts as well as rare studio and live recordings. Since then, she has released the album *trampin'* and produced *Strange Messenger*, an exhibit containing drawings, silk screens, and photographs from 1967 to 2002. Her published books include *Babel*, *Early Work*, *The Coral Sea*, *Complete,* and *The Long Road*.

Sparrow is the author of two books, *Republican Like Me* and *Yes, You ARE a Revolutionary!* He has run for president four times.

Theresa Stern is credited as the author of a book of poems, *Wanna Go Out?*—a collaboration between Richard Hell and Tom Verlaine. (The volume's frontispiece headshot of the author was printed from superimposed negatives of Hell and Verlaine in identical wig and makeup.) By the time the pamphlet appeared, the pair had started playing music together as the Neon Boys, and within a year they'd be the leaders of the first new-era band, Television, to play at CBGB's. It was in Theresa's book that the phrase "blank generation" first appeared in print.

Catherine Texier is the author of four novels, *Chloé l'Atlantique*, *Panic Blood*, *Love Me Tender*, and *Victorine*, and a memoir, *Breakup*. She was coeditor of the literary magazine *Between C & D*.

Lynne Tillman's novels are *Haunted Houses*, *Cast in Doubt*, *Motion Sickness*, and *No Lease on Life*. Her story collections are *The Madame Realism Complex*, *Absence Makes the Heart*, and, most recently, *This Is Not It*. Her nonfiction books are *Bookstore: The Life and Times of Jeanette Watson and Books & Co.*; *The Broad Picture*, an essay collection; and *The Velvet Years: Warhol's Factory, 1965–67*, with photographs by Stephen Shore. Her fifth novel, *American Genius, A Comedy,* was published by Soft Skull.

Susie Timmons was a poet in New York from 1975 to 1991. The city chewed her up and spit her out, and it felt great.

Mike Topp is the author of *I Used to Be Ashamed of My Striped Face*, *Happy Ending*, and *Where We Found You.*

David Trinidad's books include *Phoebe 2002: An Essay in Verse* and *Plasticville*. He teaches poetry at Columbia College in Chicago, where he also directs the graduate poetry program and coedits the journal *Court Green*.

Anne Turyn worked at Hallwalls, where she started *Top Stories,* which was published for thirteen years. She lives in New York, is a photographer, and teaches photography.

Carl Watson has published books and chapbooks of poetry and fiction, including *Anarcadium Pan*, *bricolage ex machina*, *Beneath the Empire of the Birds*, and *hotels des actes irrevocable*.

Bruce Weber is the author of four published books of poetry, most recently *The First Time I Had Sex with T. S. Eliot*. He performs regularly in the New York area with his group, the No Chance Ensemble. He is the organizer of the Unorganicized Sunday Reading at ABC No Rio, the editor of the broadside *Stained Sheets*, and the producer of the Alternative New Year's Day Spoken Word/Performance Extravaganza.

Bob Witz is a visual artist who has exhibited widely. He is the editor and publisher of *Appearances* magazine and has published work in *Public Illumination Magazine* and various Unbearables anthologies.

An important figure in New York's East Village art scene of the 1980s, David Wojnarowicz is known for several volumes of fiction and memoir, and for his artwork in various media, including painting, photography, installation, sculpture, film and performance. His most celebrated collection of writing, *Close to the Knives: A Memoir of Disintegration,* was recently translated into French. Wojnarowicz died of complications due to AIDS in 1992.

Emily XYZ is a writer, performer, and vocalist best known for her rhythmic poems for two voices. As part of the seminal spoken-word groups the Nuyorican Poets Cafe Live! and Real Live Poetry, and on their own, XYZ and her longtime partner, Myers Bartlett, have appeared across the United States and in Canada, Germany, and Australia. Her two-voice works are collected in *The Emily XYZ Songbook*, which includes an audio CD of studio and live recordings.

New York–based filmmaker and author Nick Zedd coined the term "Cinema of Transgression" in 1985 to describe a loose-knit group of like-minded artists, utilizing shock value and humor in their works. Among his directorial works are the motion pictures *Police State*, *War Is Menstrual Envy*, *Ecstasy in Entropy*, *Lord of the Cockrings*, and *Thus Spake Zarathustra*. Additionally, he is the co-creator, with Reverend Jen, of the television series *Electra Elf* and the author of two autobiographical books, *Bleed* and *Totem of the Depraved*.

Poet, essayist, fiction writer, art critic, and contributing editor to *NY Arts* from Paris, Nina Zivancevic is the author of nine books of poetry published in Serbian and English; she has also written three books of short stories and two novels. She has lectured at Naropa University, New York University, the Harriman Institute, and St. John's University in the United States, and at numerous universities and colleges in Europe.

TEXTUAL CREDIT LINES

(In Alphabetical Order by Author's Last Name)

Selection from *I Dreamt I Was a Nymphomaniac! : Imagining*, originally published in San Francisco: Empty Elevator Shaft Press (1974), then reprinted in *Portrait of an Eye* (1992). Copyright © 1974 the Estate of Kathy Acker. Used by permission of the Estate of Kathy Acker.

"New York City in 1979" was originally published in its entirety in the periodical *Crawl out Your Window* No. 7 (1979), then as the Top Stories pamphlet of the same name (1981), and later reprinted in *Hannibal Lecter, My Father* by Semiotext(e) Native Agents (2002). Copyright © 1979, 1981 the Estate of Kathy Acker. Used by permission of the Estate of Kathy Acker.

"The Wound," "Imposter," and "The Pact" by Roberta Allen are from *The Traveling Woman*, originally published by Vehicle Editions. Copyright © 1986 Roberta Allen. Used by permission of Vehicle Editions.

"Black Story + White Story," "Green Story," "(one) Blue Story," "(two) Blue Story," "(three) Blue Story," and "Red Story" by Holly Anderson originally appeared in various hand-drawn formats in a variety of publications, but never together. Copyright © 1984 Holly Anderson. Used by permission of the author.

"Lower East Side Mesostics 81–82" by Holly Anderson first appeared in *Redtape* No. 6. Copyright © 1986 Holly Anderson. Used by permission of the author.

"Words in Reverse" by Laurie Anderson was originally published as the Top Stories pamphlet of the same name. Copyright © 1979 Laurie Anderson. Used by permission of the author.

"While You Were Out" by Penny Arcade aka Susana Ventura originally appeared in *Out of Character: Rants, Raves, and Monologues from Today's Top Performance Artists*, edited by Mark Russel, published by Bantam Books. Copyright © 1982 Penny Arcade aka Susana Ventura. Used by permission of the author.

"The New School 1990" by Richard Armijo first appeared in *Redtape* No. 7. Copyright © 1992 Richard Armijo. Used by permission of the author.

"A Visit from Mom" by Bruce Benderson appeared in *Pretending to Say No*, published by Plume. Copyright © 1990 Bruce Benderson. Used by permission of the author.

"Cardiac" (1989) and "Gathering Bruises" (1984) by Max Blagg. Copyright © max blagg, used by permission.

"Competition," "How to Pick Up Impotent Men," and "The Couple" by Lisa Blaushild. Copyright © Lisa Blaushild. Used by permission of the author.

"In The Dark" was first published as a Wedge Press pamphlet (1983). A later version appears in *The Essential Bogosian: Talk Radio, Drinking in America, Funhouse, & Men Inside*, published by the Theater Communication Group, 1994. Copyright © 1994 by Eric Bogosian. Used by permission of Theatre Communications Group.

"Lecture on 3rd Avenue (After V-Effect)" by Michael Carter. Copyright © 1982 Michael Carter. Used by permission of the author.

Selection from *Bagatelles* by Peter Cherches, originally published in full by Benzene Editions. Copyright © 1981 Peter Cherches. Used by permission of the author.

"Title Page" and "Italian Food" from *Colorful Tales*, published by Purgatory Pie Press. Copyright © 1983 Peter Cherches and Purgatory Pie Press. Used by permission of the author and Purgatory Pie Press.

"GEORGE: Wednesday, Thursday, Friday" later appeared as a part of *Closer*, published by Grove Press. Copyright © 1989 Dennis Cooper. Used by permission of the author.

From *The Colorist* by Susan Daitch, originally published by Vintage Press. Susan Daitch edited this particular selection for this anthology. Copyright © 1990 Susan Daitch. Used by permission of the author.

Haiku from *Public Illumination Magazine* by mr. basho originally appeared in various issues of *Public Illumination Magazine*. Copyright © 1982–1989 Steve Dalachinsky. Used by permission of the author.

"Part One, Book One" from *Modern Love*. *Modern Love* originally appeared in serial form as books 1–5 of *The Complete Works of Constance DeJong*, published and distributed by the author, September 1975–July 1976. Copyright © 1975 Constance DeJong. Used by permission of the author.

"G-39" by Tim Dlugos from *Powerless: Selected Poems, 1973–1990*, published by High Risk Books/Serpent's Tail. Copyright © 1996 by the publisher and the Estate of Tim Dlugos.

"North of Abysinnia" is from *Weep Not My Wanton* by Maggie Dubris, published by Black Sparrow Press. Copyright © 2001 by Maggie Dubris. Reprinted by arrangement with Black Sparrow Books, an imprint of David R. Godine, Publisher, Inc.

"Beauties Who Live Only for an Afternoon" originally appeared in *Smile*, published by Warm

Spring Press. Copyright © 1990, 1993 by Denise Duhamel. Used by permission of the author.

"Fear on 11th Street and Avenue A, New York City" is from *Queen for a Day*, by Denise Duhamel, © 2001. Reprinted by permission of the University of Pittsburgh Press.

"On the Side of the Road" by Janice Eidus from *Vito Loves Geraldine*, published by City Lights. Copyright © Janice Eidus. Used by permission of the author.

"This Is It?" by Barbara Ess originally appeared in *Just Another Asshole #6*, edited by Glenn Branca and Barbara Ess, published by Just Another Asshole. Copyright © 1983 Barbara Ess. Used by permission of the author.

Lisa B. Falour's untitled interview with Gerard Malanga appeared in *Bikini Girl* No. 8 from the collection of Lisa B. Falour. Copyright © Lisa B. Falour 1981, 2004. Used by permission.

"Folk" by John Farris is from *It's Not about Time*, edited by Jenny Seymore, published by Fly By Night Press/A Gathering of Tribes. Copyright © 1993 John Farris. Used by permission of the author.

"Poem with a Title at the End" by Jim Feast from *National Poetry Magazine of the Lower*

East Side, vol. 1, no. 2, 1986. Copyright © 1986 Jim Feast. Used by permission of the author.

The story "Baby Birds" by Karen Finley first appeared in this form in *Blatant Artifice 2/3: An Anthology of Short Fiction by Visiting Writers, 1985–1987*, edited by Edmund Cardoni (Hallwalls Contemporary Arts Center, Buffalo, NY, 1988). It appeared in slightly different form in *Shock Treatment*, published by City Lights. Copyright © 1990 by Karen Finley. Reprinted by permission of City Lights Books.

Selection by Mary Gaitskill reprinted with the permission of Simon & Schuster Adult Publishing Group, from *Two Girls, Fat and Thin* by Mary Gaitskill (USA). Extract from *Two Girls, Fat and Thin* by Mary Gaitskill, published by Chatto & Windus. Reprinted by permission of the Random House Group Ltd. Copyright © 1991 by Mary Gaitskill. All rights reserved.

"War Stars" is an excerpt from the unpublished fictional memoir "Giving Up the Ghost" by Mike Golden from the collection of Mike Golden. Copyright © 1991–2005 Mike Golden. Used by permission.

"TV" by Brad Gooch appeared in *Jailbait and Other Stories*, published by the Seahorse Press. Copyright © 1984 Brad Gooch. Reprinted by permission of the author.

**PICTORIAL
CREDITS**
(IN CHRONOLOGICAL ORDER)

1970S

"The East Village 1970–71" by Richard Kostelanetz appeared in its entirety in *I Articulations/Short Fictions*, published by Kulchur Foundation. Copyright © 1974 Richard Kostelanetz. This excerpt reprinted with permission of the author.

Cover of *Punk Magazine* No. 2, 1976. Copyright © Punk Magazine 1976/ 2005. Used by permission of Punk Magazine.

Cover of *Modern Love*, a novel by Constance DeJong

(Standard Editions: 1977). Used by permission of Constance DeJong.

Johnny Rotten T-Shirt from *Koff* No. 1, 1977, from the collection of Maggie Dubris, Elinor Nauen, and Rachel Walling. Used by permission.

Richard Hell & the Voidoids, Lautréamont flyer, CBGB's, 1978.Design by Richard Hell; Photo by Roberta Bayley. Copyright © Richard Hell. Used by permission of Richard Meyers.

Manifesto from *Koff* No. 2, 1978, from the collection of Maggie Dubris, Elinor Nauen, and Rachel Walling. Used by permission.

"Fuck Frank O'Hara" letter from *Koff* No. 2, 1978 from the collection of Maggie Dubris, Elinor Nauen, and Rachel Walling. Used by permission.

Cover of *dodgems* No. 2, 1979. Copyright © Eileen Myles. Used by permission of Eileen Myles.

Cover of *Koff* No. 3, 1979, from the collection of Maggie Dubris, Elinor Nauen, and Rachel Walling. Used by permission.

Cover of *Words in Reverse* by
Laurie Anderson, Top Stories
No. 2, 1979. Editor: Anne Turyn;
Photo of Laurie Anderson by Marcia
Resnick. Used by permission.

Cover of *East Village Eye,* Vol.
1, No. 1, 1979. Art by Dana
Gilbert; Art Director Christof
Kohlhoefer. Copyright © Leonard
Abrams/EVE. Reprinted by
permission of Leonard Abrams.

"Wall Eye" (Slum Journal No. 1,
first page) from *Hot and Cold* by
Richard Hell. Copyright © 2001
by Richard Meyers. Originally
published in the *East Village Eye*,

October 1979. Reprinted by permission of powerHouse Books.

Cover of *New York City in
1979* by Kathy Acker, Top
Stories 9, 1981. Editor: Ann
Turyn; Photographer: Anne
Turyn. Copyright © 1981 Anne
Turyn. Used by permission
of Anne Turyn/Top Stories.

Cover of *Tear to Open (This This
This This This)* by Bob Holman,
1979. Designed by Joe Chassler/
PowerMad Press. Copyright
© 1979 Joe Chassler/PowerMad
Press. Reprinted by permission
of Barbara Barg.

Cover of *Bikini Girl*, Vol. 1,
No. 2, 1979. Editor: Lisa B.
Falour. From the collection
of Lisa B. Falour/Bikini Girl.
Copyright © 1979 Lisa B.
Falour. Used by permission.

Cover of *Bikini Girl*, Vol. 1,
No. 3, 1979. Editor: Lisa B.
Falour. From the collection of
Lisa B. Falour/Bikini Girl.
Copyright © 1979 Lisa B.
Falour. Used by permission.

Photobooth pictures of David
Wojnarowicz, ca. 1979. Used
by permission of the Estate
of David Wojnarowicz.

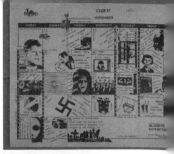

1980S

Cover of *East Village Eye*, Vol. 2, No. 12, 1980. Art by John Holmstrom; art director: Gaby Moritz. Copyright © 1980 Leonard Abrams/EVE. Reprinted by permission of Leonard Abrams.

"Torso Tied" (Slum Journal No. 5) by Richard Hell. Copyright © 1980 by Richard Meyers. Originally published in the *East Village Eye*, April 1980. Reprinted by permission of Richard Meyers.

Cover of *Soho News*, November 5–11, 1980. Photo of Laurie Anderson by Jimmy DeSana. Reprinted by permission Laurie Anderson and the Estate of Jimmy DeSana.

Leif Garrett collage from the *Tenderness of Wolves/Safe* scrapbook by Dennis Cooper, 1980. Artist: Dennis Cooper. Reprinted by permission of Dennis Cooper.

Cover of *Soho News*, October 22, 1980, from the collection of Allen Tannenbaum. Photographer:

Allan Tannenbaum. Copyright © 1980 Allan Tannenbaum. Used by permission.

Club 57: September schedule, 1980. Used courtesy of the Fales Library, NYU.

3rd Annual AMES, Poetry Project Flyer, 1980. Used courtesy of the Fales Library, NYU.

The Kitchen, Aluminum Nights Flyer, 1981. Used courtesy of the Fales Library, NYU.

Cover of *Bomb,* Vol. 1, No. 1, 1981. Artwork by Sarah Charlesworth, cover design by Mark Magill. Copyright © New Art Publications, Inc./Bomb Magazine. Reprinted by permission.

Max Blagg and Jim Farmer flyer, 1981. Used by permission of Max Blagg.

Photo [*L to R*] Dennis Cooper, Tim Dlugos, and Bob Flanagan on NYC Subway, ca. 1981. Photo credit: Sheree Rose. Copyright © Sheree Rose. Courtesy of Sheree Rose.

"Graffiti" from *Public Illumination Magazine* No. 13 ("Civilization"), March 1981. Artist: Kip Herring. Copyright © 1981 Public Illumination Magazine. Reprinted by permission of PIM.

Cover of *Public Illumination Magazine*, No. 17, "Excess," September 1981. Artist/Designer: Prof., Dr., Dr. Zagreus Bowery. Copyright © 1981 Public Illumination Magazine. Reprinted by permission.

Cover of *The Low Tech Manual*, ed. Ron Kolm. Copyright © 1981 by Art Spiegelman, reprinted with the permission of the Wylie Agency, Inc.

Eileen Myles, Attitude Art flyer/postcard, 1981. Used courtesy of the Fales Library, NYU.

Cover of *Zone* No. 7, Spring/Summer 1981 ("Collaborations"). Editor: Peter Cherches; Artist: Michael Madore. Copyright © Michael Madore. Used by permission of the publisher and the artist.

Cover of *Benzene/Zone*
No. 10, the Nothing Issue
(Part One), 1981–1985.
Artist/Designer: Allan Bealy.
Copyright © Allan Bealy.
Reprinted by permission.

Com Press Benefit, Harkness
Theater at Butler Library
Flyer, 1981. Used courtesy
of the Fales Library, NYU.

Handbill for *Appearances*
No. 8 release party December
11, 1982, at Art et Industrie.
Reprinted by permission
Bob Witz.

Cover of *Benzene* No. 4,
1982. Art by Robert Younger,
design by Allan Bealy.
Copyright © Allan Bealy.
Reprinted by permission.

Flyer for Bomb publishing party
at Danceteria, 1982. Artwork by
Mary Heilman, Design by Mark
Magill. Copyright © New Art
Publications, Inc./Bomb Magazine.
Reprinted by permission.

Flyer for 3 Teens Kill 4 at the
Underground, 1982. Used courtesy
of the Fales Library, NYU.

Cover of *Adulterers Anonymous*,
1982. [*L to R*] Lydia Lunch and
Exene Cervenka. Photographer:
David Arnoff, Designer: Roy
Colmer. Copyright © 1996 Lydia
Lunch and Exene Cervenka. Used
by permission of Lydia Lunch.

"To Bruce with Love" by Scott
Neary, 1982 (drawing accompanying
Ursule Molinaro's "AC-DC" in
Benzene No. 5/6 Double Issue,
Spring/Summer 1982). Copyright
© 1982/2005 Scott Neary. Used
by permission of the artist.

"National Reflexology" from *Public
Illumination Magazine* No. 19,
"Technique," February 1982.
Author/Artist: Paula Clark as told
to Dr. Bowery. Copyright © 1982
Public Illumination Magazine.
Reprinted by permission.

Cover of *Public Illumination
Magazine*, No. 21, "Contraception,"

June 1982. Artist/Designer: Prof.,
Dr., Dr. Zagreus Bowery Copyright
© 1982 Public Illumination
Magazine. Reprinted by permission.

Cover of *Redtape* No. 2, 1982:
Assemblage Issue. Editor:
Michael Carter; Artwork: Michael
Carter. Copyright © Michael
Carter. Reprinted by permission.

Flyer for Black Market Press,
2nd Annual Feast of the
Unbraining, St. Clements Church,
May 24, 1982. Reprinted by
permission of Mike Golden.

Seduction of Chaos, poster
for an event organized by
Barbara Ess and Lynn
Holst, May 1982. Designer:
Barbara Ess. Reprinted by
permission of Barbara Ess.

Poster for *Zone* Magazine's
"Benefit for Nothing," 1982.
Artist/Designer: Dikko Faust/
Purgatory Pie Press, © Dikko
Faust. Used by permission Dikko
Faust/Purgatory Pie Press.

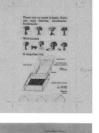

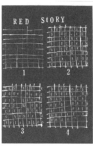

Handbill for *Redtape* No. 3, 1983, Benefit at Danceteria, decorated with image of "car accident victims" by Greer Lankton. Artist: Greer Lankton. Reprinted by permission of the Estate of Greer Lankton.

Cover of *Benzene* No. 7, 1983. Editor: Allan Bealy; Photo of Judy Lopatin: Anne Turyn. Copyright © 1983 Anne Turyn. Reprinted by permission.

Flyer for a poetry reading by Michael La Bombarda, Robert Lunday, Ron Kolm, Hal Sirowitz, May 7, 1983. Used courtesy of the Fales Library, NYU.

Cover of *Appearances*, November 10, 1983. Editor: Bob Witz; Photographer: Richard Sandler. Copyright © 1983. Used by permission of Bob Witz and Richard Sandler.

Cover of *Public Illumination Magazine*, No. 24, "Vermin," February 1983. Artist/Designer: Prof., Dr., Dr. Zagreus Bowery.

Copyright © 1983 Public Illumination Magazine. Reprinted by permission.

Cover of *In the Dark*, Eric Bogosian, Wedge Press, 1983. Editors: Phil Mariani, Brian Wallis; Photo: Paula Court. Copyright © Paula Court. Reprinted by permission of Paula Court and Brian Wallis/Wedge Press.

Peter Cherches: "Italian Food" from *Colorful Tales,* 1983, published by Purgatory Pie Press. Copyright © 1983 Peter Cherches and Purgatory Pie Press. Used by permission of the author and Purgatory Pie Press.

Cover of *Just Another Asshole* No. 6, 1983. Editors: Glenn Branca and Barbara Ess; Artist/Designer: Barbara Ess. Copyright © Barbara Ess 1983. Reprinted by permission.

Cover of *Wedge* 3/4/5, *Partial Texts: Essays & Fictions,* Winter/Spring/Summer 1983. Editors: Phil Mariani, Brian Wallis. Copyright © 1983. Reprinted by permission of Brian Wallis/Wedge Press.

Cover of Roberta Allen, *Partial Portraits* from *Wedge* 3/4/5, *Partial Texts: Essays & Fictions*, Winter/Spring/Summer 1983. Editors: Phil Mariani, Brian Wallis. Copyright © 1983. Reprinted by permission of Brian Wallis/Wedge Press.

Original art work for *Blood and Guts in High School* by Kathy Acker from the Kathy Acker papers at Duke University. Drawings: Kathy Acker, ca. 1984. Copyright © the Estate of Kathy Acker. Used by permission of the Estate of Kathy Acker.

Hal Sirowitz, "Crumbs." Copyright © 1984 Hal Sirowitz and Purgatory Pie Press. From the collection of Purgatory Pie Press. Used by Permission.

Flyer for *Redtape* No. 4 Benefit at Danceteria, 1984. Artist: Patrick Howe. Courtesy of Patrick Howe.

"Black Story + White Story," "Green Story," "(one) Blue Story," "(two) Blue Story," "(three) Blue Story," and "Red Story" by Holly Anderson originally

appeared in various hand-drawn formats in a variety of publications, but never together. They are from the collection of Holly Anderson. Copyright © 1984 Holly Anderson. Used by permission.

5 Plus 5 Announcement, Low Tech Press, 1984. Artist: Jörga Cardin. Used by permission of the artist.

Dennis Cooper and Alice Notley, The Poetry Project, 1984. Used courtesy of the Fales Library, NYU.

Cover of *How to Get Rid of Pimples* by Cookie Mueller, Top Stories 19–20, 1984. Editor: Anne Turyn; Photo credit: David Armstrong. Copyright © 1984. Reprinted by permission.

Cover of *The Underground Film Bulletin*, Vol. 1, No. 1, 1984. Editor: Nick Zedd; Illustration of Donna Death: Nick Zedd. Artist/Designer: Nick Zedd. Copyright © 1984 Nick Zedd. Used by permission.

Cover of *Blatant Artifice: An Annual Anthology of Short Fiction, Visiting*

Writers, 1984–1985, Volume II. Editor: Edmund Cardoni; Artwork: Paul Kalinowski. Copyright © 1986 by Hallwalls, Inc. Contemporary Art Center. Reprinted by permission Hallwalls Contemporary Art Center.

Flyer for *Wallpaper* Extravaganza, November 1984. Artist: Peter Bernard. Reprinted by permission.

Photograph of Kathy Acker by Robert Mapplethorpe, from the collection of the Estate of Kathy Acker. Copyright © 1984 Robert Mapplethorpe. Used by permission of the Estate of Kathy Acker.

Cover of *Between C & D*, Vol. 1, No. 2, Summer 1984. Editors: Joel Rose and Catherine Texier; Artist: Rick Prol. Copyright © 1984. Reprinted by permission.

Front and Back Cover of *Portable Lower East Side*, Vol. 1, No. 1, 1984. Editor: Kurt Hollander; Cover design: Kurt Hollander. Reprinted by permission Kurt Hollander.

Ground Zero, Installments 1–4, 1984 (from the *East Village Eye*), from the collection of Marguerite Van Cook and James Romberger. Authors: Marguerite Van Cook and James Romberger. Copyright © 1984/2005 Marguerite Van Cook and James Romberger. Used by permission.

Mockup for the cover of *Redtape* No. 4, 1984. Editor: Michael Carter; Artist: Michael Roman. Reprinted by permission.

Flyer for Hi Tech Low Life "film, discourse, and dance" at Darinka, August 18, 1984. Used courtesy of the Fales Library, NYU.

Cover of *New Observations*, No. 26, "Critical Love," 1984, ed. Lynne Tillman. Artist/Designer: Mark Magill. Used by permission Lucio Pozzi/New Observations.

Cover and two inside pages from *Madame Realism*, 1984 (Brooklyn: Print Center). Author: Lynne Tillman, Artist: Kiki Smith. Used by permission.

"Jealousy & Sunstroke" by Max Blagg, 1984. (Photo of *Safe* by Dennis Cooper with a knife in it.) Used by permission Max Blagg.

Flyer for a reading by Max Blagg, Ron Kolm, and Lynne Tillman (with a William Anthony slide show) at the Living Theater, 1984. Copyright © David Sandlin. Used by permission.

Cover of *Soho Arts Weekly*, No. 1, September 25, 1985. Copyright © 1985 by Art Spiegelman, reprinted with permission of the Wylie Agency, Inc.

Flyer for *Avenue E* benefit featuring Cookie Mueller and Gary Indiana at Neither/Nor, 1985. Used courtesy of the Fales Library, NYU.

Cover of *Between C & D,* Fall 1985, Vol. 2, No. 2. Editors: Joel Rose and Catherine Texier; Artist: Barbara Kruger. Copyright © 1985. Reprinted by permission.

Flyer for *Between C & D* readings at Darinka/ABC No Rio, 1985. Used courtesy of the Fales Library, NYU.

Photograph of Bruce Benderson, 1985, from the collection of Bruce Benderson. Photographer: Scott Neary. Used by permission.

Cover for *Anarcadium Pan* by Carl Watson (Erie Street Press, 1985). Artist: Matt Straub. Used by permission.

Cover for *Soho Arts Weekly*, No. 9, December 4, 1985. Photo of Karen Finley: Mark Jenkinson. Reprinted by permission.

Cover of *Soho Arts Weekly*, No. 8, 1985. Photo credit: Elaine Ellman. Copyright © 1985. Reprinted by permission.

Cover of *Between C & D*, Vol. 1, No. 4, Winter 1985. Editors: Joel Rose and Catherine Texier; Artist: David Wojnarowicz. Copyright © 1985. Reprinted by permission.

Flyer for *Portable Lower East Side* Benefit Party at the Gas Station, 1985. Reprinted by permission of Kurt Hollander.

Cover of *Wild History*, Tanam Press, 1985. Edited by Richard Prince. Used by permission of Reese Williams.

Flyer for *Right Side of My Brain* at the Pyramid Club, 1986. Used by permission of Lydia Lunch.

Lisa Blaushild, "The Other Woman" postcard, front/back, Purgatory Pie Press, 1985/86, from the collection of Purgatory Pie Press. Reprinted by permission.

Cover of *Condensed Book* by Peter Cherches, Benzene Editions 1986. Artist/Designer: Allan Bealy. Copyright © 1986 Allan Bealy. Used by permission.

Flyer for Max Blagg's Chocolate Daydreams at Madam Rosa's, 1986. Used by permission of Max Blagg.

SOHO ARTS WEEKLY

Avenue E

featuring
Gary Indiana
Cookie Mueller

with
Steve Cee
Tony Clay
Ann Craig
Kate Dillon
Frank Green
Robert Kaplan
Anole Rubin

music by
Stephanie Crawford

at
neither/nor

703 East Sixth Street
just east of Avenue C
475-9758

Benefit Party #5.
Sunday, March 17th 9:00 PM

ANARCADIUM PAN

Carl Watson

Fall 1985   Volume 2 Number 2

BETWEEN C AND D
Post-Literate Lower East Side Fiction Magazine

You are the perfect crime

BIRTH
REBIRTH
AFTER BIRTH
STILL BIRTH
COMPUTING

$4.00 $5.00 OUTSIDE NEW YORK CITY

BETWEEN C AND D
Lower East Side Fiction Magazine
Presents
Two Readings

Sunday, March 10, 8:30 PM   Sunday, March 31, 3:00 PM
at   at
DARINKA   ABC NO RIO
118 East 1st Street   156 Rivington Street

Bina Sharif   Darius James
Gary Indiana   Joel Rose
Catherine Texier   Dennis Cooper
Peter Cherches   Lisa Blaushild
Lynne Tillman   Reinaldo Povod
Patrick McGrath   David Wojnarowicz

$3.00 $2.50

saw
ARTS WEEKLY

SOHO ARTS WEEKLY

BETWEEN C AND D

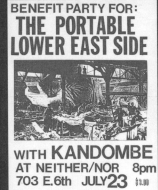

BENEFIT PARTY FOR:
THE PORTABLE
LOWER EAST SIDE

WITH KANDOMBE
AT NEITHER/NOR 8pm
703 E.6th JULY 23 $3.00

WILD HISTORY

RIGHT SIDE OF MY BRAIN
by R. KERN   starring LYDIA LUNCH
PYRAMID CLUB FEB 18 1986 11 PM Rated X

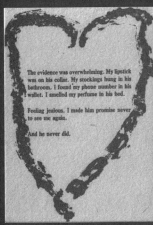

The evidence was overwhelming. My lipstick
was on his collar. My stockings hung in his
bathroom. I found my phone number in his
wallet. I smelled my perfume in his bed.

Feeling jealous, I made him promise never
to see me again.

And he never did.

Condensed Book

PETER CHERCHES

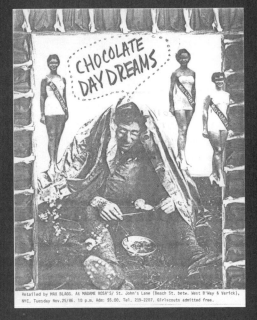

CHOCOLATE DAY DREAMS

Retailed by MAX BLAGG. At MADAME ROSA'S/ St. John's Lane (Beach St. betw. West B'Way & Varick),
NYC, Tuesday Nov.25/86. 10 p.m. Adm: $5.00. Tel. 219-2207. Girlscouts admitted free.

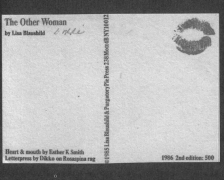

The Other Woman
by Lisa Blaushild

©1985 Lisa Blaushild & Purgatory Pie Press 238 Mott #B NY 10012

Heart & mouth by Esther K Smith
Letterpress by Dikko on Rosaspina rag

1986 2nd edition: 500

Cover of *Downtown Magazine* No. 34, 1986. Depicted: Mickey Yo and Alphabet Town Boogie Band. Reprinted by permission.

Cover of *Redtape*, No. 6, 1986, depicting "sissy" by Greer Lankton. Artist: Greer Lankton. Reprinted by permission of the Estate of Greer Lankton.

Cover of *Five*, Top Stories, No. 23–24, 1986. Editor: Anne Turyn; Artist: Gail Vachon. Copyright © 1986. Reprinted by permission.

Flyer for a Richard Bandanza, Carmelita Tropicana, and Ron Kolm Performance/Reading at St. Mark's Church, 1986. Artist: Mark Kostabi. Used by permission of the artist.

Cover for *Between C & D,* Vol. 2, No. 4, 1986. Editors: Joel Rose and Catherine Texier; Artist: Kiki Smith. Copyright © 1986. Reprinted by permission.

Flyer for Poetry Project's Marathon Reading Benefit, 1986. Used courtesy of the Fales Library, NYU.

Ron Kolm/*Public Illumination Magazine* parody, 1986. Artist: Thomas Zummer. Used by permission of Thomas Zummer.

Flyer for "Hot Season" at Poetry Project Flyer, ca. 1987. Used courtesy of the Fales Library, NYU.

Cover for *East Village Eye*, Vol. 8, No. 72, 1987. Photographer: Isabel Snyder; Art Director: Donald Schneider. Copyright © 1987. Reprinted by permission of Leonard Abrams/*East Village Eye*.

Cover for *Portable Lower East Side*, Vol. 4, No. 1, 1987. Editor: Kurt Hollander; Cover Design: Kurt Hollander. Reprinted by permission Kurt Hollander.

Photo of Lynne Tillman, 1987, from the collection of Lynne Tillman. Photographer: Nan Goldin. Used by permission of Lynne Tillman and the artist.

Cover of *Cover*, Vol. 1, No. 7, September 1987. Depicted: Guerrilla Girls. Used courtesy of the Fales Library, NYU.

Flyer for James Strahs and Peter Cherches Book Party at La Mama La Galleria, 1987. Used courtesy of the Fales Library, NYU.

Cover for *Bomb* No. 20, 1987. Artwork: Nan Goldin, Cover design: Stanley Moss. Copyright © New Art Publications, Inc./Bomb Magazine. Reprinted by permission.

Photo [*L to R*] Susie Timmons and David Trinidad at the Cuz Poets' Banquet, St. Mark's Church, 1988. Photo credit: Chris Stein. Copyright © courtesy of Richard Meyers.

Photo [*L to R*] Various Diners. Cuz Poets' Banquet Table by unknown, 1988. Copyright © courtesy of Richard Meyers.

Photo [*L to R*] Richard Hell, Dennis Cooper and Ishmael Houston-Jones at the Cuz Poets' Banquet, St. Mark's Church, 1988. Photo credit: Chris Stein. Copyright © courtesy of Richard Meyers.

Photo [*L to R*] Dennis Cooper, Michael DeCapite, Lee Ann Brown, Eileen Myles, Richard Hell, Amanda Uprichard. Posed Group shot by Chris Stein, 1988. Copyright © courtesy of Richard Meyers.

Photo of Sparrow on Broadway, 1988. Photo credit: Frederick Wasser. Used by permission.

Cover of *Bomb* No. 22, 1988. Artwork: Jimmy DeSana; Cover design: Stanley Moss. Copyright © New Art Publications, Inc./Bomb Magazine. Reprinted by permission.

Cover of *Big Cigars* No. 3, Winter 1988. Editors: Michael Randall and Jose Padua; Artist/ Designer: Michael Randall. Used by permission.

Flyer for Staten Island Poetry Festival, 1988. Used courtesy of the Fales Library, NYU.

Cover for *Paper Magazine*, October 1988. Photo credit: Richard Pandiscio. Used by permission Paper Magazine.

Flyer for Mexico City Blues by Jack Kerouac at Knitting Factory, 1988. Used courtesy of the Fales Library, NYU.

The Unbearable Beatniks of Life, Life Café flyer, 1989. Used courtesy of the Fales Library, NYU.

Flyer for Hanuman Books reading at St. Mark's Church, 1989. Designer: Raymond Foye. Reprinted by permission.

Cover of *God with Revolver*, Rene Ricard, Hanuman Books, 1989. Cover design: C. T. Nachiappan. Reprinted by permission.

Cover of *Plastic Factory* by Ron Kolm, published by Red Dust, 1989. Artist: Michael Randall (from his painting, "Untitled 1987"). Used by permission.

Cover of *New Observations*, "Bitten by a Monkey," ed. Mike Topp, No. 66, 1989. Artist: Ida Applebroog. Used by permission of Lucio Pozzi/ New Observations.

Cover of *Nationalistic Poetry Magazine of the Lower East Side*, Vol. 4, No. 1, Issue 14, Winter 1989. Editors: Jim Feast, Stephen Paul Miller, Carol Wierzbicki; Artist: Unknown. Used by permission of the editors of *National Poetry Magazine of the Lower East Side*.

Flyer for Carl Watson and Sharon Mesmer at St. Mark's Church, 1989. Drawing by Sharon Mesmer. Used by permission.

James Romberger, "The Triumph of Death (after Brueghel)," 1989. In the collection of the Newark Museum, reprinted by permission of the artist.

Flyer for Poets and Painters at Blue Mountain, 1989–90. Used courtesy of the Fales Library, NYU.

In the Tradition of Lincoln, Twain & Roosevelt

Panic DJ! at The Cooper Union

A DAY IN THE LIFE

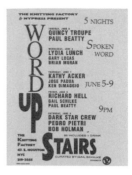

THE KNITTING FACTORY & NYPRESS PRESENT 5 NIGHTS

WORD UP

QUINCY TROUPE
PAUL BEATTY
SPOKEN WORD

LYDIA LUNCH
GARY LUCAS
BRIAN MORAN

KATHY ACKER
JOSE PADUA
KEN DIMAGGIO JUNE 5-9

RICHARD HELL

DARK STAR CREW
PEDRO PIETRI
BOB HOLMAN 9PM

STAIRS

THE KNITTING FACTORY
47 E. HOUSTON
NYC
219-3055

A Celebration for Scarlet

Our Phone Flea Market Begins

DOWNTOWN

Justice At Tompkins Square

1990S

EPIPHANY ALBUMS
"THE ALBUM THAT CHANGED MY LIFE"

READINGS BY LENNY KAYE, IRWIN CHUSID,
LINDA YABLONSKY, FRANK NIMS, SILVIA
GANZA, ED FRIEDMAN, JOSE PADUA, J.P.
...LSON, DARIUS JAMES, SHANNON KETCH
& CARL WATSON

FRIDAY, OCTOBER 9TH AT 10:30
THE POETRY PROJECT
ST. MARK'S CHURCH
SECOND AVENUE & TENTH STREET
674-0910
$5 SUGGESTED CONTRIBUTION

Flyer for Panic DJ! at the Cooper Union. Photographer: Michael Wakefield; Design: Jonathan Andrews. Copyright © 1990 Bob Holman. Reprinted by permission.

Flyer for Instant Classics Reading at Nosmo King, 1990. Used courtesy of the Fales Library, NYU.

Advertisement for *A Day in the Life* and related event, 1990. Artist: Seth Tobocman. Used by permission.

Flyer for Image Brilliance, Dalachinsky and Rower at the Knitting Factory, 1990. Used courtesy of the Fales Library, NYU.

Flyer for Word Up at the Knitting Factory, 1990. Used courtesy of the Fales Library, NYU.

Original art from *Memories That Smell Like Gasoline*, ca. 1990. Artist: David Wojnarowicz. Used by permission the Estate of David Wojnarowicz.

Flyer for Scarlet Benefit at Nuyorican Poets Café, 1991. Used courtesy of the Fales Library, NYU.

Cover of *Downtown Magazine* (Tompkins Square Riots), No. 249, June 19–26, 1991. Used courtesy of the Fales Library, NYU.

Flyer for a reading by Janice Eidus, Ron Kolm, and Geoffrey O'Brien at the Knitting Factory, 1991. Artist: William Anthony. Reprinted by permission.

Flyer for the Unbearables, Madonna/Bukowski Flyer, Max Fish, 1991. Designer: bart plantenga. Used courtesy of the Fales Library, NYU.

Photo [*L to R*] Gary Indiana, Ira Silverberg, David Trinidad, and Bob Flanagan, ca. 1991. Photo credit: Sheree Rose. Used by permission of Sheree Rose.

Illustrated version of Ron Kolm's "Suburban Ambush." Artist: Michael Madore, ca. 1991. Copyright © Michael Madore. Used by permission of the artist.

Photo of David Rattray, ca. 1991. Photographer: Lynne Tillman. Used by permission the photographer and the Estate of David Rattray.

"Letter Bomb" by Walter Sipser, 1992, from the collection of Walter Sipser. Copyright © Walter Sipser. Used by permission.

Flyer for Epiphany Blues at the Poetry Project, 1992. Used by permission.

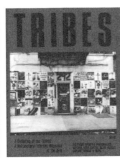

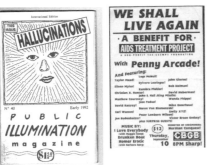

"Dope Brands, 1981–1992" by Walter Sipser, 1992, from the collection of Walter Sipser. Copyright © Walter Sipser. Used by permission.

Cover of *Gathering of the Tribes*, No. 2, 1992. Photo credit: Ari Marcopoulos, Bullet Space. Copyright © 1992 A.G.O.T.T. Reprinted by permission.

Flyer for *Redtape* "Tragicomix" Gala at CBGB's, 1992. Art: Eric Drooker. Used by permission.

Flyer, "8 Reasons Why You Should Write in Eileen Myles for President in '92," 1992. Author: Eileen Myles. Copyright © Eileen Myles. Used by permission.

Cover of *National Poetry Magazine of the Lower East Side*, Vol. 7, No. 24, 1992. Editors: Jim Feast, Stephen Paul Miller, Carol Wierzbicki; Artist/ Designer: Catherine Sand. Copyright

© 1992 Catherine Rutgers (Sand). Used by permission of the artist.

Untitled, inside of the back cover of *Redtape* No. 7, 1992. Editor: Michael Carter; Artist: Kaz. Copyright © Kaz. Used by permission of the artist.

Cover of *Public Illumination Magazine*, No. 40, "Hallucinations," Early 1992. Artist/Designer: Prof., Dr., Dr. Zagreus Bowery. Copyright © 1992 Public Illumination Magazine. Reprinted by permission.

Flyer for We Shall Live Again at CBGB's, 1992. Used courtesy of the Fales Library, NYU.

Flyer for *Beet* Magazine Benefit at Biblios, 1992. Used courtesy of the Fales Library, NYU.

Flyer for the Unbearables at Fez, 1992. Designer: bart plantenga.

Used courtesy of the Fales Library, NYU.

Flyer for David Wojnarowicz Memorial, 1992. Used by permission the Estate of David Wojnarowicz.

Photo of the Unbearables (with notations by Ron Kolm), ca. 1992, from the collection of Ron Kolm. Photographer: Unknown. Used by permission.

Cover of *Rant* No. 3, ca. 1992. Editor: Alfred Vitale; Artist: Shalom Neuman. Used by permission the artist and publisher.

Advertisement for Janice Eidus's *Urban Bliss*, ca. early '90s. Artist: Susan Weinstein. Used by permission of the artist.

Flyer for Poetry at Mona's, ca. 1994. Used courtesy of the Fales Library, NYU.

ABOUT THE EDITOR

After finishing graduate school in Buffalo, Brandon Stosuy moved to New York City to work as an archivist in the Fales Library's Downtown Collection. He is currently a staff writer at *Pitchfork* and contributes to *The Believer*, *Magnet*, and the *Village Voice*. Stosuy has published essays in a monograph on Sue de Beer and a book about Dennis Cooper and has written for *Bomb*, *Bookforum*, *L.A. Weekly*, *Prague Literary Review*, *Slate*, and *Time Out*, among other publications. He curated Kathy Acker's "Discipline & Anarchy" at New York University's Tracey/Barry Gallery and organized "Prose Acts," a three-day New Narrative festival at Hallwalls in Buffalo. In the early to mid-'90s, Stosuy edited fifteen issues of the fanzine, white bread, and co-operated the noise label, Sweet Baboo. Today, he lives in Brooklyn where he is writing his first novel.

ABOUT THE DESIGN

For over 20 years, Yolanda Cuomo Design and her staff have created a range of projects for leading publishers, museums, authors, editors, artists and photographers. The firm's work includes: book and exhibition design for *Diane Arbus Revelations*; book design for *Pre-Pop Warhol* (1988) and collaboration with numerous renowned artists including Paul Simon, Laurie Anderson, Twyla Tharp, Gilles Peress and Sylvia Plachy.